CHAWTON HOUSE LIBRARY SERIES

MEMOIRS OF WOMEN WRITERS

Contents of the Edition

PART I

PART II

PART III

CHAWTON HOUSE LIBRARY SERIES: WOMEN'S MEMOIRS

Series Editor: Jennie Batchelor

TITLES IN THIS SERIES

Women's Theatrical Memoirs
Women's Court and Society Memoirs
Memoirs of Scandalous Women

www.pickeringchatto.com/chawtonhouse

MEMOIRS OF WOMEN WRITERS

EDITED BY

Gina Luria Walker

NS FACULTY

Volume 10

Mary Hays, *Female Biography; or, Memoirs of Illustrious and Celebrated Women, of All Ages and Countries* (1803)
Volume VI

LONDON
PICKERING & CHATTO
2014

Published by Pickering & Chatto (Publishers) Limited
21 Bloomsbury Way, London WC1A 2TH

2252 Ridge Road, Brookfield, Vermont 05036-9704, USA

www.pickeringchatto.com

BRITISH LIBRARY CATALOGUING IN PUBLICATION DATA

Hays, Mary, 1759 or 60–1843.
Memoirs of women writers. Part 3. – (Chawton House library series. Women's
memoirs)
1. Women authors – Biography. 2. Women – Biography.
I. Title II. Series III. Fitzer, Anna M. IV. Walker, Gina
Luria, 1942–
828.6'09-dc22

ISBN-13: 9781848930537

∞

This publication is printed on acid-free paper that conforms to the American
National Standard for the Permanence of Paper for Printed Library Materials.

Typeset by Pickering & Chatto (Publishers) Limited
Printed and bound in the United Kingdom by Berforts Information Pres

CONTENTS

FEMALE BIOGRAPHY;

OR,

MEMOIRS

OF

ILLUSTRIOUS AND CELEBRATED

WOMEN,

OF ALL AGES AND COUNTRIES.

Alphabetically arranged.

———

BY MARY HAYS.

═══════

IN SIX VOLUMES.

═══════

VOL. VI.

———

LONDON:

PRINTED FOR RICHARD PHILLIPS, 71, ST. PAUL'S
CHURCH-YARD.

By Thomas Divison, White-Friars.

———

1803.

MEMOIRS

OF

DISTINGUISHED WOMEN.

━━━━━━━━

OCTAVIA,
WIFE TO ANTONY.

OCTAVIA, grand-niece of Julius Cæsar, and sister to Augustus, was the daughter of Caius Octavius and Atia, Romans of distinguished birth and virtue. She received in the house of her parents a strict and exemplary education; she was early accustomed to control her feelings, to discipline her imagination, to sacrifice her inclinations to others, and to impart the benefits she received. The modesty of her deportment, her unaffected and simple manners, the beauty of her person, her virtues and fine qualities, rendered her the boast and ornament of the court; while her splendid connections, and affinity to the adopted son of Cæsar, procured her the devotion of

2   OCTAVIA.

the Roman youth, who eagerly aspired to her alliance. Octavia, humble and unambitious, shunned
the public homage; dreading to be made a sacrifice
to political motives, she sighed after that purer happiness, which, seated in the mind, gratifies the heart
and its affections. It was proposed, during the civil
war between Cæsar and Pompey, that Octavia should
be given to the latter as a pledge of union, and that
a period might be put to the dissensions which deso-
lated Rome: but other circumstances arising, interrupted this negociation, and, for the present, delivered the princess from a destiny which, however
adverse to her feelings, she had determined not to
oppose. That the happiness of individuals should
yield to the public welfare, was a principle which
had been early impressed upon her mind.

Claudius Marcellus at this time possessed the con-
sular dignity, and with it the respect and confidence
of the citizens. The reputation of his virtues had
attracted the attention of Octavia; by a farther acquaintance with his character, esteem was softened
into tenderness; the princess rejoiced when she
found herself destined, by her brother, to be the
wife of a man whom her judgment and her heart
equally approved. Marcellus united to an agreeable
person and engaging manners, the qualities of a Roman citizen, of a hero, and of a sage. In these
nuptials, Octavia found realised the most sanguine

OCTAVIA. 8

wishes of a virtuous and tender heart. Marcellus loved his wife with entire affection, and confided in her as a friend: they seemed animated but by one soul; while their affections, their pursuits, their taste, and their judgment, were in perfect unison.

This harmony received no other interruption than from the calamities with which the state was torn, when the proscription of the triumvirs deluged Rome with blood. Octavia exerted on this occasion her influence with her brother to humanise his heart, and put a stop to the effusion of Roman blood: she refused her protection and good offices to no one, while her house was the refuge of the unfortunate. When these troubles were in some degree allayed, Octaviva requested permission to retire, with her husband, from the tumults of the city, to devote themselves to the leisure of a tranquil and studious life: but the pleasure which Octavius experienced in their society frustrated the execution of this plan, and still detained them in the capital. Octavia took no share in the dissipations of the court, or the amusements common to her sex and rank: secluded in her house, and devoted to her husband, she assisted him in his serious occupations, shared his pleasures, and passed in his society her most delightful hours.

Weeks and months thus glided away in delicious

4   OCTAVIA.

tranquillity, when Marcellus was suddenly seized with a fever, which, in its commencement, exhibited the most malignant symptoms : his physicians, at the expiration of two days, despaired of his recovery, and exhorted him to settle his affairs. Marcellus, receiving the sentence of his death with manly fortitude, employed the short remainder of an useful and exemplary life, in consoling his beloved wife, in entreating her to support with firmness their separation, and to transfer to the pledges of their affection her cares and tenderness. The best support of his dying moments, he assured her, would be the conviction, that she would bear with resignation her loss ; that she would not indulge in weak because fruitless sorrow ; but look forward to new scenes of happiness, which her virtues merited, and of which her youth, her rank, and the vicissitudes of human affairs, gave her a reasonable prospect. Having breathed his last, the sorrow which, while her services might be yet useful, Octavia had stifled in her bosom, burst forth uncontrolled, while overpowered by the acuteness of her anguish, she sunk into a trance, and remained for some hours insensible to her loss. Time only could soften a grief so sincere and reasonable : Octavia found in her widowhood no mitigation of her affliction, but in calling to mind the dying injunctions of her husband, and in the duties and cares which her children demanded. With

OCTAVIA.　　　5

the consent of her brother she retired from Rome, for the purpose of devoting herself to the education of her offspring, the only object which now attached her to life.

Soon after this period, the civil war having commenced between Octavius and Antony, it was proposed, by the common friends of the triumvirs, that, as a pledge of conciliation, the widow of Marcellus should be bestowed on Antony. Octavia heard this proposal with horror and repugnance; she knew not how to promise to Antony, whose infatuation to the queen of Egypt and whose neglect of his former wife had been notorious, that affection and respect which the tenderness and virtues of Marcellus had made not less her duty than her happiness. She felt the dissimilarity of her own character to that of the man who now demanded her, and the sacrifice which was exacted from her; she foresaw the misery into which she was about to be plunged, while the peace of Rome, and the duties which she owed to her distracted country, struggled with her repugnance: after a severe internal conflict, hopeless of happiness, she determined to become a victim to the public safety.

By the Roman laws, widows were forbidden, within the first ten months of their widowhood, to contract a new engagement; but from motives of

6   OCTAVIA.

state, a dispensation was on this occasion granted for the marriage of Octavia. A renewal of the civil war was dreaded by the people ; the most auspicious hopes were, from the beauty and fine qualities of Octavia, entertained from this union; common forms appeared comparatively unimportant; the nuptials were accordingly hastened, and celebrated in Rome, in the year 714, amidst the joyful acclamations of the nation. The sadness which clouded the brow of the bride, seemed to yield to the public demonstrations of satisfaction : conscious of having bestowed on Antony, with an alienated heart, a reluctant hand, she determined to make up, by the attentive discharge of her duties, for the absence of those sentiments over which she felt she had no control.

A peace being thus concluded between the triumviri, Augustus continued in Italy, while Antony, with Octavia, passed into Greece, and remained during the winter at Athens. The Athenians omitted no respect due to the rank and virtues of Octavia, who, observing her husband at times emerging from the licentious habits in which he had but too habitually indulged, and seeking the society of men of science and learning, began to be better reconciled to her situation, and to cherish hopes of his reformation. While her youth and beauty, her gentleness, her complaisance, and watchful attentions, appeared to gain an influence over the mind of An-

OCTAVIA. 7

tony, and to banish from his recollection his Egyptian mistress, the grateful sense which he manifested of her conduct awakened a real tenderness in the sensible heart of Octavia.

These promising appearances were of no long duration; the gentleness and affection of Octavia were of a nature too uniform for senses accustomed to the stimulus of licentious gratification : her virtues, her ingenuousness, her simplicity, were feeble attractions to a debauched imagination, corrupted by meretricious arts ; even the zeal with which she entered into his interest, and the frankness with which she suggested plans for his advantage, disgusted the self-love of Antony : in the clear judgment and admirable understanding of his wife, he seemed to fear a rival, while the homage which her virtues exacted appeared a tacit reproach to his vices. Cleopatra had governed him by artifice and flattery; the sincerity of Octavia was offensive to his vanity.

Augustus, still engaged in a war with the son of Pompey, demanded succours from Antony, who, under pretence of assisting him, but for the real purpose of informing himself of the state of affairs at Rome, and of deriving from them advantage, returned to Italy. A mutual jealousy and coldness ensued ; Antony, refused entrance into the haven of Brundusium, put into Tarentum, whence,

8 OCTAVIA.

at her request, he sent Octavia to her brother. Augustus, touched by the remonstrances and supplications of a beloved sister, consented to wave the cause of his contention with her husband, and to return with her to Tarentum. On this occasion, reciprocal demonstrations of reconciliation and friendship, through the mediation of Octavia, passed between the princes.

After this interview, Antony, leaving Octavia with her brother in Italy, returned into the East, where he again fell into the snares of Cleopatra. While, occupied in the duties of her family (to which she had added the children of Antony, by his former marriage), Octavia continued at Rome, she heard with sorrow, but without anger, of the infatuation of her husband, and of the disastrous issue of the Parthian campaign. Having vainly attempted to palliate to her brother his conduct, alarmed for the safety of this unworthy husband, she resolved to return into the East, and to make a last effort to avert from him the evils by which he was menaced. Having prepared to execute her determination, she received letters from Antony, who had been informed of her design, commanding her to stop at Athens, where she soon learned that, absorbed in his passion for the queen of Egypt, he was solicitous to avoid the presence of his wife. To the harsh mandate which stopped her progress, she returned an answer

OCTAVIA. 9

full of meekness and submission, requesting direc-
tions in what manner to dispose of the presents she
had brought with her, and of which she solicited
Antony's acceptance. By an answer still more
severe and peremptory, her immediate return to
Rome was commanded; proper orders, it was added,
would be given for the disposal of the presents,
which she might leave behind her in Athens. On
receiving these commands, Octavia, without a murmur at the indignities which she had suffered, returned to Rome; and, taking up her residence in the
house of her husband, notwithstanding the remonstrances and intreaties of her brother, who urged
her to leave him to his fate, devoted herself to the
education of her own and his children. She omitted no endeavours to soothe the pride and the resentment of Augustus, while she implored him not to
make her wrongs, which she could sustain with
fortitude, a pretence for involving Rome in the miseries of a civil war. When at length, at the insti-
gation of her rival, she was, by the orders of Antony, compelled to quit his house, her tears flowed
for the fatal consequences which she apprehended
from this insult, rather than from her own peculiar
sorrows.

Her heroic conduct tended but to accelerate those
evils to her country which she was solicitous to avert.

10   OCTAVIA.

The contempt and indignation of the people were roused by the infatuation of Antony, whom the artifices of a voluptuous woman held in disgraceful bondage, blinding him to the merits of his admirable wife, who surpassed her rival, not merely in the qualities of the heart and mind, but in the attractions of youth and beauty. In proportion as she exerted herself to lessen, by patient cheerfulness, and in kind offices to the children and friends of her husband, the public sense of her injuries, she added, without intending it, fuel to the hatred and rage of the nation. Being desirous of making one more effort to recal by her personal influence the affections of her husband, she obtained permission of her brother to execute her purpose, in the secret hope that, by the multiplied insults of Antony to his incomparable wife, the Romans might be roused to vengeance. Cleopatra, informed of the design of her rival, and dreading the effect of her merit and perseverance, put in practice every artifice to induce her lover to forbid her approach. She represented to him, that it was sufficient glory for Octavia to bear the title of his wife, while herself, a sovereign princess, submitted to that of mistress : nor, so ardent was the passion with which he had inspired her, could she think herself degraded by the proofs she had given him of her affection, while he did not, by separating himself from her, plunge her

OCTAVIA.   11

into despair. The friends of Antony, on the other side, pressed him to send back Cleopatra from Ephesus, whither she had followed him, and to avert, by this measure, the storm which threatened him from Rome. But the influence of his mistress triumphed over the subjected mind of her lover, whom she prevailed on to take her with him wherever he should remove. On their arrival at Athens, where Octavia had been received with peculiar distinction, the queen of Egypt courted popularity by the most lavish generosity.

The war which the imprudence of Antony at length provoked, terminated in his ruin. After the battle of Actium, in which, betrayed by Cleopatra, he fled covered with disgrace, Octavia, by repeated messages, intreated him to authorise her mediation with her brother, and to allow her to be the pledge of his future conduct, while she assured him of her forgiveness of the past, and her determination never, by recrimination or reproach, to revive the memory of his disasters. But vain were all the efforts of this heroic and unfortunate woman; Antony, deaf to her supplications, chose rather to die with her perfidious rival.

Octavia, illustrious in virtue and in descent, to whom nature and fortune had been equally lavish, the dawn of whose life promised a brilliant and unclouded day, beheld the sun of her prosperity set

at noon : over the remainder of her life thick darkness rested; while, towards its close, the gloom
deepened.   Marcus Claudius Marcellus, her son by
her former marriage, who inherited the virtues of
his parents, was the pride and boast of Rome; while,
united to the daughter of Augustus, he was regarded
as presumptive heir to the empire.   This son, so
dear to Octavia, in whom his father appeared yet to
survive, died in the flower of his age.   From a blow
thus severe, which seemed to fill up the measure of
her calamities, Octavia never recovered.   The eulogy
of Marcellus, composed by Virgil, is inserted in the
Æneid, book vi. verse 860, &c.   On its recital by the
poet, in the presence of Augustus and his sister,
the emperor melted into tears, and the unhappy mother swooned away.

Octavia gave up the remainder of her life to solitude, in which, brooding incessantly over her misfortunes, her temper became soured, and her mind
broken : cherishing a spirit of misanthropy, she even
sickened at the glory of her brother.   She could not
endure to hear any woman named who possessed the
happiness of being a mother; she would suffer no
person to speak to her of her son, on whom, notwithstanding, her thoughts perpetually dwelt; she
rejected all comfort and amusement, appeared buried in the most profound sadness, and sought darkness and solitude : clothed in deep mourning, she

OCTAVIA. 1**5**

appeared to have lost all interest in life, and to become indifferent respecting the fate of her children who survived. Repeated sorrows had exhausted her fortitude: the spring of her mind was weakened by suffering: if at times she returned to the studies in which she had before delighted, philosophy was found ineffectual to heal the wound of a deeply lacerated spirit.

In this situation, she suffered life thirteen years, and died, universally esteemed and pitied, in 744, at Rome. She left two daughters, the offspring of her union with Antony, who formed advantageous alliances. A temple, it is said by Pausanias, was erected at Corinth, in honour of her constancy and virtues. She took into her own family the children of Antony by Cleopatra, whose daughter she gave in marriage to the king of Mauritania, celebrated for his wisdom and knowledge of the sciences.

Lives of Cleopatra and Octavia, by Sarah Fielding—— Bayle's Historical Dictionary—Biographium Femineum, &c.

OCTAVIA,

WIFE TO NERO.

Octavia, the daughter of Claudius and of Mes salina, born in the 795th year of Rome, maintained, in despite of the vices of her parents, and of the

14   OCTAVIA.

contagion of a corrupt age and court, in the midst of licentiousness, and of unmerited misfortunes, the simplicity and innocence of an unsullied life. To personal charms, she added modesty, sweetness, beneficence, purity of manners, talents, and an irreproachable conduct. Her life was a series of calamities; a dark and deep cloud obscured her fate, through which a beam of joy scarcely ever penetrated. She was betrothed in early youth, by the emperor her father, to Lucius Silanus, a noble and illustrious Roman, great-grandson to Augustus. Claudius, who entertained for his intended son-in-law the esteem which his merit justified, lavished on him honours and privileges.

On the death of the empress Messalina, who perished violently, a victim to her vices, the emperor espoused his niece Agrippina, whose ambitious projects for the aggrandisement of her family, led her, with a view of uniting the princess to Domitius (her son by a former marriage), to oppose the fortune of Silanus. To effect this purpose, it was necessary to injure his credit with the emperor, by calumniating his character, and misrepresenting his actions. However atrocious their designs, the rich and powerful are seldom at a loss for instruments to assist in their accomplishment: Vitellius, the censor, a corrupt magistrate, sacrificed without scruple, for the advancement of his interest, and the favour of the new

OCTAVIA.   **15**

empress, the laws of honour and of humanity. The reputation of Silanus was blasted by falsehoods; accusations the most odious were brought against him; which, though destitute of proof or rational evidence, terminated in his ruin. He was declared unworthy of his employments, and deprived of the prætorship, the duties of which he had discharged with fidelity and popular esteem. The weak emperor suffered his judgment to be imposed upon, and his affections alienated from a man who had, by a series of services, merited the distinctions he held. Silanus was disgraced, the nuptial contract cancelled, and the lovers torn asunder.

Pollio, a Roman nominated to the consulate, was, by the flatteries and promises of Agrippina, induced to propose a marriage between the princess and Domitius, to which the indolent and unsteady Claudius with facility yielded his assent. Silanus, on the day of these inauspicious nuptials, terminated, in despair, his existence.

Agrippina, encouraged by the weakness of the emperor, whose incapacity prevented him from penetrating her views, set no limits to her ambition. Having represented to him the infirm state of his health, the weight of government, and the youth of his son Britannicus, which required a support, she prevailed upon him, after the example of Augustus, who had adopted the sons of Livia, to receive Domitius into his family, by adopting him under the name of Nero. While every man of integrity reprobated a step so pernicious to the interest of the heir, a venal senate confirmed the decree. Octavia wept in secret over the violence done to her heart, the fate of her lover, and the threatening destiny of her brother. By a mock adoption, she was herself engrafted on another family; a superstitious farce, to prevent the scandal of the supposititious affinity between her and her husband. Agrippina, triumphing in the success of her arts, bent all her intrigues for securing the succession to her son, which she at length effected. The emperor having fallen a victim to poison, Nero was declared his successor, to the prejudice of the rights of Britannicus.

Octavia, an alien in the palace of her father, the victim of an ambitious step-mother, the wife of a profligate, from whom she experienced neither tenderness nor confidence, bereaved of the man she had loved, indignant at the injustice suffered by her brother, and trembling for his fate, was compelled to stifle, in the bottom of her heart, a grief too poignant for words. Her unaffected beauty, her pure and simple manners, had no charm for the heart of Nero, vitiated by meretricious allurements : the wanton beauty of a slave, a woman of licentious manners and ignoble birth, had wholly fascinated his senses. The corruption of his manners had been

OCTAVIA.   17

encouraged by his preceptors and counsellors, with a view of opposing to the authority of Agrippina the blandishments of the new favourite. In vain were the remonstrances of a few individuals, who, observing with apprehension the licentious propensities of the emperor, sought to stem the tide of corruption, by representing to him the merits and the claims of Octavia. Listening only to his appetites, Nero treated as enemies all who opposed them : he even meditated a divorce from his blameless consort : when Burrhus, his governor, bluntly reminded him, that, should he repudiate Octavia, it would be necessary to restore her dowry; thus intimating, plainly, that it was to her he owed the diadem. The wandering of her husband's affections was regarded by Octavia with indifference : she disdained any competition with her rival ; and considered her injuries as sufficiently avenged in the contempt which, in every worthy mind, the conduct of the emperor excited. Not satisfied with supplanting the princess in the heart of her husband, his mistress meditated a more glorious triumph, and aspired to ascend the throne. With this view she redoubled her allurements, practising with success every fascination that might tend to increase and to secure her influence.

Nero, plunged in sensuality, and surrounded by dissolute companions, became every hour more insensible to the dictates of honour, and more callous

to the feelings of humanity : at length, throwing off
all restraint, he abandoned himself to the most odious
depravity.   The ascendancy of his mother, who opposed his passion for Acte, had for a time obliged
him to practise some reserve.; till, wearied by constraint, impelled by the impetuosity of his character,
and determined to burst every barrier, he prepared
to repudiate his wife, and to raise her rival to the
throne.   But before these measures could be put in
execution, his safety imposed on him the necessity
of reflection.   The senate and people, devoted to the
family of the Cæsars, and with whom the virtues of
Octavia had acquired popularity, might, it was probable, by a divorce, be incited to revolt : a marriage
with Acte, a slave of obscure birth, would doubtless
be considered as a degradation of the majesty of the
purple : the hearts of the citizens would by such a
step become alienated, and their views turned towards their rightful sovereign.   By these ideas,
which obtruded themselves on his mind, his purposes were suspended, and his passions checked.   To
gain over a venal senate, did not appear to be an enterprise of difficulty; persons might be suborned,
nay, such had actually offered themselves, to fabricate, from a race of kings, a genealogy for the
favourite.   But Britannicus must first be removed,
who had now entered his thirteenth year, and whose
personal merit added claims to his birth.   To these

OCTAVIA.   **19**

considerations were joined the threats of Agrippina, who, incensed at the conduct of her son, scrupled not to declare her intention of disclosing the frauds which had advanced him to the throne, and of conducting to the Roman legions Britannicus their rightful master.

Urged by motives thus pressing, Nero hesitated not in the career of crimes, but determined on the destruction of his rival. Pollio, tribune of a prætorian cohort, retained in prison a woman named Locusta, famed for her skill in preparing the most subtle poisons. To this wretch, through the connivance of the tribune, freedom was offered upon condition of the murder of the prince. A potion was, by his preceptors, administered to the ill-fated Britannicus : whether its operation was too tardy for the impatience of the tyrant, or whether the vigour of the prince's constitution resisted its venom, it seemed to produce but little effect. Enraged at the disappointment of his barbarous purpose, Nero threatened with vengeance his infamous associates, who, to appease his fury, promised to procure a more potent drug, by which an instantaneous death should be produced. This engagement was but too well performed. The poison was prepared in the chamber, and in the presence of the emperor, and administered to the victim at table. To avert suspicion, when the prince called for liquor, it was brought to

him boiling, and tasted, according to the custom of
the court, by the person who presented the cup.
Britannicus, as had been foreseen, complaining of
the heat, water, in which the poison had been previously infused, was brought to mingle with the
beverage. The prince had scarcely taken the vessel
from his lips, when he fell from his seat, and instantly expired. Octavia, who was present at this
catastrophe, abandoned herself, in the first moment
of surprise and horror, to grief and despair. Nero
sought to persuade her, that her brother was merely
seized with an epilepsy, to which, he affirmed, he
had been subject. The unhappy Octavia, without
doubting the truth, was compelled to smother her
emotions, and to affect an acquiescence which did
equal violence to her understanding and her heart.
She saw, in the fate of Britannicus, the family of
the Cladii extinct, and her own last hope and resource blasted. Her injuries had excited general
sympathy, yet her friends were powerless to assist
her; impotent pity and good wishes were all that
remained to her.

Agrippina, unaffectedly shocked at an event which
gave to her influence the finishing stroke, and in
the barbarity of her son anticipating her own destiny, mingled her sorrows, whose source was less
pure, with those of Octavia: she soothed the princess, with whom a similarity of fate seemed to unite

OCTAVIA. 2I

her, with every testimony of apparent affection and sympathy.

The capricious Nero had, in the mean time, become disgusted with the mistress for whom he had steeped his hands in blood, having conceived a new passion for Sabina Poppæa, whom he determined to espouse. Considering his mother as the only obstacle to this design, he revolved in his thoughts, now familiar with crimes, the monstrous project of shedding the blood of her to whom he owed life. This atrocious action, at which nature sickens, instigated by Poppæa, he at length perpetrated: habituated to the vicious indulgence of every passion, nature and human feeling had become extinct in his heart. To the vices she had herself implanted in his mind, Agrippina was at length the victim: in raising him to the throne she had violated every principle of justice and humanity, and, by her own example, prepared the way for that monstrous corruption which terminated in her own destruction.

Octavia now found herself alone and unprotected, exposed to the savage fury of her husband, and the vindictive malice of a jealous rival. Nero, not daring to commit open violence against a princess, whose birth, whose misfortunes, and whose virtues, rendered her the idol of the people, determined to be himself her executioner, and to strangle her in private with his own hands: but, by the danger and difficulty attending this project, he was at length induced to abandon it, and to content himself with procuring a divorce from his blameless wife. This idea was suggested to him by Tigellinus, the parasite of his vices, and the companion of his debaucheries, a man of mean birth, destitute of education, of talents, and of virtues, a compound of every vice, and of every odious quality. The exemplary conduct of Octavia leaving her husband without a pretence for the injustice he meditated, it was determined to allege, as a ground for the separation, that she was incapable of giving an heir to the empire. On this pretext, she was deprived of the privileges of her rank and station, and, instead of the empire which she had brought as a dowry to Nero, the estate of Plautus, and the house of Burrhus, who had been governor to the emperor, were assigned to her use.

Poppæa, not satisfied with the degradation of her rival, and impatient of the vicinity of her virtues, was intent on convicting her of some misconduct, which might afford a pretence for exiling her from Rome. In this infamous purpose she was aided by Tigellinus, who suborned a domestic of the devoted princess, to accuse her of a criminal commerce with Eucer, an Alexandrian slave, and a maker of musical instruments. With this charge, destitute of probability as of proof, was the daughter of Claudius insulted. Her women and servants un-

OCTAVIA. **23**

derwent an examination, and, menaced with the torture, were exhorted to depose against her. If, among her domestics, the weakness of some induced them to subscribe implicitly to all that was demanded of them, others sustained with intrepidity the malice of her accusers, and, in the midst of the most cruel pangs, bore testimony to the worth and purity of their mistress. The innocence of Octavia acquired, in every unprejudiced eye, new lustre by this infamous transaction : the machinations of her enemies, predetermined to condemn her, nevertheless prevailed ; she was banished to Campania as a state-prisoner, and a guard set over her.

An oppression so glaring did not escape the censures of the people, who loudly expressed their indignation : the murmurs of the populace, and their invectives against his mistress, to whom Octavia had been sacrificed, reached the ear of the tyrant : apprehensive of the consequences which seemed to menace the throne, and overwhelmed with the terrors of a base mind, Nero repealed the unjust sentence, and recalled from exile his injured wife. She was received by the people with acclamations and triumph : the statues erected to Poppæa were overthrown, and those of the empress, crowned with flowers, carried through the streets, and placed in the temples. The city was in a tumult of joy, the streets resounded with mirth and festivity, while even the emperor acquired a momentary popularity for an act of justice to which he had been compelled.

Poppæa, irritated to fury by the insults of the populace and the honours paid to her rival, and aware that Nero had yielded but to his fears, determined on a last effort for the destruction of the empress. Bathed in tears, she rushed into the presence of her lover, and, prostrate at his feet, represented in language to which passion gave force, the indignities offered to his authority, the shameful pusillanimity of thus yielding to the tide of popular clamour, and suffering the woman whom he loved, helpless and unprotected, to become the scorn of a rabble, whose insults to his mistress were but the prelude of those they were about to shower upon himself. She insisted, that the power of Octavia, thus permitted to establish itself, would proceed to impose laws on the throne, the safety and honour of which were concerned in opposing barriers to a frenzy, to which, if suffered with impunity, it would become difficult to assign limits. Nero, weak and capricious, overpowered by the blandishments and expostulations of his mistress, allowed himself to be prevailed upon to sign the sentence of death, pronounced by Poppæa on her rival. As a prelude to this tragedy, it was resolved that Octavia should be again removed from Rome, when measures should be concerted for accomplishing, without hazard, their cruel purpose.

OCTAVIA.   **25**

Solicitous to gloss over their barbarity with some colour of justice, the enemies of the empress were at a loss for an excuse : to their former calumnies no credit had been given; the testimony of her women, added to her unexceptionable manners, had evinced its falsehood.   To the charge of incontinence, it was now determined to add that of treachery against the state, and to suborn in evidence some person, whose office should favour the accusation. Anicetus, commander of the galleys, the assassin of Agrippina, who hesitated at no crime by which his interest was advanced, was selected as a fit agent for the occasion.   To this wretch the emperor, in person, imparted his design, observing, that having owed to him a deliverance from the treason of his mother, the benefit was yet imperfect, while he remained exposed to the more dangerous machinations of his wife. In the present case, neither blood nor violence were required of him ; it was sufficient that he should declare the empress an adultress, and himself her paramour : on his compliance, he might rest assured of a magnificent recompence for the service exacted of him, while any hesitation must of necessity be followed with death, as security for a secret involving the safety of the emperor.   Anicetus, whom no scruples of honour or humanity withheld, readily acceded to the proposal : in the pre-

VOL. VI.   C

sence of the companions and flatterers of the tyrant, assembled for the purpose, he asserted his criminal intercourse with the empress, and thus filled up the measure of his infamy. The innocent victim of a prejudiced tribunal, on the single testimony of an unprincipled ruffian, whose evidence, unsupported by circumstances, unestablished by even the shadow of fact, criminated himself, was at once accused, tried, and condemned ; and, after this mockery of justice, again romanded into exile. The fictitious partner of her offence was, to save appearances, banished to Sardinia, where the means of an indolent and licentious life were amply afforded to him. No one gave credit to the farce, though the public indignation, exhausted perhaps by its former intemperance, for the present slumbered.

The next measure adopted by the tyrant and his adherents, was to fabricate and publish a project, which was attributed to the royal exile, of having bartered her honour to the commander of the galleys, for the purpose of having at her devotion the naval force. To this was added another charge, equally curious and consistent: it was pretended that Octavia, recently divorced from the throne on the pretence of sterility, had, to conceal her connection with Anicetus, and cover her shame, used means to procure an abortion, lest her pregnancy should announce to the public her incontinence.

OCTAVIA. 27

Thus, overwhelmed with injury, and branded with infamy, alike unmerited, this unhappy princess was driven from her natal city and the throne of her ancestors; and, on her way to Pandataria, the place allotted for her retreat, exposed, amidst a guard of brutish soldiery, to every insult which wanton malignity could devise. Her misfortunes, her youth, her beauty, yet in its early bloom, failed to move the savage nature of her conductors, who were commissioned to aggravate her distress.

Scarcely had she reached the place of her destination, when she was warned to prepare for death, of which these insults had been but the prelude. In vain the innocent victim to the vices of her persecutors, timid in youth, her fortitude exhausted by suffering and fatigue, humbled herself before the barbarians into whose power she had been committed. In vain she declared her resignation to the injustice she had suffered, and to the triumph of her rival, with whom, content to be considered as the sister of Nero and cheerfully resigning every other claim, she wished not to dispute the heart of the emperor. As vainly she invoked the manes of her ancestors, and called on the name of Agrippina, the original cause of all her sorrows, whose severities, she declared, compared with her present sufferings, were tender mercies. Her supplications, her

appeals, her despair, her streaming eyes, her up-
lifted hands, availed her not.   Having been seized
and bound, her veins were opened, while the blood,
which terror had congealed round her heart, flowed
slowly and with difficulty.   At length, suffocated in
the bath, her miseries and her life were terminated
together.   She expired beneath the hands of these
merciless barbarians, on the 11th day of June, having but just completed her twentieth year.

Poppæa glutted her malignity by viewing the head
of her illustrious rival, which she caused to be sent
to her for the purpose.   The fate of Octavia plunged the city in sorrow and mourning : " curses deep
not loud" were muttered ; every heart was penetrated, every eye bathed in tears !   Retribution was
not far distant: Poppæa perished miserably by the
brutal caprice of a monster who disgraced the throne
and human nature, and who, exactly six years after
the murder of his wife, became his own executioner.

*Lives of the Roman Empresses, &c.—Bayle's Histo-
rical Dictionary.*

MRS. OLDFIELD.

THIS lady, so celebrated in the annals of the
drama, was born in Pall-Mall, London, in 1683.
Her father had been an officer in the Guards, and

MRS. OLDFIELD.   29

possessed a competent estate, which he squandered
in dissipation, leaving at his death an helpless and
unprovided family.   In these circumstances, his widow was necessitated to accept the offer of residing
with a sister, who kept a tavern in St. James's market; while her daughter was placed with a sempstress, in King-street, Westminster. The young lady
had a particular predilection for reading plays; and
was one day amusing her relations at the tavern by
the exercise of her talent, when her voice reached
the ear of captain George Farquhar, who happened
to dine there, and who, struck with the flexibility
and sweetness of her tones, and with her agreeable
figure and air, immediately pronounced her admirably
fitted for the stage.   Her own inclinations concur-
ring with this decision, her mother consulted sir
John Vanbrugh on the occasion, who was a friend
to the family.   Sir John, finding upon trial her
qualifications very promising, recommended her to
Mr. Rich, patentee of the King's-theatre, who immediately received her. It was some time before her
powers displayed themselves, till, in 1703, she established her reputation in the character of Leonora,
in " Sir Courtly Nice." The following year she
appeared with equal advantage in Lady Betty Modish, in " The Careless Husband."   About this period she attracted the attention of Arthur Maynwar-

ing, esq. who greatly interested himself respecting her performance, and took pains to improve her natural genius. This gentleman dying in 1712, she afterwards entered into a connection with brigadier-general Churchill. She had one son by her former lover, and another by the brigadier. To both of these gentlemen she is said to have behaved with the fidelity, duty, and attachment, of a wife. Among many humane and generous actions for which Mrs. Oldfield was respected, may be mentioned the annuity of fifty pounds, which she allowed to Savage the poet, so celebrated for his genius, his misfortunes, and his imprudence. This annuity was regularly paid during her life. Mrs. Oldfield's talents in her profession rendered her a distinguished favourite with the town; while her taste in dress, elegance of manners, and powers of conversation, threw a veil over those parts of her conduct which were considered as reprehensible.

She died, October 23d, 1730; her body lay in state, in the Jerusalem-chamber, whence it was conveyed to Westminster-abbey. Her pall was borne by gentlemen of high rank and character. Her eldest son, Arthur Maynwaring, esq. was chief mourner. She was interred towards the west end of the south aisle, between the monuments of Mr. Craggs and Mr. Congreve. She was elegantly dressed in her coffin in fine Holland and Brussels

lace. She left the bulk of her fortune to her eldest
son, through whose father she had received and acquired it; yet she did not neglect to shew a proper
regard to her second son, Charles Churchill, and to
her own relations.

Biographium Fæmineum.

MARIA PACHECO PADILLA.

DURING the civil wars in Castile, under the reign
of the emperor Charles V. don John de Padilla,
eldest son of the commendator of Castile, a young
and gallant nobleman, distinguished for his talents,
his ambition, and his courage, was the chief leader
of the insurgents. In the course of their hostile
operations against the government, they stood in need
of money to satisfy their troops; a difficulty from
which they were relieved by the boldness of the
wife of their chief, donna Maria Pacheco Padilla,
a woman of noble birth, high spirit, and great abilities, animated with an ardent zeal for the liberties of
her country, and superior to those superstitious fears
to which the dependent state of her sex, by weaken-
ing their minds, renders them peculiarly liable: donna
Maria proposed that they should seize and appropriate
the rich and magnificent ornaments in the cathedral
of Toledo. But, lest this apparent sacrilege should

give offence to the prejudices of the people, the wife of Padilla, with her retinue, clad in mourning habits, their eyes filled with tears, and their hair dishevelled, marched in solemn procession to the church, where, falling on their knees, they implored pardon from the saints whose shrines they were compelled by necessity to violate. Under this artifice, they stripped the cathedral, appeased the populace, and procured for their cause the aid of a considerable sum.

In a subsequent engagement between the two parties, which a combination of circumstances had rendered disadvantageous to the insurgents, Padilla, determined not to survive a defeat and the ruin of his party, rushed into the thickest of the enemy, and, being wounded and dismounted, fell into their hands. His execution quickly followed, to which he submitted with the dauntless spirit of a man and a hero. One of his companions having expressed some indignation at hearing himself proclaimed a traitor, Padilla calmly observed, ' that yesterday was the time to have displayed the spirit of gentlemen, the present day to die with the meekness of Christians !' Being permitted to write to his wife, and to the community of Toledo, his native city, previous to his ascending the scaffold, he addressed and consoled the former in a strain of virtuous and manly tenderness, and the latter with the exultation of a martyr to freedom.

PADILLA.   33

The dejected commons of Castile, depressed by
this defeat, lost with their leader all their spirit and
their zeal. Toledo alone, animated by the widow of
Padilla, who despised unavailing lamentations, prepared, in prosecuting the cause in which their general
had fallen, to redress their country and avenge his fate.
Respect for her talents, admiration of her courage,
sympathy with her misfortunes, and tenderness for
her sex, combined to secure to donna Maria the
same ascendant over the minds and affections of the
people, which her husband had so recently possessed. Nor did she fail to justify by her conduct their
attachment and confidence. She wrote to the French
general in Navarre, whom, by an offer of powerful
assistance, she sought to encourage to the invasion
of Castile ; while, by her letters and emissaries, she
endeavoured to revive the hopes and the spirits of its
cities. She raised soldiers, and, in order to defray
the expence of keeping them on foot, exacted a
large sum from the clergy belonging to the cathedral.
To interest and excite the populace, she employed
every artifice which could rouse or inflame. She
ordered crucifixes instead of colours to be used by
the troops, as if they had been at war with the enemies of their church. Seated on a mule, clad in
deep mourning, her son in her arms, and having a
standard borne before her on which was depictured

34   PADILLA.

the fate of her husband, she marched solemnly
through the city, in mournful pomp. The passions
of the people, kept by these methods in continual
agitation, had not leisure to subside: animated by
a spirit of enthusiasm, they became insensible to the
danger of their situation, and stood alone in opposition to the power of the throne.

While their army was employed in Navarre, the
attempts of the enemy to reduce Toledo by force
proved fruitless: neither were their endeavours to
diminish the credit of donna Maria with the people,
nor to gain her, through the influence of her
brother*, by solicitations and promises, more successful. The French, at length, being expelled
from Navarre, part of the army returned into Castile, and immediately invested Toledo. The obstinate courage of donna Maria was not yet subdued; she defended the town with vigour, while her
troops, in several sallies, beat the royalists. No
progress was made towards reducing the city, till
the clergy, whom the invasion of their property had
offended, withdrew their support from the citizens.
Having soon after received information of the death
of the archbishop † of Toledo, whose possession of

---

* The marquis de Mondeiar.
† William de Croy, a foreigner,

PADILLA.

that see had been their principal grievance, and that the emperor had named a Castilian as his successor, they openly turned against donna Maria, whom, by the most absurd legends, they injured in the esteem of the people. The credulous multitude were taught to believe, that the influence which the widow of Padilla had acquired over them was by the force of enchantment; that a familiar demon, in the form of a negro maid, assisted her councils; and that it was by infernal suggestions that her conduct was regulated. Thus instigated, impatient of a long blockade, despairing of succours from the French, and from the other cities, their former confederates, the populace took up arms, and, having driven donna Maria from the city, surrendered it to the royalists. Retiring to the citadel, the widow of Padilla, with astonishing fortitude, defended it for four months longer; till, reduced to the last extremities, she was compelled to escape in disguise, and to flee to Portugal, in which she had many relations. After her flight, the citadel surrendered; tranquillity was re-established in Castile; and the power of the crown, from the unsuccessful opposition of the commons, confirmed and extended.

Robertson's History of Charles V.

[36]

DOROTHY, LADY PAKINGTON.

DOROTHY, LADY PAKINGTON, wife to sir John Pakington, baronet, and daughter of Thomas lord Coventry, keeper of the great-seal, was born in London, about the middle of the reign of James I. This lady, distinguished for her virtues and talents, is the reputed author of " The Whole Duty of Man." Of the circumstances of her private life, except as connected with the evidence for this opinion, we have little account. " The Whole Duty of Man" has been attributed to four different persons beside lady Pakington.—

To Mr. Abraham Woodhead, of whom it is sufficient to observe, that he lived and died a zealous Roman-catholic. To Mr. William Fulman, a learned clergyman of Penshurst in Kent, who died June 28th, 1688. In 1684, bishop Fell, in a preface to the folio edition of " The Works of the Author of The Whole Duty of Man," observes, " that, if God had given longer life to this eminent person, the world would have been benefited by a new work, a treatise designed and promised, " On the Government of the Thoughts." Mr. Fulman survived the date of this publication four years.

The third person to whom this celebrated production has been attributed, was Dr. Richard Sterne, archbishop of York. It is observed by Mr. Drake, his biographer, that the archbishop was suspected of being the author of " The Whole Duty of Man." This suspicion seems to have been ill founded. The archbishop owned himself the writer of a book " On Logic," and "A Comment on the 103d Psalm;" why then should he affect concealment respecting a work of greater merit and celebrity ? To this supposition there are also some chronological objections : when the treatise " On the Government of the Thoughts" was promised to the public, the archbishop had attained the advanced age of 87. "The Whole Duty of Man" likewise differs in its style and orthography from the writings of the archbishop. The fourth reputed author of the work in dispute was archbishop Frewen. In objection to this, among other reasons, it is remarked, that in a preface to " The Causes of the Decay of Christian Piety," a production allowed to be written by the author of " The Whole Duty of Man," merition is made of the plague and fire of London, whence it appears that the writer was living at the latter end of the year 1666, whereas archbishop Frewen died in 1664.

By the adversaries of lady Pakington it is objected, that the learning displayed in "The Whole Duty of Man" can scarcely be attributable to a woman. " A learned man has observed to me in a letter," says Ballard, " that 'The Whole Duty of Man' could not have been the production of a woman, from the great variation of style, and different manner of treating the subjects, which it contains ; beside the many quotations from Hebrew writers, with which every page abounds. In the Christian's Birth-right, through which a close thread of logical reasoning runs, the language is particularly exalted. Both the arguments and diction of this work are such as the profoundest scholars would use." In reply to this, it may be recollected that, during the age of Elizabeth and James, it was the fashion to give to women a learned education ; that the study of the languages, and even of the abstruse sciences, was the occupation of the most illustrious ladies of the court ; and that in no period were there more numerous examples of female excellence and worth. Of the endowments and erudition of lady Pakington there are also various testimonies. Dr. George Hickes, a man of known probity, and intimate with the family, thus speaks of this lady, in a preface to his " Anglo-Saxon, and Mæso-Gothic Grammars," printed before his " Thesaurus," and inscribed to sir John Pakington, the descendant of lady Pakington: " Your grandmother, the daughter of Thomas lord Coventry, &c. was illustrious for every virtue, more especially such as consist in the practice of a christian life. She had moreover an excellent judgment, and a talent of speaking correctly, pertinently, clearly, and

LADY PAKINGTON.　　39

gracefully; in which she was so accomplished, particularly in an evenness of style and consistent manner of writing, that she deserved to be called and reputed the author of a book concerning the duty of man, published anonymously, and well known through the christian world for its extraordinary completeness. Hammond, Morley, Fell, and Thomas, those eminently learned men, averred that she was as great an adept in the Scriptures as themselves, and as well versed in divinity, and in all those weighty and useful notions relating to DUTY, which have been recommended and handed down to us either by profane or christian philosophers. " She was also so far from being unacquainted with the antiquities of her own country, that she knew almost as much as the greatest proficients in that kind of knowledge. Nor is this to be wondered at; since she had in her youth the most excellently learned sir Norton Knatchbull for her tutor and preceptor; and, after she was married, the famous Hammond, and others, his contemporaries, very celebrated men, for her companions and instructors."

It was declared by a lady, not long deceased, that Dr. Hickes had assured her, he had himself seen " The Whole Duty of Man" in manuscript, written in the hand of lady Pakington, with many erasures, alterations, and interlineations. Various passages in

40   LADY PAKINGTON.

the work itself afford a presumption of the sex of the writer, who contends for the intellectual privileges of women and the equality of the sexes. The following are the direct evidences in favour of this opinion.

By the author of the "Baronettage," lady Pakington is spoken of as a bright example to her age, and one of the most learned and accomplished of her sex. " Her letters," says he, " and other discourses, still remaining in the hands of her family and friends, are an admirable proof of her genius and capacity. She had the reputation of being the writer of ' The Whole Duty of Man,' the truth of which none who knew her, or were competent judges of her abilities, would call in question. Though her modesty would not suffer her to claim the honour, yet as the manuscript, in her handwriting, now remains with the family, there is scarcely room for doubt. By her virtues and attainments she acquired the esteem of all our learned divines, who confessed themselves edified by her conversation, and instructed by her writings. These gentlemen never failed of an agreeable retreat and sanctuary at Westwood, as far as those dangerous times would permit. It ought to be remembered, to the honour of this lady and her husband, that Dr. Hammond found in their family a comfortable sub-

LADY PAKINGTON.   41

sistence for several years, and at last reposed his bones in their burial-place at Hampton-Lovett, in a chapel built by sir Thomas Pakington, in 1561."

Farther proofs respecting the subject in dispute may be found in " A Letter from a Clergyman in the Country, to a dignified Clergyman in London ; vindicating the Bill brought the last Session of Parliament, for preventing the Translation of Bishops ;" printed in London, 1702. The writer of this letter, after an eulogium on the ancestors of sir John Pakington *, adds, " but his grandfather's spending 40,000l. and being tried for his life during the late civil wars, because he vigorously endeavoured to prevent the martyrdom of king Charles I. and the destruction of episcopacy; the uninterrupted correspondence of his grandmother with the learned and pious Dr. Morley, bishop of Winton, and Dr. Hammond, and who is, by several eminent men (archbishop Dolben, bishop Fell, and Dr. Abbestry, declared this of their own knowledge after her death, which she obliged them to keep private during her life) allowed to be the author of the best and most masculine religious book extant in the English tongue, called 'The Whole Duty of Man;' will serve instead of a heap of instances to shew how great

---

* By whom the bill was brought into the house.

regards this family have formerly paid to the church and kingly government."

A transcript is also given, by Ballard, from a paper said to be in the possession of Dr. Snape, provost of King's-college, Cambridge, in which is the following attestation: "October 19th, 1698, Mr. Thomas Caulton, vicar of Worksop in Nottinghamshire, declared on his death-bed, in the presence of William Thornton, esq. and his lady, Mrs. Heathcote, Mrs. Ash, Mrs. Caulton, and others, as follows: viz. ' On the 5th of November, 1689, at Shire-Oaks, Mrs. Eyre * took me up into her chamber after dinner, and told me that her daughter Moyser of Beverly was dead. Afterwards, among other private affairs of the family, she told me who was the author of The Whole Duty of Man; at the same time pulling out of a private drawer a manuscript tied together, and stiched in octavo, which she declared was the original, written by

---

* The wife of Anthony Eyre, esq. of Rampton in Nottingham, who, after the revolution, wrote and published a pamphlet entitled, " The Opinion of Mrs. Eyre, Daughter of the excellent Lady Pakington, concerning the Doctrine of Passive Obedience, as the distinguishing Character of the Church of England; in a letter to a friend, occasioned by bishop Lake's declaration, that he died in the belief thereof:" London, 1689 and 1710, 8vo.

lady Pakington, her mother, who disowned ever having written the other books attributed to the same author, excepting The Causes of the Decay of Christian Piety. She added, that the manuscript had been perused by Dr. Covil, master of Trinity college, Cambridge; Dr. Stamford, prebend of York; and Mr. Binks, rector of the great church of Hull.'"

By lady Pakington's disowning the works attributed to her, it seems merely to be implied, that she did not directly avow or claim them. "The Whole Duty of Man," was published by bishop Fell, with other treatises, as declaredly the production of the same author. Having thus stated the evidence on this subject, the decision must be left with the reader. The underwritten is a catalogue of the works attributed to the author of "The Whole Duty of Man," which was first printed in 1657, and translated into Latin by Dr. Richard Lucas, and into Welsh by Dr. William Bell.

"The Causes of the Decay of Christian Piety, or an impartial Survey of the Ruins of the Christian Religion undermined by unchristian Practices," London, 1725.

"The Gentleman's Calling," London, 1725.

"The Lady's Calling, in two Parts," London, 1725.

44 LADY PAKINGTON.

" The Government of the Tongue," London, 1725.

" The Art of Contentment," London, 1725.

" The lively Oracles given to us, or the Christian's Birthright and Duty in the Custody and Use of the Holy Scriptures," London, 1725.

" A Prayer for King Charles II. in his Banishment," and a " Prayer for Resignation," are given by Ballard, copied by a lady from a manuscript of lady Pakington's at Westwood. She had, some time before her death, been engaged in a work entitled " The Government of the Thoughts," which was mentioned by Dr. Fell in high terms, but never finished. The following eulogium is given by Dr. Fell to the writer of these treatises : " She was wise, humble, temperate, chaste, patient, charitable, and devout; she lived a whole age of great austerities, and maintained in the midst of them an undisturbed serenity."

Lady Pakington died May 10th, 1679, and was interred in the church at Hampton-Lovett in Worcestershire; a memorial of her is inscribed at the bottom of a monument erected to her husband. Sir John Pakington expended the greater part of his fortune in the service of king Charles I. in adhering to whose cause he was tried for his life.

Ballard's British Ladies—The Female Worthies.

[43]

ANNE DE PARTHENAI.

ANNE DE PARTHENAI, wife to Anthony de Pons, count de Marennes, was the daughter of John de Parthenai l'Archenesque, and of Michelli de Sorbonne, a lady of Bretagne. Michelli, the mother of Anne, was a woman of wit and talents, and lady of honour to Anne of Bretagne, wife to Lewis XII. by whom she was appointed governess to her daughter, Renata, duchess of Ferrara. Anne received, under the superintendance of her mother, a learned education; she made great progress in the knowledge of the languages, and became a student in theology, respecting which she took a pleasure in reasoning and disputing with the most celebrated theologians of the times. She was also skilled in music, and an accomplished performer both vocal and instrumental. Her interest and favour with the duchess of Ferrara, added to her theological studies, drew on her, from the catholics, the suspicion of calvinism. On this subject we have from Theodorus Beza, in his "Ecclesiastical History," a direct testimony. By him we are informed, that Antony de Pons, count de Marennes, during the life of his firſt wife, the lady Anne de Parthenai, sister to the lord of Soubise, was a lover of truth and virtue, and particularly conversant with

46   ANNE DE PARTHENAI.

the Scriptures, himself instructing, with great zeal and labour, his subjects and officers in the city of Pons. But that, after the decease of his excellent and amiable consort, " God so took away his understanding, that he espoused one of the most defamed ladies of France, Mary de Monchenu, the lady de Massey; and became, from that period, an enemy and persecutor of the truth, which he had before studiously promoted."

The influence of Anne de Parthenai over the mind of her husband, is also mentioned by Gregory Gyraldus, who testifies, that the count de Marennes and his wife pursued the same studies, with the same success. Count Marennes was first gentleman of the bedchamber to the duke of Ferrara, to whom Gyraldus dedicated the fourth dialogue of his " History of the Poets." Soubise, brother to Anne de Parthenai, was one of the principal supports of the huguenot party. The count de Marennes was obliged to leave the court of Ferrara, for presuming to compare the dignity and antiquity of his own family with that of the duchess of Ferrara, whom he served.

Bayle's Historical Dictionary, &c.

[47]

CATHERINE DE PARTHENAI.

CATHERINE, daughter and heiress of John de Parthenia lord of Soubise, and niece to Anne de Parthenai, was born in 1554. In 1568 she married Charles de Quellence, baron de Pons, who, three years afterwards, fell in the general massacre of the huguenots on the fatal night of St. Bartholomew, 1571. He fought bravely on this occasion, and sold his life dear. Catherine deplored his loss in several elegiac poems. In 1573, she entered a second time into the married state, and espoused Renatus viscount Rohan, the second of that name, by whom she had several children. In 1586, she was again left a widow, at thirty-two years of age. She refused to enter into any new engagement, determined to devote the remainder of her life to the care and education of her family.

Her maternal affection and solicitude were amply rewarded. The celebrated duke de Rohan, her eldest son, supported with great spirit and bravery the cause of the Reformation, during the civil wars, in the reign of Lewis XIII. Her second son was the duke of Soubise. She had three daughters: Henrietta, who died in 1629, unmarried; Catherine, who gave her hand to a duke of Deux-Ponts, and

48   CATHERINE DE PARTHENAI.

who is celebrated for her reply to Henry IV. who, enamoured of her charms, solicited her love: ' I am too poor,' said she, ' to be your wife, and too nobly descended to be your mistress.' Her third daughter Anne, who also lived single, and who survived all her brothers and sisters, inherited the genius and magnanimity of her mother, with whom she bore all the calamities of the siege of Rochelle. The courage of Catherine de Parthenai, on this occasion, was the more worthy of admiration for her advanced age, being then in her seventy-fifth year. Reduced, for three months, to the necessity of living upon horse flesh and four ounces of bread a-day, in this situation she wrote to her son ' to go on as he had begun, nor suffer any extremities to which she might be reduced, however severe, to induce him to take measures that might prejudice the cause he had espoused.' Having, with her daughter, refused to be included in the articles of capitulation, they were conveyed, prisoners of war, to the castle of Niort, in 1628. She died at Poitou, 1631, greatly lamented.

She possessed a taste for poetical composition, and published some poems in 1572, when only eighteen years of age. In 1574, a tragedy of her composing, entitled " Holofernes," was represented on the theatre at Rochelle. " She understood poetry," says La Croix du Main*, " and is much to be esteemed for the excellency of her wit, which her writings sufficiently testify. She composed several tragedies and comedies in French, among others the tragedy of Holofernes, publicly acted at Rochelle. She wrote also several poems or elegies, on the death of her first husband, who lost his life in the massacre of St. Bartholomew; likewise upon the admiral and other great and illustrious persons who perished on the same occasion. She translated the precepts of Isocrates to Demonicus, not yet printed. She is in great repute," continues he, " this year (1584)." If it be true, as asserted by a learned man, that madame de Parthenai, lady of Soubise, was spoken of as an author before madame de Rohan was known, she must indeed have written very young, since she married at fourteen years of age. A concealed but keen satire upon Henry IV. under the title of an apology, is generally attributed to this lady, and in the new edition of the Journal of Henry III. it is printed as hers. D'Aubigné thus speaks of this work: " The king shewed it some, as being in the style of madame de Rohan. It is a prevaricating apology, of which Roquelaire cried out, ' Oh, how well the authors of that piece

---

* La Croix du Main, Biblioth. Francoise, p. 478. Baillet.

are informed of what we do !'" Bayle declares, that whoever composed the *Apology* was a person of wit and talents.

Bayle's Historical Dictionary—Biographium Fæmineum.

PAULINA.

Seneca having been condemned to death, his wife Paulina opened her veins, that she might die with her husband ; but, having been compelled to live, she appeared (says Tacitus) the few years she survived, with an honourable paleness, which attested her conjugal attachment, and that a part of her blood had flowed with that of her husband.

PERILLA,

A Roman lady, who, in the age of Augustus, was distinguished for her erudition and poetical talents. She is celebrated by Ovid, whose scholar in poetry she appears to have been. Her reputation for chastity is, notwithstanding, unblemished.

[51]

SUSANNA PERWICH.

SUSANNA, daughter of Robert Perwich of Hackney, Middlesex, was born September 23d, 1636, in the parish of Aldermanbury, London. She displayed almost in infancy an uncommon capacity and thirst of knowledge. When under seven years of age she appeared eager for instruction, and delighted in acquiring information by her own exertions. In the eighth year of her age, her father undertook the superintendance of a school at Hackney, whither he removed his residence. In this situation, Susanna made rapid improvements in every accomplishment usually taught to her sex. She devoted herself more particularly to music : at fourteen years of age she was a perfect mistress of the treble viol, on which she played, whether singly or in concert, with exquisite skill and effect, giving promise of extraordinary musical powers. Her judgment and knowledge of the theory of music was not less excellent than her ear and execution : she studied her favourite art as a science, and was skilful in composition. She played also on the lute with great taste and sweetness, accompanying the instrument with her voice, which was fine and melodious. She learned some lessons on the harpsichord, on which she wanted only leisure and practice to become a proficient. She was a graceful and incomparable dancer, and carried to excellence every thing which she undertook.

The fame of her musical powers attracted the connoisseurs and masters of the art, both foreigners and natives, who visited her in great numbers, and to whom she gave by her performance universal satisfaction. She excelled likewise in needlework, in writing, in arithmetic, and in domestic order and management. Nor was she less distinguished for intellectual powers, for quickness of apprehension, wit, imagination, judgment, memory, invention, and taste. To these advantages she added a sweetness and gentleness of temper, modesty, courtesy, prudence, and good sense. Her person was beautiful, and her manners graceful and engaging.

She suffered an early disappointment in her affections, from the death of a young man to whom she was tenderly attached, and to whom she was about to have been united. This misfortune seized on her spirits, while grief and sensibility prepared her mind for the reception of ardent devotional impressions. Her education and habits had been pious, and her heart, disappointed in its object, yielded itself to that sublime and flattering enthusiasm so congenial to fervent and susceptible tempers. Neglecting those elegant and liberal pursuits which had former-

SUSANNA PERWICH. 53

ly engaged her time and attention, she devoted herself wholly to those studies and observances which
she fondly believed would fit her to meet the friend she
had lost in a world of more stable enjoyment. The
fanatic character of the times gave strength to these
dispositions, and tinged her ideas with its sombre
colouring; dwelling on the calvinistic notions of
original sin, predestination, and sovereign grace, she
tortured her pure and innocent mind with fancied
sins, doubts, and omissions. Among the books
which she perused with the greatest avidity were
" Shepard's True Convert" and " Sound Believer,"
" Baxter's Call to the Unconverted," " Goodwin's
Triumph of Faith," " Brooke's Riches of Grace,"
and others of a similar character. As her scrupulosity increased with these pursuits, she denied herself the recreation of music, or practised it only for
spiritual uses and occasions. The necessary and
daily occupations of the family at length became
burthensome to her, as an interruption of her pious
exercises. She abjured all innocent relaxation, nor
could longer be prevailed upon to join in the dance,
or in the amusements of her young companions.
Rigidly severe to herself, she dreaded lest vanity, or
complacency in her acquirements, should unwarily
obtrude itself on her mind; she renounced every
ornament of dress, and imposed on herself the most

austere observances : all the energy of her character was directed against her own happiness ; she seemed to believe that the God of Nature required of his creatures a moral martyrdom, and a perpetual suicide of every natural and laudable propensity. But this morose and cruel system, to which she offered herself a voluntary victim, was yet insufficient to sour the natural amenity and sweetness of her temper : amidst the sacrifice of her reason, her duties, and her happiness, she was still gentle, amiable, and affectionate.

She rejected several solicitations of marriage, declaring that no worldly advantages should induce her to change her situation : she required a certain spiritual perfection in the person to whom she should give her hand, that probably was not easily to be met with.

In June, 1661, during the Whitsuntide vacation, she was prevailed upon to visit a friend in London, where, from sleeping in damp linen, she contracted a cold, that brought on a fever, which terminated in her death. On the 8th of June she returned to the house of her father, fully persuaded, from the symptoms she experienced, that the hour of her dissolution approached : as her disorder increased she displayed great fortitude, patience, and resignation, conversing calmly with her friends on religious subjects, and distributing to them small presents to

PHILA.

be kept as memorials of her. She gave orders respecting her funeral, and preserved, notwithstanding severe sufferings, her gentleness and equanimity to the last. She died with courage and composure, in the twenty-fifth year of her age, lamented by her family and regretted by her friends. Her relations and the young ladies her companions, six of whom bore up the pall, attended her remains to the grave, which were followed by persons of the first rank and respectability in the neighbourhood. Her funeral sermon was preached by Dr. Spurstow, from 1 Cor. iii. 22. Her praises were celebrated in verse and prose, in elegy, acrostic, and anagram.

> *The Life of Mrs. Susanna Perwich, written in Prose and Verse, by John Batchiler, London, 1661, and dedicated to "all the young Ladies of the several Schools in and about London, more particularly to those of Mrs. Perwich's School at Hackney."*

PHILA.

PHILA, the daughter of Antipater, governor of Macedonia during the absence of Alexander, was the most beautiful and accomplished women of the age. The dignity of her manners and the lustre of her charms, were softened by an air of modesty and sweetness that engaged all hearts. She possessed, with uncommon prudence and judgment, a superior genius, and a capacity for the most important affairs. Her father never engaged in any enterprise without consulting her; while she used her influence with him in the cause only of virtue and humanity. Her liberality procured her absolute power among the troops; all cabals were dissolved in her presence, and all revolts appeased by her mediation. By her knowledge of the human heart, her address, and facility of accommodating her measures to various tempers and characters, she prevented an insurrection in an army full of turbulence and faction. Nor was her administration in civil affairs less skilful and admirable. She portioned young women at her own expence, protected innocence, and opposed oppression. She seems to have been but little indebted to experience for her capacity; her father, distinguished for his political abilities, entrusted to the management of Phila, when at a very early age, the juridical affairs of the kingdom.

She gave her hand to Craterus, one of the captains of Alexander, and the most popular among the Macedonians. Craterus fell in battle, and, after his decease, his widow became the chief wife of Demetrius, who, according to the custom of the East, in which polygamy was allowed, possessed several of inferior merit and quality. This marriage proved unhappy: Phila suffered, not merely from the di-

PHILA. 57

vided affections of her husband, but by his dissolute conduct. Attached to the celebrated Lamia, and corrupted by her seductions, Demetrius treated his wife with coldness and disrespect. Yet he confided in her abilities, and deputed her to Cassander, her brother, to justify his conduct towards Plistarchus, whom he had offended. He also shewed high indignation against the Rhodians, who had presented to the king of Egypt a ship which they had captured, in which was a letter, accompanied by a magnificent present, addressed to him by Phila.

Demetrius having lost his dominions, the fortitude of Phila sunk under the prospect of impending calamities: unable to see the husband, who had treated her unworthily, a fugitive and an exile, she swallowed poison, and terminated her sorrows with her life. She left by her second marriage two children, a son and a daughter, the celebrated Stratonice, wife to Seleucus, and by him yielded to his son Antiochus, who had conceived a passion for his stepmother.

Rollin's Ancient History—Bayle's Historical Dictionary—Biographium Fœmineum.

[58]

PHILIPPA.

PHILIPPA, daughter to the count of Hainault, was espoused to Edward III. king of England. During the absence of Edward in France, David king of Scotland, with 50,000 men, invaded the northern counties of England. Philippa, superior to the weakness of her sex, prepared, on this occasion, with spirit, to repel the enemy. Having assembled an army of 12,000 men, and appointed lord Percy to the supreme command, she rode through the ranks, and, in person, exhorted the troops to fulfil, with courage, their duty ; nor would she be persuaded to retire from the field, till the armies were on the point of engaging. In this battle the king of Scots was taken prisoner. Philippa, having secured her royal captive, crossed the sea at Dover, and was received at Calais with triumph and enthusiasm.

The story of the burghers of Calais, who had devoted themselves for the salvation of their fellow-citizens, and who were indebted for the mercy of Edward to the tears and supplications of Philippa, appears to have been romantic and ill-founded. It accords but little with the temper of the times, or with the brave and generous character of Edward. Many

KATHERINE PHILLIPS. 59

extraordinary women appeared with lustre at this period, which was the reign of gallantry and chivalry.

Hume's History of England.

KATHERINE PHILLIPS.

KATHERINE, celebrated under the poetical name of Orinda, daughter of John Fowler, of Bucklers-bury, London, merchant, and of Katherine, daughter of Daniel Oxenbridge, M.D. was born in the parish of St. Mary Wool-church, London, January 1, 1631. A female relation, Mrs Blacket, had the charge of her infancy and early childhood. At eight years of age, she was placed in a school at Hackney, under the care of Mrs. Salmon, where her improvements were singular and rapid. She displayed an early taste for poetical composition, and a devotional turn of mind, somewhat enthusiastic, originating probably in the sensibility of temper inseparable from genius, and in the spirit and manners of the times. She had perused the Bible throughout before she was four years of age, and had committed to memory many passages and chapters. At ten years of age she would repeat, with scarce any omissions, entire sermons, of which she was a frequent hearer. She also began early to exercise her fancy in poetical composition. She acquired a perfect knowledge of the French language,

60   KATHERINE PHILLIPS.

and applied herself successfully to the Italian, with
the assistance of an ingenious friend, sir Charles
Cotterel. She was educated in the principles of the
presbyterian dissenters, but became afterwards a pro-
selyte to the established church, and the royalist party.

In the year 1647, she gave her hand to James
Phillips, esq. of the priory of Cardigan. A son
and a daughter were the fruit of this union : the
former died in his infancy, the latter became the
wife of —— Wogan, esq. of Pembrokeshire. The
fortune of Mr. Phillips being encumbered and embarrassed, Mrs. Phillips, by her economy, prudence,
and excellent management, added to her interest
with sir Charles Cotterel, whose friendship for her
rendered him zealous in the cause of her husband,
nearly extricated him, in the course of a few years,
from the difficulties in which he had been involved.
Mrs. Phillips, in a letter to sir Charles, after speaking of her husband with respect and attachment,
adds, " and I hope God will enable me to answer
his expectations, by making me an instrument of
doing him essential service, which is the only ambition I have in the world, and which I would purchase with the hazard of my life. I am exceedingly obliged to my lady Cork, for remembering me
with so much indulgence ; but above all for her
readiness to assist my endeavours for Antenor *,

---

* Mr. Phillips.

which is the most generous kindness that can be done to me."

During her retirement at Cardigan, she cultivated poetry as an amusement, to beguile her solitary hours. Copies of her poems being dispersed among her friends, they were collected and published anonymously, in 8vo. 1663, without the knowledge or consent of the author. Mrs. Phillips's vexation at this circumstance, which she appears acutely to feel, and sensibly laments in a letter to sir Charles Cotterel, occasioned her a severe fit of illness.

The charms of her conversation, her modesty, sweetness, and unassuming manners, rendered her the delight of her acquaintance, while her genius and talents procured her the friendship of men distinguished for their merit, their talents, and their rank, among whom may be mentioned the earls of Ormond, Orrery, and Roscommon. The affairs of Mr. Phillips having rendered the presence of his wife necessary in Ireland, she accompanied thither the viscountess Dungannon, and was received with distinction and esteem. During her residence in that kingdom, she was induced, by the importunity of the before-mentioned noblemen, to translate into English, from the French of Corneille, the tragedy of Pompey, which was acted with applause on the Irish stage, in 1663, also in 1664, when it was printed and given to the public. It was likewise again performed, with considerable success, at the duke of York's theatre, in 1678. This play, to which a prologue was added by lord Roscommon, was then published, dedicated to the countess of Cork.

Mrs. Phillips also translated, from the French of Corneille, the tragedy of Horace, to which a fifth act was added by sir John Denham, and which was represented by persons of rank at court, with a prologue, spoken by the duke of Monmouth.

In Ireland, Mrs. Phillips renewed a former friendship with the celebrated Dr. Jeremy Taylor, bishop of Down and Connor, who some time previously had published and inscribed to her, " A Discourse of the Nature, Offices, and Measures, of Friendship, with Rules of conducting it; in a Letter to the most ingenious and excellent Mrs. Katherine Phillips." In this production many high compliments are paid to the sex, to their capacity for friendship, and the more elevated virtues, exemplified by allusions to the celebrated characters of antiquity.

July 15th, 1663, Mrs. Phillips left Ireland, and returned to Cardigan, where she appears to have laboured under a depression of spirits, occasioned by some untoward circumstances in her husband's affairs. She continued in the country through the remainder of that year, and a part of the following,

KATHERINE PHILLIPS. 63

when she made a visit to London, with a view of
unbending her mind, and softening her anxieties, in
the society and conversation of her friends. In
London she was unfortunately seized with the small-
pox, which proving fatal, she expired, universally
regretted, in apartments in Fleet-street, June 22,
1664, in the thirty-fourth year of her age, and was
interred in the church of St. Bennet Sheer-hog, in
her family vault, under a large monumental stone.

She was of middle stature, as described by Mr.
Aubry, inclining to fat; her complexion was fair
and ruddy. Her poems and translations were, after
her decease, collected and published in one volume
folio, 1667, and entitled " Poems, by the most deservedly admired Mrs. Katherine Phillips, the matchless Orinda: to which are added, M. Corneille's
Pompey and Horace, Tragedies, with several
other Translations from the French; and her picture
before them, engraved by Faithorre." A second edition was printed in 1678, in the preface to which
the reader is told, " that Mrs. Phillips wrote familiar letters with facility, in a very fair hand, and
perfect orthography ; which, if collected, with the
excellent discourses written by her on various subjects, would make a volume much larger than her
poems." In 1705, a small volume of her letters to
sir Charles Cotterel was published, under the title
of " Letters from Orinda to Poliarchus." In one

64   KATHERINE PHILLIPS.

of these letters, Mrs. Phillips mentions the insertion
of some of her Poems in a miscellaneous collection published in Ireland. The following testimony
to the merit of the Letters of Orinda to Poliarchus,
is given by major Puck, in his Essay on Study :
" The best letters I have met with in our English
tongue, are those of the celebrated Mrs. Phillips,
to sir Charles Cotterel. They are all addressed to
the same person, so they run all in the same strain,
and seem to have been employed in the service of a
refined and generous friendship. In a word, they
are such as a woman of spirit and virtue should
write to a courtier of honour and true gallantry."
Mrs. Phillips is said, by Mr. Langbain, to have
equalled the Lesbian Sappho in genius, and the Roman Sulpicia in virtue. To this he adds, " as they
were praised by Horace, Martial, Ausonius, and other
eminent poets, so was this lady commended by the
earls of Orrery and Roscommon, by Cowley, and
other eminent men." An anonymous writer, in the
second volume of the duke of Wharton's works,
thus speaks of Mrs. Phillips : " I have been
looking into the writings of Mrs. Phillips, and have
been wonderfully pleased with her solid and masculine thoughts, in no feminine style. Her refined
and rational ideas of friendship, a subject she delights in, shew a soul above the common level of
mankind, and raise my desire of practising what is

LÆTITIA PILKINGTON.   65

thus nobly described. Though I know nothing of Mrs. Phillips but what I have learned from her Poems, I am persuaded she was not less discreet, good-humoured, modest, constant, and virtuous, than ingenious. Her " Country Life" is a sweet poem, sprinkled with profound philosophical thoughts, expressed in very poetical language."

To the praise of talents, universally allowed to this lady by her contemporaries, is added that of generosity and benevolence. The qualities of the heart, united to those of the mind, form a combination equally admirable and rare. Four letters from Mrs. Phillips to the hon. Berenice, are inserted in a collection of letters published by Mr. Thomas Brown, 1697. A tribute of respect is paid to her memory by Mr. Thomas Rowe, in his " Epistle to Daphnis."

Ballard's British Ladies—Biographium Fæmineum, &c.

LÆTITIA PILKINGTON.

LÆTITIA, the daughter of Dr. Vanlewin, a physician, was born in Dublin, 1712. She married young to the rev. Matthew Pilkington, a poet. This union was not happy. Mr. Pilkington was jealous of his wife, in whose chamber he one day found a gentleman, and from whom he obtained a separation. Mrs. Pilkington, in her Memoirs, not-

66   MRS. PIX.

withstanding that appearances were against her, asserts her innocence. She had afterwards recourse
to her pen for her support, and raised a considerable
subscription on her Memoirs, in which many anecdotes are given of Dr. Swift, with whom the writer was intimately acquainted. She died in poverty,
in July, 1750, in consequence of the pernicious habit of intoxication, into which she had fallen, to
lose the sense of her misfortunes. She left several
children, whom her husband renounced. John, the
eldest, was the author of some poems; he also wrote
his own Memoirs, and died in 1763. Mrs. Pilkington, beside her poems and Memoirs, wrote a burlesque piece, entitled " The Turkish Court, or
the London Prentice," acted in Dublin, 1748. She
also wrote one act of " The Roman Father," which
is printed in her Memoirs.

Biographium Fæmineum.

MRS. PIX.

MARY GRIFFITH, the daughter of a clergyman,
and descended on the side of her mother from the
family of Wallis, was born at Nettlebed, in Oxfordshire, in the reign of William III. She was a contemporary with Mrs. Manley, and with Mrs. Cockburne, and was satirised with them in a little dramatic
piece, called " The Female Wits." She was the

DIANA DE POITIERS. 67

author of the following plays : " The Spanish
Wives," 4to. 1696 : " Ibrahim XIII. Emperor of
the Turks," 4to. 1696 : " The Innocent Mistress,"
4to, 1697: " The Deceiver deceived," 4to. 1698 :
" Queen Catherine, or the Ruins of Love," 4to.
1698 : " The False Friend, or the Fate of Disobedience," 4to. 1699: " The Czar of Muscovy,"
4to. 1701 : " The Double Distress," 4to. 1701 :
" The Conquest of Spain," 4to. 1705 : " The
Beau defeated, or the Lucky Younger Brother,"
4to*. She married a Mr. Pix, by which name only
she was known.

DIANA DE POITIERS.

JOHN DE POITIERS, seigneur de St. Vallier, was
in 1523 condemned to die, as an accomplice in the
revolt of the constable of Bourbon. His sentence
was however changed; he escaped with life, and
suffered a degradation from his rank, with the confiscation of his estates. According to Mezerai, the
president Henault, and other writers, the life of
her father was saved by Diana de Poitiers, by the
sacrifice of her chastity to Francis I. from whose
embraces she passed into those of his son, Henry II.
This story is, however, very doubtful, and most

---

* The latter is in some catalogues ascribed to Mr. Barker.

68 DIANA DE POITIERS.

probably false, as, at the time of her father's disgrace, Diana had been married ten years to Louis de Breze, count de Maulevrier, and grand-senechal of Normandy, to whom she bore two daughters. Beside which, the punishment of St. Vallier, though delivered from death, was commuted into one not less terrible: he was sentenced, after his degradation, to be perpetually immured between four walls, in which was only one small window, through which he might receive his provisions. The horror he experienced at the idea of his fate, brought on a fever, which in a short time terminated his life.

Diana had been married to the senechal of Normandy, in the last year of the reign of Lewis XII.: at what time her connection with Henry II. commenced, is uncertain; but, before he had completed his eighteenth year, her ascendency over him was established. To personal endowments she added talents, vivacity, and a cultivated understanding: she was warmly devoted to her friends, but a dangerous and implacable enemy: her spirit was high and unyielding, and she transfused into the mind of her lover the firmness and vigour of her own character. Not more fond of power than of flattery and homage, she received with pleasure the adulation of the court, while the nobles crowded around her to express their devotion. Even the constable Montmorenci, notwithstanding his severe and haughty

DIANA DE POITIERS.   69

manners, condescended to mix in her train. In vain had the duchess d'Estampes*, during the life of Francis, essayed every art of hatred and of rivalry to disunite from Diana her youthful lover : in vain did she publish, that the mistress of the prince was married in the same year which gave birth to herself : the passion of Henry, which was carried to the utmost extravagance, appeared to be increased rather than diminished by these efforts.   He seemed to delight in giving testimonies of his attachment, both in public and in private, and in displaying to the world the influence of Diana.   The furniture of the palace, after he ascended the throne, the public edifices, his own armour, were all ornamented and emblazoned by a " moon, bow and arrows," the emblems and the device of his mistress.   Through her mediation every favour was obtained : at her request Brassac, a gallant and amiable nobleman, who was supposed to stand high in her favour, was created grand-master of the artillery.   She may be said to have divided the crown with her lover, of whose council she was the directing principle, and of whose tender and ardent attachment she was the sole object.   Her influence, both personal and political, was carried to an unbounded extent.   Time

---

* The favourite mistress of Francis I.

seemed to have no power over her attractions: her beauty appeared undiminished even in the autumn of her life: she was forty-eight years of age when Henry had scarcely attained his twenty-ninth year.

After the death of Francis, the duchess d'Estrampes was compelled to quit the court, but Diana, who succeeded to her honours, had either the magnanimity or the prudence to forbear to deprive her of the possessions lavished on her by the late monarch: she was content to suffer her to retire, disgraced and neglected, to one of her country seats, where she lived in obscurity many years.

While the duke of Guise and the constable Montmorenci were in Guienne, employed in quelling an insurrection, festivals and carousals engaged the court, in which Diana de Poitiers (created by her lover duchess de Valentinois), in whose honour they were given, presided as a tutelar deity. On these occasions the young queen, Catherine de Medicis, whose genius, taste, and beauty, rendered her inferior to no one, acted a subordinate and humiliating part. Catherine, notwithstanding her talents and superior powers of mind, was never admitted by her husband to any real participation in the government. These entertainments and tournaments were, in the spirit of the age, succeeded by spectacles of a very different nature. A number of proselytes to

DIANA DE POITIERS.   71

the doctrines of the Reformation were publicly and solemnly burnt at the stake, while the court attended these barbarous exhibitions.

The house of Guise, which had firmly united itself with the duchess de Valentinois, whose ascendancy over the king seemed daily to acquire strength, continued to establish and aggrandise itself. The profusion of the court, added to the expence of the wars in which France was engaged, rendered it necessary to increase the revenues by taxes and imposts; while the odium of these exactions chiefly rested on the duchess. Henry, amiable, magnificent, and flexible to those he loved, was wholly governed by the suggestions of his mistress, whom he enabled to erect the superb palace of Anet, to which the lovers frequently retired. The people, ignorant and superstitious, attributed to magic and sorcery the attachment of the king, and the fascinations of Diana: it was reported that she wore magical rings, which preserved her beauty from decay, and kept alive the passion of her lover. This opinion, so soothing to her own pride, was supported and confirmed by Catherine de Medicis. Anet was situated near Dreux, in the Isle of France, upon the river Eure. Philibert de Lorme was the architect employed in its construction: the emblems and devices of the duchess de Valentinois were exhibited in every part. Voltaire, in the ninth canto of the Henriade, depictures love as on his flight to the palace of Anet.

Brantome, who was personally acquainted with the duchess, describes her beauty in its most advanced periods. " I beheld Diana," says he, " only six months before her death. Even then she was so lovely, that the most insensible could not behold her without emotion. She was recovering from a severe indisposition, occasioned by the fracture of her leg, which had been broken by a fall from her horse in riding through the streets of Orleans : yet neither the accident nor the pain had diminished her charms." The duchess was at this time sixty-five years of age.

After the death of Henry, who was accidentally killed in a tournament, his mistress received orders from the queen to retire to her own house, which command she thought proper to obey. A second mandate followed, enjoining her to deliver up the jewels of the crown, with other rich effects in her possession. She enquired if the monarch yet breathed, ' for know,' said she, ' so long as he shall retain the appearance of life, I neither fear my enemies, however powerful, nor will shew any deference to their menaces or commands. Carry this answer to the queen.' The duchess had borne to her lover no children. The Guises, after the death of the king, sacrificed Diana to make their court to the queen; while, abandoned by the flatterers and parasites who had surrounded her, the duchess in her turn suffered humiliation. She retired from a situation where her power was extinguished, and her presence become odious, and passed the remainder of her life at the palace of Anet. Catherine, from respect to the memory of her husband, permitted her rival to retain the rich presents which his bounty had lavished upon her.

The maréchal de Tavannes, with a brutal and unmanly adulation, offered to the queen to cut off the nose of Diana; while the Guises, connected with her by marriage, and principally indebted to her for their elevation and favour, became her open enemies. The cardinal of Lorrain * would have been her bitterest persecutor, had he not been restrained by his brother, the duke of Aumale, who had married the daughter of the duchess, and who reminded him, that he would by such conduct draw down infamy upon himself. The constable of Montmorenci alone remained faithful to her, and, from respect to the memory of the king his benefactor, withstood the enemies of his beloved mistress. Diana expressed her gratitude for the queen's forbearance, by presenting to her the palace of Chaumont sur

---

* One of the princes of the house of Guise.

VOL. VI.   E

74   PORCIA.

Loire, and received from her in return the castle of
Chenonceaux.

The last public act of the duchess of Valentinois
was the being recalled to court, by Catherine, to try
her powers of persuasion upon Montmorenci, whom
the queen was desirous of attaching to her party.
Diana succeeded, and, after this proof of her influence over the constable, returned to Anet. She
survived this event five years, and died in the sixty-
seventh year of her age, April 26, 1566. Her
body reposes under a marble mausoleum, in the centre of the choir of the great chapel of Anet, which
she had herself erected.

*Wraxall's History of the House of Valois—Bayle's
Historical Dictionary—History of France.*

PORCIA.

Porcia, the daughter of Cato of Utica, inherited
the virtues and the magnanimity of her father. She
strengthened her mind, and cultivated her understanding, by the study of philosophy. She married
Bibulus, and, after his death, gave her hand to Brutus,
of whom she was worthy, and to whom she proved
her fidelity and courage. Having observed that her
husband appeared to be meditating some important
enterprise, she was solicitous to share in his glory, or
in his cares, and to deserve his confidence, which

PORCIA.

she resolved not to ask till she had made trial of her own fortitude. With this view, she inflicted a deep wound on her thigh, the pain of which, added to the loss of blood, brought on a dangerous malady. She carefully concealed for some time the cause of her illness; till, observing her husband overwhelmed with grief and concern on her account, she seized this opportunity of addressing him. As the daughter of Cato, she told him, she had a claim to expect, not merely the common courtesies and civilities of an ordinary wife or concubine, but to share in the thoughts and counsels, in the good and evil fortune, of her husband : and that, whatever weakness might be imputed to her sex, her birth, education, and honourable connections, had strengthened her mind, and formed her to superior qualities. But, though the daughter of Cato, and the wife of Brutus, titles in which she gloried, she had not boasted of her fortitude, but upon trial, that had proved her invincible to pain and inconvenience. Having thus spoken, she discovered to Brutus her wound, and related the cause in which it had originated.

Brutus, affected, and struck with tenderness and admiration, raised his hands to heaven, and implored the gods to assist his enterprise, that he might live to prove himself worthy a wife like Porcia. He then imparted to her the project of fleeing Rome, and restoring the republic, by the death of Julius Cæsar.

The courage which had sustained the daughter of Cato under her own sufferings, deserted her in the danger of her husband. On the day appointed for the assassination of Cæsar, Porcia, previous to its execution, sunk under the agitation of her spirits: she was seized with a succession of fainting fits, when her attendants, believing her dead, abandoned themselves to grief and lamentation. The rumour of her death reached Brutus, who, notwithstanding his grief and concern, shrunk not from the purpose he had undertaken. Cæsar fell, a victim to a virtuous, but mistaken, patriotism: a combination of causes had conspired to the ruin of the republic, and to the subjugation of the Roman people, which the death of an individual was insufficient to counteract.

Brutus, perceiving he had failed in the end for which means so questionable had been adopted, resolved to leave Italy: passing by land through Lucania to Elea, by the sea-side, he there took leave of his wife, it being judged necessary that she should return to Rome. The daughter of Cato, struggling with her feelings, assumed on this separation an appearance of firmness; but a picture which hung on the wall, representing the parting of Hector and Andromache, accidentally meeting

MODESTO POZZO.   **77**

her eyes, overcame her resolution. Gazing earnestly on the figure of Hector, delivering the young
Astyanax into the arms of his mother, she melted
into tenderness and tears. A friend of Brutus, who
was present on this occasion, repeated from Homer
the address of the Trojan princess to her husband—

" Be careful, Hector, for with thee my *all*,
  My father, mother, brother, husband, fall."

Brutus replied, smiling, ' I must not answer Porcia
in the words of Hector to Andromache,

" Mind you your wheel, and to your maids give law."

For, if the weakness of her frame seconds not her
mind, in courage, in activity, in concern for the
cause of freedom, and for the welfare of her country, she is not inferior to any of us.'

When Porcia was informed that her husband had
fallen by his own hand, she determined not to survive
him. Being watched by her friends, who sought to
prevent her fatal purpose, she snatched burning
coals from the fire, and held them in her mouth till
they produced suffocation.

Plutarch's Lives—Bayle's Historical Dictionary.

MODESTO POZZO.

Modesto Pozzo, born at Venice, 1555, and left
early an orphan, was educated in the convent of St.

Martha of Venice, where she studied Latin and
poetical composition. She possessed extraordinary
powers of memory, and was able to repeat literally
the sermons on which she was obliged to attend.
She married Philip de Georgiis, with whom she lived
happily twenty years, and died in child-bed, 1592.
She was the author of an Italian poem, entitled
" *Floridoro;*" also of a poem upon the passion and
resurrection of Christ. She published a prose composition, entitled " *De Meriti delle Donne,*" in which
she contended for sexual equality. In her publications, she assumed the name of Moderata Fonte *.
Her book On the Merit of Women appeared not till
after her death. Her husband raised a monument
to her memory, on which was engraven a Latin
epitaph in her praise. N. di Lorzi, her daughter,
wrote a preface to her works. A panegyric on her
learning and talents is inserted by Peter Paul Ribera,
in his " Theatre of Learned Women " She is also
mentioned by father Hilarion de Coste, in his
" *Eloges des Dames Illustres.*"

Bayle's Historical Dictionary, &c.

---

* Moderata answers to Modesto, and Fonte to Pozzo.

[79]

PRAXILLA.

PRAXILLA, a Sycionian dithyrambic poetess, is said to have flourished in the 32d Olympiad; and is reckoned among the nine most celebrated lyrics. There is a work of hers entitled *" Metrum Praxilleum."*

———————

PROBA.

PROBA (Valeria Falconia), was the wife of Adelphus the Roman proconsul, in the reigns of Honorius and Theodosius, junior. She composed a Virgilian cento upon the Books of the Old and New Testament, which was printed at Frankfort, 1541. She also wrote an epitaph upon her husband.

Biographium Fœmineum.

———————

RENATA,
DUCHESS OF FERRARA.

RENATA, daughter of Lewis XII. and of Anne of Bretagne, was born at Blois, October 25, 1510 In 1513, she was engaged to Charles of Austria; and, in 1515, promised to Joachim marquis of Brandenburg; but, in 1527, she was married to Hercules d'Este, the second of that name, duke of Ferrara and of Modena. She is said to have possessed " a refined and delicate wit;" and to have acquired, without difficulty, the most abstruse sciences. M. Varillas declares, that she had great erudition, that she excelled in every branch of the mathematics, particularly in astronomy. Her person was somewhat deformed: but elegant manners, and a graceful and flowing eloquence, more than compensated for this disadvantage. She bore to her husband five beautiful children. She was no less distinguished for learning and talents, than for her virtues and attachment to the Reformation. It is said by Varillas, that Calvin was accessary to the conversion of this princess from the errors of the church of Rome; but it is believed that Marot, who had before been a refugee in her court, had a still greater influence over her mind and principles. Resentment for the ill offices which her father had received from the papal court, might probably, as alleged by Brantome, lay the foundation for her abjuration of popery.

In the year 1559 she lost her husband, whose neglect and infidelities she had supported with exemplary mildness. In 1560 she left Italy, on the account of her religion, where she had been permitted, as a princess of the blood, to profess Huguenotism. She retired to her castle at Montargis, where she afforded protection and an asylum to the reformed, who flocked to her from all quarters.

RENATA.   **81**

The duke of Guise, who had married her daughter, Anne d'Este, sent John de Sourches Milicovne, with four troops of horse, in 1569 *, who summoned her to deliver to him the chiefs of the factions, who had taken refuge at Montargis, threatening, in case of her refusal, to bring his cannon before the castle and take them by force. ' Take care what you do,' replied the spirited Renata, 'and learn that the king only hath a right to command me. Should you proceed to extremities, I will myself stand in the breach, and try if you will dare to murder the daughter of a king, whose death heaven and earth will avenge upon you, and upon your children.' Checked by her resolution, John de Sourches desisted from his purpose.

At the same time, it was represented to the duchess, by the duke of Alençon, that her castle being a harbour for heretics, where plots against his majesty were daily devised, she must either send from her the huguenot ministers, and forbear the exercise of their religion, or depart to some other abode. To this she answered, ' that she was too nearly related to the crown to treat it with disrespect; that the persons with her were a poor

---

* Some historians place this event in 1562; and, in 1569, the actual departure of the Protestants.

harmless people, who troubled not themselves with the affairs of the state; that she would not quit a place that belonged to her, and in which she was resolved to live and die, even in the exercise of that religion which the king had permitted her to profess.' She was, however, afterwards obliged, with whatever reluctance, to withdraw her protection from the fugitives; and, in dread of having an immediate garrison brought into the town, to send from her castle four hundred and sixty persons, two thirds of whom were women and children. She dismissed them with tears, in carts and travelling coaches, which she had provided for their acommodation. These poor people escaped with difficulty a stratagem planned to destroy them on the road.

The duchess had always manifested a laudable desire to succour the distressed. In Ferrara, the subjects of her husband loved and praised her for her bounty and goodness. She displayed her tenderness and compassion more particularly towards her countrymen: every Frenchman, who in travelling through Ferrara was exposed to want or sickness, experienced her benevolence and liberality. After the return of the duke of Guise from Italy, she saved, as the army passed through Ferrara, more than ten thousand of the French from perishing by want and hardships. Her steward representing to her the enormous sums which her bounty thus expended—

RENATA.   83

' What,' replied she, ' would you have me do ?
These are my countrymen, who would have been my
subjects, but for the vile Salic-law *.' During the
civil wars in France, when retired into her city and
castle of Montargis, she received and supported
numbers of distressed persons, who had been driven
from their homes and estates.

" I myself," says Brantome, " during the second
period of these troubles, when the forces of Gas-
cogne, consisting of eight thousand men, headed
by Messrs. De Terrides and De Monsales, were
marching towards the king, and passing by Montargis, stopped, as in duty bound, to pay my respects to her. I myself saw in her castle above three
hundred Protestants, who had fled thither from all
parts of the country. An old steward, whom I had
known at Ferrara and in France, protested to me,
that she fed daily more than three hundred people,
who had taken refuge with her."

It is also related by the same author, that when
the prince of Condé was imprisoned at Orleans,
during the early part of the reign of Francis, she
came from Ferrara to court, to intercede for his release : she was, on this occasion, met by the king
and his train, and received with honour and respect.
She expressed to the duke of Guise, her son-in-law,

---

* Brantome.

in strong terms, her concern for the imprisonment
of the prince; adding, ' that whoever had advised
the young king to this measure was very reprehensible; that it was no small matter to treat in this
manner a prince of the blood.' This incident is also
mentioned by Thuanus. " Having come to Orleans," says he, speaking of this princess, " to compliment the king, after deploring the melancholy
aspect of his affairs, she warmly reprimanded the
duke of Guise, respecting the imprisonment of the
prince of Condé; declaring, that had she arrived
earlier, she would have prevented it, and advising
him for the future to use more moderation towards
princes of the blood : she added, that this wound
would not soon heal; and that few men had pro-
spered, who, without provocation, offered violence
to those allied to kings." Notwithstanding the interest she took in the prince of Condé, she afterwards broke with him, disapproving of the huguenots taking up arms.

Henry II. and the duke of Ferrara had in vain
used every method to engage the duchess to relinquish the cause she had espoused, and to abjure the
doctrines of the Reformers. She resisted with equal
firmness their persuasions and menaces. A curious
account has been published by M. Laboureur, respecting the commission given by Henry II. to Dr.
Oriz, one of the pope's penitentiaries, whom he

RENATA. 85

sent to Ferrara to convert the duchess. He was ordered to inform her, 'that the king had, to his inexpressible sorrow, learned that she had suffered herself to be entangled in the labyrinth of those wicked
and damnable opinions, which are repugnant to the
holy faith. That, could he hear of her reconciliation with the church, and that she had returned to
true obedience, it would afford him not less satisfaction and joy, than were he to see her raised from
death to life. But that if, instead of treading in
the footsteps of her progenitors, who by their exemplary zeal had protected the holy catholic faith,
she still remained stubborn and obstinate, nothing
could more offend and displease the king; who, in
that case, would be obliged wholly to forget the respect and duties of a kinsman; as nothing was
so odious to him as those reprobate sects,' of which
he declared himself the mortal enemy. Should
these remonstrances fail to produce the desired effect,
Dr. Oriz had orders to preach before the duchess on
polemical questions, which she and her household
should be compelled to attend. Should the lady,
after these methods had been pursued some days,
still prove contumacious, the doctor was to declare,
before the duke her husband, 'that it was the will of
his majesty, that he should separate his duchess
from all company and conversation, by immuring
her in some place at a distance from her children,

from her friends, and those of her servants, of whatever nation, who were suspected of heresies and
false doctrines. That such delinquents should be
brought to justice, and, after sentence passed upon
them, be delivered over to exemplary punishment.'

All these sagacious methods of convincing the
judgments of the duchess and her household proved
abortive: she persevered in her heretical opinions;
in consequence of which an alienation, for a period,
ensued between her and the duke, who took from
her the education of her children. Her daughter,
Anne d'Este, notwithstanding these rigorous proceedings, betrayed a predilection for the new doctrines :
her mother, who had caused her to be instructed in
the sciences, had given her for the companion of her
studies Olympia Fulvia Morata, a young woman of
talents, who afterwards imbibed the lutheran faith.
John Sinapius, a man of eminence, was their tutor.
The duchess, in placing Olympia with her daughter,
wished to inspire her with a generous emulation.
This young woman lived several years at court
greatly esteemed. From her conversation, Anne
was led to exercise her understanding on theological
subjects, and to sympathise with the new sect in
their afflictions and persecutions.

Thuanus informs us, that Anne d'Este, wife to
the duke of Guise, who from her infancy had, by
her mother, been predisposed to the tenets of the

ANNE DE ROHAN. 87

Reformers, a disposition that had been strengthened by her intercourse with Olympia Morata, interceded, with tears, with Catherine of Medicis, in behalf of the oppressed Huguenots, while she entreated the queen, as she tendered the welfare of the king and kingdom, to divert his majesty from shedding innocent blood. Yet this princess, during the League, was zealous against the Protestants; family interest, and the assassination of her husband, having combined to effect a change in her feelings.

The duchess, her mother, Renata of Ferrara, died at Montargis, June 12th, 1575, in the profession of the protestant faith.

Bayle's Historical Dictionary—Biographium Fœmineum, &c.

ANNE DE ROHAN.

ANNE, daughter of Renatus de Rohan, and of Catherine de Parthenai, heiress of the house of Soubise, and sister to the duke of Rohan, was not less distinguished for her virtues and talents than for her illustrious descent. She was the support of the reformed religion during the civil wars of Lewis XIII. in which period she sustained with heroic constancy the hardships of the siege of Rochelle; when the inhabitants lived three months on the flesh of horses, and four ounces of bread per day. Anne and her mother refused to be comprehended in the

88   MARIE ELEONORE DE ROHAN.

capitulation, choosing rather to remain prisoners of war. She was celebrated among her party for her piety and courage, and generally respected for her learning and capacity. She was also admired for her poetical talents; particularly for a poem written on the death of Henry IV. of France. She studied the Old Testament in the original language, and used in her devotions the Hebrew Psalms. She died unmarried, September 20, 1646, at Paris, in the sixty-second year of her age. The celebrated Anna Maria Shurman addressed some letters to this lady, which are in the collection of her works.

Bayle's Historical Dictionary, &c.

MARIE ELEONORE DE ROHAN.

THIS lady, celebrated for her piety and her talents, was the daughter of Hercule de Rohan-Guémené, duke de Montbazon. She was born in 1628, and educated in a convent, where she contracted a predilection for the monastic life. Of high birth and fortunes, beautiful and accomplished, the young Eléonore, at the age of eighteen, withstood the solicitations of her friends, the tears of her father, and the allurements of the world, to devote herself to a studious and secluded life. She was professed in the benedictine convent at Montargis, where, by her virtues, the sweetness of her manners, her ge-

MARIE ELEONORE DE ROHAN. 89

nius, and her talents, she extorted the respect and affection of the community. She was soon after named abbess of La Trinité de Caen. This dignity her humility led her to decline, till compelled to accept it by the entreaties of the superiors of the convent. Without ambition, she fulfilled the duties of her charge with gentleness, propriety, and wisdom. Her heart was tender, susceptible, and kind; her temper sweet and modest; her mind elevated, sublime, and firm, of which she gave singular proofs in maintaining the rights and privileges of the abbey.

The air of the sea, near which the convent was situated, being unfavourable to her health, she became languid and weak: her physicians declared that a change of air only could restore her. On this occasion she was with difficulty prevailed upon to exchange her abbey for that of Malnoue, near Paris. Her distress on her separation from her charge, to whom she was affectionately attached, was affecting and extreme. Incapable of speaking, she embraced them with tenderness, and bedewed them with her tears. Attestations of the piety and virtue of our amiable enthusiast were sent to Rome, where a declaration was made by the pope of his intention to canonise so young and so exemplary an abbess.

In 1669, madame de Rohan was solicited by the religious of the Benedictines *de Notre Dame de Consolation du Chasse-midi*, to take upon her the government of their community; to which request, without neglecting the management of De Malnoue, she was induced to consent   In the intervals of her duties, she exercised her talents, and applied herself to study.   She composed, under the title of "*Morale de Salomon*," a Paraphrase on the Proverbs, a Discourse on Wisdom, and various other tracts, in which proofs were manifested of a superior understanding.   It was said of this lady, " *que le sang des rois avoit trouvé en elle une ame royale.*"   To the modesty and softness of her own sex, she united the wisdom and learning of the other.   She died 1681, in the convent Du Chasse-Midi, generally beloved, and sincerely regretted.

*Anne Thicknesse's Sketch of the Lives and Writings of
the Ladies of France.—Dictionnaire Historique des
Femmes Célèbres.*

MARGARET ROPER.

In favour of the liberal cultivation of the minds of women, it may be observed, that at no period of the English history does there appear to have been greater attention paid to the culture of the female mind, than during the age of Elizabeth; and at no time has there existed a greater number of amiable and respectable women.   Even the domestic affections and appropriate virtues of the sex, modesty, prudence, and conjugal fidelity, far from being su-

MARGARET ROPER. 91

perseded by study and the liberal sciences, are, on the contrary, both strengthened and embellished. The habits of reflection and retirement which grow out of the exercise of the understanding, are equally favourable to virtue and to the cultivation of the heart. While the mind, by seeking resources in itself, acquires a character of dignity and independence, a sentiment of grandeur and generosity is communicated to its affections and sympathies. Dissipation and frivolous pursuits, by enfeebling the understanding, have a tendency to harden and to narrow the heart. If the concentrated passions of stronger minds, and these examples among women, are rare, have sometimes been productive of fatal effects, an impressive and affecting lesson, as in the sublimer devastations of nature, may be derived even from their failures. But the being, restless in the pursuit of novelty, irritable, dependent, unstable, and vain, who lives only to be amused, becomes necessarily selfish and worthless, the contempt and burthen of society, the reproach of one sex and the scorn of the other. Among women distinguished for their virtues and acquirements, in the 16th century, the three daughters of sir Thomas More hold an elevated rank.

Margaret, eldest daughter of sir Thomas More, lord high chancellor of England, and of Jane, daughter of Mr. John Colte of Newhall, Essex, was born

in London, in the year 1508. She received, in the
fashion of the times, a learned education, while
men of the first literary reputation were procured
by her father for her preceptors. The following interesting and patriarchal description of the family of
the chancellor, is given by Erasmus. " More," says
he, in a letter to a friend, " has built, near London,
on the banks of the Thames (Chelsea), a commodious
house, where he converses affably with his family,
consisting of his wife, his son and daughter-in-law,
his three daughters and their husbands, with eleven
grandchildren. There is no man living so fond of his
children, or who possesses a more excellent temper.
You would call his house the academy of Plato.—
But I should do it an injury by such a comparison :
it is rather a school of christian goodness ; in which
piety, virtue, and the liberal sciences, are studied by
every individual of the family. No wrangling, or intemperate language, is ever heard ; no one is idle ;
the discipline of the household is courtesy and benevolence. Every one performs his duty with cheerfulness and alacrity, &c." What a charming picture, contrasted with modern seminaries of vanity
and dissipation !

Margaret, the eldest daughter of this amiable family, was more peculiarly distinguished for her talents and genius. Dr. Clement, and Mr. William
Gonell, who ranked with the most celebrated lin-

MARGARET ROPER.   9:3

guists of the age, were her tutors in the languages :
from Mr. Drue, Mr. Nicolas, and Mr. Richard
Hart, she acquired a knowledge of the arts and
sciences. Under the care of these gentlemen, she
became mistress of the Greek and Latin ; and made
considerable progress in astronomy, philosophy, physics, logic, rhetoric, music, and arithmetic. Sir
Thomas, to whom all his children were dear, regarded his eldest daughter, in whose attainments
and powers he felt a laudable pride, with peculiar
tenderness. She is said to have written a pure and
elegant Latin style : her father delighted in holding
with her an epistolary correspondence : some of her
letters, which he communicated in confidence to
persons of the most distinguished abilities and learning, received high and just praise. The erudition
and talents of these admirable sisters were celebrated, in a Latin epigram, by Mr. John Leland the antiquarian poet. The affection of the chancellor for
his daughter Margaret, is particularly mentioned in
Mr. More's Life of sir Thomas, and in Lewis's edition of the same Life, by Roper.

During the extraordinary malady called the sweat-
ing-sickness, which commenced in the army of Henry
VII. 1483, and, spreading its contagious influence
to London, appeared again at intervals, five times,
till 1528, Margaret was seized with this disorder :
her father, while her recovery was doubtful, aban-

doned himself to the most violent sorrow; and protested, on her restoration to health, that had the
malady proved fatal, it was his determination to
have resigned all business, and for ever to have abjured the world.

In 1528, in the twentieth year of her age, Margaret gave her hand to William Roper, esq. of Well-
hall, Eltham in Kent, a man of talents and learning,
amiable, and accomplished, whose congenial qualities had united him with the family of the chancellor, by the most cordial and indissoluble ties. The
young couple continued to live at Chelsea, with the
family, till its worthy head, after being taken into
custody, was confined in the Tower. Two sons
and three daughters were the fruit of this marriage,
whose education was superintended by their mother
with the most assiduous care. Drs. Cole and Christopherson, afterwards bishop of Chichester, men eminent for their skill as Grecians, were procured by
Mrs. Roper, as preceptors to her children. This
lady corresponded, and was personally acquainted,
with Erasmus, the restorer of learning, by whom
she was styled *Britanniæ decus*, and in whose estima-
tion she held a high place. Sir Thomas having presented to Erasmus a valuable picture, drawn by
Hans Holbein, in which he was himself represented,
surrounded by his children, Erasmus returned his
acknowledgments in a Latin epistle, which he ad-

MARGARET ROPER.   95

dressed to Margaret.   In his letter he expresses the
pleasure he felt in receiving a representation of a
family which he so truly respected; and more especially that of a lady, whose resemblance could not be
beheld without being reminded of her excellent and
admirable qualities.   Margaret replied to this compliment in an elegant Latin epistle; in which,
after expressing her pleasure in the satisfaction the
picture had afforded to her learned friend, she acknowledges him as an instructor to whom she
should ever feel herself grateful.

At different periods, Erasmus addressed himself
also to her sisters, Elizabeth and Cecilia, but Margaret, to whom he dedicated some hymns of Prudentius, appears to have been his favourite. Having,
in the early part of her life, applied herself to the
languages, she now prosecuted, with no less assiduity, the study of philosophy, of the sciences, of
physics, and of theology. The two latter branches
of knowledge were more particularly recommended
to her by her father. Till this period, her life
glided on serenely, a calm unruffled stream, in
the acquisition of science, and in the bosom of her
family. It became now agitated and perturbed,
by the tragical fate of her beloved and invaluable
father.

The chancellor, having disapproved the conduct
of Henry VIII. in the business of his divorce from

Catherine, his first wife, thought proper to resign
the seals, and incurred, by this measure, the displeasure of a capricious tyrant.   Sir Thomas, living
under the same roof and in the midst of his family,
the expences of which he had hitherto defrayed from
his revenue, knew not how, on the resignation of his
office, to support the idea of a separation from them.
Having assembled his children together, he advised
with them respecting the measures which it would be
necessary to pursue : and, while they listened to him
in mournful and respectful silence, thus addressed
them : " I have been brought up at Oxford, at an
inn of Chancery, at Lincoln's Inn, and in the king's
court, from the lowest degree to the highest; and
yet have I, in yearly revenues, at this present time,
little left me above one hundred pounds a-year.   If
therefore we continue to live together, we must all
become contributers.   But my counsel is, that we
descend not to the lowest fare first: we will not yet
comply with Oxford fare, nor that of New-inn ; but
we will begin with Lincoln's-inn diet, where many
persons of distinction live very agreeably.   And,
should we find ourselves incapacitated from living
thus the first year, we will, the next, conform ourselves to that of Oxford. Should our purses not even
allow us that, we may afterwards, with bag and wal-
let, go and beg together—hoping, that, for pity,
some good people will give us their charity ; and,

MARGARET ROPER. 97

at every man's door, we will sing a *salve regina*, whereby we shall still keep company, and be merry together." This excellent family was soon after dispersed; but Margaret and her husband still continued to reside near their father.

Sir Thomas refusing to take the oath of supremacy, the prospect now became darker; he was committed to the custody of the abbot of Westminster, whence, continuing inflexible, he was removed to the Tower. Overwhelmed with grief, his daughter was, through incessant importunity, at length allowed to visit him: admitted to his presence, she left no argument, expostulation, or intreaty, unessayed, to induce him to relent from his purpose. But her eloquence, her tenderness, and her tears, proved alike ineffectual; the principles and constancy of this great, but unfortunate man, were not to be shaken. Margaret, less tenacious, or less bigotted, had herself taken the oath, with the following reservation—" *As far as would stand with the law of God.*"

The family, on this affecting occasion, seem again, from a letter addressed by Mrs. Roper to her father, to have assembled at Chelsea. "What think you, my most dear father," says she, " doth comfort us, in this your absence, at Chelsea? Surely, the remembrance of your manner of life passed among us, your holy conversation, your wholesome counsels, your examples of virtue; of which there is hope, that they do not only persevere with you, but that they are, by God's grace, much more increased.' During the imprisonment of sir Thomas, a frequent intercourse of letters passed between him and this beloved daughter; and, when deprived of pen and ink, he contrived to write to her with a coal. These letters are of an affecting nature, and are printed at the conclusion of the works of sir Thomas More, published by his nephew, Mr. Rastell: many of them are also reprinted by the last editor of the Life of sir Thomas, Mr. Roper, 1731.

It is related by Dr. Knight, in his Life of Erasmus, that sentence having been passed on the chancellor, his daughter, as he was returning towards the Tower, rushing through the populace and guards, threw herself upon his neck, and, without speaking, in a stupor of despair, strained him closely in her arms. Even the guards, at this affecting scene, melted into compassion, while the fortitude of the illustrious prisoner nearly yielded. ' My dear Margaret,' said he, ' submit with patience, grieve no longer for me, it is the will of God, and must be borne.' Tenderly embracing her, he withdrew himself from her arms. He had not proceeded many paces, when she again rushed towards him ; again, in a paroxysm of sorrow more eloquent than words, threw herself on his bosom. Tears flowed down the venerable cheeks of sir Thomas, while he gazed

MARGARET ROPER.   99

on her with tender earnestness; yet his heroic purpose continued unmoved. Having intreated her prayers for him, he bade her affectionately farewel, while every spectator dissolved in tender sympathy.

The cares of Margaret extended to the lifeless remains of her beloved parent: by her interests and exertions, his body was, after his execution, interred in the chapel of St. Peter's *ad vincula*, within the precincts of the Tower; and was afterwards removed, according to the appointment of sir Thomas during his life, to the chancel of the church at Chelsea. His head, having remained fourteen days exposed upon London bridge, in conformity to his sentence, was about to be cast into the Thames, when it was purchased by his daughter. Being, on this occasion, inhumanly summoned before the council, she firmly avowed and justified her conduct. This boldness did not escape the vengeance of the king; she was committed to prison; whence, after a short restraint, and vain attempts to subdue her courage by menaces, she was liberated, and restored to her husband and family.

The remainder of her life was passed in domestic retirement, in the bosom of her family, and in the education of her children. She is described by Mr. More, in his Life of sir Thomas, as a woman of singular powers and endowments, and as chosen by her father, for her sagacity and prudence, as his friend

and confidant. She corrected, by her own discernment, without the assistance of any manuscript, a
corruption in St. Cyprian, restoring *nervos severitatis*, for *nisi vos severitatis*, as testified by Pamelion
and John Coster. She composed many Latin epistles,
poems, and orations, which were dispersed among
the learned of her acquaintance. She wrote, in
reply to Quintilian, an oration, in defence of the
rich man, whom he accuses of having poisoned,
with certain venomous flowers in his garden, the
poor man's bees. This performance is said to have
rivalled in eloquence the production to which it was
in answer. Two declamations were likewise written
by her, and translated both by herself and her father, with equal spirit and eloquence, into Latin.
She also composed a treatise, " *Of the four last
Things*," with so much justness of thought, and
strong reasoning, as obliged sir Thomas to confess
its superiority to a discourse in which he was himself employed on the same subject, and which, it is
supposed, on that account, he never concluded.
The ecclesiastical history of Eusebius was translated
by this lady from the Greek into Latin : its publication was superseded by that of bishop Christopherson, a celebrated Grecian of that period. This labour of learning was afterwards translated from the
Latin into English by Mary, the daughter of Margaret Roper, who inherited the talents of her mother.

Mrs. Roper, whose learning and genius procured

MARGARET ROPER.   101

her the respect and admiration of the most distinguished characters of her country, and of the age in
which she lived, survived her father only nine years:
she had been a wife sixteen years, and died in 1544,
in her thirty-sixth year. In compliance with her
desire, the head of her father was interred with her;
in her arms, as related by some; or, according to
others, deposited in a leaden box, and placed upon
her coffin. She was buried in St. Dunstan's church,
in the city of Canterbury, in a vault under a chapel
joining to the chancel, the burying-place of the
Roper family. Her husband remained a widower
thirty-three years after his irreparable loss; when
he expired January 4th, 1577, and was interred with
his beloved wife.

The following is a translation of a Latin inscription to the
memory of Mr. and Mrs. Roper.

" Here lieth interred William Roper, esq. a venerable and
worthy man, the son and successor of the late John Roper,
esq.—Also, Margaret his wife(daughter of sir Thomas More,
knight, once high-chancellor of England), a woman excellently well skilled in the Greek and Latin tongues. The
above-mentioned Wilham Roper succeeded his father, John
Roper, in the office of prothonotary of the high court of
King's-bench ; and, after having discharged the duties of it
faithfully fifty-four years, he left it to his son Thomas. The
said William Roper was liberal both in his domestic and
public conduct. Kind and compassionate in his temper, the
support of the prisoner, the poor, and the oppressed. He
had issue by Margaret, his only wife, two sons and three
daughters, whose children and grandchildren he lived to see.

102   ISABELLA DE ROSANES.

He lost his wife in the bloom of his years, and lived a widower thirty-three years. At length (his days being fulfilled
in peace) he died, lamented by all, in a good old age, on the
4th day of January, in the year of our redemption 1557, and
of his age eighty-two."

     Ballard's British Ladies—Biographium Fœmineum, &c.

MARY ROPER.

Mary, youngest daughter of Margaret Roper,
and grand-daughter of sir Thomas More, was educated by her mother, whose talents she emulated.
Under the tuition of doctors Cole and Christopherson, and Mr. John Morwen, a celebrated Grecian,
she became mistress of the Greek and Latin languages, in which she composed orations highly
commended by Mr. Morwen, and translated by him
into English. She translated into English her mother's Latin version of Eusebius's Church History,
which she dedicated to queen Mary. She also
translated a part of sir Thomas More's Latin exposition of the passion of Jesus Christ, imitating the
style of her grandfather so successfully, that her
production has been mistaken for an original. Mr.
Roger Ascham styles this lady an ornament of the
court and of her sex. She was one of the ladies of
the queen's privy-chamber. She was twice married;
first to Mr. Stephen Clarke, and, after his decease,
to Mr. James Basset.

     Ballard's British Ladies—Biographium Fœmineum.

[103]

MADAME ROLAND.

IT is a task not less painful than difficult to *abridge* the memoirs of this admirable woman, the heroine of the French revolution, and the martyr of liberty, to rob them of those graces, that spirit and interest, that glow through every page, and awaken in the heart of the reader the most affecting and elevated sentiments.

Born in an obscure station, the daughter of Gatien Phlipon, an artist, and of Margaret Bimont, his wife, madame Roland passed her youth in the bosom of retirement, occupied in acquiring those virtues and talents by which she became afterwards so eminently distinguished. M. Phlipon was, by profession, an engraver; he also practised painting and enamelling, but the heat which the latter required, proving prejudicial to his sight, he determined to relinquish it, and to confine himself wholly to the art of engraving, in which he employed, in an extensive business, a considerable number of workmen. By the desire of making a rapid fortune, he was also induced to enter into trade; to purchase diamonds and other jewels, for the purpose of acquiring a profit by their sale. Active and vain, but without erudition, he possessed that degree of taste and superficial knowledge which an employment connected with the

104   MADAME ROLAND.

arts seldom fails to inspire, and which led him to court the acquaintance of professional men. While his ambition, kept within limits, had not yet injured his circumstances, he led a temperate, regular life, and piqued himself on his honour and commercial punctuality.

His wife, with a small fortune, brought him a charming figure, and a " celestial mind *." The eldest of six children, to whom she had been a second mother, she resigned, at six-and-twenty, her place to her sister, and married M. Phlipon, whom her parents presented to her as an honest man, whose talents ensured her subsistence, and whom her reason, rather than her heart, accepted. " It is a proof of wisdom," observes madame Roland, " to be able to contract our desires: enjoyments are more rare than is imagined ; but virtue is never without its consolation."

Madame Roland was the second of seven children, and the only one who survived: her mother frequently remarked, with pleasure, that, of all her children, she alone had never caused her sorrow or regret: her pregnancy and her delivery of this beloved daughter had been equally happy ; and had even appeared to contribute towards the re-establishment of her health.   The

---

* The language of madame Roland will be adopted in this memoir whenever it is practicable.

MADAME ROLAND.   105

nurse selected by madame Besnard, an aunt of M. Phlipon's, in the neighbourhood of Arpajon, to take the charge of the infant, was a healthy and well-disposed woman, much esteemed for the propriety of her conduct in an unhappy marriage with a man of brutal temper. Madame Besnard had no children ; her husband stood godfather to their little niece, whom they both loved as a daughter, with constant and invariable affection. Their kindness recompensed the vigilance of the nurse, whose zeal and success procured for her the friendship of the whole family of her charge. Madame Roland preserved through life an affectionate intercourse with her foster-mother, to whose simple and tender tales, of the little incidents and frolics of her infancy, she never failed to listen with patience and pleasure. This good woman never suffered two years to elapse without taking a journey to Paris to visit her foster-child.

The little *Manon*, for so was she called, was brought home to her father's at two years of age, a lively little brunette, with dark hair falling in graceful ringlets over an animated and glowing face. The prudence and fine qualities of madame Phlipon soon gave her an ascendancy over the mild and affectionate temper of *Manon*, whom it was never found necessary to punish, otherwise than by gravely applying to her the title of *mademoiselle*, which was substituted by her mother, with heart-rending dignity, for kinder and more familiar appellations. Lively without being turbulent, and of a reflective temper, *Manon* desired only to be employed, while she quickly seized every idea that was presented to her. " This disposition," says madame Roland, " was turned to so good an account, that I never remember having been taught to read."—" At four years old the business was in a manner completed; all that was necessary in future was only to supply me with books, which, whenever they were put into my hands, were sure to engross all my attention; which nothing but a nosegay could divert." —" Under the tranquil shelter of my paternal roof, I was happy, from my infancy, with flowers and books. In the narrow confines of a prison, amidst chains, imposed by the most shocking tyranny, I forget the injustice of men, their follies, and my own misfortunes, with books and flowers."

The parents of mademoiselle Philpon availed themselves of her studious turn, to put into her hands the catechisms, with the Old and New Testaments; while she learned with facility every thing which was taught her. Guibol, a painter, whose panegyric on Poussin obtained the prize from the academy at Rouen, frequently visited at

MADAME ROLAND.   197

M. Phlipon's; where he delighted in amusing the little *Manon* with extravagant and marvellous tales. " I think I see him now," says she, " with a figure bordering on the grotesque, sitting in an armed chair, taking me between his knees, and making me repeat the creed of St. Athanasius : then rewarding my compliance with the story of *Tanger;* whose nose was so long, that he was obliged, when walking, to twist it round his arm."

At seven years of age *Manon* was sent to the parish church to attend *catechism,* in order to prepare her for *confirmation.* The children, on this occasion, repeated, as their weekly task, the epistle and gospel, a portion of the catechism, and the collect for the day. A young priest gave them instructions, and explained to them the questions necessary to the subject. The pastors were also sometimes seen among their youthful flock, whom they interrogated respecting the progress they had made. Mr. Garat, the rector of the parish, accosted *Manon* on one of these days, in order to sound the depth of her erudition, and to display, at the same time, his own sagacity. ' How many orders of spirits are there,' enquired he, with an ironical tone and air, ' in the celestial hierarchy ?' ' Though many,' replied the little theologist, with a smile, ' are enumerated in the preface to the Missal, I have found, from other books, that there are only nine—*angels, arch-angels, thrones, dominions,'* &c. She went on, marshalling the spirits in their proper order, and establishing her reputation, as a chosen vessel, among all the devout matrons in the neighbourhood.

Possibly the good sense of madame Phlipon might have operated against these public exhibitions, and lessons of vanity and superstition, had not these ceremonies been committed to the care of her younger brother, an ecclesiastic belonging to the parish, who found, in the presence of his niece, a stimulus to persons, above the inferior ranks, who, by this example, were induced to send their children also. The capacity of mademoiselle Phlipon, and even the neatness and elegance of her appearance, were additional sources of gratification to the pride of her indulgent parents. At the distribution of prizes, at the end of the year, mademoiselle Phlipon appeared without a competitor; her uncle was congratulated on the talents of his niece, and obtained, through her means, greater notice and distinction. The eagerness of *Manon* to learn, suggested to her uncle the idea of teaching her Latin; while, delighted with a new study, she received his instructions with ardour. At home, masters for geography, for writing, for music, for dancing,

MADAME ROLAND. 10§

were provided for her : she received from her
father also lessons in drawing. Amidst these various occupations she still found time for her lessons
and her books : rising at five iu the morning,
when a profound repose reigned throughout the
house, she was accustomed to steal softly, regardless of stockings or shoes, with a night-gown thrown
over her, to the chamber of her mother, in a
corner of which, on a table, her books were deposited. In this situation she either read or repeated and copied her lessons, with an assiduity
that surprised her teachers. Her diligence and
rapid progress rendered her the favourite of her
masters ; while the interest and pleasure they felt
in assisting her, redoubled her industry and attention. Her tutors, at length, flattered by the
capacity of their scholar, universally agreed, that
their instructions were no longer necessary, and
that they ought not to be paid, though they
should gladly continue to visit at the house, to
converse with their pupil, and, as friends, to behold her progress.

The influence of M. Phlipon, over the education of his daughter, was fortunately but slight,
as that little was calculated to do mischief. *Manon*
was somewhat obstinate, or rather she did not
readily submit to authority or caprice, when her
judgment resisted its dictates. Her mother, who

had studied a temper, which doubtless she had contributed to form, governed her by reason, or drew her by the chords of affection; nor did she often experience opposition to her will. Her father, who issued his mandates in a higher tone, found them sometimes disputed, and seldom obeyed without reluctance. If, on these occasions, he attempted force, the affectionate and gentle *Manon* was converted into a lion. More than once, during the operation of a whipping, she bit the thigh across which she was laid, protesting, with violence, against a chastisement so degrading. One day, being a little indisposed, it was thought proper that she should take medicine. The draught was accordingly presented, and, from its nauseous scent, rejected with abhorrence: madame Phlipon tried to overcome the repugnance of her daughter, and, by her expostulations, inspired her with the desire of obedience. But, her senses still revolting, the effort proved vain. M. Phlipon, on hearing what had passed, put himself in a rage, and, ascribing to stubbornness the resistance offered to the medicine, had once more recourse to his remedy of the rod. The resolution of *Manon* was, from that instant, taken; she determined against a compliance that was to be thus extorted. A violent struggle ensued, followed by new menaces and a second whipping. The mischief was increased:

MADAME ROLAND. 111

Manon, more indignant and more resolved, uttered terrible shrieks, and, raising her eyes to heaven, prepared to throw from her the bitter potion. Her gestures indicated her design, and her father, in a transport of fury, threatened a third flagellation. All at once her tears ceased to flow, she sobbed no longer, her passions were concentrated in a single resolution. Fortitude was developed by the extremity of injustice. Turning to the bed-side, and leaning her head against the wall, she presented herself to the rod in silence and meek determination. " My father," said she, " might have killed me on the spot, but he would not have drawn from me a single sigh." Her mother, dreadfully agitated by the scene, at length drew her husband from the room, and, without uttering a word, put to bed the refractory daughter, and left her to repose. Having returned at the end of two hours she conjured her, while her eyes were filled with tears, to comply with their wishes. *Manon,* looking steadfastly in the face of her mother, made an extraordinary effort, and swallowed the medicine at a draught. In a quarter of an hour it was, however, thrown back; a violent paroxysm of fever ensued, for the cure of which it was necessary to have recourse to other means. Mademoiselle Phlipon was, at this time, but little more than six years of age. After relating this

112   MADAME ROLAND.

anecdote, she thus observes: " I experienced the same inflexible firmness that I have since felt on great and trying occasions; nor would it at this moment cost me more to ascend undauntedly the scaffold, than it then did to resign myself to brutal treatment, which might have killed, but could not conquer me." This anecdote is related at large, as an affecting lesson to parents and tutors.

The conduct of his daughter seemed to have produced on M. Phlipon its proper effect. From that instant she never received another blow, nor did he even undertake to control her: on the contrary, he caressed her frequently; taught her to draw; took her out to walk; and treated her with a kindness that ensured her respect and submission. The seventh anniversary of her birth was celebrated as the attainment of the age of reason; when it was intimated to her, that she was expected to follow its dictates. This politic compliment, without increasing her vanity, gave her confidence in herself. The discretion of children is increased by an obligation to its early exercise.

Her days now glided on in domestic peace and mental activity. Her mother, almost always at home, received but little company. Two days were however appropriated to going abroad: one to visit the relations of her father; and the other,

MADAME ROLAND.

which was Sunday, to go to church, to take a walk, and to see her maternal grandmother, who, from an attack of the palsy, had gradually declined into a state of dotage. This, to the lively spirits of *Manon*, was rather a painful task: no books were to be found at her grandmother's, or none but the Psalter; which, for want of other amusement, she used to read over twenty times in French, and chant the Latin. When she was gay the old lady would weep, and laugh if she happened to get a blow or a fall. This, though told it was the effect of disease, did not please *Manon*: she could have borne with the laughter of her grandmother; but her grievous and imbecile cries rent her heart, and inspired her with terror. Madame Phlipon, who considered these visits as an indispensable though a painful duty, refused to yield to the weariness and disgust of her daughter, whom she laboured to convince of the propriety of her conduct. " I know not how she managed it," says this daughter, " but my *heart* received her lessons with emotion." Happy, thrice happy and respectable mother! When her uncle Bimont (the young ecclesiastic) met *Manon* at his mother's, her joy was inexpressible: with him she danced, sung, played, and romped.

The studies which occupied her time rendered

the days short: she soon exhausted, with the elementary books, the little family library. When new books were not to be procured, the old ones were devoured again and again. Two folio Lives of the Saints, a Bible, in an old version of the same size, a translation of Appian's Civil Wars, and a description of Turkey, written in a wretched style, were thus read. Also the comical romances of Scarron, a collection of pretended *bon mots* (which however were perused but once), the Memoirs of the brave De Pontis (a great favourite), those of mademoiselle de Montpensier, whose pride did not displease the young lady, with several other antiquated works. In her passion for knowledge, she picked up a treatise on heraldry, which she instantly began to study; its little figures and coloured plates having excited and amused her curiosity. Her father was, soon after, astonished on her giving him a specimen of her science, in some remarks on a seal not engraven according to the rules of art. She became afterwards, on this occasion, his oracle, nor did she ever mislead him. A treatise on contracts fell into her hands, which she likewise endeavoured to understand, but, from weariness, soon resigned her purpose. The Bible, of which she frequently returned to the perusal, had, for her, peculiar attractions: if, by the simplicity of

MADAME ROLAND. 115

its language, it gave her on some subjects premature information, it at least exercised her
thoughts, without seducing her imagination. In
searching the house for books, she at length discovered a new and unforeseen supply. The work-
shop of her father joined to the room in which
she sat with her mother : in this apartment,
which was handsome and neatly furnished, she
was accustomed to receive her lessons. A recess,
on one side the fire-place, was converted into a
light closet, in which stood a bed, a chair, a small
table, and a few shelves. This was the sanctuary
of *Manon*. In an evening, or at hours when the
workmen were absent, she used to steal into the
shop, where the different instruments of her
father's art, and various pieces of sculpture, were
deposited. One day she remarked there a recess,
in which one of the young men kept his books.
Volume by volume was carried off by *Manon* to
her little closet, eagerly read, and again, in silence,
deposited in its place. Fortunately these books
were inoffensive, and generally well chosen.
Madame Phlipon had made the same discovery ;
and *Manon* one day recognised in the hands of
her mother a book which had previously passed
through her own. No longer considering herself
as under any restraint, she felt emancipated by
this example from all future compunction. The

young man took no notice of the occasional
disappearance of his books; all parties seemed
agreed by a tacit convention. In this way *Manon*
perused many volumes of travels, of which she
became passionately fond; and also some plays
of second-rate authors, and the Plutarch of Dacier. This last work proved more to her taste
than any thing she had yet read, without excepting even pathetic histories, with which however she was greatly affected. "Plutarch,"
says she in her Memoirs, "was the intellectual
food that exactly suited me. Never shall I forget the Lent of 1763, at which time I was nine
years of age: I carried Plutarch with me to
church, instead of the Exercises of the Holy
Week. It is from that period that I may date the
impressions and ideas which, without my dream-
ing of ever becoming one, made me a republican." Telemachus, and the Jerusalem Delivered,
impeded for a time the current of these sublime
impressions, by a majesty of a different kind: the
tender Fenelon touched her heart; while Tasso
fired her imagination. Sometimes, at the request
of her mother, she read aloud; but this, by diverting her from that close attention in which she
delighted to indulge, proved irksome. "Rather,"
says she, "would I have plucked out my tongue,
than have so read the episodes of the island of

Calypso, and a number of passages in Tasso.—
With Telemachus I was Eucharis, and with Tancred, Erminia. Completely metamorphosed into
these heroines, I thought not as yet of being,
with some other personage, something myself.—
None of my reflections came home to me.—I was
the very identical characters, and saw only, on
their account, the objects which existed."

A young painter, notwithstanding, named *Tu-
beral*, with a soft voice, languishing features, and
a fine complexion, who came about this period
occasionally to the house of M. Phlipon, seems
to have called, in some degree, the contemplation of his daughter from fictitious heroes: but
this emotion, neither strengthened by indolence,
nor improper society, was transient and fleeting.

The powerful impressions produced on the
mind of mademoiselle Phlipon by the works enumerated, were soon after diverted by different
productions, among which may be named the
writings of Voltaire. Employed one day in perusing Candide, a lady who had just laid down
her cards, with which she had been playing in the
same room, desired to see the book which engaged the attention of her young friend. On the
return of madame Phlipon, who had quitted the
apartment, she expressed her surprise at the subject of her daughter's studies. *Manon* was

ordered by her mother, who to the observation of her visitor had made no reply, to replace the book where she had found it. From that day forward never was the officious lady favoured with one smile from our little student. The conduct of madame Phlipon was unaltered by this incident: her daughter was allowed to read all the books which came in her way, not without the knowledge, but without the interference, of her mother. No mischief appears to have ensued from this privilege; *Manon* read no immoral publications, which were probably withheld from her; but the taste which she acquired from intellectual improvement superseded the necessity of any particular watchfulness.

Her father also, perceiving her love of letters, presented her with books; of which, piquing himself on confirming the serious habits of her mind, his choice was curious: Fenelon on the education of females, and Locke on that of children in general, were put into the hands of a student who was herself a child. But this incongruity was not without its benefits. " I loved to reflect," says this truly admirable woman : " I seriously desired to improve myself:—I studied the movements of my mind :—I felt that I had a destination which it was requisite I should enable myself to fulfil. Religious notions began to fer-

MADAME ROLAND. 119

ment in my brain, and soon produced a violent explosion."

The progress of mademoiselle Phlipon in the Latin seems not to have been very great; " her little uncle," as she was accustomed to call the abbé Bimont, young, indolent, and sprightly, took more pleasure in prattling and sporting with his niece, than in teaching her to decline nouns, and conjugate verbs: she however acquired sufficient Latin to chant and understand the psalms, and to give her facility in the study of language: a few years after she learned the Italian, without a master, and with little difficulty. In drawing, her father rather amused himself with her aptitude, than cultivated her talent in the art, in which her mother, from prudential motives, was not desirous that she should excel. " I would not have her become a painter," said she; " it would require an intercommunity of studies and of connections, that we can well dispense with." She also was taught to hold the graver, of which she soon overcame the first difficulties. Her drawings and engravings served for little presents to her relations on the anniversary of their birth-days, kept with great solemnity.

Little *Manon* was fond of dress, and her mother, though plain in her own attire, took pleasure in adorning her daughter, whom she clothed with a degree of richness and elegance not perfectly suited to her condition. On a Sunday this finery was exhibited in the *Tuilleries*, where the *bourgeoise* of Paris were accustomed to parade; and, on other occasions, at festivals and family visits. The vanity of youth is content with simple gratifications. Contrasted with these exhibitions, the young lady, so elegant on a Sunday, at church, and in the public walks, with a demeanor and language suited to her appearance, would, nevertheless, during the week, attend her mother to market in a linen frock; or step out alone to purchase any little article that had been omitted or forgotten. This contrast was yet farther extended: the child who was set to study science and systems; who could explain the circles of the spheres, and enumerate the celestial hierarchy; who handled the crayon and the graver; and who, at eight years of age, was the best dancer in the youthful parties that met on extraordinary occasions;—this child, so intelligent and accomplished, knew how, in the kitchen, to make an omelet, to pick the herbs, or skim the pot. Happy simplicity! in which the useful, the ornamental, the gay, and the serious, so delightfully blend. " It was this mixture of occupation," says madame Roland, " properly ordered, and rendered agreeable by my mother's good

MADAME ROLAND. 121

management, that made me fit for every thing, that seemed to forbode the vicissitudes of my fortune, and enable me to support them."

Madame Phlipon, who was serious without bigotry, who conformed to the rules of the church, and endeavoured to believe, did not neglect to present to her daughter religious considerations, which were received with respect and attention. " These notions," says madame Roland, " were of a nature calculated to impress a lively imagination, notwithstanding the doubts suggested by my infant reason, which regarded with surprise the transformation of the Devil into a serpent, and thought it cruel in God to permit it." Having received confirmation with the temper of a mind that reflects on its duties, *Manon* prepared herself, with real awe and sacred terror, to receive her first communion. Being well read in books of devotion, her thoughts were wholly occupied with the importance of a future state, unalterable, and eternal. The age of sentiment was by religious fervors prematurely brought forward ; an extraordinary revolution agitated her feelings, and introduced into her mind a timid scrupulosity. Watching over her thoughts, lest any profane image should introduce itself, these solicitudes were also extended to her studies : for the rational desire of acquiring know-

ledge was substituted the feelings of a devotee.

But a life which became every day more strict
and retired, appeared yet too worldly for the first
ardours of a young enthusiast, who had acquired
a taste for divine communications, who passed
her hours in perusing the lives of the saints, and
the explanation of the church ceremonies, with
all their mystic signification; and who unfeignedly
regretted, that the persecuting fury of pagans
no longer conferred the crown of martyrdom
on heroic christians. After profound meditation,
Manon began to think seriously of embracing a
new vocation: the idea of parting with her
mother had, till this period, never failed to overwhelm with affliction her affectionate and susceptible mind; but now the silence and solitude of
a cloister presented a grand and romantic image
of sacrifice and seclusion, which seized on her
imagination, and captivated her senses. In this
disposition of mind, one evening after supper,
falling at the feet of her parents, she shed in
silence a torrent of tears. Alarmed at this sudden
emotion, they earnestly intreated her to explain
the cause of her distress; when, in a voice interrupted with sobs, she implored them to send her
to a convent; a measure which, however painful
to her feelings, her conscience irresistibly demanded. Her excellent mother, much affected

MADAME ROLAND.   **123**

at her request, having raised her from the ground, enquired what it was that made her desirous of leaving them; while she observed, at the same time, that they had never refused to her any reasonable demand. *Manon*, in reply, declared it was her wish to communicate, for the first time, in a disposition suited to the solemnity of the occasion. M. Phlipon, having commended her zeal, and expressed his readiness to comply with her desire, she was accordingly placed in a respectable house, of a mild order, in which the education of youth was professed by the nuns. " While pressing my dear mother in my arms," says she, " at the moment of our first separation, I thought my heart would have burst; but I was acting in obedience to the voice of God, and passed the threshold of the cloister, offering up to him with tears the greatest sacrifice I was capable of making. This was the 7th of May, 1765, when I was eleven years and two months old."— " How," adds she, " shall I recal to my mind, in the gloom of a prison, and amidst commotions which ravage my country, and sweep away all that is dear to me, that period of rapture and tranquillity? What lively colours can express the soft emotions of a young heart, endued with tenderness and sensibility, greedy of happiness,

awakening to the feelings of nature, and perceiving only the Deity ?"

The scholars of the cloister were, from the age of
six to that of seventeen or eighteen, divided into
two classes, which took their meals at separate
tables. The capacity and gravity of the little
Manon secured her, notwithstanding her youth,
a place in the first. The regularity of a life
which the variety of her studies only diversified,
was suited to her active, yet methodical mind :
her diligence still left her leisure, while she improved every moment of her time. In the hours
set apart for recreation, she was accustomed to
retire from the crowd, to read or reflect in some
solitary spot. " Every-where," said she, " I
perceived the hand of the Deity ; in the beauty
of the foliage, the breath of the zephyrs, and the
fragrance of the flowers. I was sensible of his
beneficent care, and I admired his wonderful
works." The majestic sounds of the organ, with
the melodious voices of the nuns, chanting their
devotions, completed the transport of a young
enthusiast. Beside the mass, to which the
boarders, in the morning, were regularly conducted, half an hour in every day was consecrated to meditation, to which those only who
appeared capacitated to improve it were admitted. This privilege was conferred with zeal

MADAME ROLAND.   125

upon mademoiselle Phlipon, who, not content
with this distinction, earnestly intreated to receive her first communion at the approaching
festival of the Assumption. This request, notwithstanding her short residence in the convent,
was, with the unanimous consent of the superiors,
readily granted. The monk who officiated at
the cloister, an upright and enlightened man,
whose good sense and mildness of temper softened the austerities of his demeanor, was well
fitted for his office. While he directed the
pious affections of his new charge to all that was
great and sublime in morality, he took a pleasure
in developing the germs of virtue, by the in-
strumentality of religion, without any mixture
of its absurd mysticism. Mademoiselle Phlipon
loved him as a father, and during the three years
that he survived, after she had quitted the convent, went regularly to confess to him, from a
considerable distance, at the eve of great festivals.

A young novice took the veil soon after the
arrival of mademoiselle Phlipon at the convent,
whose sensations on this occasion were affecting,
mingled, and acute. " I was myself," said she,
" the very victim of the sacrifice. I thought they
were tearing me from my mother ; and I shed a
torrent of tears. With sensibility, that renders

MADAME ROLAND.

impressions so profound, and occasions so many things to strike us, that pass like shadows before common eyes, our existence never becomes languid. If life be measured by the sentiment which has marked every moment of its duration, I have already lived to a prodigious age "

Prepared by every means which the catholic religion, so striking and so impressive, can devise to raise the imagination, and move the senses of a youthful votary, the little *Manon* was called to communicate at the altar; while transported with divine love, and bathed in tears, two nuns were obliged to support her to the sacred table. These unfeigned marks of devout sensibility obtained her great consideration among the pious sisterhood, who failed not to recommend themselves to her prayers. " Dwell with me awhile," says she, " in those peaceful days of holy delusion. Think you, that in an age so corrupt, and in a social order so perverse as the present, it is possible to taste the delights of nature and innocence ? Vulgar souls may find pleasure in such an age; but those for whom pleasure alone would be too little, impelled on the one hand by passions that promise them more, and restrained on the other by duties which, however severe or absurd, they are bound to respect, their enjoyments consist of little else than the dear-bought glory of sacrificing the feelings of nature to the tyrannical institutions of mankind." Some months had elapsed since the residence of mademoiselle Phlipon at the cloister: once a-week she was visited by her parents, who took her out on a Sunday, after service, to walk in the *Jardin du Roi.* Though she never parted from them without tears, she yet returned with pleasure to the cloister, which she walked through with measured steps, the better to enjoy its solitude, while a melancholy, full of charms, penetrated and absorbed her soul.—" I longed," said she, " to be received into the bosom of the Deity ; where I hoped to find that perfect felicity of which I felt the want."

The arrival of two young ladies from Amiens, about this period, gave a turn to her thoughts. In the society of the youngest, about three years older than herself, who possessed a sedate and reflecting temper, she first experienced the charms of confidence and friendship. Sophia Cannet, with feelings less acute than those of her new friend, possessed a cool and composed mind : gentle, without being forward in her demonstrations of kindness, she courted the good-will, of no one ; but, when opportunities occurred, obliged every body. She was fond of working, of reading, and of reasoning : she was of a pious turn, and, with less tenderness than mademoiselle Phlipon, was equally sincere. Sophia loved to analyse, to discuss, to know every thing: she was fond of talking, and spoke fluently. The two friends, though different in temper, yet united by a congeniality of character, shared in the occupations and pursuits of each other; and, in the transports of a common zeal, and a common affection, assisted each other in the attainment of all that was praise-worthy. Mademoiselle Phlipon had also inspired in the breast of a nun a very tender attachment. Angelica Bouffliers, who had taken the veil at seventeen: full of vivacity and sensibility, the acuteness of her feelings, and the sentiments of her heart, were exalted by compression and restraint. Born to no inheritance, the want of fortune had placed her in a state of servitude among the lay-sisters, with whom she had nothing but her station in common. Her active disposition, and superior qualities of mind, rendered her, in the convent, equally useful and respectable: while she enjoyed the esteem that was her due, she was appointed to offices of distinction and trust. Her affection for mademoiselle Phlipon was not less tender than constant; it followed her through life, and rendered her a sincere participator in all the vicissitudes of her fortune.

MADAME ROLAND.

At the entrance of *Manon* into the cloister, it had been determined that she should remain there only a twelvemonth; the time having elapsed, she took leave of her companions, with a promise of frequent visits. Some family circumstances induced her parents to place her for the present with her paternal grandmother; a lively, good-humoured, and agreeable woman, who with pleasure accepted the charge. A little estate, which, devolving by inheritance to the elder madame Phlipon, had rendered her independent, enabled her, with a younger sister, a devout, simple, and worthy woman, to occupy decent apartments in the island of St. Louis, whither she had retired after the death of her husband. Pleased with the society of young people, of whose attentions she was proud, with her *Manon* lived happy; while, from her lively and polished manners, she received considerable improvement. Her promise of visiting the convent was too dear to the heart of mademoiselle Phlipon to be easily forgotten; thither, accompanied by her aunt, or her father, who took a pleasure in indulging her, her walks were frequently directed. In the intervals of these visits, she entered into an epistolary correspondence with her friend Sophia. " This correspondence," says she, " was the origin of

my fondness for writing; and one of the causes of
the facility which I acquired in composition."

Mademoiselle Phlipon had completed her
twelfth year, and the thirteenth glided tranquilly
away under the roof of her grandmother; the
quiet of whose house accorded admirably with
the tender and contemplative disposition which
Manon had brought with her from the convent.

She accompanied her aunt every morning to
mass, where her gravity and devotion obtained
the notice of those who hope to gratify the Deity
by peopling the cloisters with victims, and violating the first principles and duties of nature.
Though the piety of *Manon* was sincere, her
understanding was too good to suffer her to be a
bigot; nevertheless, she secretly cherished in her
heart a design of taking the veil. St. Francis de
Sales, one of the most amiable of the saints in the
calendar, had made a conquest of her affections;
and the ladies of the Visitation, of which he was
the founder, were already her adopted sisters.
Lest she should give pain to her parents, whose
consent, during her minority, she was assured
would be withheld, she was unwilling yet to
disclose to them her plan: beside, should her resolution fail during the days of probation, she
felt that to reveal it would be giving a triumph
to the profane.

MADAME ROLAND.   131

Her grandmother's little library was laid by her under contribution, while the *Philotée* of St. Francis de Sales, and the Manual of St. Augustin, became her favourite studies. Delicious aliment for a fervent spirit abandoned to celestial illusions! The controversial writings of Bossuet, which, about this period, fell into her hands, furnished fresh food for her mind; while, in defending the faith, they let her into the secret of the objections opposed against it, and led her to investigate the grounds of her belief. This first step gradually conducted her, in a course of years, after having been Jansenist, Cartesian, Stoic, and Deist, to complete scepticism. " What a route," observes she " to terminate at last in patriotism, which has brought me to a dungeon !" In the intervals of her theological studies, she amused herself with some old books of travels, and mythology in abundance: but the Letters of madame de Sevigné, by their ease, their elegance, their vivacity, and their tenderness, fixed her taste.

Her grandmother saw but little company, and seldom went from home, but her vivacity animated their domestic circle: the old lady, who set a high value upon the graces, and upon every thing that embellishes social life, was delighted with the complaisance, the desire of pleasing, and the gentle and amiable manners of her pupil, who, placed in the midst of *kind hearts* that studied her happiness, became every day more affectionate and docile.

The following curious account is given by madame Roland of a visit paid, with her grandmother, to a distant and opulent relation, whose children had been placed under the care of madame Phlipon. ' I am very glad to see you,' cried this voluble lady (madame de Boismorel) on their entrance, in a loud and frigid tone. ' And who is this fine girl? Your grand-daughter, I suppose ? She promises to make a pretty woman ! Come hither, my dear, and sit down by my side. She is a little bashful. How old is she? She is somewhat brown, to be sure; but her skin is clear, and will grow fairer a year or two hence. She is quite the woman already. I will lay my life that hand must be a lucky one. Did you ever venture in the lottery ?' ' Never, madam; I am not fond of gaming.' ' I dare say not: at your age, children are apt to think their game a sure one. What an admirable voice !—So sweet, and yet so full-toned. But how grave she is. Pray, my dear, are you not a little of the devotee ?' ' I know my duty to my God; which I endeavour to fulfil.' ' That's a good girl! You wish to take the veil, don't you ?' ' I know not what may be my de-

MADAME ROLAND.   **133**

stination; nor do I seek as yet to divine it.'
' Very sententious, indeed ! Your grand-daughter
reads a great deal, does she not?' ' Reading,
madam, is her greatest delight; she always de-
votes to it some part of the day.' ' Ay, ay, I
see how it is : but take care she does not turn
author; that would indeed be a pity.' *Manon*
felt as much joy when an end was put to this
visit, as if relieved from some grievous suffering.
' Mind now,' said the lady, at parting, ' that
you don't forget to buy me a ticket in the lottery;
and, do you hear, let your grand-daughter choose
the number. I am determined to try her hand.
Come, give me a kiss, my little dear; and don't
look so much upon the ground. You have very
good eyes; even your confessor will not blame
you for opening them. Yes, yes, many a fine
bow will come to your share, take my word for
it, and that before you are much older.'

This behaviour appeared to our little philosopher very strange; she asked her grandmother
many questions respecting this fashionable lady.;
but kept to herself the impressions which had
been made on her mind. With the son of this
lady, who afterwards visited them, a sensible and
amiable man, of a gentle and serious character,
Manon was much better pleased. This gentleman was suspected of derangement, from his

conduct in bringing up his son, whose education, which he superintended himself, was directed by philosophical views. " I began," says madame Roland, " to suspect that there were two sorts of reason; one for the closet, another for the world : a morality of principle, and a morality of practice; from the contradiction of which resulted many absurdities, which did not escape my observation. In short, it appeared to me, that persons of the gay world call every one insane who is not affected with the common. madness. Thus did materials for reflection gradually accumulate in my active brain."

The year allotted for mademoiselle Phlipon to remain with her grandmother passed away ; and she returned to the arms of her excellent mother. It was not without regret that she quitted the isle of St. Louis, its pleasant quays, and the tranquil banks of the Seine, where she met no objects to interrupt her meditations, as, in the fervency of her zeal, she repaired with her aunt to pour forth her devotions at the foot of the altar. Notwithstanding her attachment to her mother, whose merit, accompanied with reserve, was of a more solid kind, she took leave of her kind hostess with a torrent of tears. It was still upon the banks of the Seine that she was to reside ; but the house of her father was not quiet

MADAME ROLAND. 135

and solitary like that she had quitted : the moving picture of the Pont-Neuf varied the scene every moment. In returning to the parental roof, she seemed literally to be entering the world : yet a free air, and an unconfined space, still gave scope to the reveries of a romantic imagination ; while her sensibility, which power-fully contributed to develope her mind, gave to every object, and to every situation, a more striking and vivid hue. She still continued to to take lessons in music; her master, who, though somewhat of a composer, understood but little of science, was ambitious of communicating to his pupil all he knew. ' Put soul into it !' he was frequently exclaiming ; not less afflicted at her want of expression in singing, than at the facility with which she pursued a chain of rea-soning. ' You sing an air,' said he, ' as nuns chant an anthem.' He perceived not that his scholar possessed too much genuine feeling to be able, thus mechanically, and without embarrass-ment, to give to the sentiment of the song its proper tone. Her geography, history, arithmetic, writing, and dancing, were resumed : her father also made her again take up the graver, to which he wished to attach her by the tie of interest, sharing with her, at the end of the week, the pro-fits of some trifling details in the art. But of this occupation she soon became weary; nor did she conceal her disgust. No restraints being imposed upon her inclinations, she quickly threw aside the graver, which she never resumed. In the morning she accompanied her mother to hear mass, and when the hours devoted to her masters were over, retired to her closet to read, write, and meditate. In the long evenings she joined her mother, who read to her while she employed herself with the needle. For the purpose of digesting what she had heard, she committed to paper, on the succeeding mornings, what had most forcibly struck her in the evening readings, and returned to the book to copy the passage, or to recover the connection. This habit becoming a passion, she borrowed and hired books, which she returned not till she had made their best passages her own. In this manner she went over *Pluche*, *Rollin*, *Crevier*, the *Père d'Orleans*, *St. Real*, the abbé *de Vertot*, and *Meseray*, the driest of writers, but the historian of her country; with the annals of which she wished to acquaint herself. Her uncle, the ecclesiastic, who had formerly taught her Latin, had improved his situation: he boarded with the first vicar, the abbé le Jay; at whose house *Manon*, with her parents, was accustomed to pass the evenings on Sundays and holydays. The abbé received his company in a

MADAME ROLAND.   137

large library, which afforded to mademoiselle Phlipon a new and delightful resource.

With her friends, at the convent, she still kept up her intercourse: Sophia had returned to her family; but, before her departure, had prevailed on her mother to meet madame Phlipon. In this interview the friendship of the young people was consecrated and confirmed, while their parents smiled at their promises of perpetual amity; which were, however, never violated. A correspondence was settled between them, in which they mutually imparted their observations and reflections.

By the death of the abbé Jay, *Manon* was deprived of the use of his library, in which she had found literati and historians, mythologists, and fathers of the church. This source failing, she was obliged to have recourse to the booksellers, where her father, ill qualified himself for selection, asked for whatever his daughter pointed out; whose choice generally fell on works respecting which her curiosity had been excited by quotations or extracts. She thus perused translations of Diodorus Siculus, and other ancient historians; the abbé Velly's history of France, with the continuations; Pascal, Montesquieu, Locke, Burlamaqui, and the principal French dramatists. To improve herself, and to acquire knowledge, were the only ends which she had in view. " I felt," says she, " a sort of necessity of exercising the activity of my mind, and of gratifying my serious propensities. I panted after happiness, which I could find only in the powerful exertion of my faculties. Placed in the hands of a skilful preceptor, and applying solely to a particular study, I might have extended some branch of science, or have acquired talents of a superior kind. But should I have been better or more useful? Certainly, I should not have been more happy. I know of nothing comparable to that plenitude of life, of peace, of satisfaction, to those days of innocence and of study."

On holidays, in fine weather, mademoiselle Phlipon was taken by her father to the public walks, where he was proud of displaying his daughter: he accompanied her also to every exhibition or work of art, in those days of luxury, so frequent in Paris. On these occasions, while he pointed out to her what was worthy of notice, he visibly enjoyed his own superiority. These worldly amusements, and the images they called up, agreed but ill with the devotion and studies of a sober recluse, upon whose mind, accustomed to reflection, they could not fail of producing a contrariety of impressions. Mademoiselle Phlipon, while she opposed to the principles she had acquired in the closet the maxims and manners of

MADAME ROLAND. 139

the world, became disturbed and uneasy; her reason received a shock that urged her to the investigation of the grounds of her faith. The first thing which confounded her in the religion which she professed, was the universality of its pretensions, which condemned to destruction all those by whom it was denied, or to whom it remained unknown. When, instructed by history, she considered the extent of the earth, the succession of ages, the diversities of human character, and of human opinion, the absurdity of this idea forcibly struck her mind, to which it appeared not less impious than absurd. " I am deceived," says she, " in this article of my creed, it is evident; am I not in some other equally wrong ? Let me examine"—From this moment she was lost to the church : when an enthusiast begins to reason, emancipation is not far distant. Next to the cruelty of damnation came the folly of infallibility, which was also in its turn disapproved and rejected. What then remained ? The search went on, through a number of years, with an activity and anxiety not difficult to conceive by those who have traced a similar path. Critical, moral, philosophical, and metaphysical writers, next engaged the attention of our young student; while comparison and analysis became her employment. She had lost her good confessor, the monk of the convent; it was necessary to make another choice. The abbé Morel, who belonged to the parish, was selected on this occasion : with austere principles, the abbé was not wanting in good sense. When informed of the doubts of his penitent, he was eager to put into her hands the apologists and champions of the christian church. "Behold me, then," says she, "closetted with the abbés *Gauchet* and *Bergier*, with *Abbadie, Holland*, and *Clarke*, with the rest of the reverend phalanx. I perused them with critical severity, sometimes making notes, which I left in the books when I returned them to my spiritual guide. The abbé enquired, with astonishment, if I had written and conceived these notes ! But the most whimsical part of the story is, that from these works I first got an idea of those they pretended to refute, and noted down their titles in order. In this way did the treatise on *Toleration*, the *Dictionnaire Philosophique*, questions concerning the *Encyclopédie*, the *Bon Sens* of the marquis d'Argens, the *Jewish Letters*, the *Turkish Spy, Les Mœurs, L'Esprit*, Diderot, d'Alembert, Raynal, and the *Système de la Nature*, pass in succession through my hands."

While thus exercising her understanding on important subjects, the person of mademoiselle Phlipon approached fast towards maturity : her serious and studious habits had given to her cha-

MADAME ROLAND. 141

racter a certain rectitude and severity, which a timid and scrupulous conscience had confirmed: she became mistress of her imagination by learning to control it, and to resist the first impulse of what appeared dangerous or wrong. " Pleasure, like happiness," said she, " I can see only in the union of what charms the heart with the senses, and leaves behind it no regret. With such sentiments, it is difficult to forget, and impossible to degrade oneself."—" In the mean time that renunciation of the world, and contempt for its pomps and vanities, so strongly recommended by christian morality, accorded but ill with the feelings of nature. These contradictions at first tormented me, but my reasoning necessarily extended itself to rules of conduct, as well as to articles of faith. With equal attention I applied myself to the investigation of what I ought to *do*, and the examination of what it was possible for me to *believe*. The study of philosophy, considered as the moral science and the basis of happiness, became now the only one to which I referred my reading and observations."

In philosophy, as in poetry, the lively imagination of mademoiselle Phlipon converted her into a personage of the drama: in reading Telemachus, she was Eucharis; and in Tasso, Erminia. In controversy she took the part of the authors of

Port Royal, whose logic and austerity agreed with her temper : her aversion to the jesuit character, sophistical, evasive, and flexible, was strong and instinctive. Among the sects of the ancients she gave the palm to the stoics, and, like them, absurdly endeavoured to consider pain as no evil. In studying *Descartes* and *Malebranche*, she beheld in every animal a machine, mechanically performing its evolutions. While delighted with the sagacity of Helvetius, his system of self-interest excited her disgust. She persuaded herself that he delineated mankind not from nature, but as corrupted by society ; she studied him that she might not become the dupe of the world, but without adopting his principles as the standard for her own actions ; she opposed to his system the sublime traits of history, and the virtues of its heroes. " It is thus," said she, " on the recital of a glorious deed, that I should have acted." She became a passionate admirer of republics, because it was in them that she found the most heroic actions, and the men most worthy of respect. She rejected, with disdain, the idea of uniting herself to an inferior man ; and asked, with a sigh, why she was not born a republican?

She made, with her family, a journey to Versailles, and, for one entire week, was a spectator of the court ; where her reason was offended by

MADAME ROLAND.   143

the homage paid to rank, and the exclusive privileges of the great.   When asked, by her mother,
if she was pleased with her excursion—' Yes,'
replied she, ' if it terminate speedily; but should
we remain here a few days longer, I shall so perfectly detest the people whom I see, that I shall not
know what to do with my hatred.'   ' Why, what
harm do they do you ?' enquired madame Phlipon.   ' They give me a feeling of injustice, and
oblige me every moment to contemplate absurdity.'   She recollected Athens, where, without
the spectacle of despotism, she might have admired
the fine arts : she thought of Greece, and sighed :
fancy transported her to the Olympic games, and
she lost all patience at being a Frenchwoman.
Dazzled by the history of the golden periods of
republics, she forgot their storms, their errors, and
their crimes; to which she was at length fated to
become a victim.   " The sphere of my ideas,"
says she, " continually enlarged.   At an early
period of my life, my own happiness, and the
duties to which it might be attached, occupied my
mind; afterwards, the love of knowledge made me
study history, and turn my thoughts to all that
surrounded me: the relation of my species to the
Deity, so variously represented, disfigured, and
caricatured, next attracted my attention ; but the
welfare of man, in society, fixed it to a determi-

nate point." Amidst investigation and uncertainty the following conclusions were impressed on her mind : that individual consistency, or an entire harmony between our principles and our actions, is necessary to personal happiness : that it is incumbent on every man, as a justice due to him-self, so to regulate his affections and habits, that he may not become the slave of any one : that a being is *good* in itself, when all its parts concur to its preservation, its maintenance, or its per-fection;—a principle not less true in the moral, than in the physical world. She believed that the due proportion of our desires, and the harmony of the passions, formed the moral constitution, of which wisdom only could secure the excellence and duration. That virtue and prudence, as it respected the individual, was nothing more than good sense, applied to moral purposes. But that virtue, properly so called, could spring only from the relation of a being with his fellows : " a man, therefore," said she, " is prudent as far as self is concerned, and virtuous in what regards others. In society there is no independent happiness; there every thing is relative; we sacrifice a part of our enjoyments that we may not risk the whole. But even here the balance is in favour of reason. If the life of the honest is laborious, that of the vicious is still more so : the man who stands

MADAME ROLAND. 145

in opposition to the interest of the majority, can seldom be tranquil, because he is surrounded by enemies; a situation, always painful, however flattering in appearance. To these considerations may be added that sublime instinct, which corruption may mislead, but which no sophistry can annihilate; which impels us to admire wisdom and generosity of conduct, as we do grandeur in nature, and symmetry in the arts. These principles appeared to our young philosopher, to comprise the whole of human virtue, independent of all systems, whether religious or metaphysical. "Having combined and demonstrated these truths," says she, "my heart expanded with joy; they offered me a port in the storm, where I could now examine with less anxiety the errors of national creeds and social institutions."—"It was not all at once," adds she, "that I fixed myself in this firm and peaceful seat, in which, enjoying the truths demonstrated to me, I am content to remain ignorant of what cannot be known, giving myself no disturbance about the opinions of others. I have here comprised, in a few words, the result of the studies and meditations of several years; in the course of which, if I have sometimes shared in the sentiments of the deist, sometimes in the incredulity of the atheist, and sometimes in the sceptic's indifference, I have been always *sincere*, because I had no inducement to change my faith, in order to relax my morals, which were fixed upon a foundation that no prejudice could shake. 1 therefore sometimes felt the agitation of doubt, but never the torment of fear." Thus reasoning, mademoiselle Phlipon thought fit to conform to the established worship, and to go to confession, for the edification of her neighbour, and to preserve the peace of her mother, while she frankly declared to her confessor, that she scarcely knew of what to accuse herself, so moderate were her desires, and so quiet was her life. The worthy priest, who, to keep his charge in the faith, had exhausted his library and his rhetoric, had the good sense not to complain, while he contented himself with exhorting her to distrust the spirit of pride. Satisfied with her attendance at the holy table three or four times a-year, he thought proper, in a spirit of philosophical toleration, to give her absolution. On these occasions, mademoiselle Phlipon recollected the words of Cicero, who observes, " that to complete the folly of mankind, with respect to the Deity, it remained only for them to transform him into food, and then to devour him."

The abbé le Grand, the friend of her uncle, frequently visited at the house of M. Phlipon.

MADAME ROLAND. 147

The abbé, who, with an excellent understanding, had little of his profession besides the gown, was fond of talking with the daughter of his host, to whom he brought books and works of philosophy, the principles of which he discussed with great freedom. " Philosophy," says madame Roland, " in calling forth the powers of my soul, and giving firmness to my mind, did not diminish the scruples of sentiment, or the susceptibility of my imagination, against which I had reason to be so much on my guard." From morals mademoiselle Phlipon turned her attention to physics, to which the mathematics succeeded. She amused herself with geometry, while there was no need of algebra; with the dryness of which, or the absurd contradictions in which it has been involved, she soon became disgusted.

Her correspondence with Sophia, was still one of her greatest pleasures; several journeys which had been made by her friend to Paris, had drawn closer between them the bonds of amity. Thus in offices of social kindness, or in solitary studies, transported by her imagination to distant ages, the days of this admirable young woman glided tranquilly away. Sundays and holidays were devoted to bodily exercise; to an excursion in the country, or a parade in the public walks. " During these walks," says she, " in which my vanity, power-

fully excited, was on the watch for whatever
might shew me off to advantage, an insupportable
vacuity, uneasiness, and disgust, made the pleasure
purchased seem always too dear.   Accustomed to
reflect, and to render to myself an account of my
sensations, I enquired into the cause of this inquietude—Is it, said I to myself, to please the
eye, like the flowers of a parterre, and receive a
few transient praises, that persons of my sex are
brought up in the practice of virtue, and that their
minds are enriched with talents?   What means
this desire of pleasure, so intense, which preys
upon me, and even when it should seem that it
ought to be most gratified, fails to make me
happy '   What are to me the admiration or the
compliments of a crowd of persons, of whom I
have no knowledge, and whom, did I know, I
should probably despise?   Is it to waste my existence in frivolous cares, or tumultuous sensations,
that I am placed in the world? No! I have doubtless a nobler destination. That admiration which
I so ardently feel for whatever is excellent, generous, and exalted, tells me, that it is to practise these
things I am called. The sublime and affecting duties of a wife and a mother will, on some future
day, be mine: it is in rendering myself capable of
fulfilling these, that my early years should be employed: by keeping within bounds my own inclina-

tions, I shall learn to direct those of my children. By the habit of governing my passions, and by the care of cultivating my mind, I shall secure to myself the means of giving happiness to the most delightful of societies; of providing for the man who shall deserve my heart a never-failing source of felicity, and of communicating to all about us a portion of the same bliss. Such were the thoughts that agitated my bosom. Overcome by my emotion, I shed a flood of tears, while my heart exalted itself to the supreme Intelligence, the principle of thought, and the source of sentiment—'Oh, thou, who hast placed me on the earth, enable me to fulfil my destination, in the manner most conformable to thy will, and most beneficial to my fellow-creatures!' This unaffected prayer, simple as the heart that dictated it, is now my only one. In the tumult of the world, in the depths of the dungeon, I have pronounced it with equal fervor. I have pronounced it with transport in the most brilliant circumstances of my life. I repeat it, in fetters, with resignation.—Persuaded that, in the course of these things, there are events which human wisdom cannot prevent; and convinced that the most calamitous are impotent to overturn the firm mind; that peace at home, and submission to necessity, are the ele-

ments of happiness, and constitute the true independence of the hero and the sage."

In the country, mademoiselle Phlipon found
objects more analogous to her turn of mind, to her
tender and serious temper. In the wild woods of
Meadon, amidst its avenues of pines and tower-
ing trees, she experienced, accompanied by her
parents, her sweetest recreation and most delightful moments. At five o'clock on a Sunday morning, simply dressed, and carrying a few books,
this happy family would frequently embark, in a
little boat, on the Seine, which, in the silence of a
smooth and rapid navigation, carried them to the
Shores of Belle-vue, whence, by a steep ascent,
they procceded to Meudon. At a cottage on the
way, they breakfasted on a bowl of milk, and, at
the lodge of one of the porters in the park, took
their humble dinner, rendered delicious by exercise and temperance. " Delightful Meudon," exclaims madame Roland, in her Memoirs, " how
often, beneath thy refreshing shade, have I blessed the Author of my existence, desiring what, at
some future period, might render it complete.
But this desire was without impatience; it was
that charming sentiment that serves to gild, with
the rays of hope, the clouds of futurity. How did
I love to rest myself under the lofty trees, bordering the glades, through which the swift and

MADAME ROLAND.

timid doe bounded along! I recollect also the more
sombre spots, whither we retired during the heat
of the day.   There, while my father stretched on
the turf, and my mother softly reclined on a heap
of leaves, which I had collected for the purpose,
enjoyed their afternoon's repose, did I contemplate the majesty of thy silent groves, admire the
beauties of nature, and adore the Providence
whose benefits I felt.   The glow of sentiment
heightened the colour of my humid cheeks, while
my heart enjoyed all the delights of a terrestrial
paradise!" Happy those, whose pure and undebauched minds are susceptible of these exquisite
and simple pleasures!

An account of her excursions, and the sentiments which they excited, found their way into
the letters of mademoiselle Phlipon to her friend,
sometimes in prose, and sometimes intermingled
with verse; the easy and happy effusions of a
mind to which " all was picture, life, and happiness."   Such, oh nature and virtue! such are thy
charms, and such thy rewards! From Sophia she
received, in return, a description of the persons
with whom she associated at Amiens, and a sketch
of their characters, by which she was enabled to
judge of their general insignificance. It appeared
to her, on striking a balance at the end of the

year, that, in her solitude, she had seen more
persons of merit, than had her friend amidst
routs and assemblies. This, perhaps, may be accounted for, from the profession of her father as
an artist, and from his residence in the capital.
The situation of Sophia, at Amiens, among provincial gentry, and commercial men, in haste to
acquire wealth, was less advantageous. The circumstances in which mademoiselle Phlipon was
placed, her education, her studies, by making her
feel the injustice, or observe the folly, of a variety
of privileges, and political distinctions, combined
to awaken in her mind a republican ardour, and
to prepare her for the part she afterwards performed. In all her readings she was the champion
of democracy; at Sparta, Agis and Cleomenes
were her heroes, and the Gracchi at Rome. " I
retired," says she, " with the plebeians to the
Aventine-hill, and gave my vote to the tribunes."
She candidly adds—" Now that experience has
taught me impartiality, I see, in the enterprise of
the Gracchi, and in the conduct of the tribunes,
crimes and mischiefs of which I was not then
aware." When present at the spectacles which
the capital so frequently afforded, she compared,
with grief, this parade and luxury with the ab-
ject misery of the degraded populace, who worshipped idols of their own making, and applauded

MADAME ROLAND.   153

the ostentation for which they paid by the sacrifice of the necessaries of life. The dissolute conduct of the court, and that contempt of morality which pervaded all ranks, filled her with surprise and indignation. She perceived not in these excesses the germs of revolution. While the French laughed and sung at their own miseries, she conceived the English justified in regarding them as children. She attached herself to those neighbours; de Lolme had familiarised her with their constitution; she sought an acquaintance with their literature, which she yet only studied through the medium of translations.

About this period, having completed her eighteenth year, she caught the small-pox, her parents having unfortunately cherished prejudices against inoculation. The affecting solicitude of her mother, on this occasion, made an indelible impression on her affectionate heart. She recovered slowly, after severe suffering and imminent danger, though without any detriment to her beauty: the disorder, which had been combined with a putrid and miliary fever, the eruption of which had checked the pustules, left behind it no vestiges. The doctor, finding, in one of his visits, the *Récherche de la Vérité* of Malbranche laying on the bed of his patient, chid her for wasting her spirits at such a time in study. ' Why, my good sir,' replied she, ' did all your patients thus amuse themselves, instead of getting angry with the disease and the doctor, you would have much less to do.' Some persons in the chamber were conversing on public affairs; all Paris was running, they said, to some new loan, or edict, which had just appeared. ' The French,' observed the doctor, ' take all upon *trust*.' ' Say rather,' replied his patient, ' upon *appearances!*' ' True,' said he, ' the expression is just and profound.' ' Do n't chide me then for reading Malbranche,' answered she eagerly; ' you see my time is not thrown away.'

An excursion to the country being necessary for the re-establishment of her health, mademoiselle Phlipon repaired to the house of her relations, M. and madame Bernard, with whom two years before she had passed a month. This situation was particularly calculated to fix her attention on the vices of civilised life. Madame Bernard had married the steward of a *fermier-général*, whose house she superintended. This man, when dying, had left a large fortune to his son, who lived at a great expence, and who spent a small part of the year at his château at *Soucy*, whither he carried the manners of the town. With a view of keeping his estate in order, he

MADAME ROLAND.　　　**155**

had requested M. and madame Bernard to lodge there during a part of the summer. They were well accommodated, and enjoyed the pleasures of a park, whose wildness formed an agreeable contrast with the gardens and the château. The sister-in-law and step-mother of its owner resided with him, and did the honours of the house. To this family mademoiselle Phlipon was introduced, and, to a mind like hers, their haughty condescension and insignificant character, their luxury, caprice, and extravagance, could not fail of affording materials for reflection. She recollected, on this occasion, the expression of Montesquieu, " That financiers support the state as the cord supports the criminal."

In the little library of her relations, she found the works of Puffendorf, the poems of Bernis, and a life of the English Cromwell. She observes, that in the multitude of books which chance or circumstances threw in her way, she had not yet met with the writings of Rousseau. " The truth is," adds she, " I read him late, and it was well for me that I did so : he would have turned my brain, and I should have read nothing else." Her mother, she had reason to believe, kept his writings out of her way: she had given no opposition to her critical and philosophical researches, however bold or free ; but she sagely concluded, that

to a *heart* so susceptible, stimulants were not necessary. With the same ideas, she opposed her
application to painting and music. " As to me,"
says this amiable daughter, " I was so much accustomed to love her person, and to respect her
decisions, that I never importuned her on any
subject. Beside, study, in general, afforded me
so large a field of occupation, that I was a stranger
to the pain of *ennui.* When I become a mother,
in my turn, said I to myself, it will be my business to make use of what I have acquired; I shall
then have no leisure for farther studies: I was
earnest to turn my time to account, and afraid of
losing a single moment."

Though living in a narrow sphere, and in comparative solitude, mademoiselle Phlipon, on the
confines of the great world, saw a variety of objects, on which she had leisure to observe.

At eighteen years of age, she had been only
once to the opera, and once to the *Théatre Fran-
cais.* She was sometimes taken by her father to
the inferior theatres, where the mediocrity of the
performance inspired her with disgust, and made
her content with studying, in her closet, the works
of the great masters of the drama. Happily placed
out of the vortex of dissipation, and at a distance
from temptation, with her mind busily employed,
her principles took deep root, and her virtues ac-

MADAME ROLAND.   157

quired an habitual firmness.   Thus progressively advancing in every valuable attainment, she had reached that critical period when new duties and new prospects expanded themselves before her. The propriety of her conduct, the reputation of her fine qualities, an agreeable person, and the bloom of youth, procured her a variety of suitors, who sought to obtain her favour, and the approbation of her parents.   These offers frequently involved her in disputes with her father, who, esteeming commerce as the source of riches, espoused the cause of those whose actual possessions, or hopes of acquiring property, promised his daughter an advantageous establishment. The young lady, less solicitous on this subject, occupied by her studies, happy at home, and detesting trade as the foundation of avarice and fraud, uniformly persisted in rejecting her mercantile admirers.   " My father," says she, " was sensible that I could not accept an artisan, properly so called : his vanity would not suffer him to entertain such an idea of life : but the elegant jeweller, who touches nothing but fine things, from which he derives great profits, appeared to him a suitable match, more especially when already established in business, and in a fair way of making a fortune.   But the mind of the jeweller, no less than that of the mercer, whom he looks upon as be-

158   MADAME ROLAND.

neath him, and also of the rich woollen-draper, who regards himself as superior to both, appeared to me to be alike engrossed by the lust of gold, and by mercenary calculations and manœuvres. Such men must necessarily be strangers to those elevated ideas and refined sentiments by which I appreciated existence: occupied from my infancy in considering the relations of man in society, brought up in the strictest morality, and familiarised with the noblest models, had I then, I asked myself, lived with Plutarch and the philosophers to no better purpose than to connect myself for life with a petty shopkeeper, incapable of entering into my ideas, or of justly appreciating my value." ' Tell me,' said her father, in a conversation upon this subject, ' who it is that will suit you?' ' Tell me also,' replied she, ' why, in bringing me up, you taught me to think, and suffered me to contract habits of study. I know not what kind of a man I shall marry, I know, only, it must be one who can share my sentiments, and to whom I can communicate my thoughts.' ' There are commercial men who possess both politeness and information.' ' Yes, but not of the kind I want: their politeness consists in a few phrases and bows, and their knowledge relates to the strong box, and would assist me but little in the education of my children.'

MADAME ROLAND.   159

'You might educate them yourself.' ' The task would appear laborious, if not shared by the man to whom they would owe their existence.' ' Do you suppose that *l'Empereur*'s wife is not happy? They have just retired from business, are buying capital places, keep an excellent house, and receive the best company.' ' I am no judge of the happiness of other people; but my own affections are not fixed upon riches. I conceive that the strictest union of hearts is necessary to conjugal felicity; nor can I connect myself with a man who does not resemble me. My husband must even be my superior; for, since both nature and the laws give him pre-eminence, I should be ashamed of him if he did not in reality deserve it.' ' You want a counsellor I suppose? But women are not very happy with these learned gentlemen; they have a great deal of pride, and very little money.' ' My God, sir! I do not judge of a man's merit by his cloth, nor have I ever told you that I affect such or such a profession: I want a man I can love.' ' And, according to you, such a man is not to be found in trade?' ' I confess, I do not think it probable. I have never seen a tradesman to my liking; and the profession itself is my aversion.' ' It is however a pleasant thing for a woman to sit at her ease, in her own apartments, while her husband is carry-

ing on a lucrative commerce.   Now, there is madame d'Argens, &c. &c.'   ' But, my father, I
have too well perceived, that the only way to
make a fortune in trade, is by selling dear what
you have bought cheap, by overcharging the cus-
tomer, and beating down the poor workman.   I
should never be able to descend to such practices,
nor to respect a man whose occupation they
were.   It is my wish to be a virtuous wife ; but
how should I be faithful to a husband who would
hold no place in my esteem ; even admitting the
possibility of my marrying such a man.   Selling
diamonds and selling pastry seem to me nearly
the same thing ; excepting, indeed, that the latter
has a fixed price, and, if it soils the fingers more,
requires less deceit.   I have no preference between them.'   ' Do you then suppose that there
are no honest tradesmen ?'   ' I will not absolutely
affirm it ; but I am persuaded the number is small ;
and the few who are honest possess not all I require in a husband.'   ' You are extremely fasti-
dious, methinks : but if you should not find the
idol of your imagination ?'   ' I will die a maid !'
' That would, perhaps, be a harder task than
you imagine : *ennui* will come at last ; the crowd
will be gone by ; you know the fable.'   ' Oh ! I
would take my revenge, *by deserving happiness,*
from the very injustice that would rob me of it.'

MADAME ROLAND.   161

—" I experienced," said she, " a slight sensation of melancholy, when, on casting my eyes about me, I could perceive nothing suitable to my taste. But the feeling soon subsided. I was sensible of my present comforts, and, over futurity, hope threw its enlivening beams. It was the plenitude of happiness overflowing its banks, and clearing away from my future prospects every thing unpleasant."

A young physician, from the south, well educated, of a lively disposition, and some talents, made his pretensions. ' Well,' said madame Phlipon to her daughter, in a tone of tender enquiry, ' what think you of this man? Will *he* suit you?' ' My dear mother, it is impossible for me yet to tell. Gardanne, with his three tails, his medical look, his southern accent, and his black eyebrows, seems more likely to allay than to excite a fever.' ' But you can certainly tell whether he has inspired you with dislike.' ' Neither dislike nor inclination: which of the two may come hereafter I cannot say.' ' We ought to know, however, what answer to give when a proposal shall be made in form.' ' Is the answer to be binding?' ' Assuredly, if we pass our word to a decent man, we must adhere to it.' ' And, if I should not like him?' ' A reasonable young woman, not actuated by caprice, after having once maturely weigh-

ed the motives that determine her in so important
a resolution, will never change her mind.' ' I am
to decide then upon the strength of a single interview.' ' Not exactly that; the intimacy of M.
de Gardanne with our family enables us to judge
of his conduct and way of life; and, by means of
a little enquiry, we shall easily learn his disposition. These are principal points—the sight of the
person is of much less moment.' ' Ah, mamma,
I am in no haste to marry.' ' I believe it, daughter; but, at some time or other, you must settle
yourself in the world; and you have now attained
the proper age. You have refused offers from
many tradesmen, and they are the people from
whom your situation makes offers the most likely
to come. You seem determined not to marry a
man in business: the present match is in every external point of view suitable. Take care then not
to reject it too lightly.' ' It appears to me there
is time enough yet to think about it. M. Gardanne is not, perhaps, himself decided, since it is
certain he has seen me but once.' ' True, but if
that is your only excuse, it possibly may not be
of long duration. Revolve the matter in your
mind, and two days hence let me know your opinion.' Thus ended the dialogue, when her mother kissed her forehead, and left her to reflection.

MADAME ROLAND.   163

These arguments made on the mind of her to whom they were addressed some impression, they at least determined her not to form a precipitate conclusion.   A second interview with M. de Gaidanne made, however, but little difference in her feelings.

Her mother, from some observations that she had made, believed that she saw, in the suitor of her daughter, symptoms of an imperious disposition ; a discovery that failed to alarm the philosophical *Manon*, who, accustomed to watch over herself, to regulate her affections, and to restrain her imagination, and impressed with a strong sense of the rigour and sublimity of the duties of a wife, was not aware of the importance of temper to domestic happiness.   " I reasoned like a recluse," says she, " equally a stranger to the passions and to mankind.   I took my own tranquil, affectionate, generous, and candid heart, as a common measure of the moral qualities of my species."   This connection had nearly taken place, but the minute enquiries of M. Phlipon respecting his intended son-in-law gave offence   M. Gardanne complained of this inquisitorial scrutiny : mademoiselle Phlipon seized the opportunity with engerness to dissolve the engagement, and an end was put to the negociation.   The young lady rejoiced in her escape, and her mother, who had

been alarmed by the vehemence of the lover's remonstrances, readily acquiesced in the decisions
of her daughter.

The health of madame Phlipon began to decline; she had a stroke of the palsy, which, with
affectionate fraud, she represented to her daughter
as a rheumatic affection: the precarious tenure of
her life rendered her doubly anxious for that
daughter's establishment. One day, in particular,
she urged her with melancholy earnestness to accept an honest jeweller, who demanded her hand.
' He has in his favour,' said she, ' great reputation for integrity, habits of sobriety, and mildness
of disposition, with an easy fortune, which may
become brilliant. He knows that yours is no
common mind, professes great respect for you,
and will be proud of following your advice. You
might lead him any way you like.' ' Why, mamma, I do not want a husband who is to be led; he
would be too cumbersome a child for me.' ' Do
you know that you are a very whimsical girl?
For, after all, you would not like a master.'
' My dear mother, let us understand each other:
I should not like a man who would give himself
airs of authority; he would only teach me to resist; but, neither should I like a husband whom
it would be necessary to govern. Either I am
greatly mistaken, or these beings, five foot and

a half high, with beards upon their chins, seldom fail to make us perceive that they are the stronger. Now, if the good man should think proper to remind me of that superiority, he would provoke me; and, if he should submit to be governed, I should be ashamed of my power.' ' I understand you ; you would like a man to think himself the master, while obeying you in every thing.' ' No, it is not that neither: I hate servitude, but I do not think myself made for empire ; it would only embarrass me; my reason finds it quite enough to take care of myself. I should wish to gain the affections of a man so completely worthy of my esteem, that I might be proud of my complaisance; of a man who would make his happiness consist in contributing to mine, in the way that his good sense and affection might think meet.' ' Happiness, daughter, does not always consist in that perfect conformity of ideas and affections which you imagine: were it so, a happy couple would be a phenomenon.' ' Neither do I know any whose happiness I envy.' ' Perhaps so ; but still, among those matches, there may be many preferable to a life of celibacy.' This affectionate mother went on to hint at the probability of her own decease, of its consequences to her daughter, and her anxiety to see her, before that event, the wife of a worthy man. These images overwhelmed mademoiselle Phlipon with grief, and drew from her a flood of tears. ' What,' said her mother, smiling, ' you are alarmed, as if, in taking our resolutions, we ought not to calculate all possible chances. An honest worthy man offers you his hand; you are turned of twenty, and will no longer see so many suitors as have, during the last five years, paid you their homage. I may be snatched away, do not then reject a husband, who has not, it is true, the delicacy on which you set so great a value—a quality rare, even where we look for it most: but he is a man who will love you, and with whom you may be happy.' ' Yes, mamma,' replied she with a sigh, ' happy as you have been.' Madame Phlipon, disconcerted at this remark, remained silent, nor from that moment renewed the subject. " A stranger," observes her daughter, " might, at the first glance, have perceived the great difference between my father and mother; but who, like me, could *feel* all the excellence of the latter? I had not, however, fully calculated all she must have had to suffer. Accustomed from my childhood to see the most profound peace prevail in the house, I could not judge of the efforts it might cost to maintain it."

During later periods of her life, mademoiselle Phlipon was more quick-sighted; she had gained

MADAME ROLAND.   167

an ascendancy over her father, of which she always availed herself in favour of her mother: but,
in private, not a word passed between the mother and daughter on the subject: respecting the
husband and the father they were mutually reserved and silent, excepting when any thing could
be said in his praise.

M. Phlipon had lost, by degrees, his habit of
industry; parish business had first called him
from home; sauntering abroad had afterwards
become his passion; a rage for gaming next
assailed him; connections formed at a coffee-house
led him elsewhere; and the lottery held out al-
lmements too great to be resisted.   The desire of
making a fortune, engaged him in speculations
foreign to his profession, speculations in which he
was not always successful. He was disgusted
with labour, and the thirst of riches made him
set every thing at hazard. As his art was less
exercised, his talents diminished; while an irregular life impaired his faculties his sight became
weak, and his hand tremulous. His pupils, without the superintendance of their master, were
less capable of supplying his place; it became
necessary to diminish their number, and the tide
of business turned into other channels. These
changes had gradually taken place; madame Phlipon perceived them, and grew pensive; some-

times she imperfectly intimated the state of affairs to her daughter, who concealed the observations she had made, lest they should add to the inquietude of a mother whom she tenderly loved. Thus clouds gathered over their domestic happiness; and, though the peace of the family appeared unchanged, its cheerfulness and confidence was no more.

Madame Phlipon had, for more than a year, been declining in her health: after various remedies, administered by the physicians in vain, they prescribed exercise, of which she was no longer capable, and country air. Just before Whitsuntide 1775, it was agreed that the family should pass the holydays at Meudon. Madame Phlipon appeared relieved by this little excursion, and resumed a portion of her accustomed activity. Her daughter, on their return to town, proposed a visit to the convent, where she had promised, after the holydays, to call on her friends. At the moment of setting out, her mother, a little fatigued by the exertions of the preceding day, declined accompanying her: mademoiselle Phlipon would then have broken her engagement, but this her mother would not permit. Her visit to the convent was short. ' Why are you in such haste?' said her friend, St. Agatha; ' does any one expect you.' ' No, but I am anxious to return to my

mother.' ' Why, you told me she was better?'
' I did so ; nor does she expect me so soon : but
I know not what it is that torments me ; I shall
not be easy till I see her again.' " On saying
this," says she, " I felt my heart swell, as it were,
in despite of me."

On the subject of these *presentiments*, to which,
on other occasions, madame Roland alludes in
her Memoirs, she justly observes, that they can
be nothing more than rapid glances, caught by
persons of quick perception and exquisite feelings, of a multitude of things, in themselves undefinable and scarcely perceptible, which are *felt*
rather than understood; and whence an emotion results, for which, at the time, it would be
difficult to account, although afterwards justified
by the event. This perception is lively in proportion to our sensibility, and to our interest in
the object of our anxiety.

On the return of mademoiselle Phlipon, who
had hurried from the convent, she found, standing
at the door of the house, a little girl, the child of
a neighbour, who exclaimed on her approach :
' Ah, mademoiselle! your mamma is taken very ill ;
she has sent for my mother, who is gone up stairs
with her to her apartment.' Struck with terror,
she uttered, in reply, some inarticulate sounds,

and rushed towards her mother's chamber. She found her recliningin an arm-chair, her head fallen on her shoulder, her eyes wild, her mouth open, and her arms hanging lifeless. Her countenance brightened on seeing her daughter, while she spoke with difficulty a few half-formed words. She made an effort to raise her arms, but one only obeyed the impulse. Laying her hand on the face of her daughter, she wiped away the tears with which it was bedewed, tapped her gently on the check, and tried to smile. Again she endeavoured to speak: vain attempt! palsy had annihilated half her frame. Mademoiselle Phlipon, overwhelmed with grief, had in an instant dispatched messenger, for her father and the physician, while she flew herself to a neighbouring apothecary. The disorder increased with a rapid and dreadful progress, while the short and convulsive breathing of the invalid indicated approaching dissolution. Her daughter, with excessive activity, ordered every thing; and, before it could be done by others, did every thing herself. At ten in the evening, the physician, taking aside M. Phlipon, proposed to send for a priest, who, according to the forms of the catholic church, might administer to the patient extreme unction. Mademoiselle Phlipon, standing with a light, which she held mechanically at the bed's-feet of her dying

MADAME ROLAND.   171

mother, appeared as if in a stupor, a waking
and terrible dream, that suspended all her faculties. Her eyes were fixed on one spot, her
heart was occupied by one sentiment. At length,
letting the candle fall from her hand, she fell
senseless on the floor. On her recovery, she
found herself in the parlour, surrounded by the
family. Turning her eyes towards the door, she
rose from her seat, and, with supplicating gestures,
while she was held back, implored permission to
return to the chamber of her mother. The constraint which was opposed to her, and the mournful silence that prevailed, but too well expressed
that all was over. Her father at that instant
entered the room, pale and speechless with sorrow.
His appearance drew forth a general exclamation
of grief. His daughter, in a sort of frenzy, broke
from those who withheld her, and rushed im-
petuously forth. Having reached the chamber,
she threw herself on the bed of her mother, in a
transport of anguish and despair. It was with
difficulty, after acting a thousand extravagances,
that she was separated from the corpse, and
carried into the house of a neighbour, whence her
relation, M. Besnard, took her in a carriage and
conveyed her to his own. She fainted on alight-
ing, and being put to bed, passed a fortnight be

tween life and death, in terrible convulsions;
struggling with a continued sense of suffocation.
A strong constitution, and the unwearied attentions which she received from her relations, could
only have preserved her from falling a victim in
this first trial of sorrow.   Eight days elapsed before she experienced the relief of tears, the sluices
of which were at length opened by a letter from
Sophia; the soothing tenderness of friendship
recalled her faculties, and melted, while it consoled, her heart: it produced an effect which the
warm bath and medical skill had essayed in vain.
To moral disorders moral remedies can only be
administered with success.   As her tears flowed
freely, the convulsions abated, their paroxysms
became less frequent, the sense of suffocation
ceased, and her health began to amend.   Her
father presented himself before her in the garb
of sorrow: he undertook to comfort her by those
common-place expressions and sentiments to
which the understanding attends with disgust,
and which the heart repels as an insult.   " I felt,"
says she, " the inefficacy of this pretended consolation, so little adapted to my turn of mind;
and, for the first time, perhaps, measured the distance that separated my father from myself.   It
seemed as if he was tearing away the reverential
veil under which I had hitherto considered him

MADAME ROLAND.   173

I found myself, by the loss of my mother, completely an orphan: my father could never understand me: a new kind of grief oppressed my
afflicted heart: I fell again into the deepest despair. The tears and sorrows of my worthy
relations, however, still offered me occasions of
tender emotion; they had their effect, and I was
snatched from the perils that threatened my existence. Why, alas! did it not then terminate?
It was my first affliction; by how many others has
it been followed!"

Madame Phlipon was only fifty years of age,
when an imposthume in her head, which had long
been forming, and which discovered itself, after
her decease, by the flux that took place through
her nose and ears, put an end to her existence.
" On the day that she was snatched from me,"
says her daughter, " I left her, at three o'clock
in the afternoon, apparently well. I returned
at half past five. She had been struck with the
palsy. At midnight she no longer appertained to
me. Feeble toys of a pityless destiny! why are
such lively sentiments, and projects so grand,
connected with an existence so frail!" The character of the deceased had been more amiable than
brilliant. " Naturally wise and good," observes
her daughter, " virtue did not seem to cost her

any effort; she knew how to render it mild and easy
like herself. Prudent and calm, tender without passion, her pure and tranquil spirit respired gently, as
flows the docile stream, that bathes with equal complacence the valley which it embellishes, and the
foot of the rock by which it is restrained." With a
temperament sanguine and ardent, like that of mademoiselle Phlipon, most fortunate for her youth
was the possession of such an instructress.

'It is charming,' said the abbé Legrand, mourn-
fully, at the bed-side of this affectionate daughter,
whom he came to visit at the house of her relations—
'It is charming to possess sensibility, but unfortunate to have so much of it!' As mademoiselle
Phlipon began to recover, her kind friends were
eager to receive in succession the persons who came
to visit her, in the hope of diverting the melancholy
that had seized her spirits. "I seemed not to exist,"
says she, "in the world where I was placed. Absorbed in grief, I scarcely paid attention to what
was passing around me. Recalling by starts the
frightful idea of my loss, shrieks all on a sudden
would escape me, my outstretched arms stiffened,
and I swooned away."

During the intervals of these transports, she recollected the cares and the kindness of her relations,
and sought to alleviate their concern and anxiety.
The abbé Legrand talked to her of her mother, in

MADAME ROLAND.   175

order to rouse her attention, and to lead her insensibility to other objects and ideas. When he believed her sufficiently recovered to attend to a book, he brought to her the celebrated Heloise of Rousseau. " The perusal of this," says she, " was my first employment. I was then twenty-one years of age; I had read a great deal; I was acquainted with a considerable number of writers, historians, learned men, and philosophers; but Rousseau made on me an impression similar to that which Plutarch had done when I was eight years of age. It appeared to me that this was the proper food for my mind, and the interpreter of those ideas which I had before entertained, but which Rousseau alone knew how to explain to me. Plutarch had prepared me to become a republican; had roused that strength and grandeur of character by which a republican is constituted; had inspired me with a real enthusiasm for public virtue and liberty. Rousseau pointed out to me the domestic happiness to which I could aspire, the ineffable enjoyments I was capable of tasting. Ah! if he is able to protect me from follies, could he arm me against a passion? Amidst the corrupt age in which I was destined to live, and the revolution which I was then far from anticipating, I acquired beforehand all that could render me capable of great sacrifices, and expose me to great misfortunes. Death will only be to me the term of both. I expect it; nor would I have filled the short interval which separates me from it with the recital of my private history, had calumny not dragged me upon the stage, for the purpose of making on those whom she would ruin a more cruel attack. I love to publish truths, that interest not myself alone; and I wish to conceal none, that their connection may serve towards their demonstration."

The return to her father's was a new trial for the affectionate sensibility of mademoiselle Phlipon. They had taken the ill-judged precaution of removing her mother's portrait, as if the place where it had hung would not more painfully recal her loss. She instantly demanded it, and it was restored to its situation. The domestic cares now devolved on mademoiselle Phlipon. " I have never been able to comprehend," observes she, " how these cares can absorb the attention of a woman, however considerable may be her household, who possesses method and activity; a little vigilance, and a wise distribution of employments, are all that is necessary*. Lei-

---

* Madame Roland's acquaintance with her sex could not have been very extensive. Has their education been such that we may reasonably expect from them method, activity, vigilance, and wisdom? Alas, no! These are great qualities, and rarely combined.

MADAME ROLAND. **177**

sure," adds she, " will always be found by persons
who know how to employ their time. Those who
want time are the people who do nothing. Nor is
it surprising that women who receive and pay useless visits, or think themselves ill dressed unless
many hours are consecrated to the science, find their
days long from mere lassitude, and yet too short for
the performance of their duties."

The studies of mademoiselle Phlipon became
every day more dear to her, and constituted her
only consolation. " Left more than ever by myself," says she, " and often in a melancholy humour, I felt the necessity of writing. I loved to
render to myself an account of my own ideas, and
to enlighten them by the intervention of my pen.
When not employed in this way, I revised still more
than I meditated. I pursued a chain of reasoning,
and by these means bridled my imagination." She
entitled her performances, of which she began to
make some collections, " The Works of Leisure
Hours, and different Reflections." Her intention
was by this means to fix her opinions, and to possess
a register of her sentiments and the progress of her
mind. " Never," says she, " did I feel the slightest
temptation to become an author. I perceived, at a
very early period, that a woman who acquires this
title, loses more than she gains. The men do not

like, and her own sex criticise, her. If her works
are bad, she is ridiculed; if good, she is bereaved
of the reputation annexed to them. If the public are
forced to acknowledge that she has talents, they sift
her character, her morals, her conduct, and balance
the reputation of her genius by the publicity which
they give to her errors*. Beside," adds she, with
truth, " my *happiness* was my chief concern, and I
perceived that the public never interfered with the
happiness of any one without marring it. Ah, my
God! what an injury did those persons do to me,
who took it upon them to withdraw the veil under
which I loved to remain concealed. During twelve
years of my life, I have laboured along with my
husband in the same manner as I ate with him, because the one was as natural to me as the other.
During his administration, if it was necessary to
express great or striking truths, I employed the
whole bent of my mind; that its efforts should be
preferable to those of a secretary, was but natural.
I loved my country†; I was an enthusiast in the

---

* Madame Roland might have added, And if they cannot find any real blemishes in her conduct, they are ingenious to substitute fiction for facts; the more absurd, the
more credible and the more eagerly received.

† Fickle people, and frivolous as light! unworthy of the
sacrifices that have been made for them!

cause of liberty; I was unacquainted with any interest, or with any passions, that could enter into competition with these; and my language, which was that of the heart and of truth, ought to have been pure and pathetic." But to return.

Monsieur Phlipon, for some time after the death of his wife, endeavoured to remain more at home with his daughter; but of this constraint he soon became weary. The means of rendering his house agreeable to him, by drawing a circle of acquaintance round him, were not in her power, since she had no other society than that of her old relations. " If I wished to converse with him," said she, " we had but few ideas in common, and he then probably hankered after a mode of life, with which he did not wish that I should become acquainted. Become a widower at the very moment when he stood in need of new chains to confine him at home, my poor father kept a mistress, that he might not present to his daughter a step-mother: he had recourse to play to indemnify himself for the loss of business; and, without ceasing to be an honest man, he ruined himself insensibly, and without making any noise."

The relations of mademoiselle Phlipon, confiding in her father's affection for her, believed that to his guardianship her interest might safely be entrusted. If she felt the contrary, filial delicacy and respect

MADAME ROLAND.

kept her silent. " Behold me then," says she, " alone in the house, my time divided between my work and my studies." Her servant, a little woman, lively and gay, and fifty-five years of age, attached herself to a mistress who rendered her life happy and comfortable. This woman attended her, during the absence of her father, in her walks abroad, which seldom extended beyond the church, or the residence of her relations. " I carried with me to church," says she, " if not the tender piety I formerly possessed, at least a sufficiency of decency and recollection. I no longer accompanied the *ordinary of the mass.* I read some christian work : I had preserved a great passion for St. Augustine ; and assuredly, there are fathers of the church whom one may peruse without being devout : there is food in them both for the heart and the mind."

Mademoiselle Phlipon wished to study the eloquence of the pulpit, and for this purpose to go through a course of sermons. With Bossuet and Flechier she was already acquainted ; Bourdaloue and Massillon followed. In the memorandum-book of this young philosopher might be seen the names of these celebrated divines by the side of those of Paw, of Raynal, and the author of the System of Nature. Unfettered by systems, truth and improvement were the objects of her pursuit. From reading sermens, a natural transition, she passed to com-

MADAME ROLAND.   181

posing one. Wearied with the constant recurrence
of mysteries, she determined to draw up a moral
discourse, in which the incarnation and the devil
should not be mentioned. She took for her subject,
the love of her neighbour. Her little uncle, become a
canon of Vincennes, whom she amused with her
performance, blamed her for not taking up this employment earlier, that he might have availed himself.
of her talent.

The grief and sensibility displayed by mademoiselle
Phlipon at the death of her mother, attracted notice, and procured her many marks of regard. M.
de Boismorel, whom she had not seen since his visits
at her grandmother's, came to pay his respects to
her at the house of her father. He repeated his visit,
during her absence from home, and was taken by
her father into her little apartment, on a table in
which her compositions were lying. Monsieur
Phlipon, proud of the genius of his daughter, talked
to his guest of her studies, and, having excited his
curiosity, took upon himself to gratify it by communicating to him some of her writings. Mademoiselle Phlipon was, on her return, on learning
what had passed, displeased and offended. But her
anger was appeased the next day, by the receipt of
a well-written letter from M. Boismorel, with an
offer of the use of his library, expressed in the
most obliging and flattering terms. A correspond-

ence, from this incident, commenced between them, which afforded to our young student both instruction and pleasure.

A visit to the family of M. Boismorel followed, who resided in a charming house, near the banks of the Seine, at a little distance from Paris. Mademoiselle Phlipon and her father were received by the ladies of the family in a summer saloon. ‘ How well your dear daughter looks !’ exclaimed the mother of M. Boismorel, whom the reader may probably recollect ; ‘ but, do you know, that my son is enchanted with her ? Tell me, mademoiselle, do you not wish to be married ?’ ‘ Others have already thought for me on that subject, madam, but I have not as yet seen reason to come to any determination.’ ‘ You are difficult, I suppose ; have you any repugnance to a man of a certain age ?’ ‘ The knowledge I might have of a person would only determine my attachment, my refusal, or my acceptance.’ ‘ Those kinds of marriages have most solidity ; a young man often escapes through our fingers, when one thinks him most attached.—She is dressed with taste,’ observed the old lady, turning to her daughter-in-law. ‘ Ah, extremely well, and with so much modesty !’ replied the young lady, who was a devotee, and whose agreeable face was shaded with the curls of her hair, disposed with much nicety and art. ‘ How different,’ added she, ‘ from that

MADAME ROLAND.   **183**

ridiculous mass of plumage we see fluttering above
empty heads! You do not love feathers, mademoiselle?' 'I never wear them, madam; because, being the daughter 'of an artist, and on foot, they
would seem to announce a rank which does not belong to me.' 'But would you wear them, were you
in a different situation?' 'I do not know; I attach but little importance to trifles: I estimate, in
regard to myself, these matters by convenience only,
and am careful never to judge respecting any one
in consequence of the first glimpse of her toilette.'
This severe observation was pronounced with mildness. 'A philosopher!' exclaimed the lady, with
a sigh, recollecting that her guest belonged not to
her own sect. M. Boismorel put an end to this
personal inquisition, by conducting mademoiselle to
visit his garden and library. Here she recovered
her ease and her spirits, while she pointed out the
volumes, and collections of works, with the perusal
of which she wished her obliging host to favour her.
Among these were Bayle, and the *Memoirs* of the
academies. On another visit to this family, in
which mademoiselle Phlipon met a large company,
she observes: "Those points of view in which I
consider the world, and examine it unperceived by
any one, serve but to disgust me, and to attach me
still more to my own manner of living."

M. de Boismorel carried his young friend to the

meeting of the French academy, on the anniversary of St. Lewis, where she listened with pleasure to a discourse of the abbé de Besplas, who mingled with his subject some bold philosophical opinions, and oblique satires upon government. At the theatre mademoiselle Phlipon appeared with the same unaffected ingenuous character: without considering those who were around her, she smiled and wept at the various incidents and sentiments pourtrayed or expressed on the stage, with the happy simplicity of uncorrupted youth.

The eulogy on Catinat, by La Harpe, which had gained the prize at the academy, inspired M. de Boismorel with the desire of making a visit to St. Gratien, where Catinat had, at a distance from the court and its honours, ended his days in retirement. He proposed this pilgrimage to M. Phlipon and his daughter, who agreed with pleasure to accompany him. On the morning of a Michaelmas-day, they proceeded to the valley of Montmorency, and visited the borders of the lake by which it was embellished. They then ascended to St. Gratien, and reposed under the shade of the trees which Catinat had planted with his own hand. After a frugal repast, they spent the remainder of the day in the park of Montmorency, where they beheld the cottage which had been inhabited by J. J. Rousseau.

Through M. Boismorel mademoiselle Phlipon be-

MADAME ROLAND. 185

came acquainted with all that was novel and interesting in the republic of letters. " I saw him but seldom," said she, " but I heard from him every week. His conduct was that of a man of sense and sensibility, who honoured my sex, esteemed my person, and, as it were, protected my taste. His letters resembled himself: an agreeable seriousness characterised them; they bore the stamp of a mind superior to prejudices, and of a respectful friendship." This gentleman, greatly attached to literature, and admiring the talents of his young *protegée*, pressed her to choose a subject, and to make an essay of her genius in composition. Thus urged, mademoiselle Phlipon explained to him her disinterested attachment to study, which she wished to render serviceable to her happiness, without the intervention of any kind of glory, which she justly considered as calculated only to trouble her repose. With her arguments on this subject, she mingled extempore verses, which her correspondent replied to in the same style.

Calling on her one day, he informed her that he was desirous of practising a stratagem to quicken the industry of his son, a youth of seventeen years of age, whose application to his studies had lately begun to give way to a taste for dissipation, and who took more delight in the Italian opera than in the mathematics. ' It is necessary,' proceeded mon-

sieur de Boismorel, ' that you should reprimand
my son in a letter full of wisdom and penetration:
in short, write in such a manner as your own mind
shall dictate; stimulate his self-love, and awaken generous resolutions.' ' Me, sir! me? and in what
manner, I beseech you, shall I be able to preach to
your son?' ' Adopt any mode you please; your
name shall not appear; it shall be so contrived as if
some person, acquainted with his conduct and interested in his welfare, takes this method to warn
him of his danger. I will get the letter conveyed
to him at a moment when it shall produce its full
effect. At a proper opportunity he shall be informed to what physician he is indebted for his
cure.' ' Oh! you must never mention my name!
But you have other friends, who can do this service
better.' ' I think otherwise; and I demand of you
this favour.' ' Very well; I renounce every other consideration, to demonstrate my desire of obliging you.
I shall transmit to you the rough draught of my letter, of which you shall give me your opinion and
corrections.' On the same evening mademoiselle
Phlipon drew up a pointed and somewhat ironical
epistle, calculated to flatter the self-love, and excite
the reason of a young man, and to recal his attention
to serious subjects, by considerations in which his
happiness was involved. The father, delighted with
this production, besought his young friend to send

MADAME ROLAND. 187

it without the alteration of a word. It was accordingly inclosed in a letter to Sophia, to be put into the post-office at Amiens. Several circumstances were, previous to its reception, arranged by monsieur Boismorel, for the purpose of insuring its effect. The young man received it, was touched by its contents, attributed it to the celebrated Duclos, and went to thank him for his kindness. Deceived in this conjecture, he makes farther guesses with no better success; and, at length, in some measure, resumes his studies.

Not long after this circumstance, M. de Boismorel walking with his son on a very hot day, from Bercy to Vincennes, where mademoiselle Phlipon was then with her uncle, and whither he brought to her the abbé Delisle's translation of the Georgics, was struck with a *coup de soleil.* Having treated it lightly, a fever ensued, followed by a coma *, which carried him off, in the vigour of his age, after a few days' illness. Mademoiselle Phlipon wept bitterly the death of her kind friend and valuable instructor; " nor can I ever recollect him," says she, " without experiencing that mournful regret, that sentiment of veneration and tenderness, which always accompanies the remembrance of a good man." When time had in some degree softened her sorrow,

---

* An apoplectic disorder.

she composed a monody to his memory, which, without disclosing it to any one, she sung, accompanied by her guitar. On a visit of condolence, which her father paid to the son of their lost and valued friend, the young man told him in a vacant tone of voice, that he had found and thrown into a corner the letters of mademoiselle Phlipon to his father, to be restored to her if she should wish it; and that among them he had discovered the original of a certain epistle, which he had himself received. His guest, sensible of what was alluded to, said but little in reply. The youth appeared to be piqued, " whence," says his fair monitress, " I concluded that he was a fool, and troubled myself no more about him.'

Many circumstances less interesting, and less important to the formation of the mind of this truly admirable woman, this martyr to humanity and virtue, whose untimely fate can never be sufficiently lamented, are here omitted, lest this article should be extended to an unreasonable length.

In speaking of Saint-Lette, one of the members of the council of Pondicherry, and who, on his return to Paris, in 1776, brought letters from a friend to M. Phlipon and his daughter, which introduced him to their acquaintance—" Those," says the latter, " who have seen much, are always worth hearing; and those who have felt much have always seen more than others, even when they have tra-

MADAME ROLAND.   189

velled less than Saint-Lette. He presented me
with several of his performances : I communicated
to him some of my reveries; and, in a prophetical
tone of voice, and with a full persuasion of the
event, he repeated to me several times, ' You are
in the right, mademoiselle, to be on your guard,
for all this will end in your writing a book.'" ' It
shall then be under another person's name,' replied
the young lady, ' for I will sooner eat my fingers
than become an author.'

Saint-Lette met at M. Phlipon's a man destined to
have a powerful influence on the fate of his daughter, and with whom she had been acquainted for
some months.

Her friend Sophia, whose situation led her into
mingled society, had frequently mentioned in her
letters a man of merit, who, on account of his
place, occasionally resided at Amiens, where he visited at her mother's, and who came every winter to
Paris, and often in the spring made still longer journeys. Sophia, pleased with a man whose instructive
conversation, amidst the frivolous crowd by which
she was surrounded, appeared to her with peculiar
advantage, whose austere and simple manners inspired confidence, and who, without being beloved
by the world, to which he bore but little resemblance, was yet generally respected, talked to him
of her *dear friend*; while in the family, the warmth

and constancy of an attachment formed in a convent, and to which time had given respectability,
was a perpetual theme. M. Roland had also been
shewn the portrait of this dear friend. ' Why
then,' said he frequently, ' do you not make me acquainted with her? I go to Paris every year, cannot I carry to her a letter?'

The desired commission was at length obtained,
in September, 1775. " I was still in mourning
for my mother," says the friend of Sophia, " and
in that mild, melancholy, state of mind, which suc-
ceeds to violent grief. Whoever presented himself
from Sophia could not fail to be well received."

" This letter," observes Sophia, in her introductory epistle, " will be delivered by the philosopher
whom I have already mentioned to you, M. Roland de la Platiere, an enlightened man, of pure
morals, and who cannot be reproached with any
thing but his great admiration of the ancients, at
the expence of the moderns, whom he despises, and
the foible of loving to speak too much of himself."
" I beheld," says her *dear friend*, to whom this description was addressed, " a man somewhat more
than forty years of age, tall, negligent in his appearance, and with that kind of formality contracted
by study ; but his manners were simple and easy,
and, without possessing the polish of the world,
they connected with the gravity of a philosopher the

MADAME ROLAND. 191

politeness of a man of birth. His person was lean, his complexion accidentally yellow ; his forehead, sparingly furnished with hair and very open, did not injure the regularity of his features, which, however, it rendered more respectable than seductive. When he became animated in conversation, or with the idea of any thing that pleased him, an extremely subtle smile, and a lively expression which pervaded his countenance, made him appear quite another person. His voice was masculine, his sentences short, like those of a man whose respiration is not very long. His discourse, full of facts, from a head replete with ideas, occupied the judgment rather than flattered the ear. His language was sometimes poignant, but harsh and destitute of harmony*."

La Blancherie, about this period, returned to Paris, whence he had been for some time absent. On his visit to mademoiselle Phlipon, where he learned the death of her mother, he manifested a degree of surprise and grief, that, while it affected,

---

* It is justly observed by madame Roland, that the charms of the voice possess a powerful influence over the senses ; and that this charm does not merely belong to the quality of the sound, but results still more from that delicacy of sentiment which varies the expression, and modulates the accent.

pleased her. He repeated his visits, and was received with pleasure. M. Phlipon, whose continual absence from home rendered his daughter's situation delicate, and who disliked the trouble of
performing the office of a duenna, announced to her
his intention of desiring La Blancherie to desist from
his visits. Mademoiselle heard this resolution with
some degree of chagrin : interested in favour of La
Blancherie, she had begun to believe it possible to
love him. " The head, I believe," says she, " was
only at work; but it was making some progress."
Having formed the resolution of softening in some
degree her father's prohibition, by imposing the in-
junction herself on La Blancherie, she addressed to
him a polite letter of dismission, which, while it
deprived him of all hope of replying, did not destroy that of having pleased. This circumstance
gave rise to some melancholy, but not unpleasing,
reflections in the mind of the fair writer ; which
were, however, suspended by the arrival of Sophia
at Paris, who remained some time in the capital,
with her mother and her sister Henrietta. " The
latter," says mademoiselle Phlipon, " being now
more on a level with us, in consequence of the age
she had attained, and the sedateness she had acquired, became also my dear friend. The charms
of her lively imagination darted coruscations around,
and animated the ties which she had formed."

MADAME ROLAND.   193

The friends, with mademoiselle d'Hangard, often repaired to the Luxembourg, where they met La Blancherie, whose respectful salute was by one of the party returned with some emotion. ' You then know this gentleman ?' says mademoiselle d'Hangard, who had at first imagined the salute intended for herself. ' Yes, and do not you?' ' Oh ! certainly ; but I have never spoken to him. I visit the mademoiselles Bordenave, the youngest of whom he demanded in marriage.' ' Is it long since ?' was a question asked by one of the ladies with some degree of earnest curiosity. ' A year, perhaps eighteen months. He found means to get himself introduced into the house : he went thither from time to time, and at length made a declaration. These young women are rich, the youngest is handsome. He has not a farthing, and is in search of an heiress, for he made a similar demand in respect to another person of their acquaintance, of which they were informed. The ladies dismissed him ; and we call him *the lover of the eleven thousand virgins.* How did you know him ?' ' By seeing him often at madame l'Epine's concert,' answered mademoiselle Phlipon, while she bit her lips and withheld any farther information, chagrined at the idea of having thought herself beloved by a man who, in soliciting her hand, had probably been influenced only by sor-

did motives : while yet more mortified by the recollection of the letter she had written to him, she
found in what had passed a subject for meditation
and future caution.

A few months after this adventure, a little Savoyard came one day to tell the maid of mademoiselle,
that some person wanted to speak to her. The servant went out, and returning informed her mistress,
that M. la Blancherie intreated to see her. It was
on a Sunday, when mademoiselle Phlipon expected
her relations. ' Yes,' replied she, ' let him come
immediately ; go, find and bring him with you.'
The lover of the eleven thousand virgins enters ; the
lady was seated in a corner near the fire-side. ' I
did not dare, mademoiselle, to present myself to
you, after your prohibition. I was extremely desirous to speak to you, and I cannot express what I
felt in consequence of the dear and cruel letter which
you then addressed to me. My situation is since
altered ; I have projects at present with which you
must not remain unacquainted.' He then began to
unfold to her the plan of a moral and critical work,
to which he invited her approbation and concur-
rence. He was allowed to go on for some time
without interruption, and, even after he had finished
speaking, to make some little. pause. Mademoiselle
then began to observe to him, with calm politeness,
that she had herself taken the trouble to request the

MADAME ROLAND.   195

discontinuance of his visits, on account of those sentiments respecting her, which he had thought proper to declare to her father, and for which she was desirous of demonstrating her gratitude. That, at her time of life, the vivacity of the imagination was but too apt to mingle itself with every transaction, and even sometimes to change their appearance. But that error was not a crime, and she had already recovered from hers with too good a grace to give herself any more concern on that subject. She admired his literary projects, she added, but without wishing to participate in them, or in those of any other person. She must, therefore, confine herself to wishes for his success, and it was to tell him this that she had consented to see him, and also that he might hereafter avoid every similar attempt. Having thus spoken, with great composure, she besought him to conclude his visit.

Surprise, grief, agitation, were all about to be displayed, when a stop was put to the exhibition by an observation of the lady, ' That she was ignorant whether the mademoiselles Bordenave, and others whom he had honoured with his addresses, nearly at the same period, had expressed themselves in regard to him with equal frankness; but that hers was unbounded, nor did the resolutions she had taken in consequence admit of any explanation.' At

the same time she rose, bowed, and made a motion with her hand towards the door. One of her
relations entering at that moment, the lover of the
eleven thousand virgins retreated in silence, and made
his appearance no more, " Who," says the lady,
" has not since heard of the *agent-general of the correspondence of the arts and sciences ?*" But to return
to M. Roland.

During the last eight or nine months, he had several times visited at M. Phlipon's, where, though
his visits were not frequent, neither were they
short; they appeared also to be paid with pleasure.
With his frank and instructive conversation, mademoiselle Phlipon was never wearied, while the attention with which he found himself listened to by
a sensible and amiable young woman, interested and
gratified his feelings. It was on the eve of his return from Germany that this acquaintance commenced; he was then preparing for a tour into
Italy, and, in the arrangement of his affairs previous
to his journey, he chose to deposit his manuscripts
with his new and amiable friend, who, should any
misfortune happen to the author, was to remain
mistress of their disposal. This mark of confidence
and esteem was not received without gratitude and
pleasure. On the day of his departure, M. Roland,
accompanied by Saint-Lette, dined at mademoiselle
Phlipon's. On taking leave, he asked permission to

MADAME ROLAND.   197

salute his fair friend, a privilege which was not granted without a blush. ' You are happy in departing,'
said Saint-Lette to him, gravely ; ' but make haste
to return, in order to demand another.'

During the stay of Saint-Lette in France, his
friend Sevelinge became a widower. Saint-Lette
repaired to him at Soissons, where he resided, and
brought him back with him to Paris, in the hope of
diverting his grief.   They visited mademoiselle Phlipon together.   Sevelinge possessed a cultivated
mind, and a taste for letters.   Saint-Lette in leaving France felt a pleasure in having introduced his
friends to each other.   Saint-Lette at length reim_
barked for Pondicherry, where he arrived ill, and
died within six weeks.   His death was regretted by
his friends in France, and more especially by Sevelinge.   A correspondence had taken place between
the latter and mademoiselle Phlipon.   " His letters,'
says she " which were written in a good style, and
abounded in agreeable description, afforded me great
pleasure.   They wore an appearance of a mild philosophy, and a melancholy sensibility, for which I
always possessed a great inclination.   What Diderot
has said on this subject is exceedingly just, ' That
great taste supposes great sensibility, delicate or-
gans, and a temperament inclined to melancholy.'"

K 3

Monsieur Phlipon at length began to discover, that it was useless to display abilities at the expence of postage. His daughter, chagrined at this intimation, communicated her perplexity to her little uncle, who authorised her to cause the letters of Sevelinge to be addressed to his house. Some manuscripts which, at the desire of Saint-Lette, had been entrusted to the perusal of Sevelinge, were returned to the author, with critical observations; " of which," says she, " I was exceedingly vain; for I did not suppose my *works* worth examination. They were in my own eyes reveries, sage enough, but common, and relating to things with which it appeared to me every one was acquainted. The only merit which I thought they possessed, was their originality, in having been composed by a young maiden. The events of the revolution, the change of affairs, the variety of my situations, the frequent comparisons with a great crowd, and with people esteemed on account of their merit, were all necessary, in order to make me perceive, that the platform on which I stood was not encumbered by numbers."

The academy of Besançon proposed, as the subject for a prize, the following question : " In what manner can the education of women contribute to render men better ?" Mademoiselle Phlipon, struck

MADAME ROLAND. 199

with the idea, seized her pen, and composed a discourse, which she sent without a name, but which
was not judged worthy of the reward; an honour
which no one obtained. The question was proposed
anew for the following year. " In wishing to treat
on this subject," says she, " I deemed it absurd to
determine on a mode of education unconnected
with general manners, which depend on government, and conceived that we ought not to pretend
to reform one sex by the other, but to ameliorate
the species by means of good laws. Accordingly,
I mentioned what it appeared to me that women
ought to be; but added, that it was impossible to
render them such but by a new order of things.
This notion, certainly philosophical and just, did
not come within the plan of the academy. Instead
of solving, I reasoned on the problem."

A copy of this discourse was sent to M. Sevelinge,
who confined his remarks to the style. "My head,"
says the author, " became cool, I discovered my
work to be defective in the very foundation, and I
amused myself with criticising it, as if it had been
the production of another."

In this communication of talents between the
correspondents, more than a twelvemonth elapsed.
Sevelinge appeared at length to be uneasy respecting
the situation of his young friend, and weary himself

of living alone *. He made many reflections on the charms of a rational society; his correspondent agreed with him; and they reasoned for some time on the subject. The gentleman soon after made a journey to Paris, and presented himself at M. Phlipon's, incognito, as if upon business. Mademoiselle, though she received him herself, did not recollect her friend, who withdrew with a mortified air. This circumstance recalled his features to her memory; but still she remained doubtful as to his identity. His letters at length made the discovery. The singularity of the adventure produced on the mind of the lady a disagreeable, though undefinable, impression. The correspondence relaxed, and after a time entirely ceased.

Mademoiselle Phlipon went sometimes to Vincennes, to visit her uncle at his canonical residence, where the walks were delightful, and the society agreeable. The castle of Vincennes was inhabited by a number of persons, whom the court gratified with apartments. " My uncle," says his niece, " was well received every-where, but visited little, and saw at home only a small number of persons. But on our return from a walk, we usually stopped in the evening at the pavilion on the bridge, belong-

---

* Sevelinge was fifty-three years of age, possessed a small fortune, and held a place in the department of the provincial finances.

MADAME ROLAND.   201

ing to the park, where the women assembled. There I found new pictures to paint. The tragedies of Voltaire, which she read and rehearsed with her uncle, occupied a part of the days: " and those lame concerts," says she, " after supper, when, on the table which they had just cleared, muff-cases served by way of pulpit to the good canon Bareux, in spectacles, snoring in a thorough-bass, while I scraped on the violin, and my uncle made a noise with his flute. Ah ! I shall recur to these gentle scenes, if they permit me to live."

The manuscripts left by M. Roland under the care of mademoiselle Phlipon, during the eighteen months which he passed in Italy, made her better acquainted with the author than even a personal intercourse could have done. They consisted of travels, plans of works, reflections, and anecdotes respecting the writer, whose strong mind, austere probity, strict principles, knowledge, and taste, thus discovered themselves. Born amidst opulence, he was descended from an ancient family, whose fortunes had been melted away by prodigality and disorder. The youngest of five brothers, who had been made to enter the church, he had left his parental mansion at the age of nineteen, to avoid taking orders or entering into commerce, to both of which he was equally averse. He had formed a

project of going to the Indies, which the state of his
health had prevented.　M. Godinat, a relation and
inspector of manufactures at Rouen, proposed to
him to engage in that part of the administration.
The young man complied, distinguished himself by
his activity, and at length became advantageously
settled.　Travelling and study divided his time.
Before he set out to Italy, he brought to M. Phlipon's his best-beloved brother, a benedictine and a
prior, a man of talents and amiable manners, who
sometimes visited mademoiselle, and read to her the
notes which M. Roland transmitted to him, and
which contained the observations made on his
journey.

On the return of the traveller, mademoiselle Phlipon found in him a valuable friend.　" His gravity,
his manners, his habits," said she, " made me consider him only as a philosopher who existed by reason.　A sort of confidence established itself between us, and, in consequence of the pleasure
which he experienced in my society, he contracted
by degrees the desire of visiting me more frequently."　Near five years elapsed, from the commencement of the acquaintance, before M. Roland
declared other sentiments than those of friendship.
He was esteemed by the lady more than any man
whom she had hitherto known, yet she had remarked an external unsuitability both in the lover

and in his family. She told him frankly, that he
did her honour in his addresses, to which she would
consent with pleasure, had she thought it an advantageous connection for him. She then discovered
to him the state of her father's affairs, who had
completely ruined himself. " I had saved," says
she, " in consequence of the accounts, which I had
at length taken upon me to demand of my father
at the risque of experiencing his hatred, five hundred
livres of yearly income, which, with my wardrobe,
formed the remainder of that apparent affluence in
which I had been brought up." She dissuaded M.
Roland from thinking of her, as a third person
might have done. He however persisted, and, affected by his disinterestedness, the lady consented
that he should disclose his sentiments to her father:
but, preferring to express himself on paper, it was
determined that his explanation with M. Phlipon
should not take place till after his return to the place
of his residence. During the remainder of his stay
in Paris, the friends met daily, and mademoiselle
Phlipon, considering him as the being to whom she
was about to unite her destiny, became attached to
M. Roland.

On his return to Amiens, he explained to M.
Phlipon his wishes and his designs. His letter did
not please. The person to whom it was addressed
had no inclination to accept for his son-in-law an

austere man, in whose looks he had felt a censor.
He replied to the address of M. Roland with harshness, and even with impertinence, nor did he communicate what had passed to his daughter till he
had dispatched the answer.   She instantly took her
resolution.   Having informed M. Roland, that the
event had but too well justified her apprehensions,
and entreated him to abandon his design, that it
might not occasion to him farther mortification, she
declared to her father her intention of retiring to a
convent; a measure which his conduct had rendered
necessary.   Before her departure, she resigned to
him the portion of plate that belonged to her in
right of her mother, that he might be able to satisfy some debts that pressed for payment.   She
then hired a small apartment at the *Congregation*, to
which she retreated, with a resolution to circum-
scribe her wants within the limits of her scanty income.

After severely calculating her expenditure, she
laid aside something for presents to the servants of
the house.   Potatoes, rice, and beans, stewed with
a little butter and a few grains of salt, formed the
principal articles of her diet.   She went out only
twice a-week, once to visit her relations, and once
to her father's, where she cast an eye over his linen,
and carried back with her what wanted repairing.
The remainder of her time " inclosed," says she,

MADAME ROLAND.   205

" within my roof of snow, for I lodged near to heaven, and it was winter," was passed in solitude and in study, to which she resigned herself. The affectionate Agatha spent with her half an hour every evening, and softened the severe lot she had chosen, with the tender sympathy of friendship. This consolation, and a walk in the garden when every one had retired, were the only relaxations which our admirable young philosopher allowed to herself. " I fortified my heart," said she, " against adversity, by deserving happiness, and thus I avenge myself on that fortune that refuses to grant it. The resignation of a strong mind, the peace of a good conscience, the elevation of a character that defies misfortune, those laborious habits that make the hours fly swiftly away, that delicate taste of a sound understanding which finds in the sentiment of existence, and in the idea of its own value, indemnifications unknown to the vulgar :—such were my treasures ! I was not always free from melancholy, but this had its charms ; and, if I was not happy, I had within my own bosom all that was necessary to be so."

M. Roland, surprised and distressed at what had passed, continued to write to his respectable friend, as a man who ceased not to feel for her all the sentiments she deserved, but who had been hurt by the conduct of her father. Near six months thus wore

away, when he returned, and visited her at the
grate, " where," says she, " I still retained the
countenance of prosperity." Having offered to her his
hand anew, he pressed her to leave her retreat. "I reflect," says she, " profoundly on what I ought to do.
I do not conceal from myself, that a man less than
forty-five years of age would not have waited several
months to prevail upon me to change my resolution, and I readily allow that this idea had reduced
my sentiments to a state in which there was no
illusion. But, on the other hand, I consider that
this offer, so maturely reflected upon, ought to convince me that I was esteemed. In fine, marriage
was, as I believed, a severe tie, an association, in
which the wife usually charges herself with the
happiness of two individuals. Was it not better for
me then to exercise my faculties and my courage
in this honourable task, than in the retirement in
which I lived ?" These and other reflections determined her conduct, and she at length became the
wife of a worthy man, who understood and prized
her value. " To him," says she, " I devoted myself with an excess more enthusiastic than discreet.
In consequence of considering nothing but the felicity of my partner, I perceived that something was
wanting to the completion of mine. I have not
ceased, however, for a single moment, to behold in
my husband one of the most estimable of men, and

MADAME ROLAND.   207

to whom I deem myself honoured to belong.   But I have often felt that parity did not exist between us, and that the ascendancy of a predominating character, added to twenty additional years, rendered one of these superiorities too great.   If we lived in solitude, I might have many unpleasant hours to pass ; if we mixed with the world, I might be beloved by others, and some might affect me too much : I therefore plunged myself into study along with my husband; another excess which had its inconvenience also, and I accustomed him not to know how to do without me during a single instant."

The first year of their marriage was spent at Paris, whither business, which respected the manufactures, called M. Roland.   He employed his wife as his *amanuensis*, and the corrector of his proofs, a task, however little suited to her cultivated mind, which she fulfilled with humility and exactness.   "I respected my husband to so great a degree," says she, " that I easily supposed he knew every thing better than I did.   I was so fearful of a cloud upon his brow, and he was so tenacious of his opinions, that it was not until long after that I acquired confidence enough to differ from him."   After the business of a secretary and a housekeeper was finished, this excellent and attentive wife, finding the state of her husband's health to be delicate, condescended to prepare for him, with her own hands, the viands that suited him best; she filled up the remainder of her time with the study of botany and natural history, of which she entered into a course.

After leaving Paris, they spent four years at Amiens, where madame Roland performed the duties of a mother and a nurse, without ceasing to participate in the labours of her husband, who was charged with a considerable portion of the New Encyclopedia. " We never quit our study," says she, " but to walk in the neighbourhood of the town : I form an herbal of the plants of Picardy, and a taste for aquatic botany gives rise to *l'art du tourbier*. Frequent maladies render me uneasy respecting Roland's preservation ; my cares were not useless to him ; this constituted a new tie : he loved me because I was devoted to him ; my attachment to him was strengthened by the services I rendered to him."

During their stay at Amiens, Sophia gave her hand to the chevalier de Gomicourt, who lived six leagues from the town, and farmed his own estate. Henrietta, who had been partial to M. Roland, to whom her family had wished her to have been united, loudly approved of the preference which he had given to her friend, to whom the generosity and affecting sincerity of her character doubly endeared her. This charming young woman was sacrificed to an old man, who, at seventy-five years of age, was

MADAME ROLAND. 209

advised by his physician and his confessor to take another wife. Both the sisters became widows. Sophia grew devout, and fell into a languishing state of health. " The difference of our ideas," says madame Roland, " in respect to pursuits and opinions, added to absence and business, have re-laxed without dissolving our attachment. Hen-rietta, always frank, lively, and affectionate, has come to visit me during my captivity, and would have occupied my place to have ensured my safety." Roland, after their marriage, wished his wife to see her friends but seldom. She complied with this re-quest, till time and confidence in her character had removed from her husband all injurious apprehen-sions respecting rivalship in her affection. " This prohibition was ill judged," says she; " marriage is grave and austere *; if you deprive a woman of sensibility of the pleasures of friendship with per-sons of her own sex, you diminish a necessary ali-ment, and expose her to temptation."

In 1784, M. and madame Roland removed to the generality of Lyons, and settled at Villefranche, in the paternal habitation of the former, where an an-cient mother still resided, with her eldest son, a canon and a counsellor. The philosophy of madame

---

* To this austerity inequality of age must doubtless con-tribute.

Roland was here put to the proof, by the terrible temper of her mother-in-law. In the autumn they repaired to Thezée, two leagues from Villefranche, where, after the decease of their mother, they passed the greater part of the year. This country, arid in respect to its soil, was rich in vines and in woods. " It was there," says madame Roland, " my simple taste became conversant in all the details of rural economy : it was there that I employed for the relief of my neighbours some acquired knowledge : I became the physician of the village, so much the more beloved as giving succour instead of demanding retributions, while the pleasure of proving useful rendered these cares agreeable."

In 1789 madame Roland snatched her husband from the grave, during a frightful malady, from which her cares only could have saved him. She passed twelve days without sleep, and without undressing, and six months in all the anxiety of a perilous convalescence. " Yet," says she, " I was not even indisposed ; so much does the heart confer strength, and double our activity."

The revolution ensued, that extraordinary epoch in human affairs: the friends of liberty and humanity, in the hope of beholding the regeneration of their species, and meliorating the lot of the lower and more unfortunate classes of mankind, rejoiced and triumphed. Respectable but mistaken

MADAME ROLAND.   **211**

transport! M. and madame Roland gave, by their opinions, offence at Lyons to many individuals, " who," observes the latter, " habituated to commercial calculations, could not conceive how any one should be induced, through mere philosophy, to provoke and applaud changes, which could only prove useful to others." M. Roland, elected a member of the municipality on its first formation, distinguished himself by his inflexible justice.

Being deputed to the constituent assembly in behalf of the interest of Lyons, he repaired to Paris, where they passed nearly a year. It was at this period that they connected themselves with those respectable but unfortunate men, destined, with themselves, to become the martyrs and the victims of the sacred cause of humanity and freedom.

In 1784 they had made the tour of England, and in 1787 that of Switzerland, an interesting account of which has since appeared in the posthumous works of madame Roland. During these journeys they acquired some valuable and interesting friends. They also visited several parts of France, and had projected a visit to Italy.

M. Phlipon had been prevailed on by his daughter and son-in-law, who paid the few debts which he had contracted, to retire from business: they at the same time settled on him an annuity. His proud heart was hurt at this obligation. He died, during the severe winter of 1787, at sixty-three years of age, in consequence of a catarrh with which he had been long affected. The uncle of madame Roland expired at Vincennes, in 1789. They lost also soon after her husband's favourite brother.

Public affairs now absorbed their attention, and swallowed up all their time, while they resigned themselves to the passion of serving their country, and thus benefiting the human race.

M. Roland had executed the office of inspector of commerce and manufactories in the *generalty* of Lyons, with knowledge, activity, and probity. He had digested in his closet, during this period, the materials with which his experience furnished him, and continued the dictionary of manufactures for the " New Encyclopedia." A correspondence' had also taken place about this time between him and Brissot, whom congenial principles had mutually attracted. This correspondence was, by the revolution, still farther encouraged. Brissot, at this juncture, having begun a periodical paper, M. and madame Roland (who assisted her husband in all his literary labours) frequently contributed towards it. They became thus, without any personal intercourse, intimate and confidential friends. Notwithstanding his situation in life, his family, and his connections, which might be supposed to attach him to the aristocracy, Roland was, by his turn of mind and character, rendered interesting to the popular party. Amidst the political struggles of the revolution he was elected a member of the municipality of Lyons: in this situation his inflexible integrity led him to lay open, without reserve, the numerous abuses that had crept into the administration of the finances; a conduct by which his enemies were multiplied. The debt of the city of Lyons, which exhibited an epitome of the disorders of the state, was found, on examination, to amount to the sum of forty millions of livres *. To solicit assistance for the manufactures, which had suffered in the revolution, it became indispensable to commission a deputy-extraordinary to the constituent assembly; and M. Roland was the person chosen for the purpose.

On the 20th of February, 1791, he arrived with his family at Paris. Madame Roland, who had been five years absent from the place of her birth, and who had watched with a lively interest the progress of the revolution and the labours of the assembly, whose characters and talents she had anxiously studied, seized this opportunity to attend their sittings. " Here," says she, " I saw the powerful Mirabeau, the only man in the revolution

---

* 1,666,667l.

whose genius could guide the others, and sway the
assembly; the astonishing Cazalés, the daring Maury,
the artful Lameths, and the frigid Barnave. I remarked
with vexation that kind of superiority on the side of
the court party, which dignified habits, purity of language, and polished manners, cannot fail to give in large
assemblies.   But strength of reason, and the courage of integrity, the lights of philosophy, the fruits
of study, and the fluency of the bar, could not fail
to secure the triumphs of the patriots, if they were
all honest, and could but remain united."   At Paris
they were visited by Brissot, with whose mind and
writings they were already conversant.   Brissot introduced to them several of the other members,
whom similitude of principles, or zeal for the public
good, drew frequently together.   It was even agreed
that they should meet four evenings in the week in
the apartment of madame Roland, whose lodgings
were conveniently situated for the purpose.   By this
arrangement she became acquainted with the progress of affairs, in which, from her taste for political
speculation, and for the study of mankind, she was
deeply interested.   " I knew," says she, " the part
which became my sex, and never stepped out of it.
I took no share in the debates which passed in my
presence.   Sitting at a table, without the circle, I
employed myself with my needle, or in writing letters: yet, if I dispatched ten epistles, which was some-

MADAME ROLAND. 215

times the case, I lost not a syllable of what was passing, and more than once bit my lips to restrain my impatience to speak. What struck me most, and distressed me exceedingly, was that sort of light and frivolous chit-chat, in which men of sense waste two or three hours without coming to any conclusion. Taking things in detail, you would have heard excellent principles maintained, and some good plans proposed ; but, on summing up the whole, there appeared to be no path marked out, no fixed result nor determinate point, towards which the views of each individual should be directed. Sometimes, for very vexation, I could have boxed the ears of these philosophers, whom I daily learned to esteem more for the honesty of their hearts and the purity of their intentions. Excellent reasoners all, and all philosophers, and learned theoretical politicians; but, totally ignorant of the art of managing mankind, and consequently of swaying an assembly, their wit and learning were too generally lavished to no end."

Robespierre was sometimes of these parties. Persuaded, at that time, of his zeal for liberty, the usual penetration of madame Roland was suspended in his favour, while she was inclined to attribute his faults to an excess of patriotism. " That kind of reserve," observed she, " which seems to indicate either the fear of being seen through, because we

can get nothing by being known ; or the distrust of
a man who finds in his own bosom no reason for
giving credit to the virtue of others ; that kind of
reserve for which Robespierre is remarkable, gave
me pain, but I mistook it for modesty.   Thus it is
that, with a favourable prepossession, we transform
into symptoms of the most amiable qualities, the
most untoward dispositions.   Never did the smile
of confidence rest on the lips of Robespierre ; while
they were almost always contracted by the malignant
grin of envy, striving to assume the semblance of
disdain.   His talents as an orator were below mediocrity ; his vulgar voice, ill-chosen expressions,
and faulty pronunciation, rendering his discourse
extremely tiresome.   But he maintained principles
with warmth and perseverance ; and there was some
courage in doing so, at a time when the defenders
of the popular cause were greatly diminished in
numbers : on this account I esteemed Robespierre."

   At a juncture when the fears of Robespierre were
greatly roused for his safety, M. and madame Roland drove to his house, near midnight, to offer him
an asylum.   He had already quitted his habitation :
they proceeded therefore to Buzot's, whom they
wished to interest in his favour. 'There is nothing,'
said Buzot, after some hesitation, ' that I would not
do to save that unhappy young man ; though I am

MADAME ROLAND.   217

far from thinking of him as many others do : he thinks too much of himself to be greatly in love with liberty ; but he serves its cause, and that is enough for me.'

The mission of Roland having detained him seven months at Paris, he quitted it in the middle of September, after obtaining for Lyons every thing that it could desire; and passed the autumn in the country, employed in the vintage.

One of the last acts of the constituent assembly was the suppression of inspectors. M. and madame Roland considered whether it would be better to remain in the country, or to pass the winter in Paris, where Roland might prefer his claim to a pension, as a recompence for forty years' service ; where at the same time he could continue his labours for the Encyclopedia, in the focus of science, amidst artists and men of letters. In the month of December they accordingly returned to Paris. The members of the constituent assembly had retired to their several homes ; and Petion, who had been chosen mayor, was occupied with his office : they also saw Brissot less frequently. Their attention was now wholly engaged with the plan of establishing a journal of the useful arts ; and of diverting their minds by study from public affairs, which exhibited a melancholy aspect.

About the middle of March, they were informed by one of their friends, that the court, full of perplexity and alarm, was desirous of doing some popular act, and had even an idea of appointing patriot ministers. Several persons, he added, had turned their thoughts towards M. Roland, whose literary reputation, administrative knowledge, justice, and vigour of mind, afforded a prospect of stability. Roland, at that time, frequented the jacobin society, and was employed in its committee of correspondence *. The 21st of the same month, Brissot called upon madame Roland, and repeated, in a more positive manner, the same intimation, while he enquired whether her husband would take on himself the burthen of administration. Madame Roland replied, that she had mentioned the affair to him, when it was first started, in the course of conversation, and that it appeared to her, that, after

---

* Madame Roland read these letters, and often undertook to answer them. She considered that the society might exert its influence in disseminating good principles. " Persuaded," says she, " that a revolution is no better than a terrible and destructive storm, if the improvement of the public mind keep not pace with the progression of events ; and sensible of the good that might be done by taking hold of men's imaginations, and giving them an impulse towards virtue ; I employed myself with pleasure in this correspondence."

MADAME ROLAND.   219

taking into the account all the dangers and difficulties, his zeal and activity would not object to such
a field for exertion ; but that it was a business that
required farther consideration.   Roland did not
shrink from the task proposed to him; his confidence in his own abilities inspired him with the desire of being serviceable to his country, and to the
cause of freedom.   Such was the answer that, on
the following day, was given to Brissot.

On Friday the 23d, Brissot and Dumouriez came,
on the breaking up of the council, to inform Roland that he was appointed minister for the home
department, and to salute him as their colleague.
They staid but a few minutes, while they appointed
an hour, in the ensuing day, for Roland to take the
oaths. ' There goes a man,' said madame Roland,
speaking of Dumouriez, whom she had then seen
for the first time, as they went out—' there goes a
man of a subtle mind, and a deceitful look ; against
whom it will perhaps behove you to be more upon
your guard than against any other man whatever :
he expressed great pleasure at the patriotic choice
he was employed to announce, and yet I shall not
be surprised if, on some future day, he brings about
your dismission.'   It appeared to her impossible
that Dumouriez and Roland could act long in concert. " On one side," says she, " I beheld inte-

grity and frankness personified, with rigid justice, devoid of all courtly arts, and of all the dextrous manœuvres of a man of the world. On the other, I fancied I could recognise a libertine of great parts, a determined adventurer, inclined to make a jest of every thing except his own interest and fame."

Roland, by his indefatigable industry, readiness in business, and methodical habits, was soon enabled to arrange in his head the various branches of his department ; but the principles and manners of his chief clerks opposed to him formidable obstacles. For the first three weeks he was enchanted with the apparently excellent disposition of the king, to whose professions he gave entire credit. ' Good God !' said his wife to him, ' when I see you and Claviere * set out for the council with all that delightful confidence, it always seems to me that you are on the point of committing some egregious folly.' " I never," observes she, " could bring myself to believe in the constitutional vocation of a king, born and brought up in despotism, and accustomed to arbitrary sway. Had Lewis been sincerely the friend of a constitution that would have restrained his power, he must have been a man above the common race of mortals; and had he been such

* One of his colleagues in office.

MADAME ROLAND.   221

a man, he would never have suffered those events to occur that produced the revolution."

The first time Roland appeared at court, the simplicity of his apparel excited the surprise and indignation of the court satellites, who, deriving from *etiquette* their sole importance, believed the state depended on its preservation. ' Oh, dear sir,' said the master of the ceremonies, with a countenance of alarm, whispering Dumouriez, and glancing at Roland, ' he has no buckles in his shoes.' ' Oh lord!' answered Dumouriez, with comic gravity, ' we are all ruined and undone.' A council being held four times a-week, the ministers agreed on those days to dine by turns at each other's houses. They were received by madame Roland as her guests every Friday. Dumouriez, she observed on these occasions, had more of what is called *parts* than all his colleagues put together, and less *morality* than any one of them. " He wanted nothing," says she, " but strength of mind in proportion to his genius, and a cooler head to execute the plans he conceived."

In the mean time, the troubles respecting religion, and the preparations of the enemy, called for decisive measures, while the refusal of the king to sanction the decrees, tore off the veil with which he had sought to conceal his purposes. At first this refusal was evasive; the ministers complained of the delay; Roland and Servan, in particular, remonstrated incessantly, and spoke with becoming spirit the most striking truths. Their situation had become critical; the public weal was in danger; it was incumbent on the ministers, who professed patriotism, either to provide the means of safety, or to relinquish their office: Roland proposed writing a letter to the king to this purport; his colleagues, unwilling to lose their places, objected and demurred; while Dumouriez, intent on playing at leisure his own cards, left them to settle the business.

The postponement of the sanction had reached its utmost limits: sensible that the council had neither the firmness nor the unanimity to act collectively, it was determined between M. and madame Roland, that it became the integrity and courage of the former to step forward alone. The question was no longer to resign, but to deserve a dismission. Madame Roland composed the celebrated letter on this occasion. " Studious habits," says she, " and a taste for letters, made me participate in the labours of my husband, as long as he remained a private individual: I wrote with him as I ate with him, because one was almost as natural to me as the other, and because my existence being devoted to his happiness, I applied myself to those things which gave him the greatest pleasure. Ro-

MADAME ROLAND. 223

land wrote treatises on the arts, I did the same, although the subject was tedious to me. He was fond of erudition. I helped him to pursue his critical researches. Did he wish, by way of recreation, to compose an essay for some academy, we sat down to write in concert, or else separately, that we might afterwards compare our productions, choose the best, or compress them into one. If he had written homilies, I should have done the same. When he became minister, I did not interfere with his administration; but, if a circular letter, a set of instructions, or an important state paper were wanting, we talked the matter over with our usual freedom, and, impressed with his ideas, and pregnant with my own, I took up the pen, which I had the most leisure to conduct. Our principles and turn of mind being the same, we were agreed as to the form, and my husband risqued nothing in passing through my hands. I could advance nothing, warranted by justice and reason, which he was not capable of realising, or supporting by his energy and conduct. But my language expressed more strongly what he had done or promised to do. Roland *without me* would not have been a worse minister; his activity, his knowledge, his probity, were all his own : but *with me* he attracted more attention; because I infused into his writings that

L 4

mixture of spirit and of softness, of authoritative reason and of seducing sentiment, which are perhaps only to be found in a woman endowed with a clear head and a feeling heart. I composed with delight such pieces as I deemed likely to be useful; and felt in so doing greater pleasure than had I been known as the author. I am avaricious of happiness, and with me it consists in the good I do."

While M. and madame Roland were reading over this letter, *Pache** came in. ' 'T is a very bold step,' observed he. ' Very bold, without doubt,' answered madame Roland, 'but just and necessary : what signifies any thing else ?' The letter was carried to the council, with the intention of being read aloud; but the king, when pressed anew for his sanction, waved the discussion, and required from each of his ministers their written opinion on the following day. Roland returned home, added to his letter a few introductory lines, and delivered the whole into the hands of the king on the morning of the next day, the 11th of June. On the 12th, Servan, one of his colleagues, walked into his apartment, with a cheerful countenance : ' Congratulate me,' said he, ' I am turned out.' ' I am much mortified,' replied madame Roland, ' that you

---

* A man raised to office by Roland, whose calumniator he afterwards became.

MADAME ROLAND. 225

should have that honour first; but I hope ere long it will be awarded to my husband.' Servan went on to inform them, that it was Dumouriez who had, in his majesty's name, demanded from him his *portfolio*, of which he was going to take charge himself. ' Dumouriez !' exclaimed madame Roland; ' his conduct surprises me but little ; yet it is infamous, and the other ministers in that case ought not to wait for their dismission.' The three preceding days, Dumouriez had held long and frequent conferences with the queen. The opinion of Roland coincided with that of his wife, that the ministers ought not to wait till they were dismissed. He communicated to his colleagues the letter he had sent to the king in the morning, from which he expected to meet with treatment similar to that experienced by Servan. After a long debate, it was agreed that they should meet early on the next day, and that Roland should, in the mean time, prepare a letter for them all to sign. The ministers having assembled at the appointed hour, expressed their doubts respecting the letter, and concluded that it would be better to declare their sentiments to the king in a personal conference. While they deliberated, a messenger from the king ordered one of them (Duranthon) to repair alone to his majesty. ' We will wait for you at the Chancery,' said Roland and Claviere. Scarcely had they reached it when Duranthon returned, and, with an hypocritical face of concern, drew slowly from his pocket an order for the discharge of his two colleagues. ' You make us wait a long while for our liberty,' said Roland with a smile, ' I perceive that our delays have made us lose the start.' ' Well,' said he, on his return to madame Roland, ' I also am turned out.' ' I hope,' replied she, ' it is better deserved on your part than on that of any one else. But one thing remains to be done ; that you should be the first to acquaint the assembly with your dismission, and to send them a copy of its cause, your letter to the king : since he has not profited by the lesson it contained, you ought to render that lesson useful to the public.' This idea was immediately executed : it answered a double purpose. " Utility and glory," says madame Roland, " were the consequences of my husband's retreat. I had not been proud of his elevation to the ministry, but I was proud of his digrace." Thus did Roland and his wife return to private life.

While her husband remained in the ministry, madame Roland determined neither to pay nor to receive visits, nor to invite any female to her table. " I had," said she, " no great sacrifices to make on this occasion, for my acquaintance was not extensive ; beside, my love of study equals my detestation of cards ; and the society of silly people affords me no amusement. Accustomed to spend my days in domestic retirement, I shared the labours of Roland, and pursued the studies suited to my own particular taste. Twice a-week indeed I gave a dinner to some of the ministers, a few members of the assembly, and persons with whom my husband had business ; but I had not the rage of interfering. Out of all the rooms of a spacious apartment, I chose for myself the smallest parlour, which, by removing into it my books and bureau, I converted into a study. It often happened that the friends and colleagues of Roland, when they wished to speak to him confidentially, instead of going to his apartment, where he was surrounded with clerks, would come to mine, and request me to send for him. Thus, without intrigue, or idle curiosity, I found myself drawn into the vortex of public affairs. Roland, with that confidence which ever subsisted between us, had a pleasure in afterwards conversing with me, in private, respecting what passed on these occasions ; an intercommunity of knowledge and opinions was thus established between us."

With the revolution of the 10th of August every one is acquainted : Roland was at that period recalled to the ministry, which he re-entered with renovated hopes. ' It is a great pity,' said madame Roland, on this occasion, ' that the council should be contaminated by that Danton, who has so bad a reputation." ' What can we do?' said some friends, in reply to this remark; ' he has been useful in the revolution, and the people love him: there is no prudence in making malecontents: it will certainly be better to make the most of him as he is." " There was some reason in this," observes madame Roland; " still it is easier to deny a man the means of influence, than to prevent his putting it to a bad use. Here began the faults of the patriots. The instant the court was subdued, an excellent council should have been formed, the members of which, being distinguished for knowledge, and irreproachable in their manners, would have given dignity to the government, and impressed foreign powers with respect. The thing which most surprised me," says she, " after the elevation of my husband gave me an opportunity of becoming acquainted with a number of persons, particularly those employed in important affairs, was the universal meanness of their minds: it surpasses all that can be imagined, and pervades every rank. But for this experience, never should I have thought so poorly of my species, nor was it till then that I assumed any confidence in myself. In this scarcity of able men, the revolution having driven away successively those whose birth, fortune, education, and circumstances, had rendered them, by a somewhat higher cultivation, superior to the mass of the people,

it is no wonder if we fell gradually into the hands
of the grossest ignorance, and the most shameful
incapacity." Speaking again of Danton, who visited almost daily at the minister's hotel : " While I
contemplated his forbidding and atrocious features,
I could not bring myself to associate the idea of a
good man with such a countenance. I never saw
any aspect so strongly expressive of the violence of
brutal passions, and the most astonishing audacity,
half disguised by a jovial air, an affectation of frankness, and a sort of simplicity. My lively imagination represents every person, with whom I am
struck, in the action that I conceive suitable to his
character. In this manner have I often figured
Danton, with a dagger in his hand, encouraging by
his voice and example a band of assassins, more
timid or less ferocious than himself : or else, when
satiated with his crimes, indicating his habits and
propensities by the gestures of a Sardanapalus."
Danton, and Fabre d'Eglantine, an unprincipled hy-
pocrite, sought, by vaunting their own patriotism,
to throw madame Roland off her guard, and make
her speak out. " It was a subject," says she, " on
which I had nothing to conceal or dissemble. I
avow my principles equally to those whom I suppose
to participate in them, and to those whom I suspect
of cherishing sentiments less pure. In regard to the
former, it is confidence : to the latter, pride. I dis-

dain to disguise myself, even under the pretence, or
with the hope of being better able to fathom the
minds of others. I lay open my whole soul, and
never suffer a doubt to exist of what I really am."

Danton and Fabre ceased to visit at Roland's towards the latter end of August; cautious, no doubt,
of exposing themselves to attentive eyes, on the
approaching matins of September. Preparations
were made, by public commotions and alarms, for
this dreadful tragedy, on the first symptoms of
which, Roland took every step, in his office of minister, to avert the coming storm, which the most
vigilant humanity could devise. At five in the evening of Sunday, nearly at the moment when the
prisons were invested, about two hundred men proceeded to the hotel of the home department. Madame Roland, who was sitting in her own apartment, rose at the noise, of which, stepping into the
anti-chamber, she enquired the cause. Roland was
from home, but the persons who asked for him, dissatisfied with this information, insisted on speaking
to the minister. Madame Roland perceiving the
assurances of her servants ineffectual, sent to invite,
in her own name, ten of the malecontents to walk up
stairs, of whom she calmly enquired what they
wanted? They informed her, that they were honest
citizens, ready to set off for Verdun, but who, in
want of arms, came to ask the minister, whom they

MADAME ROLAND.   231

were resolved to see, for a supply. She observed to them, that the minister of the interior never had arms at his disposal, and that it was to the war-office that they should address their request. They had already been there, they said, and had been repulsed: all the ministers, they added, were rascally traitors, and they wanted Roland. ' I am sorry he is out; for his arguments would have had weight with you : come with me, and search the hotel, and you will be satisfied that he is from home, and that there are no arms here; nor indeed ought there to be any, as on reflection you must needs be convinced. Return, I pray you, to the war-office, or complain to the commune; and if you wish to speak to M. Roland, repair to the hotel of the marine, where the council is assembled.' On this remonstrance, the band withdrew; but, from a balcony over the court, madame Roland beheld a furious fellow in his shirt, his sleeves tucked up to his shoulders, and a broad sword in his hand, declaiming against the treachery of the ministers. They carried with them, on their retreat, the valet de chambre of M. Roland, by way of hostage.

Madame Roland instantly got into a coach, and hastened to the admiralty, to inform her husband of what had passed. Danton was, in the mean time, at the residence of the mayor, in the committee of vigilance as it was styled, whence issued the orders

of arrest, that had for some days past been so numerous. A reconciliation had just taken place between him and Marat, after a parade of a feigned
quarrel. Going up to the apartment of Petion, he
took him aside, and, in his customary language, in-
terlarded with oaths, ' Can you guess,' said he,
' what they have taken in their heads ? Why, may
I die, if they have not issued a warrant against Roland !' ' Who do you mean ?' ' Why, that mad-
headed committee to be sure. I have the warrant in
my possession. Look, here it is. We can never
suffer them to go on at this rate. What, the devil !
against a member of the council !' Petion, having read the warrant, returned it to him with a
smile ; ' Let them proceed,' said he, ' it will have
a good effect.' ' A good effect !' exclaimed Danton, examining with an earnest eye the countenance of the mayor : ' Oh ! no, I can never suffer
it ; I 'll find means to make them listen to reason.'
The warrant was not executed ; but it was evident
that the two hundred men were sent to the minister's hotel by the devisers of that warrant. " Who
so dull," says madame Roland, " as not to suspect,
that the failure of that attempt, by delaying the execution of the project, might allow those who had
conceived it time to pause ? And who so wanting
in penetration as not to perceive in Danton's conduct to the mayor, that of a conspirator, endeavour-

ing to discover what effect such a blow would produce, or, in its failure, to take to himself the honour of having parried it ?"

It was past eleven when Roland left the council,
nor was it till the ensuing morning that he learnt
the horrors of the night. Distressed beyond measure at these abominable crimes, and his incapacity
of preventing them, it was agreed between M. and
madame Roland, that there remained nothing for an
honest minister to do, but to denounce them in the
most public manner, to rouse the indignation of all
men of honour, and, if necessary, to expose himself
to the dagger of the assassins, rather than to incur
the guilt and shame of being in any way their accomplice. ' It is equally true,' observed madame
Roland to her husband, ' that a courageous determination is not more consonant to justice, than conducive to safety. Firmness only can repress audacity. If the denunciation of these enormities were
not a duty, it would be an act of prudence. The
people who perpetrate them must necessarily hate
you, for having endeavoured to obstruct their proceedings. Nothing remains for you, but to inspire
them with fear.' Roland wrote to the assembly his
letter of the 3d of September; a letter not less
celebrated than that addressed to the king. The
assembly having ordered it to be printed, posted up,

and sent to the departments, applauded a courage it dared not to emulate.

The massacres continued four whole days; and curious people went to the spectacle. All Paris witnessed these horrible scenes, perpetrated by a small number of cut-throats: so small indeed as not to exceed a dozen at the *Abbaye*. " All Paris," says madame Roland, " looked on: all Paris was accursed in my eyes: I could no longer entertain hopes of the establishment of liberty among *cowards*, insensible to the last outrages that can be committed on nature and humanity, and coolly contemplating enormities, which fifty armed men might have prevented with ease. I know of nothing in the annals of the most barbarous nations comparable to these atrocious acts." From the most authentic accounts, it appears that there were not two hundred villains concerned in the whole of these infamous transactions; but the people were terrified with rumours, and rendered stupid by horror and surprise.

The health of Roland was impaired by these proceedings; the bile, obstructed in its course by the derangement of his system, spread itself over the skin: he became yellow and emaciated, but, though unable to eat or sleep, continued his labours. He was still ignorant of a warrant having been issued against him; a secret which his wife had been care-

MADAME ROLAND.   235

ful to keep from his knowledge. Somebody, however, in the following week, took it into his head to inform him of this circumstance.

The gold, jewels, and other valuables, which, from the rank and condition of the captives, abounded in the prisons at the time of the massacres, were of course pillaged: still more considerable had been the plunder, collected by the members of the commune, after the struggle of the 10th of August: but the minister of the interior, who had a right to make the demand, could obtain no information concerning these transactions. The assembly to which he complained, commended as usual his zeal, but took no measures to support him: while millions fell into the hands of those who would naturally employ them to perpetuate the anarchy from which they derived all their power. Marat, who had been refused by Roland the disposal of a sum of money, allotted to the minister by the assembly, for the expence of printing useful works, became from that moment his enemy and calumniator. Madame Roland, unacquainted with Marat, and who had sometimes doubted whether he was indeed a real or a fictitious being, expressed to Danton a curiosity to see him, and desired he would bring him to the hotel. This request Danton declined, as a measure not only useless, but which could not fail of proving disagreeable, since Marat was an original, like no-thing else in the world.

Three weeks had passed away since the tragedy of September. Marat complained bitterly of the incivism of the minister, in refusing him the sum demanded: he also, in a bill which he had stuck up, attacked by name madame Roland, who perceived in this measure the hand of Danton. ' Intending to attack you,' says she, to her husband, ' they begin by prowling around your house. Danton, with all his sense, has the folly to imagine that I shall be hurt by his abuse ; that I shall take up my pen to answer it ; that he will have the pleasure of bring-ing a woman forward upon the stage ; and thus ex-pose to the shafts of ridicule the man to whom she is allied. These people may form a tolerable opi-nion of my talents, but they are utterly incapable of judging of the temper of my soul. Let them continue their calumnies as long as they please ; they will never make me stir a step, nor excite my uneasiness.'

On the 22d of September, Roland made an exact and spirited report of the state of Paris, its dis-orders, and insubordination : the assembly, sound in judgment, but weak in resolution, ordered the report to be printed, but rectified nothing. The depart-ment of the Somme, in which Roland resided, elected

MADAME ROLAND.   237

him as a member of the convention ; a choice which excited almost general regret. To take from the helm a man of talents and courage, whom it would be difficult to replace, in order to put him in an assembly where many others, by their votes, might equally serve the state, was a measure to be deprecated. An outcry was raised on all sides, while a motion was made, that Roland should be invited to remain in the ministry. Danton, who was present in the convention, rose to oppose this invitation with vehemence and rancour, observing, among other malicious remarks, that the address ought also to be extended to the wife of the minister, as a person by no means useless to the administration. Murmurs of disapprobation repelled this invidious insinuation ; but, though the general wish was strongly expressed, the decree did not pass. Neither was the resignation of Roland accepted. A crowd of members repaired to his house, pressing him to remain in office, as a sacrifice due to his country. These solicitations lasted two days, when news was brought, that an error had attended his election, which rendered it void: of course, that he had no excuse for quitting the ministry. Having therefore resolved on keeping his place, he wrote to the assembly in a courageous and dignified style, that confounded his enemies.

The party of Danton had endeavoured to conceal
the circumstance that set aside his election, till he
had resigned the administration, in the hope of
throwing him out on all sides. At length, no longer
giving him quarter, every day produced some fresh
attack; while incessant calumnies and accusations,
each more atrocious and absurd than the other, followed in rapid succession. They even imputed to
him as a crime, his care to inform the public mind.
" It requires," observes madame Roland, " no profound skill in politics to know, that the strength of a
government depends on opinion. All the difference,
in this respect, between a just and a tyrannical administration, is, that while the former is employed
in diffusing truth, and enlarging the sphere of knowledge, it is the business of the latter to suppress the
one, and to contract the other." The *patriotic correspondence* of Roland had produced the most admirable effects, and remained a monument, attesting his
enlightened vigilance, and the purity of his principles.
From that instant the minister was represented as a
dangerous man, who had offices of public spirit :
soon after, as a corruptor of the opinions of the
people, and a man ambitious of the supreme power ;
and last of all, as a conspirator. The departments
returned him for his letters the warmest thanks, but
the banditti of Paris continued to calumniate and

abuse him: a distrust was excited in the public mind, which the jacobins seconded with all their power, while the Dantons, the Robespierres, and the Marats, bore all the sway.

Madame Roland was accused, during the administration of her husband, of giving sumptuous entertainments, where, like another Circe, she corrupted all those who came to the banquet. From the following account of her habitual conduct at the hotel, the reader may form a judgment of the truth of this accusation : " Twice a-week, only, I gave a dinner, once to my husband's colleagues, and once to a mixed company, composed either of national representatives, of first clerks in the offices, or of persons concerned in the business of the state. Taste and neatness presided at my table, to which profusion and the luxury of ornament was unknown. Without devoting much time to conviviality, for I gave only one course, every one was at his ease. Fifteen was the usual number of the guests, which seldom amounted to eighteen, and only once to twenty. After dinner we conversed for some time in the drawing-room, and then every one took his leave. We sat down to table about five; at nine not a creature remained : yet this was the court of which they made me queen; and thus, with the doors wide open, did we carry on our dark and dangerous conspiracies. On other days, confined to our family, my husband and myself usually sat down to table alone; delaying, for the transaction of public business, our dinner to a very late hour : my daughter dined with her governess in her own room. Those who saw me at that time, will bear witness in my favour, whenever the voice of truth can make itself heard. I shall then perhaps be no more ; but I shall go out of the world with the persuasion, that the memory of my persecutors will be lost in maledictions, while my name will sometimes be recollected with a sigh."

In the latter period of the administration of Roland, conspiracies and threats succeeded each other so fast, that his friends often pressed him and madame Roland to leave the hotel during the night. Two or three times they yielded to these intreaties, but, soon tired of this daily removal, they observed, that if destined to fall, it would be more conducive to public utility and to personal glory, for the minister to perish at his post. They accordingly no longer slept from home. Madame Roland, that she might suffer the same hazard as her husband, had his bed brought into her room ; while she kept under her pillow a pistol, not to use for a vain defence, but to save herself, should she perceive them approach, from the outrages of assassins. In this situation she passed three weeks, during which the hotel was twice beset.

MADAME ROLAND.   241

" To-day on a throne, to-morrow in a prison :"

" Such," observes madame Roland, " is the fate of virtue in revolutionary times. Enlightened men, who have pointed out its rights, are, by a nation weary of oppression, first called into authority. But it is not possible that they should maintain their places: the ambitious, eager to take advantage of circumstances, mislead the people by flattery, and, to acquire consequence and power, prejudice them against their real friends. Men of principle, who despise adulation and contemn intrigue, meet not their opposers on equal terms; their fall is therefore certain: the still soft voice of sober reason, amidst the tumult of the passions, is easily overpowered."

The resignation of Roland appeased not his enemies; his very name, which was become the signal of discord, could not be pronounced without confusion. If a member, less venal than the rest, ventured to speak in his defence, he was reduced to silence, and treated as an instrument of faction. His continuation in the ministry, which could no longer be productive of utility, had become an additional source of disorder in the convention ; he deemed it therefore prudent to resign. In his retirement, he gave a terrible blow to his enemies, by publishing such accounts as no minister before him had furnished ; but to have them examined and sanctioned by a report, was an act of justice for which he solicited in vain. Such a proceeding, by giving a proof of his meritorious conduct, would have confounded the malice of his detractors, whose interest it was to blind and to mislead the people. In vain, seven times in four months, did he intreat, publish, and write, to the convention, whose weakness would not permit them to undertake his defence. The jacobins continued to denounce him as a traitor; and Marat to prove to his adherents, that the head of Roland was necessary to the tranquillity of the republic.

The eighth time he wrote to the convention, which deigned not even to peruse his letter: his wife, in the mean while, was preparing with her daughter to go into the country, whither domestic business, with other motives, rendered her desirous of retiring. Should the enemies of her husband proceed to the last extremities, it would be easier, she considered, for him to escape alone, than when embarrassed with his family; while prudence pointed out the propriety of diminishing the number of points in which he might be attacked. Her passports had been delayed at the section, through the management of some *Maratists*, in whose eyes she had become an object of suspicion: scarcely were they delivered to her, when she was seized with a nervous colic, attended with convulsions, the only malady to which she was subject, and to which the vehement affections of a strong mind acting upon a

MADAME ROLAND.   243

robust frame, particularly exposed her. Being compelled to take to her bed, in which she passed six
days, on the seventh she proposed to go out in order
to shew herself at the municipality; when, by the
sound of the alarm-bell, her purpose was suspended.
Every thing seemed to foretel an approaching crisis.
The commotions which succeeded excited in the
mind of madame Roland that interest and curiosity
which great events cannot fail to inspire. The de-
basement of the convention appeared to her so dis-
tressing, that she scarcely considered as dreadful the
worst excesses, that might tend to open the eyes of
the departments, and to determine their conduct.
Roland was pressed by some persons, who came to
confer with him on what was passing, to make his
appearance at his section, by which he was greatly
esteemed. It was agreed, however, though nothing
but the good intentions of the citizens were talked
of, that he should not sleep at home on the following night.

At half past five the same evening, six armed
men appeared at his house, when one of them read
an order of the *revolutionary committee*, by virtue of
which they were come to apprehend him. ' I know
of no laws,' replied Roland, ' which constitute the
authority you mention, nor shall I obey the orders
which it issues. If you employ force, I can only

oppose to it such resistance as a man of my years is capable of making. But I shall protest against it to the last moment of my life.' ' I have no order,' said the spokesman, ' to use violence. I shall return, therefore, and communicate your answer to the council-general of the commune : in the mean time, I will leave my colleagues here.'

It immediately occurred to madame Roland, that it might not be amiss to denounce, in the most public manner, these proceedings to the convention; either to prevent by that means the arrest of her husband, or to obtain his prompt release. In a few minutes this idea was communicated to Roland, a letter was written to the president, and the courageous wife of the ex-minister was on her way to the convention. Her servant being absent, she left a friend with her husband, and, having stepped alone into a hackney-coach, ordered it to proceed as fast as possible to the Carousel. The court-yard of the Tuilleries, which she swiftly crossed, was filled with armed men. Having arrived at the doors of the outer halls, which were all closed, she found sentinels placed at the entrance, who allowed no one to pass, and who sent her by turns from door to door. In vain did she insist on admission ; till, as an expedient to overcome the resistance of the sentinels, she determined to affect the language of a disciple of Robespierre. 'Citizens,' said she, address-

MADAME ROLAND.   **245**

ing them, ' why in this day of salvation for our country, and in the midst of the traitors from whom we have so much to fear, do you prevent me from transmitting to the president some papers of the last importance? Send at least for an usher to whose care I may entrust my credentials.'

The doors instantly flying open, madame Roland walked into the petitioners' hall, where having enquired for an usher, she was desired by a sentry to wait for some moments, till one should come out. A quarter of an hour had elapsed, when she perceived Ross*, of whom she solicited permission to appear at the bar, and to plead the cause of Roland as connected with the public weal. Ross, conceiving at once the subject of the letter, of which he took charge, and the impatience which the writer must necessarily feel, requested that the paper which he carried in, and laid upon the table, might be read without delay. An hour passed heavily away, while madame Roland paced backwards and forwards, her eyes cast towards the door of the hall, which was several times opened and closed by the guard. A dreadful noise from time to time assailed her ears. Ross at length appeared. ' Well!' enquired the wife of the ex-minister, with breathless impatience. ' Nothing

---

* A Scotchman, usher to the convention.

has yet been done. An indescribable tumult prevails in the assembly. Some petitioners, at this moment, demand at the bar the confinement of the *twenty-two*: I have just assisted Rabaud in getting out unseen. Several others are making off; nor can any one say what may be the event.' 'Who is president?' 'Hérault Séchelles.' 'Ah! my letter will not be read. Send to me some member with whom I may speak a few words.' 'Whom shall I send?' 'Indeed I am little acquainted, or have little esteem for any of them, excepting those who are proscribed. Tell Vergniaux I wish to see him.'

Ross went in search of him. At the end of a considerable period, Vergniaux appeared, and talked with madame Roland for seven or eight minutes. He then went back to the hall, and again returned. 'In the present state of the assembly,' said he, 'I dare not flatter you; you have no great room for hope. You may obtain, if you get admission to the bar, a little more favour as a woman; but the convention is no longer able to do any good.' 'It is able to do any thing it pleases;' replied madame Roland, with quickness: 'the majority of Paris only desire to know how they *ought* to act. If I am admitted to the assembly, I will venture to say what you could not utter without exposing yourself to impeachment. As to me, I fear nothing; and if I cannot save Roland, I will speak some homo

MADAME ROLAND. 247

truths, which will not be altogether useless to the republic. Inform your worthy colleagues of my desire; a courageous sally may yet have an effect, it will at least serve to set a great example.'

" I was indeed," says she, " in that temper of mind which imparts eloquence ; warm with indignation, superior to fear, my bosom glowing for my country, the ruin of which I foresaw : every thing dear to me at stake ; feeling strongly, expressing those feelings fluently, and too proud not to utter them with dignity, I had the most important interests to discuss, possessed some means of defending them, and was in a singular situation for doing so with advantage." ' But at any rate,' said Vergniaux, ' your letter cannot be read for some hours ; think what a tedious time you will have to wait !' ' I will go home, then, to know what has been passing there, and will immediately return : you may tell our friends that this is my intention.' ' Most of them are absent ; they behave with courage when they are here ; but they are deficient in assiduity.' ' That, alas ! is but too true.'

Madame Roland, quitting Vergniaux, flew to Louvet's, whence, having left a note to inform him of what was passing, she threw herself into a coach, and ordered it home. The wretched horses not keeping pace with her feelings, and some battalions of national guards impeding the way, she jumped out of the coach, which she discharged, and, rushing through the ranks, hastened forwards.   Having reached her house, the porter whispered her that Roland was at the landlord's at the bottom of the court.   Thither she immediately hastened, and there she learned, that the bearers of the warrant, not being able to procure a hearing at the council, and Roland persisting in protesting against their orders, they had, after demanding his protest in writing, withdrawn themselves; in consequence of which Roland had retired through the back-door.   Being found by his wife at the second house in which she sought him, she informed him of what she had done, and the measures she meant to pursue.

From the solitude of the streets she perceived that it was late; she prepared nevertheless to return to the convention, without recollecting her recent illness, which demanded quiet and repose.   On approaching the Carousel, she found the sitting was at an end; from which she augured the subjugation of the assembly.   A few men still remained at the gate of the national palace: ' Citizens,' said she to some *sans-culottes* collected round a cannon, ' has every thing gone well ?'   ' O ! wonderfully: they embraced each other, and sang the *Marseillois* hymn, there, under the tree of liberty.'   ' What, then, is the right side ap-

MADAME ROLAND.   249

peased ?' ' Faith ! it was obliged to listen to reason.'
' And what of the committee of twelve ?' ' It is
kicked into the ditch.' ' And the *twenty-two?*'
'The municipality will have them taken up.'   ' Aye,
but *can* the municipality ?' ' Why, body o' me, is
not the municipality the sovereign ? It is high time it
should, to set those b——s of traitors to rights, and
support the commonwealth.'   ' But will the departments be pleased to see their representatives—'
' What are you talking about ? the Parisians do nothing but in concert with the departments : they said
so to the convention.'   ' That however is not quite
so certain ; for, to know their will, the primary assemblies were wanting.'   ' Was there any want of
primary assemblies on the 10th of August ? Did
not the departments then approve what Paris did ?
They will do so now : it is Paris that is saving
them.'   ' Or rather say, it is Paris that is ruining
itself.'

While concluding this dialogue she crossed the
court, and returned to the coach which waited :
' You will set me down,' said she to the coachman,
' at the galleries of the Louvre.'   There she meant
to call on a friend, and concert with him the. means
of Roland's safety.   Pasquier had retired to bed :
he rose ; and madame Roland submitted to him her
plan.   It was agreed that they should meet the

next day. She stepped into her coach, and was proceeding home, when she was stopped by the sentry who stood on his post. ' Have a little patience,' said the coachman in a whisper, turning round on his seat; ' it is the custom at this time of night.' The serjeant advanced and opened the door: ' Whom have we here?' ' A woman.' ' Whence come you?' ' From the convention.' ' It is very true,' said the coachman, as if he feared her assertion would need confirmation. ' Whither are you going?' ' Home.' ' Have you no bundles?' ' None, as you may see.' But the assembly is broken up.' ' Yes; to my sorrow, for I had a petition to present.' ' A woman, at this hour! it is very strange; very imprudent.' ' It certainly is not a very common occurrence; nor is it with me a matter of choice: I must have had strong reasons for it.' ' But, madam, *alone!*' ' How, sir, alone! Do you not see that I have *innocence* and *truth* for my companions? what would you have more?' ' Well, I must be content with your reasons.' ' You are quite right,' in a gentle tone, ' for they are good ones.'

Having at length reached her house, she had ascended eight or ten steps, when a man, who was close behind her, and who had slipped in unperceived by the porter, begged her to conduct him to citizen Roland. ' To his apartment, with plea-

sure, if you have any thing advantageous to impart ;
but to *him* it is impossible.' ' I came to let him
know, that they are absolutely determined on con-
fining him this very evening.' ' They must be sagacious if they accomplish their purpose.' ' I am
happy to hear it, for it is an honest citizen to whom
you are speaking.' ' Well and good,' replied she,
as she proceeded up stairs, perplexed what opinion
to form.

" I may be asked," says she, " why, under such
circumstances, I returned to the house. Nor is
the question irrelevant. I have a natural aversion
to every thing inconsistent with the grand, bold,
and ingenuous proceedings of innocence : an effort
to escape from the hand of injustice, would be to
me more painful than any thing it could inflict.
During the last three months of Roland's administration, our friends often urged us to quit the hotel;
but it was always contrary to my inclinations. It
was incumbent on the minister to be at his post ;
for there his death would cry aloud for vengeance,
and prove a lesson to the republic.. It was possible
to reach his life when abroad, with equal advantage to the assassins, less benefit to the public, and
less glory to the victim. Such reasoning will be
deemed absurd by those who prefer life to all
things ; but he, who in a period of revolution sets

any value on existence, will set none on virtue, his honour, or his country."

Madame Roland acted upon these principles , she refused to leave the hotel in the month of January, determined to share the fate of her husband. When Roland was no longer in office, she thought him justified in shunning his enemies. For herself she believed she had less to fear; or even should they wish to begin the business by subjecting her to an examination, she doubted not of being able to confound them, and that her answers might even serve to dispel more rapidly the delusion of those who had suffered themselves to be misled. Should they proceed to another 2d of September, it would prove that all was lost in Paris ; in which case she preferred death to living a witness of her country's ruin ; while she felt, that she should glory in being found among the victims sacrificed to a guilty fury.

That fury, she also believed, glutted with her destruction, would be mitigated against Roland; who, if saved from this crisis, might yet be reserved to benefit France. Her imprisonment and trial might therefore be productive of advantage to her husband and her country; or, if destined to perish, it would be under circumstances in which life itself would have become a burthen. Thus magnanimously reasoned this admirable woman !

MADAME ROLAND. 253

Having, on her return home, quieted the fears of her family, she took up a pen for the purpose of writing a note to her husband. Scarcely had she seated herself at the desk, before she was disturbed by a loud knocking at the door. It was about mid-night. A numerous deputation of the commune appeared, and enquired for Roland: ' He is not at home.' ' But where can he be?' said a person who wore an officer's gorget: ' when will he return? You are acquainted with his habits, and doubtless can judge of the hour of his return.' ' I know not whether your orders authorise you to ask such questions; but this I know, nothing can compel me to answer them. As Roland left the house while I was at the convention, he had it not in his power to make me his *confidante*. This is all I have to say.'

The party withdrew much dissatisfied, leaving a sentry at the door of madame Roland's apartment, and a guard at that of the house. Overcome with fatigue, and determined to brave the worst, she ordered supper; and, having finished her letter, and entrusted it to the care of a faithful domestic, she retired to rest. She slept soundly for about an hour, when she was awakened by a servant, and informed that some gentlemen of the section requested her to step into the adjoining room. ' I understand what it means,' replied she calmly: ' go, child,

I will not make them wait.' Having sprung from
the bed, she was dressing, when her maid came in,
and expressed her surprise that she should be at the
pains of puting on more than a morning-robe:
' When people are going abroad,' replied she, ' they
should at least be decent.' The poor woman, looking in the face of her mistress, burst into tears.
Madame Roland walked into the next apartment.
' We come, *citoyenne*, to take you into custody, and
to put seals upon your property.' ' Here,' said a
man, taking out of his pocket a warrant from the
revolutionary committee, which ordered the wife of
Roland to be committed to the Abbaye, without specifying any motive for her arrest. ' I have a right
to tell you,' said she, ' like Roland, that I know
nothing of your committee; that I will not obey
its orders; and that you shall not take me hence
unless by violence.' ' Here is another order,' said
a little hard-featured man, in a hasty and commanding tone of voice, reading to her one from the
commune; which also directed, without specifying
any charge, the commitment of monsieur and madame Roland. The latter deliberated whether she
should still resist, or resign herself into their hands.
She had a right to avail herself of the law which
prohibits nocturnal arrests; and, if the law by which
the municipality were authorised to seize suspected
persons were urged, to retort the illegality of the

MADAME ROLAND.   255.

municipality itself, cashiered and created anew by an arbitrary power.   But *law* was become no more than an empty name to cover oppression and abuses; and had she compelled these men to resort to force, she justly dreaded their brutality, and the indignities to which she might expose herself.

‘ How do you mean to proceed, gentlemen ?’ said she.   ‘ We have sent for a justice of peace of the section; and you see here a detachment of his armed force.’   The justice of the peace arrived, and put his seal upon every thing, even on the drawers which contained the linen.   One of the men insisted on the *piano-forte* being sealed up also ; but, on being informed it was a musical instrument, he drew out a rule and took its dimensions, as if he designed it for a particular place.   Madame Roland asked leave to take out the clothes of her daughter, and made up a small packet of night-clothes for herself.   During these transactions, fifty or a hundred people passed backward and forward, completely filling the apartments : persons malevolently disposed might, without difficulty, have deposited or have carried away any thing.   The officer, not daring to lay his commands upon this crowd, gently requested them to withdraw; but their places were soon occupied by new comers. The prisoner, sitting down at her bureau, wrote to a friend concerning her situation, with a recommendation of her daughter to his care. She was folding up the letter, when the officer informed her it was necessary that he should see what she had written, and know to whom her letter was addressed. ' I have no objection to read it to you, if that will satisfy you.' ' No, it will be better to let us know to whom you are writing.' ' I shall do no such thing : the title of my friend is not at present of a nature to induce me to name the person on whom I bestow it.' Thus speaking, she tore in pieces the letter. As she turned from them they gathered up the fragments, in order to seal them up. She smiled at the precaution, the letter being without an address.

At seven in the morning she left her daughter and her domestics, after exhorting them to calmness and patience. ' You have people here who love you,' said one of the commissioners, observing the tears of her family. ' I never had any about me who did not,' replied she, while walking down stairs ; from the bottom of which to the coach, drawn up on the opposite side of the street, stood two ranks of armed citizens. She proceeded gravely, with measured steps, while her eyes were fixed on these deluded men. The armed force followed the coach in two files, while the miserable populace, attracted by the sight, stopped to gaze as it passed. ' *Away with her to the guillotine !*' exclaimed several women.

MADAME ROLAND. 257

' Shall we draw up the blinds?' said one of the commissioners, civilly. ' No, gentlemen; innocence, however oppressed, never puts on the guise of criminality: I fear not the eye of any one, nor will I conceal myself from any person's view.' ' You have more strength of mind than many men; you wait patiently for justice.' ' Justice! were justice done, I should not be now in your hands. But should an iniquitous procedure send me to the scaffold, I shall walk to it with the same tranquillity and firmness as I now pass to prison. My heart bleeds for my country, while I regret my mistake in supposing it qualified for freedom and happiness: but life I appreciate at its due value. I never feared any thing but guilt;—injustice and death I despise.'

Having arrived at the Abbaye, that theatre of massacre and blood, five or six field-beds, with as many men stretched upon them, in a dark and dreary apartment, were the first objects that struck the eye of the prisoner. Her guides made her ascend a dirty and narrow staircase. They came at length to the keeper's apartment, which was tolerably clean, and where a seat was offered to her. ' Where is my room?' said she to the wife of the keeper, a corpulent woman, with an agreeable countenance. ' Madam, I did not expect you, I have no room as yet; but in the mean time you will remain here.' The commissioners in an adjoining

room gave their verbal orders, which they dared not
commit to writing, and which were very severe,
and often afterwards renewed.   The keeper, an
active, obliging, humane man, observed not literally
what he was under no obligation to perform.
' What would you choose for breakfast?' said he.
' A little capillaire and water.'   The commissioners
withdrew, observing to madame Roland, that if
her husband were not guilty, there could be no occasion for him to abscond.   ' It is so extraordinary,'
replied she, ' to suspect a man who has rendered
such important services to the cause of liberty!
Just as Aristides, and severe as Cato, it is to his
virtues he is indebted for his enemies.   Their fury
knows no bounds; let them satiate it on me: I
defy its power, and devote myself to death.   It is
incumbent on *him* to save himself for the sake of his
country, to which he may yet be capable of rendering important services.'   An awkward bow was the
only answer which these gentlemen, whose confusion was evident, thought proper to make.

   The wife of the keeper made some civil observations, expressive of the regret which she felt when
a prisoner of her own sex arrived, ' for,' added she,
' they have not all your serene countenance.'   Madame Roland thanked her with a smile; while she
locked her into a room hastily put in order for her
reception.   ' Well then,' said she, seating herself,

MADAME ROLAND.   259

and falling into a train of reflections, ' I am in prison.' The moments that followed, she declares,
she would not have exchanged for those which
might be esteemed by others as the happiest of her
life. Her situation rendered her sensible of the
value of integrity and fortitude, united with an ap-
proving conscience. " I recalled the past to my
mind," says she; " I calculated the events of the
future. I devoted myself, if I may so say, voluntarily to my destiny, whatever it might be: I de-
fied its rigour, and fixed myself firmly in that state
of mind, in which, without giving ourselves concern for what is to come, we seek only employment for the present." But this tranquillity in regard to her own fate extended not to that of her
country and her friends. She waited for the evening paper, and listened with extreme anxiety to
every noise in the street. She wished to ascertain
what portion of freedom was yet left to her. ' May
I write? May I see any body? What will be my
expences here?' were her first questions. The
keeper informed her of the orders he had received,
and how far he could venture to evade or modify
them. She wrote to her faithful maid to come to see
her; but it was agreed that this indulgence should
be kept a secret.

The first visit she received was from Grandpré,
on the day of her arrival. ' You shall write to the

assembly,' said he ; ' have you not yet been thinking of it ?' ' No ; and now you remind me of it, I do not see how I shall be able to get my letter read.' ' I will do all I can to assist you.' ' Very well; then I will write.' ' Do so : I will return in two hours.' He departed, and madame Roland took up her pen to address the national convention. She complained of the treatment she had received, and remonstrated respecting the injustice and illegality of the proceedings. She demanded justice and pro-tection in a high tone. " If the convention," added she, " confirms my arrest, I appeal to the law which ordains the declaration of the crime, and the examination of the prisoner, within four-and-twenty hours after his capture. In the last place, I de-mand a report on the accounts of that irreproach-able man, who exhibits an instance of unheard-of persecution, and who seems destined to give to all Europe the terrible lesson of virtue proscribed by the blindness of infuriate prejudice. If to have shared the strictness of his principles, the energy of his mind, and the ardour of his love of liberty, be crimes, I plead guilty and await my punishment. Pronounce sentence, legislators ! France, freedom, the fate of the republic and of yourselves, depend on this day's distribution of that justice which it is yours to dispense."

From the agitation in which she had passed the

MADAME ROLAND. 261

preceding night, she felt extreme fatigue. She desired to have a chamber, of which, at ten o'clock, she took possession. When, on entering it, she found herself surrounded by four dirty walls, in the midst of which was a bed without curtains ; when she observed a double-grated window, and was assailed by a close and offensive smell; she felt indeed sensible of the change in her situation. The room however was of a tolerable size, it had a fire-place, and the bed-clothes were not bad : she deemed herself therefore, without dwelling on comparisons, not altogether ill accommodated. She retired to bed, and was not risen at ten in the morning, when Grandpré returned. He appeared more uneasy than the preceding evening, while he cast a mournful look around the wretched apartment. ' How did you pass the night?' said he, his eyes filled with tears. ' I was repeatedly awakened by the noise, but fell asleep again as soon as it ceased, in despite even of the alarm-bell, which I thought I heard this morning.—Ha! is it not sounding still ?' ' Why, I thought so; but it is nothing.' ' Be it as is pleases Heaven : if they kill me, it shall be in this bed; for I am so weary, that here I will expect my fate. Is any thing new brought forward against the members ?' ' No, I have brought back your letter. It is my opinion, and also that of Champagneux, that the beginning should be softened. Here is what we propose to substitute: and then you should write a line or two to the minister of the home department, that he may transmit your letter officially, which would enable me the better to solicit that it should be read.' 'If I thought,' replied she, taking the paper and looking over it, ' that my letter would be read as it now stands, so it should remain, even were I sure it would be productive of no advantage to myself; for it is scarcely possible to hope for justice from the convention. The truths addressed to it are not for an assembly incapable, at present, of putting them in practice: but they should be uttered, that they may be heard by the departments.' At length, convinced that her exordium might prevent the reading of the letter, she omitted the first paragraphs, substituting in their stead what had been proposed by her friends. She also wrote a few lines to the minister, in order to render the proceeding regular.

Rising about noon, she busied herself in arranging her apartment. She had in her pocket Thomson's Seasons, a work of which she was peculiarly fond: she made a memorandum of such other books as she should wish to procure. Among these were the Lives of Plutarch, Hume's History of England, and Sheridan's Dictionary. " I would rather," says she, " have continued to read

MADAME ROLAND. 263

Mrs. Macaulay, but the person who had lent me the first volumes was from home." While employed in these peaceful preparations, she heard the town in a tumult, and the drums beating to arms. She could not help smiling at the contrast. ' At any rate,' said she to herself, ' they will not prevent my living to my last moment more happy in conscious innocence than my persecutors with the rage that animates them. If they come, I will advance to meet them, and go to death as a man would go to repose.'

The keeper's wife came to invite her prisoner to her apartment, that she might dine in a better air. Here she found her faithful domestic, who, bathed in tears, and nearly suffocated with grief, threw herself into the arms of her mistress, who, on this occasion, could not avoid melting into tenderness and sorrow. She even almost reproached herself with her previous tranquillity, when she reflected on the anxiety of those who were attached to her. She endeavoured to prove to this affectionate servant, who was desirous of remaining in the prison, that she would be more useful to her without; that by giving way to her grief she would incapacitate herself from serving her ; and that upon the whole she was far from being so unfortunate as might be imagined : and this indeed was true. " Whenever I have been ill," observes madame Roland, "I have experienced a particular kind of serenity, proceeding unquestionably from my mode of thinking, and from the law I have laid down for myself of always submitting quietly to necessity instead of revolting against it. The moment I take to my bed, every duty and every solicitude seems at an end: I am bound only to remain there with resignation and with a good grace. I call up agreeable impressions, pleasing remembrances, and ideas of happiness. All exertions, all reasonings, and all calculations, I discard ; giving myself up entirely to nature : peaceful like her, I suffer pain without impatience, and seek repose or cheerfulness. I find that imprisonment produces on me nearly the same effect . I am only bound to be in prison, and what great hardship is there in that ? I am not such very bad company for myself."

A multitude of new victims being brought to the Abbaye, madame Roland was informed she must change her situation, as her chamber would contain more than one bed. To be alone, she was obliged to be confined in a small closet, the window of which was over the sentry, who guarded the prison-gate. *Who goes there ? Kill him ! Guard ! Patrole !* called out in a thundering voice, were the sounds that annoyed her through the night. The houses were illuminated, and from

MADAME ROLAND.   265

the number and frequency of the patroles, it was easy to infer some commotion. She rose early and employed herself in making her bed, cleaning her little room, and in rendering her person, and every thing around her, as neat as it was in her power. " Had I desired these things to be done for me," says she, " I must have paid for them dearly, waited a long time, and had them performed in a slovenly manner. By taking on myself the office, I was sure to be a gainer, and that the trifling presents I might make would be rated higher, because they would be altogether gratuitous."

Madame Roland had listened impatiently to hear the bolts of her door drawn back, that she might ask for a newspaper. She read in it the decree against the twenty-two: the paper fell from her hands, while she exclaimed, in a transport of grief, ' My country is undone !' Firm and tranquil herself, beneath the yoke of oppression, she could not see the triumph of guilt and error, the national representation violated, the torch of civil discord lighted up, the enemy about to avail himself of the divisions of the people, freedom lost to the north of France, probity and talents proscribed, and the republic a prey to the most dreadful dissensions, without poignant

sorrow. ' Farewel, my country !' exclaimed she ;
' sublime illusions, generous sacrifices, hope and
happiness, farewel !   Splendid chimeras! from
which I reaped so much delight, ye are all dis-
pelled by the horrible corruption of this vast city.
I despised life : the loss of you makes me detest
it, and defy the utmost fury of the men of blood.
Anarchists, savages, for what do you wait ? You,
who have proscribed virtue, why do you not spill
the blood of those who respect her laws ? When
shed upon the earth, it will make her open her
devouring jaws, and swallow you up.'   A sullen
indignation succeeded in her mind to these emotions ; indifferent to what concerned herself, and
almost hopeless for others, she waited for events
with curiosity rather than with concern.   "I no
longer live to *feel*," says she, " but to *know*."
She soon learned, that apprehensions had existed
the preceding night for the fate of the prisons:
hence the strict and noisy guard ; hence the motive of Grandpré's inquietude.   He had, for eight
successive days, in vain endeavoured to obtain of
the assembly the reading of madame Roland's
letter.   On finding, by the *Moniteur*, that her
section had expressed itself in her favour, she determined to address it, and to recapitulate the circumstances that had passed.

Several days elapsed, and still she underwent

MADAME ROLAND.   267

no examination. To the administrators, who had visited her on different pretences, she uniformly expressed herself with force and dignity: among them, two or three men of sense appeared to understand her, without however daring to take her part. She was at dinner, when five or six persons were at once announced to her. ' Good-morrow, *Citoyenne*,' said one who advanced before the rest, and who assumed the office of spokesman. ' Good-morrow, sir.' ' Are you satisfied with this house? Have you any reason to complain of your treatment, or any particular demand to make?' ' I complain of being here; and demand my enlargement.' ' Is your health impaired? or does solitude affect your spirits.' ' I am in good health, and not at all out of spirits. *Ennui* is the disease of hearts without feeling, and of minds without resource in themselves. But I have a strong feeling of injustice, and protest against the lawless oppression which arrested me without cause, and has detained me without examination.' ' Why, in a period of revolution, there is so much to be done, that there is not time to attend to every thing.' ' A woman, to whom king Philip made nearly the same reply, answered him, " If thou hast not time to do me justice, thou hast not time to be a king." Take care you

MADAME ROLAND.

do not oblige oppressed citizens to use the same language to the people, or rather to the arbitrary authorities, by which the people are misled.' ' Adieu, *Citoyenne*,' said the flippant officer, confounded by her spirit, and unable to reply.

Madame Roland had been induced by her love of order, and habits of regularity, to enquire into the customs and expences of the prison, which she was desirous rigidly to observe. She seemed to take a pleasure in making trials of her fortitude, and in enuring herself to privations. She determined therefore to make an experiment how far the human mind is capable of diminishing gradually the wants of the body. She began by substituting, in the place of coffee and chocolate, bread and water for breakfast. For her dinner, she desired to have one plain dish of meat, with a few vegetables; and vegetables also for her supper without a dessert. She likewise relinquished both wine and beer. As her purpose in adopting this conduct was moral rather than economical, she appropriated the sums thus saved for the relief of those miserable wretches who were lying upon straw, that, while eating her dry bread in the morning, she might have the pleasure of reflecting that, by this deprivation, she was adding to their dinner. " If I remain here six months," said she, " I will engage to leave the place with

MADAME ROLAND.   269

a healthy complexion, and a body by no means
emaciated, having reduced my wants so far as to
be satisfied with bread and soup, with a few benedictions *incognito*." She also made little presents
to the servants of the prison, that her economy
might not prove injurious to them. By these
means she considered that she rendered her independence more perfect, and was at the same time
a gainer in good-will.

Her section, in the mean while, actuated by
the best principles, had come to a resolution to
protest against arbitrary imprisonment, and even
to resist it when attempted. The letter of madame Roland was there read, and listened to with
concern. The debate that ensued being prolonged till the next day, the mountain party took the
alarm, while a host of furious deputies from the
different sections hastened to suppress, in its birth,
this struggle for justice. Urged by Grandpré,
madame Roland again addressed herself to the
ministers of justice and of the home department.
Her letters were conceived in terms but little conciliating, and not less forcible than severe. " Factions pass away," said she, " justice only remains : of all the faults of men in place weakness
is the least pardonable, because it is the source
of the greatest disorders, particularly in times of

trouble." From the men who had neglected the decrees, by which they were enjoined to prosecute the authors of the massacre of September, she expected nothing: she was aware of their weakness and perfidy; and the truths she addressed to them were meant but to point out to them their duties and their failures.

Every person distinguished for virtue or talents must have experienced the malignity of the *mob* of little minds, and the arts to which they descend to lower in the public opinion those whose characters they despair of emulating, and whose excellences they feel as a tacit reproach. Of the truth of this reflection the public prints, on the present occasion, afforded an example. In the Thermometre, for the 9th of June, there appeared a series of questions, under the title of An Examination of L. P. d'Orleans, among which was the following charge: " That the prisoner had been present at secret cabals, held by night in the apartment of the wife of Buzot, in the Fauxbourg St. Germain, whither Dumouriez, Roland and his wife, Vergniaux, Brissot, Petion, Louvet, &c. were accustomed to repair." It displays a curious instance of effrontery in wickedness, that the very deputies, thus calumniated, were precisely those who voted for the banishment of the Bourbons, and to whom d'Orleans never ap-

MADAME ROLAND.   271

peared as a leader possessed of capacity, but always as a dangerous tool : it was they who were among the first to dread his vices and his ascendancy, to denounce the latter, and to hunt down those who appeared to be his agents. Neither M. nor madame Roland ever met d'Orleans, they even refused to associate with those in any degree connected with him. Indignant at these vile absurdities, madame Roland took up her pen to write to the editor of the paper, of whom she had conceived a favourable opinion, and with whom she had been on friendly terms till his seduction by the Mountaineers. She represented to him the audacity and infamy of this proceeding; the cruelty and injustice of loading with calumny those who were already entangled in the trammels of persecution. She exhorted him to give the answers that must have been made to these questions, and to do justice to those whom he had injured.

During her confinement in the Abbaye, this courageous and unfortunate woman beguiled her imprisonment by books and literary labours; particularly in writing *Memoirs* of the times, the loss of which can never be sufficiently regretted. The insurrection of the 31st of May, and the outrages of the 2d of June, had filled her with indignation; yet, persuaded that the departments would in the end make the good cause triumphant, while indulging this hope, she was careless of her own safety. " The success of my friends," said she, " and the triumph of true republicans, in the anticipation, consoled me for every thing. I could have suffered the execution of an unjust sentence, or have sunk under the stroke of some unforeseen atrocity, with the calmness, the pride, and even the joy of innocence, which despises death, and knows that its wrongs will be avenged."

About this period the publication of a gross libel, proclaimed loudly by the hawkers under her window, persuaded her that some new outrage was in contemplation. In one of the numbers of the *Père Duchesne*, an abominable print, it was pretended that its author had paid a visit, disguised as a Vendean, to madame Roland, and obtained her confidence : that she had confessed to him the connections of Roland and the Brissotines with the rebels of Vendée and the English government. In this ridiculous story, in which physical and moral facts were alike disregarded, madame Roland heard herself metamorphosed into an old toothless hag, who was exhorted to weep for her sins, till they should be expiated on the scaffold. The hawkers, who, doubtless as they were instructed, left not the vicinity of the prison for a moment, accompanied their proclamations by the most sanguinary advice to the populace. Madame Roland, thus outraged, took up her pen, and wrote a few lines to the minister*, pointing out to him the infamy of an administration which exposes innocence, already oppressed, to the blind fury of a misguided people.

About the same time a young woman, a friend to madame Roland, found means to make her way into the prison. " How was I astonished," says she, " to see her sweet countenance, and to feel myself pressed to her bosom, and bathed in her tears. I took her for an angel, and an angel she was, for she is good and handsome, and had done all that she could to bring me news of my friends: she furnished me also with the means of informing them of my situation."

This consolation had almost made her forget her captivity, when on the 24th of June, about noon, the gaoler's wife entreated her to step into her apartment, where an administrator was waiting to see her. She was in pain, and in bed ; she rose, however, and followed her conductress. On entering the room, she perceived a man walking backward and forward, while another sat writing,

---

* Garat.

neither of whom seemed to observe her. ' Am I
the person, gentlemen, for whom you asked ?'
' You are the wife of citizen Roland ?' ' Yes,
Roland is my name.' ' Be so good as to sit
down. The one continued to write, and the
other to walk. At length, while she was endeavouring to divine the meaning of this farce, the
writer addressed her : ' I am come,' said he, ' to
set you at liberty.' ' Why, indeed,' replied she,
with but little emotion, ' it is very right to remove me from this place ; but that is not all : I
wish to return home, and the door of my apartment is sealed up.' ' The administration will
have it opened in the course of the day : I am
writing for an order, because I am the only administrator here, and two signatures are necessary
for the gaoler's discharge.' He rose, and having delivered his message, turned towards madame Roland with the air of a person who wishes
to inspire confidence. ' Do you know,' said he,
suddenly, as without design, ' where M. Roland is
at present ?' She observed, smiling, that the
question was not sufficiently candid to deserve an
answer, and retired to prepare for her departure.
Her first idea was to dine quietly, and not to remove till the evening, but a moment's reflection
convinced her of the folly of remaining in a prison, whence she was free to depart ; the gaoler

MADAME ROLAND.   275

also appeared impatient to take possession of her lodging. It was a small closet, with dirty walls, close gates, and in the neighbourhood of a pile of wood, where all the animals of the house deposited their ordure. The gaoler, who had never seen it occupied by any person so tranquil as the present inhabitant, who was accustomed to arrange in it her books, and to adorn it with flowers, called it the pavilion of Flora. As it contained but one bed, it was generally allotted to a new comer, or to an individual desirous of solitude. " I was ignorant," says madame Roland, " that the gaoler, at the very moment he was speaking, intended it for Brissot, whom I did not even suppose to be my neighbour: and that, soon after, it would be inhabited by a heroine worthy of a better age, the celebrated Charlotte Cordey."

Madame Roland's servant, who had just arrived to vist her mistress, wept for joy while she packed up her things in preparation for their removal. The order for her liberation, founded upon want of evidence of any crime, was shewn to the prisoner, who, having settled her accounts, distributed her little favours to the poor, and to the servants belonging to the prison. On her way out, she met the prince of Linanges, one of the hostages, who obligingly congratulated her upon her enlargement. She replied, ' that she should be happy to pay him the same compliment, as it would be a pledge of the release of the commissioners, and of the return of peace.' Then sending for a hackney-coach, she walked down stairs, surprised at finding the administrator, who came to see her into the carriage, had not yet left the prison.

Driving home, with the intention of leaving there a few things, and then proceeding to the house of the worthy people who had adopted her daughter, she jumped lightly from the coach, and flew, as on wings, under the gateway. ' Good morrow, Lamarre,' said she to the porter, cheerfully, as she passed. She had scarcely proceeded up four or five stairs, when she heard herself called by two men, who had kept close behind her. ' What do you want ?' said she, turning round. ' We arrest you in the name of the law.' Her feelings, at this moment, may be easily conceived. She desired the order to be read to her, and taking an immediate resolution, stepped down stairs, and walked hastily across the yard. ' Whither are you going ?' ' To my landlord's, where I have business; follow me thither.' The mistress of the house opened the door with a smile. ' Let me sit down and breathe,' exclaimed madame Roland, ' but do not rejoice at my being set at liberty : it is only a cruel artifice : I am no sooner released from the Abbaye than I am ordered to St. Pelagie. As I am not ignorant of the

MADAME ROLAND. 277

resolutions entered into of late by my section, I am determined to put myself under its protection, and I will beg you to send thither accordingly.' The landlord's son*, with all the honest indignation of youth, immediately offered to go. Two commissioners from the section returned with him, desired to see the order, and made to it a formal opposition. They afterwards begged madame Roland to accompany them to the mayor, where they were going to assign the reasons of their conduct; a request which she could not refuse. The intermediate time she employed in writing notes to her friends, to inform them of her new destination, and in taking leave of the family, whom this scene had filled with surprise and consternation. On being conducted to the house of the mayor, she was put into a small antechamber, with inspectors charged with the care of her person, while the commissioners proceeded to the office of the police. The debate continued for some time, and became warm. Ill at ease, and indignant, while thus obliged to act the part of a criminal, at being exposed to inquisitive eyes, madame Roland rose, and opened the door of the office. ' There can certainly, gentlemen, be no harm in my being present at a discussion of which I am the sub-

---

* He was, on this account, dragged to the scaffold, and his father died with grief.

ject.' ' Get you gone,' cried a little man, whom
she recognised for the person by whom she had
been so awkwardly examined at the Abbaye. ' But,
gentlemen, I have no intention to commit any act
of violence, I am not prepared for it; I do not
even ask to be heard; I only desire to be present.'
' Get you gone, get you gone !—*Gendarmes*, come
hither.' " Any one," observes she, " would have
supposed the office was besieged, because a woman
of common sense wished to hear what they were
saying of her." It was however vain to resist. Soon
after she perceived them making signs, running backwards and forwards, and sending for a coach. An
inspector of the police, at length, desired her to
follow him. Turning to the door of the office, and
setting it wide open, ' Commissioners of the section
of Beaurepaire,' said she, ' I give you notice that they
are taking me away.' ' We cannot help it : but the
section will not forget you ; it will take care that you
shall be examined.' ' After having been set at liberty
at one o'clock, because *there was no evidence against me*,
I should be glad to know how I could become *a suspected person* in my way home from the Abbaye, and
thus give cause for a new detention.' One of the
administrators, not less stupid than awkward, confessed, in a magisterial tone, that the first arrest was
illegal, and that the prisoner had been enlarged, that
she might be afterwards taken according to the forms

MADAME ROLAND.   279

of the law. This avowal opened to madame Roland
a field of which she was about to avail herself: but
tyrants, even when they suffer the truth to escape
them, refuse to hear it from others, or to abide by
its consequences. Perceiving that expostulation
would be vain, she suffered herself to be conveyed
to the prison of *St. Pelagie.*

This house had, under the old government, been
inhabited by nuns, to whose charge was committed
the female victims of *lettres-de-cachet:* it was situated in a remote quarter of the town, the inhabitants
of which were of a low order, and well known for
the ferocious spirit which they had manifested in the
month of September, by the massacre of so many
priests. This, on the present occasion, was not a
consolatory circumstance. While a note was taking
of the entrance of the prisoner, an ill-looking man
began to examine the bundle which contained her
night-clothes, with apparent curiosity. On her expressing indignation at this impropriety, he was ordered to desist. " Twice a-day," says she, " was
I doomed to see the horrible countenance of this
man, who was turnkey of the corridor in which I
lodged." She was asked if she chose a room with
one or two beds. ' I am alone, and want no company.' ' But the room will be too small.' ' It is
all the same to me.' Upon enquiry, it was found
they were all full; madame Roland was therefore

conducted to a two-bedded room, six feet by twelve,
so that with two small tables, and two chairs, it was
sufficiently crowded. She was then informed, that
she must pay the first month's lodging in advance,
fifteen livres for one bed, and double this sum for
the two. As she wanted only one, and had preferred a single-bedded room, they agreed to take the
fifteen livres. ' But there is no water-bottle, nor
other conveniences.' ' You must purchase them,'
replied they. To these she added an ink-stand, pens
and paper, and established herself in her new residence. The mistress of the house came to visit her
charge, who enquired of her the customs of the
place. She was informed in reply, that the state
allowed nothing to the prisoners. ' How then do
they live ?' They receive only a plate of kidney-
beans, and a pound and a half of bread per day; but
you would not be able to eat of either.' I can easily
believe that they are not such as I have been accustomed to ; but I wish to know what belongs to every
situation, and will make a trial.' She did so, but
without success: her health would not bear the
prison diet, and she was obliged to have recourse to
the kitchen of madame Bouchaud, who made an offer
of boarding her. This fare was both comparatively
good and economical : a mutton-chop and a few
vegetables for dinner, a sallad for supper, and bread
and water for breakfast, the diet to which she had

been accustomed to at the Abbaye. Notwithstanding this simplicity and temperance, reports were raised of her expences at *St. Pélagie,* where, it was said, she was seeking to corrupt the gaoler by giving treats to his family. Hence arose great indignation among the *Sans-culottes,* and a proposal from some of them to dispatch her to the other world. To this other calumnies were added, equally absurd and ill-founded.

Her courage sunk not under these new trials, but the refinement of cruelty which had attended her removal from the Abbaye, filled her with indignation. " Feeling myself," says she, " in that state of mind when every impression becomes stronger, and its effects more prejudicial to health, I went to bed : I could not sleep, and it was not possible to avoid thinking. This violent state, however, never with me, lasts long. Being accustomed to govern my mind, I felt the want of self-possession, and thought myself a fool for affording a triumph to my enemies, by suffering them to break my spirit. They were only heaping on themselves fresh odium, without greatly altering the situation I had already found means so well to support. Had I not here, as at the Abbaye, books and leisure ? I began, indeed, to be angry with myself for having allowed my peace of mind to be disturbed : I no longer thought of any thing but of enjoying existence, and of employing my faculties with that independence of spirit which a strong mind preserves in the midst of fetters, and which thus disappoints its most determined enemies."

In pursuance of these admirable resolutions, she purchased crayons, and had recourse to drawing, to vary her occupations. Fortitude, she justly conceived, consisted not merely in an effort of the mind to rise above circumstances, but in maintaining that elevation by suitable conduct. " I am not content," says she, " with calling up, under unfortunate events, the maxims of philosophy to support my courage ; but I provide for myself agreeable amusements : neither do I neglect the art of preserving health, to keep myself in a just equilibrium." She divided her days with a certain kind of order. In the mornings she studied English in Shaftsbury's Essay on Virtue, and in the poetry of Thomson, by whom she was transported by turns to the sublime regions of intellect, and to the affecting scenes of nature. With Shaftsbury she strengthened her reason, with Thomson she charmed her imagination, and delighted her feelings. Afterwards she employed herself with her crayons till the hour of dinner, and repeated with pleasure, though with less skill, an art which in her youth she had practised with success. It is those only who have acquired the habit of exerting their faculties, and of exercising over themselves a voluntary control, that evade the malice of fortune, and escape from a languor

MADAME ROLAND.   283

scarcely less cruel, and the most destructive of mental disorders : it is thus, also, that the seductions of vice, or of a dissipation scarcely less pernicious, are stripped of their allurements, and assail us in vain.

It is impossible to withhold our respect from a mind, that, rich in its own resources, could calmly pursue its course, in a situation like that in which this deserving woman was so unworthily placed. The wing of *St. Pelagie*, appropriated to female prisoners, was divided into long and very narrow corridors, on one side of which were the cells. Under the same roof, and upon the same line, separated only by a thin plaster, did the respectable wife of the virtuous Roland dwell in the midst of murderers, and women of ill-fame : by her side was one of those wretches who make a trade of seduction, and a sale of youth and innocence : above her was a woman who forged assignats, and, with a band of savages to which she belonged, tore in pieces upon the highway an individual of her own sex. The door of each cell was secured on the outside with an enormous bolt, and opened every morning by a man, who stared indecently into the room, to see whether the prisoners were up or in their beds. The inhabitants of the cells then assembled in the corridor, upon the staircases, or in a damp and noisome room. Their distance from the lodging of madame Roland was insufficient to preserve her

ears from the contamination of the grossest obscenities.   Nor was this all: the wing in which the
men were confined, had windows which fronted
those of the women, the consequences of which,
among persons of such a description, may be easily
conceived.   " If this," observes the heroic sufferer,
be the reward of virtue on earth, who will be astonished at my contempt of life, and at the resolution
with which I shall be able to look death in the face?
It never appeared to me formidable : at present it is
not without its charms, and I could embrace it with
pleasure, did not my daughter invite me to stay a
little longer with her; and if my voluntary exit would
not furnish calumny with weapons against my husband, whose glory I ought to support, would they
dare to summon me before a tribunal."

The keepers of *St. Pelagie*, doubtless moved by
the merit of their prisoner, were at pains to render
her situation less disagreeable.   The excessive heats
of July rendering her cell, upon the white walls of
which the sun fiercely struck, scarcely habitable, the
wife of the gaoler invited her charge to spend the
days in her apartment.   Her acceptance of this
offer was limited by madame Roland to the afternoons.   It was then she thought of sending for her
piano-forte, with which she sometimes beguiled the
heavy hours.   At this period, her moral situation
had also become less dreadful.   The rising of some

MADAME ROLAND. 285

of the departments revived her hopes ; her husband was in a safe and peaceful retreat ; her daughter in the house of her venerable friends, continued, under their inspection, and with their children, her exercises and her education ; while the fugitives, her friends, welcomed at Caen, were there surrounded by a respectable force. She flattered herself that the salvation of her country was growing out of events, and, resigned to her own fate, was still happy, while, as usual, she employed her time in useful or agreeable occupations. She sometimes saw the persons who were accustomed to visit her at the Abbaye; the worthy Grandpré, the faithful Bosc, who brought her flowers from *le Jardin de Plantes*, which, with their brilliant colours, and fragrant perfumes, diminished the horrors of her gloomy abode. With them came an amiable woman, and the kind Champagneux, who persuaded her to continue her historical memoirs. She therefore resumed her pen, and laid by her Tacitus and Plutarch, to which she was accustomed to devote the afternoons.

Madame Bouchaud, perceiving that she availed herself with great reserve of the offer of her apartment, removed her altogether from her cell into a comfortable room, on the ground-floor, underneath her own chamber. Thus was she delivered from the shocking company, that had for three weeks been her greatest torment. The good-nature of madame

Bouchaud extended itself to the minutest details, even to the very jasmine carried up before her window, round the bars of which it wound its flexible branches. She looked upon herself as the boarder of this good and humane woman, and forgot her captivity. All the articles of her study and amusement were now united around her; her *piano-forte* was by her bedside, and recesses in the wall afforded her the means of arranging her little furniture with that neatness which was her characteristic, and in which she took delight.

But, alas! this gleam of sunshine was soon overclouded: intrigue and arms were, not without success, employed against the departments: soldiers deluded, or brought over, betrayed the brave Normans; Caen abandoned the members to which it had afforded a refuge; they were declared, by a domineering banditti, traitors to their country, their persons outlawed, their property confiscated, and their wives and children arrested. Guilt triumphed over unfortunate virtue. "That cowardice," observes madame Roland, "which marks the selfishness and corruption of a degenerate people, too debased to be reclaimed by reason; that cowardice delivers over to terror the perfidious administrators, and the ignorant multitude." A rod of iron was, in the mean time, held over Paris, which famine threatened, and on the vitals of which poverty prey-

MADAME ROLAND. 287

ed. The reign of proscriptions flourished, and the prisons overflowed. At this season of violence and terror, when the friends of madame Roland were all fugitives or proscribed, Champagneux, who was in possession of almost the whole of her *Historical Memoirs*, was threatened with an arrest: uneasy, agitated, and convinced that the principles which they contained would, if found, be a passport to the scaffold, he committed them to the flames.

In the midst of these alarms, madame Roland still enjoyed the pleasant room allotted to her by her kind hostess, and here she occasionally, though by stealth, had the pleasure of seeing her friends. This apartment adjoined to a large room called the council-chamber, where the administrators of the police met to examine prisoners. Madame Roland was indebted to this circumstance for the knowledge of some curious scenes. Here also they sometimes held their orgies with some favourite prisoners, consuming, at the expence of the gaoler, cordials, wine, capons, chickens, &c. in lavish profusion. When this company assembled, Bouchaud or his wife never failed to withdraw the key from the door of their charge, and to give her notice of their arrival. "At last," says she, " I took a resolution, and shut my ears against their noise. I even found a pleasure in continuing my *Historical Memoirs*, and in writing vigorous passages in the neighbourhood of wretches, who, had they heard only a single phrase, would have torn me in pieces."

The 10th of August approached, and fears were entertained of the renewal of the carnage of the 2d of September; the administrators therefore found means to withdraw from St. Pelagie the rogues of their acquaintance, and the civic feasts were held no more. " Could I persuade myself to speak on subjects so disgusting," says madame Roland, " I could give shocking accounts of the abuses prevailing in prisons. Every thing gets tainted, or completely spoiled, in these infectious places, under a vicious administration, actuated by passion only, careless of correcting, and desirous to destroy."

On her first coming to St. Pelagie, madame Roland had accepted the services of a woman confined for some trifling offence. " Not," says she, " but I was well able to be my own servant. *Tout sied bien au généreux courage**, was said of Favonius, who performed for Pompey, in his misfortunes, the offices of a domestic. This may, with equal truth, be applied to the unfortunate man, stripped of his possessions, and providing for his own wants; and to the austere philosopher, disdaining every superfluity. But, as in fetching water, and articles of a

---

* Every thing becomes a noble spirit.

MADAME ROLAND. 289

similar kind, it was necessary at St. Pelagie to pass through long passages, and mix with their inhabitants, I was not sorry to have a person whom I could oblige by sending her on such occasions."
This woman was, one morning, going into the room of madame Roland at the very instant that an administrator was at the door of the council-chamber. He enquired who lodged there, went in, and cast around him an angry glance. On quitting the room, he complained to the wife of the keeper of the degree of comfort she allowed the prisoner to enjoy. ' Madame Roland was indisposed,' replied madame Bouchaud ; which was true ; ' and I put her more in the way of receiving such assistance as she might require. Beside, she sometimes amuses herself with a *piano-forte*, for which there is not room in the cell.' ' She must do without it : send her this very day into a corridor : it is your business to maintain equality.'

Madame Bouchaud, exceedingly distressed at this inhuman interference, went to communicate to her charge the orders that had been given ; but she felt consoled by the tranquil resignation with which her commission was received, and it was agreed between them, that madame Roland should come down in the course of every day, to change the air, and resume her studies, the materials for

which were to be left in her present apartment.
" Thus, once more," says she, " am I destined to
see the turnkeys, to hear the creaking of the bolts,
to breathe the fœtid air of a corridor, sadly illumined
of an evening by a lamp, of which the thick smoke
blackens all the walls, and suffocates the neighbourhood! Insolent comedians! you are playing your
last part : the enemy is at hand. By the enemy I
mean the departments, who will ultimately ensure
the triumph of reason and of true liberty, and prepare for your destruction. Mine, no doubt, is
inevitable : I have deserved the hatred of all tyrants;
but I only regret the ruin of my country, which
your chastisement will console, but cannot save."

Oppression had filled the corridor with women
in whose society madame Roland could remain without shame. There she found the wife of a justice
of the peace, whose neighbour ascribed to her un-
civic expressions. There also was the wife of the
president of the revolutionary tribunal; and there
was madame Petion. ' I little thought,' said madame Roland, accosting her, ' when I was sharing
your uneasiness at the *Mairie**, on the 10th of August (1792), that we should keep our sad anniversary at St. Pelagie; and that the fall of the throne
would lead to our disgrace.'

---

* The residence of the mayor.

MADAME ROLAND. 291

The first part of madame Roland's captivity had been employed in the composition of her Historical Memoirs. " My pen," said she, " proceeded with so much rapidity, and I was in so happy a disposition of mind, that in less than a month I had manuscripts sufficient to form a duodecimo volume. These memoirs, or historical notices, contained a variety of particulars relative to all the facts, and all the persons, connected with public affairs, that my situation had afforded me an opportunity of knowing. I related them with all the freedom and energy of my nature, with all the openness and unconstraint of an ingenuous mind, setting itself above selfish considerations ; with all the pleasure that results from describing what we have experienced, or what we feel ; and lastly, with the confidence that, happen what would, the collection would serve as my moral and political testament." The destruction of these writings, by the arrest of the friend to whom they were confided, severely distrest the writer. " This," says she, " may easily be conceived, when it is remembered, that I may be murdered to-morrow; and that these writings were the anchor to which I had committed my hopes of saving from reproach my own memory, with that of many deserving characters. As we ought not, however, to sink under any event, I shall employ my remaining time in setting down, without form or order, whatever may occur to my mind. These fragments will not make amends for what is lost, but they will serve to recal it to memory, and assist me in filling up the void, on some future day, should the means of so doing remain in my power."

It was about this period that, to divert the vexation of her mind, she determined on writing a narrative of her life. " I should despise myself," says this truly philosophical and heroic woman, " did I suffer my mind to sink in any circumstances. In all the troubles I have experienced, the most lively impression of sorrow has been almost immediately accompanied by the ambition of opposing my strength to the evil, and of surmounting it, either by doing good to others, or by exerting to the utmost my fortitude. My *Historic Notices* are gone: I mean to write my Memoirs; and, prudently accommodating myself to my weakness, at a moment when my feelings are acute, I shall talk of my own person, that my thoughts may be the less at home. I shall exhibit my virtues and my faults with equal freedom. He who dares not speak well of himself, is almost always a coward, who knows and dreads the ill that may be spoken of him : and he who hesitates to confess his faults, has neither spirit to vindicate, nor virtue to repair them."

Near five months had madame Roland passed

within the walls of St. Pelagie, in silent resignation, when a stranger appeared before her. It was a physician brought by the friendly care of her keepers. When informed of her name, he told her he was the friend of a man whom perhaps she did not like. ' How can you know that? and who is the person you mean?' ' Robespierre!' ' I once knew him well, and esteemed him much: I thought him a sincere and zealous friend of freedom.' ' Why, is he not so?' ' I am afraid that he loves power: perhaps from an idea that he knows how to do good as well as any man, and desires it no less. I am afraid that he is very fond of revenge, and inclined to exercise it particularly upon those whom he considers as blind to his merit. I believe that he is very susceptible of prejudices; that his resentment is easily excited; and that he is too ready to think every one guilty who subscribes not to his opinions.' ' You never saw him more than once or twice in your life.' ' I have seen him much oftener! Ask him; let him lay his hand upon his heart; and you will see whether he has it in his power to say any thing to my disadvantage.'

Madame Roland conceived, on this occasion, the idea of addressing Robespierre through this man, who called himself his friend. From this long and eloquent letter, my limits, which I have already exceeded, will not allow of more than an extract: "I write not," says she, " to entreat you.   Prayer becomes the guilty, or the slave : innocence vindicates herself, which is sufficient; or complains, as she has a right to do, when the object of persecution. But even complaints accord not with my temper: I can suffer, and dare look in the face any shape of misfortune.   Besides, I know that at the birth of republics, revolutions, which are almost inevitable, and which give to the passions of mankind too great a scope, frequently expose those who have best served their country to become the victims of their own zeal, and of the delusion of their countrymen.   A good conscience will be their consolation, and history their avenger."   She goes on to enquire, why a *woman*, incapable of action, is exposed to these storms, that burst generally upon the heads only of efficient individuals ?   And what is the fate which she has to expect ?   These questions, she declares, are deemed by her but of small personal importance. " For what," says she, " is a single emmet, more or less, crushed by the foot of the elephant, in the general system of the world ?"   She proposes them only because they are of infinite interest in regard to the present liberty, and future happiness, of her country.   She next adverts to her respectable husband, the probity of his character, and to the injustice of which he was the victim.   Her own implication in his imputed guilt, she treats with contempt. " Brought up in retirement," says she; " devoted from my youth to those serious studies, which have given to my mind some degree of force; blessed with a taste for simple pleasures, which no change of circumstances has been able to pervert; an enthusiastic admirer of the revolution, and giving way to the generous sentiments it inspired; kept a stranger to public affairs by principle, as well as by my sex, yet conversing about them with warmth, because the public weal, as soon as it exists, takes the lead of all other concerns; I regarded the first calumnies invented against me as contemptible follies: I deemed them the necessary tribute levied by envy upon a situation, which the imbecility of the vulgar led them to consider as exalted, and to which I would have preferred the state in which I had passed so many happy days." She enumerates her consequent injuries, and her courage and patience under them. " I have wearied no one," says she, " with my remonstrances: wanting many things, I have asked for nothing. I have made up my mind to misfortune, proud of trying my strength with her, and of trampling her under my feet."—" It is not," adds she, " to excite your compassion, which I am above asking, that I present you with a picture less melancholy than the truth: it is for your instruction." She reminds him of the instability of popular favour, and of the fate that may overtake him. She declares her own determination to await, after the honours of persecution, those of martyrdom, but she wishes to know her destiny. " Speak," says she, " it is something to know our fate ; and a soul like mine is capable of looking it in the face*."

After the two-and-twenty deputies were condemned to the scaffold, madame Roland considered theirs as a presage of her own fate. Though resigned to death, she felt repugnant to becoming a spectacle to the savage curiosity of a ferocious multitude. Under this feeling she caused laudanum to be procured for her, that she might remain mistress of her own destiny. " It was not," said she to a friend, who reproved her on this occasion, " my intention to depart at that moment, but to procure the means of doing so, when it should appear to me that the most proper period was arrived. I wished to pay homage to truth, as I well knew how, and then to take my departure immediately before the appointed ceremony. I thought it noble thus to disappoint my tyrants. It seemed to me, that there was a degree of weakness in receiving the *coup-de-grâce* when I could give it to myself, and in exposing myself to the insolent clamours of madmen, as unworthy of

---

* This letter was not sent.

MADAME ROLAND.   297

such an example, as incapable of deriving from it any advantage."

She however made no use of the resource she had provided, being persuaded by her friends that her execution might prove useful to her country. She beheld its approach with unaffected tranquillity. She suffered her hair to be cut off, and her hands to be bound, without a murmur, or a complaint. She traversed Paris amidst the insults of the populace, and received death with heroic firmness. She seemed even to experience a degree of pleasure in this last sacrifice to her country. She expressed, in dying, a wish to transmit to posterity the new and extraordinary sensations which she experienced in her road from the *Conciergerie* to the *Place de la Révolution*. For this purpose, when at the foot of the scaffold, she demanded pen and paper, which were refused to her. Her last moments are thus described by Riouffe, who was detained in the *Conciergerie*, when madame Roland arrived there.

" The blood of the twenty-two was not yet cold, when citizeness Roland was brought to the *Conciergerie* : aware of the fate that awaited her, her peace of mind remained undisturbed. Though past the prime of life, she was still a charming woman ; her person was tall and elegantly formed, her countenance animated, and very expressive ; but misfortune and confinement had impressed on her aspect traces of melancholy, which tempered its vivacity. In a body moulded by grace, and fashioned by a courtly politeness, she possessed a republican soul. Something more than is generally found in the eyes of women was painted in hers, which were large, dark, and full of softness and intelligence. She often spoke to me at the grate with the freedom and firmness of a *great man;* while we all stood listening around her in admiration and astonishment. Her conversation was serious without coldness, and she expressed herself with a correctness, a harmony, a cadence, that made her language a sort of music, with which the ear was never cloyed. She spake not of the deputies who had suffered death but with respect, and yet without effeminate compassion : she even reproached them for not adopting measures sufficiently strong. She generally styled them *our friends,* and often sent for Clavières for the purpose of conversing with him. Sometimes her sex recovered its ascendancy, and it was easy to perceive, that conjugal and maternal recollections had drawn tears from her eyes. This mixture of fortitude and softness, served but to render her the more interesting. The woman who waited on her, said one day to me, ' Before you, she summons all her courage, but in her own room she sometimes stands for three hours together, leaning against her window and

weeping.' The day on which she was called up to be
examined, we saw her pass with her usual firmness,
but when she returned, it was not with dry eyes:
she had been treated with harshness, and questions
had been put to her injurious to her honour. In
expressing her indignation, she had not been able to
suppress her tears. A mercenary pedant coldly insulted this admirable woman, celebrated for the excellence of her understanding; and who at the bar
of the national convention had, by the graces of her
eloquence, compelled even her enemies to admire
her in silence. She remained a week at the *Con-
cærgerie*, where her gentleness endeared her to all
the prisoners, who sincerely deplored her fate. On
the day of her condemnation, she was neatly dressed in white, her long black hair flowing loosely to
her waist. She would have melted the most savage nature, but these monsters were without hearts.
Her dress was chosen, not to excite pity, but as a
symbol of the purity of her mind. After her condemnation, she passed through the wicket with a
quick step, bespeaking something like cheerfulness,
and intimating by an expressive gesture that she was
condemned to die. She had for the companion of
her fate a man, Lemarche, director of the fabrica-
tion of assignats, whose fortitude equalled not her
own. She found means, however, to inspire him

with a certain degree of courage; and this she did with a gaiety so cheering, so real, as several times to force a smile in his countenance. At the place of execution she bowed before the statue of liberty, while she exclaimed, ' *Oh, liberty! what crimes are committed in thy name!*' She had frequently said that her husband would not survive her; and, soon after, we learned in our dungeons, that her prediction was accomplished. The virtuous Roland killed himself on the public road, thereby indicating his wish to die irreproachable, without endangering courageous hospitality. My heart, though suffering many torments in that horrible abode, felt nothing more severely than the pang occasioned by the death of this woman, *whose fame can never die.* The remembrance of her murder, added to that of my unfortunate friends, will make my mind a prey to sorrow till the latest period of my existence."

A few days before madame Roland was dragged to the scaffold—' If fate,' said she, ' had allowed me to live, there was one thing only of which I should have been ambitious, that of writing the annals of the present age, and of becoming the Macaulay of my country. I have, during my confinement, conceived a real fondness for Tacitus, and cannot go to rest till I have read a passage of his work. It seems to me, that we see things in the

MADAME ROLAND.   301

same light; and that in time, and with a subject equally rich, it would not have been impossible for me to imitate his style.'

She passed five months in prison, and, with the exception of two or three real friends, whom the terrors of the place did not prevent from coming to bewail with her the misfortunes of France, no one expressed the least degree of pity or interest in her fate. Neither in the journals, nor in the publications of the day, was a single remonstrance, or a single word, written in her favour.

On the 30th of May, 1790, the day of the federation of Lyons, madame Roland, who was present, gave (in a journal conducted by Champagneux) a description of the *fête*, with a spirit and energy that affected every heart. Upwards of sixty-thousand copies of the paper were distributed. The writer secretly enjoyed the triumph of her eloquence, but without suffering her name to be divulged.

It has been falsely asserted, that the wife of Roland was minister under the name of her husband. But, on the contrary, it is declared by those who were best acquainted with facts, that she took no share in the routine of his department; that she resisted the solicitations with which she was daily importuned, or when prevailed upon (which was very rarely) to engage in any affair, she indorsed the petitions in such a manner, as to caution the offices against partiality. Every sentiment in her mind was subordinate to the love of justice, and the maintenance of principle. But, though a stranger to what passed in the office of her husband, she was interested in his glory: when circumstances required a writing dictated by feeling, it was to her that the task was entrusted. It was on these occasions that, preserving the genius and character of M. Roland, she threw into the composition a force and passion that gave soul and animation to the arguments. It was the peculiar characteristic of her language to re-animate by confidence, and to convince by energetic reasoning: she knew the springs of the human heart, which she never failed to move. When the ruin of the minister was determined, his wife was involved in the proscription; a period in which her courage was severely tried, more particularly during the months of December, 1792, and of January, 1793, when every day brought to light new dangers, and every night threatened assassination. Perpetually harassed with alarms, she was entreated by her friends to sleep out of the minister's hotel; but, incapable of pusillanimity, she yielded not to this advice without indignation. One evening, at ten o'clock, she was informed that armed men, of a suspicious appearance, lurked around the house, with an apparent intention of forcing an entrance. Every one present exhorted her on this intelligence to leave the house in disguise, till, unable to resist their united solicitations, she consented to put on the dress of a peasant girl. The clothes having been procured, the cap was objected to by some one present, as not sufficiently coarse and ordinary : it was proposed to substitute for it another. ' I am ashamed,' exclaimed she, in a burst of indignation, ' at the part I am made to act. I will neither disguise myself, nor go out of the way. If I am to be assassinated, it shall be in my own house. I owe to my country this example of firmness, and I will give it.' This was pronounced with so much confidence and vivacity, that no one presumed to reply. From that day, till Roland resigned, she never quitted the hotel for a moment. Her enemies might with ease have ridded themselves of her, but they dreaded the consequences, and wished to effect their purpose under a legal sanction : careless of personal danger, she trembled only for the safety of her daughter, whom she dared not to expose to hazard. In concert with her husband, arrangements were made for the preservation of their child, who, with her governess, she wished to confide to the protection of her husband's brother, who resided at Villefranche, in the department of the Rhine, near the landed estate, whither they wished to send Eudora. To this gentleman she addressed a letter full of courage, of patriotism, and of resignation to the fate hanging over them; recommending her daughter to his paternal care. " To-morrow," says she, in this letter, " according to the accounts brought us from all quarters, and the preparations made long since, may be the last day of our lives: at all events our fate will not be useless to the safety of the republic: our fall will teach the departments what dangers they have to combat....I am what you have always known me, devoted to my duties which I love, appreciating life for the blessings of nature, and the enjoyments of virtue....I am too much habituated to despise death, to fear, or to fly from it. I leave my daughter good examples, and a memory ever dear to her. ....May she judge, feel, and avail herself of every thing, with a conscience always as pure, and a soul as expansive, as have been those of her parents."

All these precautions were of no effect, the Rolands were given to understand, that, in the retreat intended for her, their daughter would be still more exposed, and that even in the journey there would be danger. The brother, to whom the letter was addressed, was guillotined by the temporary commission established at Lyons. Mademoiselle Mignot, the governess of Eudora, betrayed her benefactress, from whom she had received a thousand kindnesses, and appeared before the tribunal as a witness in the affair, which led the mother of her pupil to the scaffold. Roland was reduced to con-

MADAME ROLAND.   305

seal himself by flight from his enemies; his wife had in her power the same resource, but she refused to employ it. She sought to turn aside the mischiefs which threatened her husband, by offering herself as a victim to their enemies. She was thrown into the dungeons of the Abbaye, June 1, 1793, and a short time after transferred to St. Pelagie. In prison she comported herself with a dignity which extorted the respect of all who approached her; while, by her conciliating manners, she softened all the officers of the prison. The wife of the keeper more particularly distinguished her by her attentions; her extreme kindness and benevolence gave birth to the idea of a project for the escape of her illustrious charge, by whom this plan was after some consideration rejected, lest it should again rouse the fury of her husband's enemies, which for the present appeared to slumber. ' While they keep me in prison,' said she, ' they will leave him at quiet; it is of more importance to the public weal that he should escape than that I should. If reason and justice should ever resume their empire, would not the nation be happy to find Roland alive, and to place him at the helm of affairs? Beside, I am determined not to expose any one; I cannot enjoy a liberty which would involve the safety of others; I will therefore remain here. Such is my resolution.'

It was about this time that Marat was stabbed by

Charlotte Cordey. Madame Roland admired this personal sacrifice, but observed, that the stroke had not been aimed at the right person. An extreme indignation seized her on hearing of the honours paid to the memory of Marat, and of the baseness of the representatives, whose probity had till then inspired her with some hope. Depression succeeded to these transports; the political atmosphere appeared in her apprehension overspread with a thicker gloom. ' I shall not,' said she, ' leave this place, but to go to the scaffold. I am, however, less tormented by my own fate, than by the calamities which will overwhelm my country, which is ruined and undone.' After a long and melancholy pause, she again broke silence, to speak of Brissot, a prisoner at the Abbaye, and whose death she foresaw to be nearer at hand than her own. ' He is confident !' said she; ' he sees not that the fury of his enemies can be glutted only with blood. He must be apprised of this......Brissot, the most ardent apostle of liberty, must not be stabbed in the dark. He has useful truths to tell his contemporaries, and important lessons to give to posterity. He must fulfil this task, it will be sweeter to him when he is invited to it by me.' Having formed this resolution, she found means to execute it; she addressed to Brissot a letter, in the sentiments of which was combined all that is most sublime in philosophy,

MADAME ROLAND. 307

and consolatory in friendship.' In consequence of her exhortations, Brissot composed his *Testament Politique*, which was considered by those to whom it was confided as superior to all that had before come from his pen; events had tempered the fire of his enthusiasm, while experience and misfortune had enlightened his judgment. This work passed the gates of the prison, and had gone through the press, when both the impression and the MS. were destroyed by Robespierre.

Although madame Roland had no faith in the justice either of the committees or the convention, she took every proper step, by remonstrance and petition, to free herself from confinement, but without effect. She transmitted, in a memorial addressed to her section, an account of the injustice and oppression under which she laboured. The president, to whom this paper was addressed, durst not cause it to be read, such progress had been made in the reign of terror. In a letter to Champagneux, who had himself become a prisoner, a victim to the jealous despotism of the day, madame Roland congratulates herself upon having been called as a witness on the trial of the deputies. " But," adds she, " there is an appearance that I shall not be heard. These executioners dread the truths which I have to tell them, and the energy with which I should publish these truths. It will be easier to them to put us to death

unheard. You will see no more either Vergniaud or
Valazé. We shall all perish, my friend. Without
this, our oppressors would not think themselves in
safety.....We shall perish victims of the weakness
of honourable men, who imagined it sufficient for
the triumph of virtue to place it in contrast with
vice....I write to you by the side, and almost under
the eye, of my executioners. I take a pride in
braving them."

A great part of the Memoirs of madame Roland,
written during her confinement, and entrusted to
Champagneux, were destroyed by the timidity of a
woman, to whose care he had confided them, previous
to his imprisonment. Madame Roland, when informed of this event, could repair only in part the loss.

The following character is given of madame Roland, by M. Champagneux, the intimate friend of
her husband:

" During the first twenty-five years of her life,
she had read and studied with attention every work
of celebrity, both ancient and modern; from the
greater number of which she made extracts. She
wrote with ease and grace, both in English and
Italian; her thoughts always outstripping her pen
and her words. She was mistress of several sciences,
and particularly skilled in botany. By her travels
she had acquired experience and improvement. She
was remarkable for her penetration, her sagacity,

and her judgment. In private and domestic life she practised every virtue; her filial piety was exemplary; and, united to a man twenty years older than herself, she made his constant happiness. As a mother, she was exquisitely tender. Order, economy, and foresight, presided over her domestic management; her servants seemed to partake of her excellences, and served her from attachment and respect, rather than from interest; this was manifested by their affection and courage at the time of her apprehension. The worthy Lecoq, the faithful Fleury, were ambitious of following her to the scaffold : Lecoq succeeded, but Fleury failing, grief at the loss of her mistress threw her into a state of mental derangement : she was dismissed from before the revolutionary tribunal as a woman insane. She was afterwards protected and sheltered by the daughter of madame Roland, with whom she mingled her tears and her regret."

At the news of the death of his wife, Roland, in his retreat, fell into a crisis, in which it was believed he would have expired. His senses at length returning, he abandoned himself to despair, and determined not to survive his misfortune. From the fear of exposing to mischief the kind friends who had given him shelter, he resolved on quitting their house for the execution of his purpose. When these respectable friends found every effort vain to dissuade him from his resolution, they deliberated with him on the best means of effecting it. The first idea of this unfortunate husband was to repair privately to Paris, to throw himself into the middle of the convention, to force them to hear truths which might be useful to their country, and afterwards to request death on the scaffold, where his wife had been previously sacrificed. He was induced to abandon a plan so heroic, by considerations which respected his daughter, who, by his legal murder, would suffer the confiscation of her property. He therefore adopted his second plan, that of retiring a few leagues from the house of his female friends (at Rouen), and dying by his own hand. At six in the evening, November 15th, 1793, he left his asylum, and took the road to Paris. At Bourg-Baudoin, four leagues from Rouen, he entered an avenue leading to the house of citizen Normand, where, sitting down on a bank, he plunged into his breast a sword which he had provided for the purpose. He received his death so composedly, that he was found the next day by some passengers, in the same attitude, sitting and leaning against a tree, as if in a slumber. In his pockets were discovered papers, containing an apology for his life and death, a few prophetic imprecations, and an address to those by whom his body might be found.

Eudora, the daughter of M. Roland, became af-

ELIZABETH ROWE. 311

terwards wife to one of the sons of Champagneux, the faithful friend of her parents.

Mémoires of Madame Roland, written by herself—Champagneux's Preliminary Discourse, prefixed to the Posthumous Works of Madame Roland.

═══════════

ISABELLA DE ROSARES.

ISABELLA DE ROSARES preached in the great church of Barcelona in Spain. In the reign of Paul III. she repaired to Rome, where, by her eloquence, she converted the Jews in that city.

═══════════

ELIZABETH ROWE.

ELIZABETH, eldest daughter of Mr. Walter Singer, was born Sept. 11th, 1674, at Ilchester, in Somersetshire. Mr. Singer's first residence in Ilchester was in imprisonment for non-conformity, during the reign of Charles II. Mrs. Portnell, the lady who became afterwards his wife, and the mother of Mrs. Rowe, visited him during his confinement, from motives of sympathy, of principle, and of charity: an acquaintance was thus commenced, which terminated in a lasting and affectionate union. Three daughters were the fruit of this marriage. Mr. S. continued to reside at Ilchester till the death of his wife, when he removed into the neighbourhood of Frome, in the same county, where he was respected for his good sense, his simplicity of manners, and the virtues of his life. He died April 19th, 1719.

Elizabeth, his eldest daughter, gave early pro-mise of those talents and amiable qualities by which she was afterwards distinguished. Her father, who beheld with pleasure the fertility of her mind, spared no pains in its cultivation. She imbibed from her parents devotional sentiments, which, operating upon a susceptible temper, a lively imagination, and an affectionate heart, gave an enthusiastic turn to her character and compositions. She displayed in her childhood a taste for the arts; painting, drawing, and music, alternately engaged her time and attention; but the bent of her genius was more particularly directed towards the cultivation of poe-try. She began to write verses at twelve years of age; and, in her twenty-second year, she published, at the desire of two of her friends, a collection of poems, on various occasions. These productions were principally on religious subjects; and those of a lighter cast were unexceptionable for the purity of their sentiment; yet, so scrupulous did the author become as she advanced into life, that she recollected with regret and uneasiness the sportive sallies of her youthful muse. Her moral sense was so exquisitely delicate, that, not to have

ELIZABETH ROWE.   313

injured the cause of virtue, appeared to her an insufficient plea; while she cherished a species of remorse for having written any thing by which it was not directly promoted.

Her poetical talents introduced her, before she had completed her twentieth year, to the family of lord Weymouth, who became her kind and liberal patrons, and whose friendship she enjoyed through life. Her paraphrase of the 38th chapter of Job, by which she acquired reputation, was written at the request of bishop Ken, who resided at that time in the Weymouth family. The hon. Mr. Thynne, son to lord Weymouth, took upon himself the task of instructing her in the French and Italian languages. She improved rapidly from the lessons of her noble and friendly preceptor, being, in a few months, enabled to read with great ease the Jerusalem of Tasso.

In the year 1710, she married Mr. Thomas Rowe, son of the rev. Benoni Rowe, a nonconformist minister. Mr. Rowe, who was thirteen years younger than his bride, possessed with a superior understanding, considerable learning, a highly cultivated mind, and an amiable temper. A marriage between two persons, united by congenial acquirements, sentiments, and virtues, notwithstanding the disparity of years, could scarcely fail of proving happy. Mr. and Mrs. Rowe passed five years in the most perfect harmony, confidence, and affection.

The constitution of Mr. Rowe was originally delicate; a sedentary life and intense application to study, had contributed to weaken it; his health began to decline towards the end of the year 1714. His disorder, which was of a consumptive nature, put a period to his life, May 13th, 1715, in the twenty-eighth year of his age. He died at Hampstead, whither he had removed for the benefit of the air, and was interred in his family vault in Bunhill-fields. His name, and the dates of his birth and death, were engraven on his tomb. His afflicted widow, after the first tumult of grief had subsided, composed an elegy to his memory, full of passion, tenderness, and sorrow, and continued to the latest periods of her life to testify the same respect and affection for his memory: nor could she ever mention his name without tears.

> " In all the countless numbers of his kind,
> Man rarely meets with one congenial mind:
> If haply found, death wings his fatal dart,
> The tender union breaks, and breaks his heart.*"

Mr. Rowe, from every account of him, appears to have been a young man of genius and distin-

---

* Langhorne.

ELIZABETH ROWE.   315

guished worth, deserving of the tenderness and
fidelity of his wife. Mrs. Rowe, on all occasions,
took peculiar pleasure in shewing respect and friendship to the relations and family of her husband.
On the anniversary of the day of his death, she again
commemorated, in elegiac verses, the melancholy
event.

> " Unhappy day, be sacred still to grief,
> A grief too obstinate for all relief!
> On thee my face shall never wear a smile,
> No joy on thee shall ere my heart beguile."
>   *   *   *   *   *   *   *   *

In complacence to her husband, Mrs. Rowe had,
after her marriage, resided with him in London
during the winter season. On his decease, her
love of solitude revived, and having settled her
affairs, she removed to Frome, in Somersetshire,
the scene of her youthful pleasures, in the neighbourhood of which lay the greater part of her property. She left the metropolis with a determination
to return to it no more, but to devote the remainder
of her life to study and retirement. Her principles
afterwards, in some few instances, induced her to
deviate from this plan. In compliance with the
solicitations of the hon. Mrs. Thynne, she passed
with her some months in London, after the death of
the lady Brooke, her daughter. And, on the decease of

Mrs. Thynne, she complied with the request of the countess of Hertford (afterwards duchess of Somerset), who earnestly requested her company for some time at Marlborough, to soften, by her friendship and conversation, her affliction on the loss of her excellent mother. The same lady, once or twice, on other occasions, prevailed on Mrs. Rowe to spend a few months with her at one or other of her country seats. Mrs. Rowe, even at the call of friendship, never quitted her retreat without regret, nor returned to it but with satisfaction.

In this seclusion, she composed her " *Friendship in Death,*" in twenty letters from the dead to the living, 1728. Also her " Letters, Moral and Entertaining," in prose and verse, Part 1. 1729; Part 2. 1731; Part 3. 1733. These productions, which display great sensibility of heart, a lively imagination, and a visionary turn of mind, were translated into French, and published at Amsterdam, in 1740, in two vols. 12mo. All the writings of Mrs. Rowe breathe a spirit of benevolence, of purity, and of virtue, animated by a raised and enthusiastic devotion.

In the year 1736, she was prevailed upon by some friends, to whom she had imparted her History of Joseph in manuscript, to give it to the public. It was with unfeigned reluctance that she yielded her assent: this piece had been written in her youth,

ELIZABETH ROWE. 317

and carried no farther than the marriage of the hero: at the request of the duchess of Somerset, she added to it two books, including Joseph's discovery of himself to his brethren. This addition is said to have been composed within three or four days. This was her last work: it was published but a few weeks preceding her death.

Her constitution was uncommonly good; she had passed a long series of years in almost uninterrupted health. Half a year before her decease, she was attacked with a disorder, attended with threatening symptoms. She complained, during this malady, that her mind was less serene and prepared to meet death, than she had flattered herself it would have been: this depression, probably the physical consequence of her situation, she struggled against and subdued. She experienced in this conquest a lively satisfaction, and repeated, in a pious and poetical transport, Mr. Pope's " Dying Christian's Address to his Soul." Though advanced in years, she recovered from this indisposition to her usual state of health: her exact temperance, added to the calmness of her mind and disposition, encouraged her friends to hope that she might yet live many years. On the day previous to her decease, she appeared in perfect health and vigour; and, after conversing with a friend with unusual vivacity, retired to her chamber early in the evening. About ten o'clock, her servant, hearing a noise as of something falling in the apartment of her mistress, found, on entering it, that she had fallen on the floor, speechless, and apparently dying. A physician and surgeon were immediately summoned; but all aid proved ineffectual; she expired with only one groan, before two o'clock the ensuing morning, Feb. 20, 1736-7, in the 63d year of her age. Her disorder was pronounced to be an apoplexy. Religious books and pious meditations were found lying by her. Her life had been tranquil, and, except in the loss of her husband, unclouded; and her death was happy. She had always been apprehensive of the effects which might be produced upon her mind by the pain and languor of a sick-bed, which she thus fortunately escaped; and, on various occasions, had expressed to her friends her desire of a sudden death.

She was buried, according to her request, under the same stone with her father, at Frome. Her death was regretted by her friends, to whom her virtues, and the gentleness of her manners, had endeared her; and lamented by the poor, to whom she was a kind benefactress.

In her cabinet were found letters addressed to several of her friends; to the countess of Hertford, the earl of Orrery, Mr. James Theobald, and Mrs.

ELIZABETH ROWE.   319

Sarah Rowe. These letters *, which breathed an affectionate and pious temper, were superscribed, to be delivered to the respective persons after her decease. She left also a letter to Dr. Watts, accompanying her papers containing her Devout Exercises, which were, by the doctor, afterwards published.

Beside the productions of Mrs. Rowe already mentioned, there are two volumes of her miscellaneous works, consisting of poems and letters, to which are added (by her desire) several poems and essays written by her husband. " The softness of her sex, and the fineness of her genius," says Matthew Prior †, " conspire to give her a very distinguishing character."

She is said (by the writers of her Life) to have possessed a command over her passions, and a constant serenity and sweetness of temper, which neither age nor misfortune could sour or ruffle. It is questioned whether she had ever been angry in her life; a proof that the tender and gentle sensibilities may exist independent of the irascible passions. Her servant, who lived with her near twenty years,

---

* They are published in her Life by Mr. Theophilus Rowe, and prefixed to her works.

† In his Preface to his Poems.

gave a testimony to the kind and even tenor of her mistress's temper. She knew not indignation, except against vice, where indifference is almost criminal. To firm principles, and an elevated mind, she added the softness and graces of her sex. She expressed, on all occasions, an aversion to satire, so rarely free from malice and personality : her conversation, like her writings, was the effusion of a benevolent and amiable mind : she fortified her resolutions against a severe and acrimonious spirit, by particular and solemn vows. " I can appeal to you," said she, in a letter to an old and intimate friend, " whether you ever knew me make an envious or an ill-natured reflection on any person upon earth ? Indeed, the follies of mankind would afford a wide and various scene ; but charity would draw a veil of darkness here, and choose to be for ever silent, rather than expatiate on the melancholy theme." Detraction appeared to her an inhuman vice, for which no wit could atone. She loved to praise, and took a pleasure, on all occasions, in doing justice to merit; she was ever the advocate for the absent, and extenuated where she could not excuse. If compelled to reprove, gentleness and delicacy softened her reprehension. She possessed peculiar powers of conversation, an inexhaustible fancy, flowing language, the most perfect ingenuousness, with unaffected sweetness and ease. " It was not possible

ELIZABETH ROWE. 321

to be in her company," says her biographer, "without becoming wiser and better, or to quit it without regret." Accustomed from her youth to admiration and distinction, she preserved a perfect humility and unaffected modesty: she rarely mentioned her productions even to her most intimate friends; neither was she, in the least degree, elated by their success, nor by the compliments of the most distinguished writers of the age. " It is but for Heaven," said she, " to give a turn to one of my nerves, and I should become an ideot." She never dictated to others, nor arrogated to her own sentiments any deference or respect: she was amiable, affable, and accessible, a stranger to that insolent intellectual fastidiousness affected by pedants and despised by the truly enlightened. She had no taste for what is called pleasure; she mixed in no parties of dissipation, was ignorant of any game, and avoided formal and insipid visitings. Temperate, cheerful, friendly, and affectionate, she sought and found her happiness in intellectual pursuits, the exercise of her affections, and the enjoyment of simple pleasures. She had a contempt for riches, was content with a moderate income, nor would avail herself of those pecuniary advantages to which by her labours she was justly entitled. She refused to publish her works by subscription, nor would suffer them to be collected by the bookseller, who offered her liberal terms. She let her estates below their value: she abhorred exaction and oppression; while to her tenants she was an indulgent and kind benefactress. Indifferent to fame, and fond of solitude, she shunned rather than sought applause. Her modesty followed her to the tomb, and even appeared afterwards in the orders she left respecting her interment Having desired that her funeral might be by night and attended only by a small number of friends, she added, " Charge Mr. Bowden not to say one word of me in the sermon. I would lie in my father's grave, and have no stone nor inscription over my vile dust, which I gladly leave to corruption and oblivion, till it rise to a glorious immortality."

As a daughter, as a wife, as a friend, as a mistress, her conduct was exemplary: her taste for letters led her not to neglect the duties and occupations of her sex. During the lingering illness of her husband, she attended him with patient affection and tender solicitude; while she consecrated to his memory the remainder of her life. " The solitude in which I have spent my time," said she, in one of her posthumous letters, " since the death of Mr. Rowe, has given me leisure to make the darkness of the grave, and the solemnity of dying, familiar to my imagination. Whatever such distinguished

ELIZABETH ROWE. 323

sense and merit could claim, I have endeavoured to pay to the memory of my much-loved husband. I reflect with pleasure on my conduct on this occasion; not merely from a principle of justice and gratitude to him, but from a conscious sense of honour, and love of a virtuous reputation after death. But if the soul, in a separate state, should be insensible to human censure or applause, yet there is a disinterested homage due to the sacred name of virtue." It is observed greatly to her honour, by her biographer, that no one of her domestics ever left her, except with a view of changing their condition by marriage.

Her charities, considering the mediocrity of her fortune, bordered on excess: she consecrated, by a solemn vow, the half of her income to benevolent purposes. To enable herself to fulfil this engagement, she retrenched all superfluous expences, and practised a rigid economy. The first time she accepted any acknowledgment from her bookseller for her writings, she bestowed the whole sum on a distressed family : another time, on a similar occasion, she sold a piece of plate to relieve an exigency for which she was not sufficiently provided. It was her custom on going out, to furnish herself with pieces of money of different value, to relieve such objects of compassion as might fall in her way. Her munificence was not confined to the place in which she

ELIZABETH ROWE.

lived, nor to any sect or party. " I never," said she, " grudge any money, but when it is laid out upon myself; for I consider how much it would buy for the poor." Nor did she confine her charities to money; she gave to the distressed her time, her labour, her sympathy, often of infinitely greater value. She caused the children of the neighbouring poor to be instructed; and herself assisted in forming their minds and principles. Nor was her beneficence limited to the lower ranks. " It was one of the greatest benefits," she was accustomed to say, " that could be done to mankind, to free them from the cares and anxieties that attend a narrow fortune." The delicacy and sweetness of her manner, on all occasions, doubled the bounties she conferred. The calm and uniform tenor of her life, her active virtue and happy constitution, produced a perpetual sunshine of the mind, that diffused itself on all around her.

The most distinguished characters of the age were among the friends of Mrs. Rowe: by the countess of Hertford, who composed an elegy on her death, she was more particularly lamented. A large collection of poems to her honour, is prefixed to her miscellaneous works. *Philomela* was the poetical name given to Mrs. Rowe, in allusion to her maiden name of Singer, and to the softness and harmony of her verses. Her person is thus described by her biographer, Mr. Theophilus Rowe,

CLAUDIA RUFINA—LADY RUSSEL.   325

the brother of her husband: " Her stature was moderate, her hair of a fine auburn colour; her eyes darkish grey, inclining to blue, and full of fire. Her complexion was exquisitely fair, and a natural blush glowed in her cheeks. She spoke gracefully, her voice was sweet and harmonious, suited to the gentle language which always flowed from her lips. But the softness and benevolence of her aspect were beyond all description: they inspired irresistible love, yet not without some mixture of that awe and veneration which distinguished sense and virtue, apparent in the countenance, are wont to create."

Memoirs of Mrs. Rowe—Gibbons's Memoirs of Pious Women—Female Worthies.

CLAUDIA RUFINA.

THE poet Martial, who extols this lady for her virtues, her learning, and her beauty, was the friend of her husband, Aulus Rufus Pudens, a Bononian philosopher, and of the Roman equestrian order. Claudia Rufina was a noble British lady, and the author of a book ef epigrams, an elegy on the death of her husband, and other compositions, both in verse and prose.

LADY RUSSEL.

ELIZABETH, third daughter of sir Anthony Cooke, was born in 1529, and was instructed, with her sisters, in every elegant and liberal acquirement:

she even surpassed them in her progress, and was celebrated by the first scholars of the age. She married sir Thomas Hobby, and accompanied him into France, where he was sent by the queen on an embassy to the court. Sir Thomas died in Paris, April 13th, 1566, leaving his widow in a state of pregnancy. She accompanied the body of her husband to his native land; and having erected a chapel, on the south side of the chancel of the church at Bisham, in Berkshire, she deposited his remains with those of his brother, sir Philip Hobby, and placed on the tomb inscriptions, in Latin and English verse, of her own composition. Sir Thomas left on his decease four children, Edward, Elizabeth, Anne, and Thomas posthumous, who, it appears from a letter * addressed by his mother to her brother-in-law, lord treasurer Burleigh, gave her great anxiety by his wild and irregular conduct.

Some years after the decease of sir Thomas Hobbey, his widow espoused lord John Russel, son and heir to Francis Russel, the second earl of Bedford of that name. Lady Russel became a widow a second time, in 1584: her husband died before his father, and was buried in the abbey church of Westminster, where a monument is erected to his memory, with inscriptions by his widow, in Latin,

---

* In the possession of the hon. James West.

LADY RUSSEL.   327

Greek, and English. One son was the fruit of this marriage, who died young in 1580, and two daughters, Anne and Elizabeth. The latter survived her father but a short time. It is this lady of whom it is reported, that she died in consequence of wounding the fore-finger of her left hand by a needle; a tale or legend which the attitude of her figure, placed on the monument, within the same grate with that of her father, is thought to intimate. Her statue of alabaster is placed on a pedestal of black and white marble, in imitation of a Roman altar : it appears seated in a wrought osier chair, in a melancholy position, the head inclined towards the right hand, with the fore-finger of the left extending downwards, pointing to a death's-head under its feet. Admitting the story of her death to have been well founded, it is probable that some nerve or tendon might be wounded by the accident, or that from the state of her blood, or habit, a gangrene might have ensued. Yet it is certain that the tale wears the appearance of fiction. The attitude of the statue is capable of a moral and religious interpretation, and it is by no means in proof of this popular tradition. The monument was erected to her memory by Anne, her only surviving sister.

Lady Russel translated from the French a religious tract, originally written in German, entitled " A way of Reconciliation of a good and learned Man, touching the true Nature and Substance of the

Body and Blood of Christ in the Sacrament," printed
1605, and dedicated to her only daughter, Anne
Herbert, wife to lord H. Herbert.   This dedication
breathes the tenderest affection for her daughter, to
whom the work is presented as a new-year's-gift.

The time of her death is uncertain ; but it appears that she was living, though very infirm, in
August, 1596 ; and in the ensuing year, she complains, in a letter to her nephew Cecil, of declining
health, and the infirmities of old age.—The letter
thus concludes : " Your lordships owld awnt of
compleat 68 years, that prays for your long lyfe,
Elizabeth Russel, Dowager."   She was probably
buried with her first husband at Bisham, in Berks,
in the chapel founded by herself, in which a magnificent monument is erected against the south wall,
and in the middle a large arch, raised on four pil-
lars, under which is placed her statue, kneeling, and
having on its head the coronet of a viscountess.
The figure of an infant lies on the cushion on which
she rests, and behind her kneel three daughters.
Westward, without the arch, are the statues of two
men in armour, and eastward, the statue of a lady
in a robe lined with ermine, a coronet on her head.
On a block marble tablet, at the foot of the monument, is a Greek inscription, and on another tablet
is an inscription in Latin.   Lady Russel lived to
write the epitaphs, in the Greek, Latin, and English languages, for both her husbands, for her

LADY RACHEL RUSSEL. 329

son, her daughter, her brother, sister, and friend, Mr. Noke, of Shottesbrooke.

Ballard's British Ladies—Biographium Fæmineum.

LADY RACHEL RUSSEL.

RACHEL, daughter of Thomas Wriothesley, earl of Southampton, was born in 1636. Her mother, first wife to the earl, was the daughter of Henry de Massey, baron of Rovigny. The earl of Southampton, distinguished for his talents and independent spirit, was an enemy to the arbitrary measures pursued by the crown, during the administration of the earl of Strafford. In the subsequent prosecution of that nobleman, he opposed himself with equal firmness to the parliament, which had, he believed, exceeded the limits of justice and the constitution. He became eminently serviceable to the king on this occasion, whose cause he adopted against the popular proceedings. He is styled by Burnet, " A fast friend to the public, the wise and virtuous earl of Southampton, who deserved from the king every thing which he could bestow." At the Restoration he was made lord high-treasurer, an office which he filled with ability and integrity. He died May 16th, 1667, leaving by his first wife two daughters ; Elizabeth, married to Edward Noel, baron Wriothesley, of Titchfield, &c. &c. and Ra-

chel, wife to Francis lord Vaughan, eldest son of
the earl of Rocraw, earl of Carberry. After the
death of lord Vaughan, his widow, in 1669, espoused William lord Russel, son of William earl
of Bedford : one son and two daughters were the
fruit of this union.

In the struggle against the encroachments of the
crown, under Charles II., during a fit of sickness
which seized the king at Windsor, the duke of
Monmouth, lord Russel, and lord Grey, instigated
by the earl of Shaftesbury, agreed, should the disorder of Charles prove mortal, to oppose in arms
the succession of the duke of York. The king recovered ; but their projects were not laid aside. The
imprisonment of Shaftesbury gave a check to these
machinations, which new encroachments on the liberties of the people had revived. The train was
laid and ready to take fire, when Monmouth was
induced by lord Russel to delay the enterprise. At
length the conspirators were, by their common
views and common apprehensions, induced to form
a regular plan of insurrection. A council of six
was formed, consisting of Monmouth, Russel, Essex,
Howard, Algernon Sidney, and John Hambden,
grandson to the celebrated patriotic Hambden.
These men, though united in a common cause, were
instigated by motives widely different. Sidney desired a commonwealth ; Essex was animated by the

same principle; Monmouth aspired to the crown; while Russel and Hambden, attached to the ancient constitution, proposed only the redress of grievances, and the exclusion of the duke from the succession. Howard, an unprincipled man, had his own interest only in contemplation.

An inferior order of malecontents were also in the habit of meeting, who indulged themselves, wholly unknown to the council of six, in planning criminal and desperate measures. In this cabal the assassination of the king and of the duke was freely discussed, and even a project proposed for the purpose. But the plan, however plausible, was loose and wild; neither were there persons, arms, nor horses, provided for its execution. Among those who composed this faction, Keiling, a man who for some bold measures had rendered himself obnoxious to a prosecution, determined to purchase his safety by revealing the conspiracy. The council of six, though guiltless of the assassination plot, became involved in this discovery. Monmouth absconded; Russel was sent to the Tower; Howard saved himself by basely impeaching his colleagues; while Essex, Sidney, and Hambden, were apprehended upon his evidence. The English laws of treason, under the act of Edward III., were mild and equitable : they required proof of having compassed or intended the king's death, or of having actually levied war against him; greater latitude had been afterwards introduced both in the proof and definition of the crime. Soon after the restoration of Charles a law had passed, by which the consulting or intending a rebellion was declared treason; but which required that the prosecution should take place within six months after the commission of the crime. Under this statute the offence of Russel fell. The facts, however, sworn against him, were beyond the limit of the time required by law: to make, therefore, the indictment more extensive, the intention of murdering the king was comprehended in it, by a refinement in law.

Russel, perceiving this irregularity, desired to have the point argued by counsel; but this privilege was refused to him, excepting on condition of his previously confessing the facts laid to his charge, The confounding the two species of treason, a practice supported by precedents, was not the only hardship of which Russel had to complain. Too candid to deny his share in the conspiracy for an insurrection, he contented himself with protesting, truly, that he had never formed any design against the life of the king. A defence so feeble availed him little: his jury, zealous royalists though men of fair character, after a short deliberation, brought him in guilty.

The day previous to his trial, he had asked leave

of the court that notes of the evidence might be taken for his use. By the attorney-general he was informed in reply, that he might if he pleased use one of his servants for the purpose. ' I ask no assistance,' answered the prisoner, ' but that of the lady who sits by me.' At these words the spectators, turning their eyes on the daughter of the virtuous Southampton, who rose to assist her husband in his distress, melted into tears. The old earl of Bedford, the father of lord Russel, offered to the duchess of Portsmouth a hundred thousand pounds to procure her interest with the king for the pardon of his son. But every application proved vain. The independent spirit, the patriotism, the popularity, the courage, the talents, and the virtues, of the prisoner, were his most dangerous offences, and became so many arguments against his escape. Charles could be prevailed on only to remit the more ignominious part of the sentence which the law requires to be pronounced against traitors.

Lady Russel threw herself at the feet of the king, and pleaded with tears the merits and loyalty of her father, as an atonement for those offences into which her husband had been drawn, by honest though erroneous principles. Charles beheld unmoved the daughter of his best friend weeping at his feet: he even rejected her petition for a respite of a few weeks. ' Shall I grant that man,' said he, ' six

weeks, who, had it been in his power, would not
have granted me six hours ?' These tears and these
supplications were the last instance of feminine sorrow which lady Russel betrayed on so trying an occasion. On finding every effort fruitless for saving
the life of her husband, she collected her courage,
and fortified her mind for the fatal stroke, confirming by her example the resolution of her lord.

No one doubted the innocence of Russel respecting the charge of conspiring against the life of the
king, which he solemnly denied with his dying
breath. The witnesses who deposed against him,
made no mention of any such design: his principal guilt had been his opposition in parliament to
what he deemed unconstitutional measures, with his
efforts for the exclusion of the duke of York from the
throne. His friends essayed every means that money and interest could afford to preserve his invaluable life. They engaged that he should promise
on his liberation to exile himself from his native
land. Lord Cavendish offered to facilitate his escape by changing habits with him, and remaining
as his substitute. But Russel refused to save his
life by an expedient that might subject his friend to
hazard. The duke of Monmouth sent to him a
message, that, if he thought it would avail any
thing towards his safety, he would deliver up himself, and share the fate of his friend. To this pro-

position Russel only replied, ' that it would be of no advantage to him to have his friends die with him !' It was proposed by Cavendish that a party of horse should attack the guards, and deliver him forcibly, on his way to the scaffold; an attempt which there was great reason to suppose the people would facilitate. But lord Russel, firmly opposing any measures which might expose his friends to danger, patiently submitted to his fate.

In the journal of the duke of Monmouth, he affirms, that the king had told him he was inclined to save the life of Russel, but found it impossible without breaking with the duke of York, who, in the meanness of his vengeance, was desirous that the illustrious victim should suffer in the square before York-house; an insult to which the king would not be persuaded to submit.

An order being signed for his execution, a respite of only two days was refused to his friends. Bishops Burnet and Tillotson, with a view of serving him, tried to prevail on him to confess resistance to be unlawful. ' He could not tell a lie,' was the magnanimous reply of Russel. Tillotson observed, that he did not think resistance authorised by remote fears and consequences, or illegal practices. On this hypothesis, Russel declared he saw no difference between a lawful and a Turkish government, and that, in case of a total subversion, resist-

ance would be too late. In answer to some clergyman, who flattered him with the hope of life on
condition of his acknowledging, that subjects had
in no case a right to resist the throne, ' I can,' said
he, ' have no conception of a limited monarchy,
which has not a right to defend its own limitations;
neither will my conscience permit me to say otherwise to the king.' This firmness in refusing to purchase life by the sacrifice of his principles, affords
the best testimony to his integrity and virtue.

As his fate drew near, he expressed his satisfaction that he had chosen death rather than flight,
since he felt that, separated from his family and
friends, whose affection and society constituted all
his happiness, life would have been to him insupportable. To another project suggested by the gallant Cavendish, he replied smiling, that he thanked
him very kindly, but would not escape; adding,
he could never yet limit his bounty to his condition,
and that the only pleasure he had felt in the anticipation of a large estate, to which he was heir by
descent, was in the hope of an extension in the
means of doing good. He thanked God, who
knew the sincerity of his heart, that he had in all
things acted in conformity to the dictates of his conscience; that he could never enter into what he
thought wrong, nor could on any occasion tell an
untruth.

Tillotson informed the king that Russel had declared to him, that he had associated with those unhappy men, only to preserve the duke of Monmouth from being ensnared by them into any rash
undertaking. Being then questioned why he had
not in that case discovered their designs to the king;
he answered, he could not betray his friends, nor
turn informer while he saw no danger; yet, had
things come to a crisis, he would have contrived a
method of giving the king warning; and had violence been attempted, would have been the first to
oppose it with his sword.

On the Tuesday before his execution, after dinner, when lady Russel had left him, he spoke with
pleasure of the magnanimity she displayed; and observed, ' that a separation from her was the severest
part of what he had to undergo, since he dreaded lest
she should sink under her grief.' ' At present,' he
added, ' she was in some degree supported by her
exertions to save him, by which her mind was occupied: but when her hopes were over, he feared the
quickness of her spirits, and the poignancy of her
feelings.' On the Thursday, while she was labour-
ing to gain a respite till the Monday, he expressed
a wish that she would abandon a cause so hopeless:
yet the consideration, that her sorrow might be
mitigated by the recollection that she had spared no

possible means for his safety, prevented him from
opposing her designs.

His courage never appeared to faulter but when
he spoke of his wife; his eyes would, on such occasions, fill with tears, while he appeared eager to
fly from the subject. On the Friday night as she
left him, he embraced her repeatedly, while she restrained her grief lest it should too sensibly affect
him. The evening before his death, his children
were brought to him : he parted with them and his
friends with courage and constancy. Some of his
expressions denoted not only composure but plea-
santry. Being seized with a bleeding at his nose,
' I shall not now,' said he to Dr. Burnet, who attended him, ' let blood to divert this distemper, that
will be done to-morrow.' A short time before he
was conducted by the sheriffs to the scaffold, he
wound up his watch, observing, ' he had now done
with time, and henceforth must think only on
eternity.'

When parting from lady Russel, who commanded herself with heroic fortitude, they mutually preserved a solemn and affecting silence. He declared
when she had left him, ' that the bitterness of death
was past.' He praised her character and conduct,
while he spoke of his affection for her with eloquence and fervor. He protested that she had
ever been to him a blessing; and observed how

LADY RACHEL RUSSEL.   339

wretched it would have made him, had she not joined to tenderness and sensibility a spirit too magnanimous to desire him to be guilty of baseness, even for the preservation of his life. He expressed his gratitude to Providence, that had given him a wife, who, to birth, fortune, talents, and virtue, united sensibility of heart, and whose conduct, in the extreme crisis of his fate, had even surpassed all her other virtues. He spoke of the joy which he felt, that his family would lose nothing by his death, since he left his children in the hands of so admirable a mother, who for their sakes had promised to preserve herself.

The scaffold for his execution was erected in Lincolns-inn-fields, that the triumph of the court might be manifest, in the exhibition of the illustrious sufferer to the populaee. As he passed through the city, bishops Burnet and Tillotson accompanied him in the coach. The people, who fancied they beheld virtue and freedom suffer with him, melted into tears at the spectacle. As, on passing it, he looked towards Southampton-house, a tear started to his eye, which he instantly wiped away. He observed, 'that a cloud was hanging over the nation, to which his death would prove more serviceable than his life.' The moment before his execution, he affirmed, on the faith of a dying man, that he knew of

310   LADY RACHEL RUSSEL.

no plot against the king's person or government;
but, having submitted himself to the decision of the
laws, he was determined to abide the penalty.

The populace beheld with unfeigned grief the
fate of their beloved leader, once the object of all
their confidence : as he had been the most popular
among his own party, so was he the least obnoxious
to the opposite faction : every heart sensible to generosity or humanity united in tender commiseration
on this affecting catastrophe. Without the least
change of countenance, he laid his head on the
block : at two strokes it was separated by the executioner from his body. This tragedy took place
July 21, 1683. A paper, expressive of his innocence, was delivered by him to the sheriffs, which
gave great offence at court. Burnet was questioned
on the subject, but the widow of lord Russel, in a
letter to the king, justified and exculpated her husband. Of lord Russel, it was said by Calamy,
" that an age would not repair to the nation his loss,
and that his name ought never to be mentioned by
Englishmen without respect."

Lady Russel sustained the loss of this worthy and
beloved husband with the same heroism which she
had displayed during his trial and imprisonment.
When, in open court, attending by his side, observing and taking notes of all that passed in his favour,
when, a weeping suppliant at the feet of the king,

she pleaded for a life so precious to her, in the name, and for the services, of a deceased father; when, in meek and solemn silence, without suffering a tear to escape her, she parted for ever with a husband so deservedly beloved ; she appears equally an object of sympathy, admiration, and reverence.

After this melancholy and cruel event, the widow of the respectable and patriotic Russel proved the faithful guardian of his honour and his fame; the wise and active mother to his children; and the friend and patroness of his friends. She survived more than forty years, and died September 29th, 1723, at the advanced age of eighty-seven.

The letters of lady Russel, written after the decease of her husband, afford an affecting picture of the conjugal affection and fidelity of the writer, whom new trials yet awaited. Wriothesley duke of Bedford, her only son, died of the small-pox, May 1711, in the thirty-first year of his age. To this affliction succeeded the death of her daughter, the duchess of Rutland, who died in childbed. Lady Russel gave on this occasion a new instance of her fortitude and self command. Her daughter, the duchess of Devonshire, was also in childbed at the time of her sister's decease. The mother, after beholding one daughter in her coffin, repaired to the chamber of the other, with a composed and tranquil countenance. The duchess of Devonshire earnestly enquiring after the welfare of her sister, lady Russel evasively replied, without betraying any emotion, ' I have seen your sister out of bed to-day.'

To this instance of her fortitude an anecdote may be added, in testimony of her courage and presence of mind, displayed on a lesser and unpremeditated occasion.

" The following relation," says Mr. Selwood *, " I had from lady Russel, in Southampton-row, Bedford-house, where the accident happened. Her ladyship's own words, to the best of my remembrance, were these : ' As I was reading in my closet, the door being bolted, on a sudden the candle and candlestick jumped off the table, an hissing fire ran on the floor, and, after a short time, left some paper in a flame, which with my foot I put into the chimney to prevent mischief. I then sat down in the dark to consider whence this event should come. I knew my doors and windows were fast, and that there was no way open into the closet but by the chimney; but that something should come down

---

* Mr. Thomas Selwood lived in the family of lady Russel, copied her letters from the originals, which, having published with permission, he dedicated to the duke of Bedford.

LADY RACHEL RUSSEL.   343

there, and strike my candle off the table in that strange manner, I believed impossible. After I had wearied myself with thinking to no purpose, I rang my bell. The servant in waiting, when I told him what had happened, begged pardon for having by mistake given me a mould candle, with a gunpowder squib in it, which was intended to make sport among the fellow-servants on a rejoicing day.' Her lady-ship bid the servant not be troubled at the matter, for she had no other concern about it than that of not finding out the cause."

It is observable in the letters of lady Russel, that no expression of resentment, or traces of a vindictive spirit, mingle at any time with the sentiment of grief, by which they are uniformly pervaded, for the fate of her husband. When James H. who had been principally aiding to that fate, became a wanderer in a foreign land, driven from his throne and country, there appears no triumph in the expressions of this lady, nor even an intimation, that retributive justice had overtaken him. She also passes over in silence the tragical end of the barbarous and infamous Jefferies, who had distinguished himself against lord Russel on his trial.

It appears from several of her letters, that lady Russel experienced uneasiness, some years after the death of her husband, from dimness and weakness in her sight. From this complaint she was relieved by an operation, in June, 1694. Archbishop Til-lotson, writing to Dr. Burnet bishop of Salisbury on the 28th of June, informs him, " that the eyes of lady Russel had been couched, the preceding morn-ing, with good success." From this time till her death she enjoyed her sight without impediment, and was accustomed, at a very advanced period of life, to write without spectacles. The apprehen-sion of the loss of sight, that invaluable blessing, was sustained by lady Russel with her wonted cou-rage and resignation. The first persons of the age, both in rank and literature, did honour to themselves by their respect and friendship towards this illustri-ous and heroic woman.

Letters of Rachel, Lady Russel, from the MS in the Li-brary at Wooburn Abbey—Hume's History of England—Memoirs of Pious Women.

LAURA SADE.

AMONG writers celebrated for their learning and genius, at the revival of letters in the fourteenth century, Francis Petrarch, a Florentine poet, whose ancestors were intrusted with offices of honour in the state, holds a high and distinguish-ed rank. Petrarco, his father, having become the

LAURA SADE. 345

victim of faction, was, together with Danté*, banished from the republic, and condemned to pay
a considerable fine. After many sufferings and
struggles to regain his patrimony, tired of suc-
cessless efforts, he at length determined to repair
to Avignon, a city of France, on the banks of the
Rhone, situated between Lyons and Marseilles, to
which a Gascon pope had removed the Roman
see.

The young Petrarch was by his father destined
to the profession of the law, to which he flattered
himself, from the talents he had observed in his
son, that he would prove a distinguished ornament. This plan, however, but little accorded
with the lively sensibility and genius of the youth,
which irresistibly impelled him to more congenial pursuits. His subsequent progress in letters
and reputation, belongs not to the present memoir to narrate.

Nature had been to Petrarch lavish of her
bounties. To superior endowments, a lively
imagination, and a susceptible heart, he added a
fine person and a prepossessing countenance.
The fervor of his passions, and the impetuosity
of his youth, had, in the earlier periods of his

---

* Danté, in his works, bitterly resents this treatment.

life, and in a voluptuous and dissolute court, sometimes betrayed him into transient irregulari- ties, which his principles condemned, and which his taste abhorred. " I can aver," says he, " that from the bottom of my soul I detest such scenes." —" If I sometimes acted with freedom, it was because love had not yet become an inhabitant of my breast."

After his return from Bologna, whither he had been sent by his father to prosecute his studies, he passed a whole year, with gaiety and indifference, among the beauties of Avignon, who contended for the conquest of his heart. The Muse was the only mistress whose favours he courted. " I was as free and as wild," says he, " as the untamed stag." But the moment when his liberty was to be forfeited approached. " Love," says he, " observing that his former arrows had but glanced over my heart, called to his aid a lady against whose power neither wit, beauty, nor strength, were of any avail."

On Sunday in the holy week, at six in the morning, the time of Matins, Petrarch beheld, at the church of the monastery of St. Claire, a young lady whose charms absorbed and captivat- ed his attention. " She was dressed in green, and her robe was embroidered with violets. Her face, her air, her gait, were somewhat more than

LAURA SADE. 347

mortal. Her person was delicate, her eyes tender and sparkling, and her eyebrows black as ebony.
Golden locks waved over her shoulders, which
were whiter than snow : her ringlets were interwoven by the fingers of love. Her neck was
finely formed, and her complexion, which art
would vainly attempt to imitate, animated by the
tints of nature. When she opened her mouth,
you perceived the beauty of pearls and the sweets
of roses. She was full of graces. Nothing was
so soft as her looks, so modest as her carriage, so
touching as the sound of her voice. An air of
gaiety and tenderness breathed around her, but
so pure and happily tempered, as to inspire every
beholder with the sentiments of virtue : for she
was chaste as the spangled dew-drop of the morn.
Such was the amiable Laura !"

This lady, to whom the genius of Petrarch has
given celebrity, appears, from a comparative view
of the few particulars * which are to be found
respecting her private life, to have been the
daughter of Andibert de Novès, a chevalier, and
his wife Ermessenda. Her family held the first
rank at Noves, a town of Provence, two leagues

---

* From the archives of the house of Sade, and from the
writings of Petrarch.

from Avignon. Laura possessed a house in that
city, where she passed a part of the year. Her
father had left to her a handsome dowry, to be
given to her on her marriage, which took place
when she was very young (through the authority
and influence of her mother), with Hugues de
Sade, whose family was originally of Avignon,
where they held the first offices. It was not till
after her marriage that Petrarch beheld her, at
the church of the monastery at St. Claire; hence
his frequent remorses, and the severity of Laura's
behaviour. An old picture of Laura was, in
1642, brought to cardinal Barberini: this portrait
had been long preserved in the house of Sade at
Avignon; and Richard de Sade, then bishop of
Cavoillon, proved that this Laura, of the house
of Sade, was really the Laura of Petrarch, and
that those who had considered her as the mistress
of Petrarch at Vaucluse, or as an allegorical person, were romancers, ill-informed of real circumstances or facts.

In the sonnets of Petrarch there is a perpetual
allusion to the laurel* and Daphne, with which
he took a pleasure in associating the object of his

---

* The laurel, with which poets were crowned, was consecrated to Apollo, who was the god of poetry.

affection. " I run every-where after Laura," says he, " but she flees from me, as Daphne fled from Apollo."

On the system of Pythagoras, he supposed, with a poetical licence, that the soul of Daphne, after a long succession of transmigrations, had passed into the body of Laura. Under this illusion, he beheld not the laurel without transports, and planted it in every place. He frequently seated himself at the foot of one of those trees, on the side of a river, where Laura was accustomed to pass ; while, in her absence, every thing in this delightful spot, which was her favourite walk, presented to him her image, and rekindled his poetical raptures. " On this bank," says he, " and under the shelter of this charming tree, I sing with transports the praises of Laura. The gentle murmurs of the stream accompanying my tender sighs ; the refreshing shade tempers the ardour of my passion : these only are the objects which have power to relieve my soul."

While Petrarch concealed in his bosom the passion with which Laura had inspired him, he owns that she behaved to him with kindness ; but, when she discovered the state of his mind, she treated him with great severity. Awed by the chastity of her conduct and manners, Petrarch had not dared to speak of his feelings; but Laura,

on perceiving that he followed her every-where,
and directed towards her his ardent glances, soli-
citously avoided him, and, if by accident he approached her in public, immediately left the
place; she hastily covered herself with her veil
whenever she saw him, to defend herself from his
tender glances. Petrarch perpetually complains
of this cruel veil, which hid from his view the
charms he adored. His timidity, the characteristic of true love, was increased by the rigours of
his mistress, the magnificence of whose dress also
tended to heighten his respect." " Dazzled by
the lustre of her beauty and the splendour of her
dress, for she wore on her head a silver coronet,
and tied up her hair with knots of jewels*; terrified also with the austerity of her looks, he had
not courage to speak to her." " Was I," said he,
" to see the lustre of those bright eyes extinguished by age, those golden locks changed to
silver, the flowers painted on that complexion
faded, was I to see Laura without her garland,
without her ornamented robe, I feel I should have
more courage." Petrarch does not appear, at
this period, to have been admitted to the house of
Laura; he saw her only in public, and at festivals
where the ladies assembled. " She appeared,"

---

* An extraordinary magnificence in those times.

LAURA SADE. 351

says he, " among the beauties of Avignon, like a
fine flower, in the midst of a parterre, eclipsing,
by its lustre and by the brightness of its colours, all
those by which it was surrounded." His attachment
to her increased with his respect, while the admiration with which her virtue had inspired him, led
him to greater purity and regularity of conduct.
" I bless the happy moment," says he, " that
directed my heart to Laura. She led me to see
the path of virtue, to detach my heart from base
and grovelling objects: from her I am inspired
with that celestial flame which raises my soul to
heaven, and directs it to the Supreme Cause, as to
the only source of happiness."

Petrarch was, by the severity of Laura (who
had forbidden him to see or to speak to her), the
restless state of his mind, and the desire of acquiring knowledge, determined to travel; but,
scarcely had he quitted Avignon, before he repented of his purpose, and with difficulty could
prevent himself from returning. During his
journey, the image of Laura was ever present to
his thoughts. He passed, on his return, through
a part of the forest of Ardenne, which was rendered more peculiarly dangerous by the inroads
of troops, from a war between the duke of Brabant and the court of Flanders, who disputed
with each other the sovereignty of Moulines.

Petrarch, however, took no guard; alone and un-
armed, wholly occupied by his passion, he traversed the most gloomy recesses of the forest.
" Love," said he, " enlightened the shades of
Ardenne, where Laura appeared in every object,
and was heard in every breeze." On approaching Lyons, he beheld the Rhone with transport,
which, in its course to the sea, bathed the walls
of Avignon. He had flattered himself that absence might have softened the rigours of Laura,
and that she would have beheld him on his return
with greater complacency. Of the disappointment of this hope he bitterly complains, and compares his mistress to the snow, on which the sun
had not beamed. " It is now," says he, " seven
years that I have sighed night and day for Laura,
without hope of being able to touch her heart "

It is the natural effect of a romantic and tender
passion to render common society distasteful to
its victim : Petrarch quitted the city in despair,
and immured himself in the shades and caverns
of Vaucluse. " The more desert and savage the
scene which surrounds me, the more lively," says
he, " is the form in which Laura presents herself
to my view. The mountains, the woods, and the
streams, see and witness my anguish." The sentiment which preyed on his heart undermined his
health and sapped the springs of life : the idea of

LAURA SADE.   **353**

death and of a future state presented itself to his imagination, ever lively and enthusiastic, and opposed itself to the fervours of love : he lamented the time which he had wasted in this pursuit, and determined, in vain, to conquer a passion which indulgence, habit, and association, had too firmly interwoven with the whole texture of his mind.   To assist him in his resolution, he had recourse to a monk, Dennis de Robertis, a native of Italy, a man distinguished for his talents, and to whom Petrarch was greatly attached.   Father Dennis said all that wisdom could dictate, or that ingenuity could devise, to heal the wounded mind of his penitent, who solicited of him advice, and implored of him remedies for his passion; but the eloquence of the good father was, by one glance from Laura, obliterated from the mind of his pupil.

Avignon, about this period, was afflicted with a pestilence of a singular nature, from an extraordinary heat and drought : persons of every age and sex changed their skins, which fell from their faces and hands in scales.   The constitution of Laura was too delicate not to suffer by this state of the atmosphere; her recovery was for some tune doubtful; and Petrarch experienced all the agony which anxiety for the life of a beloved object, added to constrained absence, can inflict on a susceptible heart. Laura, however, recovered, and relieved him from his distress. "Would to God," said he, in a letter to a friend, who had rallied him on his passion, " that my Laura were indeed an imaginary person, and that my passion for her was only a jest ! alas, it is a phrensy !" Petrarch frequently retired into the deepest solitudes ; and if, by accident, he met with Laura in the streets of Avignon, he avoided her and passed swiftly on. This affectation, notwithstanding the reserve of her conduct, appeared to displease her. She wished probably to preserve a lover whose reputation flattered her pride ; or, it is possible, that in secret she was not insensible to his devotion and constancy. One day, having met him by accident, she looked on him with greater kindness. A favour so unexpected restored him to happiness, and vanquished in a moment his boasted resolution. He now again sought her in public, when she behaved to him with more ease: he wished to speak to her of his sentiments, but the dignity of her manners repressed and awed him. Laura desired to be beloved by Petrarch, but with a refinement that should prevent him from any expression of his feelings. If ever he attempted to violate this respectful silence, she treated him with the utmost severity ; but when she saw him afflicted, in despair, and too much discouraged, some trifling complacency, a word, a gesture, were sufficient to reanimate him. It was by this refined species of coquetry, if so harsh a term may be allowed, that Laura, without stain to her honour, kept alive for twenty years the passion of a man of impetuous character, whose morals, previous to his acquaintance with her, had not been irreproachable. At one period, emboldened by her complacence, and the confidence with which it inspired him, he ventured, though with hesitation and timidity, to express his feelings, and to complain of her rigour. 'I am not,' replied Laura, with visible emotion, ' I am not, Petrarch, the person whom you suppose me to be.' Struck by the manner in which she uttered this reproof, he was awed into silence. Laura forbade him to appear again in her presence, refused to receive his apologies, and avoided every occasion of meeting him. The sorrow and remorse of Petrarch seriously affected his health, he was seized with a dangerous indisposition, and Laura was persuaded to see and pardon him.

After his return from his travels, the admonitions of father Dennis raised in his mind religious scruples; Laura seemed to divide his heart with God, and to interfere with the practice of his duties. ' How much time,' said his spiritual instructor, ' have you wasted on that Laura! How many useless steps have you taken in those woods!' But the most trifling circumstance was sufficient to disturb his philosophy, and to over-throw his wisest resolutions. Having one day observed a girl washing the veil of Laura, he was seized with a sudden tremor, and, under a sultry sky, shivered as in the depths of winter. He neglected the conduct of his affairs, and became distracted and bewildered in his studies and among his books. The conflict between his reason and his feelings, injured his mind and shook his frame. " Ten years," says he, " has grief preyed upon me : a slow poison consumes me : scarcely have I strength to drag along my weakened limbs. I must get out of this terrible situation. I must regain my liberty." Again be determined to tra-vel, and to try the effects of absence. Having concealed his name, and embarked in a ship about to set sail for Italy, he assumed the charac-ter of a pilgrim, going to worship at Rome. On landing on the Italian coast, his native country, after which he had long sighed, he perceived a laurel tree, which love had associated in his mind with the idea of Laura. Too vehemently trans-ported to observe his steps, he ran towards his favourite plant, without observing a brook which impeded his way, and fell into the stream. The

fall occasioned him to swoon, and, on his recovery, to reflect with a degree of shame on his
heedlessness and infatuation.

Exercise, change, and absence, seemed to produce upon his mind a favourable effect; the idea
of Laura became less habitual, the agitation of
his feelings no longer destroyed his health, his
sleep was less unquiet, and he was more easily
amused; he believed himself cured, and even
smiled at his past extravagance. In this disposition he returned to Avignon, 1337. But no
sooner had he again beheld Laura, than his wound,
but slightly healed over, opened afresh, and his
relapse was more violent even than his original disease. " I desired death," said he; " I
was even tempted to seek it in the violence of my
anguish. Laura was sick; but the approach of
death could not diminish the lustre of her eyes.
I trembled at her shadow. The sound of her
voice deprived me of motion." He perceived
that safety could only be found in flight; he determined to leave Avignon, and to seek repose in
the lonely solitudes of Vaucluse. In this retreat,
while he indulged his taste for letters and retirement, he sought to cure himself of his passion.
" I may hide myself," says he, " in the rocks
and in the woods, but there are no places so wild
and solitary whither the torments of love do not

pursue me. Thrice in that dark and lonely hour, when nothing but ghastly shades are seen or heard, Laura, with stedfast look, approached my bed, and claimed her slave. Fear froze my limbs; my blood, forsaking my veins, rushed upon my heart. Trembling I rose ere morn, and left a house where all I saw alarmed me. I climbed the rocks, I ran into the woods, watching with fearful eyes this dreadful vision. I may not be believed, but still it followed. Here I perceive it starting from a tree—there rising from a fountain—now it descended from the rocks, or floated on the clouds. Surrounded thus, I stood transfixed with horror." The state of Petrarch's mind, his enthusiastic temperament, and the solitude in which he cherished a diseased sensibility, sufficiently account for these visionary flights. He passed near a year in this retreat, attended only by an old fisherman; his domestics, unable to sustain the severity of such a seclusion, having requested to be dismissed. After this period, he made several journeys to Avignon: sometimes he flattered himself with having conquered his passion, and again relapsed into weakness and grief. His mind, accustomed to a strong stimulus, had become restless and enfeebled; his resolution was continually fluctuating; he groaned under the weight of his chains, and yet dreaded indifference

LAURA SADE.   359

as a more terrible evil. The sonnets which he composed at this time are strongly expressive of his disordered state.

In 1342, the pope granted two favours to two of Laura's children   Her daughter Ermessenda was received into the convent of St. Lawrence, where she professed herself.   Some time after, Audibert her son was appointed to the canonship of Notre de Dame de Dons.   These children were about twelve or thirteen years of age.

Whether touched by his sufferings, his constancy, or his reputation, Laura, on the return of Petrarch to Avignon, treated him with less reserve   Avignon became from this circumstance, and from the favour of the pope, more agreeable to him; he now passed in the city the greater part of his time, and visited Vaucluse but at intervals.   The praises which Petrarch had lavished upon his mistress rendered her name celebrated throughout Europe; every person who came to Avignon was solicitous to behold these powerful charms.   Though not yet thirty years of age, the beauty of Laura was somewhat tarnished: domestic chagrins and frequent child-bearing appeared to have impaired her health; the bloom of her complexion was less vivid and fresh.   By a kind of sympathy, Petrarch had also lost that florid hue which gave vivacity to his features.

" I am not what I was," says he, in a letter to a friend, " so changed am I by the perpetual war-fare between my soul and body, that you would scarcely know me."

Some time after this he met Laura at a public assembly, where, magnificently attired, she wore on her hands silk gloves embroidered with gold. This ornament, which was in those periods ex-tremely rare and costly, seems to be in testimony of the nobility of Laura, which was also proved by her marriage contract. She happened to let fall one of these gloves, which Petrarch, whose attention was ever bent towards her, instantly picked up. Laura, on perceiving it in his pos-session, and that he had a desire to retain it, im-mediately took it from him, with some displea-sure. " It is not," said Petrarch, " the person of Laura that I adore, but that soul so superior to all others. Her conduct and her manners are an image of the life the blessed lead in heaven. Should I ever lose her (the very idea makes me trem-ble!) I would say what Lelius, the wisest of the Romans, said on the death of Scipio, ' I loved his virtue, and that shall ever live.'" " If my de-sires have ever passed the bounds which rea-son prescribes, it is no longer so. Those li-mits are now sacred. But with respect to Laura, let me ever do her justice. Never,

in the most interesting moments of our intercourse, have I seen her principles waver. Her
conduct, in the gayest hours of her life, was always uniform, always pure. How admirable is a
constancy, a resolution, so superior to the generality of her sex !" Yet he sometimes made other
reflections, not less true and just. " You cannot
deny," says he to himself, in his Confessions, in
the form of dialogues, in imitation of St. Augustin, " you cannot deny, and you indeed confess,
that this love of which you boast has made you
unhappy, and was near drawing on you a fatal
crime, of which this admirable woman was the
cause. Ought she not to have suppressed rather
than to have encouraged an inclination so fatal
to your peace? This truth she ought to have
known, and to have impressed upon you: That
of all the passions to which human nature is subject, love is the most to be feared; it makes us
forget what is due to ourselves, and it leads us
even to forget our God. Every thing serves to
nourish and increase it; and those wretched beings, whom it holds in bondage, carry a fire within them, by which soul and body will be ultimately
consumed."—" Recal the torments you have
suffered, the useless tears you have shed, and the
short pleasures you have obtained, which may be

VOL. VI.   R

compared to those light zephyrs of the summer, which refresh the air but for a moment; and then reflect on the duties you have neglected," &c.

Notwithstanding the attachment of Petrarch to Laura, the love of his country was never absent from his mind. Various circumstances combined to render him desirous of quitting Avignon, and of breathing once more the balmy air of Italy. His friends, in vain, sought to detain him. " Every thing," says he, " alters with time. My hair, which is become grey, warns me to change my manner of thinking and my life. Love suits not with one of my age: the air of Italy is purer, the waters clearer, the flowers more beautiful; it is time that I should go there to enjoy my liberty, and to take possession of my father's sepulchre." He went to take leave of Laura, who, ignorant of the motive of his visit, received him with a smiling countenance; but, when she learned his determination to depart, she changed colour, cast down her eyes, and kept silence. Her manner seemed to say: ' Alas! will you then go? shall I lose my faithful friend?'

He had not been long absent before his inquietudes revived, and he wished to return. In leaving Laura, he felt that he had left behind him the half of himself. His friends, in their letters, informed him that she appeared to suffer too much from his

LAURA SADE.   363

absence. Soon after this, under pretence of pressing business, he returned precipitately to Avignon.
Impatient for the sight of Laura, he went on horseback from Lyons to Avignon, along the banks of
the Rhone, whose current he wished to follow, that
he might the sooner behold his mistress. Laura viewed
again with pleasure the friend whom she feared she
had for ever lost: if she did not express this sentiment in words, she however mixed in her behaviour nothing that was severe. She had this year
some subject of domestic grief, respecting which,
Petrarch, who had now access to her house, went
frequently to console her. " I went," said he,
" to express my tender interest in Laura's sorrow.
Love, who was my guide, has engraven for ever on
my heart her looks and expressions."—" Tears
stood in her eyes; those eyes radiant as the sun.
She joined patience with sorrow, and the divine
harmony of virtue with every burst of woe."

Among the festivals which were given about this
period by the pope, in honour of the king of Bohemia, and Charles, prince of Moravia, his son,
the city of Avignon gave a magnificent ball, at
which the beauties of the province were assembled.
Charles, a gallant prince, sought among the ladies,
who graced the entertainment, for Laura, to whom
the genius of her lover had given so much celebrity.

364   LAURA SADE.

Having at length discovered her, he passed by all those whose rank or age gave them a title to precedence, and, casting down his eyes, paid his homage to her, by bowing his head after the French fashion. Every person was pleased at this mark of distinction paid to a lady to whose character it was justly due. Petrarch conceived from this circumstance a high idea of the discernment of the prince, and a particular interest and sympathy in his favour.

Laura had a friend, who, as far as virtue and honour would allow, was in the interest of her lover. She wished that he should be beloved, but with a pure and tender friendship. When she saw him desponding and cast down, she reanimated his spirits; and when he presumed too far, checked his confidence. She also used her influence with Laura in favour of Petrarch. One day, having represented to him the tenderness expressed in Laura's countenance and behaviour, when his conduct had merited her regard: ' Incredulous!' added she, ' and can you after this doubt of her affection?' The constitution of Laura had been always delicate, and her health began to decline. Petrarch was touched and affected by her drooping state. ' Heaven grant me,' said he, ' to die before Laura, that I may never see so dreadful an event!' A complaint in her eyes, which was extremely painful,

LAURA SADE.   365

happened to Laura this year, and threatened her sight. Petrarch went often to see her during her confinement: he found her one day cured of her complaint, which seemed by a certain sympathy to have passed into his own eyes. " I fixed my eyes on those of Laura," said he, " and, that moment, something like a shooting star darted from them into mine. I rejoice in this present from love: how delightful is it thus to cure the darling object of one's soul !"

This intercourse with Laura, in which he experienced so much pleasure, received an interruption from the officious impertinence of those persons who take a pleasure in separating hearts which friendship and affection have united. It was intimated to Laura, that Petrarch imposed upon her, and that she was not the real object of his attachment or his sonnets : under her name, it was added, he concealed a passion for another woman, who was the secret inspirer of his muse. Laura, too much interested in the intelligence that was communicated to her not to be credulous, took umbrage at the supposed duplicity of her lover, and withdrew herself wholly from him. " My joys," said he, " were like the bright days of winter, of flattering aspect, but of short duration." This circumstance sufficiently proves that Laura was far from indifferent to the attentions of Petrarch, a sensibility which she tried to conceal in the bottom of her heart, and to the forced suppression of which, and the difficulties of her situation, her declining health might be in some degree attributable. Her character appears with far greater interest and dignity upon the supposition of this sensibility, and the sacrifice of feeling to principle, than when she is considered as a vain coquet, trifling, for the gratification of her vanity, with the happiness of a man of worth, who truly loved her. She was, however, too reasonable not to allow herself to be convinced of the innocence of her lover of the crime laid to his charge, and to refuse to readmit him to her confidence and esteem.

The restlessness of Petrarch again recurred; he thought of leaving Avignon, and of revisiting Italy : the love of his country, and his dislike to Avignon, balanced in his heart his passion for Laura : with these, other motives combined to determine his departure. He passed a part of the autumn in preparation at Vaucluse, whence he went to Avignon, to take leave of Laura, whom he found at an assembly which she often frequented. " Her air," said he, " was more touching than usual. She was dressed perfectly plain, without pearls or any gay colours. Though she was not melancholy, she did not appear with her usual cheerfulness. She sung not, as usual, nor did she speak with that sweetness which charmed every one. She was serious and thoughtful: she had the air of a person who fears an evil, of the nature of which he is ignorant. I sought in her looks, in taking my leave of her, a consolation for my own sufferings. Her eyes had an expression which I had never before beheld in them. I deposited to their keeping my heart and my thoughts, as to faithful friends, on whom I could depend. Her altered dress and air, her countenance, a certain concern mixed with grief which I perceived in her aspect, predicted the sorrows that threatened me." Touched with the appearance and manners of Laura, Petrarch could, with difficulty, restrain his tears; while Laura seemed scarcely equal to sustain the idea of, perhaps, an eternal separation from so true and devoted a friend. When the hour of his departure arrived, she regarded him with a look so tender, pure, and affecting, as had nearly subdued the resolution for which he had so painfully struggled. " Must I never," says he, " see again that beautiful face, those kind looks which relieve the tender heart ?"

The situation in which Petrarch left Laura, on his departure from Avignon, filled his mind with inquietude, and haunted his imagination with terrible forebodings. The plague, which at that

368   LAURA SADE.

period ravaged Europe, and which carried off many
of his friends, added to his anxiety. His correspondents informed him, in their letters, that his
beautiful mistress was so changed since his absence,
as scarcely to be known by those who were not in
the habit of constantly seeing her. " Heretofore,"
said he, " I saw her often in my dreams. Her
angelic vision then consoled me; but at present it
overwhelms and afflicts me. I think I see in her
aspect compassion mixed with grief. I think I
hear her thus speak to me : ' Recal that night,
when, forced to part from you, I left you bathed in
tears; I was not able to tell you then, nor would I
have done so, but I will tell you at present, and you
may believe me, you shall see me no more upon
earth.' What a dreadful vision ! Shall I learn only
from dreams an account so interesting to me ? Shall
she herself come to announce it ? No : it cannot be.
Heaven and nature forbid !—Uncertain of my state,
I sigh, I write, I fear, I hope : I am no longer
what I was: I resemble a man who walks in a
path of which he is not sure. I open my ears, but
no one speaks of her I love : my soul floats between
fear and hope : cruel departure ! Why, if I am so
soon to lose her, why separate myself from her ?"

On the 6th of April, 1348, Petrarch was at
Verona, his mind occupied by these dark presages,
when, in a dream towards the morning, he seemed

to behold Laura, and held with her a long conversation. " Her appearance," said he, " was like
that of the spring, and her head was crowned with
oriental pearls. As she drew near to me she sighed,
and gave me a hand which had long been the object
of my tenderest wishes. ' Do you recollect,' she
asked, ' her, who, by engaging the affections of
your youth, led you from the common road of life ?'
While she spoke these words, which were accompanied with an air of modesty and earnestness, she
sat down under a laurel and a beech, on the side of
a brook, and commanded me to place myself by
her." Having informed her lover that she was no
longer an inhabitant of this world, and reproved him
for his grief ; " ' To the spotless soul,' continued
she, ' death is the deliverance from a darksome
prison : it is no more than a sigh, or a short passage
from one life to another. In the flower of my
youth, when you loved me most, and when life
was decked out in all its charms, then was it bitter,
compared with the sweetness of my death. I felt,
at this moment, more joy, than an exile returning to
his wished-for country. There was but one idea that
afflicted me. I was to leave you. I was moved
with compassion.' ' Ah !' replied I, ' in the
name of that truth, by which you were governed
while on earth, and which now you more clearly

distinguish, in the bosom of him to whom all things
are present, tell me, I conjure you, whether *love*
gave birth to this compassion ? Those rigours mixed
with softness, those tender angers, and those delicious reconciliations, which were written in your
eyes, have, for ever, kept my heart in uncertainty
and doubt.' Scarce had I ceased to speak, when
I beheld those heavenly smiles which have at all
times been the messengers of peace. ' You have
ever,' said she with a sigh, ' possessed my heart,
and shall continue to possess it. But I was obliged
to temper the violence of your passion by the movements of my countenance. It was necessary to
keep you in ignorance. A good mother is never
more solicitous respecting her child, than when she
appears to be most in anger with him. How often
have I said to myself, Petrarch does not love, he
burns with a violent passion, which I must endeavour to regulate. But, alas ! this was a difficult
task for one whose fears and affections were likewise
engaged. He must not, I said, be acquainted with
the state of my heart. He admires so much what
he sees without, that I must conceal from his knowledge what passes within. This has been the only
artifice which I have used. Be not offended. It
was a rein necessary to keep you in the right road.
There was no other method by which I could preserve our souls. A thousand times has my coun-

LAURA SADE. 371

tenance been lighted up with anger, while my heart
has glowed with love; but it was my determined
resolution, that reason, not love, should hold the
sovereignty. When I saw you cast down with
sorrow, I gave you a look of consolation. When you
were on the brink of despair, my glances were still
more tender; I addressed you with a softer air, and
soothed you with a kind word: my apprehensions
even altered the tone of my voice; you might see
them impressed on my countenance. When you
looked pale, and your eyes were bathed in tears,
I said, he is very ill, he will certainly die if I take
not pity on him. It was then that you had every
succour which virtue could give, and then was you
restored again to yourself. Sometimes you were like
the fiery horse, fretted with the spur; it was then necessary that you should feel the bridle, and be managed
with the bit. Such have been the innocent artifices
by which I have led you on, without stain to my honour.' ' Ah!' said I, with a faultering voice, my
eyes bedewed with tears, ' such sentiments, had I but
courage to believe them, would amply recompense all
my sufferings.' ' Faithless man!' said she, a little
angrily, ' what motive can I have for this declaration,
had it not been the true cause of that reserve and distance of which you so often complained? In all things
else we were agreed; and honour and virtue were
the bonds of our affection. Our love was mutual, at

least from the time that I was convinced of your
attachment. While one discovered, the other concealed the flame; this was the only difference between us. You were hoarse with crying Mercy!
Help! while I opened not my mouth. Fear and
modesty permitted me not to reveal my sentiments.
The flame which is confined burns more fiercely
than that which is at liberty. Recollect the day
when we were alone, and when you presented to
me your sonnets, singing, at the same time, This
is all my love dare say. I received them with kindness; and, after such a proof, could you doubt my
affection? Was not this removing the veil? My
heart was yours, but I chose to be mistress of my
eyes. This you thought unjust; and yet, with
what right could you complain? Were you not
possessed of the nobler part? Those eyes, which
have so often been withdrawn, because you merited
this severity, have they not been restored to you a
thousand times? How often have they regarded you
with tenderness? and would, at all times, have
done so, had I not dreaded the extravagance of
your passion. But the morning advances; the sun
is emerging from the ocean; it is with regret that I
tell you we must now be separated. If you have
anything more to say to me, be quick, and regulate your words by the few moments that remain to
use?" I had time only to add, ' My sufferings are

LAURA SADE. 373

fully recompensed ; but I cannot live without you :
I would therefore know, whether I shall soon follow
you ?' She was already in motion to depart, when
she said, ' If I mistake not, you shall remain a
long time upon earth.'"

The inquietude of Petrarch was redoubled from
these multiplied visions, which seemed to assure
him of the fate of Laura. He waited with impatience for news from Avignon, but the plague
had put a stop to all communications. On the 9th
of May, 1348, he received, while at Parma, a
letter from a friend, who resided in the same city
with Laura, and who informed him, that she had
died of the plague, on the 6th of April, the very
day on which the vision had appeared to him. Laura
had felt the first attacks of this disorder on the 3d
of April, when she was seized with the fever and
the spitting of blood. Being persuaded that she
should not survive the third day, she immediately
received the sacraments, and made her will ; after
which she tranquilly awaited her death. Though
attacked with a malady that terrified all the world,
her relations, friends, and neighbours, gathered
round her, so greatly had she been beloved by
those of her own sex. Seated on her bed, she appeared perfectly composed, while her companions
were overwhelmed with grief and regret. ' We
are going,' said they, ' to lose a friend and com-

panion, the soul of our innocent pleasures, who consoled us in our chagrins, and whose example was to us a living lesson. In losing her we lose all. Heaven takes her hence as a treasure of which we were not worthy.' Though not insensible to the distress of her friends, her last moments were occupied by sublimer considerations. She expired gently, and without struggle, like a lamp whose oil is gradually wasted. She appeared after her death as one who slumbers; death had not discomposed the serenity of her features. " Her road to heaven," says Petrarch, " was not to seek in death ; she had long known and walked in its paths."

She died about six in the morning, April 6th, 1348. Her body was, on the same day, at vespers, carried to the church of the Franciscans, and interred in the chapel de la Croix, built by Hugues de Sade, her husband, close to the chapel of St. Ann, which had been erected by her father. In the year 1533, the remains of Laura were found there, with an Italian sonnet of Petrarch's; a circumstance which proved that the Laura of Petrarch was the same with Laura de Noves, wife of Hugues de Sade. It appears by her will, that, after some pious legacies, she left her husband her heir, to whom she had borne ten children, six boys and four girls. She was not happy in her nuptials, and experienced some trouble with her children. She lost her eldest

LAURA SADE. 375

son in the flower of his age, and her eldest daughter gave pain to a mother so nicely sensible to her honour, by misconduct in her marriage state.

Modesty was the characteristic of Laura, whom neither her beauty, her birth, nor the fame she derived from the passion of Petrarch, could render vain or assuming. In her dress she was peculiarly elegant and magnificent, particularly in the ornaments of her head, and in the tasteful manner in which she disposed her hair : she sometimes wore a coronet of silver or gold, and sometimes, to vary her appearance, wreathes of natural flowers. Petrarch speaks of two rich dresses which she wore ; one of purple, edged with azure, and embroidered with roses, in which he compares her to the Phœnix * ; the other enriched with gold and jewels. This magnificence in her attire seems to have been adopted in conformity to her rank, and to the wishes of her family, rather than to any particular pleasure which she took in displaying her charms. She was peculiarly reserved in her behaviour towards the men, in a city in which the manners were dissolute and corrupt, and where great delicacy and caution was, on that account, the more necessary. An old lady, in her presence, once said, that life was preferable

---

* Naturalists describe the Phœnix with purple feathers, and a blue tail, strewed over with roses.

even to honour; a sentiment which Laura rebuked with becoming indignation. ' The grief of Lucretia,' she declared, ' ought to have rendered a poinard unnecessary.' But, notwithstanding the severity of her principles, her manners were courteous and elegant; she mingled with society, and in gay circles, where she knew how to unite wisdom and virtue with the graces, and to give even to austerity a charm. Her education seems not to have been superior to that of the ladies of her times, who were rarely taught either to read or write. Those who knew how to read, and who were seldom to be found but in convents, were esteemed prodigies of erudition, and treated with peculiar distinction.

Petrarch, speaking of Laura, says, " that her words had the dignity of nature, which raised her above her education; and that her voice was a source of continual enchantment, soft, angelic, and divine; that it could appease the wrath, dissipate the clouds, and calm the tempests, of the soul." Her mind was elevated, her temper sweet, and her life uniform and simple. Her health appears to have been prematurely weakened by domestic chagrins, and, probably, from an attachment which duty forbade her to encourage, and which, in secret, preyed on her heart.

The grief of Petrarch for her loss, susceptible

LAURA SADE.   377

minds may conceive. " I dare not think of my condition," says he, " much less can I speak of it." He passed several days, without nourishment, abandoned to the most poignant sorrow. On the MS. of Virgil (ornamented with paintings, by Simon de Sienna), Petrarch's favourite book, he wrote the following lines: " Laura, illustrious by her own virtues, and long celebrated in my verses, appeared to my eyes, for the first time, the 6th of April, 1327, at Avignon, in the church of St. Clair, at the first hour of the day : I was then in my youth. In the same city, on the same day, and at the same hour, in the year 1348, this luminary disappeared from our world. I was then at Verona, ignorant of my wretched situation. That chaste and beautiful body was buried the same day, after vespers, in the church of the Cordeliers : her soul returned to its native heaven. To retrace the melancholy remembrance of this great loss, I have, with a pleasure mixed with bitterness, written it in a book to which I often refer. This loss convinces me, that there is no longer any thing worthy of living for. Since the strongest cord of my life is broken, with the grace of God, I shall easily renounce a world, where my cares have been deceitful, and my hopes vain and perishing."

From the Life of Petrarch, translated by Mrs. Dobson.

[378]

SAPPHO.

SAPPHO, so celebrated for her impassioned and elegant poetry, was a native of Mitylene, in the isle of Lesbos. She lived in the forty-second Olympiad, six hundred and ten years before the Christian æra. She composed a great number of odes, elegies, epigrams, epithalamiums, &c. and received from her contemporaries the title of the tenth muse. But few of her numerous productions have descended to posterity; yet those few justify the panegyrics which have been bestowed upon her. Her Hymn to Venus was preserved by Dionysus of Halicarnassus, who inserted it in his works as an example of perfection. Her well-known amatory ode was preserved by Longinus, as a specimen of equal excellence. Her poetry was held in great and just esteem by the ancients. " In Greece," says Tanaquillus Faber, " no productions were esteemed more elegant, exquisite, and beautiful, than those of Sappho." Mitylene boasted of the honour of her birth : in testimony of their respect for her memory, the Mitylenians stamped their coin with her image. The Romans afterwards erected a statue of porphyry to her honour. Both ancients and moderns have vied with each other in enthusiastic admiration of her genius and talents. Vostius affirms,

SAPPHO. 379

that none of the Greek poets excelled Sappho for the sweetness of her verse: he adds, that she took as her model the style of Archilochus, the severity of which she softened. Critics, historians, and poets, have, in every age, united in her praise. Catullus endeavoured to imitate the verse of Sappho, but with inferior success: nature, tenderness, and passion, breathe through all her productions.

She was married young to Cercala, one of the richest inhabitants of the isle of Andros, by whom she had a daughter, named Cleïs. The parentage of Sappho is uncertain; she had three brothers, one of whom, called Charaxus *, she reproves for his infatuation with Rhodope or Doricha, a celebrated courtezan. She lost her husband not many years after their marriage, and determined against second nuptials.

She unhappily conceived a passion for Phaon, a beautiful youth, whom she followed into Sicily, where, as it is believed, she composed the Hymn to Venus. It is doubtful whether Phaon, of whom she complains with so much eloquence, was insensible to her tenderness or unfaithful to his vows: the latter, according to Ovid, appears to have been the case. Unable to recal her wandering lover, or to move his obdurate heart, she determined, by a perilous expedient, to put

---

* Charaxus sold Lesbian wines in Egypt.

an end to her sufferings and mortification, and
to extinguish, with her life, her unfortunate
passion. For this purpose she threw herself from
the promontory of Leucas into the sea. This promontory, entitled the lover's leap, was resorted to
by those who had suffered disappointment in their
affections, as an effectual cure for their sorrows.
According to tradition, though the self-devoted
victims should escape with life, which was scarcely
possible, they would experience from the leap a
cure for their passion. Sappho is said to have been
the first woman who tried the dangerous experiment,
and perished in the trial.

An expression of Sappho's is recorded by Aristotle, to prove what the stoics affected to deny,
that death is an evil. " The gods," said Sappho,
" have judged it so ; otherwise they would themselves die." Whether death is to be considered as
an evil, must depend upon the degree of enjoyment
which attends life : privation of good must always
be evil ; release from suffering desirable. Sappho
herself acted upon this principle.

Alcæus, a contemporary poet, conceived a passion
for Sappho ; he wrote to her : " I wish to explain
myself," said he, " but shame restrains me."
" Your countenance would not blush," replied she,
" if your heart were not culpable." Sappho professed to reconcile the love of pleasure and the love

SAPPHO.   381

of virtue. " Without virtue," said she, " nothing is so dangerous as riches: happiness consists in the union of both." " This person," she would also say, " is distinguished by his figure; that by his virtues : the one appears beautiful at first view; the other not less so on a second." It is possible that the licentiousness imputed to Sappho may be a calumny: the extreme sensibility of the Greeks, and the animated language in which they were, on all occasions, accustomed to express their feelings, may mislead a modern reader. Persons of licentious manners are seldom capable of the strong individual attachment which proved fatal to Sappho : neither is it, by any means, always a true criterion to judge of a writer by his works; still less of a poet, who professes to give the reins to his imagination.

After the death of her husband, Sappho devoted herself to letters, and undertook to inspire the Lesbian women with a taste for literature: many foreigners were, with her fair countrywomen, among her disciples. The Lesbian poetess was, like all persons of talents (*women* more especially), exposed to envy and slander : having neglected to conciliate her enemies, she provoked them by contempt and irony. Persecuted, and at length compelled to fly her country, she found an asylum in Sicily, where it was proposed to erect a statue to her honour.

382 ALEXANDRA SCALA.

Her poems, composed in a metre of which she was herself the inventress, abounded in a variety of novel and happy expressions, with which she is said to have enriched her native language. Of all the Grecian women who cultivated poetry, not one equalled Sappho; of men, very few, if any, surpassed her. She painted from nature and from genuine sensibility; her style was flowing and harmonious, her sentiments tender and voluptuous. From her descriptions of the symptoms and emotions of love, which were exquisite and unrivalled, the physician, Erasistratus, discovered the cause of the sickness of Antiochus, who was enamoured of his step-mother, Stratonice. In the Prytaneum of Syracuse was a beautiful statue of Sappho, the work of Silanion.

Bayle's Historical Dictionary—Biographium Faemineium, &c. &c.

ALEXANDRA SCALA.

ALEXANDRA was the daughter of Bartholomew Scala, a learned Florentine in the fifteenth century, who, by his talents, raised himself from a low origin to rank and honours. Alexandra, who displayed early a superior capacity, received from her father a learned education, in which she made an extraordinary proficiency. She married Michael

ALEXANDRA SCALA. 383

Marullus, a man of letters, a scholar, and a poet. The motive ascribed to Marullus in his choice of a bride is somewhat curious and singular. " He was not satisfied with being master of the Greek tongue, unless he could join to it the Roman elo‑ quence; for which reason he married, at Florence, Alexandra Scala, a young woman of talents and learning *."

Politian, notwithstanding a literary animosity be‑ tween himself and the father of Alexandra, which had been maintained with mutal bitterness, cele‑ brated her praise in Greek verse; to which she replied in the same language, acknowledging her sense of his civilities. These verses appeared in print.

Marullus does not seem to have repented of his choice of a learned wife: among his poems are several written in her praise, both before and after marriage. Of one of these poems the following is a translation :

" My Scala, while I mark and trace
Your every charm, and every grace,
I own such beauty to be rare ;
Yet others may be found as fair.
But, when your heav'nly charms I see,
From all immodest tincture free,
Then, let me perish, but I find
Scala the Phœnix of her kind.

---

* Paul Jovius, Elo. cap. xxviii.

384　　ANNA MARIA SCHURMAN.

While, last, as president of wit,
I see you with the muses sit ;
Scala, no more a Phœnix, is
A goddess mixed with goddesses."

Alexandra Scala died in 1506.

Bayle's Historical Dictionary.

ANNA MARIA SCHURMAN.

The learned and ingenious Anna Maria Schurman was born at Cologn, Nov. 5th, 1607. Her parents were descended from noble protestant families. Anna Maria discovered from her early childhood extraordinary ingenuity. At six years of age she cut, with her scissars, without pattern or model, a variety of curious figures in paper. Two years afterwards, she learned in a few days to design flowers with great perfection ; and, in her eleventh year, acquired, in three hours, the art of embroidering. She afterwards received instructions in music, in painting, in sculpture, and in engraving ; in all of which she was admirably successful. It is observed, by Mr. Evelyn, in his History of Calcography, " That the very knowing Anna Maria Schurman is skilled in this art, with innumerable others, even for a prodigy of her sex !" Her hand-writing, specimens of which have been preserved by the curious in their cabi-

ANNA MARIA SCHURMAN. 385

nets, was in all languages inimitably beautiful. Mr. Joby, in his journey to Munster, speaks of the beauty of her penmanship in Greek, Hebrew, Syriac, Arabic, and French, of which he had been an eye-witness: he also mentions her skill in miniature-painting; and in drawing, with the point of a diamond, portraits upon glass: she painted her own picture. She possessed the art of imitating pearls, which could not be distinguished from the originals, but by piercing them with a needle.

The powers of her understanding were not inferior to her ingenuity. At eleven years of age, being occasionally present at the lessons of her brothers, she frequently set them right by a whisper, when examined in their Latin exercises. Her father, observing her genius for literature, resolved to cultivate a capacity so uncommon: a foundation was thus laid for her future acquirements. Her proficiency in the Hebrew, Greek, and Latin languages, in which she wrote and spoke fluently, astonished the learned. She made great progress also in the oriental languages, the Arabic, Ethiopic, Chaldee, and Syriac. With the living languages, English, Italian, and French, she was not less conversant. She studied the sciences with equal success; geography, astro-

386　　ANNA MARIA SCAURMAN.

nomy, and physics. Her temper having early acquired a devotional cast, she at length exchanged for theology the more liberal pursuit of learning.

Her father had, during her infancy, settled at Utrecht, whence, for the improvement of his children, he removed to Franeker; where, in 1623, he died. On this event, his widow returned to Utrecht, where Anna Maria continued to devote herself to her studies. Her predilection for letters prevented her from engaging in more active life, and induced her to decline an advantageous establishment. Mr. Cots, pensionary of Holland, and a celebrated poet, who, when she was only fourteen years of age, had written verses in her praise, offered her his hand and heart.

Her modesty, no less singular than her knowledge, rendered her desirous of burying her acquirements in obscurity: it was in despite of her inclination that Rivetus, Spanheim, and Vossius, brought her forward to notice. To these may be added, Salmasius, Huygens, and Beverovicius, who, holding with her a literary correspondence, spread her fame through foreign countries. Her reputation, thus extended, procured her letters from Balzac, Gassendi, Mercennus, Rochart, Contart, and other men of eminence: while she was visited by princesses, and persons of the first dis-

ANNA MARIA SCAURMAN. 387

tinction, cardinal Richclieu also honoured her with marks of his esteem.

About the year 1650 her religious sentiments underwent a revolution. Having declined attendance on public worship, she performed her devotions in private. It was reported that she meant to embrace popery. The truth was, she had attached herself to Labadie, the celebrated quietist, whose principles she embraced, and whom she accompanied wherever he went. She resided with him for some time at Altona, in Holstein, where she attended him at his death, in 1674. She retired afterwards to Wiewart, in Friesland, where she was visited by William Penn, in 1677. She died at Wiewart, the following year, May 5th, 1678. She chose for her device the words of St. Ignatius, " *Amor meus crucifixus est*," i.e. " My love is crucified."

Her works are, " De vitæ humanæ termino," *Ultrajact*, 1639. " Dissertatio de Ingenii muliebris ad doctrinam & meliores literas aptitudine," *Lugd. Bat.* 1641. These pieces, with letters in Greek, Hebrew, Latin, and French, to her learned correspondents, were printed at Leyden, 1648, in 12mo. under the title of " A. M. a Schurman Opuscula, Hebræa, Græca, Latina, Gallica: prosaica & metrica," enlarged in the edition of

s 2

Utrecht, 1652. She wrote likewise, " Eukleria, seu melioris partis electio." This work, a defence of her attachment to Labadie, was, while she resided with him, printed at Altona, 1673.

Biographium Fæmineum—The Female Worthies.

MADELIENE DE SCUDERY.

MADELIENE DE SCUDERY, descended from an ancient and honourable house, was born at Havre de Grace, 1607. Educated with care under a sensible mother, she was distinguished while in her childhood for intellectual acuteness, for a lively imagination, and a just and delicate taste. In the endowments of her person, nature had been less liberal. By her wit, and the disadvantages of her figure, she obtained the name of Sapplio, whose genius she emulated, with greater purity of manners. She came early to Paris, where her talents excited attention, and procured her admittance into the first literary circles. At the Hotel de Rambouillet, the centre of wit and knowledge, she was admitted a member, and soon celebrated as one of its brightest ornaments. Her fortune being limited, necessity first induced her to turn her thoughts to the press. Romances were the taste of the age, to which mademoiselle de Scudery gave a new and more refined turn.

MADELIENE DE SCUDERY. 389

Sentiments of honour, of heroism, and of virtue, were substituted for dissolute scenes and descriptions of intrigue; female manners were pourtrayed with delicacy and chasteness, and the passions refined from their grossness. Her books, which formed a new era in that species of writing, were bought with avidity, and read eagerly by persons of all ranks. To the name of Scudery, which her brother had already rendered celebrated, Madeliene added new lustre. The academy of the Ricovrati, at Padua, complimented her with a place in their society, in which she succeeded the learned Helena Cornaro. Every other academy, in which women were admitted, became ambitious of enrolling her among their members; while her merit and reputation procured her from all ranks and orders of people the most flattering testimonies of esteem and admiration. From the prince of Paderborn, bishop of Munster, she received, with a medal, a present of his works. Christina, queen of Sweden, with whom she corresponded, sent her her picture, and settled on her a pension. Cardinal Mazarine left her by his will a handsome annuity; as did also the chancellor Boucherat; and Lewis XIV. at the solicitation of madame de Maintenon, in 1683, settled on her a pension of 2000 crowns, which was punctually paid. In a special audience, appointed by the monarch to receive her acknowledgments for this donation, he paid her many flattering compliments.

A curious accident befel this lady in a journey which she made with her brother. At a great distance from Paris, their conversation one evening, at an inn, turned upon a romance which they were then jointly composing, to the hero of which they had given the title of prince Mazare. 'What shall we do with prince Mazare?' said mademoiselle Scudery to her brother : ' is it not better that he should fall by poison, rather than by the poinard?' ' It is not time yet,' replied her companion, ' for that business; when it is necessary, we can dispatch him as we please; but at present we have not quite done with him!' Two merchants in the next chamber, overhearing this conversation, concluded they had formed a conspiracy for the murder of some prince, whose real name they disguised under that of Mazare. Full of this important discovery, they imparted their suspicions to the host and hostess, when it was unanimously determined to inform the police officer of what had happened. The officer, happy to shew his diligence and activity, put the travellers immediately under an arrest, and had them conducted, with a strong escort, to Paris.

MADELIENE DE SCUDERY. 391

It was not without difficulty and expence that they procured their liberation, and permission for the future to hold an unlimited right and power over all the princes and personages in the legends of fiction.

At Paris, the house of mademoiselle Scudery was the court of the muses, where all the talent and genius in the capital assembled. She died at the advanced age of ninety-four, 1701, of a rheumatic fever. Two churches contended for the honour of her remains, a point at length decided by the authority of the cardinal de Noailles, to whom the dispute was referred.

Her works were numerous: it is said by M. Coster, that she composed eighty volumes, an undoubted proof of great fertility of invention. She also acquired the first prize of eloquence in the academy of Paris. Her stories were generally founded on facts, disguised and intermingled with fiction. In her " Cyrus" is drawn the character of Louis de Bourbon, prince of Condé. In the romance of " Clelie," many circumstanees are related which occurred about that period in the court of France. Her narratives are tedious, and her descriptions prolix ; but the praise of ingenuity, of elevated sentiment, and of purifying and enno-

s 4

392   ANNE DE SEGUIER.

bling that species of writing, cannot be denied to her.

The Female Worthies, or Memoirs of the most illus-
trious Ladies of all Ages, Nations, &c.—Ann
Thicknesse's Sketch of the Lives and Writings, &c.

ANNE DE SEGUIER.

ANNE, daughter to Pierre Seguier (whose family gave to France so many illustrious magistrates), lord of Verriere, lieutenant-criminal au châtelet de Paris, married Francis du Prat, baron de Thiers, to whom she bore two daughters, Anne and Philipine, who were educated in the court of Henry III. Anne de Seguier inherited the talents of her family, and devoted her leisure to the cultivation of sacred poetry. Her poems are preceded by a prose dialogue between Virtue, Honour, Pleasure, Fortune, and Death. Her daughters emulated their mother in the cultivation of their minds, and were celebrated for their skill in the Greek and Latin languages, for their knowledge, and for their attainments in general literature.

Dictionnaire Historique, &c.—Ann Thicknesse's Sketch
of the Lives and Writings of the Ladies of France.

[393]

SEMIRAMIS.

THE account of the wonderful actions of Ninus and Semiramis, the period of whose existence and reign it would be difficult to determine, abounds in absurdity and contradiction. Semiramis, according to historians, was the wife of an officer, in the army of Ninus, king of Assyria, who, attracted by her beauty and artifices, married her, after the decease of her husband. Having gained over to her interest the principal men of the state, Semiramis, it is said, prevailed on Ninus to invest her with the sovereign power for five days. A decree was accordingly issued that, during this period, the nation should implicitly obey the commands of the queen. Semiramis began the exercise of the authority imprudently entrusted to her by causing her husband to be put to death, that she might secure to herself the sovereignty. This account is denied by some historians, but all are agreed that she succeeded Ninus in the empire; when, ambitious of immortalising her name, she built Babylon in one year, and employed two millions of men in accomplishing so stupendous and magnificent a work. Her statue was erected in the famous temple of Hierapolis, where divine honours were paid to her memory.

s 5

394   SEMIRAMIS.

Other writers are of opinion, that the preceding circumstances have, without any other foundation, been extracted from terms improperly
understood. Semiramis, according to these, signifies a people called Semarim, a title assumed
by the ancient Babylonians from Semarim, whose
badge, a dove (expressed Semramas), was used
as an object of worship, and considered to be the
same as Rhea, the mother of the gods. It was a
common mode with the ancients to call a tribe
or family by the name of its founder, and a nation by the head of the line. When the Ninevites performed a great action, it was ascribed to
Ninus, supposed founder of Ninevah. Thus, as
by Ninus the Ninevites are to be understood, so
by Semiramus is meant a people called Semarim.
In the history of those personages are recorded
the great actions of the two nations: historians
have thus been involved in difficulties and contradictions, by limiting to the life of individuals
an historical series of ages. All that is attributed
to Semiramus and Ninus was actually performed
by Semarim, and the Ninivites, who conquered
the Medes and Bactrians, and extended their dominions. These events, which took place ages
after the foundation of the kingdoms, began under Pul of Nineve, and were carried on by Assur,

SEMIRAMIS.   395

Adon, Salmanassar, Sennacherib, and others. Nineve was at last ruined, and the kingdom of Assyria was united to Babylon; an union alluded to
in the supposed marriage of Semiramis and Ninus.   It was then that Semarim accomplished the
works attributed to Ninus and Semiramis.   " Besides Babylon, which they built, there are," says
Strabo, " almost over the whole face of the
globe, vast mounds of earth *, walls, and ram-
parts, attributed to Ninus and Semiramis, in
which were subterraneous passages of communication, banks for water, and staircases of stone:
also vast canals to direct the course of rivers,
with lakes to receive them; likewise highways
and bridges of wonderful structure.   They built
the famous terraces at Babylon, and the beautiful gardens at Ecbatana: they discovered the art
of weaving cotton, an invention attributed to
those of their family who passed into Egypt.
The Samarim of Egypt and of Babylonia were of
the same family, sons of Chus, who came and
settled among the Mizraim, under the name of
shepherds."

By some historians, Semiramis is represented
as a woman and a princess, who reigned in Babylon; by others as a deity.   She was, says Athe-

---

* These were high altars, in which the people sacrificed
to the sun.

nagoras, esteemed the daughter of Dercetus, the same as the *Suria Dea, Rhea,* &c. Thus by many *Rhea, Isis, Astarte, Atargatus,* and *Semiramis,* are one and the same deity. We have the testimony of Lucian, that they were so accounted by the Syrians of Hierapolis, who regarded them as different symbols relating to the same object. Semiramis was said to have been changed into a dove, because she was under that form depicted and worshipped. Hence it appears that Semiramis was merely an emblem, the name compounded of Sama-Ramas, or Ramis, which signified *the divine token,* the type of providence; or as a military ensign, interpreted, with some latitude, *the standard of the Most High.* The emblem consisted of the figure of a dove, probably encircled with the Iris, which is frequently represented with the dove. All who went under the standard, or worshipped this emblem, were styled Semarim. The title of Samarim, or Semiramus, did not relate to one person, but to many, and was particularly assumed by princes. The Cuthites, settled about Cochin and Madura, in India, and the great kings of Calecut, were styled Samarim, even in later times, when the countries were visited by the English and Portuguese. It is reported of this ideal personage, that she was exposed among the rocks, preserved

MADAME SETURMAN.   397

by a shepherd, and afterwards married to Menon. She is also said to have constructed the first ship. Simma is a personage made out of Sema, or Sama, *the divine token*; Menon is the *deus Lunus*, under which type the ark was reverenced in many regions. The ark being the first ship constructed, with which the dove was connected, the merit of building it was given to Semiramis, a name which, according to Hesychius, and others, signified a wild pigeon.

The critical and ingenious reader will probably extract some degree of interest and amusement from the preceding curious research into antiquity.

Bayle's Historical Dictionary, &c. &c.

MADAME SETURMAN.

MADAME SETURMAN, a native of Cologne, excelled in the arts, and acquired great reputation. She was a painter, a musician, an engraver, a sculptor, a philosopher, a geometrician, and a theologian. She understood and spoke nine languages.

New Biographical Dictionary.

[398]

THE MARCHIONESS DE SEVIGNE.

MARIE DE RABUTIN, daughter and heiress of
the baron de Chantal, Bourbilli, &c. and of Mary
de Coulanges, his wife, was born February 5th,
1626. While yet in her infancy, she was deprived of her father, who was killed July 22d,
1627, at the descent of the English upon the isle
of Rhée, where he commanded a squadron of
gentlemen volunteers. This loss was supplied to
her by the cares and attentions of an affectionate
and sensible mother, and of her uncle, Christopher de Coulanges, who superintended her education, and implanted in her mind the purest
principles. She was early instructed in the Latin, Spanish, and Italian languages, and familiarised with the writings of the best authors. At
eighteen years of age, she married Henry, marquis de Sévigné, descended from one of the most
ancient houses of Brittany, to whom she bore a
son and a daughter. Tenderly attached to her
husband, whose disposition was gay and incon-
stant, she experienced many domestic sorrows,
which were aggravated by the untimely death of
the marquis, who fell in a duel with the chevalier d'Albret.

Thus left a widow in the bloom of her youth,
she determined against a second engagement, and

THE MARCHIONESS DE SEVIGNE. 399

devoted herself with exemplary attention to the duties of a mother. She was assisted in these cares by her uncle, a man of merit and talents, who attached himself through life to his neice, with whom he wholly resided, and who, on her part, repaid his kindness with the most grateful affection. The talents of madame de Sévigné, the propriety of her conduct, and the charms of her conversation, procured her the respect and esteem of the most distinguished persons of the age : her house was the resort of literature, and the temple of the muses. She is said to have decided the famous dispute between Perrault and Boileau, respecting the ancients and the moderns. ' The ancients,' said madame de Sévigné, ' are the finest, and we are the prettiest.'

Her children did credit to such a mother, who loved them with more than maternal tenderness : Charles, marquis de Sévigné, her son, was not less distinguished for his military talents, than for his engaging manners and elegant address: her daughter inherited the virtues and fine qualities of her mother. Mademoiselle de Sévigné married Francis de Castellane-Adhémar de Monteil, count de Grignan, lieutenant-general of the king's forces, and governor of Provence.

In giving her daughter to a nobleman of the court, madame de Sévigné flattered herself with

400   THE MARCHIONESS DE SEVIGNE.

the hope of passing the remainder of her life near this beloved child. This expectation was, however, frustrated: monsieur de Grignan received an order from the king to repair to his government, where, in the absence of the duke de Vendome, he was obliged to command. The separation was equally affecting to the mother and daughter, in whose intercourse the charm and tenderness of equal friendship had been substituted for the authority and reserve of the parental and filial characters. It is to this absence that the world is indebted for those charming letters, so generally and deservedly admired and celebrated. Madame de Sévigné made long and frequent visits to her daughter.

Her last journey into Provence, in 1695, was to be present at the marriage of her grandson, the marquis de Grignan, with mademoiselle de St. Amant. Of these nuptials some account is given in her letters. Soon after this event, a long and dangerous illness of madame de Grignan deeply affected her mother, whose inquietude, at a period of life so advanced, undermined her health, and brought on a fever; when, after a sickness of fourteen days, she expired, Aug. 6th, 1696, at the age of seventy, under the roof of madame de Grignan.

The enlightened mind and admirable talents

THE MARCHIONESS DE SEVIGNE. 401

of this amiable woman, proved insufficient to preserve her from the influence of superstition, and the contagion of the times.   She appears to have exulted in the extirpation of protestantism in Provence, by the power of her son-in-law, count de Gregnan; she even speaks with levity of the sufferings of the huguenots, *dragooned* into the bosom of *the true church*.   If in a mind of high cultivation, superior refinement, and exquisite sensibility, such is the effect of fanaticism, who shall calculate its ravages, marked as they have ever been with desolation and blood.

Madame de Sévigné left a valuable collection of letters, the best edition of which is that of 1754, at Paris, 8 vols. 12mo.

" These letters," says Voltaire, " filled with anecdotes, written with freedom, in an easy animated style, are an excellent criticism upon studied letters of wit, and still more upon those sublime fictitious letters, which aim to imitate the epistolary style by false sentiments, and a recital of feigned adventures to imaginary correspondents."   To this may be added, the testimony of two men of the first literary rank, by one * of whom madame de Sévigné is declared to merit a place among the most illustrious women of her

---

* See Bayle's Letters, p. 652. Rotterdam, 1714, 12mo.

402   LADY ARABELLA SEYMOUR.

time. The other * declares himself her most zealous admirer, and " that her letters are, in his opinion, master-pieces in that species of writing, not to be paralleled by either ancients or moderns." Tenderness and sensibility are the characteristic of these letters, in which the sentiment is expressed with equal delicacy and vivacity. " The true mark of a good heart," says madame de Sévigné, " is its capacity for loving."

Dictionnaire Historique—Biographium Fœmineum—Ann Thicknesse's Sketch of the Lives and Writings of the Ladies of France—Letters from the Marchioness de Sévigné to her Daughter.

LADY ARABELLA SEYMOUR.

ARABELLA, daughter of Charles Stuart, earl of Lenox (youngest brother of lord Darnley, who espoused Mary queen of Scots), was born in 1577. Her mother was the second daughter of sir William Cavendish, of Chatsworth, in the county of Derby, knt. The earl of Lenox died in his 29th year. Arabella, who had been his only child, was educated with extraordinary care : she possessed talents above the common order, and had a facility in poetical composition. Her papers are still preserved in the Harleian and

---

* The president Bouhier.

LADY ARABELLA SEYMOUR. 463

Longbeat libraries. Her affinity to the crown involved her in perpetual misfortunes. It appears, from a passage in Mr. Ogleby's Negociations in Spain, in 1596, that she was under restraint during the latter period of the reign of Elizabeth. He observes, that the queen of England refused to deliver her up to the king of Scots, who purposed marrying her to the duke of Lenox, in Scotland, with an intention, having at that time no issue, of making the duke his heir and successor. The pope also formed a design of raising her to the throne of England, by espousing her to cardinal Farnese, brother to the duke of Parma. This project seems to have been favoured by Henry IV. of France, from an apprehension lest England, when united to Scotland, under the same monarch, should become too powerful. Soon after the accession of James, a conspiracy was entered into by some English lords, through jealousy of the Scots, to kill the king, and bestow the crown on Arabella. This transaction, which was discovered and the conspirators punished, appears to have occasioned the confinement of Arabella to her own house, and to have ultimately proved destructive both to her health and fortunes. She was, however, restored to favour, and received from the king, as a new-year's gift, a service of plate, worth 200l.

and a thousand marks to pay her debts, with a
yearly addition to her income. She was soon
after, without the consent of James, privately
married to Mr. William Seymour, second son to
the earl of Hertford, afterwards earl and marquis
of Hertford, and at length restored to the duke-
dom of Somerset. On the secret of their marriage being divulged, they were both committed
to the Tower. After the imprisonment of a year,
they contrived, though under the charge of different keepers, to escape at the same time. The
court was on the intelligence seized with an
alarm, and a proclamation was issued for their
apprehension. Arabella had escaped in man's
apparel, from a house near Highgate, whence
she was to have been sent the next day to Durham. Having arrived at Blackwall, about six in
the evening, a boat was prepared ready to receive her, and another filled with baggage for
herself and her husband. They rowed first to
Woolwich, and then proceeded to Gravesend.
At the dawn of day they had reached Lee, when
they discovered at anchor, a mile beyond them,
a French barge, which waited their coming.
Here the lady Arabella was desirous of waiting
for her husband; but, through the importunity
of her companions, was induced to go on. Mr.
Seymour, by this circumstance, missed the vessel

LADIES SEYMOUR.   405

A pinnace was, in the mean time, dispatched by government in pursuit of the fugitives. The barge, lingering in expectation of Seymour, was overtaken, and, after enduring thirteen shot from the pinnace, compelled to strike. Arabella, who was brought back to the Tower, rejoiced in the midst of her distress at the probable escape of her husband. The remainder of her life was spent in close and melancholy confinement, which at length deprived her of reason. Death, after a period of four years, put an end to her sorrow. She expired, not without suspicion of poison, Sept. 27th, 1615, and was interred with Mary queen of Scots, in Henry VIIth's chapel.

Ballard's British Ladies—History of England, &c.

LADIES ANNE, MARGARET, AND JANE SEYMOUR.

THESE ladies, sisters, were celebrated for their learning in the sixteenth century. They composed four hundred Latin distichs on the death of the queen of Navarre, Margaret de Valois, sister to Francis I. These verses were soon after translated into Greek, French, and Italian, and printed at Paris in 1551, under the title of " Tombeau de Marguerite de Valois, Reine de Navarre." Nicholas Denisot, preceptor to the learned sisters,

made a collection, containing a translation of the
distichs, with other verses on the same subject,
and also in honour of the fair writers, which he
dedicated to Margaret de Valois, duchess of
Berri, sister of Henry II. The distichs are
called by Ronsard, who celebrates the sisters, " a
christian song." They are said by Bayle to contain more pious and moral reflections than poetical images : yet it is affirmed by Ronsard,
with poetical licence, that, had Orpheus heard
them, he would have been ambitious to become
the scholar of their authors.—

> " If that harper so renown'd,
>   Could these charming Syrens hear
> From the shores of Albion sound,
>   Wonder would perplex his ear,
> He would break his pagan lyre, &c."

These sisters are also celebrated by Nicholas de
Henerai, sieur des Essars, who translated into
French the Amadis de Gaule. By the authority
of Mr. Fulman* we are informed, that these ladies
were the daughters of Edward Seymour, duke of
Somerset and uncle to Edward VI. by Anne his
second wife, daughter of sir Edward Stanhope :
six daughters had been the fruit of this marriage,
who all received a learned education. Anne, the
eldest, was first married to John Dudley, earl of

---

* XV. vol. MS. collections in the archives of Corp. Chr. college.

Warwick; and, after his death, to sir Edward
Unton, knight of the bath. It appears, from a
letter in her own hand, that she was living towards the latter end of the reign of Elizabeth.
Margaret died unmarried, though addressed by
the lord Strange, in the year 1551, as is proved
by a letter dated July, from the king and council
to the earl of Derby, the father of lord Strange,
signifying his majesty's satisfaction in the intended nuptials. The misfortunes and disgrace which
soon after befel the duke probably prevented the
marriage. Jane also, whom her father aspired
to unite to Edward VI. died unmarried, March
19th, 1560, in the twentieth year of her age. She
was maid of honour to Elizabeth, and high in her
favour. She was interred, with great solemnity,
in St. Edmund's chapel, in Westminster. On the
east side of the chapel is a plain monument, containing little more than an enumeration of the
titles and dignities of the family. A copy of
Latin verses, in commendation of lady Jane Somerset, composed by Dr. Haddon, are preserved
by Mr. Camden, of which the following is a translation:

" For genius fam'd, for beauty lov'd,
    Jane bade the world admire:
Her voice harmonious notes improv'd,
    Her hand the tuneful lyre.

Venus and Pallas claim'd this maid,
  Each as her right alone ;
But death superior power display'd,
  And seiz'd her as his own.

Her virgin dust this mournful tomb
  Its kindred earth contains ;
Her soul, which fate can ne'er consume,
  In endless glory reigns."

Bayle's Historical Dictionary—Biographium Fæmineum.
—Ballard's British Ladies, &c.

CATHERINE SFORZA.

CATHERINE, grand-daughter of Francis Sforza, duke of Milan, and natural daughter of Galeazzo Maria Sforza, is renowned for her courage and great qualities. She espoused Jerom Riario, lord of Forli and of Imola, the lordship of which she brought to her husband as a dowry, her father having possessed himself of it by taking advantage of the dissensions between Tadeo Manfredi, lord of Imola, and his son, in 1472. Several children were the fruit of these nuptials, among whom Octavio Riario inherited the estates of his parents, which he held of the see of Rome. Catherine, left a widow at two-and-twenty years of age, with an infant son, held, during his minority, the reins of government with equal vigour and address. In the tumults occasioned by the expedi-

CATHARINE SFORZA. 409

tion of the French into Italy, 1494, Catherine neglected not to advance the interests of her states.
Forli was, in the year 1500, besieged by the duke
of Valentenois, son of Alexander VI. Catherine,
with great intrepidity, defended the fortress, but,
unable to resist the superior force of the enemy,
she was at length compelled to surrender, made
prisoner, and sent to Rome, where she was confined in the castle of Angelo.

She was soon after liberated, at the intercession
of Ives d'Allegre, and privately married to John
de Medicis, on whose account she performed great
services to the Florentines, and to Ludovic Sforza,
duke of Milan, a friend of the Medici family.
She is commended by Varillas, a French historian,
for her talents, her courage, her policy, her
beauty, and the military powers she displayed
during the siege of Forli. Her estates, taken by
the duke of Valentenois, were never recovered,
but, after the death of Alexander VI. were reunit-
ed to the holy see.

Bayle's Historical Dictionary, &c.

[410]

ISABELLA SFORZA.

ISABELLA SFORZA, who deserves a place in the catalogue of learned women, lived in the sixteenth century. Some of her letters are inserted in a collection published at Venice, by Hortensio Lando, 1549. Among these is a letter of consolation, written to Bonna Sforza, widow of the king of Poland, lately deceased. Also one to Margaret Bobbia, in vindication of poetry. This collection of letters is referred to by Christofano Bronzini, in a dialogue, in which one of the speakers is represented as denying the capacity of women to put together in writing two words (*i. e.* sentences more probably was meant by this man of straw). His adversary, in reply, quotes the collection of female letters, published by Hortensio Lando, the propriety, ingenuity, elegance, and elocution of which he praises, distinguishing more particularly those of Isabella Sforza.

Bayle's Historical Dictionary.

[**411**]

FRANCES SHERIDAN.

In the family of this lady, wit and genius appear to be hereditary. Frances, descended from an English family, and grand-daughter of sir Oliver Chamberlaine, was born in Ireland, in 1724. During the disputes relative to the theatre, in which Mr. Thomas Sheridan (son of Dr. Thomas Sheridan, the friend and biographer of Swift) had embarked his fortune, Miss Chamberlaine distinguished herself by a small pamphlet, which excited the attention of the public, and the curiosity of Mr. Sheridan to be introduced to his fair champion. An attachment afterwards took place, which terminated in a matrimonial engagement. Mrs. Sheridan, with superior talents and engaging manners, was exemplary in every relative duty. Her admirable Domestic Tale of Sydney Biddulph is well known, and justly esteemed by the public. She was also the author of a small romance, entitled Nourjahad, which possesses considerable merit. She likewise wrote two comedies, " The Discovery," cr. 8vo. 1763; and " The Dupe," cr. 8vo. 1765. After lingering some years in ill health, she died at Blois, in the south of France, 1767.

New Biographical Dictionary.

T 2

[412]

SOPHRONIA.

SOPHRONIA, a name given to the lady of a Roman governor, commended by Eusebius, and other
writers, for her courage and chastity. The tyrant,
Maxentius, was in the habit of sending his soldiers
into the houses of his subjects, to bring forcibly to
him the wives or daughters of the citizens, whose
beauty or accomplishments had captivated his licentious fancy. A permission having been extorted
from the husband of Sophronia, the soldiers brought
to her the royal summons. Under pretence of
adorning her person to appear before the emperor,
Sophronia was permitted to retire alone to her
chamber, where she plunged a sword into her bosom; justly preferring death to submitting to the
brutal lust of a despot.

The Female Worthies, &c.

SULPICIA.

SULPICIA, or SULPITIA, a Roman lady, daughter of Sulpicius Parterculus, and wife to Fulvius
Flaccus, is celebrated for the purity of her manners.
Great dissoluteness having prevailed among the
women of Rome, the books of the sybils were consulted for a remedy to these disorders, when, from

COUNTESS OF SUNDERLAND.   413

the report made by those appointed to the office, it was decreed by the senate, that a statue should be erected to *Venus Verticordia*, or the converter of hearts, and that the most virtuous of the Roman ladies should consecrate the statue of the goddess. For this purpose, an hundred women were first selected; from this number ten were chosen, all of whom were unanimous in appointing Sulpicia for the sacred office. This event took place in the year 639 of Rome. It does not appear that the honour conferred upon Sulpicia proved efficacious in the reform of female manners. A temporary incitement to laudable ambition was quickly overpowered in the luxury and corruption of the times, which continued to increase, till Julius Cæsar, in a revolution of the state, made himself master of the commonwealth. The moral and political barometer of nations will ever rise and fall in exact proportions.

Bayle's Historical Dictionary—Biographium Fæmineum.

DOROTHY,
COUNTESS OF SUNDERLAND.

DOROTHY, daughter of Robert Sidney, earl of Leicester, married Henry lord Spencer, of Wormleighton, during his minority. On the 8th of June, 1643, he was created earl of Sunderland; and, in the same year, killed at the first battle of Newbury,

in the twenty-third year of his age.   His widow afterwards gave her hand to Robert Smythe, esq. of
the Bounds, in the parish of Bidborough, in Kent,
whom she also survived.   One son was the fruit of
her second marriage, Robert Smythe, governor of
Dover castle in the reign of Charles II.   This lady
was the sacharissa of Waller : she was an amiable
woman, and fond of retirement.   Having met Waller one day, when she was far advanced in life, she
asked him ' when he would write such fine verses
upon her again ?'   ' When your ladyship,' he replied, ' is as young again.'   She survived her husband forty years, and was buried with him, in the
same vault, at Brington, in Northamptonshire, Feb.
25, 1683-4.

            Granger's Biographical History of England.

THE COUNTESS DE LA SUZE.

Born in Paris, 1618, daughter of the count de
Coligni, a marshal of France, and grand-daughter
of the famous admiral Coligni, this lady was first
married to Thomas Hamilton, a Scotch nobleman,
and after his decease to the count de la Suze, with
whom she led a wretched life.   His unhappy temper, and extreme jealousy, induced him to seclude
from society a woman who was formed to be its
delight and ornament.   Shut up in a country-house,
at a great distance from the capital, the countess,

impatient of constraint, determined, as a means of eluding the tyranny of her husband (who professed the huguenot faith), to abjure her religion, and take shelter in the catholic church. It was on this occasion said by Christina of Sweden, that Henriette de la Suze changed her religion, that she might escape the society of her husband both in this world and the next.

This schism for a time appearing to aggravate the misery of her situation, she solicited a divorce, and, to procure the consent of the count, offered him 25000 crowns. The terms were accepted, and the marriage dissolved by the parliament. In consequence of this event the pecuniary affairs of the countess became involved in embarrassment, an evil light in comparison with those she had escaped, and to which she submitted with fortitude. On this subject a whimsical anecdote is related. One morning, at eight o'clock, an execution was brought into her house. Being informed by her woman of this circumstance, she desired to speak with the officer. Having not yet risen, the man was introduced into her bed-chamber. ‘ Sir,’ said she, ‘ I have had very little sleep the past night, and I must entreat your patience an hour or two longer.’ ‘ Certainly, madam,’ replied the officer, politely, and immediately withdrew. The countess then

416   COUNTESS DE LA SUZE.

composed herself to sleep, and awoke not till ten o'clock, when she arose and dressed to fulfil an engagement to dinner. She thanked the officer for his civility, as she passed out of her apartment, and, tranquilly hastening to her appointment, left him master of the house.

Having a suit at law with madame de Châtillon, madame de la Suze pleaded her cause before the parliament of Paris. These two ladies meeting one day in the court, monsieur de la Feuillade, who accompanied the former, thus addressed the latter, who was escorted by Benserude and several other poets of reputation, ' You, madam, have rhyme on your side, and we have reason.' ' It cannot be said, then,' replied the countess, with an air of contempt, ' that we plead without rhyme or reason.'

Madame de la Suze, unfortunate in her domestic connections, became melancholy and attached to solitude. She indulged her feelings in plaintive and elegiac effusions, full of tenderness and passion. Her thoughts are said to have been just and elevated, and her language poetical, but her rhymes inharmonious. Her songs, madrigals, and odes, were inferior to her elegies, which abounded in delicate and fine turns of sentiment. Her poems are printed in a collection in four vols. 12mo. with those of Pelisson and madame de Scudery. She died at Paris, esteemed and lamented, in 1673.

MARY SYDNEY.   417

She was the subject of many eulogiums. Madamoiselle de Scudery, in her romance of Clelia, thus describes her: " Hesiode, sleeping upon Parnassus, sees the muses in a dream, who shew to him the poets in their order of succession. ' Behold,' says Calliope, speaking of the countess de la Suze, ' behold a woman who, with the form of Pallas, the beauty, the softness, the expression, and the air of Venus, possesses yet more wit than beauty, though adorned by a thousand charms.' " Charleval, one of the most celebrated wits of his age, addressed to madame de la Suze a copy of verses, in which he highly extols her genius, and compares her to Sappho.

Biographuim Fœmineum—The Female Worthies, &c.—Ann Thicknesse's Sketch of the Lives and Writings of the Ladies of France—Dictionnaire Historique des Femmes Célébres.

MARY SYDNEY,
COUNTESS OF PEMBROKE.

MARY, daughter of sir Henry Sydney, knight of the Garter, lord deputy of Ireland, and lord president of Wales, and of his wife the lady Mary, eldest daughter of John duke of Northumberland, was born about the middle of the sixteenth century, and lived during the reigns of Elizabeth and of James. Sir Philip Sydney, the celebrated author of the

418 MARY SYDNEY.

Arcadia, was brother to this lady, who, in 1576, married Henry earl of Pembroke. Three children were the fruit of this marriage ; William, who succeeded to the titles and estates of his father, and from whom the present family is descended ; Philip and Anne, who died young. These nuptials were projected by Robert Dudley, earl of Leicester, uncle to the countess, whose fortune, on this occasion, he increased.

The countess of Pembroke had received a liberal education, and was distinguished among the literary characters of the age for a highly cultivated mind and superior talents. Congenial qualities and pursuits united her with her brother, sir Philip Sydney, in bonds of strict friendship. Sir Philip dedicated to his beloved sister his Arcadia, under the title of " The Countess of Pembroke's Arcadia." To her also Mr. Abraham Fraunce devoted his poetic and literary labours. The countess possessed a talent for poetical composition, which she assiduously cultivated. She translated from the Hebrew into English verse many of the Psalms, which, bound in velvet, are said to be preserved in the library at Wilton. She is represented in her picture holding in her hand a book of Psalms. She also translated and published " A Discourse of Life and Death, written in French by Philip Morney, done into English by the Countess of Pembroke, dated May 13, 1590,

MARY SYDNEY. **419**

Wilton: printed at London for William Ponsonby, 1600, 12mo." Likewise, " The Tragedie of Antonie: done into English by the Countess of Pembroke, 12mo. London, 1595." This little work contains, though not paged, fifty-four leaves. She loved learning, and was a patroness of letters. Dr. Mouffet was allowed by her a yearly pension: her liberality and her taste for letters are also spoken of by Mr. Giles Jacob.

She survived her husband twenty years, and, having lived to an advanced age, died at her house in Aldersgate-street, London, Sept. 25, 1602. She was interred with the Pembroke family, in the chancel of the cathedral at Salisbury, without any monument. The following lines, designed as an inscription for her tomb, were written by the celebrated Ben Johnson:

" Underneath this sable herse,
Lies the subject of all verse ;
Sydney's sister, Pembroke's mother ;
Death, ere thou hast kill'd another,
Fair, and learn'd, and good as she,
Time shall throw a dart at thee.
Marble piles let no man raise
To her name, for after-daies
Some kind woman, born as she,
Reading this, like Niobe,
Shall turn marble, and become
Both her mourner, and her tomb."

420 **MARY SYDNEY.**

Sir Francis Osborn, in his Memoirs of the Reign of James, thus speaks of the countess of Pembroke: " She was that sister of sir Philip Sydney to whom he addiessed his Arcadia, and of whom he had no other advantage than what he received from the partial benevolence of fortune (i. e. *nature*) in making him a man, which yet she did, in some judgments, recompence in beauty, her pen being nothing short of his, as I am ready to attest, so far as so inferior a reason may be taken, having seen incomparable letters of hers. But lest I should seem to trespass upon truth, which few do unsuborned (as I protest I am, unless by her rhetoric), I shall leave the world her epitaph, in which the author doth manifest himself a poet, in all things but untruth."

Wood * ascribes to sir Philip Sydney the translation of the Psalms, which he says are in manuscript in the library of the earl of Pembroke, at Wilton, bound in crimson velvet, and left by the countess; some Psalms by whom are however printed in Mr. Hartington's Nugæ Antiquæ, 3 vols. 12mo.

Ballard's British Ladies—Biographium Fœmineum, &c.

---

* Athen. Oxon. vol. I. p. 184.

[421]

TANAQUIL.

TANAQUIL, wife to Tarquinius Priscus, king of Rome, was born at Tarquinii, in Tuscany. She married Lucumon, whose father being expelled from Corinth, his native city, fled to Tarquinii: his wealth, which was confiderable, was inherited by his son. Lucumon, who, in espousing Tanaquil, became allied to the noblest families in Tarquinii, flattered himself with being raised to the first dignities of the city: this ambition was defeated by his birth and foreign extraction. Tanaquil, humiliated by losing her rank, and incensed at the indignities suffered by her husband, determined to quit her native city, and to seek a place where she would be less subjected to mortification. She pressed her husband to go to Rome, where, without respect to adventitious circumstances, preferment waited on merit. Lucumon listened to her representations, and consented to her wishes.

A presage of good fortune is said to have attended them on their journey. As they arrived at mount Janiculus, before they entered Rome, an eagle gently alighted upon their chariot, and, taking off the cap of Lucumon, hovered for some time over the carriage: at length, with a loud outcry, he restored the cap to the head of its master, and took his flight. Tanaquil, embracing her husband, congratulated him on this incident, which she assured him forboded great fortune. Elated with hope, they entered Rome, where Lucumon assumed the name of Tarquinius. Having gained the esteem of the Romans, he insinuated himself into the favour of the king, who advanced him to the highest offices. He at length aspired to the throne, and succeeded in his ambition: he reigned thirty-seven years, and in the thirty-eighth was assassinated in his palace.

Tanaquil suffered not herself to be overwhelmed by this blow, however severe: by her address and influence she secured the succession to her son-in-law, Servius Tullius, whose elevation she had before predicted. Servius Tullius was born and educated in the palace of the king. A flame, according to the legend, was seen one day hovering over his head as he slept: the attendants, alarmed, were about to extinguish it, but Tanaquil prevented them, and, taking her husband aside, told him that this child would one day support the royal family in their adversity, and that care ought to be taken of his education. When the infant awoke, the flame disappeared. The advice of Tanaquil was followed; Servius received a princely education, and espoused the daughter of his benefactor. The father of the prince, it is believed, was Servius Tullius, who was slain in defending his principality of Corniculum, a

TANAQUIL.   423

town of Italy, besieged and taken by Tarquinius. His mother, who was taken captive in a state of pregnancy, gave birth to a son in the palace of Tarquinius, to whom the youth succeeded.

The memory of Tanaquil, whose history is thus mingled with fable, was long held in veneration at Rome, where the work of her hands was sacredly preserved. Varro, a contemporary with Cicero, assures us, that he had seen, in the temple of Sangus, the distaff-spindle of Tanaquil, with the wool with which she had been spinning: also, that a royal robe which she had wrought, and which was worn by Servius Tullius, was preserved in the temple of Fortune. Pliny adds, that, on this account, young women were, at their nuptials, followed by a person bearing the distaff and spindle with wool and yarn. He affirms likewise, that Tanaquil was the first who wove the garments which were given to the youth of Rome when they attained the age of manhood, and to the maidens on their espousals.

Though illustrious as a queen and as a politician, Tanaquil, as these emblems seem to imply, neglected not the humbler duties of domestic life. Great virtues were ascribed to her girdle. The Romans had a tradition, that Tanaquil having made important discoveries in medicine, had enclosed or incorporated with her girdle certain drugs or remedies, which the sick were solicitous to procure. This girdle was placed around her statue in the temple of San-cus, a Roman deity known by the name of *Dius Fidius*. Tarquinius, or Tarquin, was less known to fame than his wife, by whom it appears he ac-quired the regal dignity. " The admirable virtues of that queen," says St. Jerom, " are too deeply impressed upon the memory of all ages ever to be forgotten." If some satirists (as Juvenal) have ridiculed Tarquin for the ascendancy which his wife possessed over his mind, it should be remembered, that to this ascendancy he was indebted for his good fortune.

Bayle's Historical Dictionary—Biographium Fæmineum.

TELESILIA,

A noble poetess of Argos, who being advised by the oracle (which she consulted respecting her health) to the study of the muses*, attained in a short time such excellence, as to animate, by the power of her verse, the Argive women to repel, under her con-duct, Cleomenes the Spartan king, and afterwards king Demaratus, from the siege of Pamphiliacum, with great loss.

---

* This prescription properly intimates, that by the acti-vity of the mind the body is invigorated.

[425]

THEANO.

A TRIPLE name of considerable celebrity. The first of this name was Theano Locrencis, a native of the city of Locri, and surnamed Melica, from the melody of her songs and lyric poems. The secoud was a poetess of Crete, said by some historians to have been the wife of Pythagoras. The third, Theano Thuria, or Metapotino, the wife of Carystius, or, according to others, of Brantinus of Cretona, and daughter of the poet Lycophron. The three are mentioned by Suidas. There are three epistles by Theano (but which of the Theanos is not determined) published, with the epistles of several ancient Greek authors, at Venice, by Aldus.

MRS. THOMAS.

THE life of Mrs Thomas, known to the public by the poetical name of Corinna, affords an interesting picture, and displays a tissue of calamities that can scarcely fail to excite the sympathy and commiseration of the reader. Born in 1675, she seems to have inherited from her father, who was far advanced in life, and whose health had been long infirm, an unhappy constitution, rendered yet more delicate and feeble by the injudicious tenderness with

MRS. THOMAS.

which she was nurtured. From her infancy she was afflicted with fevers and defluxions; but, with these physical disadvantages, she possessed a gay and lively temper, and gave early promise of a vigorous intellect. Before she had completed her second year, the death of her father, of whose circumstances his family, from his expensive manner of living, had formed an erroneous calculation, involved them in embarrassment and distress. Her mother had, at the age of eighteen, from motives of ambition and avarice, sacrificed her youth and beauty to infirmity and age: but on the decease of her husband, it was not without difficulty that she was enabled to defray the expences of an ostentatious funeral. Having, in this reverse of her situation, disposed of her house in town, and another in Essex, she prudently retired, with her infant daughter, and the small remnant of her effects, into economical lodgings in the country.

In this situation she unfortunately formed an acquaintance with a pretender to alchymy, by whom, under the pretence of preparing an apparatus for the discovery of the philosopher's stone, or the art of transmuting metals into gold, she suffered herself to be defrauded of three hundred pounds. In the moment of the expected projection, the works were blown up, and the golden dreams of the credulous widow rudely dissipated.

The projector had, in the intervals of his labour,

MRS. THOMAS.   427

officiated as tutor to the young Corinna, whom he instructed in the rudiments of Latin, arithmetic, and the mathematics, for which she discovered a particular predilection. The widow was for some time so much affected by the dissolution of her emperical visions, added to her loss and mortification, that she suffered her health to be impaired by the indulgence of her grief: time, at length, softening the keen sense of her folly, she determined to make those exertions for herself and her child which were become more than ever necessary. Having made application to the friends and clients of her late husband, and received a promise of their services, she took a house in Bloomsbury, where, by economy and a genteel appearance, she concealed the state of her finances.

Being one day visited by the duke of Montague, he advised her to let a part of her house. She appeared not averse to this idea, but objected to receiving ordinary lodgers, for which she conceived her former habits had unfitted her: yet she intimated, that she should not object to accommodating a respectable family. The duke offered to become himself her tenant. ' Be assured,' said he, observing her smile incredulously, ' I am serious. I want more freedom than my rank will allow me at home; I could wish occasionally to come here unrestrained, with some honest fellows of my acquaintance, whose society I love, and eat a bit of mutton.' The arrangement, under which the duke concealed deeper views, was immediately concluded upon: it was agreed that her noble lodger should pass at Bloomsbury for a Mr. Freeman, of Hertfordshire.

In a few days a dinner was ordered for himself and his friends, under the familiar appellations of Jack and Tom, Will and Ned, plain honest country gentlemen. At the time appointed the widow was introduced, not without surprise, to the duke of Devonshire, lords Buckingham and Dorset, a viscount and his son, William Dutton Colt. Several meetings had taken place, when the hostess was informed by her noble guest, who had conceived a high and just opinion of her integrity, that the subject of these conferences was a projected revolution in the state. This event being at length effected, the rendezvous was broken up, and the widow, on parting with her guests, received a promise of obtaining either a pension, or a place in the household, as a recompence of her zeal and services, and a compensation for the loss of the shattered wreck of her fortune by the closing of the Exchequer.

The dreams of the alchymist, and the courtiers' promises, proved alike illusive: in the change of measures and circumstances the widow was quickly forgotten. The duke of Montague, it is true, continued to make flattering professions of service; and

MRS. THOMAS.   429

when his late hostess solicited him, as captain of the band of pensioners, to bestow a post on a Mr. Gwynnet, a young gentleman who had long addressed her daughter, actually assented to her request, on condition that the bride elect should apply to him in person.   The guileless mother overwhelmed her generous benefactor with grateful acknowledgments, and instantly hastened to inform her daughter of their flattering prospects, when, to her extreme surprise, she received from Corinna, who had been accustomed to yield to her commands an implicit obedience, a peremptory refusal to avail herself of the bounty of the noble duke.   Compelled at length to explain the motives for a conduct so unreasonable and extraordinary, the young lady confessed that his grace had, as a recompence for the hospitality and fidelity he had uniformly experienced under their roof, attempted to allure her from the paths of chastity. To this she added, that in the condition he had annexed to his services to her lover, she had but too just cause to fear a renewal of his dishonourable purposes.   The feelings of a mother upon such an occasion require no description : equally unnecessary is it to comment upon the *generous* conduct of the courtier.

The mind of Corinna had been highly cultivated by a perusal of the best authors, while, as her taste refined, her sentiments became delicate and elevated,

and her character strongly tinctured with those virtues which

"The sons of interest deem romance."

Their circumstances becoming daily more perplexed and involved, she remonstrated with her lover
on the inequality of their fortunes and prospects,
and the imprudence of the connection which he
solicited. The attachment of Mr. Gwynnet, who
was already in a great degree independent of his
family, was increased by the delicacy and disinterestedness of his mistress ; nor was it long before he
gained the consent of his father to an union in which
his happiness was so deeply involved. With this
sanction he returned to London, to claim the reward
of his affection and fidelity.

Mrs. Thomas being at this time in an infirm state
of health, her amiable daughter refused, in her own
better prospects, to abandon her mother to the care
of strangers. She replied to the solicitations of her
lover, that as she had not thought sixteen years too
long a period to wait for him, she hoped he would
not consider six months as tedious, in expectation of
receiving, at the end of that time, the recompence
of his generous constancy. ' Six months at present,
my Corinna,' he replied, with a sigh, ' are more
than the sixteen years that are passed—you now
defer our union, and God will put it off for ever.'
His words were prophetic. The next day he re-

turned into the country and made his will, by which he bequeathed to Corinna six hundred pounds: he sickened shortly after, and expired April 16th, 1711. To express the feelings of his mistress on this event language is inadequate :—' Sorrow,' said she, ' has been my portion ever since.'

The deed of conveyance, by which the father of Mr. Gwynnet had empowered his son to dispose of his effects, with the will which he had in consequence made, were suppressed by his brother.   Corinna was impelled to seek a legal resource.   Her adversary, not satisfied with the injury he had already done her in defrauding her of her right, added baseness to injustice, endeavouring, by the vilest means, to suborn persons to blast the character of the innocent victim of his rapacity ; but, in this instance, to the credit of human nature be it spoken, he could find no agent, or probably his bribes were not sufficiently high, to aid his barbarous and atrocious purpose.

Corinna, from respect to the memory of her deceased lover, offered terms of accommodation, and, on condition of receiving two hundred pounds immediately, and two hundred more at the end of the year, consented to relinquish the remainder of her claim.   The first payment was accordingly made, which she instantly divided among the creditors of her mother.   When the second payment became due, Mr. G. bid her defiance, and stood a suit on his own bond, which was carried on through four terms, from court to court, and at length brought to the bar of the house of lords. Here Gwynnet, aware of the infamy which awaited him, thought proper to stop and pay the money before the cause was brought to a hearing. Corinna had, in the course of the suit, been obliged to sign an instrument to empower the lawyers to receive the money, and pay themselves the costs. The consequences may be foreseen: thirteen pounds sixteen shillings was the residue which these conscientious gentlemen, who sell justice very dear, paid into her hands.

Reduced by this event to the necessity of retiring from her creditors to obscurity and want, she was betrayed by a pretended friend, and thrown into prison. But the measure of her misfortunes was not yet filled up. In April, 1711, she accidentally swallowed, while speaking hastily, the middle bone of the wing of a fowl, which being of a large size, the bone was more than three inches in length. For the first few days she felt no inconvenience from this accident; at length she became sensible to a weight and oppression at her stomach, and was seized with a dysentery, attended with violent and constant pain, fainting fits and convulsions, which were followed by a malignant fever. For two years these deplorable sufferings continued to harass her without

MRS. THOMAS. 433

intermission, and baffled the skill of the faculty. She was at length ordered to Bath, where she experienced a temporary relief, and where she continued for some years in a state of comparative health and ease, though involved by an unjust executor in an eight-years' suit of law.

Deprived from repeated acts of cruelty and injustice of the means of support, she suffered a close imprisonment, in want even of the necessaries of life, and for two years was obliged to lie on the boards. During this period she experienced no inconvenience from the bone she had swallowed. But on recovering her liberty, and beginning to take the exercise of which she had been so long deprived, her stomach and head began to swell, and rapidly increased to an alarming size. After having tried in vain the efficacy of medicine, her case was pronounced to be an incurable dropsy. Nature, at this crisis, unexpectedly relieved itself; in twelve hours she voided or threw up about five gallons of water, and for some days experienced a considerable mitigation of her sufferings, but the water gathering again, she was afflicted with a perpetual hectic and sense of suffocation.

These successive and cruel calamities did not shield her from the petulance of vanity and the shafts of malignity. Mr. Pope had once paid her a visit, in company with Henry Cromwel, esq. whose let-

ters, with some of Mr. Pope's, afterwards fell accidentally into her hands. On the death of Henry
Cromwel, Curl, the bookseller, found means to
get from her these letters, which he immediately
committed to the press. The enraged wit avenged
himself of this injury, magnified by self-love into an
enormous crime, by placing Corinna in ludicrous
circumstances in the Dunciad.

After her liberation from confinement, Mrs.
Thomas resided in a small and humble lodging in
Fleet-street, where she died, February, 1730, in
the fifty-sixth year of her age. She was interred
in the church of St. Bride's.

Her productions, though not entitled to rank in
a high class of poetical compositions, possess softness and delicacy. They were published after her
death by Mr. Curl, with two volumes of letters
which passed between her and Mr. Gwynnet.

Biographium Fæmineum, &c.

THYMELE.

A MUSICAL composer, and a poetess, mentioned
by Martial, and reputed to have been the first who introduced into the scene a kind of dance, called by the
Greeks, from this circumstance, Themelinos. From
Thymele also, an altar, used in the ancient theatres,
is supposed to have taken its name.

[435]

CATHERINE TISHEM.

THIS lady, who about the middle of the sixteenth century married Gualtherus Gruter, a burgomaster of Antwerp, to whom she bore a son, James Gruter, celebrated for his erudition and his voluminous productions, is said to have been an Englishwoman. Being persecuted, on the account of her religion, by the duchess of Parma, governess of the Netherlands, she took refuge in England, with her son, in 1565. It is observed to her honour, by Balthasor Venator, that she was her son's chief instructor ; and it is certain that she bore the character of one of the most learned women of the age. She was acquainted both with the ancient and modern languages, and read Galen in Greek, which few physicians were then able to do. She also superintended the studies of her son during his residence at Cambridge, whence he went to Leyden in 1579.

Biographium Fæmineum.

ELIZABETH TOLLET.

ELIZABETH, daughter of George Tollet, esq. commissioner of the navy in the reigns of William and of Anne, was born in 1694. Her talents were assiduously cultivated by her father, under whose

U 2

436   ELIZABETH TOLLET.

superintendance she received every advantage of
education. She spoke fluently and correctly the
Latin, Italian, and French languages , she was conversant in history, cultivated poetry, and studied the
mathematics. She had great taste and skill in music,
and excelled in drawing and designing. She was
exemplary in her conduct and in the relative duties of
life. The former periods of her life were passed in
the Tower, where her father had a house ; the latter
at Stratford and Westham. She died February 1st,
1754, and was buried at Westham. In 1755 a volume of her poems was printed, among which appeared a musical drama, entitled " Susanna, or
Innocence Preserved." She was favoured with the
friendship of sir Isaac Newton, who was much
pleased with some of her first essays. Several of
her poems are on philosophical subjects, and display
profound thinking. Her Latin poems are said to be
written with classical taste. She would not suffer
her productions to appear till after her decease. Her
estate, which was considerable, she left to her
youngest nephew. Her eldest nephew, George
Tollet, of Betley in Staffordshire (previously of
Lincoln's Inn), was known as the author of Notes
on Shakspeare. He died October 21, 1779.

[437]

TYMICHA,

A Lacedæmonian lady, who became the wife of Myllias, a native of Crotone. She is placed by Jamblicus, in his Life of Pythagoras, first in the list of female Pythagoreans. When summoned, with her husband, before the tyrant Dionysius, he proffered to them honours and fortune, on condition that they should reveal to him the mysteries of their sect. His offers being rejected with contempt, he drew Myllias aside, and promised to him an honourable deliverance if he would only reveal to him why the Pythagoreans would rather suffer death than trample over a field of beans. The sturdy disciple of Pythagoras replied, that as his sect preferred death to treading upon beans, so would be rather tread on beans than gratify the curiosity of Dionysius. The desire of the tyrant being inflamed by this opposition, he determined, if possible, to extort the secret from Tymicha, who was far advanced in pregnancy, by the menace of torture; relying for success on her situation, and on the weakness and timidity of her sex. Tymicha (observing this confidence), with more than masculine resolution, bit off her tongue, and spit it in the face of the tyrant, who was convinced, when too late, of the fallacy of his calculations, and that courage and heroism are not sexual virtues.　　　*Biographium Fœmineum.*

[438]

VALERIA.

DIOCLETIAN*, emperor cf Rome, having associated with himself in the government Constantius and
Galerius (surnamed Armentarius, from his original
profession of a herdsman), gave to the latter his
daughter Valeria in marriage.   This princess, whose
misfortunes inight afford a subject for a tragedy,
fulfilled and even surpassed in her conjugal state the
duties of a wife.   Having no children of her own,
she adopted the illegitimate son of her husband,
towards whom she invariably displayed a truly maternal tenderness.   After the death of her husband
her possessions provoked the avarice, and her beauty
excited the passions, of Maximin, his successor:
the wife of Maximin being still living, the tyrant,
availing himself of the Roman laws, determined to
divorce her.

Valeria, the daughter and the widow of emperors,
answered to his suit as became the dignity of her
rank and character, but, aware of her defenceless
situation, she tempered her rejection with mildness.
To the persons commissioned to treat with her on
the subject, she replied, ' That, even could honour
permit a woman of her character and rank to
entertain a thought of second nuptials, decency
would at least forbid her to listen to the addresses of

---

* March 1st, 292

VALERIA.

his successor, while the ashes of her husband, and of his benefactor, were yet warm, and while the sorrow of her heart was yet expressed by her mourning vestments.' She also ventured to add, ' That she could place but little confidence in the professions of a man whose cruel inconstancy was capable of repudiating a faithful and affectionate wife.'

This repulse converted the love of the tyrant into fury , and, having witnesses and judges always at his command, he found it not difficult to cover his rage and vexation under a legal exterior, and to assault at once the peace and the fame of his destined victim. By a horrible abuse of justice, the estates of Valeria were confiscated, her domestics devoted to the torture, and her friends, among whom were several respectable matrons, condemned to death. The princess herself, on a false accusation of adultery, was, with her mother Prisca, sentenced to exile, ignominiously hurried from place to place, and at length confined to a sequestered village, in the deserts of Syria, where their shame and distress were exposed to the provinces of the East, which had during thirty years respected their dignity.

Diocletian, the father of Valeria, who, having abdicated the purple, had retired to a private condition in Dalmatia his native country, made several ineffectual efforts to alleviate the misfortunes of his daughter , and entreated Maximin, that, at a last acknowledgment for an empire resigned, he would allow her to share with him his retreat, and to close the eyes of her afflicted father. Since he could no longer command, his supplications produced no effect ; the pride of the tyrant was gratified by the humiliation of the man to whom he owed the power of insulting him, whose prayers were received with coldness, and answered with scorn, and whose daughter was treated as a criminal.

The death of Maximin seemed at length to promise the princesses a more favourable destiny. The vigilance of their guard having relaxed in the public disorders, they contrived to effect their escape, and repaired, though in disguise and with precaution, to the court of Licinius, who succeeded to the empire, and whose conduct for the first few days of his reign had revived their confidence. But the bloody executions which quickly followed filled them with horror and astonishment, and convinced them that the throne was filled by a monster, not less inhuman than him by whom he had been preceded. Valeria, still accompanied by her mother, consulted her safety by a precipitate flight : concealed in plebeian habits, they wandered for fifteen months through the provinces of the empire.

At Thessalonica they were at length discovered, and the sentence of death, already pronounced, in-

LA VALLIERE.   441

flicted upon them: their bodies, having been beheaded, were thrown into the sea.   The people
gazed at the tragical spectacle, but were compelled
by a military guard to stifle their grief and indignation.   Such was the fate of the wife and daughter
of the emperor Diocletian: their crimes have never
been discovered, but their misfortunes are worthy of
sympathy and commemoration.

Gibbon's Decline of the Roman Empire.

MADEMOISELLE DE LA VALLIERE.

MADEMOISELLE DE LA VALLIERE, mistress
of Lewis XIV. deserves to be distinguished from
those women, whom ambition has led to prefer
to the domestic duties, and the honourable obscurity of a private life, a state of venal and
splendid degradation.   The tender and unfortunate
La Valliere was the daughter of the principal maitre-d'hotel to the lady of Gaston.   Her
mother, becoming a widow, took for her second
husband St. Remi, chief maitre-d'hotel to Monsieur (brother of Lewis XIV.) who introduced his
daughter-in-law into the family of Henrietta*, as
one of her maids of honour.   La Valliere, when at

---

* Daughter of Charles the First of England, and wife to
Monsieur.

U 5

Blois, in the court of Gaston, had been asked in marriage by a gentleman of Bragela; a circumstance which afterwards gave some umbrage to the pride and delicacy of Lewis, who wished to believe that no other man had ever excited in the heart of his fair mistress sentiments of tenderness or partiality. La Valliere is thus described by contemporary writers: " She was a most lovely woman; the lucid whiteness of her skin, the roses on her cheeks, her languishing blue eyes, and her fine silver-coloured hair, were altogether captivating." To her person and face Choisy applies the following line :

" And grace still more charming than beauty."

" That La Valliere (says Anquetil in his Memoirs) who was so engaging, so winning, so tender, and so much ashamed of her tenderness, who would have loved Lewis for his own sake had he been but a private man ; and who sacrificed to her affection for him her honour and conscientious scruples, with bitter regret and remorse." The king is said to have first conceived a passion for her, from having accidentally heard her, from the back of an arbour, confessing to one of her companions, the emotions which she felt in his presence, and the impression which he had made on her heart. The certainty of finding, what he had long sought in vain, a heart attached to him for his own sake, attracted him to-

LA VALLIERE. 443

wards her. Other circumstances also combined to draw closer the union between them. Philip duke of Orleans * had espoused Henrietta of England, in whose society, from a similar turn of mind and sentiment, the king took great delight, and at whose apartments he first saw La Valliere. Monsieur became jealous of his brother's attentions to his wife, and complained to the queen-mother, who remonstrated with her son on the occasion: to avoid the lectures of the queen, and the jealousy of monsieur, it was concerted between madame and the king, that the latter should affect a passion for one of her maids of honour. Mademoiselle La Valliere was for her simplicity, her gentleness, and her artless character, selected for the purpose. Henrietta flattered herself, that should the monarch actually become attached to her, it would not be difficult, whenever she should think proper, to divert his inclinations. Such is the account of madame De la Fayette.

According to others, while the king frequented the apartments of madame and the countess de Soissons, in order to obtain a glance of La Valliere, these ladies considered his attentions as addressed only to themselves: they interpreted in the same manner the feasts, the tournaments, and the balls, of

---

* Monsieur, the king's brother.

which La Valliere was the real object, and for which her heart, that understood that of her lover, thanked him. In the distribution of ribands, feathers, toys, diamonds, and expensive articles of dress, among the ladies of the court, they suspected not that the monarch, by this lavish generosity, sought only to present to his mistress what otherwise she would have refused to receive. This modest reserve was long maintained by La Valliere, who, a stranger to ambition, and not less timid and scrupulous than tender, avoided the monarch, while she cherished in her heart an affection for the man. At a review, the king, who watched her with a jealous eye, observed her smile on a young man, who saluted her familiarly in return. The same evening Lewis enquired, in a tone of disquietude and anger, the name of the person whom she had thus distinguished. La Valliere discovered some confusion at this address, but at length replied that it was her brother who had saluted her. The monarch, on receiving this information, heaped on him favours and honours : it was this gentleman who was father to the first duke De la Valliere.

Fouquet, the superintendant of the finance, whose profligacy was equalled only by his prodigality in his pleasures, was captivated by the charms of La Valliere, to whom he caused it to be intimated, that he had at her service twenty thousand pistoles.

LA VALLIERE. 445

This offer, which was treated with becoming disdain, was thought to have accelerated the fall of the inspector.

Proofs at length exhibited themselves of the weakness of La Valliere, who had yielded to love what interest and ambition had demanded in vain: humbled at her situation, she retired in confusion from the public eye, and injured her health by confinement, to avoid those observations which filled her with remorse and shame. Her penitence, her anguish, and her despair, embittered the triumph of her lover, who was harassed at the same time by the jealousy of the young queen, and the reproaches of his mother. The connection of Lewis with La Valliere was but yet imperfectly rumoured, when, by her own imprudence and scruples, it became revealed to the public. In a fit of repentance and despondency, mingled with jealousy, from slight and accidental circumstances, she, one day, quitted the court, and shut herself up in a convent at St. Cloud. The king, when apprised of what had passed, without listening to the reproofs of his mother, who remonstrated with him on his conduct, seized the first horse that came to hand, and, on full speed, rode after his mistress. Having ordered the convent to be opened to him, he expostulated with the lady, reproached and importuned her, prevailed over her pious resolutions, and carried her back with him in triumph to court

' Adieu, sister,' said she to the nun who opened the
gate for her, as, with a fluttering heart and swim-
ming eyes, she passed the threshold of the cloister;
' you shall soon see me again !' During the most
intoxicating moments of her passion, her pleasures
were mingled with contrition, and resolutions to
expiate, by the severity of the future, the frailty of
the present moment.

From the time that La Valliere, shunning he public gaze, lived in retirement, the king mixed but
little with the circles of the court. The ladies,
piqued at his conduct, determined to detach him
from his mistress, for which purpose they sought to
sow discord in the royal family. They contrived,
by a stratagem, to inform the young queen of the tri-
uimph of her rival, in the hope that she would complain to the king's mother, and that by their joint
attacks they would oblige him to abandon La Valliere,
or that, ashamed of exciting uneasiness in the family
of her lover, she would herself return to the convent.
A forged letter, fabricated for this purpose, with an
intention that it should fall into the hands of the
queen, was, through an accident, delivered to Lewis,
who, astonished at the perfidy of the transaction,
and unable to guess at the agents, applied for information to a man in the plot of the ladies, and who
artfully contrived to fix the suspicions of the monarch on madame de Navailles, who had not long

LA VALLIERE. 447

since incurred his displeasure by the severe propriety and rectitude of her conduct.

The duchess of Navailles had been lady of honour to the queen, in which situation she had watched over the conduct of the young ladies* committed to her charge. Some steps which the king had taken, led her to suspect him of designs which she considered it her duty to prevent. She addressed him on the occasion, and remonstrated respecting the impropriety of his behaviour, in terms at once firm and respectful. Lewis shewed at first no displeasure at these lectures ; he, however, became at length dissatisfied by precautions that continually frustrated and interfered with his inclinations. He expressed this dissatisfaction, but with a politeness and delicacy that gave the lady no cause to fear his resentment. His vexation after some time growing stronger, he hinted to the duchess that she was risking his displeasure, and forbade her to interfere so officiously in what respected the maids of honour. By his command, several methods were proposed to her of preserving appearances, without opposing his wishes. The duchess replied magnanimously to these representations, that, without persisting in the strict discharge of her duty, she could not fulfil her obligations , and that

---

* Maids of honour.

so long as his majesty should be pleased to continue
her in her office, she should certainly exert the same
vigilance. The king thoroughly irritated by this answer, bade her reflect on what she might suffer from
his resentment, and, as she regarded her own interest, to beware of disobeying him. ' I have, sire,'
returned she nobly, ' fully considered this subject; I
perceive clearly the disadvantages which the loss of
your favour may produce to me. It is to your majesty that both my husband and myself owe our
rank and fortune; he, the lieutenancy of the light
horse and the government of Havre; and I, my
place in her majesty's household. You may deprive us of these. But even such a prospect shall
not induce me to alter my resolution of satisfying
my principles by the discharge of my duty. I entreat you, sire,' continued she, kneeling before him,
' to look out for objects to gratify your desires elsewhere than in the household of the queen.' The
king replied with severity; but, the next day, came
up to the duchess, in the apartment of the queen-mother, and took her kindly by the hand, in token of
reconciliation. But the proper reflections of the
monarch on this incident, and his good dispositions,
were dissipated and perverted by the raillery of the
countess of Soissons, an intriguing and unprincipled woman, who was desirous of superseding the
duchess in her office. By this lady the honourable

LA VALLIERE. **449**

conduct of madame de Navailles was branded as a pretence, and the patience of Lewis, who suffered her to lay a restraint on his pleasures, treated with ridicule. Assisted by the passions and the vanity of the king, and intent on humbling her rival, she prevailed by her insinuations over his better resolutions, and laid a train for the fall of the duchess.

In the mean time, madame de Navailles, fearful, in a situation of so much delicacy, of trusting wholly to her own judgment, solicited the advice of a virtuous and learned man, who confirmed her in her duty, and determined her against a criminal complaisance to the monarch. " I saw her," says madame de Motteville, from whose Memoirs this account is extracted, " under the impression of that advice. I was witness of her anxiety and distress. She shed many tears, and felt the utmost agony at the hard alternative, before she could determine on following counsel so dangerous to her worldly interest." Her resolution being at length fixed, she no longer preserved any measures, but caused all the private passages, by which Lewis might steal into the apartments of the maids of honour, to be barricaded with iron grates. The consequences which she expected from this conduct did not immediately follow ; the king satisfied himself with depriving her of her office of governess, which he conferred on her more accommodating enemy. The courtiers were divided in their opinions on this subject : by some the conduct of the duchess was blamed, as an imprudence which made public the foibles of majesty , by others it was highly applauded ; but all agreed in doing justice to the rectitude of her intentions [*]. It was upon this lady that the cabal against La Valliere, of which the countess of Soissons was the principal instrument, prompted the vengeance of the monarch to fall. The king, with a mind poisoned by the insinuations that were artfully distilled into his ears, was persuaded with little difficulty to punish a woman, who had more than once placed herself in opposition to his inclinations. The duke and duchess of Navailles were, in despite of the entreaties of the queen-mother, who pleaded their cause with her son, deprived of all their employments, and exiled to their estates.

But the malice of which they became the victims remained not unrecompensed. The bonds which unite the unprincipled are of an unstable natuie : some intrigues among the cabal terminated in a rupture ; the king was informed of all that had passed, and the countess of Soissons banished for ever fiom

---

[*] This episode in the life of madame de la Valliere is not irrelevant to the nature of the present work. The conduct of madame de Navailles, in a dissolute court, justly entitles her to a rank among illustrious women.

LA VALLIERE. 451

court. The duke and duchess of Navailles were not, however, recalled, although the mother of Lewis solicited on her death-bed their reception to favour. The monarch contented himself with naming the duke governor of the district of Aunis, Brouage, and Rochelle, and, some years after, without having the favour demanded, created him a marshal of France. After the perfidy to which he had been a witness, it was remarked that Lewis became suspicious, reserved, and jealous of those who surrounded him. " Had kings," observes Anquetil in his Memoirs, " none about them but men of virtue, even though that virtue were obstinately rigid, and did they but know the worth of such men, they would be less frequently exposed to those perplexities which continually harass them, and which surround a throne."

The death of the queen-mother, who expired in Jan. 1666, and whose influence had in some measure restrained the levities of the court, was sincerely lamented by her son. But love healed his afflictions, and consoled him for his loss: La Valliere, in obedience to her lover, and from tenderness to her children, ventured once more to appear in public, and accepted the title of duchess, with the honours annexed -to the rank. Mademoiselle de Blois, her daughter, and M. de Vemandois, her son, were brought up openly under the eye of then mother.

452   LA VALLIERE.

La Valliere is accused, and not without cause, of having treated with disrespect the queen, to whose court she belonged. Maria Teresa, following the king on a journey towards the frontiers, forbade any person to go before her, that she might herself have the pleasure of coming up first to her husband. La Valliere, imprudently contemning this order, made her carriage withdraw from the line of procession, and cross the fields, that she might first reach the monarch. The queen, incensed at this temerity, was about to have her stopped; but the ladies of her train, laying before her the probable consequences of such a step, and properly blaming the conduct of the favourite, prevailed on her to let it pass. ' For my part,' observed one lady *, ' God keep me from becoming mistress to his majesty ! Were I so unfortunate, I should never have the effrontery to appear in the presence of his queen.'

Madame de Montespan, daughter to the duke de Mortemart, had obtained, by the interest of her husband with monsieur, the place of a lady of the palace. Her beauty, though faultlessly perfect, added to an extraordinary share of wit and address, did not for some time attract the notice of the amorous monarch. *The tongue of the Mortemarts* was a pro-

---

* The celebrated madame de Montespan, who soon succeeded to the situation of La Valliere.

LA VALLIERE. 453

verbial expression at court, the whole family being distinguished for the felicity of their language. Madame de Montespan had formed a habit of passing her evenings with the queen, when she was waiting on the king. Lewis was insensibly attracted towards her by her powers of entertainment, her talent of mimicry, her addiess in relating a story, the poignancy of her replies, and the satirical turn of her conversation. The queen, confiding in the professions of the lady, observed without alarm this growing intimacy, which had already become the theme of the court. La Valliere, whose discernment affection had quickened, was not ignorant of what was passing, far less could she observe it with indifference; but if she formed schemes of vengeance, they were directed only against herself. She once more retired from court, and shut herself up among the nuns of Chaillot. Lewis did not, as before, immediately follow her ; he contented himself with sending to her Colbert, to whose care her children were entrusted, and Lazun, who was master of the arts of persuasion. La Valliere sent a message to the king, importing, that, after having lost the honour of his good graces, she should much earlier have quitted the court, had she been able to prevail on herself to see him no more; but that her weakness on that subject was so great, that she was scarce capable of making a sacrifice of it to God:

but she was now resolved the remains of that
passion she had once felt for him should make a part
of her penance, and that, as she had devoted to him
her youth, it could not be thought unreasonable if
the rest of her life was spent in cares for her own
salvation.   The king wept bitterly on receiving
this message, and entreated the fair penitent to return immediately to Versailles, that he might speak
to her once more.   She obeyed this summons, unable to resist the importunity of the man she loved.
She had an hour's conversation with the monarch,
during which they both shed tears.   Her rival, madame de Montespan, ran to meet her on her return,
and received her with open arms.   Several inter-
views followed between Lewis and the unhappy La
Valliere, who suffered herself to be prevailed upon
to resume those chains, the weight of which had
already become galling, and to continue to drag on
a life of pain and conflict.

   The queen was still lulled in security respecting
the ascendancy of madame de Montespan. ' I have
a letter by the post,' says she, writing to mademoiselle, ' informing me that the king is no longer attached to La Valliere, but has transferred his attentions
to madame de Montespan.   I do not believe a syllable of it.'   This letter was sent by her majesty to
her husband : thus was the aim of the writer defeated.   La Valliere, though not absolutely deserted,

LA VALLIERE.

retained over the mind of the monarch the influence only of habit, and regard for their mutual offspring. She felt this too sensibly, but love taught her resignation, and at length made her suffer with patience the avowed preference to her rival. A desire to please the king made her carry her complaisance yet farther, even to ornament with her own hands the woman who had robbed her of his affection. Madame de Montespan, incapable of generous sympathy, abused her triumph, and added insult to cruelty. Affecting to admire the taste and dexterity of the humbled La Valliere, she frequently declared maliciously, that she could never be pleased with her dress unless assisted by this unfortunate woman, who shewed the utmost solicitude to please her. Lewis knew that it was only as a pretence still to linger in his presence, that La Valliere paid these attentions to her rival: he saw the secret inquietude which consumed her, but he saw it with little emotion. sensuality had hardened his heart. An expression of her uneasiness once escaped La Vallieie, in the piesence of another lady, who, with her, witnessed the dalliance of the monarch with his new favourite. ' When any thing occuis,' said she, ' among the Carmelites to give me pain, I will then think of what these people have made me suffer.'

But the period approached when, by a last heroic effort, she broke from her fetters, and bade a final

adieu to the court. She had long deliberated respecting this measure, the execution of which had
been delayed by various obstacles. The devotees
advised her to set a signal example of penitence: the
more moderate wished her merely to retire to a
cloister, without taking the vows. Her mother, an
ambitious woman, was desirous that her daugher, still
retaining her rank and household, should live with
her and educate her own children. The king, who
esteemed not the mother, doubted whether La Valliere would be safe under her protection: and La Valliere herself timidly believed that she needed, to attach her irrevocably to virtue, some powerful obligation. It was then proposed, that if she assumed the
veil, she should make choice of an order in which
she might be raised to the dignities consistent with
the retirement of a cloister. ‘ Alas !’ replied she,
‘ having shewn myself unable to regulate my own
conduct, shall I presume to direct that of others?’
Propositions of marriage were offered to her ; but
St. Simon attributes to the king the proud delicacy,
‘ that she who had once been his, should never after
belong to any but God.’ Rendered selfish by the
indulgence of his inclinations, and by his devotion to
the object of a new passion, he consigned, without
compunction, to a convent, in the bloom of her
youth and beauty, the victim of his caprice. In
this decision she cheerfully acquiesced.

LA VALLIERE.   457

On the 19th of April, 1674, she received the fare-wel compliments of the court ('Happy region!' exclaims madame de Sevigné, 'where the unfortunate are so soon forgotten!') and supped at madame de Montespan's. The next morning, after hearing mass in the king's chapel, she threw herself into her carriage, and proceeded, at thirty years of age, with her beauty yet unimpaired, to bury herself in a cloister. The convent of the Carmelites was made choice of for her retreat. On the 4th of June, in the following year, she took the vows in the presence of the queen and the whole court, under the name of sister Louisa, of the order of Mercy. She survived this sacrifice six-and-thirty years, devoted to the performance of the regular austerities of the conventual life, and not without the consolations which arise out of the tender enthusiasm of a susceptible heart. Madame de Montespan went sometimes to visit her. 'Are you really so happy,' said she to her one day, 'as people tell?' 'I am not happy,' replied the gentle Carmelite, 'but content.' In the calm of the passions, or in the new direction which devotion had given to them, she probably found comparative repose.

Madame de la Valliere left in the world one daughter, mademoiselle De Blois, afterwards married to the prince of Conti, and a son, Lewis of Bourbon, count de Vermandois, whom, according to some, an

acute distemper cut off at the siege of Courtrai, in
1683. Others assert, that, having struck the dauphin
in a dispute, he was condemned to death, but
snatched from his fate by the paternal kindness of
the king, and conveyed secretly to the Bastille, where
he was living in 1703, and known by the appellation
of *the man with the iron mask.* But this tale abounds
with improbabilities. M. Bonnet was deputed to
inform his mother of his decease. ' Alas, my God!'
said she, prostrating herself before the cross, ' must
I weep for his death, before my tears have expiated
his birth?' After the retreat of La Valliere, the
king appeared wholly devoted to madame de Montespan, whom jealousy instigated to use her influence
with her lover to suppress the establishment of the
queen's maids of honour. ' A dangerous cavern,'
' says madame de Sevigné, ' whence issued a hydra
with heads constantly multiplying.' Their place
was supplied with *ladies of honour,* a substitute which
did not prove particularly favourable to the morals
of the court: in young hearts even vice is timid,
and over those yet unestablished in life the terrors
of infamy have their full force.

Madame de Sevigné, speaking of the duchess de
Fontange, another transient favourite of the voluptuous Lewis, thus contrasts her with La Valliere:
" She was so elated with the splendor of her situation, that we may consider her character as the very

VETURIA. 459

reverse of that gentle creature, who, like the humble violet, sought only to conceal her beauties, and who, far from being vain of the honours conferred upon her, blushed at the titles of a mistress, a mother, or a duchess. Never shall we again see her match!"

Anquetil's Memoirs of the Court of Lewis XIV.—Marchioness de Sevigné's Letters, &c. &c.

VETURIA.

VETURIA, the mother of Coriolanus (who had joined the Volsci), with the Roman matrons, prevailed on her son to lay aside his resentment, and to return to the bosom of his country. The senate having requested that Veturia and her companions would ask their reward, they only solicited permission to build, at their own expence, a temple to the Fortune of Women. This edifice was, by the orders of the senate, erected on the spot where the circumstance it was designed to commemorate had taken place. On its completion, Veturia was consecrated perpetual priestess.

Roman History.

[460]

MADEMOISELLE DE LA VIGNE.

ANNE DE LA VIGNE, daughter to a physician at *Vernon*, was boin 1634. Celebrated for her poetical taste and genius, she holds a distinguished place among French literary women. Her ode, entitled " *Monseigneur le Dauphin au Roi,*" obtained great reputation, and was praised by the poets and wits of the age.

Soon after the publication of this piece, she received from an unknown hand a little box, containing a lyre richly enamelled, ornamented with gold; and a complimentary ode accompanied this elegant present, in which were the following lines:

> " Reçois donc, belle héroine !
> Une lyre qu' Appollon,
> Pour ce dessein te destine.
> Souvent son illustre son
> A, sous une main divine,
> Charmé le sacre vallon :
> Trop heureuse, qu'elle obtienne,
> De résonner sous la tienne."

Anne de la Vigne also addressed a congratulatory ode to mademoiselle de Scudery, on her obtaining the prize from the French Academy. The ode, with the reply of M. de Scudery, were published. The answer of mademoiselle de la Vigne to a gallant

MARY, COUNTESS OF WARWICK.   461

letter addressed to her, from *Les Champs Elisées* *, on her recovery from a dangerous sickness, was greatly admired, as were several other
poems, written by this lady, of equal merit. Her
father, a man of learning, and eminent in his
profession, who had a son *un peu borné* †, was
accustomed to say of his children—' Quand j'ai
fait ma fille, je pensois faire mon fils; & quand
j'ai fait mon fils, je pensois faire ma fille."

This lady died in Paris in 1684.

*Dictionnaire Historique, &c.—Ann Thickness's Sketch,
&c.*

MARY, COUNTESS OF WARWICK.

MARY was the thirteenth of the fifteen children
of the great earl of Cork, founder of the illustrious house of Boyle. Her mother was second
wife to the earl, and daughter of sir Geoffry Fenton. Mary married Charles earl of Warwick,
whom she survived five years. From her liberality to the poor, the earl her husband was said
to have left his estate to charitable uses. The
fame of her hospitality and benevolence advanced
the rent of the houses in her neighbourhood,

---

* The Elysian Fields.   † Of confused intellects.

x 3

where she was the common arbitress of all differ-
ences. Her awards, by the judgment and sagacity which they displayed, prevented many law-
suits. The earl her husband, alluding to her
economy and other admirable qualities, was accustomed to declare, that he would have chosen
her, upon a mere prudential calculation, with five
thousand pounds, in preference to any other woman with twenty thousand. She died April 12,
1678. Her funeral sermon was preached at Felsted in Essex, April 30th, 1678, by A. Walker,
D.D. rector of Fyfield, and published in 8vo.

ELIZABETH JANE WESTON.

THIS lady, who was born about the beginning
of the reign of Elizabeth, is supposed by Dr.
Fuller to have been a branch of the ancient family
of the Westons, of Sutton in Surrey. She appears to have left England at an early age, and to
have settled at Prague in Bohemia. She was
skilled in the languages, particularly in the Latin,
in which she wrote with elegance and correctness. She was greatly esteemed by learned foreigners. She is commended by Scaliger, and
complimented by Nicholas May in a Latin epigram. She is placed by Mr. Evelyn, in his *Nu-*

ANNE WHARTON. 463

mismata, among learned women; and by Mr.
Phihps among female poets. She is ranked by
Mr. Farnaby with sir Thomas More, and the best
Latin poets of the sixteenth century. She translated several of the fables of Æsop into Latin
verse. She also wrote a Latin poem in praise of
typography, with many poems and epistles, on
different subjects, in the same language, which
were collected and published. She married John
Leon, a gentleman belonging to the court of the
emperor; and was living in 1605, as appears
from an epistle written by her, and dated Prague,
in that year.

ANNE WHARTON,

WAS the daughter and co-heiress of sir Henry
Lee, of Ditchley in Oxfordshire, who, dying
without a son, left his estate between his two
daughters; Anne, and the countess of Abingdon.
The memory of the latter is celebrated by Dryden, in a funeral panegyric entitled " Eleonora."
Anne, who was distinguished for her poetical
genius, was first wife to Thomas, afterwards
marquis of Wharton, by whom she had no issue.
Many of her poems are printed in the collections

464 ANNE, COUNTESS OF WINCHELSEA.

of Dryden and Nichols. The mother of John
Wilmot, earl of Rochester, was her aunt. " They
were allied," says Mr. Waller, speaking of Rochester, " in genius as in blood." Anne died at
Adderbury, October 29th, 1685, and was buried
at Winchenden the 10th of the following November. From a caveat entered on the books of the
Stationers'-company it appears, that she was the
author of a play entitled " Love's Martyr, or
Wit above Crowns."

Biographium Fæmineum.

ANNE, COUNTESS OF WINCHELSEA.

ANNE, daughter of sir William Kingsmill, of
Sidmonton, Hants, knight, was maid of honour to
the duchess of York, second wife to James II.
She married Heneage, second son of Heneage
earl of Winchelsea. Her most celebrated production was a poem upon the Spleen, printed in
" A new Miscellany of original Poems, on several
Occasions," published by Mr. Charles Gildon,
1701. This poem gave birth to another, by Mr.
Nicholas Rowe, entitled " An Epistle to Flavia,
on the sight of two Pindaric Odes, on the Spleen
and Vanity, written by a Lady to her Friend."
A collection of the countess's poems was printed

ZENOBIA. **465**

in London, together with a tragedy, never acted, entitled " Aristomenes." A number of her poems remain still unpublished. She died.without issue, August 5, 1720.

Biographium Fæmineum.

ZENOBIA.

ZENOBIA, the celebrated queen of Palmyra, a descendant from the Macedonian kings of Egypt, equalled her ancestor Cleopatra in beauty, and surpassed her in every admirable and heroic quality of mind. Her stature was majestic, her complexion dark, her teeth of a pearly whiteness, her large black eyes sparkled with fire, tempered by an attractive sweetness. Her constitution was robust, her habits chaste, temperate, and hardy, while she excelled in every martial exercise. Her strong understanding, improved by study, rendered her not less able in the cabinet than formidable in the field. She was mistress of the Greek, the Syraic, and the Egyptian languages, and not unskilled in the Latin. She drew up for her own use an epitome of oriental history, and, under the tuition of the celebrated Longinus, familiarly compared the beauties of Homer and Plato.

x 5

466　　　　　ZENOBIA.

Odenathus, a Saracen prince, whom she espoused, had raised himself from a private station
to the dominion of the East: the friend and companion of a hero, Zenobia greatly contributed to
the important victories gained by her husband
over the Persians, which preserved to the Romans
the empire of the East. In the intervals of war,
she delighted in accompanying Odenathus to the
chace, and pursued with ardor the lion and the
panther of the desert. Inured to fatigue, and
disdaining covered carriages, she was accustomed to appear on horseback, in a military habit,
in which she frequently performed on foot long
and toilsome marches, at the head of the troops.
In the year 264 of Rome, when Odenathus, as the
reward of his services, was made emperor by Gallienus, the title of Augusta was conferred upon
Zenobia.

To the prudence and fortitude of Zenobia,
Odenathus was, in a great measure, indebted for
his military successes: their victories over the
Great King, whom they twice pursued to the gates
of Ctesiphon, laid the basis of their united fame
and power. The armies they commanded, and
the provinces they saved, acknowledged no other
sovereigns. Odenathus at length returning to
the city of Emesa in Syria, after a successful expedition against the Gothic plunderers of Asia,

ZENOBIA. **467**

was cut off by domestic treachery. His nephew Mæonius, having, at the chace, darted his javelin before that of his uncle, was reprimanded by him for his presumption : this reproof prevented him not from repeating his temerity. Odenathus, as a sovereign and a sportsman, incensed at this pertinacity, ordered his horse to be taken from Mæonius, a mark of ignominy among barbarians, and inflicted on him a short confinement. The offence was quickly forgotten, but the punishment was remembered : Mæonius, with a few daring associates, assassinated his uncle in the midst of an entertainment. Herod, the son of Odenathus, perished with his father.

The assassin, by his crime, obtained only the transient pleasure of vengeance : he had scarcely assumed the sovereign title, before he was sacrificed by Zenobia to the manes of her husband. With the assistance of the friends of Odenathus, his widow seized the reins of empire, and governed Palmyra and the East five years with vigour and ability. By the decease of the emperor, the authority which she held, as a personal distinction, from a grant of the Roman senate, was at an end. But Zenobia, disdaining the control of Rome, and ambitious of independence, obliged one of its generals, sent against her, to retreat into Europe, with the loss of his army and reputation.

Not less prudent in peace than active in war, her steady administration was guided by the wisest maxims of policy: when mercy was expedient, she knew how to sacrifice her vindictive feelings; when severity became necessary, she imposed silence on pity. Her strict economy was by many censured as avarice, but, on proper occasions, she was liberal and munificent. The neighbouring states of Armenia, Arabia, and Persia, dreaded her power and courted her alliance. To the dominions of Odenathus, which extended from the Euphrates to the frontiers of Bithynia, she added the inheritance of her ancestors, the fertile and populous kingdom of Egypt.

The emperor Claudius, acknowledging her merit, was content that she should assert the dignity of the eastern empire, while he pursued with his legions the Gothic war. Her conduct, however, appeared equivocal to Rome, which suspected her design of erecting an independent and hostile monarchy.

Zenobia blended with the popular manners of the Roman princes, the stately pomp of the oriental courts, and exacted from her subjects the adoration that was paid to the successors of Cyrus. She gave to her three sons a Roman education, while she frequently shewed them to the troops, adorned with the imperial purple; for herself she

ZENOBIA. 469

reserved the diadem, with the title of Queen of the East.

An adversary thus formidable, notwithstanding her sex, awakened the jealousy of the Roman senate: Aurelian passed over to Asia in arms against her, and, by his presence, restored to its obedience the province of Bithvnia, subdued by the intrigues and the power of Zenobia. He also received, at the head of his legions, the submission of Ancyra, and, after an obstinate siege, was admitted by perfidy into Tyana. The traitor, receiving the reward of his crime, was abandoned by Aurehan to the rage of the soldiers, while respect for the philosopher Apollonius, born at Tyana, induced the conqueror to treat his countrymen with lenity. At the approach of the Roman army, Antioch was deserted, till, by salutary edicts, the emperor recalled the fugitives; while to those who had engaged in the service of Zenobia from necessity rather than choice, he granted a free pardon. Having by a policy thus wise and humane conciliated the minds of the Syrians, the wishes of the people, even to the gates of Emesa, seconded the terror of his arms.

Zenobia saw not inactively the advance of the western emperor towards her capital. Two great battles, one fought near Antioch, and the other near Emesa, decided the fate of the East. In

both these engagements Zenobia, by her presence, animated her forces ; the execution of her
orders was committed to Zabdas, who had in the
conquest of Egypt signalised his military talents.
The force of the queen consisted chiefly of light
archers, and heavy cavalry clothed in complete steel.
The Moorish and Illyrian horse of the enemy, unable to sustain their ponderous charge, fled in
real or feigned disorder, and, having engaged the
Palmyrenians in a laborious pursuit, harassed
them in a desultory combat, by which the un-
wieldy and impenetrable cavalry were fatigued
and discomfited.   The archers having, in the
mean while, exhausted their quivers, remained
exposed without protection to the swords of the
legions.   Aurelian had, on this occasion, selected
the veteran troops usually stationed on the Upper
Danube, whose valour the Alemannic war had
severely proved.

   After the defeat of Emesa, Zenobia found herself
unable to collect a third army ; the nations subject
to her empire, even to the frontier of Egypt, had
joined the victor, who detached from his army the
bravest of his generals to possess himself of the
Egyptian provinces.   The queen, finding in Palmyra her last resource, retired within the walls of
her capital, where, preparing for a vigorous resistance, she intrepidly declared, the last moment

of her reign and of her life should be the same. The emperor, with incessant vigour, pressed the siege in person, and was himself wounded with a dart.

" The Roman people," says he, in an original letter, " speak with contempt of the war which I am waging against a woman: they are ignorant of the character and power of Zenobia. It is not possible to enumerate her warlike preparations, of stones, of arrows, and of every species of missile weapons. Every part of the wall is provided with two or three *balistæ*, while artificial fires are thrown from the military engines. The fear of punishment has armed her with a desperate courage; yet still I trust in the protecting deities of Rome, who have hitherto favoured all my undertakings. It is, I hear, objected to me, that I acted not a manly part in triumphing over Zenobia. Those who censure would commend me, did they know the woman; what prudence in her designs, what constancy in her resolutions, with what dignity does she conduct herself towards her army, how bountiful is she upon necessary occasions, how severe where severity is requisite! It is to her that I ascribe the victories of Odenathus over the Persians. I can affirm, that she was so formidable to the eastern nations, that the Arabians, the Saracens, and the Armenians, remained quiet, and dared not oppose her, &c."

Doubtful of the event of the siege, so spirited were the efforts of the besieged, Aurelian offered terms of advantageous capitulation; to the queen a splendid retreat, to the citizens their ancient privileges. These proposals were rejected with obstinacy and insult. The hope that famine would in a short time compel the Romans to re-pass the desert, supported the spirits of Zenobia; who beside expected, and not without reason, that the kings of the East, more especially the Persian monarch, would arm in defence of their common rights. But to the perseverance of the Western emperor every obstacle was forced to yield. The Persian counsels were at this time distracted by the death of Sapor; the inconsider-able succours with which they attempted to re-lieve Palmyra, were intercepted without difficulty by the arms or the liberality of Aurelian. A ic-gular succession of convoys also, from every part of Syria, arrived safely in the camp, while the Roman forces were strengthened by the return of Probus, with the troops from the conquest of Egypt.

Thus beset, and deprived of every succour, it was now that Zenobia resolved to fly. Mount-

ZENOBIA.   473

ed on the swiftest of her dromedaries, she had already reached the banks of the Euphrates, sixty miles from Palmyra, when, pursued by the light-horse of Aurelian, she was overtaken, captured, and brought back to the emperor. Her capital, compelled to surrender, was treated by the con-queror with lenity. The arms, horses, camels, treasures of gold, of silver, of silk, and precious stones, were delivered to Aurelian, who, leaving in Palmyra a garrison of archers, returued to Emesa with the spoils; where, at the end of a war which restored to the empire its revolted provinces, he employed himself in the distribu-tion of rewards and punishments.

The captive queen having been brought into the presence of the conqueror, he sternly de-mandcd of her, how she had presumed to rise in arms against the emperors of Rome. ' Because,' replied she, with mingled firmness and respect, ' I disdained to consider as Roman emperors Aureolus or Gallienus :—*you*, alone, I acknow-ledge as my conqueror and sovereign.'

In the hour of trial, it is added with regret, the courage of the heroine deserted her: trem-bling at the clamours of the soldiers, who called loudly for her execution, she purchased life with the sacrifice of her fame and of her friends, to whose counsels sho- imputed the obstinacy of her resistance, and on whose heads she drew down the vengeance of the emperor. Among the victims of this weakness, was the celebrated Longinus, whose learning and genius failed to move the illiterate and barbarous Aurelian. The philosopher, without uttering a complaint, calmly resigned himself to his fate, pitying his unhappy mistress, and comforting his afflicted friends.

On his return from the conquest of the East, the emperor, who had already crossed the streights which separate Europe from Asia, was incensed by the intelligence that the Palmyrenians, having massacred the garrison, had already raised the standard of revolt. Once more he turned his face towards Syria, and the city of Palmyra suffered the consequences of his rage. The innocent and the guilty, old men and women, children and peasants, citizens and nobles, were involved in one undistinguishing carnage. His savage fury at length appeased, after directing his principal attention towards the re-establishment of a temple of the sun, he granted to the wretched remnant of the people permission to rebuild and inhabit the city. To restore is less easy than to destroy. The city of Zenobia, the seat of arts and commerce, sunk into an obscure town, a trifling fortress, and, at length, a miserable village.

ZENOBIA.   475

Aurchan, on his return to Rome, received the honours of a triumph, which was celebrated with superior magnificence.   Four-and-twenty elephants began the cavalcade, followed by four royal tigers, and two hundred curious animals, from every climate; sixteen hundred gladiators, devoted to the barbarous amusement of the amphitheatre, succeeded   after these were displayed the wealth of Asia, the arms and ensigns of conquered nations, with the superb plate and wardrobe of the Syrian queen, disposed with artful negligence.   Embassadors of Ethiopia, Arabia, Persia, Bactriana, India, and China, clothed in rich and singular habits, exhibited the power and fame of the Roman emperor; who also exposed to the public the presents he had received, with a number of crowns of gold, the offerings of grateful cities.   A long   train of captives, in barbarous pomp,   reluctantly   followed ;—Goths,   Vandals, Sarmatians, Alemanni, Franks, Gauls, Syrians, and Egyptians, each nation distinguished by appropriate inscriptions.   Ten martial heroines, taken in arms, of the Gothic nation, on whom the title of Amazons was bestowed, succeeded. But, disregarding inferior captives, every eye was fixed on the lovely Zenobia, who, confined by golden fetters, a gold chain (supported by a slave) encircling her neck, and almost fainting under the weight of her jewels, preceded on foot the magnificent chariot in which she hoped to have entered Rome. The chariots of Odenathus, and that of the Persian monarch, still more splendid, followed. Next came Aurelian, drawn by four elephants[*]. The most illustrious of the senate, the army, and the people, closed the procession.

The pride of Aurelian having thus ignobly indulged itself in insulting his vanquished enemies, he displayed in his future conduct a generosity more worthy of a conqueror. He presented to Zenobia an elegant villa at Tibur (or Tivoli), twenty miles from the capital, where the Syrian heroine gradually sunk into the Roman matron: her daughters contracted noble alliances, and her race was not extinct in the fifth century.

Previous to her defeat by Aurelian, in the year 272, she interested herself in the theological controversies of the times, and, either from policy or principle, protected Paul of Samoseta, the celebrated philosophical unitarian, whom the council of Antioch had condemned.

Gibbon's Decline of the Roman Empire—Bayle's Historical Dictionary.

---

[*] Or, according to some, four stags.

THE END.

T. Davison, White-Friars.   VALUABLE

APPENDIX 1

'Memoirs of Mary Wollstonecraft'
Fiore Sireci

'Memoirs of Mary Wollstonecraft', published in *The Annual Necrology 1797–8* in 1800, is a crucial document. Drawing upon the information and extant letters collected by William Godwin, Mary Hays recasts the life and work of Wollstonecraft, offering an alternative to Godwin's account. In the two texts prepared by Godwin immediately after the death of Mary Wollstonecraft, *Memoirs of the Author of a Vindication of the Rights of Woman* (1798) and *Posthumous Works of the Author of the Vindication of the Rights of Woman* (1798), Wollstonecraft's emotional, spiritual and personal life is highlighted. Godwin's *Memoirs* contains a lengthy account of her relationship with Gilbert Imlay as well as speculations on Wollstonecraft's interest in Henry Fuseli, although recent scholarship has been investigating these claims. Godwin provides a sketchy account of the composition of *A Vindication of the Rights of Woman*, one that does not engage deeply with the intellectual content of the work, and one which has proven to be misleading about how long it took Wollstonecraft to prepare and complete the work. Godwin claims it took six weeks to compose; this is all the more surprising considering the title of Godwin's text. In the *Posthumous Works*, also published by Godwin, consisting of four volumes in the first London edition, all of volume three and thirty-nine pages of volume four are devoted to Wollstonecraft's letters to Imlay.

Godwin's revelations of Wollstonecraft's affair with Gilbert Imlay, as well as her suicide attempts, produced a surge in negative public opinion about this acknowledged champion of the rights and education of women. However, considering the profound and rapid reaction of writers to Wollstonecraft in the years following her death, it is more likely that the information contained in the *Memoirs* was a pretext for harsh and sustained attacks on what was always at stake – the radical implications of her social thought. In any event, Wollstonecraft's name would henceforth be linked with sexual impropriety, an association which also limited the reception of her thought in the nineteenth century. In 1800, when the tide of public opinion had turned overwhelmingly against Wollstonecraft, Hays was one of her few remaining advocates.

The timing and structure of Hays's 'Memoirs' reveals Mary Hays's intention to play a decisive role in the struggle for Wollstonecraft's legacy, at the same time foreshadowing Hays's interest in a full-scale revision of women's history that came to fruition in *Female Biography*. At the start, Hays, like Godwin, focuses on Wollstonecraft's emotional life; Hays's 'Memoirs' contains a large proportion of the letters to Imlay. Moreover, this material was most likely taken directly from the plates used by Joseph Johnson in the publication of Godwin's two texts, judging by the similarity in typeface and punctuation. Unlike Godwin, however, Hays casts the allegedly extreme passions of Mary Wollstonecraft as part of a larger picture of personal and spiritual growth.

Early on, Hays writes that people who break rules of convention are 'vigorous minds', who 'quit beaten paths' to eventually 'acquire wisdom by an individual experience' (p. 483). Eighteenth-century readers were familiar with the concept of an alchemy of passion, which appears in Alexander Pope's *Essay on Man*: 'The surest virtues thus from passions shoot / Wild nature's vigour working at the root'.[1] Another source of the idea of self-development through trial and error is the theological writing of early eighteenth-century theologians. Joseph Butler's *Analogy of Religion* (1736) was a key work for the development of the moral philosophy of Rational Dissent and an important influence on both Hays and Wollstonecraft. In the *Analogy*, which Wollstonecraft cites throughout her works, our lifetimes are a time of 'probation', in which God intends for us to pursue the full flowering of intellectual and physical capacities. Although it was likely not Butler's intention to relate this to women's rights, Wollstonecraft begins Chapter 1 of *A Vindication of the Rights of Woman* with a concise application of this principle: 'For what purpose were the passions implanted? That man by struggling with them might attain a degree of knowledge.' It was Wollstonecraft's achievement to take up contemporary theological and philosophical concepts such as these and build her feminism upon them. For if it is divinely mandated that all human beings must develop themselves fully, then to block the development of women, or to condemn them without recourse, is to be profoundly impious, a powerful argument in the context of Wollstonecraft's time.[2] Hays's comments on the role of passion in the development of a woman's spirit reflects her understanding of the philosophical and theological underpinnings of Wollstonecraft's feminism, a set of principles which the two women held in common.

Notes
1. A. Pope, *Essay on Man*, in *Major Works* (Oxford: Oxford University Press, 2006), ll. 183–4, p. 286.
2. This has been recognized and eloquently argued by B. Taylor, 'The Religious Foundations of Mary Wollstonecraft's Feminism', in C. L. Johnson (ed.), *The Cambridge Companion to Mary Wollstonecraft* (Cambridge: Cambridge University Press, 2002), pp. 99–118, on p. 110.

THE

ANNUAL

NECROLOGY,

FOR

1797-8;

INCLUDING, ALSO,

VARIOUS ARTICLES

OF

NEGLECTED BIOGRAPHY.

LONDON:

PRINTED FOR R. PHILLIPS, ST. PAUL'S
CHURCH-YARD,

By T. Bensley, Bolt-court, Fleet-street.

1800.

PREFACE.

HISTORY has been confidered as " Philofophy teaching by example ;" and Biography, although it affects lefs dignity, and afpires to lefs diftinction, may fairly lay claim to a fimilar definition. While the former indulges in fublime fpeculations intimately connected with the happinefs and the mifery, the profperity and the misfortunes of a large portion of the human race, it is the humbler, yet no lefs ufeful province of the latter to unveil the motives and the actions, the adventures and the purfuits, the merits and the fingularities, the virtues and the vices of a few individuals. The one, therefore, being occupied with the deftiny of nations, exhibits leffons for ftatefmen ; but it is the peculiar advantage of the other, that it is adapted to perfons of all defcriptions.

It would be equally vain and fuperfluous to enumerate the benefits refulting from a faithful and impartial record of the lives of remarkable men. It is evident, however, that fomething is ftill to be wifhed for in refpect to General Biography, and it would not be difficult to mention the names of feveral eminent perfons, even of our own country, of whofe career fcarcely a trace is to be found ; while, of many others, curiofity is forced to be fatisfied with what can be gleaned from very fcanty materials.

In fine, a proper vehicle has hitherto been wanting : for the moft obvious and important occurrences, if not communicated while yet recent, foon become either obliterated by time, or obfcured by tradition, and leave only a few mutilated facts, or unconnected fragments, for the information of the future narrator, and the regret of pofterity.

A 2   The

iv   PREFACE.

The French and Germans, fully aware of this, and at the same time confcious of the many advantages refulting from *Contemporary Biography*, or memoirs written while intelligence may be eafily collected, evidence examined, and papers obtained, have of late publifhed *Annual Obituaries*, containing all the particulars that can be procured relative to fuch remarkable characters as may have died within the preceding year. It would be ungenerous to omit, that it is upon this fcheme the prefent volume is prepared for the prefs; but it may be here neceffary, on the other hand, to remark, that the plan has been extended, fo as to include *Neglected Biography*, under the general name of NECROLOGY, a Greek compound, which has been already adopted into more than one language on the continent, and it is hoped will not be confidered as improperly engrafted on our own.

It is infinitely more eafy to defcribe the importance of, than to difplay the talents neceffary for, an undertaking, calculated, like the prefent, to give a fuller fcope to the range of curiofity and inftruction. Of all the various requifites demanded for conducting fuch a work, the Editor can boaft only of induftry and good fortune. The firft has enabled him to collect many curious particulars which might have otherwife remained for ever in oblivion; and in confequence of the fecond, he has had an opportunity, partly from his own knowledge of individuals, and partly in confequence of the liberal affiftance of others *, to detail a variety of interefting facts; nor has recourfe to books

* The following articles have been contributed by various correfpondents, viz.

Mr. Bakewell,	M. Beuda.
... Bruce,	The Count de Hertzberg,
... Dupuy,	Mr. Venn.
... Mellmann,	Dr. Farmer,
Dr. Kippis,	Mr. Maion, and
M. Neubauer,	Mrs. Woolftonecraft.

Some important communications have been deferred until another opportunity, and among thefe, it would be uncandid not to particularife a variety of interefting papers by a nobleman (the earl of Buchan), who has on many occafions evinced his attachment to the caufe of literature.

been

Memoirs of Women Writers, Volume 10

been wanting, when they could afford information, or fupply de-
ficiencies of any kind.

Many important papers, never before fubmitted to public
infpection, are interfperfed with the memoirs; and it may not
be improper to remark, that either in the text, or at the bottom
of the page, of feveral of the foreign articles, will be found the
terms of art, and fcientific expreffions, exactly tranfcribed from
the language in which they were firft written. The advantages
refulting from this mode are manifeft, as it renders a reference to
the original unneceffary, and enables the fkilful reader to detect
any error that may have occurred in the tranflation.

A copious Index will be found at the end, and a Chronological and Alphabetical Table at the beginning of the Volume.
The firft and laft are calculated to afford facility of reference, and
the fecond is intended to fupply fome neceffary dates which were
not at firft afcertained with fufficient exactnefs.

As this Work is intended to be continued annually, the Editor
earneftly folicits the affiftance of all fuch as may be defirous to
co-operate in fo ufeful and important an undertaking.

London, Nov. 1799.

WOLLSTONECRAFT.   411

MEMOIRS OF

MARY WOLLSTONECRAFT.

THE intrepid fpirit, daring flights, lofty pretenfions, and difdain of fanctioned opinions, which characterize the productions of the vindicator of the Rights of Woman, have combined to excite an extraordinary degree of attention; which fome events, of a peculiar nature, in her perfonal hiftory have had a tendency to increafe. By the diftinction which the reputation of fuperior talents confers, their poffeffors are exalted to a dangerous pre-eminence: attention is roufed, curiofity excited, their claims are fubjected to a fcrutiny, in which all the nobler and all the bafer paffions become equally interefted. While, on one fide, by the partiality of affection and the blind enthufiafm of implicit admiration, their excellencies are made the theme of exaggerated panegyric: on the other, thofe errors or frailties to which they are liable, in common with their fpecies, or thofe exceffes that more peculiarly belong to ardent characters, are invidioufly fought after, propagated with malignity, amplified by envy, diftorted by prejudice, and received with triumph by the vulgar of every rank, by the interefted, the ignorant, and the malicious. Perfons of the fineft and moft exquifite genius have probably the greateft fenfibility, confequently the ftrongeft paffions, by the fervor of which they are too often betrayed into error. Vigorous minds are with difficulty reftrained within the trammels of authority; a fpirit of enterprife, a paffion for experiment, a liberal curiofity, urges them to quit beaten paths, to explore untried ways, to burft the fetters of prefcription, and to acquire wifdom by an individual experience.

The preceding reflections are not unappropriate to the fubject of the prefent narrative, in whofe character ftrong light and fhade appear to have been blended. If, by her quick feelings, prompt judgments, and rapid decifions, fhe was fometimes betrayed

trayed into falſe concluſions, her errors were expiated by ſuf-
ferings, that, while they diſarm ſeverity, awaken ſympathy and
ſeize irreſiſtibly upon the heart. Let it not be forgotten, that if
the exceſs of certain virtues encroach on the limits of vice, yet
faults of this deſcription have a generous ſource. Thoſe whom
a calmer temperament conduct in an even path, deviating
neither to the right nor to the left, will find their reward in
the ſafety of their courſe. But it is to ſpeculative and
enterpriſing ſpirits, whom ſtronger powers and more impetuous paſſions impel forward, regardleſs of eſtabliſhed uſages,
that all great changes and improvements in ſociety have owed
their origin. If, intoxicated by contemplating the grand projects in their imagination, they deviate into extravagance, and
loſe ſight of the nature of man, their theories remain to be
corrected by experience, while, in the gratitude of poſterity,
the contemporary cry of intereſt will be abſorbed and forgotten.

To advance on the ſcale of reaſon half the ſpecies, is no
ignoble ambition. The efforts of the extraordinary woman
whoſe life we are about to review, were directed to the emancipation of her own ſex, whom ſhe conſidered as ſunk in
a ſtate of degradation, glorying in their weakneſs, voluntarily ſurrendering the privilege of rational agents, and contending, in her own emphatic language, " for the ſentiment
that brutalized them."

Mary, daughter of Edward-John and Elizabeth Wollſtonecraft, was born on the 27th of April, 1759. Her mother
was of the family of the Dixons of Ballyſhannon in Ireland,
her paternal grandfather a manufacturer in Spitalfields, from
whom her father is ſuppoſed to have inherited property to a con-
ſiderable amount. Mr. Wollſtonecraft's family conſiſted of
ſix children (three ſons and three daughters), of whom Mary
was the ſecond. It does not appear that Mr. W. (who near
the period of his daughter's birth occupied a farm on Epping
Foreſt) was brought up to any profeſſion. Nor is it certain
whether the ſubject of our narration received her exiſtence in
London

London or on the Foreft, where the firft five years of her life were principally fpent.

Mary Wollftonecraft gave early indications of thofe acute feelings and vigorous powers of mind which led to the fubfequent incidents and exertions of an eventful life. It is poffible that the reftraint which fhe is faid to have experienced, and the feverity under which fhe occafionally fuffered, from the irafcible and capricious temper of her father, might tend to roufe that fpirit of refiftance, that indignant impatience of injuftice and oppreffion, which formed the diftinguifhing features of her maturer character.

Experience teaches us that, in the moral as in the phyfical world, evil is often connected with good. Suffering and oppofition, if they exceed not certain limits, have a ftimulating power: ftill they are evils, and it would be rafh to conclude, that, by the adoption of lefs exceptionable means, the fame end might not be effected. He, who has ftudied the human mind, will know how to avail himfelf of its more delicate fprings: terror and force have been proved feeble engines when oppofed to emulation and love.

As, with increafing years, the underftanding of Mary Wollftonecraft matured, it triumphed over the petty vexations of her childhood, and procured her, by its afcendancy, a confequent predominance in her family: while her influence and interpofition ferved to fcreen her mother from the confequences of her father's temper, fhe was regarded by both with an involuntary portion of affection and refpect. To the hardy habits of her childhood fhe confidered herfelf as indebted for a robuft conftitution. Sporting in the open air, and joining in the active amufements of her brothers, her health acquired a found and vigorous tone.

In 1768 Mr. Wollftonecraft removed from the Foreft to a farm near Beverly in Yorkfhire, where he refided with his family for fix years. During this interval his daughter occafionally frequented a day-fchool in the neighbourhood. What benefit fhe derived from the inftructions fhe there received, we have no account. From Beverly Mr. W. repaired to a houfe in Queen's Row, Hoxton,

near

near London, with a view of engaging in commerce. Mary Wollftonecraft had now entered her fixteenth year. About this period fhe became acquainted with a Mr. Clare, a near neighbour, a clergyman, a man of tafte, and a humorift, to whom fhe was indebted for encouragement and affiftance in the cultivation of her mind, and at whofe houfe fhe frequently paffed days and weeks. The manners of this gentleman were conciliating, and his habits peculiar.

By the wife of Mr. Clare fhe was introduced to a young per-fon of her own fex, Frances Blood, who refided in the village of Newington, and for whom, on their firft interview (in which Frances appeared peculiarly interefting, furrounded by the younger children of her family), fhe conceived a friendfhip that partook of all the fervour of her character. Frances Blood, two years older than her friend, is defcribed as an accomplifhed and exemplary young woman : an affectionate intercourfe and corre-fpondence fucceeded between them, in which the afpiring tem-per of the younger was. roufed to emulation by the fuperior attainments of the elder, who undertook to be her inftructor, and whofe leffons were received with grateful delight.

The removal of Mr. Wollftonecraft, whofe temper was reftlefs and unftable, to a farm in Wales, in the fpring of 1776, was a cruel ftroke to his daughter, whofe affection for Frances had now become the ruling paffion of her foul. In this retirement the Wollftonecrafts formed an intimate acquaintance with the family of Mr. Allen, two of whofe daughters have been fince married to the elder fons of the celebrated Jofiah Wedgewood. After remaining in Wales little more than a year, Mr. W. again re-turned to the neighbourhood of London, and, at the earneft requeft of his daughter, who panted to be near her friend, fixed his abode at Walworth.

The fpirit of independence was characteriftic of Mary Woll-ftonecraft; fhe revolved in her mind projects for quitting the parental roof, and providing for her own fupport: with this view, fhe entered into an engagement which promifed to be eligible, but was induced to relinquifh her plan by the tears and entreaties of her mother; but a defign fo congenial to the intrepidity of her character,

character, though postponed, was not abandoned. In the year 1778, it was proposed to her, to reside as a companion with a widow lady (Mrs. Dawson) of Bath, to which proposition, not discouraged by intimations which she had received of the peculiar humour of the lady, she immediately acceded. In this situation she soon acquired an influence over her patroness, extorting from her a degree of consideration which rarely attends the circumstances to which she had submitted.

After residing two years with Mrs. Dawson, she was recalled to her family, now living at Enfield, by the declining health of her mother, on whom she attended with the most affectionate assiduity, through a lingering disease, which, terminating fatally, she finally quitted her family, her health impaired by fatigue and anxiety, and fixed her residence with her friend, at Waltham-green, near the village of Fulham. In this situation their mutual attachment became more lively and confirmed. Of the manner in which she now supported herself, we have no information: her spirit would doubtless have preserved her from becoming burdensome to the industry of her friend. Two years subsequent to her attendance on the closing scenes of a mother's life, her sympathy was again excited and her attention engrossed by the affecting state of a married sister, who, in consequence of a perilous lying-in, sunk into a melancholy and lingering disorder.

During the languor and confinement of her sister, Mary Wollstonecraft, who had now entered her twenty-fourth year, had leisure for reflection. In addition to her darling plan of personal independence, her benevolence prompted her to meditate projects more arduous and extensive. The affairs of her father long declining, had at length become hopeless, involving a small independent provision made for his daughters. In conjunction with her friend and sisters, she therefore formed, and at length executed, a plan for the opening of a day-school in the village of Islington: from Islington they thought proper, in the course of a few months, to transfer their residence to Newington-Green.

Every new impression or vicissitude produced on her susceptible mind important consequences: some valuable connexions which

which she now formed, gave a tincture to her future views and character; among the most diftinguished of thefe she accounted Dr. Richard Price (equally refpected for his talents and virtues), for whom she conceived a fincere reverence and friendship, and on whofe public inftructions she occafionally attended. Poffeffing in an exalted degree thofe devotional affections fo congenial to ardent and tender natures, her religion, for she laid no ftrefs on creeds and forms, was a fentiment of humility, reverence, and love; a fublime enthufiafm, the afpirations of a fervent imagination, fhaping to itfelf ideal excellence, and panting after good unalloyed. Her active mind, confcious of its powers, exulting in its capacities, abhorred the thought of extinction, and yearned to perpetuate itfelf. She believed in a being,·higher, more perfect than vifible nature, in her own conformity to that fuperior being, in a future ftate of exercife and gratification of thofe powers and fenfibilities that, denied a fcope for exertion, too often preyed upon herfelf. Her faith refted not upon critical evidence or laborious inveftigation; it was the bold conception of a pregnant fancy; the delicious fentiment of a tender heart: she adored the Creator in the temple of the univerfe, worfhipped him amidft the beauties of nature, or, fuffering her mind to expatiate amidft ideas of fpotlefs purity and boundlefs goodnefs, humbled herfelf before him in the·ftill hour·of recollection.

About this period she acquired alfo the friendship of Mrs. Burgh, widow of the author of the Political Difquifitions, and of the reverend John Hewlett, a clergyman of the church of England. Being likewife introduced to the acquaintance of Dr. Johnfon, she was received by him with kindnefs and diftinction: his fubfequent illnefs and death fruftrated her intention of cultivating a further intimacy with this extraordinary man.

The health of her friend, Frances Blood, whofe character, though amiable, was timid and feeble, now began to decline; difappointment and indulged grief, had impaired her conftitution, and fymptoms of a confumption appeared, for which she was advifed to try the effects of a fouthern climate. In the beginning of the year 1785 she accordingly fet fail for Lifbon, having previoufly fuffered herfelf to be prevailed upon to accept, on her arrival, the hand of

Mr.

Mr. Hugh Skeys, of Dublin (then refident in Portugal), who had for fome time paft paid his addreffes to her. Mrs. Skeys, whofe health had received little benefit from the voyage, becoming pregnant foon after her marriage, the affectionate folicitude of Mary Wollftonecraft induced her to quit for a time her fchool, and to fubject herfelf to various inconveniences, for the purpofe of paffing over to Portugal, to adminifter aid and confolation to her friend. With fome pecuniary affiftance from Mrs. Burgh, fhe was enabled to accomplifh her defign, and arrived at Lifbon but a fhort period before the lady in queftion was prematurely delivered; a crifis which proved fatal both to the mother and child.

During her ftay in Portugal, the circle of her obfervation being enlarged, her active mind collected materials for reflection: the influence of defpotifm and the pernicious effects of a blind fuperftition more peculiarly impreffed her.

On her paffage to England, towards the latter end of December, a new occafion prefented itfelf for the exercife of her humanity; a French fhip, in danger of foundering, and deftitute of provifions, implored the aid of the mafter of the veffel in which fhe was a paffenger, who, fearful left his own ftores fhould fall fhort, was induced folely by her fpirited remonftrances to grant to the fufferers the neceffary relief.

Having arrived in her native land, fhe quickly perceived that the expectations fhe had cherifhed refpecting the fuccefs of her fchool were likely to prove abortive. For the bufinefs of education fhe is faid to have been peculiarly fitted, by a talent of conciliating the affections of her pupils, by a firm yet gentle difcipline, a watchful attention to their individual qualities, a promptitude in availing herfelf of them, and a careful obfervation of the fuccefs of her experiments. Hitherto difappointed in her plans, and earneftly defirous of indulging the benevolence of her temper, in affording pecuniary aid to fome relations of her deceafed friend, fhe was now induced to confider and adopt the advice of a gentleman (Mr. Hewlett), for whom fhe entertained an efteem, and who, forming a favourable and juft opinion of her talents, fuggefted literary employment as a fource of profit.

E e

Ia

In purſuance of this idea, ſhe wrote a duodecimo pamphlet of
one hundred ond ſixty pages, entitled " Thoughts on the Education of Daughters," for the copy-right of which ſhe obtained
ten guineas from Mr. Johnſon, bookſeller in St. Paul's church-
yard: this ſum was immediately applied to the purpoſe for which
the manuſcript had been written.

Diſguſted with the diſappointments that had attended her pro-
jeᴄt of public tuition, ſhe now determined to reſign her ſchool,
and accept, for the preſent, a propoſal made to her of reſiding in
the family of lord viſcount Kingſborough, of the kingdom of
Ireland, in the capacity of private governeſs to his daughters.
Her darling plan of independence, which ſhe ſtill cheriſhed a
view of realizing by literary occupation, was not given up, but
ſhe was previouſly deſirous of acquiring a ſmall ſum of money,
as a reſource in caſe of failure in her firſt attempts. Her ſitua-
tion in the family of lord Kingſborough was attained through
the medium of the reverend Mr. Prior, one of the maſters of
Eton, under whoſe roof ſhe paſſed ſome time after the reſigna-
tion of her ſchool.

She remained in the houſe of lord Kingſborough, where her
excellent underſtanding and conciliating manners procured her
the reſpeᴄt of the family and the affeᴄtion of her pupils, but
little more than twelve months. Some reſtriᴄtions which had
formerly been impoſed on the young ladies, were in a ſhort time
rendered unneceſſary by the more powerful aſcendency of their
new preceptreſs: while ſhe inſpired her pupils with a generous
confidence, ſhe found her reward in their docility and attachment. A cordial friendſhip grew up more eſpecially between
the eldeſt daughter of lord Kingſborough (afterwards counteſs
Mount Caſhel) and her governeſs, cemented by correſponding
excellencies. The dignity of her talents and the charms of her
converſation procured her, during her reſidence in Ireland, many
valuable friends.

In the ſummer of 1787, ſhe repaired with lord Kingſborough
and his daughters to Briſtol, whence they had projeᴄted a tour to
the continent ; this purpoſe was afterwards relinquiſhed, in con-

4   ſequence

fequence of which Mary Wollftonecraft, who was to have been of the party, clofed her engagements with the family*, for the execution of a fcheme fhe had long anxioufly meditated : at Briftol, the fmall volume entitled " Mary a Fiction," was compofed, in which is delineated, under fictitious circumftances, a glowing and interefting picture of the writer's fentiments and character, as connected more peculiarly with her affection for Frances Blood. Fervid feeling, a vivid imagination, a high-toned and exquifite fenfibility, a bold and original caft of thought, are the diftinguifh-ing characteriftics of this production.

Having quitted Briftol and arrived at the metropolis, fhe re-paired to her publifher, to whom, on receiving an encouraging reception, fhe frankly explained her defigns, requefting his affiftance towards their execution. Availing herfelf of his friend-ly invitation, fhe continued under his roof for fome weeks, whence fhe removed, at Michaelmas 1787, to George-ftreet, on the Surry fide of Blackfriars-bridge, where a houfe was provid-ed for her by the friendfhip of Mr. Johnfon. She now com-menced, with avidity, her literary career. Her novel, which had not yet paffed the prefs, fhe prepared for publication, and made fome progrefs towards an Oriental tale, " The Cave of Fancy," which was afterwards relinquifhed. At this period fhe alfo produced a little work, " Original Stories from Real Life," for the ufe of children. From the fuggeftion of her publifher, fhe applied herfelf to the acquifition of the French, Italian, and German languages, with a view of qualifying herfelf for tranfla-tion. In purfuance of this plan, fhe tranflated, in part, " The New Robinfon," from the French, in which, before its conclu-fion, fhe was anticipated. She alfo abridged and altered " Young Grandifon," from the Dutch ; and compiled, on the model of Dr. Enfield's Speaker, " The Female Reader."

It does not appear that fhe experienced, in thefe occupations, the relief which fhe had promifed herfelf : her *underftanding* was active, but, cut off from thofe endearing fympathies which her

---

* An abfurd report has been propagated, that Mrs. Wollftonecraft was governefs to a younger daughter of lord K———h, whofe imprudence, or misfortunes, have lately rendered her a fubject of public animadverfion. This notion will be utterly confuted by a little attention to chronology.

    feelings

feelings imperioufly demanded, her *heart* languifhed: fhe regretted the connexions of her youth, the friend over whom "the grave had clofed." Her affections, denied their proper objects, turned to bitternefs; her labours had no folace, her exertions no reward. With an underftanding highly cultivated, an imagination richly ftored, a lively tafte for nature, and a thirft for focial pleafure, fhe repined in joylefs folitude.

In the Analytical Review, inftituted by Mr. Johnfon, in the middle of the year 1788, Mary Wollftonecraft was induced to take a confiderable fhare; fhe alfo employed herfelf in tranflating from the French a work by Monf. Necker, on the importance of religious opinions; fhe abridged from the fame language Lavater's Phyfiognomy *; and compreffed Salzmann's Elements of Morality, a German production, into a publication in three volumes duodecimo, which produced a correfpondence between herfelf and the author, who, in a fubfequent period, returned the compliment, by tranflating into German the Vindication of the Rights of Woman. Thefe mifcellaneous avocations comprehended a period of three years, from the autumn of 1787 to the autumn of 1790.

The dejection of fpirits which fhe is faid to have laboured under during this interval of folitary exertion, is, in fome meafure, perhaps to be attributed to the mechanical nature of her occupations, which were little calculated to intereft an ardent temper. A confiderable portion of the profits refulting from her labours was, with a rigorous morality, devoted to purpofes of benevolence. She fought to lofe the fenfe of the languor that oppreffed her, in intereft for the well-being of others; her fifters, her brothers, every individual of her family, were indebted to her generous exertions. She took into her own hands the management of her father's affairs, which, after feveral fruitlefs efforts to arrange, fhe was compelled to refign: for many years this unfortunate man derived his principal fupport from the exertions of his daughter. To thefe charges fhe likewife added the care of an orphan, feven years of age, the child of a deceafed friend. It is impoffible not to paufe here, and pay a tribute of refpect to the powers and virtues of this ad-

* This work has not yet been publifhed.

mirable

mirable female, manifested under difadvantages too obvious to be enumerated; for the obftacles oppofed to the efforts of women, even in procuring an *individual* fubfiftence, are not to be conquered but by an energy and perfeverance, which the habits of their education are little calculated to infpire. In the intervals of her engagements, fhe enjoyed and profited by the literary fociety in which fhe occafionally mingled under the hofpitable roof of her friend Mr. Johnfon. Among whom may be mentioned, as men whofe friendfhip fhe held in high eftimation, the late Mr. George Anderfon, accountant to the board of controul; Mr. Bonnycaftle, the mathematician; Mr. Fufeli, the painter; and Dr. George Fordyce.

The literary exertions of Mary Wollftonecraft, though produfctive of fome pecuniary emolument, had not yet been of a nature to obtain public diftinction: her progrefs had been filent and unambitious; the period now arrived, when her daring genius afferted its powers and affumed its prerogatives. The rigid felf-denial, economy, and feclufion of her habits, had given to her originally fervent character a tincture of enthufiafm; brooding in folitude over her feelings, they became paffions; the felect fociety in which fhe fometimes indulged, was of a nature to roufe her emulation, to excite her intellect, and to give what is termed a mafculine tone to her underftanding.

The French revolution, in its commencement the admiration and aftonifhment of Europe, formed a diftinguifhed æra in the political world. The prejudices of thofe placed without the vortex of intereft, by whom the principle of free inquiry is admitted, and who are accuftomed to fpeculation, give way without difficulty. The high moral tone of Mary Wollftonecraft's fentiments induced her to enlift on the fide of freedom with the enthufiafm that belonged to her character. The publication of Mr. Burke's Reflections on the French Revolution, November 1790, ftimulated into action her newly acquired political ardour, while, in a ftrain of impetuous reafoning and eloquent indignation, fhe combated the arguments of this great champion of eftablifhments. Accuftomed to rapid compofition, hers appeared foremoft of the numerous anfwers provoked by this extraordinary production, and was received with applaufe by the public.

A juft

A juft confidence in her own talents, increafed probably by the fuccefs of this publication, now induced her to effay her ftrength on a fubject that affected her ftill more; a fubject which fhe had keenly felt, on which fhe had deeply meditated, which her fex, her fituation, all the circumftances of her life, irrefiftibly led her to confider,—A Vindication of the Rights of Woman.—There are few fituations in which a woman of cultivated underftanding has not occafion to obferve and deplore, the fyftematic vaffalage, the peculiar difadvantages, civil and focial, to which fhe is fubjected, even in the moft polifhed focieties, on the account of her fex. It might be difficult to convince fuch a woman, confcious of fuperiority to the majority of men with whom fhe converfes, that nature has placed between them, in what refpects intellectual attainments, an infuperable barrier: fhe would be tempted to remind fuch partial reafoners of the reply given to the philofopher who difputed the exiftence of motion, when his adverfary gravely rofe up and walked before him.

It is little wonderful that the magnanimous advocate of freedom, and the opponent of Burke, fhould throw down the gauntlet, challenge her arrogant oppreffors, and, hurried away by a noble enthufiafm, deny the exiftence of a fexual character.

In the caufe of half the human race fhe ftood forth, deprecating and expofing, in a tone of impaffioned eloquence, the various means and arts by which woman had been forcibly fubjugated, flattered into imbecility, and invariably held in bondage. Diffecting the opinions, and commenting upon the precepts of thofe writers who, having exprefsly confidered the condition of the female fex, had fuggefted means for its improvement, fhe endeavours, with force and acutenefs, to convict them of narrow views, voluptuous prejudices, contradictory principles, and felfifh, though impolitic ends. It is but juftice to add, that the principles of this celebrated work are to be found in Catherine Macauley's Treatife on Education. It may alfo be here obferved, that in the intellectual advancement of women, and their confequent

fequent privileges in fociety, is to be traced the progrefs of civili-
zation, or knowledge gradually fuperfeding the dominion of
brute-force.

A production thus bold and fpirited, excited attention and
provoked difcuffion; prejudices were fhocked, vanity wounded,
intereft alarmed, and indolence roufed: yet, amidft the virulence
of oppofition, the clamours of ignorance, the cavils of fuperftition, and the mifreprefentation of wilful perverfion, feeds
were fcattered that promifed, when the ferment had fubfided, a
rich and abundant harveft.   The high mafculine tone, fometimes degenerating into coarfenefs, that characterizes this performance, is in a variety of parts foftened and blended with a
tendernefs of fentiment, an exquifite delicacy of feeling, that
touches the heart, and takes captive the imagination.   As a
compofition it difcovers confiderable power and energy of
thought; but in perfpicuity and arrangement it muft be con-
feffed to be defective: its ftyle, though frequently rich and
glowing, is fometimes inflated, and generally incorrect.   It is
to be regretted, that the author's intention of revifing and reme-
dying thefe defects in a future edition, was protracted, and ulti-
timately defeated.   Its faults are perhaps to be attributed to the
rapidity with which it was compofed and committed to the prefs;
being, we are informed, begun and completed within a period
of fix weeks.   It would be unneceffary to comment on the
imprudence and impolicy manifefted (whatever be the talents of
the writer) by fuch precipitation.   A fecond part was promifed
to the public, for which but fcanty materials were found, after
her deceafe, among the papers of the author.

In September 1791, Mary Wollftonecraft removed from her
refidence in the Surry road, to apartments in Store-ftreet, Bed-
ford-fquare.   This period of her life appears to have been fad-
dened by an unfortunate attachment, that for a time impeded
the progrefs of her mind, corroded her peace, and ultimately
determined her to break the chain of her ideas by an entire
change of fituation and objects.   It is in feclufion only, and in
characters of energy, that ftrong paffions are generated; great
ftruggles have a tendency to increafe them; the enthufiaftic

E e 4   delufion

delufion under which Mary Wollftonecraft now fuffered, never operates but upon fufceptible minds; its feductions, in tempers of extreme fenfibility, are always dangerous, and often fatal.

The affectionate heart of this admirable woman yearned to experience the tender charities of which it was but too exqui-fitely capable; to have fulfilled the duties of wife and mother would have calmed thofe feelings which, forcibly fuppreffed, preyed upon herfelf; converting the natural and healthful pro-penfities of an undebauched mind into a fruitful fource of anguifh. Sentiments of this nature fuffer in the delineation; it is on fuch occafions that human language appears coarfe and feeble: to the few who can conceive thefe feelings no defcrip-tion is neceffary; the attempt to paint them to thofe who un-derftand them not, would be to profane them. " That ro-mantic paffion, which is the concomitant of genius,—Who can clip its wing?—Not proportioned to the puny enjoyments of life, it is only true to the fentiment, and feeds on itfelf. The paffions which have been celebrated for their durability have always been unfortunate. They have acquired ftrength by abfence and conftitutional melancholy. The fancy has hovered round a form of beauty dimly feen *."

In the clofe of the year 1792 Mrs. Wollftonecraft quitted England on a tour to France, with a view, as fhe expreffed herfelf to a friend on the eve of her departure, " to lofe in public happinefs the fenfe of private mifery." She propofed only an excurfion of a few weeks, but protracted her ftay in Paris for more than two years. During her refidence of twelve months in Store-ftreet, her literary ardour feems to have lan-guifhed: fhe produced little befide fome articles for the Analy-tical Review.

It has feldom happened that a diftempered mind has experi-enced relief from mere local change: the ftricken deer carries in its heart the barbed arrow. Monfieur Filliettaz, to whofe houfe in Paris Mary Wollftonecraft had been invited, and whither fhe repaired on her arrival, was at

* Rights of Woman.

that

that period abfent. Alone, in a ftrange country, imperfect-ly acquainted with its language and manners, far removed from thofe familiar and interefting objects, affociated with the idea of home, and to the fenfible heart endearing the recollec-tion; abruptly fevered from cherifhed habits and cordial intima-cies, a cruel languor took poffeffion of her fpirits, while the melancholy tenor of her mind gave a jaundiced hue to the ob-jects that furrounded her. In this difpofition fhe commenced, in letters, a feries of obfervations on the character of the French nation, which fhe foon afterwards difcontinued. One of thefe letters has appeared in her pofthumous works.

In Paris fhe renewed her acquaintance with Thomas Paine, whom fhe had previoufly met in London; while in the friend-fhip of Helen Maria Williams, then refident in France, fhe experienced an agreeable refource. Furnifhed with letters of recommendation to feveral refpectable families, fhe became at length perfonally acquainted with many of the leaders of the French revolution; more particularly of the Briffotine party, for which fhe always expreffed a predilection. Various acci-dents, which fhe was accuftomed to mention with regret, pre-vented her from being introduced to madame Roland, the he-roine of the Girondifts: it is little to be doubted, had thefe extraordinary women met, that they would have felt the at-traction of congenial powers and qualities.

At the houfe of Mr. Thomas Chriftie, author of a volume on the French revolution, four months after her arrival in Paris 1792, fhe commenced an acquaintance with Mr. Gilbert Imlay, a native of North America, which produced on her fubfequent life and character important confequences. With this gentle-man fhe was induced to enter into an intercourfe of the moft tender and interefting nature. To this attachment reafon and duty, as in a former inftance, no longer feemed to be oppofed. In the indulgence of a fentiment that foothed and flattered her heart, fhe was led to a connexion, that, without the forms, had with her all the fanctity and devotednefs of a matrimonial engagement. Whatever were her opinions on the fubject of marriage, as practifed in European countries, where the wife,

refigning

refigning her independence and civil exiftence, becomes the fole
property of her hufband, her conduct in the prefent inftance appears to have been dictated by lefs fpeculative motives. Mr.
Imlay, upon inquiry, fhe found poffeffed but of little perfonal
property: her liberal temper and exertions for her family had
fubjected her to pecuniary embarraffments; in which, from
confiderations more generous than prudent, fhe chofe not to
involve the man whom fhe believed worthy of her heart.
Strong minds diftinguifh between queftions of expedience and
of morality; fhe was not ignorant either of the forfeitures or
the hazards to which fhe expofed herfelf: the former fhe had
courage to contemn; the latter, credulous from inexperience,
and too ingenuous for diftruft, fhe did not, as it proved, fuffici-
ently advert to. In a cafe like this, a folitary individual affords
no example; Mary Wollftonecraft's experiment was in a high
degree perilous; it is improbable that another woman fhould
exift, equal in fortitude and refource, fimilarly circumftanced:
nor, for the credit of human nature, dare we believe, how profligate foever may be the ftate of fociety, that a conduct, originating in motives thus magnanimous, would in all inftances
have met with a fimilar reward. There are few rules fo univer-
fal as to admit of no exception. The mind of Mary Wollftonecraft was not formed on common principles. That fhe was unfortunately fallible in appreciating merit muft be allowed, and is to
be regretted: neither will the diftracted ftate of the country in
which fhe then refided, be overlooked by the candid mind when
taking a review of this part of her hiftory. Her heart was
formed for the endearments of domeftic life; in the profpect of
the gratification of this darling propenfity it refted with delight;
while the habitual melancholy of her temper gave place to ferene
confidence.

" Fatigued during my youth (faid fhe, in a letter addreffed
to this chofen friend), by the moft arduous ftruggles, not only
to obtain independence, but to render myfelf ufeful; not
merely pleafure, for which I had the moft lively tafte, I mean
the fimple pleafures that flow from paffion and affection, ef-
caped me, but the moft melancholy views of life were im-
                                                        preffed

preffed by a difappointed heart on my mind. Since I knew you, I have been endeavouring to go back to my former nature, and have allowed fome time to glide away, winged with the delight which only fpontaneous enjoyment can give."

On another occafion:—" You can fcarcely imagine with what pleafure I anticipate the day when we are to begin almoft to live together; and you would fmile to hear how many plans of employment I have in my head, now that I am confident my heart has found peace in your bofom. Cherifh me with that dignified tendernefs which I have only found in you; and your own dear girl will try to keep under a quicknefs of feeling, that has fometimes given you pain—Yes, I will be *good*, that I may deferve to be happy; and whilft you love me, I cannot again fall into the miferable ftate which rendered life a burthen almoft too heavy to be borne."

" Recollection now makes my heart bound to thee; but, it is not to thy money-getting face, though I cannot be ferioufly difpleafed with the exertion which increafes my efteem, or rather is what I fhould have expected from thy character.—No; I have thy honeft countenance before me—Pop—relaxed by tendernefs; a little—little wounded by my whims; and thy eyes gliftening with fympathy.—Thy lips then feel fofter than foft—and I reft my cheek on thine, forgetting all the world.—I have not left the hue of love out of the picture—the rofy glow; and fancy has fpread it over my own cheeks, I believe, for I feel them burning, whilft a delicious tear trembles in my eye, that would be all your own, if a grateful emotion directed to the Father of nature, who has made me thus alive to happinefs, did not give more warmth to the fentiment it divides."

" Though I have juft fent a letter off, yet, as captain ———— offers to take one, I am not willing to let him go without a kind greeting, becaufe trifles of this fort, without having any effect on my mind, damp my fpirits:—and you, with all your ftruggles to be manly, have fome of this fame fenfibility.—Do not bid it begone, for I love to fee it ftriving to mafter your features; befides, thefe kind of fympathies are the life of affection: and why, in cultivating our underftandings, fhould we try to
dry

dry up thefe fprings of pleafure, which gufh out to give a frefh-nefs to days browned by care!"

" I have juft received your kind and rational letter, and would fain hide my face, glowing with fhame for my folly.— I would hide it in your bofom, if you would again open it to me, and neftle clofely till you bade my fluttering heart be ftill, by faying that you forgave me. With eyes overflowing with tears, and in the humbleft attitude, I intreat you. - Do not turn from me, for indeed I love you fondly, and have been very wretched, fince the night I was fo cruelly hurt by thinking that you had no confidence in me——

" It is time for me to grow more reafonable, a few more of thefe caprices of fenfibility would deftroy me. I have, in fact, been very much indifpofed for a few days paft, and the notion that I was tormenting, or perhaps killing, a poor little animal, about whom I am grown anxious and tender, now I feel it alive, made me worfe. My bowels have been dreadfully difordered, and every thing I ate or drank difagreed with my ftomach; ftill I feel intimations of its exiftence, though they have been fainter.

" Do you think that the creature goes regularly to fleep? I am ready to afk as many queftions as Voltaire's Man of Forty Crowns. Ah! do not continue to be angry with me! You perceive that I am already fmiling through my tears—You have lightened my heart, and my frozen fpirits are melting into playfulnefs."

" I am afraid that I have vexed you, my own ——. I know the quicknefs of your feelings—and let me, in the fince-rity of my heart, affure you, there is nothing I would not fuffer to make you happy. My own happinefs wholly depends on you—and, knowing you, when my reafon is not clouded, I look forward to a rational profpect of as much felicity as the earth affords—with a little dafh of rapture into the bargain, if you will look at me, when we meet again, as you have fome-times greeted, your humbled, yet moft affectionate."

" What a picture have you fketched of our fire-fide! Yes, my love, my fancy was inftantly at work, and I found my head

on

on your fhoulder, whilft my eyes were fixed on the little creatures that were clinging about your knees. I did not abfolutely
determine that there fhould be fix—if you have not fet your
heart on this round number."

" You have, by your tendernefs and worth, twifted yourfelf more artfully round my heart, than I fuppofed poffible.—
Let me indulge the thought, that I have thrown out fome ten-
drils to cling to the elm by which I wifh to be fupported.—This
is talking a new language for me!—But, knowing that I am
not a parafite-plant, I am willing to receive the proofs of affection, that every pulfe replies to, when I think of being once
more in the fame houfe with you.—God blefs you!

" Yours truly."

" Believe me, fage fir, you have not fufficient refpeft for
the imagination—I could prove to you in a trice that it is the
mother of fentiment, the great diftinction of our nature, the
only purifier of the paffions—animals have a portion of reafon,
and equal, if not more exquifite, fenfes; but no trace of imagination, or her offspring tafte, appears in any of their actions.
The impulfe of the fenfes, paffions, if you will, and the con-
clufions of reafon, draw men together; but the imagination is
the true fire, ftolen from heaven, to animate this cold creature
of clay, producing all thofe fine fympathies that lead to rapture,
rendering men focial by expanding their hearts, inftead of
leaving them leifure to calculate how many comforts fociety
affords."

Thofe who can coldly regard the exquifite picture which the
preceding extracts afford, will but wafte their labour in pe-
rufing a narrative which they are little likely to comprehend:
it is not to the tribunal of their judgments that fentiments like
thefe can appeal.

A project of vifiting Switzerland, which Mrs. Wollftonecraft had meditated, was, in the change of her profpects, relinquifhed; her refidence being fixed for the prefent in Neuilly,
a village three miles from Paris, where fhe occupied apartments
in the houfe of a gardener, pleafantly fituated in the midft of
his garden. In this feclufion fhe planned and partly executed,

S

A moral

A moral and hiſtorical View of the French Revolution, one volume only of which has been given to the public. From motives of delicacy her intercourſe with Mr. Imlay, in whoſe honour and tenderneſs ſhe confided, had hitherto been conducted in privacy; till, four months after its commencement, they were induced to divulge it, by the decree of the national convention reſpecting the impriſonment of the Engliſh. That the engagement was held mutually ſacred, ſhe ſeemed to entertain no doubts, having purpoſed to repair with Mr. Imlay to ſettle in America. In conſequence of the danger which now threatened her as an Engliſhwoman, it was judged neceſſary that ſhe ſhould bear the name of Imlay, and paſs as the wife of an American, for which purpoſe a certificate was granted by the ambaſſador of the United States. Having thus publicly avowed their attachment, they thought it moſt eligible to repair to Paris, and reſide under the ſame roof.

Till the preſent period her life had been a ſeries of difficulties, ſorrows, and diſappointments, to which her acute ſenſibility had added keener pangs: the degree of calamity is to be eſtimated rather by the ſuſceptibility of the ſufferer, than by the apparent magnitude of the event. There are perſons (to adopt the language of the writer* from whoſe memoirs the materials for this narrative are principally extracted) " endowed with the moſt exquiſite and delicious ſenſibility, whoſe minds ſeem almoſt of too fine a texture to encounter the viciſſitudes of human affairs, to whom pleaſure is tranſport, and diſappointment is agony indiſcribable."

Such appears to have been the character of this ſingular woman. To her affections, long forbidden to expand themſelves, exalted to enthuſiaſm by conſtraint, ſhe now gave a looſe. Her ingenuous ſpirit, a ſtranger to diſtruſt, had yet a melancholy experience to acquire of the corrupt habits of mankind. Her confidence, her tenderneſs, was unbounded, laviſh, ineffable, combining the force, the devotion, the exquiſite delicacy and refinement, which in minds of energy, the chaſte

* Mr. Godwin.

habits

habits of female youth are calculated to infpire. Abforbed in a
delicious tranquillity, fhe fondly anticipated a period, now approaching, when to the affections of a wife would be added the
fympathies of a mother : *her heart was fatisfied*, paft forrows
faded from her memory, or were recalled only to heighten by
contraft prefent felicity.

From this vifion of happinefs fhe was awakened by the temporary abfence of Mr. I. who, having engaged in commerce,
was called from Paris, in the following September, to fuperin-
tend the fhipping of goods from Havre-de-Grace. Once more
left in folitude, a prey to her own fenfations, various inquietudes
racked her foul, as fhe vainly expected, week after week,
month after month, the return of him whofe apprehended
" tendernefs and worth had twifted him clofely round her
heart." The ferocious and fanguinary temper which the French
government at this period affumed, added to her anxiety and
deepened the anguifh which, in defpite of her efforts, again
faftened upon her fpirits. Her feelings, on the execution of
Briffot, Vergniaud, and the twenty deputies, were heightened
to indignant agony. In January 1794, finding the return of
Mr. Imlay ftill uncertain, fhe took the refolution of quitting
Paris (become, under the domination of Robefpierre, a theatre
of blood), and joining him at Havre. From January to September another interval of domeftic tranquillity enfued, during
which fhe gave birth to a daughter, on whom fhe beftowed
the name of Frances, in remembrance of the friend of her
youth.

In September Mr. I. departed from Havre and repaired to
London, while by his defire fhe returned to Paris, the death of
Robefpierre having put a period to the profcriptions that had
ftained the revolution with the blood of its moft meritorious
citizens. Mr. Imlay had promifed to rejoin her, in Paris,
within two months. This expectation, on which fhe fondly
dwelt, to foften the pain of abfence, was fruftrated; new inquietudes, conjectures, and apprehenfions, protracted the mifery
of difappointment; anxiety was continually kept alive by the
alternations of hope and fear, by fufpenfe fo intolerable to an

ardent

ardent temper; her mind became weakened, her health enfeebled, her fortitude broken, her time and talents wasted, till
despair at length seized upon her heart. She struggled for a
while to impose upon herself, to repress the convictions that
forced themselves upon her, to resist that humiliating retraction
of the judgment, respecting him on whose faith she had rested
her future hopes, which the sensible heart admits not without
agony. The fabric of rare felicity, which her fancy had busied
itself in erecting, tottered to its foundation, threatening to
overwhelm in its fall her darling plans. The following extracts
from the letters published in her Posthumous Works, afford an
affecting and lively representation of the present state of her
mind:

" I have been, my love, for some days tormented by fears,
that I would not allow to assume a form—I had been expecting
you daily—and I heard that many vessels had been driven on
shore during the late gale.—Well, I now see your letter—and
find that you are safe; I will not regret then that your exertions have hitherto been so unavailing.

—   —   —   —   —   —   —   —   —

—   —   —   —   —   —   —   —   —

—   —   —   —   —   —   —   —   —

" Be that as it may, return to me when you have arranged
the other matters, which —— has been crowding on you. I
want to be sure that you are safe—and not separated from me by
a sea that must be passed. For, feeling that I am happier than
I ever was, do you wonder at my sometimes dreading that fate
has not done persecuting me? Come to me, my dearest friend,
husband, father of my child!—All these fond ties glow at my
heart at this moment, and dim my eyes.—With you an independence is desirable; and it is always within our reach, if affluence escapes us—without you the world again appears empty to
me. But I am recurring to some of the melancholy thoughts
that have flitted across my mind for some days past, and haunted
my dreams."

" Stay, my friend, whilst it is *absolutely* necessary.—I will
give you no tenderer name, though it glows at my heart, unless
you

you come the moment the fettling the *prefent* objects permit.—
I do not confent to your taking any other journey—or the little
woman and I will be off, the Lord knows where. But, as I
had rather owe every thing to your affection, and, I may add,
to your reafon, (for this immoderate defire of wealth, which
makes ———— fo eager to have you remain, is contrary to
your principles of action), I will not importune you.—I will
only tell you, that I long to fee you—and, being at peace with
you, I fhall be hurt, rather than made angry, by delays.—
Having fuffered fo much in life, do not be furprifed if I fometimes, when left to myfelf, grow gloomy, and fuppofe that it
was all a dream, and that my happinefs is not to laft. I fay
happinefs, becaufe remembrance retrenches all the dark fhades
of the picture."

" I will own to you that, feeling extreme tendernefs for my
little girl, I grow fad very often when I am playing with her,
that you are not here, to obferve with me how her mind un-
folds, and her little heart becomes attached!—Thefe appear to
me to be true pleafures—and ftill you fuffer them to efcape you,
in fearch of what we may never enjoy.—It is your own maxim
to " live in the prefent moment."—*If you do*—ftay, for God's
fake; but tell me the truth—if not, tell me when I may expect to fee you, and let me not be always vainly looking for you,
till I grow fick at heart.

" Adieu! I am a little hurt.—I muft take my darling to
my bofom to comfort me."

" I do not like this life of continual inquietude—and, *entre
nous*, I am determined to try to earn fome money here myfelf,
in order to convince you that, if you chufe to run about the
world to get a fortune, it is for yourfelf—for the little girl and
I will live without your affiftance, unlefs you are with us. I
may be termed proud—Be it fo—but I will never abandon certain principles of action."

" I confider fidelity and conftancy as two diftinct things;
yet the former is neceffary, to give life to the other—and fuch a
degree of refpect do I think due to myfelf, that, if only probity,
which is a good thing in its place, brings you back, never re-

F f'   turn.

turn!—for, if a wandering of the heart, or even a caprice of the imagination, detains you—there is an end of all my hopes of happinefs—I could not forgive it, if I would.

" I have gotten into a melancholy mood, you perceive. You know my opinion of men in general; you know that I think them fyftematic tyrants, and that it is the rareft thing in the world, to meet with a man with fufficient delicacy of feeling, to govern defire. When I am thus fad, I lament that my little darling, fondly as I doat on her, is a girl.—I am forrry to have a tie to a world that for me is ever fown with thorns."

" You left me indifpofed, though you have taken no notice of it; and the moft fatiguing journey I ever had, contributed to continue it. However, I recovered my health; but a neg-lected cold, and continual inquietude during the laft two months, have reduced me to a ftate of weaknefs I never before experienced. Thofe who did not know that the canker-worm was at work at the core, cautioned me about fuckling my child too long.—God preferve this poor child, and render her happier than her mother!

" But I am wandering from my fubject: indeed my head turns giddy, when I think that all the confidence I have had in the affection of others is come to this.—I did not expect this blow from you. I have done my duty to you and my child; and if I am not to have any return of affection to reward me, I have the fad confolation of knowing that I deferved a better fate. My foul is weary—I am fick at heart; and, but for this little darling, I would ceafe to care about a life, which is now ftripped of every charm."

" When I determined to live with you, I was only governed by affection.—I would fhare poverty with you, but I turn with affright from the fea of trouble on which you are entering.—I have certain principles of action: I know what I look for to found my happinefs on.—It is not money,—With you I wifhed for fufficient to procure the comforts of life—as it is, lefs will do.—I can ftill exert myfelf to obtain the neceffaries of life for my child, and fhe does not want more at prefent.—I have two

or

WOLLSTONECRAFT. 435

for three plans in my head to earn our fubfiftence; for do not fuppofe that, neglected by you, I will lie under obligations of a pecuniary kind to you!—No; I would fooner fubmit to menial fervice.—I wanted the fupport of your affection—that gone, all is over!—I did not think, when I complained of ——'s contemptible avidity to accumulate money, that he would have dragged you into his fchemes."

" When you firft entered into thefe plans, you bounded your views to the gaining of a thoufand pounds. It was fufficient to have procured a farm in America, which would have been an independence. You find now that you did not know yourfelf, and that a certain fituation in life is more neceffary to you than you imagined—more neceffary than an uncorrupted heart—For a year or two, you may procure yourfelf what you call pleafure; eating, drinking, and women; but, in the folitude of declining life, I fhall be remembered with regret—I was going to fay with remorfe, but checked my pen.

" As I have never concealed the nature of my connexion with you, your reputation will not fuffer. I fhall never have a confidant: I am content with the approbation of my own mind; and, if there be a fearcher of hearts, mine will not be defpifed. Reading what you have written relative to the defertion of women, I have often wondered how theory and practice could be fo different, till I recollected, that the fentiments of paffion, and the refolves of reafon, are very diftinct."

" Society fatigues me inexpreffibly—So much fo, that finding fault with every one, I have only reafon enough, to difcover that the fault is in myfelf. My child alone interefts me, and, but for her, I fhould not take any pains to recover my health.

" As it is, I fhall wean her, and try if by that ftep (to which I feel a repugnance, for it is my only folace) I can get rid of my cough. Phyficians talk much of the danger attending any complaint on the lungs, after a woman has fuckled for fome months. They lay a ftrefs alfo on the neceffity of keeping the mind tranquil—and, my God! how has mine been haraffed!

But

But whilft the caprices of other women are gratified, " the wind of heaven not fuffered to vifit them too rudely," I have not found a guardian angel, in heaven or on earth, to ward off forrow or care from my bofom."

In the beginning of April 1795, Mr. I. ftill alledging bufinefs as an excufe for his ftay, requefted her to meet him in London.

" Here I am (fays fhe, at Havre), on the wing towards you, and I write now, only to tell you, that you may expect me in the courfe of three or four days; for I fhall not attempt to give vent to the different emotions which agitate my heart—You may term a feeling, which appears to me to be a degree of delicacy that naturally arifes from fenfibility, pride—Still I cannot indulge the very affectionate tendernefs which glows in my bofom, without trembling, till I fee, by your eyes, that it is mutual.

" I fit, loft in thought, looking at the fea—and tears rufh into my eyes, when I find that I am cherifhing any fond expectations.—I have indeed been fo unhappy this winter, I find it as difficult to acquire frefh hopes, as to regain tranquillity.—Enough of this—lie ftill, foolifh heart!—But for the little girl, I could almoft wifh that it fhould ceafe to beat, to be no more alive to the anguifh of difappointment."

From Havre fhe proceeded to London, with a foreboding heart, ftruggling to reprefs hope fo often proved delufive, yet fo congenial to her fanguine fpirit : fhe returned to her native country only to find her cruelleft apprehenfions verified, in the infidelity and fubfequent defertion of a man to whom fhe had lavifhly confided her happinefs.

" I have laboured (fays fhe, in a letter bearing the date of London) to calm my mind fince you left me—Still I find that tranquillity is not to be obtained by exertion; it is a feeling fo different from the refignation of defpair!—I am however no longer angry with you—nor will I ever utter another complaint —there are arguments which convince the reafon, whilft they carry death to the heart.—We have had too many cruel explanations,

planations, that not only cloud every future profpect; but embitter the remembrances which alone give life to affection.—Let the fubject never be revived!

" It feems to me that I have not only loft the hope, but the power of being happy.—Every emotion is now fharpened by anguifh.—My foul has been fhook, and my tone of feelings deftroyed.—I have gone out—and fought for diffipation, if not amufement, merely to fatigue ftill more, I find, my irritable nerves——

" My friend—my dear friend—examine yourfelf well—I am out of the queftion; for, alas! I am nothing—and difcover what you wifh to do—what will render you moft comfortable —or, to be more explicit—whether you defire to live with me, or part for ever? When you can once afcertain it, tell me frankly, I conjure you!—for, believe me, I have very involuntarily interrupted your peace."

" I will not diftrefs you by talking of the depreffion of my fpirits, or the ftruggle I had to keep alive my dying heart.—It is even now too full to allow me to write with compofure.— *****,—dear *****,—am I always to be toffed about thus?— fhall I never find an afylum to reft *contented* in? How can you love to fly about continually—dropping down, as it were, in a new world—cold and ftrange!—every other day? Why do you not attach thofe tender emotions round the idea of home, which even now dim my eyes?—This alone is affection—every thing elfe is only humanity, electrified by fympathy."

" Why did fhe thus obftinately cling to an ill-ftarred, unhappy paffion? Becaufe it is of the very effence of affection, to feek to perpetuate itfelf. He does not love, who can refign this cherifhed fentiment, without fuffering fome of the fharpeft ftruggles that our nature is capable of enduring*."

Near feven weeks fhe paffed under the fame roof with Mr. I. (in a furnifhed houfe which he had prepared for her reception), in vain efforts to awaken his fenfibility and revive his tendernefs. In proportion as had been her truft, was now her difappoint-

* Godwin's Memoir of the Vindicator of the Rights of Woman.

ment;

438   WOLLSTONECRAFT.

ment; she had yet to learn that sensuality hardens the heart, blasts its best affections, absorbs it in selfish gratification, rendering it callous to every sentiment of justice and humanity. The man on whose principles her mind had rested, with whom her imagination had associated every virtue, forgot in the blandishments of a young actress, from a company of strolling comedians, the sacred duties of a father, the tender endearments of a chaste ineffable affection, that during its influence, by giving a temporary dignity to his character, had concealed its grossness, and imposed on the discernment of a mind, with which his own had otherwise claimed no kindred.

The strength of a passion depends principally on the imagination of the person upon whom it operates, that sketching a grand, ideal, picture, fondly attaches itself to fancied excellence, frequently associated by slight accidents to the real qualities of its object: yet the sentiments thus produced are not the less genuine, nor the less in nature; however erroneous, they are perhaps among the sweetest and the sublimest that dignify the human character: he whom they have never subdued may boast his firmness and demand our respect; but it is to the being accessible to these delightful sensibilities that all the *interesting affections* spontaneously cling. That enthusiasm which constitutes the grander passions, is founded on *illusion*: stripped of the glowing colours in which fancy decks them, what are the objects for which ambition wades through seas of blood, for which martyrs, in all causes, for all opinions, braving destruction, press forward to the scaffold or the stake?

Exhausted by contending passions, disgusted by disappointment, loathing life, this unfortunate woman determined to die; but her purpose, for the present, was prevented by him who, absorbed in selfish indulgence, had sported with her feelings, trifled with her existence, and consigned her to anguish and despair. The woman *who loved him*, to whom he had voluntarily given the most sacred claims, the mother of his child, the friend who sought to ennoble his character, by reviving in his heart the sentiment that had purified it, was forgotten in the caprices of sensuality.

                                                          Snatched

I.

WOLLSTONECRAFT. 439

Snatched from the defperation of her own purpofes, this interefting woman once more roufed the energies of her character in the fervice of the man who had transfixed her heart with an envenomed arrow ; the man for whom *fhe had dared to die !* A commercial bufinefs in Norway, in which Mr. I——— was materially concerned, required the prefence of an active agent : Mary Wollftonecraft generoufly determined on this occafion to rifque the voyage, accompanied only by a female fervant, and the little Frances, from whom fhe could not refolve on feparating herfelf. This tour, for the purpofe of promoting the intereft of one who contemned the zeal and worth he was incapable of appreciating, gave rife to a fubfequent publication, entitled Letters from Scandinavia, a work that addreffes itfelf to the heart, and feizes on its affections.

" I am haraffed by your embarraffments (faid fhe, in a private letter addreffed to the fame perfon), and fhall certainly ufe all my efforts to make the bufinefs terminate to your fatisfaction in which I am engaged.

" My friend—my deareft friend—I feel my fate united to yours by the moft facred principles of my foul, and the yearnings of—yes, I will fay it—a true, unfophifticated heart."

" Do write by every occafion ! I am anxious to hear how your affairs go on ; and, ftill more, to be convinced that you are not feparating yourfelf from us. For my little darling is calling papa, and adding her parrot word—Come, Come ! And will you not come, and let us exert ourfelves?—I fhall recover all my energy, when I am convinced that my exertions will draw us more clofely together."

" Often do I figh, when I think of your entanglements in bufinefs, and your extreme reftleffnefs of mind. Even now I am almoft afraid to afk you, whether the pleafure of being free, does not over-balance the pain you felt at parting with me? Sometimes I indulge the hope that you will feel me neceffary to you—or why fhould we meet again ?—but, the moment after, defpair damps my rifing fpirits, aggravated by the emotions of tendernefs, which ought to foften the cares of life.—God blefs you !" .

Further extracts from letters which (though they have ap-

F f 4

peared fince her death, were not meant for the public eye) cannot fail, in this place, of interefting the reader.

" The laft time we were feparated, was a feparation indeed
on your part—Now you have acted more ingenuoufly, let the
moft affectionate interchange of fentiments fill up the aching void
of difappointment. I almoft dread that your plans will prove
abortive—yet fhould the moft unlucky turn fend you home to
us, convinced that a true friend is a treafure, I fhould not much
mind having to ftruggle with the world again. Accufe me not
of pride—yet fometimes, when nature has opened my heart to its
author, I have wondered that you did not fet a higher value on
my heart."

" What are you about? How are your affairs going on? It may
be a long time before you anfwer thefe queftions. My dear friend,
my heart finks within me!—Why am I forced thus to ftruggle
continually with my affections and feelings?—Ah! why are thofe
affections and feelings the fource of fo much mifery, when they
feem to have been given to vivify my heart, and extend my ufefulnefs! But I muft not dwell on this fubject. Will you not endeavour to cherifh all the affection you can for me? What am I faying? Rather forget me, if you can—if other gratifications are
dearer to you. How is every remembrance of mine embittered
by difappointment? What a world is this! They only feem
happy, who never look beyond fenfual or artificial enjoyments.—
Adieu!"

" This is the fifth dreary day I have been imprifoned by the
wind, with every outward object to difguft the fenfes, and unable
to banifh the remembrances that fadden my heart.

" How am I altered by difappointment! When going to
————, ten years ago, the elafticity of my mind was fufficient to
ward off wearinefs—and the imagination ftill could dip her brufh
in the rainbow of fancy, and fketch futurity in fmiling colours.
Now I am going towards the North in fearch of funbeams!
Will any ever warm this defolated heart? All nature feems to
frown—or rather mourn with me. Every thing is cold—cold
as my expectations!"

" My friend—my friend, I am not well—a deadly weight of
forrow

forrow lies heavily on my heart. I am again toffed on the troubled billows of life; and obliged to cope with difficulties, without being buoyed up by the hopes that alone render them bearable. "How flat, dull, and unprofitable," appears to me all the buftle into which I fee people here fo eagerly enter! I long every night to go to bed, to hide my melancholy face in my pillow; but there is a canker-worm in my bofom that never fleeps."

"Believe me (and my eyes fill with tears of tendernefs as I affure you) there is nothing I would not endure in the way of privation, rather than difturb your tranquillity. If I am fated to be unhappy, I will labour to hide my forrows in my own bofom; and you fhall always find me a faithful, affectionate friend.

"I grow more and more attached to my little girl—and I cherifh this affection without fear, becaufe it muft be a long time before it can become bitternefs of foul. She is an interefting creature. On fhip-board, how often, as I gazed at the fea, have I longed to bury my troubled bofom in the lefs troubled deep; afferting with Brutus, "that the virtue I had followed too far, was merely an empty name!" and nothing but the fight of her —her playful fmiles, which feemed to cling and twine round my heart—could have ftopped me.

"What peculiar mifery has fallen to my fhare! To act up to my principles, I have laid the ftricteft reftraint on my very thoughts—yes; not to fully the delicacy of my feelings, I have reined in my imagination; and ftarted with affright from every fenfation (I allude to ——), that, ftealing with balmy fweetnefs into my foul, led me to fcent from afar the fragrance of reviving nature.

"My friend, I have dearly paid for one conviction. Love, in fome minds, is an affair of fentiment, arifing from the fame delicacy of perception (or tafte) as renders them alive to the beauties of nature, poetry, &c. alive to the charms of thofe evanefcent graces that are, as it were, impalpable—they muft be felt, they cannot be defcribed.

"Love is a want of my heart. I have examined myfelf lately with

with more care than formerly, and find, that to deaden is not to
calm the mind—Aiming at tranquillity, I have almoſt deſtroyed
all the energy of my ſoul—almoſt rooted out what renders it
eſtimable.   Yes, I have damped that enthuſiaſm of character,
which converts the groſſeſt materials into a fuel, that impercep-
tibly feeds hopes, which aſpire above common enjoyment.   De-
ſpair, ſince the birth, of my child, has rendered me ſtupid—ſoul
and body ſeemed to be fading away before the withering touch of
diſappointment."

" I ſhall not, however, complain.   There are misfortunes ſo
great, as to ſilence the uſual expreſſions of ſorrow.   Believe me,
there is ſuch a thing as a broken heart!   There are characters
whoſe very energy preys upon them ; and who, ever inclined to
cheriſh by reflection ſome paſſion, cannot reſt ſatisfied with the
common comforts of life.   I have endeavoured to fly from myſelf,
and launched into all the diſſipation poſſible here, only to feel
keener anguiſh, when alone with my child.

" Still, could any thing pleaſe me—had not diſappointment
cut me off from life, this romantic country, theſe fine evenings,
would intereſt me.   My God! can any thing? and am I ever
to feel alive only to painful ſenſations?   But it cannot—it ſhall
not laſt long."

" I am now on my journey to ———.   I felt more at leaving
my child, than I thought I ſhould—and, whilſt at night I imagined every inſtant that I heard the half-formed ſounds of her
voice,—I aſked myſelf how I could think of parting with her for
ever, of leaving her thus helpleſs?

" Poor lamb!   It may run very well in a tale, that " God
will temper the winds to the ſhorn lamb !" but how can I expect that ſhe will be ſhielded, when my naked boſom has had to
brave continually the pitileſs ſtorm?   Yes; I could add, with
poor Lear—What is the war of elements to the pangs of diſap-
pointed affection, and the horror ariſing from a diſcovery of a
breach of confidence, that ſnaps every ſocial tie !

" All is not right ſomewhere !—When you firſt knew me, I
was not thus loſt.   I could ſtill confide—for I opened my heart

to you—of this only comfort you have deprived me, whilst my happiness, you tell me, was your first object. Strange want of judgment!

"I will not complain; but, from the foundnefs of your unं derstanding, I am convinced, if you give yourself leave to reflect, you will also feel, that your conduct to me, fo far from being generous, has not been just. I mean not to allude to factitious principles of morality; but to the fimple bafis of all rectitude. However I did not intend to argue—Your not writing is cruel—and my reafon is perhaps difturbed by conftant wretchednefs."

"Write to me then, my friend, and write explicitly. I have fuffered, God knows, fince I left you. Ah! you have never felt this kind of ficknefs of heart! My mind, however, is at prefent painfully active, and the fympathy I feel almoft rifes to agony. But this is not a fubject of complaint, it has afforded me pleafure,—and reflected pleafure is all I have to hope for—if a fpark of hope be yet alive in my forlorn bofom.

"I will try to write with a degree of compofure. I wifh for us to live together, becaufe I want you to acquire an habitual tendernefs for my poor girl. I cannot bear to think of leaving her alone in the world, or that fhe fhould only be protected by your fenfe of duty. Next to preferving her, my moft earneft wifh is not to difturb your peace. I have nothing to expect, and little to fear, in life—There are wounds that can never be healed—but they may be allowed to fefter in filence without wincing.

"Yes; I fhall be happy—This heart is worthy of the blifs its feelings anticipate—and I cannot even perfuade myfelf, wretched as they have made me, that my principles and fentiments are not founded in nature and truth."

"You tell me that my letters torture you; I will not defcribe the effect yours have on me. I received three this morning, the laft dated the 7th of this month. I mean not to give vent to the emotions they produced. Certainly you are right; our minds are not congenial. I have lived in an ideal world, and foftered fentiments that you do not comprehend—or you would not treat me thus. I am not, I will not be, merely an object of compaffion

—a clog,

—a clog, however light, to teafe you. Forget that I exift: I will never remind you. Something emphatical whifpers me to put an end to thefe ftruggles. Be free—I will not torment, when I cannot pleafe. I can take care of my child; you need not continually tell me that our fortune is infeparable, *that you will try to cherifh tendernefs* for me. Do no violence to yourfelf! When we are feparated, our intereft, fince you give fo much weight to pecuniary confiderations, will be entirely divided. I want not protection without affection; and fupport I need not, whilft my faculties are undifturbed."

" I am weary of travelling—yet feem to have no home—no refting-place to look to.—I am ftrangely caft off.—How often, paffing through the rocks, I have thought, " But for this child, I would lay my head on one of them, and never open my eyes again !" With a heart feelingly alive to all the affections of my nature—I have never met with one, fofter than the ftone that I would fain take for my laft pillow. I once thought I had, but it was all a delufion. I meet with families continually, who are bound together by affection or principle—and, when I am confcious that I have fulfilled the duties of my ftation, almoft to a forgetfulnefs of myfelf, I am ready to demand, in a murmuring tone, of Heaven, " Why am I thus abandoned ?"

" By what criterion of principle or affection, you term my queftions extraordinary and unneceffary, I cannot determine.— You defire me to decide—I had decided. You muft have had long ago two letters of mine, from ————, to the fame purport, to confider.—In thefe, God knows ! there was but too much affection, and the agonies of a diftracted mind were but too faithfully pourtrayed !—What more then had I to fay ?—The negative was to come from you.—You had perpetually recurred to your promife of meeting me in the autumn—Was it extraordinary that I fhould demand a yes, or no ?—Your letter is written with extreme harfhnefs, coldnefs I am accuftomed to; in it I find not a trace of the tendernefs of humanity, much lefs of friendfhip."

" The tremendous power who formed this heart, muft have forefeen that, in a world in which felf-intereft, in various fhapes,

is

is the principal mobile, I had little chance of escaping misery.—
To the fiat of fate I submit.—I am content to be wretched ; but
I will not be contemptible.—Of me you have no cause to complain, but for having had too much regard for you—for having
expected a degree of permanent happiness, when you only sought
for a momentary gratification.

I am strangely deficient in sagacity.—Uniting myself to you,
your tenderness seemed to make me amends for all my former
misfortunes.—On this tenderness and affection with what confidence did I rest !—but I leaned on a spear, that has pierced me
to the heart.—You have thrown off a faithful friend, to pursue
the caprices of the moment."

" Do not keep me in suspense.—I expect nothing from you,
or any human being : my die is cast !—I have fortitude enough
to determine to do my duty ; yet I cannot raise my depressed
spirits, or calm my trembling heart.—That being who moulded
it thus, knows that I am unable to tear up by the roots the propensity to affection which has been the torment of my life—but
life will have an end !"

" I must tell you, that I am very much mortified by your
continually offering me pecuniary assistance—and, considering
your going to the new house, as an open avowal that you abandon me, let me tell you that I will sooner perish than receive
any thing from you—and I say this at the moment when I am
disappointed in my first attempt to obtain a temporary supply.
But this even pleases me ; an accumulation of disappointments
and misfortunes seems to suit the habit of my mind."

" The grief I cannot conquer (for some cruel recollections
never quit me, banishing almost every other) I labour to conceal
in total solitude.—My life, therefore, is but an exercise of fortitude, continually on the stretch—and hope never gleams in this
tomb, where I am buried alive."

" My affection for you is rooted in my heart.—I know you
are not what you now seem—nor will you always act, or feel, as
you now do, though I may never be comforted by the change.—
Even at Paris, my image will haunt you.—You will see my pale
face

face—and fometimes the tears of anguish will drop on your heart; which you have forced from mine.

" I cannot write. I thought I could quickly have refuted all your *ingenious* arguments; but my head is confufed.—Right or wrong, I am miferable!

" It feems to me, that my conduct has always been governed by the ftrictest principles of juftice and truth. Yet, how wretched have my focial feelings and delicacy of fentiment rendered me!— I have loved with my whole foul, only to difcover that I had no chance of a return—and that exiftence is a burthen without it.

" I do not perfectly underftand you.—If, by the offer of your friendfhip, you ftill only mean pecuniary fupport—I muft again reject it.—Trifling are the ills of poverty in the fcale of my misfortunes.—God blefs you!"

" Refentment, and even anger, are momentary emotions with me—and I wifhed to tell you fo, that if you ever think of me, it may not be in the light of an enemy.

" That I have not been ufed well I muft ever feel; perhaps, not always with the keen anguifh I do at prefent—for I begad even now to write calmly, and I cannot reftrain my tears.

" I am ftunned!—Your late conduct ftill appears to me a frightful dream.—Ah! afk yourfelf if you have not condefcended to employ a little addrefs, I could almoft fay cunning, unworthy of you?—Principles are facred things—and we never play with truth, with impunity.

" The expectation (I have too fondly nourifhed it) of regaining your affection, every day grows fainter and fainter.—Indeed, it feems to me, when I am more fad than ufual, that I fhall never fee you more.—Yet you will not always forget me.—You will feel fomething like remorfe, for having lived only for yourfelf —and facrificed my peace to inferior gratifications. In a comfortlefs old age, you will remember that you had one difintereftcd friend, whofe heart you wounded to the quick. The hour of recollection will come—and you will not be fatisfied to act the part of a boy, till you fall into that of a dotard. I know that your mind, your heart, and your principles of action, are all

fuperior

superior to your prefent conduct. You do, you muft, refpect me—and you will be forry to forfeit my efteem."

Callous muft have been the heart which letters like thefe failed to move!

The perfon for whom, with a fick mind and a wafted conftitution, fhe was thus exerting herfelf, had engaged to meet her on her return from Norway, perhaps at Hamburgh, and to pafs with her fome time in Switzerland: his promifes were faithlefs, and her difappointments bitter and accumulated. The ambiguity of his conduct urged her to repair to England; her very foul fickened from thefe protracted anxities; fhe conjured him to be explicit on the fubject of their future intercourfe, but her folicitude was ftill evaded.

In the beginning of October, while refiding in lodgings in London, provided for her by Mr. I————, fhe at length obtained, through the medium of a fervant, the certainty fhe fought. In the firft tumult of her feelings on this difcovery, fhe repaired to the houfe of the woman by whom fhe had been fupplanted, where, meeting Mr. I————, fome cruel explanations enfued: fhe returned to her apartments in a ftate of mind that mocks defcription, a ftate of mind which it requires a portion of her own fenfibility even to conceive. In the agony of a broken fpirit, fhe once more meditated projects of defperation; her native courage and lofty fpirit mingled a fpecies of heroifm with the anguifh that had feized her: fhe abhorred exiftence; fhe perceived that the fervent character of her foul had in the purfuit of happinefs led her from illufion to illufion, through error into calamity; fhe had chaced a phantom, and grafping it, found it diffolve in her embrace. She felt, with all its pangs, the *mifery* which the generous, ardent, trufting fpirit, treafures up for itfelf when it " refts on human love." From the retrofpect of the paft, her thoughts recoiled—over the future a dark cloud lowered!—*Hope*, a thoufand times fruftrated, at length feemed extinguifhed; fortitude was exhaufted by fuffering; the tone of her mind deftroyed (as fhe believed) for ever. Once more *fhe refolved to die.* She addreffed on her knees the man to whofe libertine habits fhe had become a victim.

" I write

" I write to you now on my knees; imploring you to fend my child and the maid with ————, to Paris, to be confined to the care of Madame————, rue ————, fection de ————. Should they be removed, ———— can give their direction.

" Let the maid have all my clothes, without diftinction.

" Pray pay the cook her wages, and do not mention the confeffion which I forced from her—a little fooner or later is of no confequence. Nothing but my extreme ftupidity could have rendered me blind fo long. Yet, whilft you affured me that you had no attachment, I thought we might ftill have lived together.

" I fhall make no comments on your conduct; or any appeal to the world. Let my wrongs fleep with me! Soon, very foon fhall I be at peace. When you receive this, my burning head will be cold.

" I would encounter a thoufand deaths, rather than a night like the laft. Your treatment has thrown my mind into a ftate of chaos; yet I am ferene. I go to find comfort, and my only fear is, that my poor body will be infulted by an endeavour to recal my hated exiftence. But I fhall plunge into the Thames where there is the leaft chance of my being fnatched from the death I feek.

" God blefs you! May you never know by experience what you have made me endure. Should your fenfibility ever awake, remorfe will find its way to your heart; and, in the midft of bufinefs and fenfual pleafure, I fhall appear before you, the victim of your deviation from rectitude."

Quitting her lodging and walking to the river fide, fhe engaged a boat, with the deliberate purpofe of plunging from it into the Thames. On her way, fhe put feveral queftions to the perfon who rowed her, and from his replies, was induced to make fome change in her plan, left its execution fhould be prevented. Having proceeded to Putney, fhe there landed. Night drew on, a heavy rain began to fall, which fuggefted to her the idea of walking till her clothes had imbibed the moifture, with a view of accelerating her defign. For half an hour fhe continued to pace backward and forward, alone and unobferved, and at length

leaped

leaped from the top of the bridge. Her courage buoyed her up; folding her wet garments round her, she made efforts to sink, which having effected, she described herself as twice rising again as from a fainting fit, to the full sense of her situation. In these terrible moments, while her purpose remained unshaken, the idea of her child forcibly obtruded itself, awakening all the mother in her heart. To the struggles of expiring nature were added the stronger pangs of maternal tenderness. At length, resolutely imbibing the water in large quantities, she suffered a sense of suffocation, and again sunk to a temporary oblivion of her woes. A considerable period had elapsed before she was observed from the shore, floating down with the tide, and, by the methods usually adopted on such occasions, rescued from the arms of death. Whatever may be the conclusions of those who, with their passions at rest, calmly speculate on the propriety of suicide, or putting an end to sensation when become an inlet only to misery *, it is impossible not to admire the courage with which this unfortunate woman effected her purpose, or not to sympathise in the anguish of a mind wounded " there, where the heart most exquisitely feels."

Awakened into transient remorse by the consequences of the *misery* he had inflicted, even Mr. I——— betrayed, on this affecting event, some symptoms of humanity: procuring a physician to attend her, he prevailed upon her to remove from her lodgings to the house of a common friend; assuring her, " that the present wandering of his affections was of a casual nature; suggesting the idea of his return to her to whom he had given more sacred claims; and of whose faithful and disinterested tenderness he had experienced, alas! but too fatal proofs." These insinuations roused once more her languid faculties: incapable of supporting the idea of a renewal of those uncertainties which had racked her mind, she was induced to propose an expedient not less romantic than extraordinary.

" If we are ever to live together again, it must be now. We meet now, or we part for ever. You say, You cannot abruptly break off the connexion you have formed. It is unworthy of

---

* To the philosopher, *the vicissitudes of life*, perhaps, afford the only satisfactory argument on this subject.

my

my courage and character, to wait the uncertain iffue of that connexion. I am determined to come to a decifion. I confent then, for the prefent, to live with you, and the woman to whom you have affociated yourfelf. I think it important that you fhould learn habitually to feel for your child the affection of a father. But, if you reject this propofal, here we end. You are now free. We will correfpond no more. We will have no intercourfe of any kind. I will be to you as a perfon that is dead."

The impracticability of fuch a plan does not appear immediately to have occurred to Mr. I———; but a little confideration induced him to retract a confent which, with a view, perhaps, of foothing her feelings, he had haftily given. In the following month he repaired with the new object of his attentions to Paris, where he continued to refide during three months, Mary Wollftonecraft having previoufly fixed herfelf in apartments in Finfbury-place, adjoining to the refidence of the lady whofe friendly roof fhe had quitted. Secluding herfelf from fociety, her thoughts inceffantly dwelling on the circumftances of her defolate fituation, nourifhing in her heart an affection yet unextinguifhed by her fufferings, indulging in melancholy retrofpection, her foul's difeafe rapidly undermining the ftrength of her frame, her health feemed daily to decline.

On the return of Mr. I——— to England, for whofe conduct fhe was inceffantly meditating excufes, fhe determined on making one more effort for an interview, flattering herfelf, that his prefent infatuation, every way (as fhe conceived) unworthy of him, could not be of a permanent nature. The interview fhe requefted was denied to her with harfhnefs. Accidentally calling a few days after at the houfe of a common friend, fhe learned that Mr. I——— was at that time in an adjoining apartment, engaged with a party of gentlemen: confcious of the rectitude of her caufe, and emboldened by the fenfe of undeferved injuries, fhe refifted the well-meant expoftulation of her friend, who would have diffuaded her from her purpofe, and, fuddenly entering the dining room, in which the company were affembled, led her infant, now near two years of age, to the knees of its

father.

father. Confounded by her prefence and her courage, Mr. I——
retired with her to another room, and, at her requeft, promifed to
meet her at her lodgings on the enfuing day. He fulfilled his
appointment, and by conciliating language calmed the anguifh
of her fpirits ; a cheering ray of hope feemed to pierce the gloom
that furrounded her, but, like a tranfient meteor, after dazzling
her aching eye for a moment, it quickly difappeared. In this
interview he ftill affected to fpeak of returning, after the wan-
derings of libertinifm (with a debauched mind, and, probably,
a fhattered conftitution) to repofe on the tried faith of the only
woman whom he had ever *loved with diftinction*, entreating her to
continue to bear his name, to which no other, he vehemently
protefted, fhould ever have a claim. " It was not for the world
(faid fhe in a letter to a friend) that I complied with this requeft,
but I was unwilling to cut the gordian knot, or tear myfelf away
in appearance, when I could not in reality." The fucceeding
day fhe left town, paffing fome weeks in the country, in the
houfe of a female friend.

On her return from this excurfion, new circumftances occurred, bringing with them a further conviction of the duplicity and
unworthinefs of the object for whom fhe had fo perfeveringly cherifhed tendernefs ; fhe refolved therefore to roufe her powers, and
finally to rend from her heart an attachment which her reafon and
her principles equally contemned—an attachment now become
humiliating to her character, and that had but too long been productive of an immenfe overbalance of pain. Making a laft effort
for freedom and tranquillity, fhe refolutely fought to repel thofe
fatal recollections and affociations that had borne down her fpirit,
clouded her faculties, and blafted her peace. She exerted her
talents, forced herfelf into employment, changed the place of her
refidence, and addreffed, *for the laft time*, the man from whofe
inftability fhe had fo feverely fuffered.

" It is now finifhed.—Convinced that you have neither regard nor friendfhip, I difdain to utter a reproach, though I have
had reafon to think, that the " forbearance " talked of has not
been very delicate.—It is, however, of no confequence.—I am
glad you are fatisfied with your own conduct.

G g 2

" I now

" I now folemnly affure you, that this is an eternal farewell.
—Yet I flinch not from the duties which tie me to life.

" That there is " fophiftry" on one fide or other, is certain;
but now it matters not on which. On my part it has not been
a queftion of words. Yet your underftanding or mine muft be
ftrangely warped.

" The fentiment in me is ftill facred. If there be any part of
me that will furvive the fenfe of my misfortunes, it is the purity
of my affections. The impetuofity of your fenfes may have led
you to term mere animal defire the fource of principle; and it
may give zeft for fome years to come.—Whether you will always
think fo, I fhall never know.

" It is ftrange that, in fpite of all you do, fomething like conviction forces me to believe, that you are not what you appear
to be.

" I part with you in peace."

This letter, which put a period to the moft afflictive incident
in her life, was written in March 1796. However weakened
by her forrows, her active fpirit had not fuffered itfelf, as in ordinary cafes, to be engroffed by them: this capacity of exertion,
in feafons of diftrefs and difficulty, affords perhaps the ftrongeft
characteriftic of a fuperior mind. Her letters from Norway had
been written and prepared for the prefs, and a comedy fketched,
the ferious incidents of which turn upon her own ftory, within
the laft ten months, during which fhe had been twice prompted
to fuicide.

Hitherto, in recording the life of this admirable woman, melancholy has marked every page; her hiftory, with but little
variation, has exhibited a train of cares, ftruggles, difappointments, and forrows; the review of it inclines us to adopt the language of an eloquent writer *: " Of what ufe are talents and
fentiments in the corrupt wildernefs of human fociety? It is a
rank and rotten foil, from which every finer fhrub draws poifon
as it grows. All that, in a happier field and a purer air, might
expand into beauty and germinate into ufefulnefs, is thus converted into henbane and deadly nightfhade."—The cloud that

* Godwin's Caleb Williams.

had

had overshadowed her destiny at length began to disperse, the prospect brightened, and the sun of hope, diffusing his rays through the gloom, shed over the latter periods of her life (of which we shall take a brief view) a mild and benign lustre.

In the beginning of April 1796, Mrs. Wollstonecraft removed to lodgings at Pentonville, in the neighbourhood of Somer's-town, in which resided Mr. W. Godwin, a writer of distinguished talents, the boldness and singularity of whose speculations had excited attention, and provoked opposition, in the philosophic and literary world. Mr. Godwin had casually met Mrs. Wollstonecraft in a mixt company, previously to her excursion to the continent, when, from some difference in their principles, they parted with impressions mutually unfavourable. Their acquaintance was now renewed, in consequence of a meeting at the apartments of a common friend [*], who had forwarded the interview, with a view of removing their prejudices, and of diverting the melancholy of a woman whose talents and misfortunes had excited in her heart the most affectionate interest. This meeting led to a greater degree of intimacy between the parties, to which a friendly and confidential intercourse gradually succeeded, preparing the way for sentiments still more cordial and tender: sorrow softens the mind and irresistibly disposes it to the claims of sympathy.

Embittered by undeserved injuries, yearning after social and domestic affections, so dear to the sensible heart, suffering under the cruellest species of widowhood, every previous tie abruptly dissolved, darling association, not gradually dissevered, but rudely torn away without a single pleasing, recollection on which to rest, impressed by the intellectual eminence, affected by the worth and kindness of Mr. Godwin, the susceptible mind of Mary Wollstonecraft admitted, almost unconsciously, while struggling to obliterate the traces of the past, new impressions, that appeared to be more worthy of her, while they promised greater stability. Six months had elapsed, since she had resolutely banished from her soul the lingering remains of an attachment that had at length become incompatible with the respect due to

[*] The writer of the present narrative.

herself.

herſelf. The ſpeculative opinions of Mr. Godwin rendered him adverſe to marriage; the pecuniary embarraſſments of Mrs. Wollſtonecraft, it can ſcarcely be ſuppoſed, were leſſened; neither can it be believed, that, on ſuch a ſubject, a mind like hers could be capable of reſerve. Mr. Godwin, in conſideration of the inconveniences which had been already ſuſtained, and to which, from the habits of ſociety, the woman he loved might ſtill be expoſed, with a liberality which did him honour, waved his own ſcruples, and gave to the union which took place between them a legal ſanction. Their marriage was not immediately declared, Mr. Godwin indulging the delicacy of his wife, who ſhrunk from becoming again a ſubject of public diſcuſſion.

It was now that her exhauſted heart began to find repoſe, that at peace with herſelf, ſhe diffuſed around her the tranquillity ſhe enjoyed: her ideas of rational happineſs had ever been concentered in the circle of domeſtic affections; in ſeeking to realize her plans, ſhe had till this period been involved in undeſerved calumny and diſtreſs; to the calm ſatisfactions of nature and ſocial affection the beſt conſtituted minds are the moſt exquiſitely ſenſible. Had the ſenſibility of this extraordinary woman early found its proper objects, ſoftened by the ſympathies, and occupied by the duties of a wife and mother, ſhe had ſerenely purſued her courſe. The placid ſtream, that gliding through the meadows, fertilizes their banks, checked in its courſe, becomes a deſtructive torrent: thoſe ſtrong paſſions, that, ravaging the mind, afflict and deform ſociety, have their origin in oppoſition and conſtraint; if in this way talent is ſometimes generated, it ſeems to be purchaſed too dear.

The laws of nature are paramount to the cuſtoms of ſociety; its dictates will not be ſilenced by factitious precepts. Thoſe who, without guilt or imprudence, find themſelves excluded from the common ſolace of their ſpecies, will be led to conſider the reaſonableneſs of this privation, of which its injuſtice tends to aggravate its importance. From the expenſive habits of ſociety, and its conſequent profligacy, a large proportion of women are deſtined to celibacy, while their importance, their eſtabliſhment, their pleaſures, and their reſpectability, are (with few exceptions)

tions) connected with marriage. Woe be to these victims of vice or superstition, if, too ingenuous for habitual hypocrisy, they cannot stifle in the bottom of their hearts those feelings which should constitute their happiness and their glory: that sensibility, which is the charm of their sex, in such situations becomes its bitterest curse; in submitting to their destiny they rarely escape insult; in overstepping the bounds prescribed to them, by a single error, they become involved in a labyrinth of perplexity and distress. In vain may reflection enable them to contemn distinctions, that, confounding truth and morals, poison virtue at its source: overwhelmed by a torrent of contumely and reproach, a host of foes encompass their path, exaggerate their weakness, distort their principles, misrepresent their actions, and, with deadly malice, or merciless zeal, seek to drive them from the haunts of civil life.

Of the truth of these remarks the vindicator of female rights had not been without an experience.

"Those who are bold enough (said she in a letter to a friend) to advance before the age they live in, and to throw off, by the force of their own minds, the prejudices which the maturing reason of the world will in time disavow, must learn to brave censure. We ought not to be too anxious respecting the opinion of others.—I am not fond of vindications.—Those who know me will suppose that I acted from principle.—Nay, as we in general give others credit for worth, in proportion as we possess it—I am easy with regard to the opinions of the *best* part of mankind—I *rest* on my own."

Her union with Mr. Godwin, though sanctioned by *forms* which the prudent will not lightly be induced to violate, did not wholly exempt her from reproach: some nice distinctions in the circle of her acquaintance which had at first excited her surprise, not unmingled with regret, were nevertheless quickly forgotten—a mind like hers justly rested on itself. More interesting hopes and sentiments now occupied her thoughts: surrounded by respectable and intelligent friends, who knew how to appreciate her fine qualities, happy in the bosom of domestic peace, her heart once more expanded itself, her genius resumed its tone and vigour. Literary avocations, domestic pleasures, and social engagements,

occcupied

occupied and diverfified her time; while fhe anticipated with pleafure an approaching period, that, by adding to her maternal cares, would afford a new exercife to her affections.

"She was a worfhipper," fays her biographer and hufband *, "of domeftic life. She loved to obferve the growth of affection between me and her daughter, then three years of age, as well as my anxiety refpecting the child not yet born. Pregnancy itfelf, unequal as the decree of nature feems to be in this refpect, is the fource of a thoufand endearments. No one knew better than Mary how to extract fentiments of exquifite delight, from trifles, which a fufpicious and formal wifdom would fcarcely deign to remark. A little ride into the country with myfelf and the child, has fometimes produced a fort of opening of the heart, a general expreffion of confidence and affectionate foul, a fort of infantine, yet dignified endearment, which thofe who have felt may under-ftand, but which I fhould in vain attempt to pourtray."

Refting not in felfifh and indolent enjoyment, her active ta-lents ftill prompted her to various projects of ufefulnefs. A production in which fhe had for fome time been engaged, was announced to the public under the title of *The Wrongs of Woman*, being defigned to exemplify thofe evils, arifing out of the laws and cuftoms of civil inftitutions, more peculiarly appropriate to her fex—evils of which fhe was but too well qualified to fpeak. She had likewife planned a feries of letters on the management of in-fants, to be fubjected to the revifion of a medical friend, the in-troductory letter of which has appeared in her pofthumous works: alfo a feries of books for the inftruction of children, a fragment of which, found among her papers, has been fince publifhed. In the execution of her novel, there is reafon to believe, from the fketch which has appeared, that fhe had propofed to employ con-fiderable attention; aware of the difficulties which attend this fpecies of compofition, defpifed by pedants, but in which to en-fure fuccefs, powers of no common order muft combine. Im-preffed with this conviction, fhe proceeded flowly, with frequent alterations and careful revifions. In the former and moft finifhed part of the work, the Story of Jemima, an abandoned female

* Godwin's Memoirs, &c.

infant,

infant, trained up through oppreffion and calamity, to vice and infamy, is conceived and executed with originality and fpirit: the remaining volumes, which appear under great difadvantages, in a mutilated ftate, feem to allude to circumftances in the life of the author: the favourable change in her fituation, it is not improbable, had fhe lived to conclude the work, might have deducted in fome degree from its pathos.

In the midft of thefe flattering profpects, fhe felt the period of child-birth approach (Wednefday, Auguft 30, 1797), which fhe met with her ufual fortitude, and which her native courage, and the favourable circumftances attending her former experience, had enabled her to anticipate without apprehenfion: fhe had always entertained an opinion, that on fuch occafions there was more propriety in receiving the aid of a female practitioner, and that notwithftanding the defects* in their profeffional education, their fkill was adequate to *common cafes*. Her's unfortunately proved not to be a common cafe; to a protracted delivery fucceeded fymptoms of a perilous nature, alarming for her fafety the fears and tendernefs of her friends. For the few following days more promifing appearances revived their drooping fpirits; on the enfuing Sunday thefe flattering expectations gave place to the moft cruel folicitude. Every affiftance that medical fkill, or the tendernefs of friendfhip could fuggeft or afford, was adminiftered in vain: fupporting her fufferings, while fenfible of her fituation, with exemplary patience and cheerfulnefs, fhe lingered till the following Sunday, September the 10th, on which fhe expired, twenty minutes before eight in the morning. It did not appear that fhe entertained apprehenfions of death till within two days preceding the event, when fhe occafionally adverted to it, without feeming to dwell on the idea, her faculties at that time being confiderably impaired. The religious fentiments fhe had imbibed in her youth, had in them no terrours that could difcompofe a dying hour; her imagination had embodied images of vifionary perfection, giving rife to affections in which her fenfibility delighted to indulge. Her remains were

---

* Thefe defects which are to be regretted, it is hoped, will be remedied by the wifdom and delicacy of future generations.

interred

interred in the church-yard of St. Pancras, Middlesex, where a plain monument has since been erected to her memory, bearing the following inscription :

MARY WOLLSTONECRAFT GODWIN,

AUTHOR OF

A VINDICATION

OF THE RIGHTS OF WOMAN.

BORN XXVII APRIL MDCCLIX.

DIED X SEPTEMBER, MDCCXCVII.

It would be difficult to review the life of this singular woman without being impressed by mingled sentiments of tenderness and respect. The sense of her errors (and who, with feelings as acute and passions as ardent, has not committed many mistakes?) is absorbed in stronger sympathy with her sorrows and reverence for her virtues. The qualities of her heart and the attainments of her understanding appear to have been eminently her own, her errors and her sufferings arose out of the vices and prejudices of others. The powers and resources of her mind, amidst the disadvantages of her sex and station, bespeak talents of the highest order; her conceptions were bold and original, her freedom of thinking, and courage in stemming popular opinions, worthy of admiration. An obscure individual, unknown and unsupported, she raised herself by her own exertions to an eminence that excited, in an extraordinary degree, public attention, and afforded her a celebrity extending beyond the limits of the country which gave her birth. More than feminine sensibility and tenderness, united with masculine strength and fortitude, a combination as admirable as rare, were the peculiar characteristics of her mind. With an unconquerable propensity to *individual* attachment, which, concentrating its feelings, has a tendency to narrow the heart, her's cherished the most expanded philanthropy, and glowed with the warmest benevolence. She thought and felt on a comprehensive scale.

Should it be alleged, that she was unstable in attachment, let the nature, the virtue, and the reasonableness of constancy be

defined,

defined, and let the circumftances in which her affections changed their object, be brought to the teft. What " fweet remembrance" had fhe, to footh, " with virtue's kindeft thoughts,
her aching breaft, and turn her tears to rapture*?"

Doubtlefs her conduct was in many inftances imprudent, in
fome faulty; from the caprices of fenfibility and the inequalities
of genius, fhe was not exempt: a conceffion humiliating to the
pride of talent, but from which ignorance and dullnefs may extract confolation.

To expect any being merely *human* fhould, in its prefent
flate, mingle with fociety untainted by its corruptions, is to be
ignorant of the fympathetic nature of mind: he, who demands *perfection*, betrays little knowledge either of himfelf or his
fpecies: he, who looks for it in ardent tempers, has the book of
nature yet to learn. Thofe who difplay eagernefs in detecting
the weakneffes of fuperior characters, would do well to weigh
in the fame balance their own proportion of goodnefs and great-
nefs. A great character, to excite emulation and roufe the
nobler paffions, fhould be placed in a juft light and a certain
point of view. A habit of fearching for defects will infenfibly
beget imitation: he, who never warmed his heart by the
contemplation of excellence, will fcarcely rife to arduous
heights.

Her own fex have loft, in the premature fate of this extraordinary woman, an able champion; yet fhe has not laboured
in vain: the fpirit of reform is filently purfuing its courfe.
Who can mark its limits?

That fomething could be added refpecting the earlier progrefs
of a mind thus gifted, is to be wifhed rather than expected;
the growth of intellect and the rife of ideas are rarely to be
traced. On this fubject we have no authority; but are inclined
to fufpect, that, like the majority of her fex, her ftudies were
defultory and her attainments cafual, purfued with little method,
under the direction of her tafte, or as her feelings took the
lead. It does not appear that fhe was acquainted with any

* Akenfide's Pleafures of Imagination.

fcience,

science, or pretended to learning in its appropriate fenfe : her knowledge of the French language had been incidentally acquired for colloquial purpofes, and the bufinefs of tranflation; with the latter view, fhe had alfo applied herfelf to the German. Confiding in the ftrength of her faculties, and the richnefs of her imagination, fhe had paid but little attention, even in her native language, to grammatical propriety; an error of which, in the latter periods of her life, fhe became fully fenfible. Her mind probably owed its activity to the difficult circumftances in which fhe had been placed, to the force of her paffions, and to the early neceffity for the exertion of her powers.

Her perfon was above the middle height, and well proportioned; her form full; her hair and eyes brown; her features pleafing; her countenance changing and impreffive; her voice foft, and, though without great compafs, capable of modulation. When unbending in familiar and confidential converfation, her manners had a charm that fubdued the heart.

APPENDIX 2

The Sources of *Female Biography*
Mary Spongberg

> To give an account, however concise or general, of every woman who, either by her virtues, her talents, or peculiarities of circumstance, has rendered herself illustrious or distinguished, would, notwithstanding the disadvantages civil and moral under which the sex has laboured, embrace an extent, and require sources of information, which few individuals, however patient in labour or indefatigable in research, could encompass or command. Yet no character of eminence will, in the following work, be found omitted.
>
> Mary Hays, Preface, *Female Biography* (1803)

Female Biography and the Dissenting Tradition

As Hays makes clear in her preface to *Female Biography*, the task she had set herself, 'to give an account, however concise or general, of every woman who, either by her virtues, her talents, or peculiarities of circumstance, has rendered herself illustrious or distinguished', was an extraordinarily difficult one. While the lives of eminent women had been the subject of such studies before, none were as encyclopedic in scope as Hays proposed. Yet her decision to create such a monumental text, in spite of the 'patient' labour and 'indefatigable' research required, has, until recently, received little scholarly praise or interest. The dismissal of *Female Biography* as 'hack-work' in one of the first detailed studies of Hays's *oeuvre* has shaped the way this text has been received by modern scholars.[1] The idea that Hays merely plagiarized a small group of sources has framed early critical studies of *Female Biography* and ensured that it is usually seen as anticipating Victorian works of prosopography, emphatically connecting it with bourgeois ideals of domesticity and feminine piety. Read in this context, *Female Biography* has been treated as an early attempt to codify acceptable feminine behaviour through biography, rather than as a radical intervention into post-Wollstonecraftian feminism.[2] It has been assumed that *Female Biography* shared the generic quality of Victorian collective biographies, and its more radical and innovative features have generally been ignored.[3]

Recent scholarship has, however, situated *Female Biography* within an Enlightenment tradition established by the radical Protestant theologian Pierre Bayle, and extended in England by Hays's fellow Dissenters in works such as the *Biographia Britannica* and the *General Biographical Dictionary*.[4] Mary Hays was acquainted with William Enfield, Joseph Towers and John Aikin, who authored such works of collective biography, and made them a significant element of the intellectual culture of Dissent in the late eighteenth century. Dissenting scholars such as Andrew Kippis followed Bayle in using their collections as vehicles for exploring tolerance, seeking to 'rise above narrow prejudices, and to record, with fidelity and freedom, the virtues and vices, the excellencies and defects of men of every profession and party'.[5] Such texts not only inserted nonconforming lives into the national imaginary, they also functioned as a form of secularized hagiography within Dissent. As William Turner explained in his *Lives of Eminent Unitarians* (1840) many years later, '[T]he practical efficacy of Unitarian principles' is best displayed, 'in its influence on the lives and character of its most eminent professors'.[6]

Hays drew on Bayle's *Dictionnaire* as her inspiration, imitating his method and deftly sorting through his text and footnotes as sources. Hays says little about her own method in assembling the materials she used for the lives in *Female Biography*. In her introduction, however, she wrote, signaling her familiarity with Bayle, 'to abridge with judgment, is of literary labours, one of the most difficult'.[7] More significantly she suggested that she disdained the work of 'mere compilation', directly contradicting the suggestion that she chose to engage in 'hack work' rather than pursue other more controversial literary fields. Following Bayle, Hays's compilations involved more than merely 'copying' other sources. Her method is clearly evidenced in her first 'original' biography, the life of Mary Wollstonecraft, that she produced for the *Annual Necrology* of 1800 (See Appendix 1, pp. 485–534). In this 'life', she drew together a diverse range of sources including Wollstonecraft's political writings and novels, William Godwin's recently published *Memoirs*, Wollstonecraft's letters to Gilbert Imlay, as well as her own knowledge of Wollstonecraft and the crucible of Dissent that first fired their feminism. While much of Hays's text derives from Godwin's *Memoirs*, Hays's account differed from his at several key points, reflecting a desire on her part to contest his narrative, to question his authority and to recuperate the reputation of her dear friend.[8] It seems probable that she was similarly motivated to question masculinist representations of women's lives in *Female Biography*. She queried Bayle's judgment on certain subjects, illuminating how masculinist prejudices may have shaped the historical record. In an early entry on Artemisia, for instance, she questions Bayle's suggestion that 'the spirit and activity of Artemisia' was 'inconsistent with what is recorded of her conjugal tenderness and sorrow'. Echoing what she said of Wollstonecraft in her *Memoirs*, Hays observed of Artemisia, 'great passions seldom break out in weak and ignoble minds; that the benevolent affections, exalted to a certain height, have in them a strong tincture of heroism'.[9] Unlike male biographers of women who treated their subjects as extraordinary women endowed with masculine spirit, Hays foregrounded the femininity of her subjects, documenting their rise to prominence while also demonstrating the civil and moral disadvantages that framed their existence.

We know Hays wrote specifically with the female reader in mind, claiming that she needed to be 'solicitous for uniformity of language and sentiment' in order to attract and hold their attention. Accessible both in the language she used, and in its clear text and style of publication, *Female Biography* was conveniently packaged to make it easy to read.[10] Comparing Hays's entries with lives of the same women found in the *Biographium Faemineum* and Ballard's *Memoirs of Several Ladies*, it can be seen that Hays attempted to standardize by removing long quotes from other authorities, synthesizing sermons, poems and prayers into the text. Such excision made her entries more accessible to her readers, providing them with a seamless narrative rather than loading them up with 'dry information' or 'uninteresting facts'.[11] Hays's refusal to make a 'display ... of vain erudition', was perhaps more controversial to her contemporaries than it might now seem. In her rather 'querulous' preface to her *Biographical Dictionary of Women* published a year after *Female Biography*, Matilda Betham sought to clearly differentiate her work from that of Hays.[12] As Elaine Bailey has observed, this caused Betham to 'self-consciously repeat the judgments of those who came before her'. While Betham may have been more concerned to ensure 'historical accuracy' than Hays, this limited her ability to question historical authority.[13] While Betham clearly sought for her *Dictionary* to form part of the 'canon', Hays more readily questioned the authority of her sources, as she sought to create a way of viewing women's lives that had greater appeal and more efficacy to her female readers.

The relationship of women to reading is a significant theme in Hays's oeuvre and in her first major work, *Letters and Essays*, she advised women on a course of reading that seems to reflect the course she herself followed, and that provided her with the materials to write *Female Biography* a decade later. Hays believed that novels provided a useful entry point for women into more rigorous fields of study such as history. Acknowledging that women were most likely to read for their leisure novels of sensibility such as Richardson's *Clarissa* or Rousseau's *La Nouvelle Heloise*, Hays argued, 'Would it not be easy to lead young persons from these works to periodical essays, which are continually interspersed with lively, and entertaining narrations, and where instruction comes in the dress of amusement.'[14] An autodidact herself, Hays saw reading as an educational process through which women could transition from novels of sensibility to biographies such as Mrs Dobson's *Life of Petrarch* and Stuart's *History of the Unfortunate Mary Queen of Scots*, both works from which she drew material for *Female Biog-*

raphy. Biographies such as these, Hays suggested, were 'composed in a manner to amuse and instruct, and to generate a taste for historical reading'.[15] Allowed only on the peripheries of those marginal seats of learning, the Dissenting Academies, Hays developed in *Female Biography*, and in her other works, her own system of pedagogy for women, 'a virtual academy', constructed through stories of women's lives.[16] This system reflected the snippets of learning she had accrued from her encounters with men such as Joseph Priestley, but it was also derived from Hays's unique dissenting feminism, which consciously embraced the biographical as a distinctive mode of pedagogy for women.[17]

Most biographical collections were thematic, signaling clearly the parameters that framed their choice of lives in their titles (*Biographia Dramatica, Lives of French Writers, Lives of Roman Empresses*). Collections dedicated to women's lives usually focused upon especially pious women or women of a particular religious sect, and rarely looked beyond the women of a single nation state.[18] Hays followed Bayle's inclusion of women of many religions and nations. Claiming to be '[U]nconnected with any party' and 'disdainful of bigotry', she chose to represent 'Every character' in her collection, 'judged upon its own principles'.[19] Jeanne Wood has argued that *Female Biography* was the first 'biographical dictionary' of women, compiled by a woman. It was thus organized alphabetically, resisting the generic conventions of the exemplary biographies of women that had preceded it.[20] Such license accounts for the great scope of *Female Biography*, but it also ensured that contemporary reviewers regretted the inclusion of certain women whose lives 'can have no claim whatever to a place in a collection calculated for the advancement of the fair sex in the grand scale of rational and social existence.'[21] Such criticism signals the controversial nature of Hays's project, suggesting that *Female Biography* marked not a retrograde step in her politics, as certain critics have suggested, nor was Hays attempting to domesticate her feminism, but rather to extend her philosophical vision as a dissenting feminist.

Sources

It may be alleged, that but little new is brought forward in this work. Yet that novelty is more rare than the vulgar imagine, it is unnecessary to hint to the learned. Suffice it to observe, that my book is intended for women, and not for scholars; that my design was, not to surprise by fiction, or to astonish by profound research, but to collect and concentrate, in one interesting point of view, those engaging pictures, instructive narrations, and striking circumstances, that may answer a better purpose than the gratification of a vain curiosity.

Mary Hays, Preface, *Female Biography* (1803)

Most biographical dictionaries produced in the eighteenth century did not involve exacting historical scholarship. Such texts were quite idiosyncratic, combining a multiplicity of primary and secondary sources, intellectual curiosities, political argument, anecdote and extraordinary tales. According to Mark Longaker, such works had no coherent sets of rules; 'the lives of ... carelessly selected groups of men (*sic*)' were arranged in an 'arbitrary or singular manner'.[22] The creators of such collections were faced with a 'scarcity of reliable source material'.[23] Selection, thus, was largely dependent on the materials that could be found, rather than decided by plan or design. Entries varied in length and cohesiveness across collections as their compilers revised, supplemented and resupplemented.[24]

Women of eminence were rarely found as subjects in the generalist collective biographies written by men, except as addendums to the lives of great men as wives or mothers. The *Biographia Britannica*, for instance, listed a select group of seventeen women, including Arlotta, Mary Astell, Lady Anna Bacon, Elizabeth Barton, Mary Beale, Joan Beaufort, Aphra Behn, Juliana Berners, Margaret Cavendish, Susanna Centlivre, Lady Mary Chudleigh, Susannah Cibber, Catharine Cockburn, Mary Delany, Elizabeth Elstob, Lady Katherine Killigrew and Lady Elizabeth Russel. Hays included some, but not all, of these women in *Female Biography*. Hays also drew on collections specifically dedicated to women such as Ballard's *Memoirs of Several Ladies* and the *Biographium Faemineum*, but as with the *Biographia Britannica*, she only selected certain lives, and did not necessarily copy such biographies verbatim. Sometimes she tweaked these sources to change their tone or emphasis. In her entry on Catherine Bovey, for example, she takes most of the body of the text from Ballard's *Memoirs*, but she makes subtle changes that alter the way in which the life of her subject might be perceived. When Ballard reports upon Bovey's decision not to marry again after being widowed, he writes of 'her resolution not to enslave herself'. Hays, however, gives Bovey more agency, saying, 'preferring to any new engagement the freedom and independence of a single life'.[25] That in her widowhood Bovey chose to spend the rest of her days with a female companion, Mary Pope, may have inspired Hays to include her in *Female Biography*. Bovey's life demonstrated the possibility that women might resist heteronormativity, just as Wollstonecraft had imagined in her last work, *The Wrongs of Woman, or Maria*.[26]

Hays's access to source material was much more limited than her male counterparts. Not only had she been denied a formal education; her sex, class and religion precluded her admission to the great collections and libraries from which male antiquarians drew their works. From what we know of Hays's life during the period in which she wrote *Female Biography*, she could have only accessed the resources that were available in a number of small private libraries in London. For the most part these sources are written in English, but she also used foreign works in translation and a number of French works that she may have translated herself. In spite of such strictures, Hays appears to have been committed to gathering as much material as possible on her subjects. She drew on diverse sources that she cites at the end of at least half of the entries in *Female Biography*. Hays referred to around 100 specific sources in these 'endnotes'. By far the most commonly cited sources in *Female Biography* are Bayle's *Dictionnaire historique et critique*, Ballard's *Memoirs of Several Ladies* and the *Biographium Faemineum*. Deciphering Hays's use of sources is frequently complicated by the way she often refers to the same source by different names. Ballard, for instance, is referred to as *Ballard*, *Ballard's Ladies of Great Britain*, *Ballard's Lives of Illustrious British Ladies* and *Ballard's Memoirs of British Ladies*. This may have reflected common usage at the time, as often these texts went through multiple editions, each with a slightly varied title. It also probably reflected the disjointed nature of a production of this kind. Sometimes the names of authors are very similar, such as Bayle (Pierre) and Bale (John) and it is not clear to whom Hays is referring.

As was typical of other eighteenth-century biographers, Hays makes no attempt to differentiate between primary and secondary sources, often quoting directly from a source within a source. For instance, in her entry on Elizabeth Carew (Cary), Hays mentions information about her subject that she appears to have derived from the annotations that the antiquarian William Oldys made in his copy of Gerard Langbaine's *An Account of the English Dramatick Poets* (Oxford: Printed by L. L. for George West, and Henry Clements, 1691), although she references neither Oldys nor Langbaine at the end of the entry. Oldys created the first edition of the *Biographia Britannica* between 1747 and 1766, but neither Lady Carew (Cary) nor her husband, Sir Henry, is mentioned in this work.

In some entries Hays used multiple sources, often quoting directly from primary texts, such as letters or obituaries. Where possible it seems she drew upon the description of women left by themselves, from memoirs and other modes of self-writing, although in many cases they did not leave such sources, or they were unavailable to Hays. Hays often embedded detail of the literary and theological works of her subjects into her entries, thus preserving evidence of their work for posterity.

Hays also used material that she does not cite at the end of each entry, drawn from diverse sources such as individual memoirs, obituaries, sermons, satires, poems, novels, letters, scripture and psalms. While such sources allowed her to present a wide range of women's lives, it sometimes led her into error. She used 'letters' from Sarah Fielding's historical novel, *Lives of Cleopatra and Octavia* (1757), as documents in her study of the Egyptian queen. She also included the 'life' of Harriet Eusebia Harcourt, a fictional character, the subject of Thomas Amory's *Memoirs of Several Ladies of Great Britain ... In Several Letters* (London: J. Noon, 1755). Such errors might be assigned to the very fluid boundary between fact and fiction in this period, but they also reflected Hays's desire to be as inclusive as possible, even when the evidence of these lives was somewhat questionable. They also reveal the limits of her education, and the effect of this on her critical judgment.

Hays even delved into Bayle's footnotes to collect the fragments of evidence from which she built her lives. Footnotes were not particularly common in eighteenth-century texts and when they were used it was often in an unsystematic and sporadic manner. Pierre Bayle used extensive footnotes in his *Dictionnaire*, but these were used to query sources or to speculate about the veracity of certain tales. Hays used footnotes as Bayle did, to query the accuracy of a source (even Bayle) or to proffer contrary opinion. When quoting the historian William Robertson's praise of Elizabeth I's choice of ministers, Hays queries his suggestion that bestowing her favour on graceful courtiers was a sign of womanly weakness:

> Favour undoubtedly, as the word implies, is distinct from esteem. The latter is the offspring of judgment, the former of taste and feeling. Nor is it peculiar to woman to be dazzled by the qualities enumerated by the grave historian. When do men, it may be asked, where their taste and passions are concerned, turn from personal graces and captivating manners, to distinguish the endowments of the mind, or recompense the virtues of the heart?[27]

Nor was Hays immune to critiquing what she considered excessive displays of femininity in her subjects. In her entry on Madame Dacier, for instance, Hays had written 'Madame Dacier had composed observations on the Scriptures, which she refused to make public; to those who urged her on this subject, she replied 'That a woman should read the scriptures, and meditate on them as a rule of conduct, but that, agreeably on the precept of St Paul, she should keep silence'. In a footnote, however, Hays commented, 'These expressions, from a woman of professed literature, savour of affectation rather than of humility: genuine modesty neither extracts nor disclaims, but is artless, sincere and simple.'[28]

Hays also used explanatory footnotes, usually to present translations from the French or other foreign languages. In a small number of entries she used footnotes rather than mentioning the names of the texts she used in her 'endnotes'. In her entry on Hester Chapone, Hays quotes extensively from Anna Laetitia Barbauld's obituary of Chapone, alluding to it only in the text as 'the following character of this work is given by a lady highly and justly esteemed in the republic of letters'.[29] In a footnote appended to the text she identifies this 'lady' as Mrs Barbauld. Barbauld's obituary was published in the *Monthly Magazine*, in 1802, a year before *Female Biography* was published, making the Chapone entry Hays's most contemporary subject. In her entry on the 'Countess of Desmond', Hays identified three sources in the footnotes at the end of the entry, but also refers to another source, 'Lord Bacon', in her text. Known principally for her mythical longevity (some claimed she lived to 140), the Countess appears not in Ballard, *Biographium Faemineum* or other similar sources. What Hays knew of the Countess of Desmond was gleaned from several historical texts such as Sir Walter Raleigh's, *The History of the World* and Sir Francis Bacon's *History of*

Life and Death, works that referred to the Countess in passing. These footnotes suggest that this was an 'original' entry in *Female Biography*, not borrowed from another work of collective biography, but synthesized by Hays from the sources she notes in her footnotes and text.

In some entries Hays simply noted the sources she used in her text, as in the entry on Artemesia Gentileschi: 'She is spoken of by Graham, as the first paintress of her times, in his Essay towards an English School'.[30] These too might be considered original entries in the sense that Hays is not reworking secondary material from an earlier dictionary of biography, but rather extrapolating from primary texts.

Original Entries

In about fifty entries Hays does not mention her sources. In some cases this appears to have been an oversight. For example, her entry on the would-be Scottish assassin, Margaret Lambrun, mentions no sources, but an entry on Lambrun appears in the *Biographium Faemineum*. Hays's entry on Lambrun follows closely the *Biographium Faemineum*, so her failure not to reference this text was almost certainly an oversight on her part or that of the printers. A number of Hays's subjects do not appear in the works of collective biographies that she has cited. In some cases, Hays embeds her source in the text. In other cases, however, the source is not obvious. Such entries might be considered 'original' in the sense that Hays has not copied them from a similar entry in an earlier dictionary of biography, but drew together materials from primary sources such as obituaries, catalogues or genealogies, or from her reading of classical or contemporary authors.

Hays also created sources where none existed, such as in her original entry on Catharine Sawbridge Macaulay. Macaulay was one of the most contemporary figures in *Female Biography*, and with the exception of one or two review essays, had not been memorialized since her death in 1791. In order to document Macaulay's life, Hays made the acquaintance of Macaulay's sister-in-law, Mrs Arnold, and interviewed her to acquire important details of her life. This innovative early use of oral history is rare in such collections, but has proven immensely important, as few other studies of Macaulay's life were undertaken either in the period immediately after her death, or in the century that followed. Throughout the nineteenth century, Hays's life of Macaulay was regularly plagiarized in those generic works of collective biography that characterized the genre in the Victorian age.[31] More recently, Hays's life of Macaulay has become highly significant, as it has formed the substratum from which most modern biographical works on Macaulay's life are drawn.

There are a number of lives in *Female Biography* for which we have no sources and it has been impossible for our researchers to ascertain from where Hays acquired the material she used in these entries. The most intriguing example of this is Hays's entry on 'Anonymous'. This entry refers to the life of not one, but eight learned women of Bologna. Hays's entry begins with Bettina Gozzadini (Bologne, 1236–62) in the thirteenth century, and traces a tradition of female scholarship through to the renowned scientist Laura Bassi (1711–78), who held a chair in the University of Bologna during the eighteenth century. No sources are provided by Hays and our work on this entry has not thrown up any obvious sources for these women, or at least sources that may have been readily available to Hays. While some entries in *Female Biography* were clearly copied from other similar collections, entries such as Anonymous suggest that Hays was engaged in something more than mere compilation, which complicates our understanding of her access to sources and her method.

Notes

1. G. Kelly, *Women, Writing and Revolution 1790–1827* (Oxford: Clarendon Press, 1993), p. 234.
2. Most critics have followed Gary Kelly and have presented *Female Biography* as beginning the rise of female prosopographies in the nineteenth century. See, for instance, R. A. Maitzen, 'This Feminine Preserve: Historical Biographies by Victorian Women', *Victorian Studies*, 38 (1995), pp. 371–93; J. Wood, 'Alphabetically Arranged: Mary Hays's *Female Biography* and the Biographical Dictionary', *Genre,* 13 (1998), pp. 117–42; M. E. Burstein, '"Unstoried in History?": Early Histories of Women (1652–1902) in the Huntington Library Collection', *Huntington Library Quarterly,* 64:3–4 (2001), pp. 469–500; and A. Booth, *How to Make it as a Woman: Collective Biographical History from Victoria to the Present* (Chicago, IL: Chicago University Press, 2004), p. 19.
3. M. E. Burstein, 'From Good Looks to Good Thoughts: Popular Women's History and the Invention of Modernity, *c.* 1830–1870', *Modern Philology*, 97:1 (1997), pp. 46–75, on p. 48.
4. G. L. Walker, *The Growth of a Women's Mind* (Hamsphire: Ashgate, 2006); M. Spongberg, 'Mary Hays and Mary Wollstonecraft and the Evolution of Dissenting Feminism', *Enlightenment and Dissent*, 26 (2010), pp. 230–58; F. James, 'Writing *Female Biography* and the Life Writing of Religious Dissent', in D. Cook and A. Culley (eds), *Women's Life Writing 1700–1850* (London: Palgrave, 2012), pp. 133–50.
5. A. Kippis, *Biographia Britannica: Lives of the Most Eminent People who have flourished in Great Britain and Ireland*, 5 vols (London: Printed by W. and A. Strahan, 1778), vol. 1, p. xxi.
6. W. Turner, *Lives of Eminent Unitarians* (London: The Unitarian Association, 1840), p. vv.
7. M. Hays, *Female Biography*, 6 vols (London: Richard Phillips, 1803), vol. 1, p. viii.
8. M. Spongberg, 'Remembering Wollstonecraft: Feminine Friendship, Female Subjectivity and the Invention of the Feminist Heroine', in D. Cook and A. Culley (eds), *Women's Life Writing 1700–1850* (London: Palgrave, 2012), pp. 165–80.
9. Hays, *Female Biography*, vol. 1, p. 192.
10. Compare, for instance, the production values of the *Biographium Faemineum* with *Female Biography*.
11. Hays, *Female Biography*, vol. 1, p. iv.
12. M. Matilda Betham, *A Biographical Dictionary of Celebrated Women of Every Age and Country* (London: E. Crosby, 1804), pp. v–vi.

13. See E. Bailey, 'Lexicography of the Feminine: Matilda Betham's Dictionary of Celebrated Women', *Philological Quarterly*, 83:4 (2004), pp. 389–414.
14. M. Hays, *Letters and Essays, Moral, and Miscellaneous* (London: Knott, 1793), pp. 96–7.
15. Hays, *Letters and Essays*, pp. 96–7.
16. Walker, *The Growth of A Woman's Mind*, pp. 66–7.
17. Spongberg, 'Mary Hays, Mary Wollstonecraft and the Evolution of Dissenting Feminism', pp. 230–58.
18. Collections such as Ballard's and Gibbons's for instance, focused on women from the Established Church in England. Anne Thicknesse's collection of literary biographies focused solely on French women. See A. Thicknesse, *Sketches of the Lives and Writings of the Ladies of France*, 3 vols (London: Dodsley & W. Brown, 1780).
19. Hays, *Female Biography*, vol. 1, p. vi.
20. J. Wood, 'Alphabetically Arranged', pp. 123–4, fn. 1.
21. Anon., *Monthly Magazine*, 15 (June 1803), pp. 450–3.
22. M. Longaker, *English Biography in the Eighteenth Century* (New York: Octagon, 1971), p. 240.
23. D. W. Nichol, 'Biographia Britannica', in S. Serafin (ed.), *Dictionary of Literary Biography: Eighteenth Century Literary Biographers* (Detroit: Gale Research, 1994), p. 288.
24. Nichol, 'Biographia Britannica', p. 293.
25. Hays, *Female Biography*, vol. 3, p. 28.
26. See C. L. Johnson, 'Mary Wollstonecraft: Styles of Radical Maternity', in S. C. Greenfield and C. Barash (eds), *Inventing Maternity: Politics, Science and Literature 1650-1865* (Lexington, KY: The University Press of Kentucky, 1999), pp. 159–72, on p. 162.
27. Hays, *Female Biography*, vol. 3, p. 25.
28. Hays, *Female Biography*, vol. 4, p. 22.
29. Hays, *Female Biography*, vol. 2, pp. 89–90.
30. Hays, *Female Biography*, vol. 1, p. 218*.
31. S. Greentree, 'Reading the Female Historian: Representations of Catharine Macaulay 1760–1900' (PhD dissertation, Macquarie University, 2012), pp. 220–68.

EDITORIAL NOTES

p. 3, l. 6: *OCTAVIA*: Octavia Minor or Octavia the Younger (69–11 BC).

p. 3, l. 6: *Julius Cæsar*: Gaius Julius Caesar (100–44 BC), assassinated dictator of Rome.

p. 3, l. 7: *Augustus*: Gaius Octavius (63 BC–AD 14), Caesar's adopted son and heir, subsequently called Gaius Julius Caesar Octavianus, and then Augustus, emperor of Rome.

p. 3, l. 7: *Caius Octavius*: see note to p. 3, l. 7, above.

p. 3, l. 8: *Atia*: Atia Balba Caesonia (85–43 BC), daughter of Julius Caesar's sister (Julia) and Marcus Atius Balbus.

p. 3, l. 18: *adopted son of Cæsar*: see note to p. 3, l. 7, above.

p. 4, ll. 6–7: *the civil war between Cæsar and Pompey*: part of a broader conflict between two socio-political factions, the Populares and the Optimates, whose military leaders were, respectively, Gaius Julius Caesar (100–44 BC) and, initially, Pompey the Great (see note to p. 4, l. 7, below).

p. 4, l. 7: *Pompey*: Gnaeus Pompeius Magnus or Pompey the Great (106–48 BC), a military and political leader who commanded the forces of the conservative senatorial faction known as the Optimates until his assassination in Egypt (28 September 48 BC) after defeat by Julius Caesar at the Battle of Pharsalus in central Greece (9 August 48 BC).

p. 4, l. 17: *Claudius Marcellus*: Gaius Claudius Marcellus Minor (88–40 BC), Roman senator and consul.

p. 4, l. 23: *her brother*: see note to p. 3, l. 7, above.

p. 6, l. 28: *her children*: Claudia Marcella the Elder (d. *c.* 2 BC or after), Claudia Marcella the Younger (*c.* 40/39 BC–*c.* after 12 BC) and Marcus Claudius Marcellus (42–23 BC).

p. 7, ll. 5–6: *the civil war having commenced between Octavius and Antony*: the military conflict between Gaius Octavius and Marc Antony (see note to p. 7, l. 6, below), which began in 31 BC.

p. 7, l. 6: *Antony*: Marcus Antonius or Marc Antony (83–30 BC), Roman politician and soldier, renowned for his eulogy for Julius Caesar, his pursuit of Caesar's assassins, his shared triumvirate with Octavian and Lepidus and his doomed relationship with Cleopatra VII.

p. 7, ll. 11–12: *the queen of Egypt*: Cleopatra; see Hays, *Female Biography*, vol. 3, pp. 319–82.

p. 7, ll. 12–13: *neglect of his former wife*: Fulvia (see Hays, *Female Biography*, vol. 4, pp. 335–6).

p. 9, l. 17: *Cleopatra*: see note to p. 7, ll. 11–12, above.

p. 9, ll. 20–1: *the son of Pompey*: Sextus Pompeius Magnus Pius or Sextus Pompey (67–35 BC), youngest son of Sextus Pompeius Magnus (Pompey the Great). The younger Sextus fought alongside his father and older brother against Julius Caesar, and continued to rebel against the forces of the Second Triumvirate from his power base on Sicily.

p. 9, l. 27: *Brundusium*: modern Brindisi, a city on the south-east coast (the 'heel') of the Italian peninsula.

p. 9, l. 27: *Tarentum*: modern Taranto, a harbour city on the southern coast (the 'instep') of the Italian peninsula.

p. 10, l. 13: *the children of Antony*: Iullus Antonius (45–2 BC) is the only child of Antony's marriage to Fulvia who came under Octavia's care. Marcus Antonius Antyllus, Fulvia's eldest son to Antony, was executed in Egypt at Octavian's order. Clodia Pulchra, Fulvia's daughter by her first husband (Publius Clodius Pulcher), was the first wife of Octavian, who divorced her in 40 BC to marry Scribonia. Her later history is unknown.

p. 10, ll. 16–17: *the Parthian campaign*: Under Antony's command, almost 25,000 men were lost in an abortive assault on the Parthian city of Phraaspa and subsequent retreat into Armenia in 37 BC.

p. 13, l. 3: *Ephesus*: major Greco-Roman city on the western coast of the province of Asia (modern Turkey).

p. 13, l. 14: *the battle of Actium*: the decisive naval engagement between the forces of Octavian and Antony and Cleopatra (2 September 31 BC); off the coast of Actium, a promontory in western Greece.

p. 14, l. 6: *the daughter of Augustus*: Julia the Elder (39 BC–AD 14), Augustus's sole biological child; married Marcellus, her cousin, in 25 BC at the age of fourteen.

p. 14, ll. 11–12: *The eulogy of Marcellus, composed by Virgil*: Anchises, father of the eponymous hero of Virgil's epic poem set in Rome's legendary past, introduces Marcellus in terms reminiscent of a funerary epigram (Vergil, *Aeneid*, 6.854–5). According to a later commentator on the *Aeneid* (Servius, *Ad Aeneidem*, 6.861), when Virgil read this passage to the emperor Augustus and his sister Octavia, their tears almost forced him to close the book.

p. 15, l. 11: *two daughters*: Antonia the Elder (39 BC–c. AD 25) and Antonia the Younger (36 BC–AD 35).

p. 15, l. 13: *Pausanias*: Pausanias (*Description of Greece*, 2.3.1) refers to a temple of the imperial cult at Corinth in Greece, dedicated to Octavia. This may be the temple, originally built in the reign of the emperor Tiberius, identified as Temple E in modern excavations at Corinth.

p. 15, ll. 15–16: *the children of Antony by Cleopatra*: the twins Alexander Helios (40–c. 25 BC) and Cleopatra Selene or Cleopatra VIII (40 BC–c. AD 4).

p. 15, l. 17: *the king of Mauritania*: Between 26 and 20 BC, Augustus arranged Cleopatra Selene's marriage to Juba II, King of Numidia in Africa. Because Numidia had been made a Roman province in 46 BC, it could not be governed as a kingdom. Instead, Augustus sent Juba and Cleopatra to rule Mauretania, a territory in ancient Libya in need of competent administration.

p. 15, l. 22: *OCTAVIA*: Claudia Octavia. The tragic fate of Octavia was the subject of a play of uncertain authorship, but transmitted among those of Seneca the Younger. It is the only surviving play on a Roman historical subject.

p. 15, l. 23: *NERO*: Nero Claudius Caesar was emperor of Rome between AD 54 and AD 68.

p. 15, l. 24: *Claudius*: Tiberius Claudius Nero Germanicus was Roman Emperor between AD 41 and AD 54.

p. 15, ll. 24–5: *Messalina*: Valeria Messal(l)ina married her second cousin (and future emperor), Claudius, in AD 39 or 40.

p. 15, l. 25: *795th year of Rome*: This would be AD 42. In using the Roman system of dating, Hays followed Bayle who in turn followed Tacitus (*Annals*, 14.64), according to whom she died in her twentieth year. That would mean she was born either in the second half of AD 42 or the first half of AD 43, but she is recorded to have been betrothed in AD 41 (Cassius Dio, *History*, 60.5.7). She was probably born by AD 40.

p. 16, ll. 9–10: *betrothed in early youth ... to Lucius Silanus*: Her betrothed was the son of Marcus Junius Silanus (consul in AD 19) and Aemilia Lepida, granddaughter of Augustus. The betrothal took place in AD 41 (see note to p. 15, l. 25, above).

p. 16, l. 11: *Augustus*: Gaius Iulius Caesar (Octavian), Julius Caesar's adopted son and heir; by virtue of his defeat of M. Antony and Cleopatra in 31 BC, he became the sole military power in the Roman world. In 27 BC, he assumed the name Augustus, and is often deemed the first emperor.

p. 16, l. 15: *death of the empress*: In AD 48 Messalina adulterously celebrated a public marriage ceremony with the consul-designate Gaius Silius. In spite of Claudius's prevarication, his freedman Narcissus issued a death sentence and dispatched an executioner.

p. 16, ll. 15–16: *who perished violently*: Encouraged by her mother, Messalina committed suicide.

p. 16, l. 17: *his niece Agrippina*: 'the Younger Agrippina', eldest daughter of Germanicus and Vipsania Agrippina (the granddaughter of Augustus).

p. 16, ll. 19–20: *Domitius (her son by a former marriage)*: Nero Claudius Caesar, the later emperor Nero, the only son of her marriage with Gnaeus Domitius Ahenobarbus (the consul of AD 32).

p. 16, l. 26: *Vitellius, the censor*: Lucius Vitellius, censor along with the emperor Claudius in AD 48. The portrait of the self-seeking and corrupt Vitellius ultimately derives from Tacitus (*Annals*, 12.4).

p. 17, l. 3: *accusations the most odious*: namely incest with his sister Junia Calvina, a former daughter-in-law of Vitellius.

p. 17, l. 14: *Pollio*: Lucius Mammius Pollio, consul-designate in AD 49 (Tacitus, *Annals*, 12.9). He is attested as suffect (replacement) consul on an inscription of that year.

p. 17, l. 19: *on the day of these inauspicious nuptials*: Octavia married Nero in AD 53.

p. 17, ll. 21–3: *encouraged by the weakness of the emperor ... set no limits to her ambition*: The observation of Agrippina's domination ultimately derives from Tacitus (see, for example, *Annals*, 12.7) who underlines Claudius's weakness.

p. 17, ll. 25–6: *the youth of his son Britannicus*: Octavia's brother, Tiberius Claudius Caesar Britannicus, was born in AD 41 and was nine years old – three years younger than Nero.

p. 17, l. 28: *the sons of Livia*: Tiberius Claudius Nero Caesar (later emperor) and Claudius Drusus Nero were the sons of Ti. Claudius Nero and Livia, whose marriage was dissolved in 38 BC when Livia married Octavian (later Augustus). Only Tiberius was adopted by his stepfather Augustus (in AD 4). (For Livia, see also Hays, *Female Biography*, vol. 4, pp. 41–65.)

p. 18, ll. 1–2: *by adopting him under the name of Nero*: On 25 February AD 50, Lucius Domitius Ahenobarbus, at the age of twelve, was adopted by Claudius through a law of the Roman People, becoming Tiberius Claudius Nero Caesar or, as he is sometimes called, Nero Claudius Caesar Drusus Germanicus.

p. 18, ll. 3–4: *the heir*: Octavia's brother, Britannicus.

p. 18, l. 8: *a superstitious farce*: There were reportedly concerns about the appearance of Octavia marrying her adopted half-brother. Dio (*History*, 60.33.2) records that a portent was observed.

p. 18, ll. 13–14: *The emperor having fallen a victim to poison, Nero was declared his successor*: Claudius died on 13 October AD 54. Earlier that year, Britannicus turned thirteen, the age at which Nero had been allowed to assume the toga of manhood (*toga virilis*), and Claudius spoke of the former's advancement. The timing of Claudius's death led to suspicions of poisoning by Agrippina, suspicions retailed by the ancient source tradition. Nero was hailed as emperor by the Praetorian Guard and the senate followed suit, voting him the requisite powers.

548 Memoirs of Women Writers, Volume 10

p. 18, ll. 16–17: *the victim of an ambitious step-mother*: the motif of the dangerous stepmother was common in Roman literature.

p. 18, l. 26: *the wanton beauty of a slave*: Claudia Acte was a freedwoman of Nero. In AD 55, encouraged by the younger Seneca, one of Nero's advisors, and despite the opposition of Agrippina, Nero made her his mistress (Dio, *History*, 61.7.1).

p. 19, l. 11: *Burrhus*: Sextus Afranius Burrus was appointed sole prefect of the Praetorian Guard by Claudius and kept his post under Nero. He was the latter's advisor and with Seneca the Younger was chiefly responsible for the government in the early period of Nero's reign.

p. 19, l. 21: *his mistress*: see note to p. 18, l. 26, above.

p. 20, l. 4: *Acte*: see note to p. 18, l. 26, above.

p. 21, l. 1: *the threats of Agrippina*: this account derives ultimately from Tacitus (*Annals*, 13.14).

p. 21, ll. 9–10: *Pollio, tribune of a praetorian cohort*: Julius Pollio (Tacitus, *Annals*, 13.15).

p. 21, l. 11: *Locusta*: According to Tacitus (*Annals*, 12.66) she was employed by Agrippina to poison Claudius.

p. 22, ll. 7–8: *instantly expired*: Britannicus died in AD 55.

p. 22, l. 18: *the Cladii*: the Claudii. This slip appears to be Hays's or the printer's own.

p. 23, l. 6: *Sabina Poppæa*: By AD 58, Poppaea Sabina, during her marriage to the future emperor Otho, became Nero's mistress (Tacitus, *Annals*, 13.45–6; compare Tacitus, *Histories*, 1.13).

p. 23, l. 20: *terminated in her own destruction*: In March AD 59 Agrippina was murdered at Baiae by the freedman, Anicetus, acting on Nero's instructions (Tacitus, *Annals*, 14.8).

p. 24, l. 4: *Tigellinus*: Ofonius Tigellinus was a Sicilian of low birth whom Nero made Prefect of the Watch and then later Praetorian Prefect. Tacitus describes Tigellinus and Poppaea as 'intimate counsellors of the *princeps*' cruelties' (*Annals*, 15.61).

p. 24, l. 15: *the estate of Plautus*: Rubellius Plautus, on his mother's side the great-grandson of the emperor Tiberius, had fallen under suspicion of imperial designs. In AD 60, he had been advised by Nero 'to attend to his estates in Asia'. Two years later, he was executed (Tacitus, *Annals*, 14. 60).

p. 24, ll. 15–17: *the house of Burrhus ... were assigned to her use*: Burrus (see note to p. 19, l. 11, above) opposed Nero's divorce from Octavia which only occurred after his death in AD 62. Suetonius (*Nero*, 35.5) and Dio (*History*, 62.13.3) assert that he was poisoned but Tacitus (*Annals*, 14.51) expresses uncertainty.

p. 24, ll. 25–6: *Eucer, an Alexandrian slave, and a maker of musical instruments*: Eucaerus was a probably a performer rather than instrument-maker (Tacitus, *Annals*, 14.60). Not further identified.

p. 25, l. 12: *banished to Campania*: Campania is a region of west central Italy bordered by the Liris River, the Apennines and the Sorrentine peninsula.

p. 27, l. 10: *Anicetus*: see note to p. 23, l. 20, above.

p. 29, l. 4: *Pandataria*: Pandateria, an island, modernly called Ventotene. Octavia's exile was effected in AD 62.

p. 30, l. 8: *11th day of June*: AD 62. The date is supplied by Suetonius (*Nero*, 57.1).

p. 30, ll. 13–14: *"curses deep not loud"*: Probably a recollection of *Macbeth* V.iii.27: 'Curses not loud but deep'.

p. 30, l. 16: *Poppæa perished*: She died whilst pregnant in AD 65, allegedly after violence perpetrated by Nero. She was given a public funeral and divine honours.

p. 30, l. 25: *born in Pall-Mall*: Eighteenth-century biographies of Anne Oldfield agree she was born in Pall Mall in 1683. No records of her birth or her parentage have been located.

p. 30, l. 26: *Her father*: Recent research suggests her father may have been William Oldfield, but of him there are no further records. J. Lafler, *The Celebrated Mrs Oldfield: The Life and Art of an Augustan Actress* (Carbondale, IL: Southern Illinois University Press, 1989), p. 5.

p. 30, l. 23–p. 31, l. 2: *officer in the Guards ... squandered in dissipation*: That Oldfield's father lived extravagantly is a theme of all eighteenth-century biographies of the actress, though these accounts cannot be corroborated. It is unlikely her father purchased a commission in the Horse or Life Guards, given that troops were drawn from the elite or the gentry, and that financial returns from a commission were very poor; Lafler, *Celebrated Mrs Oldfield*, p. 6.

p. 31, ll. 3–4: *his widow*: New research suggests Anne Oldfield's mother may have been the Anne Gourlaw who married William Oldfield in 1681 in the parish church of St Mary le Bone, but of her there are no further records; Lafler, *Celebrated Mrs Oldfield*, p. 5.

p. 31, ll. 5–6: *sister ... in St. James's market*: Edmund Curll, whose biography of Oldfield appeared under the pseudonym William Egerton the year after her death, is the source of this story. He records that Oldfield and her mother went to live with Mrs Oldfield's sister, Mrs Voss, who kept the Mitre Tavern in St James's Market. This story is then repeated in the *Biographia Britannica*, Hays's principal source. Oldfield's recent biographer has found evidence of a Mrs Voss resident in the area, but no record of a Mitre Tavern. W. Egerton [E. Curll], *Faithful Memoirs of the Life of ... Mrs Anne Oldfield* (London: E. Curll, 1731), p. 2; *Biographia Britannica*, 7 vols (London: W. Innys et al., 1747), vol. 5, p. 3262; Lafler, *Celebrated Mrs Oldfield*, p. 6.

p. 31, ll. 6–7: *a sempstress*: identified only as Mrs Wotton by [Curll], *Faithful Memoirs*, p. 1.

p. 31, l. 11: *captain George Farquhar*: Hays follows *Biographia Britannica* in identifying George Farquhar (1677–1707) as a captain, but he was best known as a playwright and actor.

p. 31, ll. 14–15: *immediately pronounced her admirably fitted for the stage*: This story of Farquhar encountering the sixteen-year-old Oldfield in her aunt's tavern is probably apocryphal. Oldfield herself may have been its source, but it is first printed in Curll's biography of the actress. Here, it appears in a letter subscribed to Charles Taylor (*Faithful Memoirs*, pp. 76–7). Farquhar and Oldfield did know each other, and there is some speculation they had a short-lived affair. Oldfield has been identified as 'Penelope' of Farquhar's letters in *Love and Business* (London: Bernard Lintott, 1702), pp. 53–111.

p. 31, l. 17: *John Vanbrugh*: Sir John Vanbrugh (1664–1726) was a playwright and architect. He was an early member of the Kit-Kat Club, and had a total of ten plays staged in the period 1696–1707.

p. 31, l. 20: *Mr Rich, patentee of the King's-theatre*: Christopher Rich (1647–1714) was chief patentee of the King's Company. This company absorbed London's second patent troupe, the Duke's Company, in 1682 creating the United Company, a monopoly patent company housed at Drury Lane Theatre.

p. 31, ll. 21–2: *it was some time before her powers displayed themselves*: Oldfield became a member of Drury Lane in 1699. Records for this period are sparse, but her first known part was as Candiope in John Dryden's *Secret Love* in the 1699–1700 season. Hays follows eighteenth-century accounts of Oldfield's career in suggesting that she was a minor member of the company until 1703, but this was not in fact the case. For example, she was given a sole benefit of *The Pilgrim*, a play in which she played a major role, on 6 July 1700 (*The Post-Boy*, no. 818, 4–6 July 1700); she also played major roles in at least nine plays, and was chosen as prologue or epilogue speaker for three of them. By 1703, she was receiving a very respectable annual salary of £70–£80. See P. Highfill, K. Burham and E. Langham, *A Biographical Dictionary of Actors, Actresses, Musician, Dancers, Managers and other Stage Personnel in London, 1660–1800*, 16 vols (Carbondale, IL: Southern Illinois University Press, 1987), vol. 11, pp. 102–3.

p. 31, ll. 23–4: *established her reputation in … "Sir Courtly Nice"*: This play, by John Crowne, was staged in the 1703 season. Susanna Verbruggen was to have played the part of Leonora, but, when she fell ill, it went to Oldfield. Colley Cibber, part of the Lord Chamberlain's company, subsequently said of her performance: '[i]t was in the part that Mrs Oldfield surpris'd me into an Opinion of her having all the innate Powers of a good actress, though they were but yet in the Bloom of what they promis'd'; *An Apology for the Life of Colley Cibber* (London: John Watts, 1740), p. 248.

p. 31, ll. 25–6: *Lady Betty Modish, in "The Careless Husband"*: Colley Cibber's play, *The Careless Husband*, premiered at Drury Lane on 7 December 1704 with Oldfield in the role of Lady Betty Modish.

p. 31, l. 27–p. 32, l. 1: *Arthur Maynwaring*: Arthur Maynwaring (1668–1712) was a politician, pamphleteer and literary author. He was closely associated with the Whigs: he became a member of the Kit-Kat Club in *c.* 1700 and was MP from 1708 until his death.

p. 32, ll. 1–3: *greatly interested himself … her natural genius*: Maynwaring wrote more than a dozen epilogues and prologues that were spoken by Oldfield.

p. 32, l. 3: *This gentleman dying in 1712*: Maynwaring's will named three heirs: his sister, Oldfield and their son. A lump sum of £1,000 went to his sister, the remainder bequeathed to Oldfield (who he also named the will's executor) and their son. This was a striking testament of Maynwaring's regard for Oldfield, as it was virtually unheard of to name one's mistress one's executor.

p. 32, ll. 4–5: *brigadier-general Churchill*: Charles Churchill (*c.* 1679–1745) was the illegitimate nephew of John Churchill, the first Duke of Marlborough. An army officer from 1688, Churchill was created a lieutenant-general in 1739.

p. 32, l. 5: *one son*: Arthur Maynwaring (*c.* 1709–41). Oldfield was pregnant again when Maynwaring died, and appeared on stage as Cato's daughter in Joseph Addison's play until late in her pregnancy, a fact that was the subject of much contemporary comment. The child appears to have been born in May or June 1713 and, as there are no further records, it likely died at birth or in early infancy.

p. 32, l. 6: *another by the brigadier*: Charles Churchill (*c.* 1720–1812) went on to become an MP like his father. He married Lady Mary Walpole, the illegitimate daughter of Sir Robert Walpole, in 1746.

p. 32, l. 12: *Savage the poet*: Richard Savage (*c.* 1698–1743) was a poet, famous for his contested claim of aristocratic birth.

p. 32, ll. 14–15: *Mrs Oldfield's talents in her profession*: Hays follows the *Biographia Britannica* in this highly selective account of Oldfield's career. Oldfield played more than one hundred and ten roles in the course of her career, sixty-eight of these she originated. She became the highest paid actor in the Drury Lane Company, and her talents – both tragic and comedic – were widely acclaimed. Colley Cibber commended her in the preface to *The Provok'd Husband* as being, 'of a lively Aspect and a Command in her Mien, that like the principal Figure in the Finest Paintings, first seizes, and longest delights the Eye of the Spectator. Her Voice was Sweet, strong, piercing, and melodious: her Pronunciation voluble, distinct, and musical; and her Emphasis always placed where the Spirit of the Sense, in her Periods, only demanded it' (London: J. Watts, 1728), [n.p.].

p. 32, ll. 18–19: *those parts of her conduct … considered reprehensible*: Hays here alludes to Oldfield's successive extra-marital relationships with Arthur Maynwaring and Charles Churchill, both of whom she lived with openly, and to the two sons that resulted. As both Maynwaring and Churchill were unmarried, the fact that Oldfield married neither appears to have been her choice.

p. 32, l. 22: *Westminster-abbey*: Churchill was largely responsible for the details of Oldfield's funeral and for securing the honour of burial in Westminster Abbey. Only two actors before Oldfield – Thomas Betterton and his wife Mary – had received this honour. Churchill later applied for permission to erect a monument to Oldfield near the place of her burial, but was denied. See A. P. Stanley (ed.), *Historical Memorials of Westminster Abbey* (London: J. Murray, 1882), pp. 284–5.

p. 32, ll. 22–3: *gentlemen of high rank and character*: The pallbearers were the following courtiers and gentlemen: John West, Baron De La Warr, a gentleman of the royal bedchamber; George Bubb Dodington, Lord-Lieutenant of Somerset and a lord of the Treasury; John, Lord Hervey, Vice-Chamberlain of the royal household; Walter Carey, Esq.; a Captain Elliot and John Hedges.

p. 32, ll. 24–5: *eldest son ... chief mourner*: Although Churchill was responsible for Oldfield's funeral arrangements, he had no official relationship to her. Consequently, Oldfield's son, Arthur Maynwaring, led the funeral party as chief mourner.

p. 32, ll. 26–7: *Mr. Craggs*: James Craggs the Younger (1686–1721), Whig politician. He served as a resident minister in Spain from 1708–11, before being elected to the House of Commons in 1713, and remained in parliament until his death in 1721.

p. 32, l. 27: Mr. Congreve: William Congreve (1670–1729), poet and popular playwright, best known for *Love for Love* (1695) and *The Way of the World* (1700).

p. 32, l. 27–p. 33, l. 8: *elegantly dressed in her coffin ... Brussels lace*: Margaret Saunders, who claimed to have been with Oldfield during her last illness, contributed this detail to Curll's biography of the actress (*Faithful Memoirs*, p. 144). The detail is repeated in all eighteenth-century accounts of the actress, perhaps because it chimes with reports of Oldfield's vanity.

p. 33, ll. 1–4: *bulk of her fortune to her eldest son ... regard to her second son*: Oldfield left a legacy of £5,000 to Maynwaring, stipulating that he was to receive only the interest until his thirtieth birthday. To her second son, Charles Churchill, ten years old at the time of Oldfield's death, she left the deed to her house in Grosvenor Street. Her will further stipulated that her estate was to be divided when her annuants were deceased; two-thirds were to go to Maynwaring, and one-third to Churchill. The fact that Churchill stood to inherit his father's estate likely accounts for this disparity.

p. 33, l. 5: *her own relations*: To her mother, Oldfield left a bequest of ten guineas and a £60 annuity; her aunt, Jane Gourlaw, was to receive a £10 annuity.

p. 33, l. 7: *MARIA PACHECO PADILLA*: Birth name María Pacheco; born in Granada 1497, died in exile in Porto (Portugal) 1531. Her parents are Íñigo López de Mendoza, Marquis of Tendilla, and Francisca Pacheco.

p. 33, l. 9: *Charles V*: King of Castile, Aragon and Holy Roman Emperor (1500–58; r. 1516–56).

p. 33, l. 9: *don John de Padilla*: She was married to John de Padilla (1490–1521) on 18 June 1515.

p. 33, l. 10: *the commendator of Castile*: Pedro López de Padilla.

p. 34, l. 9: *the aid of a considerable sum*: The story is in Hays's sources and widely spread in chronicles, although it appears that Maria did not participate directly in this event as it took place in October 1521 after she was widowed. See F. M. Gil, *La mujer valerosa. Historia de doña María Pacheco, comunera de Castilla (1497–1531)* (Toledo: Almud ediciones, etc., 2005), pp. 186–7.

p. 34, ll. 10–11: *In a subsequent engagement between the two parties*: The battle of Villalar, which is considered to be the end of the civil wars in Castile, 23 April 1521.

p. 34, l. 18: *One of his companions*: Juan Bravo (*c.* 1483–1521), another rebel leader and Maria's cousin.

p. 34, ll. 20–2: '*that yesterday ... Christians!*': See W. Robertson, *The History of the Reign of the Emperor Charles V*, 4 vols (London: W. Strahan and T. Cadell/Edinburgh: J. Balfour, 1774), vol. 2, p. 256.

p. 35, ll. 13–14: *the French general in Navarre*: André de Foix, Lord of Lesparre (1490–1547).

p. 35, ll. 25–7: *Seated on a mule, clad in deep mourning, her son in her arms, and having a standard borne before her*: In Hays's source, Maria marched through Toledo, but it is her son who sits on a mule and has the standard carried before *him* where the fate of *his father* is represented. See Robertson, *Charles V*, p. 260. This was most likely a deliberate change as all sources agree on it. Her son was Pedro (Peter) López (11 April 1516–7 September 1523).

p. 36, ll. 12–13: *her brother*: Marquis of Mondéjar, Luis Hurtado de Mendoza (1489–1566), her eldest brother. The rest of Maria's family sided with the Royalists.

p. 36, l. 22: *withdrew their support from the citizens*: Roberston used the phrase 'ceased to support her'; see Robertson, *Charles V*, p. 261. Hays's minor change presents Maria as one of the people.

p. 36, l. 24: *the archbishop of Toledo*: William de Croy, Archbishop since 1517, died in Germany on 7 January 1521 and the news arrived in Toledo twenty days later; thus it is a mistake to attribute his death to events in October.

p. 37, l. 2: *a Castilian as his successor*: Alonso of Fonseca and Ulloa (1475–1534).

p. 37, l. 9: *a negro maid*: not further identified.

p. 37, ll. 18–19: *she was compelled to escape*: The date was 3 February 1522.

p. 38, l. 1: *DOROTHY*: Dorothy, daughter of Sir Thomas Coventry (1578–1640), lord keeper, Baron Coventry from 1628 and Elizabeth Aldersey (1583–1653): See *ODNB*. Hays's account of Pakington closely follows its sources – G. Ballard, *Memoirs of Several Ladies of Great Britain: Who Have Been Celebrated for Their Writings or Skill in the Learned Languages, Arts and Sciences* (London: W. Jackson, 1752) and *Biographium Faemineum. The Female Worthies: Or, Memoirs of the Most Illustrious Ladies, of All Ages and Nations*, 2 vols (London: S. Crowder, and J. Payne, 1766). Ballard's aim was to argue the case for Pakington's authorship of *The Whole Duty of Man* (1657). Therefore, Ballard's biography of Pakington is structured as a historiography of hearsay about the authorship after an introduction in which he stated that it was his aim to end the 'concealment' because the attribution of Pakington to the work 'is not now generally believed'. His proofs included extensive quotation from G. Hickes, *Grammatica Anglo-Saxonica ex Hickesiano Linguarum Septentrionalium thesauro excerpta* (Oxford, 1711).

p. 38, ll. 2–3: *sir John Pakington*: Sir John Pakington (1621–80) was second Baronet from 1624, of Westwood Park, Worcestershire; he was a Royalist and member of the committee of safety whose lands were sequestered in 1646. Dorothy was his father's ward; they married in the early 1640s. Details about children not fully known; three were living in 1660: see *ODNB*.

p. 38, l. 5: *about the middle of the reign*: baptized 1623.

p. 38, l. 5: *James I*: James VI and I of Scotland (1566–1625); r. 1567 Scotland and 1603 England and Ireland.

p. 38, ll. 7–8: *reputed author of "The Whole Duty of Man"*: By the eighteenth century the text was attributed to Richard Allestree (*c.* 1621/2–81), one of the Royalist circle of clergyman around the Pakingtons; elected canon of Christchurch at the Restoration, his works, *The Gentlemans Calling* (London: Printed for T. Garthwait, 1660) and *The Ladies Calling* (Oxford: At the Theater, 1673) were influential in their construction of a high church Anglican morality that was specific to the wealthy gentry. *The Whole Duty of Man* (1657) was a work delivering advice on Anglican devotional behaviour within the framework of a broad understanding of the doctrine of grace. It was also an early work to claim that 'Man, we know, is made up of two parts, a Body and a Soul' (Sig.A2). A work of immense popularity, it was written while on a Royalist circuit that included the Pakingtons. It was anonymous and Dorothy Pakington's name was widely circulated as the author; printed *c.* fifty times before 1700, including with the full title *The Practice of Christian Graces, or, the Whole Duty of Man* between 1659 and 1660. The one edition that collected all three works together was published 1682 and was described on its frontispiece as 'Necessary for all Families': see *ODNB*.

p. 38, l. 13: *Abraham Woodhead*: (1609–78), Roman Catholic controversialist; converted during the civil war and part of a scholarly religious community at Hoxton, outside London: see *ODNB*.

p. 38, l. 15: *William Fulman*: (1632–88), antiquarian and one of the circle of clergymen around Bishop Henry Hammond (1605–60): see *ODNB*.

p. 38, l. 17: *bishop Fell*: John Fell (1625–86), Bishop of Oxford; wrote a life of Richard Allestree and Henry Hammond's funeral sermon.

p. 38, ll. 19–23: *"that, if God ... the Thoughts.":* *The Works of the Author of the Whole Duty of Man* was first prepared for publication by Henry Hammond, printed by B. Haite in 1682; the 1684 edition, by Roger Norton for George Pawlett, with the preface that contains this quotation, is in the British Library.

p. 38, l. 26: *Dr. Richard Sterne*: (*c.* 1595/6–1683), Rector of Yeovilton, Somerset, 1634 and Harlton, Cambridgeshire 1642, ejected by 1645. Later Archbishop of York, 1664–83. Also a church scholar and a Laudian, Sterne was one of the bishops entrusted with revising the Book of Common Prayer after the Restoration: see *ODNB*.

p. 39, l. 1: *Mr. Drake*: Francis Drake (bap. 1696–1771), surgeon who turned to antiquarian writing; see the biography in his *Eboracum, or, the History and Antiquities of the City of York* (1736); Ballard cites p. 464: see *ODNB*.

p. 39, l. 2: *the archbishop*: Richard Sterne.

p. 39, ll. 5–6: *"On Logic," and "A Comment on the 103d Psalm"*: *Summa Logicae partim ex optimus quibusque tum antiquis tum recentioribus* (1685) and *A Brief Commentary upon the CIII Psalme with the severall axioms or doctrines therein conteined* (1649).

p. 39, ll. 15–16: *archbishop Frewen*: Accepted Frewen (bap. 1588, d. 1664), a Laudian, not a notable writer of religious works.

p. 39, ll. 17–18: *"The Causes of the Decay of Christian Piety"*: work published in 1668 with the subtitle *An Impartial Survey of the Ruines of Christian Religion, undermin'd by Unchristian Practice written by the author of The Whole Duty of Man*, Sig.A1v.

p. 39, l. 27–p. 40, l. 9: *"A learned man ... scholars would use.":* Ballard, *Memoirs of Several Ladies*, p. 320. Also attributed to R. Allestree, *The Lively Oracles given to us, or, The Christian's Birth–Right and Duty in the Custody and Use of the Holy Scripture by the author of The Whole Duty of Man* (1688). Hays omits some of the power of Ballard's argument that 'It has been surpizing to me, to hear the many shifts and evasions which have been made use of ... in order to deprive this lady, and the fair sex, of the honour of those excellent performances': Ballard, *Memoirs of Several Ladies*, p. 320.

p. 39, l. 28: *Ballard*: George Ballard (*c.* 1705/6–55), antiquarian writer of the *Memoirs of Several Ladies* (1752) which underpins much of the work of Mary Hays.

p. 40, ll. 10–11: *Elizabeth and James*: Elizabeth I of England and Ireland (1533–1603; r. 1558–1603); James VI and I of Scotland (1566–1625; r. 1567 Scotland and 1603 England and Ireland).

p. 40, l. 18: *Dr. George Hickes*: George Hickes (1642–1715), nonjuring Bishop of the Church of England and writer whose works focused on the continuity of the sacerdotal traditions of the ancient British church; also wrote anti-Catholic works of controversy.

p. 40, ll. 20–2: *"Anglo-Saxon, and Mæso-Gothic Grammars"* ... *"Thesaurus"*: Hickes, *Grammatica Anglo-Saxonica*.

p. 40, l. 23–p. 41, l. 22: *"Your grandmother ... and instructors."*: Quotation in the Preface to Hickes's *Anglo-Saxon and Maeso-Gothic Grammars* with a posthumous dedication to Sir John Pakington because Hickes was given the deanery of Westwood Park.

p. 41, ll. 7–8: *Hammond, Morley, Fell, and Thomas*: All Royalist Church of England clergymen; the list originates in the Latin, in George Hickes's *Anglo-Saxon and Maeso-Gothic Grammars*, translated by Ballard. Henry Hammond (1605–60) was with Dorothy Pakington at the Battle of Worcester, accompanying Charles II, and moved to the Pakington seat of Westwood Park in 1650; George Morley (*c.* 1598–1684), Bishop of Winchester, carrier of Royalist news and information in England in the 1650s; John Fell (1625–86), Bishop of Oxford and Dean of Christ Church at the time Charles I set up his court there, part of the Royalist Anglican 'cell' that included the Pakingtons. Thomas not further identified. See *ODNB*; Hickes, *Grammatica Anglo-Saxonica*.

p. 41, ll. 18–19: *sir Norton Knatchbull*: Sir Norton Knatchbull (1602–85), first Baronet and Biblical scholar: see *ODNB*.

p. 42, l. 6: *the author of the "Baronettage"*: Arthur Collins (*c.* 1681/2–1760), *The Baronettage of England: being an Historical and Genealogical Account of Baronets from their First Institution in the Reign of King James I*, 2 vols (London: W. Taylor, 1720).

p. 42, l. 9–p. 43, l. 3: *"Her letters ... in 1561."*: Collins, *The Baronettage*, vol. 2, pp. 202–3.

p. 43, ll. 5–8: *"A Letter from a Clergyman ... Translation of Bishops"*: Francis Atterbury's *A Letter to a Clergyman in the Country* (1701) and *A Second Letter to a Clergyman in the Country* and *A Third Letter to a Clergyman in the Country* (1702): quotation from Ballard, *Memoirs of Several Ladies*, pp. 328–9.

p. 43, l. 14: *king Charles I*: Charles I (1600–49; r. 1625).

p. 43, l. 17: *Dr. Morley*: George Morley (*c.* 1598–1684), Bishop of Winchester.

p. 43, l. 19: *archbishop Dolben*: John Dolben (1625–86), Archbishop of York and civil war collaborator with Richard Allestree and John Fell: see *ODNB*.

p. 43, l. 19: *Dr. Abbestry*: Hays's mistake for 'Dr. Allestry' in Ballard, *Memoirs of Several Ladies*, p. 329, i.e. Richard Allestree (*c.* 1621/2–81).

p. 44, l. 4: *Dr. Snape*: Andrew Snape (1675–1742), provost of King's College, Cambridge.

p. 44, l. 6–p. 45, l. 8: *"October 19th ... church of Hull."*: Holy Trinity, of Kingston upon Hull, fourteenth-century brick edifice, believed to be the largest parish church in England.

p. 44, l. 7: *Thomas Caulton*: information originates with Ballard, *Memoirs of Several Ladies*, p. 329; not further identified.

p. 44, ll. 9–10: *William Thornton ... Mrs. Ash, Mrs. Caulton, and others*: witnesses to this oral communication not further identified.

p. 44, ll. 12–20: *Mrs. Eyre ... Anthony Eyre*: Anthony Eyre's wife was Dorothy Pakington's daughter, Elizabeth, who married Anthony Eyre of the extended Eyre family of Beverley, a market town in the East Riding of Yorkshire. Anne Eyre (*c.* 1612/13–81), daughter of a London merchant, was probably another family member, her maiden name of Aldersey suggesting kinship with Dorothy Pakington's mother: see *ODNB*.

p. 44, ll. 22–7: *"The Opinion of ... belief thereof"*: Two editions of the 1710 edition are to be found in the British Library.

p. 45, l. 5: *Dr. Covil*: not identified.

p. 45, l. 6: *Dr. Stamford*: not identified.

p. 45, l. 7: *Mr. Binks*: probably Robert Banks, vicar in 1642; the name of 'Binks' originates with Ballard, *Memoirs of Several Ladies*, p. 329.

p. 45, l. 19: *Dr. Richard Lucas*: Richard Lucas (1648–9), Church of England clergyman who wrote *Enquiry after Happiness* (1685) and other works of practical divinity.

p. 45, l. 20: *Dr. William Bell*: William Bell (1625–83), Church of England clergyman whose *Joshua's Resolution to Serve God with his Family* (1671) was a work of practical divinity aimed at familial-based piety: see *ODNB*.

p. 45, l. 21–p. 46, l. 12: *"The Causes ... of the Thoughts,"*: All works that are commonly ascribed to Richard Allestree, though Ballard says 'These are all the works of this author [i.e. Pakington] which are yet known to have been published': Ballard, *Memoirs of Several Ladies*, p. 332 (Ballard quotes at length the *Prayer for King Charles the Second*). The work which Pakington is supposed to have been working on before she died was *The Government of the Thoughts, a Prefatory Discourse to the Government of the Tongue* (1694); there was a further edition in 1700.

p. 46, ll. 15–19: *"She was wise ... undisturbed serenity."*: in *The Works of the Author of the Whole Duty of Man* (1684).

p. 46, l. 21: *interred in the church at Hampton-Lovett*: The Pakington family monuments were at Hampton Lovett, where the family house was before it was burnt during the civil war.

p. 47, ll. 2–3: *Anthony de Pons, count de Marennes*: Antoine de Pons, comte de Marennes (d. 1586), a nobleman whom King Francis I appointed as *chevalier d'honneur* to Renée de France, Duchess of Ferrara. At Renée's court he met and married Anne de Parthenay (m. 1533) and adopted the Protestant ideals of the duchess's circle.

p. 47, l. 4: *John de Parthenai l'Archenesque*: Jean IV de Parthenay-L'Archevêque (d. *c.* 1512), Lord of Soubise, a French nobleman and Protestant.

p. 47, ll. 4–5: *Michelli de Sorbonne*: Michelle de Saubonne du Fresne (d. *c.* 1549) married Jean IV de Parthenay-L'Archevêque in 1507. She was a Protestant sympathizer and humanist renowned for her knowledge of art, literature and music. She was influential at the French court of Anne of Bretagne, as well as the Ferrarese court of Anne's daughter, Renée de France.

p. 47, l. 7: *Anne of Bretagne*: Anne of Bretagne, Duchess of Brittany and Queen of France (1477–1514, r. 1491–8, r. 1499–1514) (see also Hays, *Female Biography*, vol. 1, pp. 122–39).

p. 47, l. 8: *Lewis XII*: King Louis XII of France (1462–1515, r. 1498–1515), Anne of Bretagne's second husband.

p. 47, l. 9: *Renata, duchess of Ferrara*: Renée de France (1510–74), youngest daughter of Anne of Bretagne and Louis XII of France. She became Duchess of Ferrara upon her marriage to Ercole II d'Este, Duke of Ferrara in 1528 (see also Hays, *Female Biography*, vol. 6, pp. 79–87).

p. 47, ll. 14–15: *the most celebrated theologians of the times*: Hays follows Pierre Bayle's praise of Anne's intellect, command of theology and conversational skills. See P. Bayle, *A General Dictionary Historical and Critical*, trans. J. P. Bernard, T. Birch, J. Lockman, et al., 10 vols (London: James Bettenham, 1737), vol. 5, p. 158. Although neither Hays nor Bayle specify which theologians Anne frequented, it is documented that the Protestant theologian John Calvin visited the court of Renée de France at Ferrara, where Anne, her sisters and their mother, Michelle de Saubonne, resided in the 1530s. See C. J. Blaisdell, 'Renée de France between Reform and Counter-Reform', *Archive for Reformation History*, 63 (1972), pp. 196–225.

p. 47, l. 21: *Theodorus Beza*: Theodore Beza, or Théodore de Bèze (1519–1605), noted writer and theologian. He was a prominent leader in the Protestant Reformation, founding the Geneva academy with John Calvin and succeeding Calvin on his death.

p. 47, ll. 21–2: *"Ecclesiastical History"*: *Histoire ecclésiastique des églises réformées au royaume de France* (1580), a historical work in which Beza chronicles events during the French Wars of Religion and the Huguenot church in France. Bayle affirms that Anne was 'a good Huguenot' and cites a passage in Beza's work where the author praises the influence of Anne's piety on her husband, Antoine de Pons, and laments his abandonment of Protestant ideals following his second marriage. See Bayle, *A General Dictionary*, p. 158.

p. 47, l. 25: *the lord of Soubise*: Jean V de Parthenay-L'Archevêque (1512–66), son of Jean IV de Parthenay-L'Archevêque and Michelle de Saubonne. Jean V served King Henry II of France and supported the Huguenots during the Wars of Religion.

p. 48, ll. 4–9: *"God so took away ... studiously promoted."*: Hays cites Beza, *Histoire ecclésiastique*, via Bayle, *A General Dictionary*, p. 158.

p. 48, ll. 6–7: *Mary de Monchenu, the lady de Massey*: Marie de Montchenu, baronne de Macy (d. 1560) married Antoine de Pons in 1557, following the death of Anne de Parthenay. Hays seconds Theodore Beza's judgment of Marie de Montchenu. See Bayle, *A General Dictionary*, p. 158. Desmond Seward notes that Marie de Montchenu, whose husband was a friend of King Francis I, was one of the French king's many mistresses. See *Prince of the Renaissance: The Life of François I* (London: Constable, 1973), p. 69. Her status at court may account in part for the unfavourable comment in Beza's *Histoire ecclésiastique*.

p. 48, ll. 11–12: *Gregory Gyraldus*: Giglio Gregorio Giraldi (1479–1552) was an erudite scholar and poet from Ferrara.

p. 48, l. 15: *duke of Ferrara:* Ercole II d'Este (1508–59), Duke of Ferrara, Modena and Reggio (r. 1534–59), Renée de France's husband and the Pope's vicar in Ferrara.

p. 48, l. 17: *"History of the Poets"*: Giraldi's *Historiae poetarum tam Graecorum quam Latinorum* (Basel: [n.p.], 1545), in which the author praises the virtues of both Anne de Parthenay and her husband, Antoine de Pons. See Bayle, *A General Dictionary*, p. 158.

p. 48, l. 19: *huguenot party:* Huguenot is a generic term used to refer to French Protestants, many of whom were persecuted during the sixteenth and seventeenth centuries.

p. 48, ll. 20–3: *was obliged to leave ... whom he served*: Ercole II d'Este obliged his wife, Renée de France, to dismiss the members of her French entourage with Protestant leanings, including Antoine de Pons and Anne de Parthenay, who left Ferrara in 1544. See D. Bentley-Cranch, 'A Question of Patronage: The Links between Clément Marot, Antoine de Pons, Bernard Palissy and Anne de Montmorency in the Context of the Reform Movement in Sixteenth-Century France', in S. A. Stacey (ed.), *Court and Humor in the French Renaissance: Essays in Honor of Professor Pauline Smith* (Bern: Peter Lang, 2009), pp. 81–92.

p. 49, l. 1: *CATHERINE DE PARTHENAI*: Catherine de Parthenay (1554–1631) was born into a Protestant family of great literary repute. Her father, Jean V de Parthenay-L'Archevêque (1512–66), was the son of Michelle de Saubonne (dates unknown), a female humanist, and secretary to Queen Anne of Brittany (r. 1488–1514); and nominated by the latter as governess to her daughter, the Princess Renée (1510–74) de France. Her mother was Antoinette d'Aubeterre (*c.* 1530–*c.* 1580), lady-in-waiting to Catherine de' Medici in 1554, and renowned for her protection of persecuted Protestants. As well as being noted by historians as erudite in philosophy and mathematics, Catherine de Parthenay was first and foremost remembered as the distinguished and learned mother of the Rohans ('*mère des Rohans*') and as a staunch supporter of the Huguenot cause.

p. 49, ll. 2–3: *John de Parthenia*: see note to p. 49, l. 1, above.

p. 49, ll. 3–4: *Anne de Parthenai*: Anne de Parthenay (1533–86) was a woman of letters described by Pierre Bayle as 'a lady of great wit and learning' (*The Historical and Critical Dictionary of Mr Peter Bayle,* trans. Desmaizeaux (London, 1734–7), vol. 4, p. 480). She was well versed in theology and, like her mother (Michelle de Saubonne, see note to p. 49, l. 1, above), an active supporter of the Huguenot cause. For a full account, see Hays, *Female Biography,* vol. 6, pp. 45–6.

p. 49, l. 5: *Charles de Quellence, baron de Pons*: Charles de Quellenec (1542–72), baron de Pons (also spelled Pont) was a Protestant. His short-lived marriage with his teenaged wife, Catherine de Parthenay, was an unhappy one; she and her mother sued him for impotence and filed for divorce. His death on the night of the Massacre of the Huguenots (also known as St Bartholomew's Day Massacre) on 24 August 1572, put an abrupt end to the divorce case (see N. Vray, *Catherine de Parthenay, duchesse de Rohan, protestante insoumise* (Paris: Librairie Académique Perrin, 1998), pp. 45–50). However, despite their marital dispute, Catherine wrote an elegiac poem in homage to her belated husband (see note to p. 51, ll. 6–9, below).

p. 49, ll. 7–8: *St. Bartholomew, 1571*: St Bartholomew's Day Massacre in 1572 (see note to p. 49, l. 5, above).

p. 49, l. 10: *several elegiac poems*: Literary history remains vague; while the poems most probably circulated in manuscript, the first printed versions seem to date back to the nineteenth century, and were mainly published in the *Bulletin de la Société de l'histoire du Protestantisme français* (e.g. 1861, 1867): some excerpts are cited by Vray, *Catherine de Parthenay,* pp. 36–7, 121–2.

p. 49, l. 12: *Renatus viscount Rohan*: René II, Viscount of Rohan (1550–86), grandson of Catherine de Foix, Queen of Navarre (1468–1517, r. 1483–1517).

p. 49, l. 13: *several children*: two sons and three daughters; see notes to p. 49, l. 19 (the Duke of Rohan), below; p. 49, l. 23 (The Duke of Soubize), below; p. 49, l. 23 (Henrietta), below; p. 49, l. 24 (Catherine), below; and p. 50, l. 5 (Anne of Rohan), below.

p. 49, l. 19: *The celebrated duke de Rohan*: Henry II of Rohan (1579–1638) was the Huguenot leader against the Catholic Royal forces; he also left a few historical and political works, which were published posthumously: his best-selling *Mémoires du duc de Rohan* (1644) which was translated into English (1660), *Voyage du Duc de Rohan faict en l'an 1600 en Italie, Allemaigne, Pays-Bas Uni, Angleterre et Escosse* (1646), and his influential *De l'Intérêt des princes et états de la chrétienté* (1650).

p. 49, l. 22: *Lewis XIII*: Louis XIII, son to the Bourbon King Henri IV, became King of France and of Navarre in 1610 at the age of nine, and officially took power in 1617 after exiling his mother, Marie de' Medici, who acted as Queen regent during his teenage years. He ruled France until his death in 1643.

p. 49, l. 23: *The duke of Soubise*: Benjamin de Soubise (1583–1642), duke de Frontenay, and baron de Soubise, commonly named the duke de Soubise; he had served his apprenticeship as a young soldier under Maurice of Nassau, Prince of Orange (1567–1625), and was the last surviving leader of the Calvinist resistance in early seventeenth-century France.

p. 49, l. 23: *Henrietta*: Henriette de Rohan (b. 1577) died in 1624 and not 1629, as it is printed here. She was commonly referred to as 'la bossue' [hunchback], according to seventeenth-century chronicler Gédéon Tallemant des Réaux; see *Historiettes: mémoires pour servir à l'histoire du XVIIe siècle*, ed. Monmerqué, Chateaugiron and Taschereau, 6 vols (Paris: A. Levasseur, 1834–5), vol. 3, p. 66. However, despite her malformation, he describes her as more spiritual than her sister Anne de Rohan – surprisingly so, since Anne singled herself out as a well-accomplished poetess (see Hays, *Female Biography*, vol. 6, pp. 87–8). Henriette's literary talent, taste for satire, and delicate sentiments and passion can be gleaned from several poems which have survived and were reprinted in nineteenth-century studies (e.g. A. Laugel, *Henri de Rohan* [1889], cited in Vray, *Catherine de Parthenay*, p. 102; and J. Bonnet, *Derniers récits du XVIème siècle* [1876], cited in Vray, *Catherine de Parthenay*, pp. 122–3). Having remained single, possibly because of her poor health, Henriette allegedly bore a deep and exalted passion for the Duchess de Nevers (Catherine de Mayenne, also known as Catherine de Lorraine (1585–1618)); see Tallemant des Réaux, *Historiettes*, p. 66.

p. 49, l. 24: *Catherine*: Born in 1580, she was briefly married to Jean de Baviere, duc de Deux-Ponts (1569–1604) and died in labour in 1607. She too seems to have been well-versed in poetry; her last poem, written on her deathbed, was printed in the *Bulletin de la Société de l'histoire du Protestantisme français* (cited in Vray, *Catherine de Parthenay*, p. 121).

p. 49, l. 25: *duke of Deux-Ponts*: see note to p. 49, l. 24, above.

p. 50, l. 1: *Henry IV*: Henri IV, King of Navarre and France (1553–1610), who ruled from 1572 until his assassination in 1610.

p. 50, ll. 3–4: '*I am too poor ... your mistress.*': Cited from Bayle, *The Historical and Critical Dictionary*, vol. 4, p. 481. There is some dispute as to the authorship of this citation, seemingly founded on a diverging interpretation of the keys to the female-authored novel *Histoire des amours du grand Alcandre* (1651) by Louise-Marguerite de Lorraine, Princess de Conti (1588–1631), which was first published in 1620 according to literary historian Fortunée Briquet (although no library records substantiate this) under the title *Roman royal, ou les Aventures de la Cour* (*Dictionnaire historique, biographique et littéraire des Françaises et étrangères naturalisées en France*) (Paris: Treuttel and Würtz, 1804), p. 213. It was re-edited again in 1663 under a third and revised title, *Histoire des amours de Henri IV*. François-Timoléon de Choisy attributes the citation to Antoinette de Pons, Marquise de Guercheville (*c.* 1560–1632): see *Mémoires de l'abbé de Choisy* (1727) in O. Talon, *Mémoires de Omer Talon*, published in Petitot and Monmerqué (eds), *Collection des mémoires relatifs à l'histoire de France* (Paris: Foucault, 1828), vol. 63, p. 516.

p. 50, l. 5: *Her third daugter Anne*: Anne de Rohan (1584–1646), an erudite and highly regarded woman of letters, who fought for the Huguenot cause; see Hays, *Female Biography*, vol. 6, pp. 87–8.

p. 50, l. 9: *siege of Rochelle*: the siege of La Rochelle (1627–8) marked the victory of Louis XIII over the Huguenots.

p. 50, ll. 15–18: '*to go on as he had begun, ... cause he had espoused.*': Hays seems to have rephrased the citation from *Biographium Faemineum*, vol. 2, p. 189.

p. 50, l. 24: *published some poems in 1572*: see note to p. 49, l. 10, above.

p. 50, l. 26: *Holofernes*: see note to p. 51, ll. 3–5, below.

p. 50, l. 27–p. 51, l. 13: "*She understood poetry' ... this year (1584).*": This citation is slightly reworded from the translator's citation of Bayle's own quotation from La Croix du Main's work *Bibliothèque française* (see note to p. 51, l. 1, below), on p. 481, note B.

p. 51, l. 1: *La Croix du Main*: La Croix du Main (1552–92) was François Grudé's lord title; he was an erudite man of letters, and a bibliographer, especially remembered for his encyclopedic compilation of European writings into an anthology known as *Bibilothèque française* (1584).

p. 51, ll. 3–5: *several tragedies and comedies in French, among others the Tragedy of Holofernes*: The manuscript of *Holofernes* appears to have been lost; but contemporaneous and later critics seem to agree that it was performed in 1574 at La Rochelle. The comedies referred to here may well be Catherine de Parthenay's three political and allegorical court ballets, entitled *Balet, Balet de Madame* and *Autre Balet*, whose original title, *Balet de Madame de Rohan,* was anonymized (see Vray, *Catherine de Parthenay*, p. 83). The first of these plays was represented in Pau, in August 1592 (Vray, *Catherine de Parthenay*, p. 82), and all were performed by Parthenay herself, her children and friends of theirs, in front of King Henri IV and his sister Catherine de Bourbon (1559–1604). For a synopsis of these three plays see Vray, *Catherine de Parthenay*, pp. 82–3, and on her political motivations see S. Broomhall, *Women and Religion in Sixteenth-Century France* (London: Palgrave Macmillan, 2006), pp. 121–2.

p. 51, ll. 6–9: *several poems or elegies, on the death of her first husband, ... likewise upon the admiral and other illustrious persons who perished on the same occasion*: see note to p. 49, l. 10, above. Here the admiral is none other than Gaspard II de Coligny (1519–72), chief leader of the Protestant rebellion who was murdered on the night of the Bartholomew's Day Massacre (see note to p. 49, ll. 7–8, above), and among those 'illustrious persons' mentioned here is Coligny's own son-in-law, Charles de Téligny, both an accomplished soldier and man of letters (see Vray, *Catherine de Parthenay*, pp. 40, 50).

p. 51, l. 8: *the massacre of St Bartholomew*: see note to p. 49, ll. 7–8, above.

p. 51, ll. 10–12: *She translated the precepts of Isocrates to Demonicus, not yet printed.*: Literary historians, including Vray (*Catherine de Parthenay*, p. 58), mention other translations; but, as with her poems, these indications are vague on the whole; scholars do not know how veritably prolific she was, and thus far have only been able to rely on contemporaneous testimonies.

p. 51, ll. 13–18: *If it be true, as asserted by a learned man ... married at fourteen years of age.*: Here Hays paraphrases Bayle, and is just as vague about the identity of the author of this citation (*Historical and Critical Dictionary*, vol. 4, pp. 481–2).

p. 51, ll. 18–21: *a concealed but keen satire ... the Journal of Henry III*: The *Journal de Henry III, Roy de France et de Pologne: ou Mémoires pour servir à l'histoire de France* was extracted for publication in 1621 from *Registres Journaux (1574–1611)*, a chronicle of the reigns of Henri III and Henri IV, written by Pierre L'Estoile (1546–1611). Also referred to as *Le Journal of Henri IV*, it enjoyed a sustained success well into the eighteenth and nineteenth centuries.

p. 51, l. 21: *D'Aubigné*: Théodore Agrippa d'Aubigné (1552–1630) was a soldier and a Baroque poet, best known for his epic poem, *Les Tragiques* (1616), which depicted the throes and persecutions to which the Protestants were subjected. D'Aubigné had also written a *Discours par stances avec l'esprit du feu roy Henry quatrième* (cited in Vray, *Catherine de Parthenay*, p. 131), and had praised Anne de Rohan's own mourning poem on the great loss of the King of Navarre, in his *Histoire universelle depuis 1550 jusqu'en 1601* (cited by Vray, *Catherine de Parthenay*, p. 131) which was censored by the parliament of Paris.

p. 51, l. 22–p. 52, l. 1: *"The king shewed ... what we do!"*: The citation is directly copied from Bayle's *Historical and Critical Dictionary*, vol. 4, p. 482, note E.

p. 51, l. 24: *Roquelaire*: Possibly alluding metonymically to sixteenth-century writer Guillaume Du Bois, generally referred to as poet of 'le duc de Roquelaure', that is Duke Antoine de Roquelaure (1544–1624). An eminent and highly esteemed military figure, he witnessed the murder of French King Henri IV in the latter's horse carriage in 1604 while travelling with him.

p. 52, l. 1: *Bayle*: Pierre Bayle (1647–1706), an important intellectual in the history of European Enlightenment, best known for his *Dictionnaire historique et critique* begun in
1695, further augmented over several decades, and first translated into English in 1709.

p. 52, ll. 2–3: *whoever composed the* Apology *was a person of wit and talents*: Hays cites Bayle,
Historical and Critical Dictionary, vol. 4, p. 482, note E.

p. 52, l. 5: *PAULINA*: Alternately Pompeia Paulina. Pompeia Paulina was a member of the
gens Pompeia, a powerful family during the Republic. She was the daughter of Pompeius
Paulinus, who held important military and civil positions between AD 48–58, and the
wife of Seneca.

p. 52, l. 6: *SENECA*: Lucius Annaeus Seneca or Seneca the Younger (*c.* 4 BC–AD 65), philosopher, politician, playwright and satirist; ordered to commit suicide by the emperor Nero
in AD 65 for his reputed involvement in a political conspiracy.

p. 52, l. 8: *her husband*: We know that they were married by AD 42, the year he published the
first passage that mentions her (*De Ira*, 3.36.3), and that she was the mother of his son
(mentioned in *Ad Helviam*, 2.5). She may have been much younger than he, a situation
common in Roman marriages; their relationship was deeply affectionate. In a letter Seneca describes her as 'my dear Paulina, who always urges me to take care of my health. I
know that her very life-breath comes and goes with my own, and I am beginning, in my
solicitude for her, to be solicitous for myself ... therefore, since I cannot prevail upon her
to love me any more heroically, she prevails upon me to cherish myself more carefully'
(*Epistolae Morales*, 104.2). Their shared moral commitment to a life of honour is demonstrated by her offer to die with him.

p. 52, l. 9: *(says Tacitus)*: Tacitus records it in this way: 'Nero meanwhile, having no personal
hatred against Paulina and not wishing to heighten the odium of his cruelty, forbade her
death ... ordered her servants to bind up her wounds and stanched the bleeding, whether
with her agreement is doubtful. For as the gossips are ever ready to think the worst, there
were persons who believed that, as long as she dreaded Nero's relentlessness, she sought
the glory of sharing Seneca's death, but that after a time ... she yielded to the charms of
life. To this she added a few subsequent years, with a most praiseworthy remembrance
of her husband, and with a countenance and frame white to a degree of pallor which
denoted a loss of much vital energy' (*Annals*, 15.64).

p. 52, ll. 11–12: *her blood had flowed with that of her husband*: Cassius Dio, the second-century AD historian, offers another version: 'The fate of Seneca needs a few words by itself.
It was his wish to end the life of his wife Paulina at the same time with his own, for he
declared that he had taught her to despise death and that she desired to leave the world
in company with him. So he opened her veins as well as his own. As he failed, however,
to yield readily to death, his end was hastened by the soldiers; and his dying so speedily
enabled Paulina to survive' (*Roman History*, 47.49.3).

p. 52, l. 13: *PERILLA*: The Roman novelist Apuleius identifies 'Metella' as the actual, metri-
cally equivalent Roman name of the woman referred to by the Greek name of 'Perilla' in
the love poetry of Ticidas (*Apology*, 10).

p. 50, ll. 14–15: *Augustus*: Gaius Octavius (63 BC–AD 14), Caesar's adopted son and heir, subsequently called Gaius Julius Caesar Octavianus, and then Augustus, Emperor of Rome.

p. 52, l. 16: *poetical talents*: In *Tristia* 2 (a long poem addressed to Augustus), Ovid defends the
erotic verse which led to his banishment, citing a host of literary predecessors, first Greek
and then Roman, who wrote about love with impunity. In his catalogue of Roman poets,
Ovid (like Apuleius) notes that Perilla was the pseudonym for Metella; he represents
her as both a love poet and the subject of such poetry, celebrated in Ticidas's erotic and

sexually explicit verses about her. Although modern scholarship has drawn the inference that she was the daughter of Clodia Metelli, Ovid does not identify her as such (see especially M. Skinner, *Clodia Metelli: The Tribune's Sister* (Oxford: Oxford University Press, 2011), pp. 92–3).

p. 52, l. 16: *Ovid*: Publius Ovidius Naso (43 BC–AD 14), Roman poet.

p. 52, l. 17: *scholar in poetry*: In *Tristia* (3.7) (a poetic 'letter' addressed to a certain Perilla), Ovid acknowledges Perilla's poetic talent, and that he and Perilla read and criticized each other's poetry. 'Perilla' must be a pseudonym, since Ovid does not mention the names of his addressees in the *Tristia* for fear of embarrassing them: he was in exile at the time. From other hints in this poem, scholars have suggested that Perilla may have been Ovid's stepdaughter; this is uncertain.

p. 53, l. 1: *SUSANNA*: Hays heavily draws from, with revisions, J. Batchiler, *The Virgins Pattern in the Exemplary Life, and Lamented Death of Mrs. Susanna Perwich* (London: Printed by Simon Dover, 1661).

p. 53, l. 2: *Robert Perwich*: married Mary Mason, Susanna's stepmother, in March 1643 in St John's Hackney, and had several further children with her, leaving substantial wealth in his will dated 1776. See Will of Robert Perwich, Gentleman of Hackney, Middlesex (PROB 11/351/545) and Mary Perwich (PROB 11/384/201).

p. 53, l. 4: *Aldermanbury, London*: Aldermanbury was within the walls of the old city of London.

p. 53, ll. 9–10: *her father undertook the superintendence of a school at Hackney*: Hackney was a wealthy enclave on the outskirts of London where several schools were established over the course of the seventeenth century; the Perwiches' large establishment, run by Robert and Mary, in Church-Street, educated 800 girls in its first seventeen years, and employed distinguished music masters including Edward Coleman (bap. 1622, d. 1669), William Gregory (d. 1663), Simon Ive or Ives (bap. 1600, d. 1662), Stephen Bing (bap. 1610, d. 1681) and organist Albertus Bryne (*c.* 1621–68). See *ODNB*.

p. 54, l. 19: *death of a young man*: not identified.

p. 55, ll. 4–7: *The fanatic character of the times ... the calvinistic notions*: Hays is critical of the impact of 'fanatic' Puritanism on Perwich. See F. James, 'Writing *Female Biography*: Mary Hays and the Life Writing of Religious Dissent', in *Women's Life Writing, 1700–1850: Gender, Genre and Authorship*, ed. D. Cook and A. Culley (Basingstoke: Palgrave Macmillan, 2012), pp. 117–32.

p. 55, l. 12: *"Shepard's True Convert" and "Sound Believer"*: *The Sincere Convert, Discovering the Paucity of True Believers* (London: Printed by T. Paine, for Humfrey Blunden, 1640) and *The Sound Beleever* (London: Printed for R. Dawlman, 1649) by Thomas Shepard (1605–49), minister trained at Puritan Emmanuel College who emigrated to New England in 1635. His influential sermons were published as *The Parable of the Ten Virgins* (London: Printed by J. Hayes for John Rothwell, 1660) which may have influenced Batchiler's *The Virgins Pattern*, pp. 17–20.

p. 55, l. 13: *"Baxter's Call to the Unconverted"*: Richard Baxter (1615–91), ejected minister whose multiple works were influential in late seventeenth-century Protestant dissent, including *A Call to the Unconverted to Turn and Live and Accept of Mercy while Mercy May be Had* (London: Printed by R. W. for N. Simmons, 1658).

p. 55, ll. 13–14: *"Goodwin's Triumph of Faith"*: Thomas Goodwin (1600–80), nonconformist minister and writer of works of pastoral theology; Batchiler cites the work as '*Dr. Goodwin His Triumph of Faith, and Heart of Christ in Heaven, Towards Sinners Upon Earth*', probably a conflation of *Christ Set Forth ... Together with a Treatise discovering the Affectionate*

Tendernesse of Christ's Heart now in Heaven, unto Sinners on Earth (London: Printed for R. Dawlman, 1642) and *Encouragements to Faith* (London: Printed for R. Dawlman, 1645).

p. 55, l. 14: *"Brooke's Riches of Grace"*: Thomas Brooks (1608–80), Independent minister and Fifth Monarchist. His pastoral works such as *Apples of Gold for Young Men and Women* (London: Printed by R. I. for John Hancock, 1657) went through multiple reprints through the later seventeenth century. Work cited is probably *The Unsearchable Riches of Christ* (London: Printed by Mary Simmons for John Hancock, 1657).

p. 56, l. 12: *several solicitations of marriage*: not further identified.

p. 56, l. 19: *a friend*: not identified.

p. 56, l. 25: *her disorder*: not identified.

p. 57, l. 5: *twenty-fifth year of her age*: Batchiler gives the exact date of death as 3 July 1661. See *The Virgins Pattern*, p. 1; D. Lysons, *The Environs of London: Kent, Essex, and Herts*, 2 vols (London: Cadell and Davies, 1811), vol. 2, p. 322, gives burial date as 6 July 1661.

p. 57, l. 11: *Dr. Spurstow*: William Spurstowe (d. 1666), nonconformist minister of Perwich family church, St John's Hackney, and friend whom Susanna Perwich requested to preach at her funeral. One of the authors of the controversial anti-episcopal tract, *Smectymnuus* (1641); friend of Richard Baxter.

p. 57, l. 12: *I Cor. iii. 22*: 'Whether Paul or Apollos or Cephas or the world or life or death or the present or the future, all are yours'. Batchiler summarized this as 'Death is yours' to emphasize her connection to Christ. See Batchiler, *The Virgins Pattern*, p. 41.

p. 57, ll. 14–15: *The Life ... by John Batchiler*: see note to p. 53, l. 1, above. John Batchiler/Bacheler (d. 1674). Ejected clergyman, commemorated in Edmund Calamy's *Nonconformist Memorial*; prior to 1660, Parliamentary chaplain and licenser of works of divinity before teaching at Perwich's school. He describes himself as 'a neer Relation' to Perwich by marriage, but it is hard to ascertain exactly whether the Abigall Perwich that Batchiler marries in 1649 is Susanna's sister or aunt (*The Virgins Pattern*, p. 1).

p. 57, ll. 17–18: *Mrs. Perwich's School at Hackney*: The school is described by Batchiler as also belonging to Perwich's stepmother, Mary. 'Mrs' is designation of mistress, not necessarily a married state.

p. 57, l. 20: *PHILA*: Greek Φίλλα (*c.* 340–287 BC). Bayle has Philla (also Phylla) in *The Dictionary Historical and Critical of Mr. Peter Bayle* (London: Printed for J. J. and P. Knapton [etc.], 1734–8), vol. 4, pp. 620–1; *Biographium Faemineum*, vol. 2, pp. 203–4 also has Philla; Rollin prefers Phila in *The Ancient History of the Egyptians, Carthaginians, Assyrians, Babylonians, Medes and Persians, Macedonians, and Greeks By Mr. Rollin*, 13 vols (London: James, John and Paul Knapton, 1734), vol. 7, p. 48. Hays blends information from Rollin with Bayle and the *Biographium Faemineum* in this entry.

p. 57, l. 20: *Antipater*: Regent for Alexander from 334 BC; he continued to rule Greece after Alexander's death until his own death in 319 BC. He had eleven children: Cassander, Nicanor, Alexarchus, Iolaus, Perilaus, Philip, Pleistarchus (sons) and Nicaea, Eurydice and Phila (daughters); the names of their mothers and another daughter are unknown.

p. 57, l. 21: *Alexander*: 'The Great', King of Macedonia 356–323 BC.

p. 58, ll. 3–4: *Her father never ... without consulting her*: The phrase comes from Rollin and extends the idea of her wisdom and role in advising her father, Antipater, the Regent for Alexander, beyond the ancient evidence (Diodorus Siculus, 19.59).

p. 58, ll. 7–12: *cabals were dissolved ... she prevented an insurrection*: An extravagant claim found in Hays's sources that goes beyond the account in Diodorus, 19.59.

p. 58, l. 14: *She portioned young women*: Her support for the marriage of poor women by providing their dowry is attested in Diodorus, 19.59.

p. 58, l. 20: *juridical affairs of the kingdom*: derived from a claim that 'she opposed with so much vigour those that oppressed the innocent' in the *Biographium Faemineum*, vol. 2, p. 203, but it is not historical.

p. 58, l. 21: *Craterus*: One of Alexander's trusted young generals (*c.* 362–*c.* 321 BC). He was appointed to replace Antipater, but did not; instead he formed an alliance with him, sealed with the marriage to Phila, his eldest daughter (Diodorus Siculus, 18.18.7), but was killed fighting Antipater's enemy Perdiccas. There is some evidence that Phila had earlier married Belacrus, satrap of Capadoccia, around 322 BC (Antonius Diogenes in Photius, *Bibliotheca*, 166).

p. 58, ll. 24–5: *Demetrius*: (337–283 BC); 'The Besieger', son of Antigonus and Stratonice, a successful Macedonian general. He ruled Macedon briefly; his son Antigonus established the family dynasty.

p. 58, ll. 27–8: *marriage proved unhappy*: Hays's interpretation of the marriage. The *Biographium Faemineum*, vol. 2, p. 203 noted that Demetrius 'had no great affection for her'. This marriage was an important political one for Demetrius, and Plutarch notes that Phila was honoured by her husband accordingly (*Life of Demetrius*, 14). Demetrius also married Eurydice of Athens, Deidamia of Epirus, Lanassa of Syracuse and Ptolemais of Egypt.

p. 59, l. 2: *Lamia*: According to Plutarch, Lamia was taken by Demetrius from the 'possessions' of Ptolemy captured after a battle off Cypris in 306 BC. She was the daughter of Cleanor and originally a flute-player; she became the most famous courtesan of her day (*Life of Demetrius*, 16, 27). Athenaeus tells us that Lamia had a daughter to Demetrius who was named Phila (Athenaeus, 577c). Lamia was famous enough to feature in comic poetry (Athenaeus, 577d–f). Demetrius also spent time with other well-known Athenian prostitutes: Chrysis, Demo and Anticyra (*Life of Demetrius*, 24) and Leaena (Athenaeus, 577c).

p. 59, l. 5: *Cassander*: One of Phila's brothers, he became king of Macedonia after the death of his father, Antipater (305 BC), and ruled until his own death in 297 BC. According to Plutarch, Demetrius used Phila as a go-between to put his position to the king (*Life of Demetrius*, 32).

p. 59, l. 6: *Plistarchus*: One of Phila's brothers, he had been made the ruler of Cilicia in 301 BC; Demetrius took Cilicia from him the following year.

p. 59, l. 8: *the Rhodians*: Demetrius conducted a lengthy siege of Rhodes, which was allied with Ptolemy, 305–4 BC. Eventually they came to terms (Plutarch, *Life of Demetrius*, 21–2; Diodorus Siculus, 20.91–100).

p. 59, l. 10: *a letter*: Plutarch tells us that in this era it was considered highly improper to open and read a private letter from a man's wife, and it should have been returned unopened (Plutarch, *Life of Demetrius*, 22).

p. 59, ll. 13–14: *sunk under the prospect of impending calamities*: This was in 287 BC when Demetrius had been exiled and driven from the throne of Macedonia (Plutarch, *Life of Demetrius*, 45).

p. 59, l. 18: *a son*: Antigonus Gonatas, who became king of Macedonia in 277 BC and ruled until 239 BC.

p. 59, ll. 18–19: *Stratonice*: Her marriage cemented an important political alliance with Seleucus, the king of Syria, in *c.* 300 BC. Stratonice married the king's son, Antiochus, in *c.* 294 BC (Plutarch, *Life of Demetrius*, 32, 38).

p. 60, l. 2: *PHILIPPA*: Philippa/Phillipa of Hainault/of England.

p. 60, l. 2: *count of Hainault*: William I (1286–1337), Count of Holland and Hainault. Hainault is in the south of present-day Belgium.

p. 60, l. 3: *Edward III*: (1312–77) with Philippa, prime ancestors of the Wars of the Roses, being the parents of both John of Gaunt, first Duke of Lancaster (1340–99), and Edmund of Langley, first Duke of York (1341–1402), who set the wheels of rivalry turning after the deposition of Richard II.

p. 60, ll. 4–5: *David king of Scotland*: (1324–71); his invasion of England was in connection with the Hundred Years' War with France. Scotland and France were allies.

p. 60, ll. 8–9: *having assembled 12,000 men*: This was the Battle of Neville's Cross, 17 October 1346.

p. 60, ll. 9–10: *lord Percy*: Lord Percy (1299–1352) of Alnwick.

p. 60, l. 19: *story of the burghers of Calais* Hays dismisses the traditional story that Edward had demanded the Burghers' sacrificial surrender in exchange for sparing the citizenry, and that Philippa, pregnant at the time, had dissuaded him on the grounds that Calais's humiliation would bring ill fortune on the child she carried. Hays calls the story too romantic, defending Edward's 'generosity'; however, at the time, demands of surrender in this manner were not perceived as particularly unkind or unusual. Even if not true, it is not for Hays's reasons.

p. 61, l. 6: *Orinda*: the coterie name of Katherine Philips née Fowler (c. 1632–64).

p. 61, l. 6: *John Fowler*: (d. 1642), prosperous cloth merchant.

p. 61, l. 7: *Katherine*: (d. 1678) née Oxenbridge, granddaughter of an early Puritan Separatist who would marry twice more.

p. 61, l. 8: *Daniel Oxenbridge, M.D.*: (1571–1642), Puritan physician.

p. 61, l. 10: *Mrs. Blacket*: a cousin, according to John Aubrey in his *Brief Lives* (written 1679–80, published 1813).

p. 61, l. 13: *Mrs. Salmon*: Presbyterian school mistress, according to Aubrey.

p. 62, ll. 2–3: *sir Charles Cotterel*: master of Ceremonies to King Charles I, known to Philips as 'Poliarchus', and editor of a folio edition of Philips's works in 1667.

p. 62, ll. 6–7: *James Phillips*: James Philips (b. 1594), an MP from Cardigan, whom Philips married in 1648.

p. 62, ll. 7–8: *A son and a daughter*: Hector (d. 1665) and Katherine (b. 1656).

p. 62, l. 10: --- *Wogan, esq.*: Lewis Wogan of Boulston.

p. 62, l. 20–p. 63, l. 2: *"and I hope God ... done to me."*: *Letters from Orinda to Poliarchus* (London, 1705), letter 47, 'Orinda to Poliarchus, 12.3.1663/4', p. 243. Manuscript is not extant.

p. 62, l. 25: *lady Cork*: Elizabeth, Baroness Clifford, married Richard Boyle, later Earl of Burlington and Cork; friendly with Philips in Dublin.

p. 62, l. 27: *Antenor*: an elderly character in *The Iliad* who attempts to make peace and the name Philips gives her husband in her poems, perhaps because he was a moderate Welsh Cromwellian.

p. 63, l. 3: *Cardigan*: the location of her husband's family home, Cardigan Priory, in the southwestern corner of Cardiganshire.

p. 63, ll. 6–7: *collected and published ... 1663*: *Poems. By the Incomparable Mrs. K.P.* (London: Printed by J. G. for Richard Marriott, 1664).

p. 63, ll. 17–18: *earls of Ormond, Orrery, and Roscommon*: James Butler, Duke of Ormonde, Lord Lieutenant of Ireland; Orrery: Roger Boyle, Earl of Orrery; and Roscommon: Wentworth Dillon, Earl of Roscommon.

p. 63, l. 21: *the viscountess Dungannon*: Born Anne Owens and renamed Lucasia by Philips in 1651, she married Colonel Marcus Trevor who would become Viscount Dungannon. Philips composed a poem, 'To my Lord and Lady Dungannon, on their Marriage, May 11, 1662'.

p. 63, ll. 25–6: *Corneille, the tragedy of Pompey*: Pierre Corneille's *Mort de Pompée*, translated by Philips (Dublin: Printed by John Crooke for Samuel Dancer, 1663); republished as *Pompey. A Tragedy. Acted with Great Applause* (London: Printed for John Crooke, 1663).

p. 64, ll. 4–5: *countess of Cork*: also known as Lady Cork.

p. 64, l. 7: *tragedy of Horace*: Philips had begun to translate this second play by Corneille from the French before she died; it was published in 1667.

p. 64, l. 8: *sir John Denham*: playwright (1615–69) who completed Philips's unfinished *Horace*.

p. 64, l. 10: *duke of Monmouth*: James Scott, Duke of Monmouth (1649–85), illegitimate son of king Charles II, claimant to the English throne.

p. 64, l. 12: *Dr. Jeremy Taylor*: (1613–67), Episcopalian theologian known for his preaching and devotional writing. His 1662 *Measures and Offices of Friendship* was dedicated to Katherine Philips.

p. 64, ll. 26–7: *some untoward circumstances in her husband's affairs*: A Cromwellian, her husband had faced political challenges in 1660 after the Restoration, but thanks to his wife's intervention, he survived the transition. In 1663, she seems to have been unhappy because of her departure from Dublin and her return to Cardigan, which isolated her from her friends and the literati.

p. 65, l. 7: *thirty-fourth*: Contemporary biographies put her age of death at thirty-two.

p. 65, ll. 10–11: *Mr. Aubry*: antiquarian and biographer (1626–97).

p. 65, ll. 14–19: *"Poems ... Faithorre"*: *Poems. By the most deservedly Admired M^{rs}. Katherine Philips, the matchless Orinda. To which is added, Monsieur Corneille's Pompey & Horace, Tragedies. With several other Translations out of French* (London: Printed by J. M. for Henry Herringman, 1667).

p. 65, l. 19: *Faithorre*: Possibly Guillaume Faithorre.

p. 65, ll. 21–6: *"that Mrs. Phillips wrote ... her poems."*: See Philips, *Poems. By the most deservedly Admired M^{rs}. Katherine Philips, the matchless Orinda. To which is added, Monsieur Corneille's Pompey & Horace, Tragedies. With several other Translations out of French* (London: Printed for Jacob Tonson, 1710), preface (n.p.).

p. 66, l. 5: *major Puck*: Richardson Pack.

p. 66, ll. 6–13: *"The best letters ... true gallantry."*: See R. Pack, 'An Essay upon Study', *Miscellanies in Verse and Prose* (London: Printed for E. Curll, 1718/1719), p. 102.

p. 66, l. 14: *Mr. Langbain*: Gerard Langbaine (1656–92), biographer and critic best known for *An Account of the English Dramatick Poets, or, Some Observations and Remarks on the Lives and Writings of All Those that Have Publish'd Either Comedies, Tragedies, Tragi-Comedies, Pastorals, Masques, Interludes, Farces or Opera's in the English Tongue by Gerard Langbaine* (Oxford: L. L. for G. West, and H. Clements, 1691).

p. 66: l. 15: *Lesbian Sappho*: Greek lyric poet, born on the Island of Lesbos in the sixth century BC. See also Hays, *Female Biography*, vol. 6, pp. 378–82.

p. 66, ll. 15–16: *Roman Sulpicia*: classical poet praised by Martial for her wifely devotion. See also Hays, *Female Biography*, vol. 6, pp. 412–13.

p. 66, ll. 16–20: *"as they were ... eminent men."*: see Langbaine, *An Account of the English Dramatick Poets*, p. 403.

p. 66, l. 17: *Horace, Martial, Ausonius*: classical Roman poets widely admired in the seventeenth century.

p. 66, l. 19: *Cowley*: Abraham Cowley, poet (1618–67).

p. 66, l. 21: *duke of Wharton's works*: Possibly Philip Wharton; not further identified.

p. 66, l. 22–p. 67, l. 7: *"I have been ... poetical language."*: This quote originated in Richard Gwinnet's *Pylades and Corinna*, 2 vols (London, 1731), vol. 2, p. 38. Hays's version is a close paraphrase.

p. 67, l. 5: *"Country Life"*: One of Philips's earliest works, this poem celebrates the choice to retreat from the corrupt competition of the city; it may be compared to other seventeenth-century country house poems such as Ben Jonson's 'To Penshurst' and may have influenced Anne Finch's early eighteenth-century poems on retirement.

p. 67, l. 13: *hon. Berenice*: not further identified.

p. 67, ll. 14–15: *letters published by Mr. Thomas Brown*: Philips's letters were included in an anthology titled *Familiar Letters* (London: W. Onley for Samuel Briscoe, 1697); these include letters by a 'Mr. Brown'; not further identified.

p. 67, ll. 16–17: *Thomas Rowe, in his "Epistle to Daphnis"*: 'To Daphnis. An Epistle' appears in Elizabeth Singer Rowe's *The Miscellaneous Works in Prose and Verse of Mrs. Elizabeth Rowe. The Greater Part now First Published, by Her Order, from Her Original Manuscripts, By Mr. Theophilus Rowe. To which are added, Poems on Several Occasions, by Mr. Thomas Rowe. And to the Whole is prefix'd, An Account of the Lives and Writings of the Authors. In Two Volumes* (London: Printed for R. Hett, 1739), pp. 278–80.

p. 67, l. 20: *Dr. Vanlewin*: John van Lewen (1684–1737), physician and man-midwife.

p. 67, l. 21: *in Dublin, 1712*: We now know that she was probably born in 1708 or 1709, either in co. Cork or in Dublin. She herself claimed the birthdate of 1712; see *The Memoirs: of Mrs Laetitia Pilkington, Wife to the Rev. Mr Matth. Pilkington. Written by Herself*, 2 vols (Dublin: Printed for the author, 1748), vol. 1, p. 3.

p. 67, l. 22: *rev. Matthew Pilkington*: Matthew Pilkington (1701–74), poet and clergyman.

p. 67, l. 25: *a gentleman*: Robert Adair (d. 1790), later serjeant-surgeon to George III.

p. 67, l. 26: *Memoirs*: see note to p. 67, l. 21, above; in 1754 a third volume was added posthumously, edited by Laetitia Pilkington's son, John Carteret Pilkington.

p. 68, l. 5: *Dr. Swift*: Jonathan Swift (1667–1745), Anglo-Irish satirist, political pamphleteer, poet and clergyman, later Dean of St Patrick's Cathedral, Dublin.

p. 68, ll. 7–8: *the pernicious habit of intoxication*: Laetitia Pilkington is thought to have died from a digestive disorder; see N. Clarke, *Queen of the Wits: A Life of Laetitia Pilkington* (London: Faber and Faber, 2008), p. 307. Hays's source for the suggestion that she died from intoxication is unknown; her account of Pilkington is much more hostile to its subject than *Biographium Faemineum*, vol. 2, pp. 204–9. There is little contemporary evidence to suggest drunkenness as a cause of death; see *The Memoirs: of Mrs Laetitia Pilkington, Wife to the Rev. Mr Matth. Pilkington. Written by Herself*, ed. A. C. Elias, 2 vols (Athens, GA: University of Georgia Press, 1997), vol. 1, pp. xxxiv, lviii, n. 33.

p. 68, ll. 9–10: *several children*: Laetitia Pilkington had three surviving children: William (bap. 1726), Elizabeth (bap. 1729) and John (Jack) Carteret Pilkington (1730–63). For Matthew Pilkington's treatment of them, see Clarke, *Queen of the Wits*, p. 316.

p. 68, ll. 10–11: *John, the eldest*: John (Jack) Carteret Pilkington was, in fact, the youngest.

p. 68, l. 11: *some poems*: John Carteret Pilkington wrote verse for magazines in the 1750s and also *The Poet's Recantation; Humbly Inscribed to the Right Honourable Sir Edward Montague ...* (London: Printed for the author, 1755); see *ODNB*.

p. 68, l. 12: *his own Memoirs*: *The Real Story of John Carteret Pilkington, Written by Himself* (London: no pub., 1760).

p. 68, ll. 14–15: *"The Turkish Court, or the London Prentice"*: This piece was never printed.

p. 68, l. 16: *"The Roman Father"*: see *Memoirs of Mrs. Laetitia Pilkington, Wife to the Rev. Mr. Matthew Pilkington. Written by Herself* ..., 3 vols (London: no pub., 1748), vol. 2, pp. 320–40.

p. 68, l. 19: *MRS. PIX*: The exact dates of Pix's birth and death are unknown: no record of her birth or date of death have been located, although an entry in the parish register of St Clement Danes Church in London records her burial on 19 May 1709. Hays follows Giles Jacob and David Erskine Baker in suggesting Pix was related to the Wallis family, but there is no evidence of this connection.

p. 68, l. 20: *the daughter of a clergyman*: Roger Griffith.

p. 68, l. 21: *her mother*: Lucy Griffith (née Berriman).

p. 68, l. 23: *William III*: William III (1650–1702), king of England, Scotland and Ireland (1688–1702) and Prince of Orange.

p. 68, l. 24: *Mrs. Manley*: Delarivier Manley (*c.* 1670–1724) playwright, novelist, periodical writer and author of *romans à clef*. Her plays were performed in Drury Lane Theatre (*The Lost Lover: Or, the Jealous Husband. A Comedy*, March 1696 and *Lucius: The First Christian King of Britain. A Tragedy*, 1717) and Lincoln's Inn Fields (*The Royal Mischief: A Tragedy*, 1696).

p. 68, ll. 24–5: *Mrs. Cockburne*: Catharine Cockburn (née Trotter) (*c.* 16 August 1674–11 May 1749), novelist, dramatist and philosopher. Cockburn's dramatic career coincides exactly with Pix's own. See also Hays, *Female Biography*, vol. 3, pp. 402–29.

p. 68, l. 26: *"The Female Wits"*: This anonymous play, *The Female Wits: Or, the Triumvirate of Poets at Rehearsal*, was performed at Drury Lane in September 1696 and printed in 1704. The title page of the printed edition gives the author's initials as 'W. M.' The female wits satirized in this play are Delarivier Manley ('Marsilia'), Catharine Trotter ('Calista') and Mary Pix ('Mrs Wellfed'), described as 'one that represents a fat female author, a good sociable well-natur'd companion, that will not suffer Martyrdom rather than take off three Bumpers in a Hand' (*The Female Wits* (London: William Turner, 1704), sig. A4v). Pix, Manley and Trotter were again grouped together (along with six female contemporaries) in *The Nine Muses* (London: Richard Basset, 1700), a collection of poems by women commemorating John Dryden, who had died in May that year. Pix ('Mrs M. P.') contributes as 'Clio: the Historic Muse'.

p. 69, l. 1: *author of the following plays*: Hays follows Baker exactly in attributing ten plays to Pix and in omitting her other writings. Two additional plays – *The Different Widows, Or Intrigue a la Mode* (Lincoln's Inn Fields, 1703) and *The Adventures in Madrid* (1706, Queen's Theatre in Haymarket) – are also attributed to Pix. She was also the author of a novel entitled *The Inhumane Cardinal: Or, Innocence Betray'd* (London: John Harding and Richard Wilkin, 1696); an adaptation, into verse, of the eighth tale of the second day of Boccaccio's *Decameron* entitled *Violenta: Or, the Rewards of Virtue* (London: John Nutt, 1704) and several verses.

p. 69, ll. 1–2: *"The Spanish Wives"*: *The Spanish Wives* was Pix's second play, a comedy, first performed in 1696 and printed later that year by R. Wellington.

p. 69, ll. 2–3: *"Ibrahim XIII. Emperor of the Turks"*: *Ibrahim, the Thirteenth Emperour of the Turks* was Pix's first play, a tragedy, staged in May 1696. The printed version of the play, published the same year by John Harding and Richard Wilkin, contains a preface in which Pix apologizes for the error in her title: Ibrahim was the twelfth Turkish emperor, not the thirteenth. *Ibrahim* was part of the repertory of the Drury Lane Theatre, with records of performances in October 1702, January 1704, February 1704 and March

1715. See E. L. Avery, *The London Stage, 1660–1800. Part 2: 1700–1729* (Carbondale, IL: Southern Illinois University Press, 1960), pp. 27, 53, 58, 347.

p. 69, l. 3: *"The Innocent Mistress"*: *The Innocent Mistress* was staged in 1697 by Thomas Betterton's company at Lincoln's Inn Fields and published in the same year.

p. 69, l. 4: *"The Deceiver deceived"*: *The Deceiver Deceived* was staged in 1697 and printed in 1698. Pix had initially given the play to Drury Lane, but withdrew it, likely after discovering that a leading actor in the company, George Powell, had plagiarized her work. Powell's imitation of Pix's play, *The Imposture Defeated, or, a Trick to Cheat the Devil*, was staged at Drury Lane in September 1697. Pix's prologue to *The Deceiver Deceived* concentrates on this act of theft, lamenting that 'Our Authoress, like true Women, shew'd her Play / To some, who like true Wits, stole't half away' (London: R. Basse, 1698), sig. A3r. Pix's play was reprinted, and possibly also restaged at Lincoln's Inn Fields, in 1699 with a new title, *The French Beau* (London: William Brown, 1699). See G. Thorn-Drury, 'An Unrecorded Play-Title,' *Review of English Studies*, 6:23 (1930), pp. 316–18.

p. 69, l. 5: *"Queen Catherine, or the Ruins of Love"*: Hays misspells the title of Pix's play: it is *Queen Catharine: or the Ruines of Love*. This tragedy was staged in 1698 and printed in the same year by William Turner and Richard Bassett.

p. 69, ll. 6–7: *"The False Friend, or the Fate of Disobedience"*: This tragedy was staged in 1699 and printed in the same year by Richard Basset.

p. 69, l. 7: *"The Czar of Muscovy"*: This tragedy was staged in 1701 and printed in the same year by Bernard Lintott. It is generally attributed to Pix, although her name does not appear in the printed version.

p. 69, l. 8: *"The Double Distress"*: This play was staged in March 1701 and printed in April of the same year by R. Wellington and Bernard Lintott.

p. 69, l. 9: *"The Conquest of Spain"*: This tragedy was staged in 1705 at the Queen's Theatre in Haymarket and printed in the same year by Richard Wellington. It is generally attributed to Pix, although her name does not appear in the printed version. It appears to be an adaptation of William Rowley's *All's Lost by Lust* (1661).

p. 69, ll. 9–10: *"The Beau defeated, or the Lucky Younger Brother"*: This play was staged at Lincoln's Inn Fields in March 1700. Hays notes that this play is 'in some catalogues ascribed to Mr. Barker' (*Biographia Dramatica: Or, A Companion to the Playhouse*, 2 vols (London: Rivington, 1782), vol. 1, p. 358), but it can be attributed to Pix with confidence. Her name subscribes the dedication to the Duchess of Bolton prefacing the printed version (London: W. Turner and R. Basset, 1700).

p. 69, l. 11: *Mr. Pix*: The parish records of St Benet Fink, London, show that she married George Pix, a merchant tailor from Hawkhurst, Kent, on 25 July 1684. See P. L. Barbour, 'A Critical Edition of Mary Pix's *The Spanish Wives* (1696), With Introduction and Notes' (PhD dissertation, Yale University, 1979), pp. 3–4.

p. 69, l. 14: *John de Poitiers*: John of Poitiers, Lord of Saint Vallier (*c.* 1475–1539), father of Diana de Poitiers; possibly unwittingly involved in a plot led by Charles de Bourbon.

p. 69, l. 16: *constable of Bourbon*: Charles III, Duke of Bourbon (1490–1527), a well-respected military leader who led a plot against King Francis I.

p. 69, ll. 19–20: *Mezerai, the president Henault*: Possibly Charles-Jean-François Hénault (1685–1770), prominent French historian.

p. 69, l. 20: *other writers*: not further identified.

p. 69, l. 22: *Francis I*: King Francis I of France (1494–1547), Renaissance king known for his patronage of the arts and letters, as well as his persecution of French Protestants or Huguenots.

p. 69, l. 23: *Henry II*: King Henry II of France (1519–59), lover of Diana de Poitiers, and known for his harsh persecution of Huguenots.

p. 70, ll. 2–3: *Louis de Brézé*: Louis of Brézé, Lord of Anet (1463–1531), husband of Diana de Poitiers and discoverer of a plot against King Francis I.

p. 70, l. 4: *two daughters*: Françoise of Brézé (1518–74) and Louise of Brézé (*c.* 1518–January 1577).

p. 70, l. 13: *married*: 29 March 1515. See Princess Michael of Kent, *The Serpent and the Moon* (New York: Touchstone, 2004), pp. 38–42.

p. 70, l. 14: *Lewis XII*: King Louis XII of France (1462–1515), popular king who earned the title 'Father of the People'.

p. 70, ll. 27–8: *constable Montmorenci*: Anne of Montmorency (1493–1567), valued advisor to King Francis I.

p. 71, l. 2: *duchess d'Estampes*: Anne of Pisseleu d'Heilly (1508–80), favourite mistress of King François I.

p. 71, ll. 4–5: *in vain did she publish*: not further identified.

p. 71, l. 15: *"moon, bow and arrows"*: see N. W. Wraxall, *The History of France* ... (London: Printed for C. Dilly, in the Poultry, 1785), p. 6.

p. 71, l. 18: *Brassac*: Possibly Charles of Cossé, Count of Brissac (*c.* 1505–63), Marshal and Grand Master of Artillery of France.

p. 72, l. 13: *duke of Guise*: Claude of Lorraine, Duke of Guise (1496–1550), head of politically ambitious Guise family.

p. 72, l. 14: *Guienne*: province in south-west France.

p. 72, l. 19: *Catherine de Medicis*: Catherine de' Medici, Queen consort of France (1519–89), fought with the Guise family against persecution of Huguenots and ruled through her young son, King Francis II of France, after her husband's death. See also Hays, *Female Biography*, vol. 2, pp. 169–229.

p. 72, l. 24: *her husband*: Henry II.

p. 73, l. 1: *the Reformation*: the Protestant Reformation was a schism within the Christian church that produced many anti-Roman Catholic sects.

p. 73, l. 9: *the wars in which France was engaged*: The eight French Wars of Religion were fought between powerful Catholic and Protestant families.

p. 73, l. 15: *Anet*: commune in northern France.

p. 73, l. 19: *it was reported*: These were popular rumours against Diana de Poitiers because of her beauty and power over the king, not official reports. They are cited in many biographies including Bayle, *Dictionnaire historique et critique* (London: Printed for J. J. and P. Knapton, 1734–8), p. 694.

p. 73, l. 24: *Dreux*: commune in northern France.

p. 73, l. 25: *Philibert de Lorme*: Philibert of l'Orme (*c.* 1514–70), one of the masters of French Renaissance architecture.

p. 73, l. 28: *Voltaire*: François-Marie Arouet (1694–1778), French Enlightenment writer and philosopher.

P. 74, l. 1: *Henriade*: Voltaire's epic poem regarding the 1589 siege of Paris.

p. 74, l. 3: *Brantome*: Pierre of Bourdeille, Lord of Brantôme (*c.* 1540–1614), French historian.

p. 74, ll. 5–13: *"I beheld Diana ... her charms."*: see Wraxall, *The History of France*, pp. 27–8.

p. 74, l. 15: *death of Henry*: 10 July 1550: see Princess Michael of Kent, *The Serpent and the Moon*, pp. 354–9.

p. 74, ll. 22–6: *'for know … the queen.'*: paraphrased from Bayle, *Dictionnaire historique et critique*, p. 698.

p. 75, l. 10: *maréchal de Tavannes*: Gaspard of Saulx and of Tavannes (1509–75), French military leader who had a hand in the St. Bartholomew's Day Massacre on 24 August 1572.

p. 75, l. 15: *cardinal of Lorraine*: Cardinal Charles of Lorraine, Duke of Chevreuse (1524–74), French Cardinal related to the Guise family and advisor to King Henry II.

p. 75, l. 17: *duke of Aumale*: Claude of Lorraine, Duke of Aumale (1526–73), third son of Claude, Duke of Guise and Antoinette de Bourbon.

p. 75, l. 18: *daughter of the duchess*: Louise of Brézé. See note to p. 70, l. 4, above.

p. 75, l. 25–p. 76, l. 1: *Chaumont sur Loire*: commune in central France.

p. 76, l. 2: *Chenonceaux*: commune in central France.

p. 76, l. 17: *PORCIA*: Porcia Catonis, also known as Porcia or Portia, was born *c.* 73 and 64 BC. She was the daughter of Marcus Porcius Cato Uticencis and his first wife Atilia.

p. 76, l. 17: *Cato of Utica*: Marcus Porcius Cato Uticencis, or Cato the Younger (95–46 BC), a politician and famous orator. A staunch supporter of conservative socio-political traditions (notably the ideals of the Roman Republic represented by the Senate) – and therefore a vigorous opponent of Julius Caesar and his political agenda – he committed suicide at Utica two months after the final battle of the civil war between the Caesarian and senatorial forces.

p. 76, l. 21: *Bibulus*: At a young age (between 58 and 53 BC), she was married to Marcus Calpurnius Bibulus, her father's political ally, and may have had a son. During the Roman civil wars, both her father and husband allied with Pompey against Caesar. Bibulus commanded Pompey's navy in the Adriatic, capturing a part of Caesar's fleet, but died in 48 BC following Pompey's defeat.

p. 76, l. 21: *Brutus*: In June 45 BC, Brutus, Porcia's first cousin, divorced his wife and married Porcia. The marriage was scandalous as Brutus did not state any reasons for divorce, despite having been married to Claudia for many years; however, the marriage was politically advantageous since Porcia was highly favoured by people such as Cicero and Atticus.

p. 76, ll. 24–5: *some important enterprise*: Brutus attacked Caesar in 44 BC. According to Cassius Dio (*Roman History*, 44.13), he confided the assassination plot to Porcia, making her perhaps the only woman aware of the conspiracy. Some historians, including Plutarch (*Cato the Younger*, 73.4), believe Porcia might have been involved in the conspiracy itself. Both Plutarch (*Marcus Brutus*, 13.7–8) and Dio (*Roman History*, 44.13.4) describe her wounding herself to prove her womanly fortitude.

p. 78, ll. 2–3: *Julius Cæsar*: Gaius Julius Caesar (100–44 BC), assassinated dictator of Rome.

p. 78, l. 28: *Hector and Andromache*: Key figures in narrative accounts about the legendary Trojan War, Hector was the son of Priam (King of Troy); his wife was Andromache. Hector was killed by the Greek hero Achilles. After Troy's defeat, Andromache was given to Neoptolemus, Achilles's son, as a spoil of war.

p. 79, l. 3: *Astyanax*: son of Homer and Andromache, Astyanax was thrown (by Achilles or Neoptolemus, depending on the account) from the battlements of Troy after the city's defeat.

p. 79, l. 5: *Homer*: Greek epic poet (*c.* ninth or eighth century BC), presumed author of the *Iliad* and *Odyssey*.

p. 79, l. 6: *the Trojan princess to her husband*: Andromache to Hector.

p. 79, ll. 7–8: *"Be careful, Hector … brother, husband, fall."*: Homer, *Iliad*, 6.429–30.

p. 79, ll. 9–15: *'I must not answer … to any of us.'*: Homer, *Iliad*, 6.490.

p. 79, ll. 19–20: *she snatched burning coals from the fire*: The story of Porcia's suicide by swallowing hot coals in 42 BC was believed by a majority of ancient historians. Modern historians find it more likely that Porcia took her life by burning charcoal in an unventilated room, succumbing to carbon monoxide poisoning (J.-A. Shelton, *The Women of Pliny's Letters* (New York: Routledge, 2013), p. 344, n. 93). An alternate version of Porcia's death is that which is inferred from the letters of Cicero, who mentions that her death from a lingering illness occurred before Brutus died. Brutus mourned, and Cicero wrote a letter consoling him in his grief (*Letters to Brutus*, 1.9).

p. 79, l. 24: *MODESTO POZZO*: or Modesta (feminization of Modesto). She often used the pen name Moderata Fonte.

p. 80, ll. 1–2: *Latin and poetical composition*: She learned Latin and composition from her grandfather, Prospero Saraceni, a man of letters (not further identified), as well as her brother Leonardo (not further identified). At that time girls were forbidden from attending grammar school. See P. Malpezzi Price, *Moderata Fonte: Women and Life in Sixteenth-Century Venice* (Madison, WI: Fairleigh Dickinson University Press, 2003), p. 28.

p. 80, l. 5: *Philip de Georgiis*: Filippo de' Zorzi (1558–98), a lawyer and one of three civil servants in charge of the water management of the Venetian lagoon.

p. 80, l. 6: *twenty years, and died in child-bed*: Biographer Giovanni Nicolo Doglioni (1548–1629), mentor to Moderata Fonte, wrote of the four children that she left at her death in 1592: the oldest aged ten years, the second aged eight, the third aged six and the newborn, whose birth caused Fonte's death in 1592. He also mentions her publication of *Floridoro* in 1581, right before mention of her marriage. The wedding year must therefore be 1582, which means the couple had been together for ten years. See G. Doglioni, 'Vita della Sig.ra Modesta Pozzo de Zorzi nominata Moderata Fonte descritta da Gio', in M. Fonte, *Il merito delle Donne*, ed. A. Chemello (Venice: Eidos, 1988), pp. 3–10.

p. 80, l. 8: "*Floridoro*": *I tredici canti del Floridoro*, published in 1581. This is the second chivalric poem published by an Italian woman, after T. D'Aragona's *Il Meschino* (see Hays, *Female Biography*, vol. 1, pp. 216*–18*). See Malpezzi Price, *Moderata Fonte*, p. 31.

p. 80, ll. 8–9: *a poem … resurrection of Christ*: La Passione di Cristo descritta in ottava rima da Moderata Fonte (1581) and *La Resurrezione di Gesu' nostro Signore che segue alla Santissima Passione in ottava rima di Moderata Fonte* (1592).

p. 80, ll. 10–11: "*De Meriti delle Donne*,"… *sexual equality*: Il Merito delle donne berates the treatment of women by men while celebrating women's virtues and intelligence, but does not appeal for sexual equality. See Malpezzi Price, *Moderata Fonte*, p. 149.

p. 80, l. 12: *Moderata Fonte*: See note to p. 79, l. 24, above.

p. 80, l. 13: *On the Merit of Women*: published in 1600 as *Il merito delle donne* (Venice: Imberti).

p. 80, l. 14: *Her husband raised a monument*: The marble epitaph on her tomb describes Pozzo as '*femina doctissima*' [a very learned woman].

p. 80, l. 16: *N. di Lorzi*: A likely reference to Cecilia de' Zorzi (b. 1587), Pozzo's daughter.

p. 80, l. 17: *wrote a preface to her works*: Her daughter wrote the dedication of this work to the Duchess of Urbino, and her son wrote a poem in praise of their mother and her text.

p. 80, ll. 18–19: *Peter Paul Ribera … "Theatre of Learned Women"*: Peter Paul de Ribera de Valentiano, a canon from the religious order of St John Lateran (not further identified).

p. 80, ll. 20–1: *Hilarion de Coste … "Eloges des Dames Illustres."*: Hilarion de Coste (1595–1661), a French priest belonging to the religious order of Minims. *Eloges et Vies des reynes, princesses, dames et damoiselles illustres en Piété, Courage et Doctrine, qui ont fleury de nostre temps, et du temps de nos Peres* (Paris: Sébastien and Gabriel Cramoisy, 1630).

p. 81, l. 2: *Praxilla*: in Greek: Πράξιλλα. She lived in the middle of the fifth century BC.

p. 81, l. 2: *Sycionian*: Sicyon was a small Greek polis west of Corinth. Praxilla performed in Athens and she was well enough known there for Aristophanes to parody her work (*Wasps*, 1238; *Thesmophoriazusae*, 528).

p. 81, l. 2: *dithyrambic*: Dithyrambs were choral songs in honour of the god Dionysus. Competitions for dithyrambs were held at festivals. She also wrote hymns (fragment 1: *Hymn to Adonis*) and *scolia*, drinking songs (fragments 3–5). Eight fragments of her work have survived: see I. M. Plant, *Women Writers of Ancient Greece and Rome* (Norman, OK: University of Oklahoma Press, 2004), pp. 38–40.

p. 81, l. 3: *32d Olympiad*: The date (from the *Biographium Faeminium*) is incorrect. Eusebius dates her to Olympiad 82.2 which is 451/50 BC (*Chronicles*, 82.2). A vase dated to *c.* 450 BC has been found with the first four words of one of her poems written on it, and her work was parodied in the fifth century BC by Aristophanes.

p. 81, l. 4: *most celebrated lyrics*: Antipater of Thessalonica lists her first in his canon of nine 'immortal-tongued' women poets (*Anthologia Palatina*, 9.26.3). A famous sculptor from Sicyon, Lysippus, made a bronze statue of her in the fourth century BC. Later reception of her work is not as favourable. Tatian (*Against the Greeks*, 33) is critical of her work and Zenobius tells us that 'sillier than Praxilla's Adonis' had become proverbial (*Proverbs*, 4.21). These writers demonstrate that her work was still relatively well known into the second century AD.

p. 81, ll. 5–6: Metrum Praxilleum: This is not the title of a work, but a reference to a poetic metre which she invented, or at least used sufficiently for it to be named the Praxilleion after her (Hephaestion, *Handbook on Metres*, 7.8).

p. 81, l. 7: *PROBA (Valeria Falconia)*: Faltonia Betitia Proba; also, Valeria Falconia Proba, Proba Valeria Falcona, Valeria Falcona Proba. The main sources for Proba are the cento (see note to p. 81, l. 11, below) associated with her name; an epitaph referring to Adelfius (identified as Proba's husband) and his 'incomparable wife'; the testimony of Isidore of Seville (a seventh-century bishop) (see *De viris illustribus*, 22 (18) and *Etymologiae*, 1.39.36); and a Vatican manuscript of the ninth century (*Palatinus latinus*, 1753, fol. 62).

p. 81, ll. 8–9: *Adelphus*: Clodius Celsinus Adelfius (or Adelphius), city prefect of Rome in AD 351, and later proconsul.

p. 81, l. 9: *in the reigns*: Proba (*c.* AD 322–70) would have lived and written during the reigns of a variety of emperors during the troubled fourth century AD, but *not* the reigns of Honorius or Theodosius I, as Hays indicates.

p. 81, l. 9: *Honorius*: Flavius Honorius Augustus (AD 384–423), Western Roman Emperor from 395 to his death.

p. 81, l. 10: *Theodosius*: Flavius Theodosius Augustus (AD 347–95), also known as Theodosius I or Theodosius the Great, Roman Emperor from AD 379 until his death.

p. 81, l. 11: *cento*: A cento (or 'patchwork') in Latin was constructed from the poetry of Virgil. Each line of the new poem was formed from a line (or two half lines) from the source; grammatical changes were permitted, but otherwise the cento should be true to the verse of the original. As the author of *Cento vergilianus de laudibus Christi* – a Virgilian cento in hexameter verse which tells the biblical story of the creation, the fall of man, Cain's murder of Abel, the flood, and the birth, life, crucifixion, resurrection and ascension of Jesus – Proba is the first known female Christian writer.

p. 81, l. 13: *epitaph*: preserved in the collection of ancient Latin inscriptions (*Corpus Inscriptionum Latinarum*) found in Rome and its environs (vol. 6): *CIL* 6.1712 (= *ILCV* 01850 = *ICUR* 1.19 = *AE* 2006, 93). The text reads: *Clodius Adelfius v(ir) c(larissimus) ex praefectis urbis uxori inconparabili et sibi fecit.* In other words, Clodius Adelfius, formerly prefect of the city (*praefectus urbi*), made a tomb or funerary monument of some kind for his incomparable wife and himself. The order in which the names of husband and wife appear on the inscription indicates strongly that Proba had died before Adelfius. If, as some scholars suggest (see, e.g. A. Cameron, *The Last Pagans of Rome* (Oxford: Oxford University Press, 2011), pp. 335–6), Adelphius was accused of treason and subsequently executed in AD 351/2, and Proba predeceased him, then the woman who wrote the *Cento vergilianus de laudibus Christi* cannot have been Faltonia Betitia Proba. Barnes suggests the author of the cento was another woman named Proba: Anicia Faltonia Proba, wife of Petronius Probus, consul in AD 371. See T. D. Barnes, 'An Urban Prefect and His Wife', *Classical Quarterly*, 56:1 (2006), pp. 249–56, on p. 253.

p. 81, l. 17: *Lewis XII*: King Louis XII of France (1462–1515, r. 1498–1515), father of Renata (also known as Renée de France), second husband of Anne of Bretagne.

p. 81, ll. 17–18: *Anne of Bretagne*: Anne of Bretagne (1477–1514), Duchess of Brittany upon her father's death in 1488, and Queen of France upon her marriage to King Charles VIII (1470–98, r. 1483–98), which allowed France to annex Brittany. She then married her husband's successor, Lewis XII (r. 1498–1515), with whom she had two daughters, Claude de France (1499–1524) and Renée de France. See also Hays, *Female Biography*, vol. 1, pp. 122–39.

p. 81, l. 19: *Charles of Austria*: In reference to Renée's prospective husbands, Hays follows Bayle, who notes that she twice was engaged (1513 and 1515) to Charles of Burgundy (1500–58), who would become Holy Roman Emperor, Charles V (r. 1519–56). See Bayle, *A General Dictionary*, p. 209. Charmarie Jenkins Webb cites evidence that Renée's father, King Louis XII, was neither willing to hand over his lands to Charles nor to send his daughter to be educated at the Imperial court of Malines; see C. J. Webb, *Royalty and Reform: The Predicament of Renée de France 1510–1575* (Tufts University, 1969, unpublished PhD dissertation), p. 37.

p. 81, ll. 20–1: *Joachim marquis of Brandenburg*: Joachim I Nestor, Elector of Brandenburg (1484–1535, r. 1499–1535), under Holy Roman Emperors Maximilian I (1459–1519, r. 1493–1519) and Charles V. Joachim I was a French sympathizer, and though he ultimately backed Charles V, he initially supported French king Francis I in the 1519 imperial election. Here, Hays misreads Bayle, who indicates that Renée again became engaged to Charles V in 1515. Bayle notes that at some time after 1515, Renée also was promised to Joachim of Brandenburg, but does not specify a date for that engagement. See Bayle, *A General Dictionary*, p. 209. Webb notes that a 1519 treaty found in the Bibliothèque Nationale de France refers to a future alliance between Joachim of Brandenburg and Renée. See Webb, *Royalty and Reform*, p. 38.

p. 81, l. 21: *in 1527*: should be 1528. Bayle states that the couple married in 1527, but also notes that another historian (Father du Londel in his *Fastes des rois*) puts forward the date of 28 June 1528. See Bayle, *A General Dictionary*, p. 209.

p. 81, ll. 21–2: *Hercules d'Este*: Ercole II d'Este (1508–59, r. 1534–59), son of Alfonso I d'Este and Lucrezia Borgia; he became Duke of Ferrara, Modena and Reggio on his father's death in 1534.

p. 81, l. 23–p. 82, l. 1: *"a refined and delicate wit"*: Here, Hays begins citing Varillas via Bayle, who notes that the subtlety and delicacy of her wit surpassed all other women of her time. See Bayle, *A General Dictionary*, p. 209.

p. 82, ll. 2–3: *M. Varillas*: Antoine Varillas (1624–96), a French historian whose reputation was called into question by his *Histoire de l'heresie de Viclef, Iean Hvs, et Jerome de Prague*

(Lyon: Jean Certe, 1682). The edition that Bayle cites has not been identified. See Bayle, *A General Dictionary*, p. 209.

p. 82, ll. 5–6: *Her person was somewhat deformed*: Renée suffered from a congenital malformation of the legs that caused her to limp. See Webb, *Royalty and Reform*, p. 23. Varillas deems her the most physically disgraced princess of her time. See Bayle, *A General Dictionary*, p. 209.

p. 82, ll. 8–9: *five beautiful children*: The children of Renée de France and Ercole II d'Este include Anne d'Este (1531–1607), Alfonso II d'Este (1533–97), who would become Duke of Ferrara, Modena and Reggio on his father's death (r. 1559–97); Lucrezia d'Este (1535–98), Eleonore d'Este (1537–81) and Luigi d'Este (1538–86). Again, Hays follows Varillas via Bayle, who appraises Renée's children as the finest found in Christendom. See Bayle, *A General Dictionary*, p. 209.

p. 82, l. 12: *Calvin*: Jean Calvin (1509–64), theologian and prominent figure in French Protestant church reform, author of *Institutes of the Christian Religion* (1536). Calvin visited Renée at her court in Ferrara in the spring of 1536, where he remained for several weeks, using the pseudonym Charles d'Espeville and pretending to be a French nobleman. See M. A. van den Berg, 'Renée de France: A Royal Friend', in R. Bruinsma (trans.), *Friends of Calvin* (Grand Rapids: Eerdmans, 2009), pp. 48–57. See also C. J. Blaisdell, 'Politics and Heresy in Ferrara: 1534–1559', *Sixteenth-Century Journal*, 6.1 (1975), pp. 67–93.

p. 82, l. 14: *Marot*: Clément Marot (*c.* 1496–1544), celebrated court poet who served Marguerite d'Angoulême, Queen of Navarre, and later, her brother, King Francis I. Marot was suspected of Lutheranism, and was imprisoned for violating Lenten observances. Following the Affaire des Placards in 1534, a propaganda campaign criticizing the Catholic mass, Marot first sought the protection of Marguerite at Navarre, continuing on to the court of Renée de France in Ferrara. Van den Berg notes that Marot was present at Renée's court during Calvin's visit. See *Friends of Calvin*, p. 51. See also G. Defaux, 'Introduction', in *Clément Marot, Œuvres poétiques*, 2 vols (Paris: Dunod, 1996), vol. 1, pp. xvii–clxviii.

p. 82, ll. 18–19: *Brantome*: Pierre de Bourdeille, seigneur de Brantôme (*c.* 1540–1614), spent his childhood at the court of Marguerite d'Angoulême, Queen of Navarre, with his mother and grandmother. Brantôme recounts experiences and observations from his life at court and from his extensive travels and military service in *Mémoires de Messire Pierre de Bourdeilles*, printed posthumously (Leyden: J. Sambix, 1665–6). In this work, containing four books on illustrious and gallant men and women, Brantôme offers a panorama of sixteenth-century chivalry and court life, though their historical veracity is questionable. See É. Vaucheret, *Brantôme: Mémorialiste et conteur* (Paris: Champion, 2010).

p. 82, ll. 23–6: *In 1560 ... to profess Huguenotism*: On the contrary, Renée's religious views were fiercely criticized by her husband. Furthermore, Blaisdell suggests that when the succession passed to Alfonso II on the death of Ercole II in 1559, the new duke's attitude towards her perceived heresy was even more inflexible, thus motivating Renée's return to France. See Blaisdell, 'Politics and Heresy in Ferrara', p. 91. Much of the wording in this passage appears to be lifted from *Biographium Faemineum*, but the confusion may stem from the information omitted from this source: 'In the year 1559, the duke her husband died, and in 1560 she left *Italy* on account of her religion, and returned to *France*, where she was permitted to profess Hugonotism [*sic*]' (italics added; p. 205).

p. 82, l. 26: *Montargis*: the castle and domain of Montargis, near Orléans, was included in Renée's dowry. There, she welcomed Protestant refugees during the French Wars of Religion, including the noted poet Agrippa d'Aubigné. See Webb, *Royalty and Reform*, p. 452.

p. 83, l. 1: *duke of Guise*: François de Lorraine, duc de Guise and d'Aumal (1519–63) married Anne d'Este in Ferrara in 1548. He led a notable military and political career, leading the Catholic faction during the French Wars of Religion. He was killed by a Huguenot in 1563.

p. 83, l. 2: *Anne d'Este*: (1531–1607) eldest child of Renée de France and Ercole II d'Este.

p. 83, l. 2: *John de Sourches Milicovne*: Jean Chourses, seigneur de Malicorne, a lieutenant sent by the duc de Guise to gain control of Montargis and to force Renée to leave her residence and reside with the royal court. See Webb, *Royalty and Reform*, pp. 477–8.

p. 83, ll. 7–14: *'Take care ... upon your children.'*: Bayle attributes this citation to Mézeray's *Histoire de France*. See Bayle, *Dictionnaire historique et critique*, p. 457. Webb remarks that numerous contemporaries of Renée were impressed by the insistence that she placed on her rights as a royal. Webb references several works that allude to this incident, including Jacques-Auguste de Thou (*Histoire universelle*), Jean de Serres (*Histoire des choses mémorables en France depuis l'an MDXLVII jusques au commencement de l'an MDXCVII*) and Agrippa d'Aubigné (*Histoire universelle*). See Webb, *Royalty and Reform*, p. 478.

p. 83, l. 17: *duke of Alençon*: François, duc d'Alençon (1554–84, r. 1566–84) and duc d'Anjou (r. 1576–84), the youngest son of king Henri II of France and Catherine de' Medici, and a leader of the Catholic faction during the French Wars of Religion. Hays lifts this passage from d'Aubigné, as cited in Bayle. See Bayle, *A General Dictionary*, p. 211.

p. 83, l. 22–p. 84, l. 6: *'that she was too ... permitted her to profess.'*: Here, Hays cites Agrippa d'Aubigné via Bayle. See Bayle, *A General Dictionary*, p. 211.

p. 83, l. 25: *Some historians*: Webb supports the date of 1562; see Webb, *Royalty and Reform*, p. 477. Bayle notes that Agrippa d'Aubigné places the incident within the context of a massacre that occurred in Orléans in 1569, but that Varillas puts forward the date of 1562. See Bayle, *Dictionnaire historique et critique*, p. 457. Hays follows d'Aubigné's dating. It is more likely, as Bayle proposes, that these are two separate incidents: one involving Jean Chourses de Malicorne in 1562, and another involving the duc d'Alençon in 1569. See Bayle, *A General Dictionary*, p. 211.

p. 83, l. 27: *Her steward*: Although unclear, Hays may be referring to François de Balzac d'Entragues (1541–1613), whom King Charles IX (1550–74, r. 1560–74) named Governor of Orleans in 1568. Renée's chateau at Montargis fell under the supervision of d'Entragues. See A. Puaux, *La Huguenote Renée de France* (Paris: Hermann, 1997), p. 299.

p. 85, ll. 1–3: *'What ... Salic-law'*: Here, Hays cites Brantôme as referenced by Bayle, *A General Dictionary*, p. 211.

p. 85, l. 3: *Salic-law*: The Salic Law comes from the code of the Salian Franks, formalized during the reign of Clovis in the sixth century, which excludes female descendants of a sovereign from succession to the throne. The Salic Law was later cited in the fifteenth and sixteenth centuries as a means of contesting the right of women to accede to the French throne.

p. 85, ll. 8–19: *'I myself ... refuge with her.'*: Bayle cites Brantôme's *Vie des dames illustres*, from his *Mémoires de Messire Pierre de Bourdeilles*. See Bayle, *A General Dictionary*, pp. 211–12.

p. 85, l. 11: *Messrs. De Terrides and De Monsales*: Jacques de Balaguier, seigneur baron de Montsalès (d. 1569), led a notable military career, dying at the battle of Jarnac. See *Documents historiques et généalogiques sur les familles et les hommes remarquables du Rouergue dans les temps anciens et modernes*, 4 vols (Rodez: Ratery, 1854), vol. 2, p. 344.

p. 85, l. 16: *An old steward*: not further identified.

p. 85, l. 21: *prince of Condé*: Louis I de Bourbon, prince de Condé (1530–69), leader of the French Huguenot faction during the first three Wars of Religion, who died at the battle of Jarnac. He was imprisoned in October of 1560 by King Francis II and released by Catherine de' Medici on her son's death the following December.

p. 85, l. 22: *Francis*: King Francis II of France (1544–60, r. 1559–60), the eldest son of King Henri II of France and Catherine de' Medici; he acceded to the throne at the age of fifteen upon his father's unexpected death, but died soon thereafter.

p. 86, ll. 2–5: *'that whoever … of the blood.'*: Hays again follows Bayle's citation of Brantôme, who attests to having heard from a reliable source that Renée spoke before the French court on behalf of the prince de Condé. See Bayle, *A General Dictionary*, p. 212.

p. 86, l. 6: *Thuanus*: Jacques-Auguste de Thou (1553–1617), a noted French historian and statesman. Bayle often cites his *Historiae sui temporis*, first published in 1604 and first translated into French in 1734 as *Histoire universelle de Jacques-Auguste de Thou, depuis 1543 jusqu'en 1607*.

p. 86, ll. 6–17: *"Having come … allied to kings."*: Bayle cites this passage from de Thou in the Latin version. See Bayle, *A General Dictionary*, p. 212.

p. 86, l. 21: *Henry II*: King Henri II of France (1519–59, r. 1547–59), the second son of King Francis I and Renée's elder sister, Claude de France; he was thus Renée's nephew. Henri II was a staunch Catholic and the repression and persecution of Huguenots was a primary concern during his reign.

p. 86, ll. 25–6: *a curious account has been published*: Hays follows Bayle's appraisal of this work, *Les Mémoires de Messire Michel de Castelnau, Seigneur de Mauvissière*, first published in 1659. See Bayle, *A General Dictionary*, p. 212.

p. 86, l. 26: *M. Laboureur*: Jean Le Laboureur (1623–75), a French cleric and historian.

p. 86, ll. 27–8: *Dr. Oriz*: Le Laboureur indicates that Dr Oriz was a representative of the Pope, serving as an Inquisitor in France. For Le Laboureur's account of the episode, see *Les Mémoires de Messire Michel de Castelnau, Seigneur de Mauvissière*, 3 vols (Brussels: Jean Léonard, 1731), vol. 3, p. 717.

p. 86, l. 28: *the pope's*: Pope Paul III (1468–1549, r. 1534–49); during his pontificate, the Council of Trent was convened (1545–63), which identified Protestant heresies and clarified Catholic doctrine.

p. 87, ll. 2–17: *'that the king had … reprobate sects'*: Here Hays is citing (and slightly changing the wording to) Bayle's paraphrase of Le Laboureur in which the latter identifies three messages that Dr Oriz was to convey to Renée: (1) king Henri II was aware of her heresy, (2) the king would be overjoyed were she to return to the true faith, (3) the king would renounce his kinship to her if she were to persist in her error. See Bayle, *A General Dictionary*, p. 212.

p. 87, l. 25–p. 88, l. 5: *'that it was … exemplary punishment.'*: Again, Hays cites Bayle's paraphrase of Le Laboureur. See Bayle, *A General Dictionary*, p. 212.

p. 88, l. 16: *Olympia Fulvia Morata*: The daughter of a university professor, Olympia Morata (1526–55) was a scholar of Greek and Latin and invited to the court of Ferrara to continue her studies alongside Renée's daughter, Anne d'Este. She and her husband, a German Protestant, left Italy due to the difficult religious climate. See also Hays, *Female Biography*, vol. 5, pp. 506–8 and O. Morata, *The Complete Writings of an Italian Heretic*, ed. and trans. H. N. Parker, *The Other Voice in Early Modern Europe* (Chicago, IL: University of Chicago Press, 2003).

p. 88, l. 18: *John Sinapius*: a German humanist (1505–60); studied Greek in Germany with Melanchthon and medicine in Ferrara. He was the personal physician of Ercole II d'Este and Renée de France, as well as tutor to their children. Sinapius met both his wife, Françoise de Boussiron, and Jean Calvin at Renée's court, but left Ferrara in 1545 because of the religious climate, as he and Françoise also espoused Protestant ideals. See M. A. Van den Berg, 'John Sinapius: A Friend in Love', in R. Bruinsma (trans.), *Friends of Calvin*, pp. 58–67.

p. 89, l. 3: *Catherine of Medicis*: Catherine de' Medici (1519–89, r. 1547–59), daughter of Lorenzo de' Medici and wife of King Francis II of France (r. 1559–60). She arranged the marriage of her youngest daughter, Marguerite, with the Huguenot, Henri de Navarre. Catherine had considerable influence in the French Wars of Religion. See also Hays, *Female Biography*, vol. 2, pp. 169–229.

p. 89, l. 7: *the League*: The Catholic faction during the French Wars of Religion was known as la Ligue (the Catholic League or the Holy League); Renée's son-in-law, the duc de Guise, was the leader of this faction.

p. 89, l. 15: *Anne de Rohan*: Anne de Rohan (1584–1646) was born into a powerful Protestant family from Brittany (the Rohans) which had important familial connections to noble families in Poitou from her mother (see note to p. 89, ll. 17–18, below) and Aquitaine through her paternal grandmother (Isabeau d'Albret).

p. 89, l. 17: *Renatus de Rohan*: René II, Viscount of Rohan (1550–86), grandson of Catherine de Foix (1468–1517), Queen of Navarre (1483–1517).

p. 89, ll. 17–18: *Catherine de Parthenai*: Catherine de Parthenay (b. 1554) was married to Pont-Quellenac in 1568, and then to René Vicomte de Rohan in 1575. She was an accomplished woman of letters who wrote several plays, elegies and translations. See also Hays, *Female Biography*, vol. 6, pp. 47–50.

p. 89, l. 19: *the duke of Rohan*: Henry II of Rohan (1579–1638) was the Huguenot leader against the Catholic Royal forces; he also left a few historical and political works, which were published posthumously.

p. 89, ll. 21–3: *the reformed religion during the civil wars of Lewis XIII*: When in 1617, the Catholic cult was officially reinstated in the predominantly Protestant region of Aquitaine, by Richelieu, chief minister to the young King Louis XIII (1601–43), this triggered strong opposition from the Huguenots. This was to lead to the break out of a series of Huguenot rebellions in 1620. It was not until 1629 that the conflict was put to an end with the Edict of Alès, also known as the Edict of Grace.

p. 89, l. 24: *The siege of La Rochelle*: the siege of La Rochelle (1627–8) marked the victory of Louis XIII over the Huguenots.

p. 90, ll. 1–2: *prisoners of war*: they were held captive in the Château de Niort, where her mother died in 1631.

p. 90, ll. 5–6: *poem written on the death of Henry IV*: the title of her dedicatory poem reads as *Stances de Madamoyselle Anne de Rohan, sur la mort du Roy* (Paris: P. Chevalier, 1610). Her other verse includes a poem on her brother's defeat at the Siege of La Rochelle, *Les Larmes et Regrets de Madamoiselle Anne de Rohan sur la desroute de Monsieur de Soubize son frère, et sur sa rebellion contre le Roy* (Paris: N. Rousset, 1622), and obituary prayers on her sister's and mother's deaths: *Prière de Madamoiselle Anne de Rohan en son affliction pour la perte de Madame sa mère* (1632), *Vers de Madamoiselle Anne de Rohan sur la mort de Madamoiselle de Rohan sa soeur* (1624).

p. 90, l. 6: *Henry IV. of France*: King Henry IV (1553–1610), second cousin to Anne de Rohan (through their mutual great-grandmother Catherine, Queen of Navarre). Born a Catholic in the French court, he had become an icon of religious tolerance. He had converted to Protestantism, and reconverted to Catholicism to be allowed to perform his duty as head of state. He facilitated the truce between the Catholics and Protestants, and enforced the Edict of Nantes (1598) whereby freedom of religion was guaranteed. In 1610, he was assassinated by François Ravaillac, a Catholic zealot.

p. 90, l. 8: *The Hebrew Psalms*: One of her translations that has survived in print is *Paraphrase sur le Psalme, 51. Miserere mei Deus, secundum magnam misericordiam tuam* (Charenton: Louys Vandosme, 1645).

p. 90, ll. 10–11: *Anna Maria Shurman*: Anna Maria van Schurmann (1607–68) was a German-Dutch woman of letters and an artist, who was a cosmopolitan intellectual genius, renowned for her erudition across Europe. See also Hays, *Female Biography*, vol. 6, pp. 384–8.

p. 90, ll. 16–17: *Hercule de Rohan-Guémené*: (1568–1654), Comte de Rochefort, then Duc de Montabazon in 1595, he lived and served four kings, each in some official capacity.

p. 90, l. 18: *a convent*: She was sent to the Priory of Notre-Dame des Anges at Montargis at age seven. See M. Rowan, 'Between Salon and Convent: Madame Rohan, A Precious Abbess', *Papers on French Seventeenth-Century Literature*, 12:22 (1985), pp. 191–207, on p. 194.

p. 90, ll. 19–20: *Of high birth and fortunes*: Daughter of society lady Marie de Bretagne-Avaugour (1610–57), the Duchess of Montbazon, second wife of Hercule de Rohan. See B. Craveri, *The Age of Conversation*, trans. T. Waugh (New York: New York Review of Books, 2006), p. 89.

p. 91, ll. 3–6: *named abbess of la Trinité de Caen ... Without ambition*: Pierre-Daniel Huet praises her convent education, her position as Abbess at the Trinité de Caen, her erudition in literary and spiritual matters, and her humility in his *Mémoires de Daniel Huet, évêque d'Avranches*, ed. L. Hachette (Paris: L. Hachette, 1853), p. 122, 127; C.-P. Goujet Le Mercier (ed.), *Supplément au Grand dictionnaire historique, généalogique, géographique, etc. de M. Louis Moreri, pour servir à la dernière édition de l'an 1732 et aux précédentes* (Paris: Libraires associés, 1749), pp. 224–6. See also A. Shelford, *Transforming the Republic of Letters: Pierre-Daniel Huet and European Intellectual Life, 1650–1720* (Rochester: University of Rochester Press, 2007), pp. 88–90.

p. 91, ll. 5–6: *the superiors of the convent*: not further identified.

p. 91, l. 13: *unfavourable to her health*: There is no indication that health concerns were involved in her relocation to the Abbaye de Malnoue.

p. 91, ll. 23–4: *a declaration was made by the pope*: Le Mercier cites numerous attestations by visitors to Rome which caused the pope to declare, 'il y avoit là de quoi canoniser la jeune abbesse' ('there is enough there to canonize the young abbess'); however, he does not give the year or identify the pope, either Innocent X (1644–55) or Alexander VII (1655–67). See Le Mercier (ed.), *Supplément*, p. 224.

p. 91, ll. 26–8: *solicited by ... Notre dame de consolation du Chasse-midi*: Rohan's expertise was sought to restore the financial condition of this failing abbey, which she did. See Le Mercier (ed.), *Supplément*, p. 224–5.

p. 92, ll. 3–5: *In the intervals of her duties ... to study*: A collaborator with Madame de Lafayette and Huet and regular member of Mme de Sablé's Port-Royal salon, which included Pascal and La Rochefoucauld. See J. J. Conley, *The Suspicion of Virtue: Women Philosophers in Neoclassical France* (Ithaca, NY: Cornell University Press, 2002), pp. 91–2.

p. 92, ll. 5–6: "Morale de Salomon": First published anonymously (Paris: Muguet, 1665), then reprinted (Paris: Barbin, 1667) under her name with preface by Huet. See Rowan, 'Between Salon and Convent', p. 196.

p. 92, l. 7: *and various other tracts*: She published a review of major Greek poets in 1664, and *La Morale du sage* in 1667. Her literary self-portrait (along with Huet's portrait of her) was included in Madame de Montpensier's *Divers Portraits* (1659). Rohan's 1674 letter to La Rochefoucauld laments his increasing misogyny in the re-edition of his *Maximes* (1666). See F. La Rochefoucauld, *Oeuvres de La Rochefoucauld* (Paris: Hachette, 1868), pp. 387–9.

p. 92, ll. 9–10: "que le sang des rois avoit trouvé en elle une âme royale": 'that the blood of Kings had found a royal soul in her' (French). Citation from *Nouveau journal des dames* (1762), vol. 1, p. 299.

p. 92, l. 12: *She died 1681*: Occasionally noted mistakenly as April 1682, date of the funeral oration, though Hays notes the year correctly. See A. Anselme, *Oraison funèbre de... Madame Marie Eleanor de Rohan, abbesse de Malnoüe, prononcée à Paris l'onzième jour d'avril 1682 en l'église des religieuses bénédictines du prieuré du Chasse-Midy* (Paris: Sébastien Mabre-Cramoisy, 1682).

p. 92, ll. 19–23: *In favour ... Elizabeth*: Elizabeth I of England (r. 1558–1603). The education of women to which Hays refers is the humanist programme of education associated with Erasmus, More and Vives, of which More/Roper was a recipient, and this, crucially, predates Hays's association with Elizabeth I (see Hays, *Female Biography*, vol. 4, pp. 70–295). See also G. Kaufman, 'Juan Luis Vives on the Education of Women', *Signs*, 3:4 (1978), pp. 891–6, on p. 896.

p. 93, ll. 24–7: *three daughters of sir Thomas More ... and of Jane*: Thomas More (1478–1535), Lord Chancellor of England in reign of Henry VIII (1509–47); Jane Colt (1498–1511), married Thomas More in 1505; daughters were Margaret (1505–44), Elizabeth (1506–c. 1564) (see Hays, *Female Biography*, vol. 4, pp. 23–4) and Cicely (1507–fl. 1526/7) (see Hays, *Female Biography*, vol. 4, p. 434). They also had one son, John More (1509–47): see *ODNB*.

p. 93, l. 28: *Mr. John Colte of Newhall, Essex*: John Colte or Colt (dates unknown) was from Netherhall in the parish of Roydon, Essex.

p. 94, l. 1: *1508*: Actually 1505. Hays's date is wrong and comes from her source, Ballard, *Memoirs of Several Ladies*, p. 38.

p. 94, l. 6: *Erasmus*: Desiderius Erasmus (1467–1530), humanist scholar and reformer known for *The Praise of Folly* (1511); his work wielded enormous influence on English humanists: see *ODNB*.

p. 94, ll. 6–22: "*More ... has built near London ... and alacrity, &c.*": *Biographium Faemineum*, vol. 2, p. 215; Ballard, *Memoirs of Several Ladies*, pp. 86–7.

p. 94, l. 7: *a friend*: not identified.

p. 94, l. 10: *daughter-in-law*: Anne Cressacre (b. c. 1511), married John More December 1529. See M. Wood, *The Family and Descendants of Sir Thomas More*, 2009, pp. 1–12, at http://www.thomasmorestudies.org/docs/Descendants_John.pdf [accessed 24 August 2013].

p. 94, l. 11: *their husbands*: Elizabeth's husband, William Dancy (d. 1548); Cicely Heron's husband, Giles Heron (c. 1504–40, Esquire of the Body in 1532).

p. 94, ll. 11–12: *eleven grandchildren*: These are most likely Margaret and William Roper's children: Elizabeth, Margaret, Mary and Thomas; John and Anne More's eldest son John II; Cecily and John Heron's three children: Thomas, John and Anne, and Elizabeth and William Dancy's eldest two children: John and Thomas. See Wood, *Family and Descendants*.

p. 94, l. 14: *Plato*: (427–347 BC), philosopher.

p. 94, l. 27: *Dr. Clement*: John Clement (d. 1572), expert in Greek and Latin and lectured at Corpus Christi College, Oxford in Medicine: *The Correspondence of Thomas More*, ed. C. F. Rogers (Princeton, NJ: Princeton University Press, 1947), p. 79, n. 45.

p. 94, ll. 27–8: *William Gonell*: William Gonnell (d. 1560), recommended by Erasmus as a tutor to More's children: *The Correspondence of Thomas More*, p. 120.

p. 95, l. 2: *Mr. Drue*: Rogers suggests that this was Roger Drew; fellow of All Saints College, Oxford and recipient of the prebend of St Stephens, Westminster, in January 1523: See *The Correspondence of Thomas More*, p. 250, n. 9.

p. 95, l. 2: *Mr. Nicolas*: Mr Nicolas is probably Nicolas Kratzer, a German astronomer: see E. E. Reynolds, *Margaret Roper: Eldest Daughter of St. Thomas More (Margaret Roper)* (New York: P. J. Kennedy and Sons, 1960), p. 13.

p. 95, ll. 2–3: *Richard Hart*: Not further identified. Hays copied him from Ballard, *Memoirs of Several Ladies*, p. 87.

p. 95, l. 18: *John Leland*: (*c.* 1503–52), antiquary and poet: see *ODNB*.

p. 95, l. 21: *Mr More's Life of Sir Thomas*: Cresacre More (1572–1649), great-grandson of Sir Thomas More: *Life of Sir Thomas More* (Douai: *c.* 1626–31). See *ODNB*.

p. 95, ll. 21–2: *in Lewis's edition of the same Life, by Roper*: John Lewis (1675–1747), clergyman and antiquarian, published William Roper's work in 1731: see *ODNB*.

p. 95, l. 22: *Roper*: William Roper (*c.* 1495/8–1578), Sir Thomas More's son-in-law. He married Margaret More in 1521. *Life of Thomas More*, also known as *The Mirror of Virtue in Worldly Greatness,* was thought to be published in Paris in 1626: see *ODNB*; W. Roper, *Lyfe of Sir Thomas More, knt, forward by Sir Thomas Walter* (London: Burns and Oates, 1905), pp. ix–xiii.

p. 95, ll. 23–6: *sweating sickness ... Henry VII ... five times*: Research in the 1990s suggested that sweating sickness may have been Hantavirus pulmonary syndrome, the first epidemic of which was in 1485 in the reign of Henry VII (1491–1547; r. 1509), with further outbreaks in 1508, 1517, 1528 and 1551; Margaret was ill during the fourth outbreak: see Burke's *Peerage*, at http://www.burkespeerage.com/articles/roking08.aspx [accessed 1 June 2013]; A. Dyer, 'The English Sweating Sickness of 1551: An Epidemic Anatomized', *Medical History*, 41:3 (1997), pp. 362–84; and M. Taviner, G. Thwaites and V. Gant, 'Comment: The English Sweating Sickness, 1485–1551: A Viral Pulmonary Disease?', *Medical History*, 42:1 (1998), pp. 96–8.

p. 96, l. 6: *1528*: 1521 is the correct date; Hays copied the inaccurate date of 1528 from Ballard, *Memoirs of Several Ladies*, p. 94.

p. 96, ll. 7–8: *Well-hall ... Kent*: Well Hall in Eltham is now in London.

p. 96, l. 12: *Chelsea*: in west London.

p. 96, l. 14: *Tower*: The Tower of London was a royal residence that served as a prison in the sixteenth century.

p. 96, ll. 14–15: *Two sons and three daughters*: Elizabeth, Mary, Margaret, Thomas and Anthony: Ballard, *Memoirs of Several Ladies*, p. 94.

p. 96, ll. 17–20: *Drs. Cole and Christopherson ... preceptors*: tutors, Henry Cole (*c.* 1504/5–*c.* 1579/80), dean of St Paul's, London; and John Christopherson (d. 1558), Bishop of Chichester: see *ODNB*.

p. 96, l. 23: *Britanniae decus*: 'the glory of Britain': Ballard, *Memoirs of Several Ladies*, p. 95.

p. 96, l. 26: *Hans Holbein*: Hans Holbein 'the Younger' (*c.* 1497/8–1543), German artist: see *ODNB*. The picture is a pen and ink drawing of Thomas More and family (1527) in Kupferstichkabinett der Öffentlichen Kunstsammlung Basel [Collection of Public Art, Basel]: see *The Complete Works of St. Thomas More*, ed. L. L. Martz and F. Manley (New Haven, CT, and London: Yale University Press, 1976), pp. xv, xxviii.

p. 97, ll. 14–15: *hymns of Prudentius*: Aurelius Prudentius Clemens (348–*c.* 410) wrote morning and evening hymns, part of Erasmus's project of *Colloquia* and commentaries on several church fathers in the 1520s. In translating the hymns Margaret effectively worked to disseminate Erasmian scholarship amongst English humanist circles.

p. 97, l. 15: *appears to have been his favourite*: Erasmus had contact with all the sisters and considered More's daughters to have 'outstanding talents'. P. Iver Kaufman, 'Absolute Margaret: Margaret More Roper and "Well Learned" Men', *Sixteenth Century Journal*, 2:3 (1989), pp. 443–56, on p. 453.

p. 97, l. 28–p. 98, l. 1: *Henry VIII. ... divorce ... Catherine*: Henry VIII (1491–1547; r. 1509) annulled his marriage to his first wife, Catherine of Aragon (1485–1536) (see Hays, *Female Biography*, vol. 2, pp. 151–69).

p. 98, l. 12–p. 99, l. 3: *"I have been ... merry together."*: from W. Roper, *The Life and Death of Sir Thomas Moore, Knt. Lord High-Chancellor Of England, In the Reign of K. Henry the Viiith ... [1626]*, ed. J. Lewis (London, 1728), pp. 66–7. The court of Chancery was an equity court presided over by the Lord Chancellor (More was also in Star Chamber); Lincoln's Inn (also known as New Inn) was one of the London inns of court and 'the king's court' probably refers to the King's Bench on which More sat from 1518.

p. 99, ll. 6–7: *oath of supremacy*: oath introduced by Act of Supremacy 1534 swearing that the monarch was Supreme Head of the church.

p. 99, ll. 8–9: *abbot of Westminster*: William Boston was abbot in 1534, and became first Dean of Westminster (d. 1549).

p. 99, l. 20: "As far as would stand with the law of God": from Roper, *Life*, p. 80, fn*.

p. 99, l. 23–p. 100, l. 2: *"What think you ... increased."*: Cresacre More, *The Life of Sir Thomas More, Kt. Lord High Chancellour of England under K. Henry the Eighth, And His Majesty's Embassadour to the Courts of France and Germany. By His Great Grandson, Thomas More, Esq.* (London: Printed for James Woodman and David Lyon, 1726), p. 93; Ballard, *Memoirs of Several Ladies*, p. 97.

p. 100, l. 9: *Mr. Rastell*: William Rastell (1508–65) was the son of More's sister, Elizabeth, and her husband, John Rastell: see *The Correspondence of Thomas More*, p. 467, n. 1. He published *More's Englyshe Workes* (1557).

p. 100, l. 10: *last editor*: Sir John Lewis, clergyman and antiquary, was the last editor: see *ODNB*.

p. 100, l. 12: *Dr. Knight ... Life of Erasmus*: Samuel Knight (1675–1746), Prebendary of Ely, wrote *The Life of Erasmus, More Importantly the Part of It that He Spent in England ... (Erasmus)* (Cambridge: Corn. Crownfield, 1726).

p. 100, l. 20–p. 102, l. 4: *'My dear Margaret,' ... tender sympathy.*: Knight, *Erasmus*, pp. 239–41.

p. 101, l. 8: *St. Peter's* ad vincula: St Peter 'in chains'. St Peter's *ad vincula* is the parish church of the Tower of London.

p. 101, ll. 12–15: *His head ... purchased by his daughter*: It is uncertain whether this is fact or fiction. See J. Guy, *A Daughter's Love* (London: Harper, 2009), pp. 2–5, 280; J. Goodrich, 'Thomas More and Margaret More Roper: A Case of Rethinking Women's Participation in the Early Modern Public Space', *Sixteenth Century Journal*, 39:4 (2008), pp. 1021–3.

p. 101, 19: *committed to prison*: The date of her imprisonment is most likely to have been in the summer of 1537, when she was detained by Thomas Cromwell overnight, probably in a privy councillor's house, from which she was released the next day. See Guy, *A Daughter's Love*, pp. 267, 325.

p. 101, ll. 25–6: *described by Mr. More, in his Life*: C. More, *The Life of Sir Thomas More*, p. 139.

p. 102, ll. 3–4: *St. Cyprian, restoring* nervos severitatis, *for* nisi vos severitatis: St Cyprian was Bishop of Carthage who had converted to Christianity in AD 146. 'nisi vos severitatis' was untranslatable and Margaret guessed it was a mistake in the text of Cyprian's letters edited by Erasmus; the whole sentence needed to be translated: 'Far be it for the Church of Rome to relax its vigour ... *and to weaken the nerves of discipline*': Guy, *A Daughter's Love*, pp. 141–2.

p. 102, ll. 4–5: *Pamelion and John Coster*: Pamelion is not identified. John Coster of Louvain, prior of Louvain Abbey. See Ballard, *Memoirs of Several Ladies*, pp. 99, 406, no. 14; Reynolds, *Margaret Roper*, pp. 41–3.

p. 102, l. 8: *Quintilian*: (AD 35–*c.* 96), Latinist and Rhetorician. See *Encyclopaedia Britannica*, at http://www.britannica.com/EBchecked/topic/487486/Quintilian [accessed 22 June 2013].

p. 102, ll. 16–17: "Of the four last Things": This manuscript does not survive. See Reynolds, *Margaret Roper*, p. 40; Guy, *A Daughter's Love*, pp. 73–4.

p. 102, l. 22: *ecclesiastical history of Eusebius*: (*c.* 260–d. before 341), Bishop of Caesarea. *The Ecclesiastical History of Eusebius Pamphilus, Bishop of Cesarea, in Palestine*. See *Catholic Encyclopaedia*, at http://www.newadvent.org/cathen/05617b.htm [accessed 22 June 2013].

p. 102, ll. 23–5: *its publication was superseded by that of bishop Christopherson*: John Christopherson, Bishop of Chichester; Eusebius's *Historia Ecclesistica* printed in *Historiae Ecclesiasticae Scriptores Graeci* (Lovain, 1569). See J. W. Binns, 'Humanistica Lovaniensia', *Journal of Neo-Latin Studies*, 27 (1978), pp. 132–3.

p. 102, l. 27: *Mary, the daughter*: Mary (née Roper) Bassett (*c.* 1526–72). According to Guy, the birth of Mary (Margaret's second child) took place around the same time as Margaret's younger brother John was betrothed to Anne Cresacre (*A Daughter's Love*, pp. 170, 306). Guy states that Mary's translation of Eusebius is from the British Library: Harleain MS 1860, fols 1–379, *A Daughter's Love*, p. 326; *ODNB*.

p. 103, l. 5: *thirty-sixth year*: Hays has her birthdate wrong, and as such, Margaret was thirty-nine when she died. See *ODNB*.

p. 103, l. 6: *head of her father*: Guy asserts that Thomas More's head was found with her when Margaret's body was disinterred and removed from the More family vault to be buried with her husband in the Roper Chapel in St Dunstan's Church, Canterbury. The skull was then set into the wall of the vault and kept behind an iron grille as a holy relic: Guy, *A Daughter's Love*, pp. 274, 328.

p. 103, l. 14: *1577*: Hays has copied Ballard, *Memoirs of Several Ladies*, p. 100. Date is 1577 Old Style/1578 New Style.

p. 103, l. 18–p. 104, l. 5: *"Here lieth interred ... eighty–two."*: Translation by Ballard, *Memoirs of Several Ladies*, pp. 100–2 of the Latin in W. Somner, *The Antiquities of Canterbury, a Survey of that Ancient Citie, with Suburbs and Cathedral* (London: Richard Thrale, 1640), p. 342.

p. 103, ll. 23–4: *John Roper*: John Roper (d. 1524), attorney-general to Henry VIII. See *ODNB*.

p. 103, l. 28: *his son Thomas*: (1533–98): see Wood, *Family and Descendants*, p. 2.

p. 103, l. 31: *children and grandchildren*: His children and grandchildren were as follows: Elizabeth married John Stephenson (no issue) and then Edward Bray: they had one child, Reginald Bray; Margaret married William Dawtry: they had William, John, Anthony and Jane; Mary married Stephen Clark (no issue) and then John Bassett: they had Philip and Charles; Thomas married Lucy Brown: they had William, Henry, Francis, Charles, Thomas, Philip, Mary, Elizabeth, Frances, Martha, Catherine and Mabel; Anthony married Ann Cotton: they had Anthony, John, Henry, Isabel and Jane. See Wood, *Family and Descendants*, pp. 2–3.

p. 104, l. 4: *1557*: Date is 1577 Old Style/1578 New Style.

p. 104, l. 8: *MARY*: Mary Roper Clarke Basset (or Bassett) (d. 20 March 1572).

p. 104, l. 8: *Margaret Roper*: Margaret Roper (1505–44), famous for her classical learning.

p. 104, l. 9: *sir Thomas More*: Thomas More (1478–1535), executed after denying Henry VIII's supremacy over the English church.

p. 104, l. 11: *Cole*: Henry Cole (*c.* 1504/5–*c.* 1579/80), prominent clergyman during Mary's reign and Catholic controversialist after the accession of Elizabeth I.

p. 104, ll. 11–12: *Christopherson*: John Christopherson (fl. 1535–58), a staunch Catholic, translated Greek religious works into Latin.

p. 104, l. 12: *Mr. John Morwen*: John Morwen (*c.* 1519/20–fl. 1583), Catholic activist against Elizabethan Protestant reform, imprisoned by English authorities in 1583.

p. 104, ll. 12–17: *celebrated Grecian ... Eusebius's Church History*: The *Ecclesiastical History* of Eusebius (*c.* 260–*c.* 339) covers early Christian history. Roper translated portions into English and Latin (Harley MS 1860, British Library), working directly from Eusebius's Greek, not a Latin translation, as Hays's sources erroneously claim. Her *orations* are not extant.

p. 104, l. 18: *queen Mary*: Mary I (1516–58) restored English Catholicism. Hays followed closely the mistaken chronology of Ballard – Roper gave Mary the translation before her accession.

p. 104, ll. 19–20: *Latin exposition*: Thomas More's final work, *De Tristitia Christi*, was written during 1534 and 1535, while in prison, to 'take comfort in tribulation' in the suffering of Christ. Roper's English version appeared in *The Workes of Sir Thomas More*, ed. W. Rastell (London: John Cawood, John Waly, and Richard Tottel, 1557). See J. Guy, *Thomas More* (London: Arnold, 2000), p. 167.

p. 104, ll. 20–2: *imitating ... original*: see N. Harpsfield, *The Life and Death of Sir Thomas Moore*, ed. E. V. Hitchcock (London: Early English Text Society, 1932), p. 83; T. More, *The Workes of Sir Thomas More*, ed. W. Rastell (London: John Cawood, John Waly, and Richard Tottel, 1557), fol. 1350.

p. 104, ll. 22–3: *Mr. Roger Ascham*: Roger Ascham (*c.* 1514/15–68) tutored Elizabeth I in Greek and Latin and wrote *The Scholemaster* (London: J. Daye, 1570), a work that encapsulated English Christian humanist education. See *Letters of Roger Ascham*, ed. A. Vos, trans. M. Hatch and A. Vos (New York: Peter Lang, 1989), pp. 249–50.

p. 104, l. 26: *Mr. Stephen Clarke*: a clothier's son.

p. 104, l. 27: *Mr. James Basset*: Gentleman-in-waiting to Philip II, Mary I's consort.

p. 105, l. 3: *the memoirs of this admirable woman*: M. Roland, *Mémoires of Madame Roland, written by herself*. The original *Mémoires, un Appel à l'Impartiale Posterité* were subdivided as the 'Private Memoirs' (Parts 1 and 2) and 'Historical Notes' (Parts 3 and 4), published posthumously in January 1795 in France by Roland's friend, Louis-Augustin-Guillaume Bosc (1759–1828), who excised portions of the 'Private Memoirs' from the original, believing they would destroy Roland's reputation. Roland had frankly described her sexual molestation in adolescence by a teenage boy, an erotic dream, and revealed the disappointment of her wedding night. An unexpurgated version did not appear until 1864, and then only in French. The first English translation of the memoirs was published in 1795, but contained only Roland's 'Historical Notes'. The first complete translation was published in 1796 as *An Appeal to Impartial Posterity by Madame Roland, Wife of the Minister of the Interior; or, a Collection of Tracts written by her during her confinements in the prisons of the Abbey, and St. Pélagie, in Four Parts, Translated from the French Original ... Second Edition, Revised and Corrected* (London: J. Johnson, 1796). It is believed that Hays worked from this second edition and may have used the original French edition as a reference. See M. Roland, *Memoirs of Madame Roland: A*

Heroine of the French Revolution, ed. and trans. E. Shuckburgh (Mt. Kisco, NY: Moyer Bell Limited, 1990), pp. 16–17.

p. 105, l. 10: *Gatien Phlipon*: Pierre-Gatien Phlipon (d. 1788), master engraver.

p. 105, l. 10: *Marguerite Bimont*: Marie-Marguerite Bimont Phlipon (*c.* 1725–75). Roland writes that her mother, who died suddenly at the age of fifty, was 'the dearest thing in the world to me'. See Roland, *An Appeal to Impartial Posterity*, vol. 2, part 4, sec. 3, pp. 213, 216.

p. 106, l. 8: *'a celestial mind'*: Hays translates 'un ame celeste' as 'celestial mind' rather than a 'heavenly mind', as the 1796 translation does. See Roland, *An Appeal to Impartial Posterity*, vol. 2, part 3, sec. 1, p. 8.

p. 106, l. 11: *her sister*: not further identified.

p. 106, ll. 14–17: '*It is a proof ... without its consolation*': See Roland, *An Appeal to Impartial Posterity*, vol. 2, part 3, sec. 1, p. 8.

p. 106, l. 25–p. 107, l. 1: *The nurse*: not further identified.

p. 107, l. 1: *Madame Besnard*: Roland's paternal great-aunt.

p. 107, l. 2: *Arpajon*: a small city just south of Paris in the region of Île-de-France.

p. 107, l. 7: *her husband*: M. Besnard was Roland's godfather.

p. 107, l. 20: Manon: nickname of Madame Roland.

p. 108, ll. 1–2: mademoiselle: French: 'Miss', an unmarried woman.

p. 108, ll. 7–10: '*This disposition ... taught to read*': See Roland, *An Appeal to Impartial Posterity*, vol. 2, part 3, sec. 1, p. 11.

p. 108, ll. 10–15: '*At four years old ... could divert*': See Roland, *An Appeal to Impartial Posterity*, vol. 2, part 3, sec. 1, p. 11.

p. 108, ll. 16–21: '*Under the tranquil shelter ... books and flowers*': See Roland, *An Appeal to Impartial Posterity*, vol. 2, part 3, sec. 1, p. 12.

p. 108, l. 26: *Guibal*: Nicholas Guibal (1725–84), painter for the royal Württembergs, lived in Stuttgart.

p. 108, l. 27: *Poussin*: Nicholas Poussin (1594–1665), Classical French baroque painter.

p. 109, ll. 3–9: '*I think I see ... round his arm*': See Roland, *An Appeal to Impartial Posterity*, vol. 2, part 3, sec. 1, p. 13.

p. 109, l. 6: *the creed of Saint Athanasius*: Saint Athanasius (AD 296–373), member of the Council of Nicaea and later Archbishop of Alexandria. The *Creed* establishes the doctrine of the trinity as one eternal being.

p. 109, l. 7: Tanger: not further identified.

p. 109, l. 20: *Mr. Garat*: Monsieur Garat was pastor of St Bartholomew parish, called Paris la Cité in Roland's childhood; not further identified.

p. 109, l. 24–p. 110, l. 2: '*How many orders ... dominions*': See Roland, *An Appeal to Impartial Posterity*, vol. 2, part 3, sec. 1, pp. 14–15.

p. 110, l. 11: *her younger brother*: Pierre-Nicholas Bimont (d. 1790), younger brother of Roland's mother and a priest in nearby Vincennes. Bimont became the canon of the celebrated, once royal castle of Vincennes.

p. 113, ll. 12–14: '*My father, ... single sigh*': See Roland, *An Appeal to Impartial Posterity by Madame Roland*, vol. 2, part 3, sec. 1, pp. 20–1.

p. 114, ll. 1–7: '*I experienced ... conquer me*': See Roland, *An Appeal to Impartial Posterity*, vol. 2, part 3, sec. 1, p. 21.

p. 115, l. 2: *her maternal grandmother*: not further identified.

p. 115, ll. 20–2: '*I know not ... with emotion.*': See Roland, *An Appeal to Impartial Posterity*, vol. 2, part 3, sec. 1, p. 23.

p. 115, l. 24: *uncle Bimont*: Pierre-Nicholas Bimont; see note to p. 110, l. 11, above.

p. 116, ll. 4–5: *Lives of the Saints*: Book of stories of early Christians and martyrs, which Roland read in preparation of her First Communion.

p. 116, l. 6: *Appian's Civil Wars*: Appian of Alexandria (AD 95–165), Roman historian of Greek descent. His scholarly history of the Roman civil wars covers the sack of Rome in 387 BC to Caesar's conquest of Gaul and provides rich, interesting detail and descriptions of military strategy.

p. 116, ll. 8–9: *the comical romances of Scaron:* Paul Scarron (1610–60) was the author of *Le Roman comique*, a popular burlesque published in three volumes in the 1650s. He was the first husband of Françoise d'Aubigné, marquise de Maintenon (see Hays, *Female Biography*, vol. 5, pp. 316–456) who, before her introduction to the king's court, was known as 'Scarron's widow' for debts he left her when he died.

p. 116, l. 11: *the memoirs of the brave De Pontis*: Benedict-Louis de Pontis (1583–1670) Jansenist (see note to p. 133, l. 13, below) who rose through the ranks of the military, fought against Protestants and in the Thirty Years' War. His *Mémoires de Sieur de Pontis, qui a servi dans les armées cinquante–six ans, sous les rois Henri IV, Louis XIII, Louis XIV* were published in 1676.

p. 116, l. 12: *mademoiselle de Montpensier*: Anne-Marie-Louise d'Orléans, Duchess of Montpensier (see Hays, *Female Biography*, vol. 1, pp. *229–*37) composed her memoirs from 1670–3. Her memoirs are a declaration of her right to freedom of action and a record of her perceived relegation to spinsterhood and solitude.

p. 118, ll. 6–7: *the Plutarch of Dacier*: Anne Le Fèvre Dacier (see Hays, *Female Biography*, vol. 4, pp. 1–23), known as Madame Dacier, was distinguished for her translations of classical Roman military and political histories.

p. 118, l. 10: *Plutarch*: (*c.* AD 46–120) Greek historian and biographer. *Lives of the Noble Greeks and Romans*, or more commonly called *Plutarch's Lives*, written in the first century, is a series of biographies of famous men.

p. 118, ll. 10–19: *'Plutarch, … a republican'*: See Roland, *An Appeal to Impartial Posterity*, vol. 2, part 3, sec. 1, p. 27.

p. 118, l. 19: *Telemachus*: the protagonist of François Fénelon's *Adventures of Telemachus* (see p. 118, l. 22).

p. 118, l. 19: *Jerusalem Delivered*: Epic poem by Tasso (see note to p. 118, l. 22, below).

p. 118, l. 22: *Fenelon*: François de Salignac de la Mothe Fénelon (1651–1715), celebrated theologian, writer and friend of Louis XIV (see note to p. 120, l. 3, below). As tutor to the future Louis XVI (1754–93, r. 1774–92), he wrote *Les Aventures de Télémaque, fils d'Ulysses* (1699), the parable of a young man in search of his father intended to teach morality and discipline to young men destined to rule France.

p. 118, l. 22: *Tasso*: Torquato Tasso (1544–95), Italian poet and the author of *La Gerusalemme liberata* (1581), an epic poem inspired by Homer and Virgil, a romantic fiction about the Christian victory over Jerusalem in the First Crusade (1099).

p. 118, l. 26–p. 119, l. 8: *'Rather, … objects which existed'*: See Roland, *An Appeal to Impartial Posterity*, vol. 2, part 3, sec. 1, p. 28.

p. 118, l. 28–p. 119, l. 1: *the island of Calypso*: Telemachus, the protagonist of François Fénelon's *Adventures of Telemachus*, is shipwrecked on the island of the nymph Calypso, where he falls in love with Eucharis, one of her attendants.

p. 119, l. 2: *Eucharis*: see note to p. 118, l. 28–p. 119, l. 1, above.

p. 119, ll. 2–3: *Tancred*: a Christian knight, the protagonist of Torquato Tasso's *Jerusalem Delivered*.

p. 119, l. 3: *Erminia*: The Princess of Antioch in Tasso's *Jerusalem Delivered*. Secretly in love with Tancred, she nurses him back to health after he is critically wounded.

p. 119, ll. 9–10: Taberal: a young painter and friend of Roland's father; not further identified.

p. 119, ll. 21–2: *the writings of Voltaire ... perusing Candide*: The pen name of Enlightenment philosopher, critic and poet *François-Marie Arouet* de Voltaire (1694–1778). *Candide* (1759), a satirical novel of an optimistic young traveller in search of happiness, was Voltaire's cynical response to Wilhelm Leibniz's philosophy that we live in the best of all possible worlds. Roland later read Voltaire's *Dictionnaire Philosophique* (1764), *Questions sur l'Encyclopédia* (1758), *Essai sur les moeurs* (1756), *Histoire de Russie* (1759; 1763) and *Eléments de Newton* (1738) and diligently summarized them in writing. See G. May, *Madame Roland and the Age of Revolution* (New York: Columbia University Press, 1970), p. 30; and *Candide; or Optimism*, trans. J. Butt, (Middlesex: Penguin Books, 1947), pp. 9–11.

p. 120, ll. 19–20: *Fenelon on the education of females*: François Fénelon's *Traité de l'éducation des filles* (1687) was considered progressive because it advocated the education of girls as critical to their futures as virtuous wives and mothers.

p. 120, l. 20: *Locke*: John Locke's (1632–1704) *Some Thoughts Concerning Education* (1693) urged the education of children as individuals to promote the habit of independent but rational thinking.

p. 120, l. 23–p. 121, l. 2: '*I loved ... explosion*': See Roland, *An Appeal to Impartial Posterity*, vol. 2, part 3, sec. 1, p. 30.

p. 121, l. 5: '*her little uncle*': See Roland, *An Appeal to Impartial Posterity*, vol. 2, part 3, sec. 1, p. 30.

p. 121, l. 6: *the abbé Bimont*: [abbot] Pierre-Nicholas Bimont; see note to p. 110, l. 11, above.

p. 121, ll. 18–21: '*I would not ... dispense with*': See Roland, *An Appeal to Impartial Posterity*, vol. 2, part 3, sec. 1, p. 31.

p. 122, l. 3: *the* Tuilleries: The Tuileries, built in the sixteenth century, was the royal palace in Paris. Louis XIV, King of France (1638–1715, r. 1643–1715) lived there while Versailles was under construction. The gardens of the palace were designed by landscape architect Andre Le Nôtre (1613–1700) and opened to the public in 1667.

p. 122, l. 4: bourgeoise: [French: bourgeois] upper-middle of the socio-economic class.

p. 122, l. 26–p. 123, l. 3: '*It was ... support them.*': See Roland, *An Appeal to Impartial Posterity*, vol. 2, part 3, sec. 1, p. 34.

p. 123, ll. 9–15: '*These notions ... permit it.*': See Roland, *An Appeal to Impartial Posterity*, vol. 2, part 3, sec. 1, p. 35.

p. 123, l. 13: *the Devil*: Rebellious fallen angel of the Christian Bible.

p. 123, l. 14: *God*: Christian god of the Bible.

p. 125, ll. 13–20: '*While pressing ... two months old.*': See Roland, *An Appeal to Impartial Posterity*, vol. 2, part 3, sec. 1, p. 39.

p. 125, l. 21–p. 126, l. 2: '*How ... the Deity?*': See Roland, *An Appeal to Impartial Posterity*, vol. 2, part 3, sec. 1, p. 42.

p. 125, l. 2: *the Deity*: Christian god of the Bible.

p. 126, ll. 15–20: '*Every-where ... works.*': See Roland, *An Appeal to Impartial Posterity*, vol. 2, part 3, sec. 1, p. 42.

p. 127, l. 4: *festival of the Assumption*: The celebration of the Virgin Mary by the Catholic Church takes place on or around 15 August.

p. 127, ll. 7–8: *the monk who officiated at the cloister*: a colleague of M. Garat (see note to p. 109, l. 20, above), a member of the Order of St Victor; not further identified.

p. 127, l. 21: *A young novice*: not further identified.

p. 127, l. 24–p. 128, l. 6: '*I was myself ... prodigious age.*': see Roland, *An Appeal to Impartial Posterity*, vol. 2, part 3, sec. 1, p. 46.

p. 128, l. 17–p. 129, l. 3: '*Dwell with me ... institutions of mankind.*': see Roland, *An Appeal to Impartial Posterity*, vol. 2, part 3, sec. 1, pp. 48–9.

p. 129, l. 7: *the* Jardin du Roi: The garden, on the Left Bank of the Seine in Paris, is known today as the Jardin des Plantes.

p. 129, ll. 12–15: '*I longed ... the want.*': see Roland, *An Appeal to Impartial Posterity*, vol. 2, part 3, sec. 1, p. 49.

p. 129, ll. 16–17: *two young ladies from Amiens*: Henriette and Sophie Cannet, whom Roland met in convent school, became lifelong friends; not further identified. Amiens is a city on the Somme River north of Paris known for the production of textiles.

p. 129, l. 22: *Sophia Cannet*: Sophie Cannet; see note p. 129, ll. 16–17, above, the younger of the Cannet sisters. Roland's correspondence with Sophie spanned a period of twenty-five years, from about 1776 until Roland's death, but Sophie's letters to Roland apparently did not survive. The correspondence was published in 1841 as *Lettres inédites de Mlle. Phlipon, Mme Roland, addressees aux demoiselles Cannet, de 1772 à 1780*, ed. A. Breuil (Paris, 1841); and *Lettres de Madame Roland, Volume 1 (1780–1787) and Volume II (1788–1793)*, ed. Claude Perroud (Paris, 1900).

p. 130, ll. 12–13: *Angelica Bouffliers*: Angelina Bouffliers became Sister Agathe as a young novice. She supervized all the girls in the convent school and remained devoted to Roland for the rest of Roland's life.

p. 131, l. 7: *her paternal grandmother*: Madame Phlipon Besnard, not further identified.

p. 131, l. 12: *a younger sister*: Madame Angelique Rotisset, Roland's aunt, not further identified.

p. 131, l. 14: *the island of St. Louis*: the pastoral Île St.-Louis, situated in the Seine River in the heart of Paris.

p. 131, l. 15: *her husband*: M. Phlipon, Roland's paternal grandfather, who died one year after Roland's father was born, not further identified.

p. 131, l. 26–p. 132, l. 2: '*This correspondence ... composition.*': see Roland, *An Appeal to Impartial Posterity*, vol. 2, part 3, sec. 1, p. 60.

p. 132, ll. 17–18: *St. Francis de Sales*: (1567–1622) An aristocrat educated by the Jesuits in theology, the humanities and the law, de Sales became Bishop of Geneva and a renowned spiritual writer who preached a philosophy of love and kindness towards rich and poor alike.

p. 132, l. 20: *the ladies of the Visitation*: St Francis de Sales created the Order of the Visitation of Holy Mary, the convent school Roland attended.

p. 133, ll. 2–4: *the* Philotée *of St. Francis de Sales*: The *Philotée*, or *Philothea, or the Introduction to The Devout Life*, set forth de Sales's compassionate philosophy of God as love.

p. 133, l. 3: *the Manual of St. Augustin*: Augustine of Hippo (AD 354–430); this probably refers to Saint Augustine's *Confessions* (AD 397–8), a memoir of his youth, his struggle with worldly passions and his conversion to Christianity.

p. 133, l. 6: *The controversial writings of Bossuet*: French Roman Catholic theologian Jacques-Bénigne Bossuet (1627–1704) defended the rights of the French monarchy to limit papal authority and advised moderation towards Protestants, including the Jansenists, but supported Louis XIV's (see note to p. 122, l. 3, above) revocation in 1685 of the Edict of Nantes (1598), which granted French Protestants some religious liberty.

p. 133, l. 13: *Jansenist*: Jansenist doctrine espoused original sin and the attainment of salvation, exclusively by divine grace rather than good works, which was only available to a chosen few who were granted free will. Roland, concerned with achieving happiness through the practice of virtue, admired the Jansenists for their highly principled convictions but rejected their harsh doctrines. See May, *Madame Roland and the Age of Revolution*, p. 38.

p. 133, l. 13: *Cartesian*: refers to the rationalist philosophy of René Descartes (see note to p. 144, l. 7, below).

p. 133, l. 14: *Stoic*: Follower of Stoicism. Begun in classical Greece and adopted by the Romans, Stoicism was a complete belief system for the attainment of happiness, or virtue, through moral and intellectual perfection. Roland wrote an essay on Socratic virtue and the rewards of its practical application to life, in which she foreshadows her destiny as a martyr to patriotic republican ideals. Roland, 'On Socrates', in *The Works (never before published) of Jeanne-Marie Phlipon Roland, Wife of the Ex-Minister of the Interior, Containing her Philosophical and Literary Essays Written Previous to her Marriage, her Correspondence, and her Travels ...* (France: J. Johnson, 1800), pp. 140–55.

p. 133, l. 14: *Deist*: Follower of Deism, the Enlightenment belief that an omnipotent being created the universe with an orderly design and endowed mankind with the ability to reason, which man is beholden to employ in the discovery and investigation of his universe.

p. 133, l. 14: *scepticism*: philosophical approach that requires all information to be well supported by evidence.

p. 133, ll. 14–16: '*What a route ... a dungeon!*': see Roland, *An Appeal to Impartial Posterity*, vol. 2, part 3, sec. 2, p. 72.

p. 133, ll. 19–20: *Letters of madame de Sevigné*: Marie de Rabutin-Chantal, marquise de Sévigné (see Hays, *Female Biography*, vol. 6, pp. 398–402); like Roland, Madame de Sévigné read avidly to educate herself and to construct a philosophy of her own, but became and remained a devoted Jansenist, even though she was an active participant in the literary salons of the day. Her voluminous and lengthy correspondence with her adored daughter, begun in 1671, discusses her religious and philosophical beliefs. It was published in several editions in the mid-eighteenth century and is said to have been revised to suit the cultural trends of that century.

p. 134, l. 9–p. 135, l. 7: '*I am very glad to see you ... indeed be a pity*: see Roland, *An Appeal to Impartial Posterity*, vol. 2, part 3, sec. 2, pp. 76–7.

p. 134, l. 10: *madame de Boismorel*: not further identified.

p. 135, ll. 10–19: '*Mind now, ... before you are much older*': see Roland, *An Appeal to Impartial Posterity*, vol. 2, part 3, sec. 2, p. 78.

p. 135, ll. 24–5: *the son of this lady*: Roberge de Boismorel; not further identified.

p. 136, ll. 3–13: '*I began, ... my active brain.*': see Roland, *An Appeal to Impartial*, vol. 2, part 3, sec. 2, pp. 80–1.

p. 137, l. 2: *the Pont-Neuf*: a busy commercial thoroughfare in the eighteenth century. It is the oldest bridge in Paris, connecting the Right and Left Banks.

p. 137, l. 11: *her master*: Cajon (not further identified) was Roland's music teacher. He had come to Paris quite destitute with his wife and children, and often borrowed money from the Phlipons. Although he managed to publish a book, *Éléments de musique*, he remained financially unsuccessful and eventually left Paris for Russia. *Memoirs of Madame Roland: A Heroine of the French Revolution*, pp. 131–2.

p. 137, l. 14: '*Put soul into it!*': see Roland, *An Appeal to Impartial Posterity by Madame Roland*, vol. 2, part 3, sec. 2, p. 83.

p. 137, ll. 18–19: '*You sing ... an anthem.*': See Roland, *An Appeal to Impartial Posterity*, vol. 2, part 3, sec. 2, p. 83.

p. 138, l. 18: Pluche: Noël-Antoine Pluche (1688–1761), author of *Le Spectacle de la Nature* (1732), a study of life and its origins, it was translated into every European language and heightened interest in natural science.

p. 138, l. 19: Rollin: Charles Rollin (1661–1741), historian, educator and Jansenist theologian, whose texts, *Histoire Ancienne* (1730–8) and *Histoire Romaine*, begun in 1738 but not finished before his death, were widely read. He is also known for his *Traité des études* (1726–31), a proposal for a new educational system.

p. 138, l. 19: Crevier: Jean-Baptiste Louis Crevier (1693–1765), student of Charles Rollin and an historian who contributed to the completion of Rollin's *Histoire Romaine*, his own *Histoire des Empereurs jusqu'à Constantin* (1750); and *Observations sur l'Esprit des Lois de Montesquieu* (1763), which was criticized by Voltaire (see p. 119, ll. 21–2) for its conservatism.

p. 138, l. 19: Père d'Orleans: Le Père Denis Pétau d'Orléans (1583–1652), distinguished philosopher, theologian and historian of Christianity and religious dogma, including the issue of predestination as set forth by Saint Augustine (see p. 133, ll. 3).

p. 138, l. 19: St. Real: César Vichard, Abbé de Saint Réal (1639–92), Jesuit and the official historian of Savoy. Best known for his *A History of the Spanish Conspiracy of 1618 against the Republic of Venice* (1674) and *Don Carlos* (1672), a historical novel.

p. 138, l. 20: *the abbé de Vertot*: René Aubert, Abbé de Vertot (1655–1735), historian and author of *History of the Revolutions that Happened in the Government of the Roman Republic* (1732); *History of the Rrevolution of Portugal* (1735); and *History of the Revolutions in Sweden Occasioned by the Change in Religion and Alterations in the Government of that Kingdom* (1743).

p. 138, l. 20: Mezeray: François Eudes Mézeray (1610–83), appointed historiographer to the king in 1649 by Cardinal Mazarin, ruler in Louis XIV's minority. Author of *Histoire de France depuis Faramond jusqu'au règne de Louis le juste* (1643–51).

p. 138, l. 25: *abbé le Jay*: a friend of Roland's uncle. The Abbé le Jay gave Roland access to his library, but this came to an end when he died.

p. 139, l. 4: *Sophia*: Sophie Cannet; see note to p. 129, l. 22, above.

p. 139, l. 23: *Diodorus Siculus*: (90–30 BC) Greek historian whose *Bibliotheca Historica* included the history of ancient Greece and other civilizations, including ancient Egypt, Mesopotamia, India and North Africa.

p. 139, l. 24: *abbé Velly*: Paul François Velly (1710–59), Jesuit theologian and historian. Author of *Histoire de France depuis l'établissement de la monarchie jusqu'au regne de Louis XIV* (1770).

p. 139, l. 25: *Pascal*: Blaise Pascal (1623–62), zealous Jansenist and author of *Pensées de M. Pascal sur la religion et sur quelques autres sujets* (1670). *Pensées* argues that mysticism is essential to the nature of religion and reason cannot prove the existence of God. Roland read Pascal and flirted with becoming a Jansenist herself. *Memoirs of Madame Roland: A Heroine of the French Revolution*, p. 157.

p. 139, l. 25: *Montesquieu*: Charles-Louis de Secondat, Baron de Montesquieu (1689–1755), political and civil libertarian; authored *L'Esprit des Lois* (1748), advocating individual freedom enhanced by the laws of the state and the separation of powers.

p. 139, ll. 26–7: *Burlamaqui*: Jean-Jacques Burlamaqui (1694–1748). *The Principles of Natural and Politic Law* (1747) became the standard law text at University of Cambridge School of Law and leading American law schools.

p. 139, l. 29–p. 140, l. 13: '*I felt ... of study.*': see Roland, *An Appeal to Impartial Posterity*, vol. 2, part 3, sec. 2, pp. 92–3.

p. 141, ll. 13–16: '*I am deceived ... examine*': see Roland, *An Appeal to Impartial*, vol. 2, part 3, sec. 2, pp. 95–6.

p. 141, l. 28–p. 142, l. 1: *she had lost her good confessor, the monk of the convent*: See note to p. 129, ll. 7–8, above.

p. 142, l. 2: *Abbé Morel*: a parish priest (not further identified), who lent Roland the writings of 'second-rate' Christian apologists who challenged certain Enlightenment philosophers, which directed her to d'Holbach (see note to p. 142, ll. 23–4, below), Helvétius (see note to p. 144, l. 10, below), Diderot (see note to p. 142, l. 22, below) and d'Alembert (see note to p. 142, l. 23, below). S. Diaconoff, *Through the Reading Glass: Women, Books, and Sex in the French Enlightenment* (Albany: State University of New York Press, 2005), p. 62.

p. 142, ll. 8–24: '*Behold me, then, ... through my hands.*': see Roland, *An Appeal to Impartial Posterity*, vol. 2, part 3, sec. 2, p. 99.

p. 142, l. 9: *abbés* Gauchet: Abbé Gabriel Gauchet (not further identified). A religious apologist who used his monthly journal to attack Enlightenment philosophers such as Voltaire, d'Holbach (see see note to p. 142, ll. 23–4, below) and Helvétius (see see note to p. 144, ll. 10, below). S. Rosenfeld, *Common Sense: A Political History* (President and Fellows of Harvard College, 2011), p. 131.

p. 142, l. 9: Bergier: Nicholas-Sylvestre Bergier (1715–90), prominent theologian and author of texts in defence of Christianity including: *Le Déisme refuté par lui-même* (1765); *La Certitude des preuves du christianisme* (1767); and *Traité historique et dogmatique de la vraie religion* (1780).

p. 142, l. 9: Abbadie: Jakob Abbadie (*c.* 1654–1727), author of *Défense de la Nation Britannique* (1693), a defence of the Glorious Revolution, in response to Pierre Bayle's *Avis important aux réfugiés* (1690). Roland borrowed the works of French Huguenot philosopher Bayle (1647–1706) from M. Boismorel's library (see note to p. 181, ll. 12–13, below). *Memoirs of Madame Roland: A Heroine of the French Revolution*, pp. 223–4.

p. 142, l. 9: Holland: Hezekiah Holland (fl. 1638–60), Anglo-Irish Anglican clergyman; used the pen name Anglo-Hibernus for his publications; *A Christian Looking-Glasse, or, A Glimps of Christs Unchangably Everlasting Love Discovered in Several Sermons, in the Parish-church of Sutton-Valence* (London: T. R. & E. M. for George Calvert, 1649); *Anglo-Hibernus, An exposition or, A short, but Full, Plaine, and Perfect Epitome of the Most Choice Commentaries upon the Revelation of Saint John* (1650); and *Adam's Condition in Paradise Discovered Wherein Is Proved That Adam Had Right to Eternall Life, in Innocency, and Forfeited It, for Him and His* (1656).

p. 142, l. 9: Clarke: Samuel Clarke (1675–1729), most important British philosopher in the generation between Locke and Berkeley, and a leading figure in Newton's circle. His works include *Three Practical Essays on Baptism, Confirmation and Repentance and Some Reflections on that part of a book called Amyntor, or a Defence of Milton's Life, which relates to the Writings of the Primitive Fathers, and the Canon of the New Testament* (1699) and *A Paraphrase upon the Gospel of St Matthew* (1701).

p. 142, ll. 17–18: *the treatise on* Toleration: Written by Voltaire in 1763. In the wake of an incident in southern France in which Calas, a Protestant, was falsely accused of killing his son to prevent the son's conversion to Catholicism, the treatise argued that religious intolerance was against natural law. Calas protested his innocence but was brutally executed and his son was buried as a martyr. Four years later Calas's conviction was overturned.

p. 142, l. 19: *the* Dictionnaire Philosophique: Published by Voltaire (see note to p. 119, ll. 21–2, above) in 1764, the text expounded Voltaire's views on diverse subjects and attacked the Roman Catholic Church and religion in general. Banned in France, it was frequently confiscated by officials but widely distributed and remained at the top of best-seller lists from 1769–89. R. Darnton, *The Forbidden Best-Sellers of Pre-Revolutionary France* (New York: W. W. Norton & Co., Inc., 1995), pp. 65–6.

p. 142, l. 20: *questions concerning the* Encyclopédie: *Questions sur l'Encyclopédie* (1772) by Voltaire, also on France's best-seller list, was arranged by topic and 'contained something to offend practically everyone in authority under the Old Regime and at the same time appealed to the broadest range of readers'. Darnton, *The Forbidden Best-Sellers of Pre-Revolutionary France*, p. 73.

p. 142, ll. 20–1: *the* Bon Sens *of the marquis d'Argens*: Jean-Baptiste de Boyer, marquis d'Argens (1704–71), wrote *La philosophie du bon sens de Jean-Baptiste de Boyer, marquis d'Argens* (1740). He abandoned his Jesuit upbringing for the life of a libertine and philosopher critical of the Catholic Church and intolerance.

p. 142, l. 21: *the* Jewish Letters: Jean-Baptiste Boyer, Marquis d'Argens (1704–71), wrote *Les Lettres juives*, or the *Jewish Letters* (1736), an epistolary conversation among five rabbis who attack religious intolerance and the Catholic Church. Boyer was forced to go into hiding in Utrecht for the next four years as a result of the uproar created by the publication.

p. 142, l. 22: the Turkish Spy: *Letters Writ by a Turkish Spy who lived five and forty years, undiscovered at Paris* (1692–4), an epistolary novel considered the first of the foreign 'spy' genre, written by Giovanni Paolo Marana (1642–93).

p. 142, l. 22: Les Meurs: Voltaire's popular and critically acclaimed *Essai sur les moeurs et l'esprit des nations*, was written during his tenure as Royal Historiographer of France and published in 1751.

p. 142, l. 22: L'Esprit: Claude-Adrien Helvétius (1715–71) wrote *De L'Esprit* in 1758 while collaborating with Diderot (see note to p. 142, l. 22, below) on the *Encyclopédie*. It was considered heretical by the Church and state and was condemned and publicly burned.

p. 142, l. 22: *Diderot*: Denis Diderot (1713–84), French philosopher, scientist and scholar, and Jean-Le-Rond d'Alembert (see note to p. 142, l. 23, below) were the creators of the collaborative *Encyclopédie* (1751–72), to which Voltaire, Montesquieu, d'Holbach (see note to p. 142, ll. 23–4, below) and other major Enlightenment thinkers contributed. The mission of the *Encyclopédie* was to improve the human condition by enlightening its readers.

p. 142, l. 23: *d'Alembert*: Jean-Le-Rond d'Alembert (1717–83), French mathematician, physicist, music theorist and Enlightenment philosopher.

p. 142, l. 23: *Raynal*: Abbé Raynal, Guillaume-Thomas François Raynal (1713–96), *philosophe*, frequented the salons of Baron d'Holbach (see p. 142, ll. 23–4) and Helvétius (see p. 144, ll. 10), and was known for his political pamphlets championing the rights of man and individual freedom regardless of race. His *L'Histoire philosophique et politique des éstablissements et du commerce des Européens dans les deux Indes* (1770) attacked methods of European colonization.

p. 142, ll. 23–4: Système de la Nature: Paul Henri Thiry, Baron d'Holbach (1723–89), atheist and politically radical philosopher. *Système de la Nature ou Des Loix du Monde Physique et du Monde Moral*, published anonymously in 1770, challenged Christian belief. His celebrated Paris salon attracted prominent European and American intellectuals, cultural and political figures.

p. 143, ll. 5–10: '*Pleasure, ... oneself.*': see Roland, *An Appeal to Impartial Posterity*, vol. 2, part 3, sec. 2, p. 102.

p. 143, ll. 10–23: '*In the mean time ... observations.*': see Roland, *An Appeal to Impartial Posterity*, vol. 2, part 3, sec. 2, pp. 106–7.

p. 143, l. 28–p. 144, l. 1: *the authors of Port Royal*: Port-Royal was an educational convent in Paris established in 1609 and acclaimed for its work in linguistics. Run by three abbesses, Angélique Arnauld (see Hays, *Female Biography*, vol. 1, pp. 180–3), her sister, Catherine Agnès (see Hays, *Female Biography*, vol. 1, pp. 183–4), and their niece, Angélique de Saint-Jean Arnauld d'Andilly (see Hays, *Female Biography*, vol. 1, p. 184), it evolved independently of the Catholic Church into a centre for Jansenism. In 1709 a papal Bull evicted the nuns as heretics and burned the building to the ground.

p. 144, l. 2: *the jesuit character*: The Jesuits were proponents of traditional Catholicism, controlled the education of elite boys and publicly opposed Diderot's *Encyclopédia* project.

p. 144, l. 5: *the stoics*: See note to p. 133, l. 13, above.

p. 144, l. 7: Descartes: Rene Descartes (1596–1650). His *Discourse on Method* (1637) and *Meditations* (1641) set forth '*Cogito ergo sum*', or 'I think, therefore I am'.

p. 144, l. 7: Malebranche: Nicholas Malebranche (1638–1715), French Cartesian philosopher, author of *La Recherche de la Verité* (1675).

p. 144, l. 10: *Helvetius, his system of self-interest*: Claude-Adrien Helvétius (1715–71), philosopher. Roland rejected his argument that rational self-interest without feeling is the sole motivator of man's actions, in favour of the altruism of the heroes of the Roman republic. *Memoirs of Madame Roland: A Heroine of the French Revolution*, p. 173.

p. 144, ll. 18–19: '*It is thus ... acted.*': see Roland, *An Appeal to Impartial Posterity*, vol. 2, part 3, sec. 2, p. 108.

p. 144, ll. 23–4: *She rejected, with disdain, the idea of uniting herself to an inferior man*: 'How', she asks, 'could I possibly marry a merchant who would not think or feel like me about anything? ... How could I be faithful to someone for whom I had no respect, even supposing I had married him in the first place? ... I refuse to marry a man who does not suit me'. *Memoirs of Madame Roland: A Heroine of the French Revolution*, pp. 199; 201.

p. 145, ll. 3–11: '*Yes, ... absurdity.*': see Roland, *An Appeal to Impartial Posterity*, vol. 2, part 3, sec. 2, p. 111.

p. 145, ll. 11–13: *She recollected Athens ... she thought of Greece*: Roland's republican spirit was ignited by her reading of Plutarch's *Lives*. She declares, 'I was passionate for the republics of the ancient world, adorned by men and deeds I could admire, and I persuaded myself that this was the only acceptable type of regime. I felt fully up to the level of these men and lamented that I had not been born amongst them.' *Memoirs of Madame Roland: A Heroine of the French Revolution*, p. 173.

p. 145, l. 19–p. 146, l. 1: '*The sphere of ... point.*': see Roland, *An Appeal to Impartial Posterity*, vol. 2, part 3, sec. 2, p. 112.

p. 146, ll. 18–27: *But that virtue, properly so called ... in favor of reason*: Roland had adapted a philosophy of virtue for her own life, both private and public, that was founded on that of Socrates and the Stoics. Its nexus was the 'unity of one's nature ... [with] the greatest possible consistency between one's beliefs and one's actions'. She adds, 'No amount of corruption and false doctrine can drive from Man's conscience that sublime instinct which impels him to admire wisdom and generosity in deeds'. *Memoirs of Madame Roland: A Heroine of the French Revolution*, pp. 175–6.

p. 146, l. 20–p. 147, l. 9: '*a man, ... the arts.*': see Roland, *An Appeal to Impartial Posterity*, vol. 2, part 3, sec. 2, pp. 113–14.

p. 147, ll. 13–17: '*Having combined ...social institutions.*': see Roland, *An Appeal to Impartial Posterity*, vol. 2, part 3, sec. 2, p. 114.

p. 147, l. 17–p. 148, l. 6: '*It was ... torment of fear*.': see Roland, *An Appeal to Impartial Posterity*, vol. 2, part 3, sec. 2, pp. 115–16.

p. 148, l. 14: *The worthy priest*: Abbé Morel; see note to p. 142, l. 2, above.

p. 148, l. 23: *Cicero*: (106–43 BC) Roman senator, lawyer, orator and philosopher during the last years of the Republic. Cicero followed the Greek Stoics, particularly their ideals of freedom and the rule of natural law and adapted them to his own life and teachings.

p. 148, ll. 23–6: '*that to complete ... devour him*.': see Roland, *An Appeal to Impartial Posterity*, vol. 2, part 3, sec. 2, p. 117.

p. 148, l. 27: *abbé le Grand*: L'abbé Legrand; not further identified.

p. 149, ll. 6–11: '*Philosophy ... on my guard*.': see Roland, *An Appeal to Impartial Posterity*, vol. 2, part 3, sec. 1, p. 119.

p. 149, l. 27–p. 150, l. 2: '*During these walks ... the sage*.': see Roland, *An Appeal to Impartial Posterity*, vol. 2, part 3, sec. 1, pp. 124–6.

p. 152, ll. 5–6: *the wild woods of Mendon*: Meudon, a small town south-west of Paris, bordered by woods, with a sweeping view of the city.

p. 152, ll. 13–14: *the shores of Belle-vue*: The Château de Bellevue was built for Madame de Pompadour (1721–64) by Louis XV (1710–74, r. 1715–74) in 1750 on a plateau in Meudon overlooking the Seine.

p. 152, l. 19–p. 153, l. 12: '*Delightful Meudon ... paradise!*': see Roland, *An Appeal to Impartial Posterity*, vol. 2, part 3, sec. 2, pp. 131–2.

p. 153, ll. 20–1: '*all was picture, life and happiness*.': see Roland, *An Appeal to Impartial Posterity*, vol. 2, part 3, sec. 2, p. 132.

p. 154, l. 16: *at Sparta, Agis and Cleomenes*: Agis (d. 241 BC) and Cleomenes (d. 219 BC) were Stoics and honourable kings of Sparta in Greece, who preferred that men participate in public life of their own free will for the public good.

p. 154, l. 17: *the Gracchi*: Tiberius (d. 133 BC) and his brother Caius Gracchus (154–121 BC), plebian senators in the Roman Republic renowned for their social reforms and republican virtue.

p. 154, ll. 17–19: '*I retired ... to the tribunes*.': see Roland, *An Appeal to Impartial Posterity*, vol. 2, part 3, sec. 2, p. 138.

p. 154, ll. 20–4: '*Now that experience ... I was not aware*': see Roland, *An Appeal to Impartial Posterity*, vol. 2, part 3, sec. 2, p. 138.

p. 155, l. 10: *de Lolme*: Jean-Louis de Lolme (1741–1804), author of *The Constitution of England* (1771), praised the English constitution for the freedom it granted its subjects through its balance of powers.

p. 155, ll. 12–13: *she yet only studied through the medium of translations*: This statement is inaccurate. By July 1784, when the Rolands travelled to England, Roland was reading in English. See May, *Madame Roland and the Age of Revolution*, p. 128.

p. 155, l. 25: *the doctor*: not further identified.

p. 155, l. 26: Récherche de la Verité *of Malbranche*: Malebranche; see note to p. 144, l. 7, above.

p. 156, ll. 1–5: '*Why, my good sir, ... to do*.': Roland, *An Appeal to Impartial Posterity*, vol. 2, part 3, sec. 2, p. 142.

p. 156, ll. 8–14: '*The French ... not thrown away*.': see Roland, *An Appeal to Impartial Posterity*, vol. 2, part 3, sec. 2, p. 142.

p. 156, l. 18: *M. and madame Bernard*: M. Besnard, married to Roland's great-aunt, was the steward of the land of the 1640 château at Soucy.

p. 156, ll. 22–3: *fermier-général*: [Farmer-general] collected customs duties on goods entering Paris at tollbooths outside the city walls and thereby amassed great wealth.

p. 156, l. 23: *his son*: the son of M. Besnard; not further identified.

p. 156, l. 26: *château at* Soucy: located in the domain of Fontenay-lès-Briis, south of Paris.

p. 157, ll. 5–6: *The sister-in-law and step-mother*: M. Besnard's relations; not further identified.

p. 157, ll. 14–15: '*That financiers ... the criminal.*': Roland, *An Appeal to Impartial Posterity*, vol. 2, part 3, sec. 2, p. 148.

p. 157, l. 17: *Puffendorf*: Samuel von Pufendorf (1632–94), historian and political theorist who advocated individual freedom and religious tolerance.

p. 157, l. 17: *Bernis*: François-Joachim de Pierre de Bernis (1715–94), ecclesiastic, diplomat and poet.

p. 157, l. 18: *the English Cromwell*: Oliver Cromwell (1599–1668), English military and political leader. Lord Protector of the Commonwealth from 1653–8.

p. 157, l. 21: *Rousseau*: Jean-Jacques Rousseau (1712–78), Genevan philosopher and writer. Roland's education, her advocacy of women's education and, above all, her participation in the Revolution, contradict Rousseau's dictum that the only place for women was in the domestic sphere. It was well known that she was the power behind her husband's ministry, and for this she was excoriated by the press and accused of 'betraying her sex' by the Revolutionary Tribunal. Roland dared to follow Rousseau's 'bold example in the *Confessions*, ... to reveal her most intimate thoughts, feelings, and experiences ...'. M. Seidman Trouille, *Sexual Politics in the Enlightenment: Women Writers Read Rousseau* (New York: State University of New York Press, 1997), pp. 165–73; 186–92; note on p. 350.

p. 157, ll. 21–4: '*The truth is,'... nothing else.*': see Roland, *An Appeal to Impartial Posterity*, vol. 2, part 3, sec. 2, p. 152.

p. 158, ll. 3–14: '*As to me ... losing a single moment.*': see Roland, *An Appeal to Impartial Posterity*, vol. 2, part 3, sec. 1, p. 153.

p. 158, ll. 20–1: Théâtre Français: Also known as La Maison de Molière and the Comédie Française and, during the Revolution, the Théâtre de la République. It was founded by Louis XIV in 1680.

p. 159, l. 19–p. 161, l. 9: '*My father ... every thing unpleasant.*': see Roland, *An Appeal to Impartial Posterity*, vol. 2, part 3, sec. 2, pp. 165–71.

p. 161, l. 4: l'Empereur's *wife*: not further identified.

p. 162, l. 25: ennui: boredom.

p. 163, l. 10: *A young physician*: not further identified.

p. 163, l. 12–p. 164, l. 26: '*Well,'... ... know your opinion.*': see Roland, *An Appeal to Impartial Posterity*, vol. 2, part 3, sec. 2, pp. 178–80.

p. 163, l. 16: *Gardanne*: see note to p. 163, l. 10, above.

p. 165, ll. 16–21: '*I reasoned like ... of my species.*': see Roland, *An Appeal to Impartial Posterity*, vol. 2, part 3, sec. 2, p. 182.

p. 166, l. 11: *an honest jeweller*: not further identified.

p. 166, l. 12–p. 167, l. 24: '*He has in his favor ... a life of celibacy.*': see Roland, *An Appeal to Impartial Posterity*, vol. 2, part 3, sec. 2, pp. 185–7.

p. 168, ll. 2–15: '*What,'... as you have been.*': see Roland, *An Appeal to Impartial Posterity*, vol. 2, part 3, sec. 2, pp. 187–8.

p. 168, ll. 17–26: '*A stranger ... cost to maintain it.*': see Roland, *An Appeal to Impartial Posterity*, vol. 2, part 3, sec. 2, p. 188.

p. 170, ll. 13–14: *Whitsuntide*: the week following Whitsunday, the Christian festival of Pentecost which commemorates the descent of the Holy Spirit upon Christ's disciples.

p. 170, l. 26–p. 171, l. 6: '*Why are you in such haste? ... in despite of me.*': see Roland, *An Appeal to Impartial Posterity*, vol. 2, part 3, sec. 2, p. 193.

p. 170, l. 27: *St. Agatha*: Angelina Bouffliers; see note to p. 130, ll. 12–13, above.

p. 171, l. 7: presentèments: presentiments.

p. 171, ll. 24–6: '*Ah, mademoiselle! ... to her apartment.*': see Roland, *An Appeal to Impartial Posterity*, vol. 2, part 3, sec. 2, pp. 194–5.

p. 172, l. 15: *the physician*: not further identified.

p. 174, l. 22–p. 175, l. 11: '*I felt, ... it been followed?*': see Roland, *An Appeal to Impartial Posterity*, vol. 2, part 3, sec. 2, pp. 199–200.

p. 175, ll. 17–24: '*On the day ... existence so frail?*': see Roland, *An Appeal to Impartial Posterity*, vol. 2, part 4, sec. 3, p. 2.

p. 175, l. 26–p. 176, l. 6: '*Naturally wise ... it is restrained.*': see Roland, *An Appeal to Impartial Posterity*, vol. 2, part 4, sec. 3, p. 2.

p. 176, l. 10: '*It is charming,*': see Roland, *An Appeal to Impartial Posterity*, vol. 2, part 4, sec. 3, p. 3.

p. 176, ll. 13–14: '*It is charming ... so much of it!*': see Roland, *An Appeal to Impartial Posterity*, vol. 2, part 4, sec. 3, p. 3.

p. 176, ll. 18–24: '*I seemed not to exist ... I swooned away.*': see Roland, *An Appeal to Impartial Posterity*, vol. 2, part 4, sec. 3, p. 3.

p. 177, l. 4: *Heloise of Rousseau*: Roland read Rousseau's epistolary novel, *Julie, ou La Nouvelle Héloïse* (1761), at the age of twenty-one. The demand for *La Nouvelle Héloïse* was so great that booksellers rented it out by the day and even by the hour, and from its first publication in 1760 to 1800 it appeared in seventy editions. See R. Darnton, *The Great Cat Massacre: And Other Episodes in French Cultural History* (New York: Basic Books, 1984), pp. 243, 227–35.

p. 177, l. 5–p. 178, l. 9: '*The perusal of this ... toward their demonstration.*': see Roland, *An Appeal to Impartial Posterity*, vol. 2, part 4, sec. 3, pp. 3–5.

p. 178, l. 17–p. 179, l. 8: '*I have never been able ... performance of their duties.*': see Roland, *An Appeal to Impartial Posterity*, vol. 2, part 4, sec. 3, pp. 5–6.

p. 179, ll. 11–18: '*Left more than ever ... bridled my imagination.*': see Roland, *An Appeal to Impartial Posterity*, vol. 2, part 4, sec. 3, p. 7.

p. 179, ll. 20–1: "*The Works of Leisure Hours, and different Reflections.*": Roland did not allow these to be published during her lifetime, but they were published after her death as *The Works (never before published) of Jeanne-Marie* [sic] *Phlipon Roland, Wife of the Ex-Minister of the Interior, Containing Her Philosophical and Literary Essays... Her Correspondence, and Her Travels to Which are Annexed the Justificative Documents Relative to Her Imprisonment and Condemnation*, with a Preliminary Discourse by L. A. Champagneux (1800).

p. 179, l. 24–p. 181, l. 5: '*Never, did I feel ... pure and pathetic.*': see Roland, *An Appeal to Impartial Posterity*, vol. 2, part 4, sec. 3, pp. 8–9.

p. 180, ll. 14–15: *my husband*: Jean-Marie Roland de la Platière (1734–93), leader of the Girondists, a political faction that campaigned for the end of the monarchy, and served as Minister of the Interior under King Louis XVI. He was dismissed in June 1792 and reinstated in August but resigned in January 1793 when the Girondists were ousted from the Convention by the Jacobins (see note to p. 241, l. 2, above).

p. 181, ll. 13–24: '*If I wished ... making any noise.*': see Roland, *An Appeal to Impartial Posterity*, vol. 2, part 4, sec. 3, pp. 12–14.

p. 181, l. 19: *a mistress*: not further identified.

p. 182, ll. 1–3: '*Behold me then ... and my studies.*': see Roland, *An Appeal to Impartial Posterity*, vol. 2, part 4, sec. 3, p. 15.

p. 182, l. 3: *her servant, a little woman*: Roland's personal servant Fleury; not further identified.

p. 182, ll. 9–17: '*I carried with me ... the heart and the mind.*': see Roland, *An Appeal to Impartial Posterity*, vol. 2, part 4, sec. 3, p. 15.

p. 182, l. 20: *Bossuet*: Jacques-Bénigne Bossuet; see note to p. 133, l. 6, above.

p. 182, l. 21: *Flechier*: Esprit Fléchier (1632–1710), religious apologist and orator, known for his great wit, which gained him entry into the court of Louis XIV.

p. 182, l. 21: *Bourdaloue*: Louis Bourdaloue (1632–1704), Jesuit scholar and preacher whose passionate but rational rhetoric mesmerized French congregants from all walks of life.

p. 182, l. 22: *Massillon*: Jean-Baptiste Massillon (1663–1742). Hailed as the successor to Bossuet and Bourdaloue, Massillon preached at the court of Versailles under Louis XIV.

p. 182, l. 25: *Paw*: Cornelius de Pauw (1739–99), Dutch ethnologist considered an authority on the Americas although he had never been there. His study of Native Americans in 1768, written in French, claimed that Europeans who travelled there would become degenerate. He also wrote about ancient China, Egypt and Greece.

p. 182, l. 25: *Raynal*: Guillaume Thomas François Raynal; see note to p. 142, l. 23, above.

p. 182, ll. 25–6: *author of the System of Nature*: Paul Henri Thiry, Baron d'Holbach; see note to p. 142, ll. 23–4, above.

p. 183, ll. 12–13: *M. de Boismorel*: Roberge de Boismorel (not further identified). Roland affectionately called him the 'Sage of Bercy' referencing Voltaire's appellation, the 'Sage of Ferney'. May, *Madame Roland and the Age of Revolution*, p. 50.

p. 184, l. 8: *the ladies of the family*: M. Boismorel's mother and other unknown relations; not further identified.

p. 184, ll. 8–9: '*How well your dear daughter looks!*': see Roland, *An Appeal to Impartial Posterity*, vol. 2, part 4, sec. 3, p. 21.

p. 184, ll. 9–10: *the mother of M. Boismorel*: See note to p. 136, l. 10, above.

p. 184, l. 11–p. 185, l. 11: '*but, do you know, ... glimpse of her toilette.*': see Roland, *An Appeal to Impartial Posterity*, vol. 2, part 4, sec. 3, pp. 21–2.

p. 185, l. 13: '*A philosopher!*': see Roland, *An Appeal to Impartial Posterity*, vol. 2, part 4, sec. 3, p. 22.

p. 185, l. 21: *Bayle*: Pierre Bayle (1647–1706), French Huguenot philosopher best known for *Historical and Critical Dictionary* (1695), a biographical dictionary.

p. 185, ll. 21–2: Memoirs *of the academies*: *Histoire de l'Académie Royale des Sciences, Années 1699–1751. Avec les Mémoires de Mathématique et de Physique pour les mêmes années, tirez des Registres de cette Académie* (Amsterdam: Gérard Kuyper, 1706–60); and *The Philosophical History and Memoirs of the Royal Academy of Sciences at Paris ... in 5 Vols* (France: John and Paul Knapton; and John Nourse, 1742).

p. 185, ll. 24–7: '*Those points of view ... manner of living.*': see Roland, *An Appeal to Impartial Posterity*, vol. 2, part 4, sec. 3, p. 24.

p. 186, ll. 1–2: *the French Academy ... St. Lewis*: The Académie française, the learned body on matters pertaining to the French language, held annual public meetings in April on the festival of Saint Lewis (Louis IX (1214–70, r. 1226–70)).

p. 186, l. 3: *abbé de Besplas*: Joseph-Marie Anne Gros de Besplas (1734–83), Abbot of the Abbey of Épau (1781–3).

p. 186, l. 12: *Catinat*: Nicholas Catinat (1637–1712), military general under Louis XIV who was awarded the title of Marshal of France for his achievements.

p. 186, l. 12: *La Harpe*: Jean François de La Harpe (1739–1803), playwright whose successful first play, *Warwick* (1763), initiated his close friendship with Voltaire. He later wrote for *Mercure de France*, a literary magazine, and was elected in 1776 to the Académie française.

p. 186, ll. 14–15: *St. Gratien*: a small town a few miles north of Paris in the Île-de-France region.

p. 186, l. 19: *Michaelmas-day*: The Christian feast of Saint Michael the Archangel, 29 September.

p. 186, l. 27: *J. J. Rousseau*: Jean-Jacques Rousseau; see note to p. 157, l. 21, above.

p. 187, ll. 2–10: '*I saw him ... friendship.*': see Roland, *An Appeal to Impartial Posterity*, vol. 2, part 4, sec. 3, p. 28.

p. 187, ll. 11–12: protegée: one who is protected, promoted or trained by a person of experience, prominence, or influence.

p. 187, l. 24: *his son*: the son of M. de Boismorel; not further identified.

p. 187, l. 28–p. 188, l. 22: '*It is necessary ... opinion and corrections.*': see Roland, *An Appeal to Impartial Posterity*, vol. 2, part 4, sec. 3, p. 31.

p. 189, ll. 7–8: *Duclos*: Charles Pinot Duclos (1704–72), influential social critic and historian. His works include *The History of Louis XI, King of France* and his novels, *Madame de Luz* (1741) and *The Confessions* (1742).

p. 189, l. 16: *abbé Delisle's translation of the Georgics*: Jacques DeLille (1738–1813), poet and translator. His translation of Virgil's *Georgics* in 1770 received critical and popular acclaim. In 1804 he translated Virgil's *Aeneid* (29–19 BC) and in 1805, Milton's *Paradise Lost* (1667).

p. 189, l. 17: coup de soleil: 'sunburn' (French) or perhaps in the case of M. Boismorel, 'sunstroke'.

p. 189, ll. 22–5: '*nor can I ever ... a good man.*': see Roland, *An Appeal to Impartial Posterity*, vol. 2, part 4, sec. 3, p. 33.

p. 190, ll. 12–14: '*whence ... no more about him.*': see Roland, *An Appeal to Impartial Posterity*, vol. 2, part 4, sec. 3, p. 33.

p. 190, l. 21: *Saint–Lette*: not further identified.

p. 190, l. 22: *council of Pondicherry*: A city on the east coast of India, Pondicherry was passed back and forth between the British and French in the eighteenth century, depending on who controlled the colony.

p. 190, l. 25–p. 191, l. 10: '*Those ... become an author.*': see Roland, *An Appeal to Impartial Posterity*, vol. 2, part 4, sec. 3, pp. 46–7.

p. 191, ll. 11–13: *a man destined to have a powerful influence on the fate of his daughter*: Jean-Marie Roland de la Platière; see note to p. 180, ll. 14–15, above. Roland met her future husband in 1776 but they did not marry until 1780. Theirs was a meeting of the minds but not one of romantic love. She writes: 'His seriousness, his moral principles and his way of life, all dedicated to his work, made me think of him as a person without sex ... a thinker entirely devoted to reason'. *Memoirs of Madame Roland: A Heroine of the French Revolution*, pp. 242–7.

p. 192, l. 3: *M. Roland*: Jean-Marie Roland de la Platière; see note to p. 180, ll. 14–15, above.

p. 192, ll. 4–7: '*Why then ... a letter?*': see Roland, *An Appeal to Impartial Posterity*, vol. 2, part 4, sec. 3, p. 48.

p. 192, ll. 9–13: '*I was still ... well received.*': see Roland, *An Appeal to Impartial Posterity*, vol. 2, part 4, sec. 3, p. 48.

p. 192, l. 14–p. 193, l. 16: '*This letter ... destitute of harmony.*': see Roland, *An Appeal to Impartial Posterity*, vol. 2, part 4, sec. 3, pp. 48–9.

p. 193, l. 17: *La Blancherie*: Claude Mammès Pahin de la Blancherie (1751–1811), a gentleman of modest means who was educated in the law but spent his time travelling the Continent. He became a writer on Sciences and the Arts, collaborating in the 1780s with Jacques-Pierre Brissot (see note to p. 214, ll. 19–22, below) on several articles.

p. 194, l. 5: *a duenna*: an elderly woman serving as governess and companion to young ladies.

p. 194, ll. 10–11: '*The head ... some progress.*': see Roland, *An Appeal to Impartial Posterity*, vol. 2, part 4, sec. 3, pp. 51–2.

p. 194, l. 22: *her mother*: the mother of Sophie and Henriette Cannet; not further identified.

p. 194, ll. 22–8: '*The latter ... which she had formed.*': see Roland, *An Appeal to Impartial Posterity*, vol. 2, part 4, sec. 3, p. 52.

p. 195, l. 1: *mademoiselle d'Hangard*: not further identified.

p. 195, ll. 4–5: '*You then, ... this gentleman?*': see Roland, *An Appeal to Impartial Posterity*, vol. 2, part 4, sec. 3, p. 52.

p. 195, ll. 7–23: '*Yes, and do not you? ... madame l'Epine's concert*': see Roland, *An Appeal to Impartial Posterity*, vol. 2, part 4, sec. 3, pp. 52–3.

p. 195, ll. 8–9: *the mademoiselles Bordenave*: not further identified.

p. 195, l. 23: *madame l'Epine's*: not further identified.

p. 196, ll. 5–6: *a little Savoyard*: not further identified.

p. 196, l. 6: *the maid of mademoiselle*: Fleury; see note to p. 182, l. 3, above.

p. 196, ll. 11–12: '*Yes, ... with you..*': see Roland, *An Appeal to Impartial Posterity*, vol. 2, part 4, sec. 3, p. 53.

p. 196, ll. 14–21: '*I did not dare, ... unacquainted*': see Roland, *An Appeal to Impartial Posterity*, vol. 2, part 4, sec. 3, pp. 53–4.

p. 197, ll. 21–7: '*That she was ignorant ... any explanation.*': see Roland, *An Appeal to Impartial Posterity*, vol. 2, part 4, sec. 3, p. 55.

p. 198, ll. 5–7: '*Who, ... the arts and sciences?*': see Roland, *An Appeal to Impartial Posterity*, vol. 2, part 4, sec. 3, p. 55.

p. 199, ll. 2–4: '*You are happy ... demand another.*': see Roland, *An Appeal to Impartial Posterity*, vol. 2, part 4, sec. 3, p. 56.

p. 199, l. 6: *Sevelinge*: not further identified.

p. 199, l. 7: *Soissons*: located on the Aisne River in Picardy, north-east of Paris.

p. 199, ll. 18–26: '*His letters, ... inclined to melancholy*': see Roland, *An Appeal to Impartial Posterity*, vol. 2, part 4, sec. 3, p. 57.

p. 200, ll. 10–23: '*of which, ... not encumbered by numbers.*': see Roland, *An Appeal to Impartial Posterity*, vol. 2, part 4, sec. 3, p. 58.

p. 200, l. 24: *academy of Besançon*: French Academies such as those of Besançon, Lyons and Dijon participated in France's Enlightenment project in the late eighteenth century to scientifically improve the condition of mankind and generate governmental reform by holding contests for the submission of essays every year on various subjects. S. Schama, *Citizens: A Chronicle of the French Revolution* (New York: Vintage Books, 1990), p. 517.

p. 200, ll. 25–7: '*In what manner ... render men better?*': see Roland, *An Appeal to Impartial Posterity*, vol. 2, part 4, sec. 3, p. 59.

p. 201, ll. 5–17: '*In wishing to treat ... on the problem.*': see Roland, *An Appeal to Impartial Posterity*, vol. 2, part 4, sec. 3, p. 59.

p. 201, ll. 19–23: '*My head ... the production of another.*': see Roland, *An Appeal to Impartial Posterity*, vol. 2, part 4, sec. 3, pp. 59–60.

p. 202, l. 21–p. 203, l. 11: '*My uncle ... if they permit me to live.*': see Roland, *An Appeal to Impartial Posterity*, vol. 2, part 4, sec. 3, pp. 62–3.

p. 203, l. 7: *canon Baeux*: not further identified.

p. 203, l. 23: *five brothers*: Dominique, the eldest, a Canon (not further identified) at the parish church of Villefranche; Jacques-Marie, a Benedictine monk (1731–1807); Laurent [possibly] (not further identified); and Pierre (not further identified), the prior of Cluny.

p. 204, l. 2: *M. Godinat*: not further identified.

p. 204, l. 9: *his best-beloved brother*: Pierre Roland de la Platière, see note to p. 203, l. 23, above.

p. 204, ll. 16–23: '*His gravity ... visiting me more frequently*.': see Roland, *An Appeal to Impartial Posterity*, vol. 2, part 4, sec. 3, p. 65.

p. 205, ll. 6–12: '*I had saved ... I had been brought up.*': see Roland, *An Appeal to Impartial Posterity*, vol. 2, part 4, sec. 3, p. 66.

p. 206, l. 16: *the* Congregation: Roland rented a small apartment at the Convent of the Congregation in Paris.

p. 206, l. 28–p. 207, l. 2: '*inclosed ... it was winter*,': see Roland, *An Appeal to Impartial Posterity*, vol. 2, part 4, sec. 3, p. 68.

p. 207, ll. 10–23: '*I fortified my heart ... that was necessary to be so.*': see Roland, *An Appeal to Impartial Posterity*, vol. 2, part 4, sec. 3, p. 68.

p. 208, ll. 2–3: '*where, ... of prosperity.*': see Roland, *An Appeal to Impartial Posterity*, vol. 2, part 4, sec. 3, p. 69.

p. 208, ll. 4–19: '*I reflect ... the retirement in which I lived?*': see Roland, *An Appeal to Impartial Posterity*, vol. 2, part 4, sec. 3, pp. 69–70.

p. 208, l. 22–p. 207, l. 12: '*To him... a single instant.*': see Roland, *An Appeal to Impartial Posterity*, vol. 2, part 4, sec. 3, p. 70.

p. 209, ll. 18–24: '*I respected ... enough to differ from him.*': see Roland, *An Appeal to Impartial Posterity*, vol. 2, part 4, sec. 3, p. 71.

p. 210, ll. 4–5: *they spent four years at Amiens*: During the first years of their marriage, the Rolands lived in Amiens, north of Paris. Jean-Marie Roland was working on the *Dictionary of Manufacturing* for Diderot's *New Encyclopedia*, and Amiens was the center of textile manufacturing in northern France. As inspector of manufacturing for the city of Lyons, he was charged with writing two volumes of the *New Encyclopedia*, published as the *Dictionary of Manufactures, Arts and Trades* in 1784, 1785 and 1790. Madame Roland was her husband's partner in every aspect of this enterprise. May, *Madame Roland and the Age of Revolution*, pp. 108–9.

p. 210, ll. 8–9: *New Encyclopedia*: also called the *Encyclopedia Methodique*. Publisher Charles-Joseph Panckoucke created it in 1782 as an expanded edition of Diderot's *Encyclopedia*. Comprising more than 200 volumes when it was completed in 1832, it contained entries on trade, manufacturing and the industrial arts.

p. 210, ll. 9–18: '*We never quit ... I rendered to him.*': see Roland, *An Appeal to Impartial Posterity*, vol. 2, part 4, sec. 3, p. 72.

p. 210, ll. 12–13: l'art du tourbier: the method of extracting peat from the ground, which the people of Amiens used to heat their homes. *L'art du tourbier* became the title of a book written in 1782 by Jean-Marie Roland, with the assistance of Madame Roland.

p. 210, l. 20: *chevalier de Gomicourt*: not further identified.

p. 210, l. 28: *an old man*: not further identified.

p. 211, ll. 4–10: '*The difference of our ideas ... my safety.*': see Roland, *An Appeal to Impartial Posterity*, vol. 2, part 4, sec. 3, p. 73.

p. 211, ll. 15–20: '*This prohibition ... to temptation.*': see Roland, *An Appeal to Impartial Posterity*, vol. 2, part 4, sec. 3, pp. 73–4.

p. 211, ll. 23–4: *an ancient mother*: not further identified.

p. 211, ll. 24–5: *her eldest son, a canon*: not further identified.

p. 212, ll. 7–14: '*It was there ... these cares agreeable.*': see Roland, *An Appeal to Impartial Posterity*, vol. 2, part 4, sec. 3, pp. 75–6.

p. 212, ll. 20–2: '*Yet ... double our activity.*': see Roland, *An Appeal to Impartial Posterity*, vol. 2, part 4, sec. 3, p. 76.

p. 213, ll. 3–7: '*who ... useful to others.*': see Roland, *An Appeal to Impartial Posterity*, vol. 2, part 4, sec. 3, p. 76.

p. 214, l. 3: *a catarrh*: an allergic inflammation.

p. 214, l. 6: *her husband's favourite brother*: Pierre Roland de la Platière, see note to p. 203, l. 23, above.

p. 214, ll. 19–22: *Brissot ... periodical paper*: Jacques-Pierre Brissot (1754–93) was the editor of the republican newspaper *Patriote Français* and had been an epistolary friend of the Rolands' since 1784. Brissot printed several of Madam Roland's letters reporting on political and social unrest in Lyons. In early 1792 Brissot and the Rolands founded the Girondist faction together; he was condemned to death in October 1793.

p. 215, l. 25–p. 216, l. 11: '*Here ... but remain united.*': see Roland, *An Appeal to Impartial Posterity*, vol. 1, part 1, sec. 1, p. 53.

p. 215, l. 26: *Mirabeau*: Honoré-Gabriel Riqueti, comte de Mirabeau (1749–91) represented the Third Estate in the Estates-General with powerful rhetoric and bold ideas for reform of the French monarchy modelled on that of Great Britain. His pragmatic proposals led some to suspect him of Royalist tendencies. Schama, *Citizens: A Chronicle of the French Revolution*, pp. 480–2; 542–5.

p. 216, l. 2: *Cazalés*: Jacques Antoine Marie Cazalès (1758–1805), deputy to the National Assembly, a Royalist democrat who favoured a constitutional monarchy. He emigrated to Switzerland in August 1792 after the September Massacres (see note to p. 219, l. 21, below), which took place outside the Tuileries Palace where the royal family was imprisoned.

p. 216, l. 2: *Maury*: Abbé Jean-Sifrein Maury (1746–1817), member of the Académie française known for his wit. As a Royalist democrat in the Estates-General of 1789, Maury represented the clergy near Lyons, supported a constitutional monarchy and opposed the confiscation of ecclesiastical properties.

p. 216, l. 3: *Lameths*: Charles Malo François Lameth (1757–1832) and Alexandre-Théodore-Victor, comte de Lameth (1760–1829) were brothers, military men who fought in the American Revolution. They joined the moderate Feuillants and served as deputies in the French National Assembly. In 1792, as the Revolution spun out of control of the Girondists, they fled to Austria.

p. 216, l. 3: *Barnave*: Antoine Pierre Joseph Barnave (1761–93) was a member of the early Jacobin faction (see note to p. 241, l. 2, below) but later joined the moderate Feuillants. His political and oratorical skills rivaled those of Mirabeau. He was one of three revolutionaries who escorted Louis XVI and Marie Antoinette (1755–93) back to Paris after their attempted escape to Varennes in 1791. His *Introduction à la revolution française*, written in prison but not published until 1843, is considered a primary document of the Revolution. He was executed in Paris in November 1793.

p. 216, l. 23–p. 217, l. 21: '*I knew ... lavished to no end.*': see Roland, *An Appeal to Impartial Posterity*, vol. 1, part 1, p. 56.

p. 217, l. 22: *Robespierre*: Maximilien François Marie Isidore de Robespierre (1758–94) and the Rolands were intimately acquainted as Jacobins (see note to p. 241, l. 2, below) upon the Rolands' relocation to Paris in early 1791.

p. 217, l. 26–p. 218, l. 20: '*That kind of reserve ... I esteemed Robespierre.*': see Roland, *An Appeal to Impartial Posterity*, vol. 1, part 1, pp. 58–9.

p. 218, l. 25: *Buzot's*: François Nicolas Léonard Buzot (1760–93), Deputy to the National Assembly. Like the Rolands he was an early Jacobin (see note to p. 241, l. 2, below) and attended the frequent political dinners of Madame Roland. Madame Roland and the young and handsome Buzot fell passionately in love in the winter of 1792. With Buzot she found the 'intimate union of hearts' that she had always yearned for. Buzot fled to Caen when the Girondists were arrested in 1793. A year later he committed suicide when authorities began to close in on him. *Memoirs of Madame Roland: A Heroine of the French Revolution*, p. 200.

p. 218, l. 26–p. 219, l. 4: '*There is nothing ... enough for me.*': see Roland, *An Appeal to Impartial Posterity*, vol. 1, part 1, p. 64.

p. 219, l. 21: *Jerome Petion*: Prominent Girondist, Jérôme Pétion de Villeneuve (1756–94) served as Mayor of Paris from October 1791 to September 1792. He was suspended for deliberately failing to protect the royal family during the September Massacres, the wave of mob violence which resulted in the execution of half the prison population of Paris, which began on August 10 when Roland, Servan (see note to p. 224, l. 2, below) and Clavière (see note to p. 222, l. 17, below) were dismissed from the ministry. Petion committed suicide with Buzot in June 1794. See Schama, *Citizens: A Chronicle of the French Revolution*, pp. 609–11.

p. 220, ll. 22–8: '*Persuaded ... this correspondence.*': see Roland, *An Appeal to Impartial Posterity*, vol. 1, part 2, pp. 3–4.

p. 221, l. 4: *Roland*: Jean-Marie Roland; see note to p. 180, ll. 14–15, above.

p. 221, l. 10: *Dumouriez*: General Charles-François Dumouriez (1739–1823) was appointed Minister of Foreign Affairs in March 1792 but was suspected of loyalty to the King. He resigned when Roland, Servan (see note to p. 224, l. 2, below) and Clavière (see note to p. 222, l. 17, below) were dismissed but resumed his career in the military and negotiated with Austria to reinstate the monarchy with Louis XVII. See 'Biographical Notes', in *Memoirs of Madame Roland: A Heroine of the French Revolution*, p. 21; and Schama, *Citizens: A Chronicle of the French Revolution*, p. 596.

p. 221, l. 16: '*There goes a man*': see Roland, *An Appeal to Impartial Posterity*, vol. 1, part 1, p. 68.

p. 221, ll. 18–25: '*there goes ... your dismission.*': see Roland, *An Appeal to Impartial Posterity*, vol. 1, part 1, p. 68.

p. 221, l. 27–p. 222, l. 7: '*On one side, ... his own interest and fame.*': see Roland, *An Appeal to Impartial Posterity*, vol. 1, part 1, p. 68.

p. 222, l. 15–p. 223, l. 2: '*Good God! ... the revolution.*': see Roland, *An Appeal to Impartial Posterity*, vol. 1, part 1, p. 69.

p. 222, l. 17: *Claviere*: Étienne Clavière (1735–93), Genevan financier who emigrated to France in 1782 and served as Minister of Public Contributions in 1792. Louis XVI abruptly dismissed him, Jean-Marie Roland and Servan when they presented the Letter to the King of 10 June 1792 written by Madam Roland for her husband's signature. See 'Biographical Notes', in *Memoirs of Madame Roland: A Heroine of the French Revolution*, p. 20; and Schama, *Citizens: A Chronicle of the French Revolution*, p. 605.

p. 223, ll. 7–12: '*Oh, dear sir, ... undone.*': see Roland, *An Appeal to Impartial Posterity*, vol. 1, part 1, p. 70.

p. 223, ll. 19–22: '*He wanted nothing ... conceived.*': see Roland, *An Appeal to Impartial Posterity*, vol. 1, part 1, p. 71.

p. 223, l. 25: *the king*: Louis XVI; see note to p. 116, l. 22, above.

p. 224, l. 2: *Servan*: General Joseph Servan de Gerby (1741–1808) a Girondon, replaced Danton in 1792 as Minister for War. He was dismissed in June 1792 and reinstated in August. He was condemned with other Girondists in 1793 and committed suicide in prison.

p. 224, l. 21–p. 226, l. 8: '*Studious habits ... the good I do.*': see Roland, *An Appeal to Impartial Posterity*, vol. 1, part 2, pp. 17–18.

p. 226, l. 10: Pache: Jean-Nicholas Pache de Montguyon (1746–1823) succeeded Jérôme Pétion as Mayor of Paris. Pache's loyalties changed with the party in power to benefit his own interests. He was successively a Girondist, a Jacobin and an Hébertist (named for Jacques Hébert, radical extremist). See Schama, *Citizens: A Chronicle of the French Revolution*, p. 805.

p. 226, ll. 10–13: *'Tis a very bold ... anything else?'*: see Roland, *An Appeal to Impartial Posterity*, vol. 1, part 2, p. 19.

p. 226, l. 23–p. 227, l. 2: *'Congratulate me ... my husband.'*: see Roland, *An Appeal to Impartial Posterity*, vol. 1, part 2, p. 20.

p. 227, ll. 6–9: *'Dumouriez! ... their dismission.'*: see Roland, *An Appeal to Impartial Posterity*, vol. 1, part 2, p. 20.

p. 227, l. 11: *the queen*: Marie Antoinette, Queen of France; see note to p. 216, l. 3, above.

p. 227, l. 25: *Duranthon*: Antoine Duranton, appointed Minister of Justice in June 1792; not further identified.

p. 227, ll. 26–7: *'We will wait ... the Chancery,'*: see Roland, *An Appeal to Impartial Posterity*, vol. 1, part 1, p. 78.

p. 228, ll. 4–15: *'You make us ... to the public.'*: see Roland, *An Appeal to Impartial Posterity*, vol. 1, part 2, p. 21.

p. 228, ll. 17–20: *'Utility and glory, ... proud of his disgrace.'*: see Roland, *An Appeal to Impartial Posterity*, vol. 1, part 2, p. 21.

p. 228, l. 25–p. 229, l. 22: *'I had' ...established between us.'*: see Roland, *An Appeal to Impartial Posterity*, vol. 1, part 1, pp. 80–1.

p. 229, l. 26–p. 231, l. 3: *'It is a great pity, ... shameful incapacity.'*: see Roland, *An Appeal to Impartial Posterity*, vol. 1, part 2, p. 30.

p. 229, l. 28: *Danton*: George Jacques Danton (1759–94), founder of the extremist Cordeliers Club, later joined the Jacobins (see p. 241, l. 2) and became Minister of Justice in August 1792. He voted to execute King Louis XVI in January 1793 and led the Jacobins in overthrowing the Girondists in March. In 1794 Robespierre and Danton's own Revolutionary Tribunal condemned him; he was guillotined in April of that year.

p. 231, ll. 4–19: *'While I contemplated ... a Sardanapalus.'*: see Roland, *An Appeal to Impartial Posterity*, vol. 1, part 1, pp. 88–9.

p. 231, l. 19: *Sardanapalus*: Diodorus Siculus, Greek historian (fl. 60–30 BC), claimed that Sardanapalus was the last king of Assyria (seventh century BC) and was famous for his excessive lifestyle, his effeminate mannerisms, voice and dress and his love of spinning and weaving.

p. 231, l. 20: *Fabre d'Eglantine*: Philippe-François-Nazaire Fabre d'Églantine (1750–94), poet and playwright, devoted to Danton and was one of the most militant Jacobins. He earned the dubious distinction of renaming the monthly calendar in October 1793 to reflect revolutionary taste. Tried and executed with Danton in April 1794. See Schama, *Citizens: A Chronicle of the French Revolution*, pp. 630; 646.

p. 231, l. 23–p. 232, l. 4: *'It was a subject ... what I really am.'*: see Roland, *An Appeal to Impartial Posterity*, vol. 1, part 1, p. 91.

p. 232, l. 20: *the persons who asked for him*: not further identified.

p. 233, ll. 7–16: *'I am sorry ... council is assembled.'*: see Roland, *An Appeal to Impartial Posterity*, vol. 1, part 1, p. 102.

p. 233, ll. 22–3: *the valet de chamber of M. Roland*: not further identified.

p. 234, l. 3: *Marat*: Jean-Paul Marat (1743–93), French physician with a degree from St Andrews University (1775) who turned radical Jacobin leader (see note to p. 241, l. 2, above) and incited the barbarism of the working class with his newspaper, *L'Ami du Peuple*. He relentlessly demanded the execution of Louis XVI but met his own violent death when he was assassinated by Charlotte Corday d'Armont (see note to p. 277, l. 17, below), a Girondist who reviled the Jacobins and blamed Marat for the worst excesses of the Revolution. See Schama, *Citizens: A Chronicle of the French Revolution*, pp. 445; 730–1.

p. 234, ll. 6–19: '*Can you guess ...listen to reason.*': see Roland, *An Appeal to Impartial Posterity*, vol. 1, part 1, p. 103.

p. 234, l. 22–p. 236, l. 3: '*Who so dull ... having parried it?*': see Roland, *An Appeal to Impartial Posterity*, vol. 1, part 1, p. 104.

p. 236, l. 7: *the* Abbaye: The prison de l'Abbaye in Paris operated from 1522 to 1854. The Abbey Prison was the target of the first of the September Massacres on 10 August 1792. It was also where arrestees were detained before their relocation to Sainte-Pélagie Prison.

p. 236, ll. 7–16: '*All Paris, ... these atrocious acts.*': see Roland, *An Appeal to Impartial Posterity*, vol. 1, part 1, pp. 110–11.

p. 236, ll. 15–24: '*It is equally true, ... inspire them with fear.*': Roland, *An Appeal to Impartial Posterity*, vol. 1, part 1, p. 105.

p. 237, l. 9: *struggle of the 10th of August*: Fédéré [federate] militias, which were volunteer troops, with support from the Paris Commune (the government of Paris from 1789–95), stormed the Tuileries palace. Louis XVI's rule was effectively terminated.

p. 237, l. 10: *minister of the interior*: Jean-Marie Roland; see see note to p. 180, ll. 14–15, above.

p. 238, ll. 3–4: *the tragedy of September*: the September Massacres; see note to p. 219, l. 21, above.

p. 238, ll. 8–21: '*Intending to ... excite my uneasiness.*': see Roland, *An Appeal to Impartial Posterity*, vol. 1, part 1, p. 116.

p. 238, ll. 26–7: *department of the Somme*: located in Picardy, in the north of France.

p. 240, ll. 10–17: '*It requires ... to contract the other.*': see Roland, *An Appeal to Impartial Posterity*, vol. 1, part 1, pp. 119–20.

p. 240, l. 27: *the banditti*: outlaws (Italian).

p. 241, l. 2: *jacobins*: Society of the Friends of the Constitution, or Jacobin Club, was the radical, left-wing political club which implemented the Reign of Terror, a period of violence at the outset of the French Revolution.

p. 241, l. 7: *Circe*: Greek mythological goddess of magic.

p. 241, l. 11–p. 242, l. 11: '*Twice a-week, ... recollected with a sigh ...*': see Roland, *An Appeal to Impartial Posterity*, vol. 1, part 2, pp. 41–2.

p. 242, ll. 3–4: *my daughter*: Eudora Roland (1781–1858), the Rolands' daughter and only child. She was twelve years old when her mother was executed. Madame Roland stipulated that the proceeds from the posthumous publication of her memoirs go to Eudora.

p. 242, l. 4: *her governess*: Mademoiselle Mignot; not further identified.

p. 243, ll. 1–14: '*To-day on a throne ... is easily overpowered.*': see Roland, *An Appeal to Impartial Posterity*, vol. 1, part 1, p. 1.

p. 244, l. 23: Maratists: followers of Jean-Paul Marat; see note to p. 243, l. 3, above.

p. 245, l. 24–p. 246, l. 7: '*I know of no laws ... my colleagues here.*': see Roland, *An Appeal to Impartial Posterity*, vol. 1, part 1, p. 8.

p. 246, l. 19: *the Carousel*: The Place du Carrousel is a public square, located at this time between the Tuileries Palace and Garden.

p. 246, l. 28–p. 247, l. 6: '*Citizens ... entrust my credentials.*': see Roland, *An Appeal to Impartial Posterity*, vol. 1, part 1, p. 9.

p. 247, l. 11: *Ross*: not identified.

p. 247, l. 24–p. 248, l. 12: '*Well!*'... *I wish to see him.*': see Roland, *An Appeal to Impartial Posterity*, vol. 1, part 1, p. 10.

p. 248, ll. 3–4: *the* twenty-two: Girondist members of the National Convention who would be brought to trial and condemned to death.

p. 248, l. 4: *Rabaut*: Jean Paul Rabaut de St. Étienne (1743–93), Protestant leader and humanist, negotiated with Guillaume-Chrétien de Malesherbes (1721–94) and members of parliament for the civil rights of Protestants and other social reforms granted in 1787. As a deputy to the Estates-General, Rabaut was instrumental in its transformation to the National Assembly and later elected as a moderate to the Convention. He was guillotined in 1793.

p. 248, l. 7: *Hérault Séchelles*: Marie-Jean Hérault de Séchelles (1759–94), French aristocrat, Royalist lawyer and skilled orator who later turned to the Jacobin faction and lobbied for the execution of Louis XVI. He was guillotined with his compatriot Georges Danton in 1794.

p. 248, l. 12: *Vergniaux*: Pierre-Victurnien Vergniaud (1753–93), Girondist deputy in the Legislative Assembly and the National Convention. As President of the Convention he presided over the debate of the execution of Louis XVI in January 1793. He ultimately cast his vote for death but was guillotined along with other Girondist leaders on 31 October 1793.

p. 248, l. 17–p. 249, l. 22: '*In the present state ... but too true.*': see Roland, *An Appeal to Impartial Posterity*, vol. 1, part 1, pp. 10–11.

p. 249, l. 24: *Louvet's*: Jean-Baptiste Louvet de Couvrai (1760–97), Girondist deputy to the National Convention and journalist. Editor of republican newspaper *La Sentinelle*, funded by Jean-Marie Roland as Minister of the Interior, in which he accused Robespierre in October 1792 of dictatorial ambition. In 1793 Louvet advised Girondist leaders to flee Paris and later fled to Caen with Buzot, where he wrote his *Mémoires de Louvet de Couvrai*, a portrait of Girondist policy and activity, published in full in 1889.

p. 250, l. 23–p. 251, l. 19: '*Citizens'... Paris that is ruining itself.*': see Roland, *An Appeal to Impartial Posterity*, vol. 1, part 1, p. 13.

p. 250, l. 23: sans-culottes: The working-class men of France, particularly in the cities, were political radicals with whom the Jacobins joined as the Revolution descended into violence. They called themselves the *sans-culottes* because they wore *pantalons*, or long pants, instead of the *culottes*, or knee-breeches, worn by bourgeois and noblemen, however this term applied to both working men and women.

p. 250, l. 26: *the* Marseillais *hymn*: 'La Marseillaise' is the national anthem of France. Written and composed in 1792, the French National Convention adopted it as the Republic's anthem in 1795.

p. 251, ll. 22–3: '*You will ... the Louvre.*': see Roland, *An Appeal to Impartial Posterity*, vol. 1, part 1, p. 14.

p. 251, l. 27: *Pasquier*: an old friend of the Rolands; not further identified.

p. 252, ll. 3–23: '*Have a little patience' ... they are good ones.*': see Roland, *An Appeal to Impartial Posterity*, vol. 1, part 1, p. 15.

p. 252, l. 28–p. 254, l. 2: '*To his apartment ... his honour, or his country.*': see Roland, *An Appeal to Impartial Posterity*, vol. 1, part 1, pp. 15–16.

p. 254, l. 14: *2d of September*: 2 September 1792, the beginning of the September Massacres. Twenty-four priests were being transported to prison when they were attacked by a mob that killed and mutilated their bodies. Later in the day, 150 priests in the convent of Carmelites were massacred.

p. 255, ll. 7–17: '*He is not at home.*' ... *all I have to say.*': see Roland, *An Appeal to Impartial Posterity*, vol. 1, part 1, p. 19.

p. 255, l. 27–p. 256, l. 1: '*I understand what it means,*' ... *make them wait*': see Roland, *An Appeal to Impartial Posterity*, vol. 1, part 1, p. 19.

p. 255, ll. 5–6: '*When people are going ... be decent.*': see Roland, *An Appeal to Impartial Posterity*, vol. 1, part 1, p. 19.

p. 256, ll. 9–18: '*We come,* citoyenne, ... *Here is another order*': see Roland, *An Appeal to Impartial Posterity*, vol. 1, part 1, p. 20.

p. 256, l. 9: citoyenne: a female citizen of the French Republic.

p. 257, ll. 7–10: '*How do you mean ... his armed force.*': see Roland, *An Appeal to Impartial Posterity*, vol. 1, part 1, pp. 20–1.

p. 257, l. 13: piano-forte: (Italian) also called the *fortepiano*, the predecessor to the piano.

p. 258, ll. 5–10: '*I have no objection ... I bestow it.*': see Roland, *An Appeal to Impartial Posterity*, vol. 1, part 1, p. 21.

p. 258, ll. 17–20: '*You have people ... who did not,*': see Roland, *An Appeal to Impartial Posterity*, vol. 1, part 1, p. 22.

p. 258, l. 27–p. 259, l. 15: 'Away with her ... *death I despise.*': see Roland, *An Appeal to Impartial Posterity*, vol. 1, part 1, pp. 22–3.

p. 259, l. 16: *Having arrived at the Abbaye*: On 1 June 1793 Roland was arrested for treason and imprisoned in the prison de l'Abbaye.

p. 259, ll. 24–8: '*Where is my room?*' ... *remain here.*': see Roland, *An Appeal to Impartial Posterity*, vol. 1, part 1, p. 23.

p. 259, ll. 24–5: *the wife of the keeper*: Madame Lavacquerie (dates unknown), wife of the jailer at prison de l'Abbaye in 1793.

p. 260, l. 3: *The keeper*: M. Lavacquerie (dates unknown), the jailer at prison de l'Abbaye in 1793.

p. 260, ll. 6–7: '*What would you ... capillaire and water.*': see Roland, *An Appeal to Impartial Posterity*, vol. 1, part 1, p. 23.

p. 260, l. 7: *capillaire*: simple syrup flavoured with orange flowers.

p. 260, ll. 10–19: '*It is so extraordinary ... important services.*': see Roland, *An Appeal to Impartial Posterity*, vol. 1, part 1, p. 23.

p. 260, l. 13: *Aristides*: (530–468 BC) Greek statesman and champion of justice immortalized by Plutarch in his *Lives*.

p. 260, l. 13: *Cato*: Marcus Porcius Cato Uticensis or Cato the Younger (95–46 BC), a Roman Stoic and statesman revered for his defence of the Roman republic in its last years.

p. 260, ll. 24–5: '*for,*' ... *serene countenance.*': see Roland, *An Appeal to Impartial Posterity*, vol. 1, part 1, p. 24.

p. 260, l. 28–p. 261, l. 2: '*Well then ... in prison.*': see Roland, *An Appeal to Impartial Posterity*, vol. 1, part 1, p. 24.

p. 261, ll. 7–14: '*I recalled the past ... for the present.*': see Roland, *An Appeal to Impartial Posterity*, vol. 1, part 1, p. 25.

p. 261, ll. 19–21: '*May I write? ... expences here?*': see Roland, *An Appeal to Impartial Posterity*, vol. 1, part 1, p. 25.

p. 261, l. 24: *her faithful maid*: Fleury: see note to p. 182, l. 3, above.

p. 261, l. 27: *Grandpré*: As Minister of the Interior, Jean-Marie Roland appointed Grandpré (dates unknown) as prison inspector. Fearing for the lives of the prisoners of the Abbaye amid rumours of a massacre in 1793, he appealed unsuccessfully to Georges Danton, President of the Committee of Public Safety, to distinguish between different types of prisoners. *Memoirs of Madame Roland: A Heroine of the French Revolution*, n. 1, p. 43; p. 44.

p. 261, l. 28–p. 262, l. 6: '*You shall write ... in two hours.*': see Roland, *An Appeal to Impartial Posterity*, vol. 1, part 1, pp. 25–6.

p. 262, ll. 11–27: '*If the convention ... yours to dispense.*': see Roland, *An Appeal to Impartial Posterity*, vol. 1, part 1, p. 28.

p. 263, l. 16–p. 264, l. 14: '*How did you ... by the departments.*': see Roland, *An Appeal to Impartial Posterity*, vol. 1, part 1, p. 29.

p. 263, l. 27: *Champagneux*: Luc-Antoine Donin de Champagneux (1744–1807), founder of the *Courrier de Lyon*, a republican newspaper in Lyons, became a close friend of the Rolands in 1785. In 1792 Champagneux served in Paris as an official in Jean-Marie Roland's Ministry of the Interior. He was imprisoned during the Reign of Terror from June 1793 until August 1794. Eudora Roland married one of his sons in 1796.

p. 264, ll. 2–3: *the minister of the home department*: Dominique Joseph Garat (1749–1833), French Basque politician, Minister of Justice in 1792.

p. 264, ll. 22–3: *Thomson's Seasons*: James Thomson (1700–48), Scottish poet and playwright. *The Seasons* was published 1726–30.

p. 264, l. 26: *Lives of Plutarch*: see note to p. 118, l. 10, above.

p. 264, ll. 26–7: *Hume's History of England*: David Hume (1711–76), Scottish Enlightenment philosopher. His *History of England* was published in six volumes from 1754 to 1761.

p. 264, l. 27: *Sheridan's Dictionary*: *Sheridan's Dictionary: A caution to gentlemen who use Sheridan's Dictionary. To which are added, for the assistance of foreigners and natives, select rules for pronouncing ... precision and elegance. The third edition* (c. 1780).

p. 264, l. 27–p. 265, l. 2: '*I would rather ... was from home.*': see Roland, *An Appeal to Impartial Posterity*, vol. 1, part 1, p. 31.

p. 265, l. 1: *Mrs. Macaulay*: Catharine Sawbridge Macaulay Graham's (see Hays, *Female Biography*, vol. 5, pp. 287–307) *History of England from the Accession of James I to that of the Brunswick Line* (1763–83). Like Roland, Macaulay was self-educated and a serious student of classical history and philosophy.

p. 265, ll. 6–11: '*At any rate, ... would go to repose.*': see Roland, *An Appeal to Impartial Posterity*, vol. 1, part 1, p. 31.

p. 265, l. 28–p. 266, l. 18: '*Whenever I have been ill ... company for myself.*': see Roland, *An Appeal to Impartial Posterity*, vol. 1, part 1, p. 32.

p. 267, ll. 6–13: '*Had I desired ... altogether gratuitous.*': see Roland, *An Appeal to Impartial Posterity*, vol. 1, part 1, p. 33.

p. 267, l. 19: '*My country is undone!*': see Roland, *An Appeal to Impartial Posterity*, vol. 1, part 1, p. 33.

p. 268, ll. 1–12: '*Farewell, my country! ... swallow you up.*': see Roland, *An Appeal to Impartial Posterity*, vol. 1, part 1, p. 34.

p. 268, ll. 16–17: '*I no longer ... to* know.': see Roland, *An Appeal to Impartial Posterity*, vol. 1, part 1, p. 34.

p. 268, l. 24: *the* Moniteur: *Gazette Nationale ou Le Moniteur Universal*, French newspaper founded in 1789.

p. 269, l. 7–p. 270, l. 4: '*Good-morrow,* Citoyenne,' ... *Adieu,* Citoyenne': see Roland, *An Appeal to Impartial Posterity*, vol. 1, part 1, p. 37.

p. 269, l. 24: *A woman*: not further identified.

p. 269, l. 25: *King Philip*: King Philip of Macedonia (382–336 BC), the father of Alexander the Great (356–323 BC). After restoring peace in his country he conquered Greece, with the exception of Sparta, using both diplomacy and force. He established the League of Corinth with representatives from each Greek state.

p. 270, l. 27–p. 271, l. 4: '*If I remain here ... benedictions* incognito.': see Roland, *An Appeal to Impartial Posterity*, vol. 1. part 1, p. 39.

p. 271, l. 16: *the mountain party*: The Jacobins were also called the *Montagnards* or the Mountaineers because their seats were high up in the Convention hall.

p. 271, l. 21: *ministers of justice and of the home department*: George Jacques Danton and Dominique Joseph Garat.

p. 271, l. 23–p. 272, l. 1: '*Factions pass away ... times of trouble.*': see Roland, *An Appeal to Impartial Posterity*, vol. 1, part 1, p. 45.

p. 272, l. 16: *the Thermomete, for the 9th of June*: The *Thermomètre du jour* was a daily newspaper published from 1791 to 1795.

p. 272, l. 18: *L. P. d'Orleans*: Louis-Philippe Joseph II, Duke of Orléans (1747–93) was the cousin of Louis XVI. In May 1789 he represented the nobility and clergy in the Estates-General but soon defected to the Third Estate, taking the name of Philippe-Egalité to show his support for the Revolution. When the duke's son, Louis Philippe I (1773–1850), defected to the Austrians, Philippe was condemned to death in November 1793.

p. 272, ll. 19–24: '*That the prisoner ... accustomed to repair.*': Roland, *An Appeal to Impartial Posterity*, vol. 1, part 1, p. 46.

p. 272, l. 21: *the wife of Buzot*: died on 30 July 1812; not further identified.

p. 272, l. 28: *the Bourbons*: the House of Bourbon, members of the Bourbon dynasty of French kings. The family also held thrones in Spain, Naples, Sicily and Parma.

p. 272, l. 10: *the editor of the paper*: not further identified.

p. 273, l. 13: *"the Mountaineers"*: the Jacobins; see note to p. 271, l. 16, above.

p. 273, ll. 24–5: *writing* Memoirs *of the times, the loss of which ... regretted*: see note to p. 289, ll. 5–10, below.

p. 273, l. 26: *insurrection of the 31st of May*: The Revolutionary Tribunal, the court for the trial of political offenders, was suspended on 31 May 1795.

p. 273, ll. 26–7: *outrages of the 2d of June*: Twenty-two Girondists were arrested, setting the stage for the Reign of Terror.

p. 274, ll. 4–11: '*The success ... will be avenged.*': see Roland, *An Appeal to Impartial Posterity*, vol. 1, part 2, p. 50.

p. 274, l. 16: *the* Père Duchesne: Jacques René Hébert's (1757–94) extremist newspaper incited the *sans-culottes* to violence with its obscenities, its hyperbole and its hate-mongering against the royal family – Marie-Antoinette in particular and, later, the Girondists. See Schama, *Citizens: A Chronicle of the French Revolution*, pp. 602; 604; 720.

p. 274, l. 18: *a Vendean*: one from Vendée, a region in western France on the Atlantic coast.

p. 274, l. 21: *the rebels of Vendée*: In February 1793 the conscription of French citizens of this intensely religious and Royalist region into the conflict prompted them to revolt in defence of the Catholic Church and the monarchy. Vendée rebels fought for two months, moving towards Paris before they were defeated by revolutionary forces. The violence rivaled the savagery of the September Massacres; 15,000 of the 30,000 Vendée fighters were killed.

p. 275, l. 4: *the minister*: George Jacques Danton; see note to p. 229, l. 28, above.

p. 275, ll. 10–17: '*How was I astonished ... of my situation.*': see Roland, *An Appeal to Impartial Posterity*, vol. 1, part 2, p. 52.

p. 275, l. 21: *an administrator*: not further identified.

p. 276, ll. 1–17: '*Am I the person ... the gaoler's discharge.*': see Roland, *An Appeal to Impartial Posterity*, vol. 1, part 2, pp. 52–3.

p. 276, ll. 20–2: *'Do you know ... at present?'*: see Roland, *An Appeal to Impartial Posterity*, vol. 1, part 2, p. 53.

p. 277, l. 9: *pavilion of Flora*: The Pavillon de Flore, in the Palais du Louvre, was a meeting place for the Committee of Public Safety during the Reign of Terror. Robespierre used the power of this committee to repress opposition and pronounce executions.

p. 277, ll. 12–17: *'I was ignorant ... Charlotte Cordey.'*: see Roland, *An Appeal to Impartial Posterity*, vol. 1, part 2, pp. 53–4.

p. 277, l. 17: *Charlotte Corday*: Charlotte Corday d'Armont (see Hays, *Female Biography*, vol. 3, pp. 432–5). A Girondist sympathizer from Caen, she assassinated the radical Jacobin Marat on 14 July 1793 in his bath. She had hoped to create a public spectacle by killing him before the Convention. Corday was taken first to the prison de l'Abbaye, then to the *Conciergerie*, and was executed in late July. See Schama, *Citizens: A Chronicle of the French Revolution*, pp. 737; 739–41.

p. 277, l. 26: *prince of Linanges*: Frédéric-Charles-Woldemar, Prince of Linanges (1724–1807) of German nobility, whose lands in Lorraine were annexed by the French in 1793.

p. 277, l. 28–p. 278, l. 3: *'that she should be happy ... return of peace.'*: see Roland, *An Appeal to Impartial Posterity*, vol. 1, part 2, p. 54.

p. 278, l. 9: *the worthy people who had adopted her daughter*: Roland's daughter, Eudora, resided for a time with the Creuzé-Latouches (not further identified) before her mother's death but was moved for reasons of safety to a boarding house run by Madame Godefroid (not further identified). After the Terror, Louis Bosc, the Rolands' close friend, became Eudora's guardian.

p. 278, ll. 11–12: *'Good morrow, Lamarre,'*: see Roland, *An Appeal to Impartial Posterity*, vol. 1, part 2, p. 54.

p. 278, l. 11: *Lamarre*: not further identified.

p. 278, ll. 15–17: *'What do you want? ... of the law.'*: see Roland, *An Appeal to Impartial Posterity*, vol. 1, part 2, p. 54.

p. 278, ll. 21–3: *'Whither are you going? ... follow me thither.'*: see Roland, *An Appeal to Impartial Posterity*, vol. 1, part 2, p. 55.

p. 278, l. 24–p. 279, l. 3: *'Let me sit down ... send thither accordingly.'*: see Roland, *An Appeal to Impartial Posterity*, vol. 1, part 2, p. 55.

p. 278, l. 28: *St. Pelagie*: The Prison of Sainte-Pélagie, where over 600 political prisoners were sent by the Revolutionary Tribunal, was second only to the *Conciergerie* on the Île-de-la-Cité as the most desolate Paris prison. Wealthy prisoners could rent a bed but others had to sleep on straw pallets in tiny cells with little air and water, with only the floor on which to relieve themselves. *Memoirs of Madame Roland: A Heroine of the French Revolution*, p. 794.

p. 279, ll. 3–4: *The landlord's son*: not further identified.

p. 279, ll. 5–6: *Two commissioners*: not further identified.

p. 279, l. 9: *the mayor*: Jérome Pétion (1756–94), Mayor of Paris from 1791–2.

p. 279, l. 24–p. 280, l. 1: *'There can certainly ... Get you gone,'*: see Roland, *An Appeal to Impartial Posterity*, vol. 1, part 2, p. 56.

p. 280, ll. 3–11: *'But, gentlemen, ... were saying of her.'*: see Roland, *An Appeal to Impartial Posterity*, vol. 1, part 2, p. 56.

p. 280, ll. 16–24: *'Commissioners of the section ... for a new detention.'*: see Roland, *An Appeal to Impartial Posterity*, vol. 1, part 2, p. 56.

p. 280, l. 17: *Beaurepaire*: In 1790 the revolutionary government divided Paris into forty-eight sections, each with its own armed assembly. Their purpose was to suppress citizen insurgency and they were given the power to issue warrants for arrest. Beaurepaire was Madame Roland's section, and she appealed to them to take action against her arrest.

p. 281, l. 10: lettres-de-cachet: A *letter-de-cachet* was an immediate summons given by the king to a political body, or by another authority, for the detention or imprisonment of an individual. It was often used indiscriminately and there was no legal recourse against it.

p. 281, ll. 21–4: '*Twice a–day, ... in which I lodged.*': see Roland, *An Appeal to Impartial Posterity*, vol. 1, part 2, p. 57.

p. 281, ll. 25–7: '*I am alone, ... the same to me.*': see Roland, *An Appeal to Impartial Posterity*, vol. 1, part 2, pp. 57–8.

p. 282, l. 5: *livres*: currency of France from 781–1795.

p. 282, ll. 8–9: '*But there is no ... purchase them.*': see Roland, *An Appeal to Impartial Posterity*, vol. 1, part 2, p. 58.

p. 282, l. 12: *The mistress of the house*: Madame Bouchard, mistress of the St Pélagie prison; not further identified.

p. 282, ll. 15–21: '*How then ... will make a trial.*': see Roland, *An Appeal to Impartial Posterity*, vol. 1, part 2, p. 58.

p. 282, l. 24: *madame Bouchaud*: Madame Bouchard; see note to p. 282, l. 12, above.

p. 283, l. 12–p. 284, l. 2: '*Feeling myself, ... its most determined enemies.*': see Roland, *An Appeal to Impartial Posterity*, vol. 1, part 2, p. 60.

p. 284, ll. 8–13: '*I am not content ... a just equilibrium.*': see Roland, *An Appeal to Impartial Posterity*, vol. 1., part 2, pp. 60–1.

p. 284, ll. 15–16: *Shaftesbury's Essay on Virtue*: Anthony Ashley Cooper, the Third Earl of Shaftesbury (1671–1713), scholar from an important Whig family whose education was designed and managed by John Locke. His philosophy was of equating moral judgement with self-reflection and combining intuition and reason to benefit all of society.

p. 284, l. 16: *the poetry of Thomson*: James Thomson; see note to p. 264, ll. 22–3.

p. 286, ll. 6–16: '*If this ... be the reward ... before a tribunal.*': see Roland, *An Appeal to Impartial Posterity*, vol. 1, part 2, pp. 63–4.

p. 286, l. 22: *wife of the gaoler*: see note to p. 282, l. 12, above.

p. 287, l. 4: *their children*: not further identified.

p. 287, ll. 5–6: *the fugitives, her friends*: Buzot and Pétion fled to Caen upon the arrest of the Girondist leaders in June 1793 to persuade the departments of Normandy to oppose the Jacobin Convention. See *Memoirs of Madame Roland: A Heroine of the French Revolution*, p. 255.

p. 287, l. 6: *Caen*: a city in Normandy near the northern coast of France.

p. 287, l. 13: *Bosc*: Louis-Augustin Guillaume Bosc; see note to p. 105, l. 3, above.

p. 287, l. 14: le Jardin de Plantes: *Jardin des Plantes*, botanical garden in Paris.

p. 287, l. 17: *an amiable woman*: This 'amiable woman' is identified by Roland as 'my dear friend Sophie', i.e. Sophie Cannet. See *Memoirs of Madame Roland: A Heroine of the French Revolution*, p. 116.

p. 287, l. 20: *Tacitus*: Publius (or Gaius) Cornelius Tacitus (AD 56–117), Roman senator who denounced the emperors of the Roman Empire in his moral political histories.

p. 288, ll. 15–16: *the brave Normans*: people from Normandy, a region in northern France.

p. 288, ll. 21–6: '*That cowardice ... the ignorant multitude.*': see Roland, *An Appeal to Impartial Posterity*, vol. 1, part 2, p. 67.

p. 289, ll. 5–10: *her* Historical Memoirs … *to the flames*: Roland's memoirs were divided into two sections; the 'Historical Memoirs' or 'Historical Notes', written first, and the 'Private Memoirs'. The 'Historical Notes' included revealing portraits of the revolutionaries with whom Roland was intimately acquainted. Roland had been 'told that her notebooks had been thrown on the fire', leading her to rewrite them, but some of the pages were later found to have been saved. See *Memoirs of Madame Roland: A Heroine of the French Revolution*, p. 16.

p. 289, l. 23: *Bouchaud*: jailer of the Prison of Sainte-Pélagie.

p. 289, l. 25–p. 290, l. 3: '*I took a resolution … torn me in pieces.*': see Roland, *An Appeal to Impartial Posterity*, vol. 1, part 2, p. 77.

p. 290, l. 4: *The 10th of August*: the previous year, on 10 August 1792, Tuileries Palace was stormed by the Parisian mob and Louis XVI was arrested.

p. 290, ll. 9–15: '*Could I persuade myself … desirous to destroy.*': see Roland, *An Appeal to Impartial Posterity*, vol. 1, part 2, pp. 77–8.

p. 290, ll. 17–18: *a woman confined for some trifling offence*: not further identified.

p. 290, l. 18–p. 291, l. 4: '*Not, but I was well able … on such occasions.*': see Roland, *An Appeal to Impartial Posterity*, vol. 1, part 2, p. 79.

p. 290, ll. 19–20: Tout sied bien au généreux courage: 'everything becomes a generous soul' (French).

p. 290, l. 20: *Favonius*: Marcus Favonius (90–42 BC), Roman statesman during the last days of the Roman republic.

p. 291, ll. 12–19: '"*Madame Roland was indisposed*" … "*to maintain equality.*': see Roland, *An Appeal to Impartial Posterity*, vol. 1, part 2, p. 80.

p. 292, ll. 2–14: '*Thus, once more, … but cannot save.*': see Roland, *An Appeal to Impartial Posterity* vol. 1., part 2, pp. 80–1.

p. 292, ll. 17–18: *the wife of a justice of the peace*: not further identified.

p. 292, ll. 19–20: *the wife of the president of the revolutionary tribunal*: not further identified.

p. 292, l. 21: *madame Petion*: Madame Pétion (dates unknown), the wife of Jérome Pétion (see note to p. 279, l. 9, above).

p. 292, ll. 21–6: '*I little thought … lead to our disgrace.*': see Roland, *An Appeal to Impartial Posterity*, vol. 1, part 2, p. 81.

p. 292, l. 23: Mairie: town hall, mayor's office (French).

p. 293, ll. 3–16: '*My pen … political testament.*': see Roland, *An Appeal to Impartial Posterity*, vol. 1, part 1, pp. 123–4.

p. 293, l. 6: *duodecimo*: 'twelfth' (Latin).

p. 293, l. 19–p. 294, l. 6: 'This, … *remain in my power.*': see Roland, *An Appeal to Impartial Posterity*, vol. 1, part 1, p. 124.

p. 294, ll. 9–27: '*I should despise myself … nor virtue to repair them.*': see Roland, *An Appeal to Impartial Posterity*, vol. 2, part 3, sec. 1, p. 5.

p. 294, l. 17: Historical Notices: *Historical Memoirs*; see note to p. 289, ll. 5–10, above.

p. 295, ll. 2–3: *a physician*: not further identified.

p. 295, ll. 6–23: '*How can you know … to my disadvantage.*': see Roland, *An Appeal to Impartial Posterity*, vol. 1, part 1, p. 185.

p. 296, ll. 1–15: '*I write not … and history their avenger.*': see Roland, *An Appeal to Impartial Posterity*, vol. 1. part 1, p. 186.

p. 296, ll. 21–3: '*For what … system of the world.*': see Roland, *An Appeal to Impartial Posterity*, vol. 1. part 1, p. 186.

p. 296, l. 21: *emmet*: an ant.

p. 297, ll. 2–18: '*Brought up in retirement ... so many happy days.*': see Roland, *An Appeal to Impartial Posterity*, vol. 1, part 1, pp. 188–9.

p. 297, l. 20–p. 298, l. 1: '*I have wearied no one ... for your instruction.*': see Roland, *An Appeal to Impartial Posterity*, vol. 1, part 1, pp. 189–90.

p. 298, ll. 5–7: '*Speak, ...in the face*.*': Roland, *An Appeal to Impartial Posterity*, vol. 1, part 1, p. 191.

p. 298, l. 15–p. 299, l. 2: '*It was not*'... *any advantage.*': Champagneux, *The Works (never before published) of Jeanne-Marie[sic] Phlipon Roland, Wife of the ex-Minister of the Interior, containing her philosophical and literary essays ... her correspondence, and her travels to which are annexed the justificative documents relative to her imprisonment and condemnation with a Preliminary Discourse*, p. xlviii.

p. 298, l. 24: coup-de-grâce: 'stroke of grace' (French), used here to mean to quickly put an end to suffering.

p. 299, l. 15: Conciergerie: a former royal palace and prison in Paris.

p. 299, ll. 15–16: Place de la Révolution: 'Place of the Revolution' (French), renamed from Place de la Concorde, a public square in Paris, during the French Revolution. A guillotine was erected here, where King Louis XVI was executed on 21 January 1793.

p. 299, l. 19: *Riouffe*: Honoré-Jean Riouffe (1764–1813), Girondist taken in October 1793 to the Conciergerie where Madame Roland had been transported from Sainte-Pélagie, and they were sometimes able to speak to one another. The sensitive description of her in his *Mémoires d'un détenu* (1794), included here by Hays, reveals his intense admiration for her. He was released in July 1794.

p. 299, l. 21–p. 302, l. 18: '*The blood of the twenty-two ... till the latest period of my existence.*': Champagneux, *The Works*, p. xlix.

p. 301, l. 25: *LeMarche*: had been in charge of the printing of *assignats* (see note to p. 301, l. 26, below); not further identified.

p. 301, l. 26: *assignats*: 'assigns' (French), paper bills issued during the Revolution to pay down France's debt and backed by clerical lands seized by the new government. While the printing of *assignats* provided a temporary stopgap, their numbers quickly tripled, creating rapid inflation and public panic.

p. 302, l. 20–p. 303, l. 3: '*If fate had allowed me ... to imitate his style.*': see Roland, *An Appeal to Impartial Posterity*, vol. 2, part 4, sec. 3, pp. 81–2.

p. 302, ll. 23–4: *the Macaulay*: Catharine Sawbridge Macaulay; see note to p. 265, l. 1, above.

p. 303, ll. 12–13: *the 30th of May, 1790, the day of the federation of Lyons*: Parades and staged dramas celebrating the Revolution swept the country in the year following the storming of the Bastille. The federation in Lyons took place on 30 May 1790. It was a huge, neoclassical spectacle, and in spite of the rain, delegations from the regions of Brittany, Lorraine, the Mâconnais and Provence participated and 50,000 people amassed on the banks of the Rhône to watch and chant the revolutionary oath. Madame Roland's firsthand account of the celebration may have been distributed separately or printed in their friend, Champagneux's, *Courrier de Lyon*, but in either case would have been published anonymously.

p. 303, l. 15: fête: festival.

p. 305, ll. 6–12: '*I am ashamed ... and I will give it.*': see Champagneux, *The Works*, p. xxvi.

p. 305, l. 24: *her husband's brother*: Pierre Roland de la Platière, see note to p. 203, l. 23, above.

p. 305, l. 26: *Eudora*: see note to p. 242, ll. 3–4.

p. 306, ll. 2–16: '*To-morrow, ... those of her parents.*': see Champagneux, *The Works*, pp. xxix–xxx.

p. 306, ll. 23–4: *Mlademoiselle Mignot*: see note to p. 242, l. 4, above.

p. 307, ll. 18–27: '*While they keep me ... Such is my resolution.*': see Champagneux, *The Works*, p. xxxiii.

p. 308, ll. 10–14: '*I shall not ... ruined and undone.*': see Champagneux, *The Works*, p. xxxiv.

p. 308, ll. 17–25: '*He is confident! ... invited to it by me.*': see Champagneux, *The Works*, p. xxxv.

p. 309, ll. 2–3: Testament Politique: *Testament politique de l'Angleterre* (1780).

p. 309, ll. 15–16: *a memorial addressed to her section*: Roland appealed to her section, Beaure-paire, arguing the injustice of her treatment and defending Jean-Marie Roland's and her own republican patriotism.

p. 309, l. 17: *The president*: not further identified.

p. 309, l. 24–p. 310, l. 9: '*But there is an appearance ... a pride in braving them.*': see Champagneux, *The Works*, pp. xlv–xlvi.

p. 310, l. 2: *Valazé*: Charles-Eléonor Dufriche de Valazé (1751–93), one of the Girondist leaders arrested on the night of 1 June 1793 and condemned to die on 31 October 1793.

p. 310, ll. 12–13: *a woman, to whose care he had confided them*: not further identified.

p. 310, l. 19–p. 311, l. 19: '*During the first twenty-five years ... her tears and her regret.*': see Champagneux, *The Works*, pp. liii–lv.

p. 311, l. 11: *Lecoq*: not further identified.

p. 311, l. 12: *Fleury*: the maid of Roland; see note to p. 182, l. 3, above.

p. 311, ll. 16–19: '*a woman insane ... her tears and her regret.*': *European Magazine, and London Review*, vol. 44, June–December (London: Philological Society of London, 1803), p. 120.

p. 312, l. 14: *Rouen*: A city in northern France on the Seine, the historic capital of Normandy. Jean-Marie Roland took refuge with unidentified friends there when Madame Roland insisted that he leave Paris in June 1793.

p. 312, l. 18: *citizen Normand*: not further identified.

p. 313, l. 1: *one of the sons of Chmpagneux*: In 1796 Eudora married the son of Luc-Antoine Champagneux, Pierre-Léon Champagneux (1777–1864).

p. 313, l. 6: *ISABELLA DE ROSARES*: Hays conflates *Isabella (de) Rosares/Roseres/Roser/ Rosell/Rosés* with *Isabella de Josa/Iosa/Joya/Joie*. See M. Lop, *Recuerdos Ignacianos en Barcelona* (Barcelona: Cristianisme, 2005). All of the information in Hays refers to the latter, Isabella de Josa. Isabella de Rosares (Barcelona, *c.* 1491–1554), born Ferrer, daughter of Francesc Ferrer and Caterina, a member of a distinguished bourgeois family. She married Pere Joan Roser. See J. Reites, 'Ignatius and the Ministry with Women', *Way*, Sup. 74 (1992), pp. 7–19. In 1543, once a widow, she went to Rome and founded the female branch of The Society of Jesus. See J. Martínez, 'Mujeres Jesuíticas y Mujeres Jesuitas', in *A Companhía de Jesus na Peninsula Ibérica nos sécs. XVI e XVII* (Porto: Universidade do Porto, 2004), pp. 369–83. Isabella de Josa (Lérida, 1508–*c.* 1549, Rome), born D'Orrit, married Gillem Ramón de Josa i Cardona (d. 1539) in 1535. See X. Lampillas, *Saggio storico-apologetico* (Genoa, 1782). *Ensayo histórico-apologético de la literatura española*, trans. J. Amar y Borbón (Zaragoza: Blas Miedes, Real Sociedad Económica Aragonesa de Amigos del País, 1782–90). See M. Pérez-Toribio, 'From Mother to Daughter: Educational Lineage in the Correspondence between the Countess of Palamós and Estefanía de Requeséns', in A. Cruz and R. Hernández (eds.), *Women's Literacy in Early Modern Spain and the New World* (London: Ashgate, 2011), p. 72. She was a humanist, Latinist, philosopher and specialist on the theology of Dunn Scottus, author of *Tristis Isabella: De ortodoxa fide*. See M. Serrano, *Apuntes para una Biblioteca de autores españoles* (Madrid: Atlas, 1975), vol. 277.

p. 313, l. 7: *preached*: Josa preached in Barcelona, in the Church of the Angels and in the Cathedral. See R. Lull, *Exposición de los Cánticos de amor*, 2 vols (Mallorca: Frau, 1760), vol. 1, p. 98.

p. 313, ll. 8–9: *In the reign of Paul III*: Alessandro Farnese (1468–1549), the 220th pope, reigned 1534–49.

p. 313, l. 9: *she repaired to Rome*: Josa, a supporter of Saint-Ignatius Loyola, used to beg in the streets for the poor. See W. Meissner, *The Psychology of a Saint: Ignatius Loyola* (New York: Yale University Press, 1994). This being a humiliation for her wealthy relatives, she was forced to travel to Italy. She left Barcelona with Roseres in April 1543. See F. Torres, *Memorias* (Barcelona: Verdaguer, 1836).

p. 313, l. 9: *by her eloquence*: Josa defended her theological conclusions before Paul III and the College of Cardinals, arguing for a lax interpretation of Saint Paul's doctrine concerning the prohibition for women to speak at church. See J. Keyssler, *Neueste Reisen* (Hannover: Forster & Erben, 1740). The English translation is *Travels through Germany*, 2nd edn (London: Linde, 1756). The Pope ordered her not to preach, but only to read publicly. Thenceforth, she kept a book open while preaching, feigning that she was reading. See H. Rahner, *Saint-Ignatius Loyola: Letters to Women* (New York: Herder & Herder, 1960), pp. 67–70.

p. 313, l. 10: *she converted the Jews*: Hays likely took the reference, though originally noting 'many Jews', from de La Croix, *Dictionnaire historique*, vol. 3, p. 337, who likely got his information from B. J. Feijóo, *Teatro crítico universal* (Madrid: Ibarra, 1726), vol. 1, discourse 16; English translation: *An Essay on Woman, Or, Physiological and Historical Defence of the Fair Sex. Translated from the Spanish of* El Theatro Crítico (London: W. Bingley, 1765), in P. Morris (ed.), *Conduct Literature for Women 1720–1770* (London: Pickering & Chatto, 2004), vol. 6, pp. 301–418. Johan Georg Keyssler, a German intellectual, Fellow of the Royal Society in London, published *Travels through Germany, Bohemia, Hungary, Switzerland, Italy and Lorrain* (Hannover: Nicolai Forster & Johns Erben, 1740), and translated it into English in the 1740s or 1750s. About Isabel de Rosares is said, 'By her learning, piety, and munificence, she converted several Jews and hereticks to the faith' (pp. 324–5).

p. 313, ll. 12–13: *Walter Singer*: (d. *c.* 1719), a dissenting minister who was imprisoned for his beliefs.

p. 313, l. 15: *imprisonment for non-conformity*: religious dissidence.

p. 313, l. 16: *Charles II*: Charles II, King of England, Scotland and Ireland (1630–85). His authoritarian rule (1660–85) discontented the Parliament and led to the Great Revolution and the overthrow of the Stuart Dynasty in 1688.

p. 313, l. 16: *Mrs. Portnell*: Elizabeth Portnell (dates unknown), mother of Rowe. She is a person 'of great worth and piety'. See Rowe, 'The Life of Mrs. Elizabeth Rowe'. See. T. Rowe, *The Life of Mrs. Elizabeth Rowe. With Some Account of Mr. Walter Singer, Her Father, and Mr. Thomas Rowe, Her Consort* (Boston, N.E.: re-printed and sold by Rogers and Fowle, 1747).

p. 313, l. 22: *Three daughters*: Elizabeth and two others. '[O]ne died in childhood; the other survived to her twentieth year, a lovely concurrent in the race of virtue and glory'. The two others are not identified. See Rowe, *The Life of Mrs. Elizabeth Rowe*.

p. 314, l. 20: *two of her friends*: not further identified.

p. 315, l. 7: *lord Weymouth*: Possibly Thomas Thynne, first Viscount Weymouth (1640–1714), who was an English politician and educator.

p. 315, l. 9: *38th chapter of Job*: one of the books of the Old Testament. It tries to give an answer to the troubling question: why do the righteous suffer?

p. 315, l. 11: *bishop Ken*: Thomas Ken (1647–1711), a prominent Anglican cleric.

p. 315, ll. 12–13: *Mr. Thynne*: Henry Thynne (*c.* 1674/5–1708), Member of Parliament and eldest son to Thomas Thynne.

p. 315, l. 18: *Jerusalem of Tasso*: *Jerusalem Delivered*, epic written by the Italian poet Torquato Tasso (1544–95) and published for the first time in 1581.

p. 315, ll. 19–20: *Thomas Rowe*: English poet and scholar (1687–1715) who studied at Leyden, proficient in Greek, Latin and French.

p. 315, l. 20: *rev. Benoni Rowe*: (1658–1706), independent minister.

p. 316, ll. 21–4: *"In all the … breaks his heart."*: a segment from Langhorne's (see note to p. 316, l. 27, below) translation of John Milton's (1608–74) *Epitaphium Damonis* (*c.* 1646). See *The Critical Review or Annals of Literature by a Society of Gentlemen* (London: Printed for A. Hamilton, 1765), vol. 19, pp. 172–3.

p. 316, l. 27: *Langhorne*: John Langhorne (dates unknown), reverend, historian and poet.

p. 317, ll. 8–11: *"Unhappy day … heart beguile."*: From Elizabeth Rowe's poem entitled 'On the Anniversary Return of the Day on which Mr. Rowe Died'. See E. S. Rowe, *The Works of Mrs. Elizabeth Rowe in Four Volumes* (London: J. & A. Arch, 1796), vol. 3, pp. 125–6.

p. 317, l. 24: *Mrs. Thynne*: Grace Thynne (née Strode) (*c.* 1676–1725), daughter and heiress of Sir George Strode (b. before 1675) and Grace FitzJames (b. before 1675).

p. 317, l. 26: *the lady Brooke*: Mary Thynne (*c.* 1702–20), wife of William Greville, seventh Baron Brooke (1695–1727).

p. 318, ll. 1–2: *the countess of Hertford*: Frances Seymour, Duchess of Somerset (1699–1754), writer, Lady of the Bedchamber and patroness of the poet James Thomson (1700–48).

p. 318, ll. 12–13: "Friendship in Death": *Friendship in Death: in Twenty Letters from the Dead to the Living*, a popular devotional work published in 1728.

p. 318, ll. 14–15: *"Letters, Moral and Entertaining"*: published 1729–32, a series in three parts.

p. 319, l. 6: *it was published*: Actually, it was published in 1736, in eight books. Two books were added and the ten-book edition came out in 1739.

p. 319, l. 11: *a disorder*: an unidentified condition, possibly a stroke.

p. 319, l. 19: *Mr. Pope*: Alexander Pope (1688–1744), a famous neoclassical, English poet.

p. 319, ll. 19–20: *"Dying Christian's Address to his Soul"*: religious poem by Alexander Pope sometime between 1708 and 1712.

p. 319, l. 27: *a friend*: not further identified.

p. 320, l. 2: *her servant*: not further identified.

p. 320, l. 5: *A physician and surgeon*: not further identified.

p. 320, l. 28: *earl of Orrery*: John Boyle, also fifth Earl of Cork (1707–62), an Irish writer and nobleman.

p. 320, l. 28: *James Theobald*: Likely, James Theobald, F.R.S. (1688–1759), merchant and natural historian. See J. H. Appleby, 'Notes and Records of the Royal Society of London', 50:2 (July 1996), pp. 179–89.

p. 321, l. 1: *Sarah Rowe*: not further identified.

p. 321, l. 4: *Dr. Watts*: Dr Isaac Watts (1674–1748), an English reverend and writer of hymns.

p. 321, ll. 5–6: *Devout Exercises*: *Devout Exercises of the Heart in Meditation and Soliloquy, Prayer and Praise* (1737).

p. 321, ll. 9–10: *two volumes of her miscellaneous works*: E. S. Rowe and T. Rowe, *The Miscellaneous Works in Prose and Verse of Mrs Elizabeth Rowe*, 2 vols (London: Printed for R. Hett and R. Dodsley, 1739).

p. 321, ll. 12–15: *"The softness … character."*: From an unidentified poetical publication by Matthew Prior (see note to p. 321, l. 14, below).

p. 321, l. 14: *Matthew Prior*: English poet and diplomat (1664–1721) who wrote to Rowe and made declarations of love.

p. 321, l. 16: *the writers*: Alexander Pope, Samuel Richardson, Dr Samuel Johnson.

p. 321, l. 16: *her Life*: Her husband died in 1715 and Elizabeth Rowe died in 1737.

p. 322, ll. 11–18: *"I can appeal ... melancholy theme."*: From S. Burder, *Memoirs of Eminently Pious Women, A New Edition*, 2 vols (Philadelphia, PA: J. J. Woodward, 1836), vol. 1, p. 234; originally in Thomas Gibbons, *Memoirs of Eminently Pious Women who were Ornaments to Their Sex, Blessing to Their Families, and Edifying Examples to the Church and World* (London: Printed for J. Buckland, 1777).

p. 322, l. 12: *an old and intimate friend*: not further identified.

p. 322, l. 28–p. 323, l. 3: *"It was not ... regret."*: Burder, *Memoirs of Eminently Pious Women*, 2 vols (London: J. Duncan, Longman and Co., 1827), vol. 1, p. 235.

p. 323, l. 10: *her biographer*: Theophilus Rowe, the brother-in-law of Elizabeth Rowe. He wrote *The Life of Mrs. Elizabeth Rowe*.

p. 323, ll. 9–11: *"It is but ... an idiot."*: see Rowe, *The Works of Mrs. Elizabeth Rowe in Four Volumes*, vol. 4, p. 341.

p. 324, l. 1: *the bookseller*: John Dunton (1659–1733), an English bookseller and author.

p. 324, ll. 11–16: *"Charge ... immortality."*: see Rowe, *The Works of Mrs. Elizabeth Rowe in Four Volumes*, vol. 4, pp. 346–7.

p. 324, l. 11: *Mr. Bowden*: John Bowden (d. 1750), an English Presbyterian minister.

p. 324, l. 23–p. 325, l. 10: *"The solitude ... name of virtue."*: Rowe, *The Works of Mrs. Elizabeth Rowe in Four Volumes*, vol. 1, p. 138.

p. 326, ll. 1–4: *"I never ... the poor."*: Rowe, *The Works of Mrs. Elizabeth Rowe in Four Volumes*, vol. 4, p. 352.

p. 326, ll. 10–14: *"It was one ... fortune."*: not corroborated. Rowe, *The Works of Mrs. Elizabeth Rowe in Four Volumes*, vol. 4, pp. 353–4.

p. 327, ll. 1–12: *"Her stature ... wont to create."*: S. Burder, *Memoirs of Eminently Pious Women* (London: J. Duncan, Longman and Co., 1827), vol. 1, pp. 416–17.

p. 327, l. 16: *Martial*: Marcus Valerius Martialis (*c*. AD 38/41–*c*. 102/4), Latin poet.

p. 327, l. 16: *extols this lady*: Claudia Rufina is praised by Martial in a poem (*Epigrams*, 11.53) which extols her beauty, marriage and childbearing.

p. 327, l. 18: *Aulus Rufus Pudens*: According to Martial (*Epigrams*, 4.13), his friend Pudens, a Roman soldier (centurion), was married to a certain Claudia Peregrina, who may be the same person as Claudia Rufina.

p. 327, ll. 18–19: *Bononian philosopher*: Pudens was believed (from the sixteenth century) to have been an early Christian, the same person as the Pudens mentioned in the New Testament (2 Timothy 4:21).

p. 327, ll. 21–3: *author ... both in verse and prose*: Like Pudens, the name Claudia is mentioned in 2 Timothy 4:21. As a result, Claudia Rufina became a British celebrity from the sixteenth century on when texts that originally had no connection were brought together and used to further both Christian and Protestant agendas. Her alleged authorship is unconfirmed in the surviving ancient sources.

p. 327, ll. 25–7: *Elizabeth ... born in 1529 ... her sisters*: Lady Elizabeth Russell (née Cooke) (1528–1609) was the third daughter of Sir Anthony Cooke (*c*. 1505/6–76) and Anne Fitzwilliam (d. 1553), born at Gidea Hall, Essex. Hays follows Ballard's erroneous year of birth, 1529. She was one of nine children, including four other sisters. Among them were Mildred Cecil, Lady Burleigh (1526–89) (see Hays, *Female Biography*, vol. 2, pp. 55–9); Lady Anne Bacon (*c*. 1528–1610) (see Hays, *Female Biography*, vol. 1, pp. 235–8), and Katherine Killigrew (née Cooke) (1542–83) (See Hays, *Female Biography*, vol. 4, pp. 483–5). Another daughter, Margaret, died in 1558. Cooke educated all of his children in humanist languages and literatures, but his daughters were especially renowned for their intellectual talents.

p. 328, l. 3: *sir Thomas Hobby*: (1530–66), diplomat and translator, most famously of Baldassare Castiglione's *Il Cortegiano* (London, 1561). He married Elizabeth on 27 June 1558.

p. 328, l. 4: *the queen*: Elizabeth I (1533–1603; r. 1558–1603) (see Hays, *Female Biography*, vol. 4, pp. 70–295).

p. 328, l. 10: *Bisham*: a former abbey awarded to Sir Philip Hoby in 1552, inherited by Thomas Hoby; the location of the tomb designed by Elizabeth.

p. 328, l. 11: *Sir Philip Hobby*: (*c.* 1504/5–58), half-brother to Thomas, courtier, diplomat and Privy Councillor to Edward VI (1537–53; r. 1547–53).

p. 328, l. 14: *Edward*: (1560–1617), Edward Hoby was a courtier, diplomat and MP for Kent and Berkshire.

p. 328, ll. 14–15: *Elizabeth, Anne, and Thomas posthumous*: Elizabeth and Anne were born by 1564 and died in 1571, within a few days of each other; after a troublesome youth, Thomas entered Gray's Inn in 1588 to study law, and went on to become a JP and MP and the third husband of the puritan diarist and heiress Margaret Hoby (née Dakins; 1571–1633) of East Riding, Yorkshire.

p. 328, l. 17: *lord treasurer Burleigh*: William Cecil (*c.* 1520/21–98), politician, courtier and ultimately Secretary of State and Treasurer to Elizabeth I; he was husband to Elizabeth's eldest sister, Mildred.

p. 328, l. 20: *John Russel*: (1553–84), married to Elizabeth in December 1574, when she would have been thirty-four years of age and he nineteen. He predeceased his father, denying Elizabeth the title Countess of Bedford.

p. 328, l. 21: *Francis Russel*: (1526–85), second earl of Bedford, member of Elizabeth I's Privy Council, among the dozen wealthiest peers in the realm.

p. 328, l. 27: *James West*: eighteenth-century London lawyer and fellow antiquarian to Ballard.

p. 329, l. 1: *One son*: Francis Russell (1579–80).

p. 327, ll. 2–3: *two daughters, Anne and Elizabeth*: Anne Herbert (b. 1578); Elizabeth (1576–1600).

p. 329, ll. 3–4: *Elizabeth ... survived her father but a short time*: This is an error; Elizabeth (see note to p. 329, ll. 2–3, above) died in June 1600, shortly after the marriage of her sister Anne to Henry, Lord Herbert, son of the Earl of Worcester. Her father, John Russell, died in 1584.

p. 329, ll. 5–6: *she died in consequence of wounding the fore-finger*: her cause of death is unknown.

p. 329, ll. 26–7: *a religious tract*: a translation of Bishop John Ponet's (d. 1556) *Diallacticon viri boni et literati, de veritate, natura, atque substantia corporis et sanguinis Christi in eucharistia*. The original was published by Sir Anthony Cooke, Elizabeth's father, in Strasbourg in 1557, where he was in exile with Ponet during the regime of Mary Tudor. Elizabeth's translation was completed many years prior to its publication in 1605.

p. 330, ll. 2–3: *Anne Herbert*: see note to p. 329, ll. 2–3, above.

p. 330, l. 3: *lord H. Herbert*: Henry Somerset, first Marquess of Worcester (d. 1646).

p. 330, l. 9: *her nephew Cecil*: Robert Cecil (1563–1612), first Earl of Salisbury, courtier and Secretary of State under both Elizabeth I and James 1, and son to Mildred and William Cecil.

p. 330, ll. 11–13: *Your lordships ... Russel, Dowager.*: see *Biographia Britannica*, vol. 5, p. 3542.

p. 331, l. 1: *her daughter, her brother, sister*: daughter Elizabeth Russell; brother not identified; sister Katherine Cooke Killigrew.

p. 331, l. 2: *Mr. Noke*: Thomas Noke, esq. (1480–1567), a Berkshire neighbour.

p. 331, ll. 5–6: *Thomas Wriothesley, earl of Southampton*: Sir Thomas Wriothesley, fourth Earl of Southampton (1607–67), English statesman, Lord High-Treasurer (1660–7).

p. 331, l. 6: *was born in 1636*: Her date of birth is unknown. She was baptized on 19 September 1737.

p. 331, l. 6: *Her mother*: the French Huguenot Rachel de Massue (1603–40).

p. 331, ll. 7–8: *Henry de Massey, baron of Rovigny*: Henry de Massue, marquis de Ruvigny and Raineval, French general of repute, deputy-general of the Huguenots of the court of Versailles, sometime ambassador at the English court.

p. 331, l. 12: *earl of Strafford*: Thomas Wentworth, First Earl of Strafford (1593–1641), one of the main advisors to King Charles I.

p. 331, l. 17: *king*: Charles I (1600–49).

p. 331, l. 19: *Burnet*: Gilbert Burnet, also Bishop Burnet (1643–1715), Scottish theologian and historian, and Bishop of Salisbury.

p. 331, ll. 19–21: *"A fast friend ... which he could bestow."*: Hays took this quotation from the Introduction to the *Letters of Lady Russell*. There is a similar description of the Earl of Southampton in Bishop Burnet's *History of His Own Time, vol. I. From the Restoration of King Charles II to the Settlement of King William and Queen Mary at the Revolution* (London: Thomas Ward, 1724), pp. 95–6.

p. 331, l. 22: *the Restoration*: the period following King Charles II's restoration to the throne of England (1660–85).

p. 331, l. 25: *Elizabeth*: Lady Elizabeth Wriothesley, Viscountess Campden (1636–80).

p. 331, l. 25: *Edward Noel*: Edward Noel, first Earl of Gainsborough (1641–89), British peer and member of the House of Lords.

p. 331, l. 26: *baron Wriothesley, of Titchfield*: Elizabeth, as the eldest daughter of the Earl of Southampton, inherited Titchfield State (Hampshire), and her husband the title.

p. 332, l. 1: *Francis lord Vaughan*: Francis Vaughan, Lord Vaughan (*c.* 1638–67), MP for Carmarthershire (Wales), married Lady Rachel in 1654.

p. 332, l. 2: *earl of Rocraw, earl of Carberry*: Richard Vaughan, second Earl of Carbery and first Baron Vaughan (*c.* 1600–86), Welsh soldier, peer and politician. The correct spelling is Carbery, which refers to a territory in Ireland, in what is now County Cork.

p. 332, l. 4: *William lord Russel*: (also Russell). William Russell, Lord Russell (1639–83), English politician, leading member of the Country Party and conspirator.

p. 332, ll. 4–5: *William earl of Bedford*: William Russell, first Duke of Bedford (1613–1700), English politician and soldier for the Parliamentarian army.

p. 332, l. 5: *one son and two daughters*: Hays is incorrect here. The Russells had four children: Rachel Russell (1674–1725); Katherine Russell (1676–1711); Wriothesley Russell, second Duke of Bedford (1680–1711); and daughter Ann (1671–2), who did not survive infancy.

p. 332, l. 8: *Charles II*: Charles II (1630–85), King of England (r. 1660–85).

p. 332, ll. 9–10: *duke of Monmouth*: James Scott, Duke of Monmouth (1649–85), illegitimate son of king Charles II, claimant to the English throne.

p. 332, l. 10: *lord Grey*: Thomas Grey, second Earl of Stamford (*c.* 1654–1720), British peer and politician.

p. 332, l. 11: *earl of Shaftesbury*: Anthony Ashley Cooper, first Earl of Shaftesbury (1621–83), English politician, member of the Council of State during the Commonwealth, and member of Charles II's Cabinet Council and Lord Chancellor.

p. 332, l. 13: *duke of York*: King James II, also called Duke of York and Duke of Albany (1633–1701).

p. 332, l. 22: *A council of six*: The aristocratic members of the Country Party who participated in an alleged Whig conspiracy, known as the Rye House plot, to raise rebellion by
seizing the king's guards and, thereby, in law, to kill the king because of his pro-Roman
Catholic policies.

p. 332, l. 23: *Essex*: Arthur Capell, first Earl of Essex (bap. 1632, d. 1683), English statesman.

p. 332, l. 24: *Howard*: William Howard, third Baron Howard of Escrick (*c.* 1630–94), English
parliamentarian soldier and nobleman. He gave account of meetings which mainly led
to Russell's conviction.

p. 332, l. 24: *Algernon Sidney*: Algernon Sidney (1623–83), Whig politician and colonel.

p. 332, l. 24: *John Hambden*: John Hampden (1653–96), English politician.

p. 332, l. 25: *the celebrated patriotic Hambden*: John Hampden (1595–1643), puritan statesman.

p. 333, l. 7: *An inferior order of malecontents*: Non-aristocratic Rye House conspirators
including Richard Rumbold (*c.* 1622–85), John Rumsey (d. 1686), Thomas Walcott (*c.*
1625–83), Richard Goodenough (d. 1687), Robert West (1649–*c.* 1712) and Robert
Ferguson (d. 1714).

p. 333, l. 16: *Keiling*: Josiah Keeling (dates unknown), white salter or oilman of London. He
gave evidence at the trials of Sidney and Russell.

p. 333, ll. 25–6: *The English laws of treason, under the act of Edward III*: The Treason Act 1351
(25 Edw 3 St 5 c 2) is an Act of the Parliament of England which codified and curtailed
the common law offence of treason.

p. 334, l. 4: *a law had passed*: Sedition Act 1661 (13 Car 2 St 1 c 1), for safety and preservation
of the king and government against treasonable and seditious practices and attempts.

p. 334, l. 28: *trial*: The trial of Russell for high treason took place on 13 July 1683 at the Old
Bailey. On 14 July, after a final protest against the illegality of his condemnation, Russell
was sentenced to death.

p. 335, l. 2: *the attorney-general*: Sir Robert Sawyer, of Highclere (1633–92), Attorney General for England and Wales (1681–7).

p. 335, ll. 4–6: '*I ask no ... who sits by me.*': Hays might have taken this quotation from the
Introduction to the *Letters*, p. xxxv. At the end of *Lady Rachel Russell's Letters* there is
an 'Appendix with the Trial of Lord William Russell, reproduced from the State Trials,
vol. III, page 629, etc'. On page 9 of this Appendix the whole episode is reproduced as it
actually happened, which is slightly different. Hays makes the audience's reaction in this
episode more tragic since she says that the spectators in the trial 'melted into tears' (l. 9),
when her sources say that 'a thrill of anguish ran through the assembly'.

p. 335, l. 11: *duchess of Portsmouth*: Louise de Kérouaille, Duchess of Portsmouth (1649–
1734), Charles II's mistress.

p. 335, l. 28–p. 336, l. 2: '*Shall I grant ... granted me six hours.*': introduction to the *Letters*, p.
xl, taken from Paul de Rapin's *L'Histoire d'Angleterre* (1724).

p. 336, l. 12: *The witnesses*: There were three witnesses against Russell in his trial: Colonel John
Rumsey, Mr Thomas Sheppard and William Howard, third Baron of Howard of Escrick.
See 'Appendix with the Trial', pp. 66–7.

p. 336, l. 21: *Lord Cavendish*: William Cavendish, first Duke of Devonshire (1640–1707),
English soldier and Whig politician.

p. 337, ll. 1–3: '*that it would ... die with him!*': quotation from a passage in the Introduction to
the *Letters*, pp. xli–xlii, reproduced also in Hume's *History of England*, ch. 69, taken from
Bishop Burnet's *History of His Own Time*, vol. 1, p. 560.

p. 337, l. 10: *the journal of the duke of Monmouth*: This event is taken from the introduction to
the *Letters of Lady Rachel Russell; from the Manuscript in the Library of Woburn Abbey*.

To Which is Prefixed an Introduction, Vindicating the Character of Lord Russell against Sir John Dalrymple, &c., 5th edn (Dublin: E. Thomas & S. Colbert, 1775), pp. xlii–xliii.

p. 337, l. 20: *Bishops Burnet and Tillotson*: John Tillotson (1630–94), Dean of St Paul and Archbishop of Canterbury. Along with Burnet (see note to p. 331, l. 19, above), he attended Lord Russell on the scaffold. He enjoyed the friendship of Lady Russell, and some of the letters collected in her book are addressed to him. The next passage about what Tillotson told the king is taken from the introduction to the *Letters*, p. xlvii.

p. 337, l. 22: '*He could not tell a lie*': Introduction to the *Letters*, p. xliii, taken from Thomas Birch's *The Life of the Most Reverend Dr John Tillotson, Lord Archbishop of Canterbury* (London: J. and R. Tonson, et al., 1752), pp. 116–7.

p. 337, ll. 27–8: *a Turkish government*: Introduction to the *Letters*, p. xliii, taken from Thomas Birch's *The Life of the Most Reverend Dr John Tillotson*, p. 123. According to the *OED*, a definition of Turkish that might suit here is: (1b) 'Like or resembling the Turks or their character; cruel, savage, barbarous'.

p. 338, ll. 4–8: '*I can … otherwise to the king.*': Introduction to *The Letters*, p. xliii, taken from John Dalrymple's *Memoirs of Great Britain and Ireland. From the Dissolution of the Last Parliament of Charles II, until the Sea-battle off La Hogue* (London: W. Strahan, 1771–3), p. 92.

p. 339, ll. 16–23: '*that a separation … poignancy of her feelings.*': introduction to *The Letters*, p. xlvii.

p. 340, ll. 14–16: '*I shall not … done to-morrow.*': from a passage of Hume's *History of England*, ch. 69, taken from Bishop Burnet's *History of His Own Time*.

p. 340, ll. 18–20: '*he had now … only on eternity*': introduction to *The Letters*, p. lii.

p. 340, ll. 24–5: '*that the bitterness of death was past*': introduction to *The Letters*, p. xlviii.

p. 340, ll. 26–7: *he spoke of his affection for her with eloquence and fervor*: Their marriage is generally described as happy and a love match. Rachel's letters to her husband give evidence of it.

p. 341, l. 15: *Lincolns-inn-fields*: The largest public square in London. Russell's execution was not performed in Tower-hill, the common place of execution for men of high rank.

p. 341, l. 22: *Southampton-house*: Russell's family house in Bloomsbury.

p. 341, ll. 24–6: '*that a cloud … than his life.*': introduction to *The Letters*, p. liv, taken from John Dalrymple's *Memoirs of Great Britain and Ireland*.

p. 342, ll. 12–13: *the executioner*: John Ketch (d. 1686), English executioner, whose execution of Lord Russell was carried out in a clumsy way, and extant pamphlet which contains his 'Apologie': see *The Apologie of John Ketch, Esq., the Executioner of London, in Vindication of Himself as to the Execution of the Late Lord Russel, on July 21, 1683* (London: Printed for John Brown, 1683).

p. 342, l. 19: *Calamy*: Edmund Calamy (1671–1732), nonconformist churchman, Divine and historian. Calamy's quotation appears in the introduction to the *Letters*, p. lxiv.

p. 342, ll. 20–2: "*that an age … without respect.*": Introduction to the *Letters*, p. lxiv, taken from Edmund Calamy's *A Letter to Mr. Archdeacon Echard, Upon Occasion of His History of England* (1718).

p. 343, l. 14: *The letters of Lady Russel*: The first edition of the letters might be this: *Letters of Lady Rachel Russell; from the manuscript in the library at Woburn Abbey. To which is prefixed, an introduction, vindicating the character of Lord Russell against Sir John Dalrymple, &c.* (London: Edward & Charles Dilly, 1773). Years later, another series of letters was published in *Some account of the life of Rachael Wriothesley Lady Russell / By the editor of Madame du Deffand's letters …* (London: Longman, Hurst, Rees, Orme and Brown [etc.], 1819).

p. 343, ll. 20–1: *her daughter, the duchess of Rutland*: Rachel's second daughter, Catherine Russell (1676–1711), who married John Manners, second Duke of Ruthland, by whom she had nine children.

p. 343, ll. 23–4: *Her daughter, the duchess of Devonshire*: Rachel's eldest daughter, Rachel Russell (1674–1725), who married William Cavendish, second Duke of Devonshire, by whom she had five children.

p. 344, ll. 4–5: *'I have seen your sister out of bed to-day.'*: from a footnote to letter 149 (Lady Russell to Earl of Galway, June 1711) in the aforementioned *Letters of Lady Rachel Russell*, p. 224, where the whole episode is narrated.

p. 344, l. 10–p. 345, l. 11: *"The following relation ... not finding out the cause."*: The whole episode has been taken from a kind of short Appendix to the *Letters* entitled 'Courage and Mildness Exemplified', signed by Thomas Sellwood, p. 237.

p. 344, l. 10: *Mr. Selwood*: Thomas Sellwood (not further identified), Lady Russell's steward.

p. 344, l. 12: *Bedford-house*: Russell family house in Bloomsbury, previously called Southampton House.

p. 344, l. 26: *published with permission*: with permission of the Duke of Bedford (see note to p. 344, ll. 26–7, below).

p. 344, ll. 26–7: *the duke of Bedford*: John Russell, Fourth Duke of Bedford (1710–71), British statesman, Lady Russell's great-grandson.

p. 345, l. 16: *James II*: see note to p. 332, l. 13, above.

p. 345, ll. 17–18: *became a wanderer in a foreign land*: As a consequence of the Glorious Revolution (1688), King James II was overthrown by a union of English Parliamentarians with the Dutch William of Orange, and had to flee from England to France, where he was allowed to live in a royal château. William's successful invasion of England with a Dutch fleet and army led to his ascending of the English throne as William III of England jointly with his wife, Mary II.

p. 345, ll. 22–3: *the tragical end of the barbarous and infamous Jefferies*: George Jeffreys, first Baron Jeffreys of Wem (1645–89), judge, notorious for his cruelty and corruption. He was the serjeant-at-law in the trials against Lord Russell.

p. 345, l. 25: *several of her letters*: From Thomas Gibbons's *Memoirs of Pious Women*, p. 315. Some of her letters referring to her sight are letter 132 (Lady Russell to Doctor Fitzwilliam, 21 July 1692), p. 202; letter 134 (Lady Russell to Lady Sunderland), p. 206; letter 139 (Lady Russell to Doctor Fitzwilliam, 25 July 1693), p. 211; letter 142 (Lady Russell to Doctor Fitzwilliam, 18 September 1693), p. 214.

p. 346, l. 2: *an operation*: A cataract eye operation (see note to p. 346, ll. 4–6, below).

p. 346, ll. 4–6: *"that the eyes ... with good success."*: from a footnote to letter 143 (Archbishop Tillotson to Lady Russell, 13 October 1693) in the *Letters of Lady Rachel Russell*, p. 216.

p. 346, l. 21: *revival of letters*: the Italian Renaissance.

p. 346, l. 22: *Francis Petrarch*: Francesco de Petrarca (1304–74), or 'Petrarch.'

p. 346, l. 25: *Petrarco, his father*: Pietro or Petracco 'Little Pietro' Garzo (1267–1326).

p. 347, l. 1: *Danté*: Dante Alighieri (*c.* 1265–1321), the renowned Italian poet and author of Inferno, Purgatorio and Paradiso; this trilogy has come to be known as *The Divine Comedy (La Divina Commedia)*. Other noted works include *La Vita Nova*, which combines prose analysis with poetry, *De Monarchia* and *De vulgari eloquentia*.

p. 347, ll. 6–9: *Avignon ... Gascon pope ... see*: In 1309, France's King Philippe IV ('le Bel') forced the election of the Frenchman Raymond de Got as Pope Clement V, and the Papacy relocated to Avignon, where it remained for six successive papal reigns, until 1378. Detractors called the Avignon Papacy the Babylonian Captivity.

p. 348, ll. 2–3: *transient irregularities*: Despite Petrarch's claims, he fathered two illegitimate children (but not with Laura). In his old age, he lived in Arcqua, now Arquà Petrarca, with his illegitimate daughter Francesca and her husband, Francesco da Brossano. Petrarch kept his relationship with Francesca's mother a secret so successfully that her name remains unknown. See V. Kirkham and A. Maggi (eds), *Petrarch: A Critical Guide to the Complete Works* (Chicago, IL: University of Chicago Press, 2009), p. 357.

p. 348, ll. 4–8: *'I can aver... breast.'*: S. Dobson, *The Life of Petrarch Collected from Mémoires pour la vie de Petrarch*, 2 vols (London, 1797), p. 25.

p. 348, ll. 14–21: *"I was ... avail."*: Dobson, *Life of Petrarch*, p. 26.

p. 348, l. 23: *the time of Matins*: i.e., dawn.

p. 348, l. 24: *the church of the monastery of St. Claire*: Clara or Clare of Assisi (1194–1253), protégé of St Francis of Assisi and founder of the Order colloquially known as the 'Poor Clares'.

p. 348, l. 26–p. 349, l. 17: *"She was dressed in green ... Such was the amiable Laura!"*: Dobson, *Life of Petrarch*, pp. 26–7; illustrated in 'first interview between Petrarch and Laura', sculpted by Ridley, plate 6, vol. 1, p. 26v.

p. 349, l. 22: *Andibert de Noves*: typographical error for 'Audibert'; see Dobson, *Life of Petrarch*, vol. 1, p. 28. The Comtesse de Genlis speculates that he died before Petrarch met Laura, i.e., before 1327. See S. Genlis, *Petrarch and Laura, Translated from the French* (London: 1820), p. 48. Genlis provides no citation for this claim.

p. 349, l. 23: *Ermessenda*: Dobson, *Life of Petrarch*, p. 28. Dobson speculates that Ermessenda died in 1346. Dobson, *Life of Petrarch*, p. 111.

p. 349, ll. 25–6: *archives of the house of Sade*: Dobson, *Life of Petrarch*, p. 28.

p. 350, ll. 6–7: *Hugues de Sade*: ancestor of the Petrarch biographer Jacques-François-Paul-Aldonze, Abbé de Sade and his nephew Donatien Alphonse François, Marquis de Sade, Hugues survived Laura, and therefore died in or after 1348. See Dobson, *Life of Petrarch*, p. 111.

p. 350, l. 12: *an old picture of Laura*: see Dobson, *Life of Petrarch*, p. 29.

p. 350, l. 13: *cardinal Barberini*: Dobson, *Life of Petrarch*, p. 29. Pope Urban VIII, elected in 1623, had three kinsmen who were cardinals: Antonio Marcello Barberini, Francesco Barberini and Antonio Barberini. Hays's Cardinal Barberini is probably Antonio Marcello (1569–1662), as he served as Vatican librarian in the 1640s.

p. 350, ll. 15–16: *Richard de Sade, then bishop of Cavoillon*: typographical error for Cavaillon. Not further identified.

p. 350, ll. 24: *Daphne*: Classical Greco-Roman mythological figure. She rejected the advances of the god Apollo and was transformed into a laurel tree. Apollo gathered 'her' branches to symbolize possession of her in the etiology of the classical practice of crowning victors with laurels.

p. 350, l. 26: *Apollo*: Classical Greco-Roman god of music and father of the Nine Muses, personifications of the arts and sciences.

p. 351, ll. 1–3: *"I run every-where after Laura ... Daphne fled from Apollo."*: Dobson, *Life of Petrarch*, p. 46. For Hays, biographical parallels existed with her frustrated romances, especially with John Eccles and, later, William Frend.

p. 351, l. 4: *the system of Pythagoras*: transmigration of souls.

p. 351, ll. 15–21: *"On this bank ... my soul"*: Dobson, *Life of Petrarch*, pp. 47–8.

p. 352, ll. 12–17: *"Dazzled by the lustre ... he had not the courage of speak to her."* Dobson, *Life of Petrarch*, p. 49.

p. 352, ll. 17–23: *"Was I ... should have more courage."*: Dobson, *Life of Petrarch*, p. 49.

p. 352, l. 26–p. 353, l. 4: *"She appeared ... which it was surrounded."*: Dobson, *Life of Petrarch*, p. 107.

p. 353, l. 1: *beauties of Avignon*: Dobson, *Life of Petrarch*, p. 49. For Petrarch, as for Dobson and Hays, Laura is glorified by the binary paradigm that demonized the supposedly unchaste and less beautiful other women of Avignon. In Italian, Laura is a *donna angelicata* or angel-woman.

p. 353, ll. 8–14: *"I bless ... happiness."*: Dobson, *Life of Petrarch*, p. 50.

p. 353, l. 24: *the forest of Ardenne*: a notoriously dense forest in the Ardennes Mountain range of present-day Belgium, France and Luxembourg.

p. 353, ll. 26–8: *War between the duke of Brabant and the court of Flanders ... Moulines*: Dobson, *Life of Petrarch*, p. 60. An episode in the Hundred Years' War, in which the English and French regimes largely exploited Brabançon and Flemish interests, and vice versa. John III, Duke of Brabant (1300–55), son of England's King Edward I and Eleanor of Castile, fought with Flanders in order to retain for Brabant permission to import English wool, an industry formerly controlled by Flemish merchants. To intimidate the Francophile Flemings, Edward had stopped their wool imports, a key source of revenue. See Neillands, *The Hundred Years War*, pp. 75–6. Later, John III abandoned his pro-English policy, marrying his daughter into the French royal family, the Valois. From the early fourteenth century, the central French region of Moulins was the ancestral duchy of the Bourbon family. See Wagner, *The Encyclopedia of the Hundred Years War*, pp. 336–7.

p. 354, ll. 4–6: *"Love ... breeze."*: Dobson, *Life of Petrarch*, p. 61.

p. 354, ll. 15–17: *"It is now ... her heart."*: Dobson, *Life of Petrarch*, p. 62.

p. 354, ll. 22–6: *"The more desert ... anguish."*: Dobson, *Life of Petrarch*, p. 62.

p. 355, l. 9: *Dennis de Robertis*: Dionigi de'Roberti of San Sepolcro (*c.* 1300–42).

p. 355, l. 20: *pestilence*: The 'Black Death'. According to a canon of Avignon (not further identified), in 1348, this plague killed half of Avignon's population, with 11,000 corpses buried in a six-week period at one cemetery, and 62,000 casualties in a six-month period. See P. Ziegler, *Pivotal Moments in History: The Black Death* (New York: HarperCollins, 2009), p. 66.

p. 356, ll. 2–6: *"Would to God ... a phrensy!"*: Mainly paraphrasing Dobson, Hays makes one substantial change. Dobson's Petrarch *confirms* that his love is a 'frenzy'; Hays's Petrarch denies it. Dobson, *Life of Petrarch*, p. 74.

p. 356, I. 3: *letter to a friend*: Dobson, *Life of Petrarch*, p. 177.

p. 357: ll. 7–8: *morals ... had not been irreproachable*: another reference to his relationships, such as with his daughter Francesca's mother.

p. 357, ll. 13–15: *"I am not ... whom you suppose me to be."*: A powerful critique of Petrarch's construction of Laura, this ventriloquism speaks to the corrective rhetorical purpose of *Female Biography*. Mary Shelley reiterates the statement in her own Laura-centered 'Life of Petrarch' for Dionysius Lardner's *Cabinet Cyclopaedia* collection of *Lives of the Most Eminent Literary and Scientific Men of Italy, Spain and Portugal* (London: Longman, 1835), vol. 1, which, in utilizing the Abbé de Sade's *Mémoires*, often effectively echoes Hays's quotations from Dobson. See M. Shelley, 'Petrarch', in T. J. Mazzeo (ed.), *Literary Lives and Other Writings, Vol. 1: Italian Lives* (London: Pickering & Chatto, 2002), pp. 15, xlvii.

p. 357, l. 28–p. 358, l. 3: *'How much time ... have you taken in those woods!'*: Dobson, *Life of Petrarch*, p. 88.

p. 358, l. 6: *a girl*: not further identified.

p. 358, ll. 13–17: *"Ten years ... regain my liberty."*: Dobson, *Life of Petrarch*, p. 88.

p. 359, ll. 15–20: *"I desired death ... me of motion."*: Dobson, *Life of Petrarch*, p. 106.

p. 359, l. 26–p. 360, l. 14: *"I may hide myself ... transfixed with horror"*: Dobson, *Life of Petrarch*, p. 115.

p. 361, ll. 1–3: *The sonnets which he composed ... strongly expressive of his disordered state.*: *Canzoniere* 264 ('I'vo pensando, et nel penser m'assale'), 272 ('La vita fugge, et non s'arresta una hora') and 274 ('Datemi pace, o duri miei pensieri').

p. 361, l. 4: *the pope*: Innocent VI, formerly Étienne Aubert (*c.* 1282–1362; r. 1352–62).

p. 361, l. 6: *convent of St. Lawrence*: The Monastere des Dames de Saint-Laurent, a convent for aristocratic women. Destroyed in 1823; a theatre was built (1825) on its site. See F. Simone and H. G. Hall, *The French Renaissance: Medieval Tradition and Italian Influence in Shaping the Renaissance in France* (New York: Macmillan, 1964), p. 54.

p. 361, l. 9: *Notre Dame de Dons*: Cathedral of Notre Dame des Doms, Avignon.

p. 362, ll. 1–4: *"I am not what I was ... you would scarcely know me."*: Dobson, *Life of Petrarch*, vol. 1, p. 205.

p. 362, l. 17–p. 364, l. 3: *"It is not ... duties you have neglected"*: Dobson, *Life of Petrarch*, p. 237.

p. 362, l. 22: *Lelius*: Petrarch called one of his best friends Lelius. A Gaius (or Caius) Laelius, Roman warrior and companion of Scipio Africanus, fl. 210–190 BC, died in or after 160 BC, and was a source for Polybius's biography of Scipio.

p. 362, l. 23: *Scipio*: Scipio Africanus (*c.* 235–*c.* 160 BC), Roman warrior; invader of Africa.

p. 363, l. 8: *his* Confessions, *in the form of dialogues*: De secreto conflictu curarum mearum, 'Of the Secret Conflict of My Cares', also known as *Secretum Meum*. See *My Secret Book*, trans. J. G. Nichols, foreword G. Greer (London: Hesperus, 2002).

p. 363, ll. 9–10: *St. Augustin*: Aurelius Augustinus, later St Augustine of Hippo (AD 354–430). Author of the *Confessions* and *City of God,* and major contributor to the development of the confession genre.

p. 364, ll. 9–16: *"Everything ... my father's sepulcher."*: Dobson, *Life of Petrarch*, p. 273.

p. 364, ll. 22–3: *'Alas! ... lose my faithful friend?'*: Dobson, *Life of Petrarch*, p. 274.

p. 365, l. 6: *his mistress*: Laura, not Francesca's mother.

p. 365, l. 11: *some subject of domestic grief*: Dobson attributes Laura's youthful death in part to her 'many domestic sicknesses and cares,' particularly stemming from her daughter's marital misconduct. Neither Dobson nor Hays enlightens the reader about the character of Laura's husband, the father of her ten children (see note to p. 376, l. 26, below), the omission of which suggests additional domestic grievances. Dobson, *Life of Petrarch*, p. 382.

p. 365, ll. 13–19: *"I went ... every burst of woe."*: Dobson, *Life of Petrarch*, p. 288.

p. 365, ll. 21–2: *king of Bohemia*: John of Luxembourg, King of Bohemia (1296–1346, r. 1310–46), also known as Jan Lucemburský.

p. 365, l. 22: *Charles, prince of Moravia, his son*: Charles of Luxembourg, also known as Karel Lucemburský (1316–78), King of Bohemia (r. 1346–78), and, as Charles IV, Holy Roman Emperor (r. 1355–78).

p. 366, l. 11: *a friend*: not further identified.

p. 366, ll. 21–7: *"Incredulous ... so dreadful an event!"*: Dobson, *Life of Petrarch*, p. 297.

p. 367, ll. 5–9: *"I fixed my eyes ... object of one's soul!"*: Dobson, *Life of Petrarch*, p. 298.

p. 367, ll. 18–19: *a passion for another woman*: Here, Hays hints that she knows about Francesca's mother or other 'irregularities'. Mary Shelley's biography more frankly states that Petrarch 'had two children,' and 'was not attached to their mother, of which nothing more is known but ... that she was not a married woman'. See Shelley, 'Petrarch', p. 35.

p. 367, ll. 23–5: *"My joys ... short duration."*: Dobson, *Life of Petrarch*, p. 299.

p. 368, l. 23–p. 369, l. 12: *"Her air ... threatened me."*: Dobson, *Life of Petrarch*, p. 343.

p. 369, ll. 21–3: *"Must I never ... tender heart."*: Dobson, *Life of Petrarch*, p. 343.

p. 370, ll. 6–25: *"Heretofore ... separate myself from her."*: Dobson, *Life of Petrarch*, p. 370.

p. 371, l. 2–p. 375, l. 5: *"Her appearance ... time upon earth."*: Dobson, *Life of Petrarch*, p. 377.

p. 375, ll. 11–14: *a letter from a friend ... she had died of the plague*: Dobson, *Life of Petrarch*, p. 377. The letter came from the friend Petrarch calls 'Socrates', also known as Ludwig van Kempen, a singer from Flanders. See Kirkham and Maggi, *A Critical Guide to the Complete Works*, p. 22.

p. 375, l. 27–p. 376, l. 5: *"We are going ... were not worthy."*: Dobson, *Life of Petrarch*, pp. 379–80.

p. 376, ll. 11–13: *"Her road to heaven ... in its paths."*: Dobson, *Life of Petrarch*, p. 380.

p. 376, l. 16: *church of the Franciscans*: Dobson calls the order the 'minor brothers'. Dobson, *Life of Petrarch*, p. 380.

p. 376, l. 19: *her father*: Apparently an error: Dobson claims the chapel was erected by her father-in-law, de Sade. Dobson, *Life of Petrarch*, p. 381.

p. 376, l. 21: *with an Italian sonnet of Petrarch's*: Dobson, *Life of Petrarch*, p. 381. The French poet Maurice Scève's alleged 1533 discovery in Laure de Sade's tomb of proof that she was Petrarch's Laura was first reported in 1547 by the Petrarch editor Jean de Tournes. Having heard whilst studying in Avignon of the local legend that the Sade matriarch was Petrarch's Laura, Tournes claims that Scève opened the tomb and found a small coffin, containing bones, a medal depicting a woman, monogrammed 'M.L.M.I.', which Scève interpreted as 'Madonna Laura Morta Iace' ('Here lie the Remains of Lady Laura') and a parchment on which was illegibly inscribed an Italian sonnet. See E. Duperray, *L'Or des Mots: Une lecture de Pétrarque et du mythe littéraire de Vaucluse des origines a l'orée du XXe. Siècle* (Paris: Sorbonne, 1957), pp. 162–3; D. Coleman, *Maurice Scève: Poet of Love* (Cambridge: Cambridge University Press, 2010), p. 64. Never shown to the public, what precisely Scève found (or claimed to have found) in the tomb remains a matter of dispute. One critic observes that Scève's 'discovery' came at the same time as the marriage of Catherine de'Medici into the French royal family, making Catherine and her husband, the future Henri II, parallels of the French Laura and Italian Petrarch.

p. 376, l. 26: *ten children, six boys and four girls*: According to Dobson, the sons are as follows: Poulin ('architect of the Metropolitan church at Avignon') died at age twenty, before 1348; Audibert, Dean of Notre Dame de Dons (1381); Hugues (Hugonin), from whom descend the lords of Sade and the Abbe de Sade; Peter, 'canon of the Metropolitan church' designed by his precocious elder brother; and James, who died young, no issue. The daughters are Angiere; Ermessenda, a 'nun in the convent of St. Laurence, and procuratrice of that convent'; Margerita, who died before 1348; Gorcenete (married three times: to an unidentified man, then 'Berrnard Ancezuine de Caderousse', then 'Raimond de Moulsong, Lord of Menamenes'); and Janet, who died young, leaving no issue. Dobson, *Life of Petrarch*, pp. 381–2.

p. 377, ll. 1–3: *her eldest daughter ... misconduct in her marriage state*: According to Dobson, Angiere de Sade, married 'Bertrand Domicellus, lord of Bedarride', and her mother, Laura, 'let her but one florin, probably on account of her ill conduct after marriage, which was such that [Pope] Clement VI at the solicitation of her relations, commanded the nuns of St Catherine d'Apt, on pain of excommunication, to receive her, and keep her shut up for the rest of her life'. See Dobson, *Life of Petrarch*, p. 382.

p. 377, l. 15: *the Phoenix*: A mythical immortal bird alleged to self-immolate only to be reborn from its ashes.

p. 377, l. 24: *An old lady*: not further identified.

p. 377, l. 26: *Naturalists*: For example, Pliny, *Natural History*, trans. J. Bostock and H. T. Riley (London: Bell, 1890), p. 480.

p. 378, ll. 2–4: *"The grief ... unnecessary*: Dobson, *Life of Petrarch*, p. 384. This implies that the Roman matron Lucretia, who was raped by the son of Rome's last king, should have died of grief, and therefore not lived to commit suicide.

p. 378, ll. 16–21: *"that her words ... of the soul"*: Dobson, *Life of Petrarch*, p. 385.

p. 379, ll. 1–3: *"I dare not ... speak of it."*: Dobson, *Life of Petrarch*, p. 387.

p. 379, l. 5: *the MS. of Virgil*: Dobson locates this elaborately illuminated manuscript at the 'Ambrosian Library' or Library of St Ambrose, in Milan. Dobson, *Life of Petrarch*, vol. 1, pp. 143, 387. It remains in the Biblioteca Ambrosiana today, as Codex a.49.inf. Martindale, p. x.

p. 379, l. 6: *Simon de Sienna*: Simone Martini (*c.* 1284–1344).

p. 379, ll. 6–7: *he wrote the following lines*: Dobson, *Life of Petrarch*, p. 269.

p. 379, ll. 7–26: *"Laura ... vain and perishing."*: Dobson, *Life of Petrarch*, p. 388.

p. 379, l. 17: *the church of the Cordeliers*: Dobson, *Life of Petrarch*, p. 388. Built 1226–1350, in the Rue des Teinturieurs.

p. 379, l. 21: *a book*: Dobson, *Life of Petrarch*, p. 388. Apparently, Petrarch's *De secreto conflictu curarum mearum*, better known as his 'Secret Book'. Unpublished in Petrarch's lifetime, it was composed between 1342–3 in three volumes.

p. 379, l. 27: Mrs. Dobson: Susannah Dobson (d. 1795).

p. 380, l. 1: *SAPPHO*: Sappho, a lyric poet, was born on the Greek island of Lesbos in the second half of the seventh century BC. Her poetry was widely admired and no other female poet attained the same level of renown in Greek or Roman antiquity. Many of her poems speak of her female companions in erotic terms. She or her family may have been involved in aristocratic political struggles on Lesbos, and her poems mention exile (in Sicily, according to the *Parian Marble* (*Marmor Parium* Ep. 36)).

p. 380, l. 4: *the forty-second Olympiad*: The Olympic Games were held every four years. This four-year period was known as an Olympiad, and was used as a measure of time, starting from the traditional date of the first Olympic Games in 776 BC. This date (623/608 BC), which is found in the tenth-century AD reference work, the *Suda* (Σ 107), may refer either to her birth, or her floruit.

p. 380, ll. 9–10: *few of her numerous productions have descended to posterity*: Her nine books of poems are lost, and only one poem survives complete from antiquity. (See note to p. 380, l. 12, below.) Others survive in more or less fragmentary condition. A recent discovery has, however, given us a new complete poem. See D. Obbink, 'Sappho Fragments 58–59: Text, Apparatus Criticus, and Translation', in E. Greene and M. Skinner (eds), *The New Sappho on Old Age: Textual and Philosophical Issues* (Cambridge, MA: Harvard University Press, 2009), pp. 7–16.

p. 380, ll. 11–12: *Hymn to Venus*: Sappho 1 is a poem addressed to Aphrodite, in which she prays to the goddess to help with her pursuit of a reluctant woman. The goddess replies indulgently and promises that the one who now flees will soon be pursuing.

p. 380, l. 12: *Dionysus of Halicarnassus*: This historian and literary critic, who lived in Rome during the early first century AD, preserved the only complete poem of Sappho that has come down to us, quoting it in its entirety in his work on composition (*Comp.*, 173–9).

p. 380, l. 13: *his works*: see note to p. 380, l. 12, above.

p. 380, l. 15: *Longinus*: the first-century AD author of *On the Sublime*, who is responsible for the survival of most of Sappho's fr. 31, which is famous for its symptomology of desire: facing her beloved she loses the use of her senses, pales, and comes near to death (*de subl.*, 10.1–3).

p. 380, ll. 17–20: *"In Greece ... those of Sappho."*: see P. Bayle, *The Dictionary Historical and Critical of Mr. Peter Bayle* (New York: Garland, 1984), vol. 5, p. 45.

p. 380, ll. 17–18: *Tanaquillus Faber*: Tannaguy (also 'Tanneguy' and 'Tanguy') le Fèvre, a seventeenth-century French classical scholar, and father of the learned Anne Dacier (see Hays, *Female Biography*, vol. 4, pp. 1–23).

p. 380, l. 26: *Vostius*: Gerardus Johannus Vostius (1577–1649), German scholar of ancient history and classics.

p. 381, l. 3: *Archilochus*: A lyric poet, born on the island of Paros whose floruit was the middle of the seventh century. Although he composed poems about war, politics and desire, he was most known in antiquity for his iambics – which were biting and at times scurrilous attacks on his contemporaries.

p. 381, l. 6: *Catullus*: Roman lyric poet (*c.* 84–54 BC). His poem 51, an adaptation of Sappho 31, describes his reaction to the sight of his beloved Lesbia (possibly a pseudonym for Claudia Metelli, a married woman from a prominent Roman family).

p. 381, l. 9: *Cercala*: The *Suda* is alone in mentioning a husband, for whom it provides the name Kerkylas of Andros. This tradition is somewhat suspect, as the name has an obscene meaning ('Prick from the Isle of Man' – translation, D. A. Campbell, *Lyric Poetry*, 5 vols (Cambridge, MA: Harvard University Press, 1982), vol. 1, p. 5, n. 4).

p. 381, l. 11: *Cleis*: a papyrus from Oxyrhynchus dated to AD 200 (*POxy.* 1800 fr. 1) says that Sappho's mother was Kleis, and that she had a daughter of the same name. Kleis appears in the poems but in terms that could equally apply to a daughter or a young lover.

p. 381, ll. 11–12: *The parentage of Sappho*: Little about her life and parentage is certain, as the sources are late and contradictory.

p. 381, l. 12: *three brothers*: Erigyius, Larichus and Charaxus.

p. 381, l. 13: *Charaxus*: One of the three brothers mentioned by the Oxyrhychus papyrus and the *Suda*.

p. 381, l. 14: *Rhodope or Doricha*: Herodotus (*Histories*, 2.135) has the story of how Charaxus, brother of Sappho, freed the courtesan Rhodopis, and was scolded in verse by his sister. Other sources say that he was a merchant and note that Sappho herself used the name Doricha for Rhodopis (Strabo 17.1.33; Sappho fr. 15).

p. 381, l. 18: *Phaon*: The tradition that Sappho committed suicide because of her unrequited love for the ferryman Phaon is late and appears to have been invented long after her death, possibly as a means of shoring up Sappho's heterosexual *bona fides*.

p. 381, l. 24: *Ovid*: Roman poet (43 BC–AD 17) who treats the story of Sappho and Phaon in his *Heroides*, fictive letters of famous and often mythical women addressed to the men they love.

p. 382, l. 4: *promontory of Leucas*: Traditionally a spot from which unrequited lovers leapt, seeking either a cure or an end to suffering through death. A dubious tradition maintains that Sappho met her death when she jumped in despair over the indifference of Phaon (Suda Σ 108).

p. 382, ll. 14–15: *Aristotle*: Greek philosopher (384–322 BC), and the most illustrious of Plato's students. This particular quote from Sappho appears in his *Rhetoric* (1389b29–30).

p. 382, l. 15: *stoics*: Stoicism was a Hellenistic school of philosophy arising in the third century BC that emphasized the use of reason to control emotion, and among whose tenets was the idea that death was not to be feared.

p. 382, ll. 16–18: *"The gods ... themselves die."*: Cited by Aristotle (*Rhetoric* 1398b29–30).

p. 382, l. 23: *Alcæus*: lyric poet from Lesbos, a contemporary of Sappho. A poem quoted by Aristotle (*Rhet.* 1367a) purports to be a dialogue between Alcaeus, who importunes her, and Sappho, who fends off his advances. It is, however, unknown if they ever met.

p. 382, ll. 24–7: *"I wish to explain ... were not culpable."*: see Sappho fr. 137, which Aristotle (*Rhet.*, 1367a) believed to be a dialogue between the two poets.

p. 383, ll. 1–3: *"Without virtue ... union of both."*: Sappho fr. 148.

p. 383, ll. 3–6: *"This person ... on a second."*: Sappho fr. 50.

p. 383, ll. 7–8: *licentiousness ... calumny*: Sappho's poetry frequently addresses young women in erotic terms. This has given rise to suggestions of sexual promiscuity with both women and men. (The word 'Lesbian' was apparently suggestive of enthusiastic heterosexuality in antiquity. It was only later that the word took on its modern meaning.) Conversely, others promoted the idea of her as a teacher of poetry to young women, perhaps to sanitize her reputation.

p. 383, l. 22: *disciples*: Many of Sappho's poems are addressed to young women who share her interest in poetry and ritual. The exact nature of these relationships is unclear, and has given rise to a rather improbable characterization of her as a sort of 'schoolmistress'.

p. 384, ll. 1–2: *in a metre of which she was herself the inventress*: The Sapphic stanza consists of three lines of eleven syllables followed by a shorter line of five syllables. This meter was also used by the lyric poet Alcaeus and imitated by the Roman poets Catullus and Horace.

p. 384, l. 12: *Erasistratus*: Physician and scientist from the island of Keos (*c.* 315–*c.* 240 BC).

p. 384, l. 13: *Antiochus*: Antiochus I Soter, son of Seleucus I Nicator, ruled the Seleucid Empire from 281–261 BC. Erasistratus is supposed to have discovered that the cause of his wasting illness as a young man was love for his stepmother. The story is found in many ancient writers including Pliny and Plutarch.

p. 384, l. 14: *Stratonice*: The much younger wife of Seleucus, whom Seleucus renounced in favour of his son Antiochus, who was dying for love of her.

p. 384, ll. 14–15: *Prytaneum of Syracuse*: In many Greek cities, the Prytaneum was a building that housed the city's sacred fire and may have originated as the home of early rulers. It was the political center of the city and often, as at Athens, provided housing or meals for political officials. Syracuse was the largest and most impressive city of Sicily.

p. 384, l. 16: *Silanion*: Athenian sculptor of the mid-fourth century BC.

p. 384, l. 20: *Alexandra*: or Alessandra, was born in Florence in 1475 and died in the Florentine convent of San Pier Maggiore in 1506.

p. 384, ll. 20–1: *Bartholomew Scala*: or Bartolomeo Scala (1430–97). One of the most influential political members of the courts of several of the Medici's of Florence (i.e., Cosimo, Piero and Lorenzo). Today he is most remembered for his literary dispute with Angelo Poliziano (see note to p. 385, l. 9, below).

p. 384, l. 26–p. 385, l. 1: *Michael Marullus*: Michael Tarchaniota Marullus (*c.* 1458–1500), Greek Renaissance scholar.

p. 385, ll. 3–8: *"He was not satisfied with being master of the Greek tongue ... a young woman of talents and learning"*: Bayle, *Dictionary Historical and Critical* (1734–8), vol. 5, p. 75. Scala was a poet, actress and Greek scholar at the court of Lorenzo de Medici, where she associated with some of the most learned men in Renaissance Italy including Angelo Poliziano (1454–94), scholar and poet; Marsilio Ficino (1433–99), philosopher; and Pico della Mirandola (1463–94), philosopher. Marullus is said to have fallen in love with her for her intelligence rather than for her renowned beauty. This relationship set off a literary argument between Marullus and Poliziano, like that between her father and the poet. See A. Grafton and L. Jardine, *From Humanism to the Humanities: Education and the Liberal Arts in Fifteenth- and Sixteenth-Century Europe* (Cambridge: Harvard University Press, 1986) and D. Robin, A. Larsen and C. Levin (eds), *Encyclopedia of Women in the Renaissance: Italy, France, and England* (Santa Barbara: ABC–Clio, 2007).

p. 385, l. 9: *Politian*: Angelo Ambrogini; he commonly used Poliziano (1454–94). Italian Renaissance scholar at the court of Lorenzo de Medici. Scholars surmise that Poliziano was in love with Alessandra, and that his historical literary disputes with her father were partly to be blamed on this unrequited love. One of Scala's only surviving works is a letter in Greek to Poliziano, published within his work. See A. Poliziano, *Liber epigrammatum Graecorum,* ed. F. Pontani (Roma: Edizione di Storia e di letteratura, 2002), p. 200.

p. 385, l. 14: *These verses appeared in print*: In 1856, Arcangelo Piccioli wrote that 'many' of her Latin and Greek poems still exist, and only her translations from Ancient Greek are lost. Recent scholarship suggests, however, that only two of her works survive. See A. Piccioli, *I fatti principali della storia di Toscana: Narrati ai giovani,* 3 vols (Firenze: Casalanziani, 1856), p. 268 and Robin, Larsen and Levin (eds), *Encyclopedia of women in the Renaissance,* pp. 332–3.

p. 385, l. 20–p. 386, l. 4: *"My Scala ... with goddesses."*: Bayle, *The Dictionary Historical and Critical,* vol. 5, p. 75.

p. 385, l. 28: *Paul Jovius, Elogia bellica virtute illustrium cap. xxviii*: Paolo Giovio (1483–52), Italian historian and biographer.

p. 386, l. 7: *ANNA MARIA SCHURMAN*: Actually Anna Maria van Schurman.

p. 386, l. 9: *Cologn*: Cologne, Germany.

p. 386, ll. 9–10: *Her parents*: Frederik van Schurman and Eva von Harff, married in 1602.

p. 386, ll. 10–11: *descended from noble protestant families*: Frederik van Schurman, a Calvinist from Antwerp, obtained a letter of nobility from the German emperor in the early 1600s while in exile there. Eva van Harff's family was of lesser German nobility. See J. L. Irwin, 'Introduction: Anna Maria van Schurman and her Intellectual Circle', in A. M. van Schurman, *Whether a Christian Woman should be Educated and other Writings from her Intellectual Circle,* ed. and trans. J. L. Irwin (Chicago, IL: The University of Chicago Press, 1998), p. 4.

p. 386, l. 12: *At six years of age*: The exact age at which van Schurman acquired these skills is not confirmed. Surviving samples of her paper cuttings are at the Museum Martena in Franeker.

p. 386, ll. 21–2: *Mr. Evelyn, in his History of Calcography*: John Evelyn (1620–1706), English writer and diarist. See *Sculptura, Or the history and Art of Chalcography, and Engraving in Copper with an ample Enumeration of the most renowned Masters and their Works* (London: Printed by J. C. for G. Beedle, and T. Collins, 1662).

p. 386, ll. 22–5: *"That the very ... prodigy of her sex!"*: The original quote reads: 'The no lesse knowing Anna Maria a [*sic*] Schurman is likewise skilled in this Art, with innumerable others even to [*sic*] a Prodigy of her Sex' (Evelyn, *Sculptura,* book 1, p. 83).

p. 386, ll. 25–6: *Her hand-writing ... have been preserved*: A surviving sample of her calligraphic writing, a page in several non Roman scripts, is at the Royal Library in The Hague.

p. 387, l. 2: *Mr. Joby*: Claude Joly (1607–1700), *Voyage fait à Munster en Westphalie et autres lieux voisins, en 1646 et 1647* (Paris: F. Clousier, 1670).

p. 387, ll. 13–16: *At eleven years of age ... Latin exercises.*: This anecdote is recounted in van Schurman's autobiography, *Eukleria seu melioris partis election. Tractatus brevem vitae eius delineationem exhibens* (Altona: Cornelis van der Meulen, 1673), p. 16.

p. 387, ll. 14–15: *her brothers*: van Schurman had three older brothers, Hendrik Frederik, Johan Godschalk and Willem. See P. Van Beek, *First Female University Student: Anna Maria van Schurman (1636)* (Utrecht: Igitur, 2010), p. 15. No further information about Hendrik and Willem could be found. Johan was an important supporter of van Schurman's studies and facilitated the acquaintance with Jean de Labadie. He died in 1664. See Irwin, 'Introduction', *Whether a Christian Woman should be Educated,* p. 8.

p. 387, l. 24: *Arabic, Ethiopic, Chaldee, and Syriac*: van Schurman studied Semitic languages with Gisbertus Voetius (1589–1676) in Utrecht; she wrote an Ethiopian grammar in Latin which was finished in 1648, but has been lost. See P. Van Beek, *First Female Student*, p. 83.

p. 388, ll. 6–7: *for the improvement of his children, he removed to Franeker*: Her father wanted van Schurman's brother, Johan Godschalk, to study medicine at the University of Franeker (Friesland), which was the second Dutch university and operated from 1585 to 1811. See Irwin, 'Introduction', *Whether a Christian Woman should be Educated*, p. 4.

p. 388, ll. 13–16: *Mr. Cots ... verses in her praise*: Jacob Cats (1577–1660), Dutch poet, jurist and diplomat; was made Grand Pensionary of Holland in 1636; he wrote about van Schurman's linguistic accomplishments.

p. 388, l. 16: *offered her his hand*: This has not been corroborated, but his work, *Houwelijck* ('Marriage', a popular book of advice for women throughout their life cycles) (1625), has a major dedication for van Schurman. See C. Pal, *Republic of Women: Rethinking the Republic of Letters in the Seventeenth Century* (Cambridge: Cambridge University Press, 2012), p. 61.

p. 388, l. 20: *Rivetus, Spanheim, and Vossius*: Andreas Rivetus (André Rivet), French Huguenot theologian (1572–1651); Friedrich Spanheim, Calvinist theologian in Leiden (1600–49); Isaac Vossius (Isaak Voss), Dutch humanist and court librarian to Queen Christina of Sweden (1618–89).

p. 388, l. 22: *Salmasius, Huygens, and Beverovicius*: Claudius Salmasius (Claude Saumaise), French classical scholar (1588–1653), professor in Leiden 1631–50; Christiaan Huygens, Dutch mathematician and astronomer (1629–95); Johannes Beverovicius (Johan van Beverwijck), Dutch physician (1594–1647).

p. 388, ll. 26–7: *Balzac, Gassendi, Mercennus, Rochart, Contart*: Jean-Louis Balzac (1597–1654), French author, founding member of the Académie française, studied in Leiden 1613 or 1615; Pierre Gassendi (1592–1655), French philosopher, priest and scientist, travelled in Flanders and Holland 1628–31; Marin Mersennus (Marin Mersenne), French theologian, philosopher and mathematician, 'father of acoustics' (1588–1648); Rochart, not further identified; Valentin Conrart (1603–75), French writer, founder of the Académie française.

p. 388, l. 28: *visited by princesses*: Princess Elizabeth of the Palatinate (1618–80), daughter of Frederick V, and van Schurman visited each other often and van Schurman served as an academic mentor to the princess. See Van Beek, *First Female Student*, pp. 148–9.

p. 389, ll. 1–2: *cardinal Richelieu ... marks of his esteem*: Armand-Jean du Plessis, cardinal-duc de Richelieu et de Fronsac (1585–1642), chief minister to King Louis XIII; could not be corroborated.

p. 389, l. 8: *had attached herself to Labadie*: Jean de Labadie (1610–74), French pietist and founder of the Labadist Reformed movement. Labadie came to Utrecht in 1666; van Schurman became one of his closest associates. She abandoned her secular studies and followed him to Amsterdam and later exile in Altona where he died.

p. 389, l. 13: *to Wiewart*: Wieuwerd in Friesland, Netherlands; van Schurman and her Labadist community settled there in 1675 after war threatened Altona.

p. 389, l. 14: *visited by William Penn*: William Penn (1644–1718), English Quaker and founder of the American colony of Pennsylvania, visited continental Europe from 1671–7; on his visit he discussed theological issues and religious prosecution with van Schurman. See Van Beek, *First Female Student*, p. 238.

p. 389, ll. 16–18: *chose for her device ... St. Ignatius ... "Amor meus crucifixus est"*: Accurately translated by Hays. Van Schurman's father made her promise celibacy on his deathbed, and she chose this quote from St Ignatius of Antioch as her motto for friendship books. See Van Beek, *First Female Student*, pp. 25–6.

p. 389, ll. 19–22: *Her works are ... 1641: De vitae termino* (Brittenburg, Netherlands: Johannes le Mair, 1639); *The Learned Maid, or, Whether a Maid May be a Scholar?* (Leiden, 1639).

p. 389, ll. 25–7: *"A. M. a Schurman ... metrica"*: A. van Schurman, *Opuscula hebraea, graeca, latina gallica, prosaic et metrica* (Leiden, 1648).

p. 390, ll. 1–2: *"Eukleria ... electio"*: A. van Schurman, *Eukleria: seu melioris partis election. Tractatus brevem vitae eius delineationem exhibens* (Altona: Cornelis van der Meulen, 1763).

p. 390, l. 7: *MADELIENE*: 'Magdeiline' in *Biographium Faemineum*, vol. 2, p. 238 and 'Madeleine de Scuderi' in A. Thicknesse, *Sketches of the Lives and Writings of the Ladies of France*, 3 vols (London: Dodsley & W. Brown, 1780), vol. 1, p. 77.

p. 390, l. 10: *mother*: Madeleine de Martel de Goustimesnil (1569–1635), married to Georges de Scudéry (b. 1560).

p. 390, ll. 14–15: *the disadvantages of her figure*: Mlle de Scudery has not been described as an attractive woman in the sources referred to. According to Thicknesse, she was 'denied the smallest portion of *external* charms' (emphasis added). See Thicknesse, *Sketches*, vol. 1, pp. 77–8.

p. 390, l. 15: *Sappho*: Greek lyrist and female poet (630–550 BC).

p. 390, l. 20: *Hotel de Rambouillet*: the renowned Paris literary salon of Mme de Rambouillet, founded 1607.

p. 391, ll. 1–5: *Sentiments ... refined from their grossness*: The language-purifying literary movement of 'la preciosité' is associated primarily with Mlle de Scudéry. See F. E. Beasley, *Salons, History, and the Creation of 17th-Century France: Mastering Memory* (Aldershot: Ashgate, 2005), pp. 19–88.

p. 391, l. 9: *her brother*: Georges de Scudéry (1601–67), poet and dramatist.

p. 391, ll. 10–11: *academy of the Ricovrati, at Padua*: founded in 1599, one of the few with female members.

p. 391, l. 13: *Helena Cornaro*: the first woman in Europe to receive a university diploma. See also Hays, *Female Biography*, vol. 3, pp. 436–8.

p. 391, l. 19: *prince of Paderborn, bishop of Munster*: Ferdinand of Bavaria (1577–1650).

p. 391, l. 21: *Christina, queen of Sweden*: Queen Christina (1626–89), benefactress of Madeleine de Scudéry. See also Hays, *Female Biography*, vol. 3, pp. 288–314.

p. 391, l. 23: *Cardinal Mazarine*: (1602–61), Chief Minister to Louis XIV.

p. 391, l. 25: *chancellor Boucherat*: Louis Boucherat (1616–99), Chancellor to Louis XIV.

p. 391, l. 25: *Lewis XIV*: Louis XIV (1638–1715), King of France.

p. 391, l. 26: *madame de Maintenon*: official mistress of Louis XIV.

p. 392, l. 5: *A curious accident befell this lady in a journey*: The story of being mistakenly suspected of planning a murder is recounted in *Biographium Faemineum*, vol. 2, p. 238, although with fewer details.

p. 392, l. 8: *a romance*: no further information is available.

p. 392, l. 10: *Mazare*: a character with this name appears in de Scudéry's novel *Artamène ou Le Grand Cyrus* (1649–53).

p. 392, ll. 10–17: *'What shall we do ... done with him.'*: see note to p. 392, l. 5, above.

p. 393, ll. 11–12: *her remains, decided by the authority of the cardinal de Noailles*: Madeleine de Scudéry was buried at the church of Saint-Nicolas-des-Champs in Paris in 1701, at ninety-three years of age.

p. 393, l. 12: *the cardinal de Noailles*: Cardinal and Archbishop of Paris (1651–1729).

p. 393, l. 14: *Her works were numerous*: *Ibrahim or the Illustrious Bassa* (1641) was published under her brother's name. *Illustrious Women or Heroic Harangues* (1642) includes 'The Harangue of Sappho', about Scudéry's alter ego. *Artaméne or the Grand Cyrus* (1649–53), 10 vols; *Clelie a Roman History* (1654–60), 10 vols, which included her famous 'Carte Tendre' or *Arcadian love map* and *Almahide, or the Slave Queen* (1661–3), 8 vols. Later in life she wrote the novellas *Célinte* (1660) and *The Versailles Promenade* (1669). She also wrote several moral essays and dialogues: *Discours de la gloire* (1671), *Conversations Morales* (1686) and *Entretiens de Morale* (1692).

p. 393, ll. 14–15: *M. Coster*: not further identified.

p. 393, l. 20: *Cyrus*: English title, *Artaméne or the Grand Cyrus* (1649–53).

p. 393, l. 21: *Louis de Bourbon, prince of Condé*: (1668–1710), Prince of the court of Louis XIV.

p. 393, l. 22: *Clelie*: English title, *Clelia* (1661).

p. 394, l. 7: *Pierre Seguier*: Pierre Séguier (d. 1559), seigneur de La Verrière, from a younger branch of famous Chancelier Pierre Séguier's (1588–1672) family: see F. Blanchard, *Les éloges de tous les premiers presidens du Parlement de Paris* ('*Eulogies for all the First Presidents of the Parliament of Paris*') (Paris: Cardin Besongnes, 1645), p. 56.

p. 394, l. 10: *Françis du Prat*: François du Prat, Baron de Thiers (also written Thiern) and Viteaux, fourth son of Antoine III du Prat (or Duprat), Seigneur de Nantouillet, grandson of famous Chancelier Antoine Duprat (*c.* 1463–1535). Widowed *c.* 1583, Anne remarried Hugues de La Vergne, seigneur de Mouy, belonging to the household of Duke d'Anjou (Henri III's younger brother): see P. Anselme, *Histoire généalogique et chronologique de la maison de France* ('*Genealogical and chronological History of French Royal Household*'), 9 vols (Paris: La Compagnie des Libraires, 1730), vol. 6, pp. 454–6 and L. Moreri, *Le Grand Dictionnaire historique*, 10 vols (Paris: Les Libraires associés, 1759), vol. 8, p. 542.

p. 394, l. 12: *Anne*: Anne du Prat, wife of Honorat Prevost, Seigneur de Chastelier-Portaut, an anti-Guise activist in 1563, was Lady-in-waiting to the Queen Catherine de Medici (1519–89, Queen of France 1547–59, Queen regent/advisor until her death in 1589): see Hays, *Female Biography*, vol. 2, pp. 169–229; Moreri, *Grand Dictionnaire*, p. 542; J. Serres and S. Goulart, *Recueil des choses memorables avenues en France sous le règne d'Henri II* ('*Record of all the memorable events occurred in France during Henri II's reign*') (1598), p. 293.

p. 394, l. 12: *Philipine*: or Philippe (1571–1628), married to Clément, Baron de Cosnac. Jean d'Avost, a poet belonging to Marguerite de Valois's (or 'Queen Margot', King Henri IV's first wife) household, was her suitor.

p. 394, l. 15: *the cultivation of sacred poetry*: see La Croix du Maine, *Les bibliothèques françaises* (Paris: L'Angelier, 1584), p. 26: Hays's entry is an effective translation of the text of de La Porte and de La Croix, *Histoire littéraire des femmes*, vol. 1, p. 119 and *Dictionnaire portatif des femmes célèbres*, 2 vols (Paris: Belin et Volland, 1788), vol. 1, p. 571.

p. 394, l. 15: *her poems*: no trace of any kind to be found of her works.

p. 395, l. 2: *Ninus*: King Ninus, legendary founder of Nineveh, an ancient Assyrian city on the eastern bank of the Tigris River.

p. 395, l. 5: *absurdity and contradiction*: The story of Semiramis and Ninus confounds myth with historical facts. They first appear in the history of Persia, *Persica*, written by Ctesias of Cnidus (*c.* 400 BC).

p. 395, ll. 5–6: *according to historians*: According to Herodotus (I.184) Semiramis lived five generations before Nitocris, *c.* 750 BC. The historical queen has been identified with

Shammuramit or Shammuramat, married to an Assyrian ruler, Rammannirar or Sham-shi-Adad VII of Assyria, thus being Ninus son of Belus, the alleged legendary husband. The mythical queen ruled as regent for forty-two years after her husband's death for her son Nynias, who some identify with Adad-nirari IV (810–782 BC).

p. 395, l. 6: *was the wife of an officer*: called Onnes: See Diodorus (II. 5). This name evokes Oannes, the god fish originally associated with the fish form of Astarte.

p. 395, ll. 10–11: *the principal men of the state*: not further identified.

p. 395, ll. 19–20: *This account is denied by some historians, but all are agreed*: see Diodorus (II. 6; II. 20); Aelian (VII.1).

p. 395, l. 22: *she built Babylon in one year*: see Herodotus (I. 184; III. 155); Diodorus (II. 7–8); Lucian (9–14); Eusebius (17) (Armenian translation); Orosius (II. 2.1; II. 2.5; II. 6.7); Justinus (I. 2).

p. 395, ll. 24–5: *Her statue ... temple of Hierapolis*: see Lucian (33).

p. 396, l. 9: *Rhea*: Rhea or Rea Silvia, or Ilia, the mythical mother of the twins Romulus and Remus, the legendary founders of Rome.

p. 396, ll. 12–14: *When the Ninevites performed a great action, it was ascribed to Ninas, supposed founder of Ninevah*: most probably a tale created by Ctesias.

p. 396, ll. 23–4: *who conquered the Medes and Bactrians*: see Diodorus (II.2–3); Orosius (I. 4); Justinus (I. 1).

p. 396, l. 27: *Pul of Nineve*: Abbreviation for Tiglath-Pileser III, King of Assyria (r. *c.* 745–727 BC).

p. 396, l. 27: *Assur*: Highest god of the Assuri people; protector of Assyria. Assyrians were usually named after their gods, therefore no further identification of this subject.

p. 397, l. 1: *Adon*: Assyrian god; see note to p. 396, l. 27, above.

p. 397, l. 1: *Salmanassar*: Shalmaneser or Salmanasser, also called Enemessar, invaded Phoenicia and captured Samaria and Israel.

p. 397, l. 1: *Sennacherib*: son of Shalmaneser, invaded Phoenicia, attempted to invade Egypt and captured several cities of Judah.

p. 397, ll. 8–23: *"Besides Babylon ... shepherds."*: Strabo (*Geography*, XVI. 1.2).

p. 397, l. 8: *Strabo*: Greek historian and philosopher most famous for his seventeen-volume *Geographica* (*c.* 20 BC), a geographical history with descriptions of historical people.

p. 397, l. 13: *vast canals to direct the course of rivers*: see Diodorus (II. 9; II. 11).

p. 397, ll. 16–17: *the famous terraces at Babylon, and the beautiful gardens at Ecbatana*: The Hanging Gardens were attributed to other rulers by Herodotus (I. 185) and Diodorus (II. 10); on the Ecbatana, see Diodorus (II. 13).

p. 397, l. 18: *weaving cotton*: On the invention of fabrics, see Clement of Alexandria (*Stromata*, I.16).

p. 397, l. 21: *Chus*: not further identified.

p. 397, l. 26–p. 398, l. 1: *Athenagoras*: see Diodorus (II. 4); Lucian (14); Athenagoras of Athens (*c.* AD 133–90), *A Plea for the Christians*, 30.

p. 398, l. 1: *Dercetus*: In Lusitanian mythology, a mountain god.

p. 398, l. 2: Suria Dea: Suria or Syria, in ancient Celtic polytheism, the female deification of flowing water.

p. 398, l. 4: *one and the same deity*: Diodorus (II. 20); Lucian (39; 54); Aelian (*Var. Hist.* XII. 39) (depicts her chasing lions and panthers as would the goddess Artarte); Strabo (XVI. 1–27); Pliny (*Nat. Hist.* V. 19).

p. 398, l. 5: *Lucian*: Lucian of Samosata (*c.* AD 125–*c.* 180), rhetorician and satirist. Probably refers to *De Dea Syria*.

p. 398, ll. 1–28: *esteemed ... preserved*: This page of text follows J. Bryant, *A New System or Analysis of Ancient Mythology*, 2 vols (London: T. Payne, Mews-Gate, et al., 1774), vol. 2, pp. 106–9.

p. 398, ll. 11–12: *the name compounded of Sama-Ramas, or Ramis*: for *Sama-Ramas* etymology see the *Mahàbhàrata: Adi Parva*, sections LXXI and LXXII.

p. 398, l. 12: *Sama-Ramas ... signified* the divine token: Bryant, *A New System or Analysis of Ancient Mythology*, vol. 2, p. 309.

p. 399, ll. 1–14: *by a shepherd ... into antiquity*: This page of text follows Bryant, *A New System*, vol. 3, pp. 146–7.

p. 399, l. 1: *a shepherd*: not further identified.

p. 399, l. 1: *Menon*: in some myths, Menon is another name for her first husband, Onnes, see note to p. 393, l. 6, above.

p. 399, l. 3: *Simma*: not further identified.

p. 399, l. 9: *Hesychius*: Hesychius of Alexandria (fl. fifth century AD), *Lexicon*, ed. M. Schmidt (col. 1435).

p. 399, l. 17: *MADAME SETURMAN*: Anna Maria van Schurman (Dutch, 1607–78), the subject of another, more substantial *Female Biography* entry (see Hays, *Female Biography*, vol. 6, pp. 384–8), which duplicates some material from 'Seturman' and bears Schurman's correct name. Prior to the publication of *Female Biography*, there is no record of any 'Madame Seturman'; afterwards, a reference appears in the London *Athenaeum*. Uncited, it commemorates a 'Madame Seturman, who .... independent of other acquirements ... spoke nine different languages'. See [Maria Jane Jewsbury (1800–1833)], 'On Modern Female Cultivation No. iii', *Athenaeum* (25 February 1832), p. 129.

p. 399, l. 17: *Cologne*: In fact, Schurman left Cologne, spent much of her life in Utrecht, and died there.

p. 399, ll. 18–19: *a great reputation*: This 'most extraordinary lady ... surprised the most learned men.' See S. Jones, *New Biographical Dictionary*, 2nd edn (London: G. and J. Robinson et al., 1796), p. SCH–SCH.

p. 399, ll. 19–21: *painter ... theologian*: Having been 'taught music ... painting, sculpture, and engraving,' Jones claims, Schurman 'succeeded equally in all these arts'. Jones's list of other accomplishments differs from Hays's. He finds Schurman competently versed in geography, astronomy, philosophy and the sciences. Her philosophical works include the *Dissertatio de ingenii muliebris ad doctrinam et meliores litteras aptitudine* (1638), which was translated into French in 1646, and into English 1659 as *The Learned Maid, or, Whether a Maid may be a Scholar?* and in 1998 as *Whether a Christian Woman Should be Educated*. Her theological pursuits included an intense attachment to the Calvinist theologian Jean de Labadie, and she met Cardinal Richelieu, who admired her. According to Grayling, she met Descartes, who objected to her appreciation of the ideas of another Calvinist, Gisbertus Voetius, Rector of the University of Utrecht. See Schurman, *Whether a Christian Woman Should be Educated*, p. 6. She tried to reconcile medicine with metaphysics, debating with the medical doctor Jan van Beverwyck on 'whether medicine could extend life', in spite of the doctrine of predestination. Her contribution appeared in print in 1639 as *De Vito Termino* and *Paelsteen van den tijt onses levens*, both loosely translated as 'On the Boundary of Life'. See Schurman, *Whether a Christian Woman Should be Educated*, p. 6.

p. 399, ll. 21–2: *nine languages*: Jones credits Schurman with varying levels of fluency in eleven languages: her native German, as well as 'Latin, Greek, Hebrew ... Syriac, Chaldee, Arabic, and Ethiopic ... French, English, and Italian.' Her extreme multilingualism seems to be something of an urban legend, as different sources list a range of languages, often disagreeing with each other. The *Ladies' Repository* claims Schurman knew 'every European tongue' including 'Turkish' and 'Persian'. Jones, *New Biographical Dictionary*, p. SCH–SCH.

p. 400, l. 2: *MARIE DE RABUTIN*: Marie de Rabutin-Chantal, marquis de Sévigné (1626–96), was the heiress to her father's estate because one elder brother died within months of birth and the other was still-born.

p. 400, l. 3: *baron de Chantal, Bourbilli*: Celse-Bénigne de Rabutin-Chantal (1596–1627) was Burgundian nobility.

p. 400, ll. 3–4: *Mary de Coulanges*: Marie de Coulanges (1603–33).

p. 400, ll. 7–8: *the descent of the English up the isle of Rhée*: The English attacked the Ile de Ré off the coast of France in July 1627, a battle that was part of the ongoing sieges of the French king against Protestant Huguenot strongholds along the coast of France nearest England.

p. 400, l. 9: *Christopher de Coulanges*: Christophe de Coulanges, abbé de Livry (1607–87) became Madame de Sévigné's guardian in 1636 and remained a close confidant and protector throughout his life. He is referred to frequently in her letters as *Bien Bon*.

p. 400, ll. 17–18: *Henry, marquis de Sévigné*: Henri de Sévigné (1623–51). Breton nobility, the marquis de Sévigné married Marie de Rabutin in 1644, dying in a duel in 1651.

p. 400, ll. 19–20: *a son and a daughter*: her daughter, Françoise-Marguerite, was born in 1646 (1646–1705) and her son Charles (1648–1713) was born two years later.

p. 400, ll. 23–4: *untimely death of the marquis*: The marquis de Sévigné was killed in a duel on 4 February 1651 that he is said to have fought over his mistress.

p. 400, ll. 24–5: *the chevalier d'Albret*: François-Amenieu d'Albret (*c.* 1629–72).

p. 400, ll. 26–7: *a widow in the boom of her youth, she determined against a second engagement*: Twenty-five years old when her husband was killed, Mme de Sévigné never remarried, perhaps in order to maintain her independence, both personal and financial.

p. 401, ll. 2–3: *assisted in these cares by her uncle*: Christophe de Coulanges, abbé de Livry, was her protector and advisor throughout her life, and assured her an excellent education in her youth.

p. 401, ll. 9–12: *conversation … temple of muses*: The elite Parisian circle of Sévigné were termed *précieuses*, women (and men) who put great emphasis on the use of language, the arts of wit and conversation. Sévigné was at the center of this movement, along with other literate and noble women who frequented each other's homes. She frequented many important salons. See E. Goldsmith, *Exclusive Conversations: The Art of Interaction in Seventeenth-Century France* (Philadelphia: University of Pennsylvania Press, 1988).

p. 401, ll. 13–14: *famous dispute … respecting the ancients and the moderns*: Boileau defended the position of the ancients, namely that all art should imitate the perfection of Greece and Rome, while Perrault argued that contemporary culture could produce art that is equivalent to or better than ancient models, thereby arguing that contemporary France could equal or surpass those civilizations.

p. 401, ll. 13–14: *Perrault and Boileau*: Charles Perrault (1628–1703) and Nicolas Boileau-Despréaux (1636–1711); two important authors in the Republic of French letters who ultimately represented two different generations as the classical movement became more nationalistic under the reign of Louis XIV.

p. 401, ll. 15–16: *'The ancients,' … are the prettiest.'*: from *Biographium Faemineum*, vol. 2, p. 241. The original source may be Sévigné's letters, but it may also be apocryphal, originating in P. Bouhours, *Pensees Ingenieuses des anciens et des modernes* (Lyon: Guerriers, 1698), pp. 113–14.

p. 401, l. 19: *Charles, marquis de Sévigné*: Charles, Baron de Sévigné (1648–1713). Born two years after his sister, Charles married in 1684, but never had children.

p. 401, l. 23: *Mademoiselle de Sévigné*: François-Marguerite de Sévigné, the future comtesse de Grignan (1646–1705), was the recipient of many of Madam de Sévigné's letters, written with the aim of informing her of Parisian gossip while she lived with her husband in Provence.

p. 401, ll. 24–5: *Francis de Castellane-Adhémar de Monteil, count de Grignan*: François Adhémar de Monteil, Comte de Grignan (1632–1714). The couple had five children together, one of whom died at birth and another in infancy.

p. 401, ll. 25–6: *lieutenant-general of the king's forces and governor of Provence*: To Madam de Sévigné's dismay, soon after the marriage, the Count was named lieutenant general of Provence by Louis XIV and the couple had to leave Paris and live at the Count's castle in the south.

p. 402, ll. 5–6: *duke de Vendome*: Louis de Bourbon (1612–69) was the grandson of King Henry IV and his mistress, Gabrielle d'Estrées, and the husband of the Cardinal de Mazarin's niece, Laura Mancini. He was appointed the governor of Provence in 1640; upon his death the post became open, but his son was too young, at fifteen years of age, to fill it. Hence, the comte of Grignan was sent to take up the post.

p. 402, ll. 12–13: *charming letters*: Although Madam de Sévigné began writing letters much earlier, in the 1650s, the bulk of her correspondence begins with her separation from her daughter. On the mother–daughter relationship, see M. Longino Farrell, *Performing Motherhood, the Sévigné Correspondence* (Hanover, NH: University Press of New England, 1991).

p. 402, ll. 14–15: *long and frequent visits to her daughter*: Sévigné visited her daughter in Province in 1672, 1690 and 1694.

p. 402, l. 17: *last journey into Provence, in 1695*: She actually went to Provence in May 1694.

p. 402, ll. 17–18: *grandson, the marquis de Grignan*: Louis-Provence de Grignan (1671–1704).

p. 402, ll. 18–19: *mademoiselle de St. Amant*: Anne-Marguerite de Saint-Amans.

p. 402, ll. 19–20: *Of these nuptials some account is given in her letters*: Sévigné does not so much describe the marriage as the contract in a December 1694 letter to Madame de Guitaut as well as a few humorous comments about the consummation in a February 1695 letter to her cousin, Mme De Coulanges. There is some follow-up about the contract and relations with the Saint-Amans family in a September 1695 letter to her son. See Madame de Sévigné, *Correspondance*, ed. R. Duchêne and J. Duchêne (Paris: Gallimard, 1978), vol. 3, pp. 1073–4, 1082–3, 1120–1. The marriage negotiations were complex because the grandson was marrying the daughter of a financier. It was not uncommon for impoverished nobility, even from ancient families like the Grignan, to marry wealthy bourgeois in this period.

p. 402, ll. 20–1: *a long and dangerous illness of madame de Grignan*: possibly a flu or pneumonia.

p. 402, ll. 25–6: *she expired, Aug. 6th, 1696, at the age of seventy*: She died on 17 April 1696.

p. 403, ll. 2–12: *the influence of superstition ... with desolation and blood*: This entire paragraph disparages the anti-protestant attitudes of Sévigné. The first part is taken almost verbatim from a long footnote in Thicknesse, *Sketches*, vol. 1, p. 206, which parses a story told by Sévigné concerning the Bishop of Rheims.

p. 403, ll. 6–7: *count de Gregnan*: Count de Grignan; see note to p. 401, ll. 24–5, above.

p. 403, ll. 13–15: *a valuable collection of letters, the best edition of which is ... 12 mo.*: Presumably she is referring to this edition: Marie de Rabutin-Chantal, marquis de Sévigné, *Recueil des lettres de madame la marquise de Sévigné a madame la comtesse de Grignan, sa fille*

(Paris: Desprez, 1754), although it is hard to know why she favours this particular edition over others to which she might have had access.

p. 403, ll. 16–23: *"These letters ... imaginary correspondents."*: Voltaire is cited by Hays from the *Biographium Faemineum*, vol. 2, p. 241.

p. 403, l. 16: *Voltaire*: French Enlightenment Philosopher François-Marie Arouet (1694–1778) who wrote about Sévigné.

p. 403, l. 24: *two men of the first literary rank*: Pierre Bayle (1647–1706) lived in Holland after 1681 because he was a Protestant; he is best known for his four-volume *Dictionnaire Historique* (Amsterdam: Reinier Leers, 1697), a work utilized by Hays. The president, Jean Bouhier (1673–1746), was a jurist and eventual member of the French Academy.

p. 403, l. 25–p. 404, l. 1: *madame de Sévigné ... woman of her time*: From P. Bayle, *Lettres Choisies de Mr. Bayle avec des Remarques* (Rotterdam: Fritsch et Böhm, 1714), vol. 2, p. 653. Also taken from the preface to the English edition of Sévigné's letters, which is a source of much of Hays's biography. See *Letters from the Marchioness de Sévigné, to her daughter the Countess de Grignan. Translated from the French of the last Paris edition* (London: J. Coote, 1763–8), vol. 1, p. xxvi for both citations.

p. 404, l. 1: *The other*: Refers to Jean Bouhier (1673–1746); see note to p. 403, l. 24, above.

p. 404, ll. 2–5: *"that her letters ... ancient or moderns."*: From a letter written by Bouhier to D. M. Perrin, the first editor of Sévigné's letters (see Marie de Rabutin-Chantal, marquis de Sévigné, *Recueil de lettres choisies, pour servir de suite aux lettres de Mme de Sévigné à Mme de Grignan, sa fille* (Paris: Rollin, 1751)), that is quoted by Perrin in his introduction to the letters, and was available to Hays in the translations of that introduction in the English editions.

p. 404, ll. 8–9: *"The true mark of a good heart ... is its capacity for loving."*: M. de Sévigné, *Letters from the Marchioness de Sévigné to Her Daughter the Countess de Grignana*, 7 vols (London: J. Sewell, 1801), vol. 2, letter 139, p. 149.

p. 404, l. 15: *ARABELLA*: Arabella Stewart (alt. Arbella Stuart) (1575–1616), the only child of Charles Stuart.

p. 404, l. 15: *Charles Stuart*: Charles Stuart (1555–76), fifth Earl of Lenox, served as acting regent for James VI of Scotland.

p. 404, l. 16: *youngest brother*: Henry Stuart (1545–67), also first Duke of Albany and King Consort to Mary, Queen of Scots from 1565 until his death in 1567.

p. 404, l. 16: *lord Darnley*: Henry Stewart, or Stuart (1545–67) also first Duke of Albany, was King consort to Mary, Queen of Scots until his murder.

p. 404, l. 17: *Mary queen of Scots*: Mary, Queen of Scots (1542–87) was Queen regnant of Scotland from 1542–67; she was imprisoned and forced to abdicate the throne after Henry Stuart's death. See also Hays, *Female Biography*, vol. 5, pp. 1–286.

p. 404, l. 18: *mother*: Elizabeth Cavendish (1555–82) secretly married Charles in 1574; they were imprisoned in the Tower of London where Elizabeth gave birth to Arabella the following year.

p. 404, l. 19: *sir William Cavendish*: (1505–57) was an English courtier who married three times and fathered sixteen children; his third marriage to Elizabeth Talbot, the Countess of Shrewsbury (commonly known as Bess of Hardwick, 1521–1608), resulted in eight of those children, including Elizabeth Cavendish, Arabella's mother (see note to p. 404, l. 18, above).

p. 404, l. 21: *died in his 29th year*: Charles Stuart (see note to p. 404, l. 15, above) died in 1576 at age 21, not 29.

p. 404, l. 25–p. 405, l. 1: *Her papers are still preserved in the Harleian and Longbeat libraries*: The Harleian Library is now housed in the British Library (The Arabella Seymour documents are found in Harley MS 6986 and Marley MS 7003); the 'Longbeat' Library is actually the Longleat House Library, Warminster, where Arabella's papers are included in the Seymour collection.

p. 405, l. 1: *affinity to the crown*: Arabella was a great-great-granddaughter of Henry VII of England on her mother's side and cousin to James VI of Scotland and I of England (1566–1626) on her father's side.

p. 405, l. 3: *Mr. Ogleby*: John Ogleby; Scottish baron and envoy for the King of Scotland to Rome and Spain.

p. 405, ll. 5–6: *reign of Elizabeth*: Elizabeth I of England (1533–1603; r. 1558–1603).

p. 405, ll. 6–7: *He observes ... deliver her up*: Arabella was not restrained or imprisoned during Elizabeth's reign, but rather was under consideration to be Elizabeth's successor prior to the determination that James was the more suitable candidate. Elizabeth had the right to make marriage decisions for members of the royal family.

p. 405, ll. 7–8: *the king of Scots*: James VI (see note to p. 405, l. 1, above).

p. 405, ll. 8–9: *duke of Lenox*: Ludovic Stuart (1574–1624), second Duke of Lennox and first Duke of Richmond.

p. 405, l. 11: *The pope*: Pope Paul V (1552–1621), Pope from 1605.

p. 405, ll. 13–14: *cardinal Farnese, brother to the duke of Parma*: Odoardo Farnese (1573–1626), second son of Alessandro Farnese (1545–92) and brother to Ranuccio Farnese (1569–1622), Duke of Parma, following Alessandro's death.

p. 405, l. 15: *Henry IV. of France*: Henry Bourbon (1553–1610; r. 1589–1610), King of Navarre and of France.

p. 405, l. 18: *James*: James VI of Scotland and I of England; see note to p. 405, l. 1, above.

p. 405, ll. 18–23: *a conspiracy ... punished*: The Main Plot of 1603, headed by Henry Brooke, Lord Cobham (1564–1619) and Sir Walter Raleigh (*c.* 1552–1618) and funded by Spain; both were imprisoned in the Tower of London. Raleigh was released after thirteen years, but then executed in 1618; Cobham was released and died of a prolonged illness a few months later.

p. 406, l. 4: *Mr. William Seymour*: William, Lord Beauchamp and second Duke of Somerset (1588–1660). Secretly married Arabella (thirteen years his senior) on 22 June 1610.

p. 406, l. 5: *the earl of Hertford*: Edward Seymour (1561–1612), actually Viscount of Beauchamp.

p. 406, ll. 10–11: *different keepers*: Arabella was kept at the home of Sir Thomas Perry, or Parry (d. 1616) in Lambeth, and then in the custody of William James, Bishop of Durham (1542–1617); William was kept in the Tower of London.

p. 406, ll. 16–17: *Durham*: A city in northeast England; Arabella was being transferred into the custody of William James (see note to p. 406, ll. 10–11, above).

p. 406, l. 17: *Blackwall*: An area in east London on the north bank of the Thames River.

p. 406, l. 21: *Woolwich ... Gravesend*: At that time, part of Kent; Woolwich is now in southeast London.

p. 406, l. 22: *Lee*: village parish in Kent.

p. 406, l. 28: *missed the vessel*: William escaped to Ostend, in Belgium.

p. 407, l. 1: *A pinnace*: lightweight boat that could be rowed or rigged with sails.

p. 407, ll. 12–13: *not without suspicion of poison*: She suffered abdominal pain and fatigue, and may have died of porphyria, a genetic condition possibly shared with James VI and I.

p. 407, l. 14: *Henry VIIth's chapel*: Westminster Abbey; there was no mourning.

p. 407, l. 18: *These ladies, sisters*: Anne Seymour (1538–88); Margaret Seymour (b. 1540); Jane Seymour (1541–61).

p. 407, l. 20: *four hundred Latin distichs*: The *Hecatodistichon*. Hays repeated the erroneous number found in G. Ballard, *Memoirs of British Ladies, Who Have Been Celebrated for Their Writings or Skill in the Learned Languages, Arts and Sciences* (London: T. Evans, 1775) and *Biographium Faemineum*. The correct number of 104 appears in Bayle and subsequent English translations. See Hosington, 'England's First Female-Authored Encomium: The Seymour Sisters' "Hecatodistichon" (1550) to Marguerite de Navarre. Text, Translation, Notes, and Commentary', *Studies in Philology*, 93:2 (1996), pp. 117–63 and P. Demers, 'The Seymour Sisters: Elegizing Female Attachment', *Sixteenth Century Journal*, 30:2 (1999), pp. 343–65.

p. 407, l. 21: *queen of Navarre, Margaret de Valois*: Marguerite de France or Marguerite de Valois (1492–1549), Queen of the Kingdom of Navarre (area of north-west Spain merged with France in the seventeenth century); notable publications included *Mirror of the Sinful Soul*, published 1531 and 1533 and *The Heptameron*, published posthumously in 1559. See M. McKinley, 'Marguerite de Navarre (Marguerite d'Angoulême, Margaret of Navarre, 1492–1549)', in D. Robin, A. Larsen and C. Levin (eds), *Encyclopedia of Women in the Renaissance: Italy, France, and England* (Santa Barbara, CA: ABC–CLIO, 2007), pp. 228–31. See also Hays, *Female Biography*, vol. 5, pp. 456–73.

p. 407, l. 22: *Francis I*: Francis I (1494–1547), king of France, younger brother to Marguerite de Navarre.

p. 407, l. 24: *Tombeau*: tomb or shrine.

p. 407, l. 26: *Nicholas Denisot*: Nicholas Denisot (1515–59), Count of Alsinois and poet; tutor to Anne, Margaret and Jane from *c.* 1547–9.

p. 408, l. 4: *Margaret de Valois, duchess of Berri*: Margaret of France, Duchess of Berry (1523–74), daughter of Francis I and Claude, Duchess of Brittany; niece of Marguerite de Navarre.

p. 408, l. 5: *Henry II*: (1519–59), King of France, ruled from 1547.

p. 408, l. 6: *Ronsard*: Pierre de Ronsard (1524–85), French poet in the court of Henri II and Charles IX, friend to Nicholas Denisot.

p. 408, ll. 6–17: *"a christian song ... lyre, &c."*: From an ode to the three sisters by Ronsard, printed in its entirety in Bayle. Orpheus was son of Calliope and Oeagrus; he was the greatest musician and poet of Greek mythology. See Bayle, *An Historical and Critical Dictionary. By Monsieur Bayle. Translated into English, with Many Additions and Corrections, Made by the Author Himself, That Are not in the French editions*, 2nd edn, 5 vols (London: Knapton, 1734–8), vol. 5, p. 109.

p. 408, ll. 18–19: *Nicholas de Henerai, sieur des Essars*: Alt. Nicholas de Herberay, Seigneur des Essarts and Nicolas de Herberay des Essarts (d. 1552), 'acclaimed for his translation of Spanish texts, most notably the Amadis de Gaule'. See M. B. Winn, *Antoine Verard, Parisian Publisher, 1485–1512, Prologues, Poems and Presentations* (Geneva: Librairie Droz, S.A., 1997), p. 365.

p. 408, l. 20: *Amadis de Gaule*: Also known as Amadis de Gaula. English translation: Amadis of Gaul. Spanish novel *c.* 1345 that details the exploits of the chivalrous knight, Amadis. Restyled in 1505 by Montalvo and published for the first time in 1508. See *Amadis of Gaul, Books I and II (Studies in Romance Languages)* trans. G. Rodriquez De Montalvo, E. Place and H. Behm (Lexington, KY: University of Kentucky Press, 2003), pp. 10–11.

p. 408, l. 21: *Mr. Fulman*: William Fulman (1632–88); English antiquary, he obtained a Master's Degree from Corpus Christi College where the manuscript is located.

p. 408, l. 22: *Edward Seymour*: Edward Seymour, Duke of Somerset (*c.* 1506–52), Lord Protector of the Realm who was beheaded during the reign of King Edward VI.

p. 408, l. 23: *Edward VI*: Edward Tudor (1538–53; r. 1547), he was the only son of King Henry VIII and Jane Seymour.

p. 408, ll. 23–4: *Anne his second wife*: Anne alt. Ann Seymour née Stanhope (*c.* 1510–87), mother to Anne, Margaret and Jane. See A. Locke, *The Seymour Family* (Boston, MA, and New York: Houghton Mifflin, 1914), p. 34. Some sources cite date of birth as 1497.

p. 408, l. 24: *Sir Edward Stanhope*: Sir Edward Stanhope (*c.* 1462–1511), Knight of Suffolk. See R. St Maur, *Annals of the Seymours* (London: Kegan, Paul, Trench, Trubner & Co., Ltd., 1902), p. 126.

p. 408, l. 27: *John Dudley*: (*c.* 1527–54), eldest son of John Dudley, Earl of Warwick. He was first husband of Anne Seymour; they married in 1550 when she was eleven years old. See W. Seymour, *Ordeal by Ambition: An English Family in the Shadow of the Tudors* (New York: St. Martin's Press, 1972), pp. 338–9.

p. 409, ll. 1–2: *Edward Unton*: (*c.* 1534–83), alt. Edward Umpton; second husband of Anne Seymour; they married in 1555. Anne suffered from 'lunacy' beginning 1 May 1566, according to an inquest from 25 October 1583. See *The Unton Inventories Relating to Wadley and Faringdon, County Berkshire in the Years 1596 and 1620 From the Originals in the Possession of Earl Ferrers with a Memoir of the Family Unton by John Gough Nichols, Esq. F.S.A.* (London: John Bowyer Nichols and Son Publisher, 1841), pp. vliv, xxxviii.

p. 409, ll. 2–3: *a letter in her own hand*: not further identified.

p. 409, l. 4: *Elizabeth*: Elizabeth I (1533–1603; r. 1558–1603). See Hays, *Female Biography*, vol. 4, pp. 70–295.

p. 409, l. 6: *lord Strange*: Henry Stanley, fourth Earl of Derby (1531–93).

p. 409, l. 7: *a letter dated July*: not further identified.

p. 409, l. 8: *the earl of Derby, the father of Lord Strange*: Edward Stanley, third Earl of Derby (1509–72), testified against Edward Seymour at the trial resulting in Seymour's execution in 1552. See C. Markham, *King Edward VI, His Life and Character* (London: Smith, Elder & Co., 1907), pp. 61, 147.

p. 409, l. 17: *St. Edmund's Chapel, in Westminster*: Westminster Abbey.

p. 409, l. 22: *Dr. Haddon*: Walter Haddon (1516–*c.* 1572), professor at Kings College during the reign of Edward VI.

p. 409, l. 23: *Mr. Camden*: William Camden (1551–1623), English antiquary, associated with Christ Church, writer of *Britannia* (1586) and the *Annals* of Elizabeth I (1617 and 1627).

p. 409, l. 25–p. 410, l. 8: *"For genius ... reigns."*: see Ballard, *Memoirs of British Ladies*, p. 100.

p. 410, l. 1: *Venus and Pallas*: Venus, the goddess of love; Pallas, the son of Eurybia and Crius, husband of Styx, father of Zelus, Nike, Cratos and Bia.

p. 410, l. 12: *Francis Sforza*: Francesco Sforza (b. 1401), Duke of Milan (1450–66).

p. 410, ll. 13–14: *Galeazzo Maria Sforza*: Galeazzo Maria Sforza (b. 1444), Duke of Milan (1466–76). His mistress, Lucrezia Landriani (*c.* 1440/45–1507), gave birth to Caterina in late 1462 or early 1463.

p. 410, l. 15: *Jerom Riario*: Girolamo Riario (1443–88), nephew of Pope Sixtus IV and made ruler of Imola in 1473 as part of the marriage negotiations for Caterina. The couple married in 1477. In 1480, Girolamo acquired Forlì, but was brutally assassinated on 14 April 1488. See J. de Vries, *Caterina Sforza and the Art of Appearances: Gender, Art, and Culture in Early Modern Italy* (Aldershot: Ashgate, 2010), pp. 13–38; and J. L. Hairston, 'Skirting the Issue: Machiavelli's Caterina Sforza', *Renaissance Quarterly*, 53:3 (2000), pp. 687–712.

p. 410, ll. 19–20: *Tadeo Manfredi ... his son*: Taddeo Manfredi (1431–86), Lord of Imola (1448–73). His son Guidoriccio overthrew him in 1471, but he returned to power in

1472 and sold the city for 40,000 ducats to Pietro Riario, who gave it to his brother Girolamo in 1473.

p. 410, ll. 20–1: *Several children*: During her marriage to Girolamo, Caterina gave birth to seven, possibly eight, children, of which six survived infancy.

p. 408, l. 22: *Octavio Riario*: Ottaviano Riario (1479–1533). He was too young to rule in 1488, so Caterina served as regent until 1500.

p. 410, l. 24: *two-and-twenty years of age*: At the time of Girolamo's assassination, Caterina was twenty-five years old, not twenty-two, a mistake Hays has repeated from her source. See Bayle, *The Dictionary Historical and Critical of Mr. Peter Bayle* (New York: Garland, 1984), vol. 5, p. 132 and de Vries, *Caterina Sforza and the Art of Appearances*, pp. 38–48.

p. 410, l. 27–p. 411, l. 1: *the expedition ... into Italy, 1494*: Charles VIII, King of France, invaded Italy between 1494–5.

p. 411, ll. 3–4: *duke of Valentenois ... Alexander VI*: Cesare Borgia (*c.* 1475–1507) received the title Duke of Valentinois from King Louis XII of France when he renounced his vows as Cardinal in 1498. He was a son of Pope Alexander VI Borgia (1431–1503; r. 1492–1503), who is considered one of the most corrupt popes of the Renaissance era.

p. 411, l. 11: *Ives d'Allegre*: Yves d'Allegre (*c.* 1450–1512). A French commander who served with Cesare Borgia, he officially arrested Caterina Sforza in January 1500. According to French law at the time, women could not be taken prisoner, and this loophole helped Caterina's case for release in June 1501.

p. 411, ll. 11–12: *privately married to John de Medicis*: Giovanni di Pierfrancesco de' Medici (1467–98) was already dead by Caterina Sforza's release in 1501; this is a mistake Hays repeated from her source. Caterina may have secretly married him in 1498, when she was pregnant with their son, Ludovico (renamed Giovanni); he died of gout later that year. There are no records of the wedding, other than Caterina's later profession of it. This testimony was crucial in her winning custody of little Giovanni. Sforza later asserted she had also secretly married Giacomo Feo (*c.* 1470–95). She gave birth to their son, Bernardino (renamed Carlo) in 1489. Feo was assassinated in 1495 because of his threat to Ottaviano Riario's future rule. See Bayle, *The Dictionary Historical and Critical of Mr. Peter Bayle* (1984), vol. 5, p. 132 and de Vries, *Caterina Sforza and the Art of Appearances*, pp. 48–53, 61–2.

p. 411, l. 13: *Ludovic Sforza:* Ludovico Maria Sforza (1452–1508), Caterina's uncle; regent of Milan (1481–95); Duke of Milan (1495–98).

p. 411, l. 15: *Varillas*: Antoine Varillas (1624–96), French historian. He was one of many historians who extolled the valiancy of Caterina Sforza in the early modern era. See A. Varillas, *Les Anecdotes de Florence, ou l'Histoire secrète de la maison de Médicis* (La Haye: Arnout Leers, 1685) and de Vries, *Caterina Sforza and the Art of Appearances*, pp. 236–50.

p. 411, l. 18: *Her estates*: Julius II (Pope from 1503–13) took control of Forlì and Imola in 1503.

p. 412, l. 1: *ISABELLA SFORZA*: Isabella (1503–63) was the illegitimate daughter of Giovanni Sforza, lord of Pesaro, the son of a lesser branch of the Sforza family. Isabella is sometimes misidentified as Isabella d'Aragona Sforza (1470–1524), wife of Giangaleazzo Sforza. See N. Ratti, *Della Famiglia Sforza*, 2 vols (Rome: Salomon, 1795), vol. 2, pp. 172–82.

p. 412, l. 4: *her letters*: some letters published in *Lettere di molte valorose donne* (1549) were published anonymously; they were recognized as Lando's work by contemporaries such as Anton Francesco Doni, who in his *Libraria* (1550) listed them under Lando's name. See also Ratti, *Della Famiglia Sforza*.

p. 412, ll. 5–6: *Hortensio Lando*: also known as Ortensio Lando. Other than the *Lettere*, he also edited and wrote the preface to Isabella Sforza's spiritual treatise: *Della vera tranquillitá dell'animo* (Venice: Manunzio, 1544); however there is speculation that he may have authored the work himself. See M. K. Ray, *Writing Gender in Women's Letter Collections of the Italian Renaissance* (Toronto: Toronto University Press, 2009), pp. 45–80; F. Daenen, 'Isabella Sforza: Beyond the Stereotype', in L. Panizza (ed.), *Women in Italian Renaissance Culture and Society* (Oxford: University of Oxford, 2000), pp. 35–56.

p. 412, l. 7: *Bonna Sforza*: also known as Bona Sforza or Buona Sforza. She was not only the widow of the King of Poland, but also the daughter of Isabella d'Aragon-Sforza, hence the confusion with the identity of these two distinguished women.

p. 412, ll. 7–8: *the king of Poland*: Sigismund I. After his first wife died, he married Bona Sforza of Milan, who was the niece of the Holy Roman emperor Maximilian.

p. 412, l. 8: *Margaret Bobbia*: also known as Margherita Pobbia. Likely an imaginary epistolary character. See Ray, *Writing Gender*, pp. 45–80; and *Lettere di molte valorose donne*.

p. 412, ll. 10–11: *Christofano Bronzini*: also known as Cristoforo Bronzini d'Ancona. He was the author of the dialogue *On the Dignity and Nobility of Women* (Florence: Pignoni, 1622–4).

p. 412, ll. 11–12: *one of the speakers*: the cavalier Tolomei, from Ferrara, a fictitious character in the dialogue *On the Dignity*, depicted as the adversary to women.

p. 412, l. 12: *denying the capacity*: humanists pushed for better education for women, and, at times, for the 'defenses' of women as well; however, they seldom gave up notions of innate male superiority.

p. 412, l. 15: *His adversary*: refers to Onorio – the writer himself (Christofano) – in defence of women.

p. 412, l. 17: *ingennity*: ingenious. See Bayle's list of commendations towards women's writing, amongst which he lists: 'great eloquence, art, propriety, and beautiful elocution'. See end page note in Bayle, *Dictionary Historical and Critical*, vol. 5, p. 133.

p. 413, ll. 2–3: *wit and genius appear to be hereditary*: Frances Sheridan's children followed their parents in literary pursuits. Charles Francis Sheridan (1750–1806) was an author and politician, Richard Brinsley Sheridan (1751–1816) was a well-known playwright and Alicia Sheridan (later Le Fanu) (1753–1817) was a novelist and playwright.

p. 413, ll. 3–4: *descended from an English family*: Sheridan's mother, who died soon after Sheridan's birth, was Anastasia Whyte; her father was Rev. Dr Philip Chamberlaine.

p. 413, ll. 4–5: *sir Oliver Chamberlaine*: Walter Chamberlaine according to the *Dictionary of National Biography* (Errata (1904), p. 249).

p. 413, l. 6: *disputes relative to the theatre*: the so-called Cato Affair, a quarrel between Thomas Sheridan and the English actor Theophilus Cibber in 1743.

p. 413, ll. 6–7: *Mr. Thomas Sheridan*: Thomas Sheridan, actor and orthoepist (*c.* 1719–88).

p. 413, l. 7: *Dr. Thomas Sheridan*: schoolmaster and Church of Ireland clergyman (1687–1738).

p. 413, ll. 7–8: *(son of Dr. Thomas Sheridan, the friend and biographer of Swift)*: Hays is incorrect here. The father, Dr Thomas Sheridan, was the friend of Swift, while his son, Mr Thomas Sheridan, was the author of *The Life of the Rev. Dr. Jonathan Swift* (1784).

p. 413, l. 10: *a small pamphlet*: *The Owls: a Fable: Addressed to Mr Sheridan, on his late Affair in the Theatre* (1743).

p. 413, ll. 16–17: *Domestic Tale of Sydney Biddulph*: *Memoirs of Miss Sidney Bidulph, Extracted from Her own Journal*, 3 vols (Dublin: H. Saunders, 1761). This novel was influenced by Samuel Richardson's *Pamela*.

p. 413, l. 19: *Nourjahad*: an Oriental tale published posthumously in 1767.

p. 413, l. 21: *"The Discovery"*: first performed in 1763, this comic play deals with love, roles in marriage and parentage.

p. 413, ll. 21–2: *"The Dupe"*: first performed in 1763 but never successful on the stage, this play has a complicated plot spun around characters contriving to marry or to prevent each other's marriage.

p. 413, ll. 23–4: *she died at Blois, in the south of France, 1767*: correct date of death is 26 September 1766.

p. 414, l. 1: *SOPHRONIA*: The main source for Sophronia is Rufinius's Latin translation of the Greek text of Eusebius, *Ecclesiastical History*, 14.16b–17. Unnamed in the original Greek text of Eusebius's narrative where she is described as 'a very wise wife' [*sophronestate gyne*]; given the name Sophronia (a feminization of the woman's superlative descriptor in Eusebius) in Rufinus's Latin translation (786, 3–4).

p. 414, ll. 2–3: *lady of a Roman governor*: Eusebius provides his readers with a report on the Christian wife of a *praefectus urbi* (prefect of the city) in Rome who took her own life in order to avoid committing adultery with Maxentius.

p. 414, l. 3: *Eusebius*: the 'father of Church history', also known as Eusebius Pamphili (*c.* AD 260–*c.* 341); bishop of Caesarea in Palestine, Christian historian, polemicist, exegete, orator and letter-writer. His *Ecclesiastical History* in Greek was translated into Latin by Tyrannius Rufinus (*c.* AD 345–410).

p. 414, l. 5: *Maxentius*: Marcus Aurelius Valerius Maxentius (*c.* AD 278–312), Roman emperor from AD 306 until his death.

p. 414, l. 10: *the husband of Sophronia*: not further identified.

p. 414, l. 16: *brutal lust of a despot*: the parallel to the account in Livy (1.57) of Lucretia's suicide is clear.

p. 414, l. 19: *Sulpitia*: Hays relies here on Bayle, *An Historical and Critical Dictionary* (London: James Bettenham, 1737), vol. 5, p. 268, who includes the name 'Sulpitia' as an alternative spelling in the heading of his item. Valerius Maximus's Latin text – cited in Bayle's commentary – also includes reference (incorrectly) to 'Sulpitia' (p. 268).

p. 414, l. 20: *Sulpicius Parterculus*: Servius Sulpicius Paterculus – Sulpicius Paterculus (Bayle, p. 268); Servius Paterculus (Valerius Maximus, *Memorable Deeds and Sayings*, 15.12). Female children would acquire the feminine form of the father's clan name – in this case, Sulpicia, giving us Paterculus's second name. The *gens Sulpicia* (Sulpician clan) was one of the most ancient patrician (elite) families at Rome, producing a number of prominent military and political leaders.

p. 414, ll. 20–1: *Fulvius Flaccus*: Quintus Fulvius Flaccus, otherwise unknown. The *gens Fulvia* (Fulvian clan) was a plebeian (non-elite) family which gained patrician patronage and produced a number of distinguished politicians and military commanders.

p. 414, l. 23: *books of the sybils*: the Sibylline Books were a collection of written oracles thought to comprise texts of the utterances of the Sibyl of Cumae, an inspired prophetess. They were kept at Rome under the charge of the *quindecimviri*.

p. 415, l. 1: *office*: the *quindecimviri sacris faciundis* were fifteen (*quindecim*) magistrates with priestly duties (Ln. *collegium*), including oversight of the Sibylline Books. At the request of the senate, they consulted and interpreted the sacred texts (*sacris faciundis*).

p. 415, l. 2: *senate*: Rome's premier political institution, which advised the Roman people on political issues, foreign affairs, and ancestral custom (*mos maiorum*), including civic cult. Based on the interpretation of a sacred text, the senate's advice to erect the 'statue' of a goddess falls under the last category.

p. 415, l. 2: *statue*: according to the ancient sources, the senate recommended that an 'image' (*simulacrum*) be consecrated to the goddess. The cult associated with this image – most likely a statue – was inaugurated during the period or just before the Hannibalic War.

p. 415, l. 3: Venus Verticordia: Venus, 'Turner of Hearts'. Valerius Maximus states explicitly that the function of this goddess was to turn the minds of virgins and women away from illicit sexual desire to sexual chastity. According to the second-century AD writer Plutarch (*Roman Questions*, 83), a temple to Venus Verticordia was built – again after consulting the Sibylline Books. According to Julius Obsequens (*Prodigies*, 37), we can date the temple's construction to 114 BC.

p. 415, l. 7: *ten were chosen*: not further identified.

p. 415, ll. 9–10: *the year 639*: 639 years after the foundation of Rome in 753 BC, i.e. 114 BC. Hays – following the *Biographium Faemineum*, and misreading Bayle, *Dictionary Historical and Critical*, vol. 5, p. 239 – assigns the date for building the temple of Venus Verticordia (Obsequens) to the erection of the original 'image' (sometime before 204 BC).

p. 415, l. 15: *Julius Cæsar*: Gaius Julius Caesar (100–44 BC), assassinated dictator of Rome.

p. 415, l. 22: *DOROTHY*: Dorothy (alt. Doll) Spencer (née Sidney) (alt. Sydney) was born in October 1617. She was renowned for her beauty, which she inherited from her mother, Dorothy Percy Sidney, Countess of Leicester; her grandmother, Dorothy Devereux Percy, Countess of Northumberland; and her famous great-grandmother, Lettice Knollys Devereux Dudley, Countess of Leicester.

p. 415, l. 22: *Robert Sidney*: Robert Sidney (1595–1677), second Earl of Leicester; he secretly married Dorothy's mother in 1615.

p. 415, ll. 23–4: *Henry lord Spencer, of Wormleighton*: She married Henry Lord Spencer (1620–43) at the Sidney family home of Penshurst Place on 20 July 1639. They had four children: Dorothy (1640–70), who married Sir George Savile, marquess of Halifax; Robert, later second Earl of Sunderland (1641–1702); and two children who died young, Penelope (1642–c. 1667) and Henry or Harry (1643–9). Wormleighton is in Warwickshire.

p. 415, l. 26: *first battle of Newbury*: Newbury, Berkshire, first Royalist defeat of the first civil war.

p. 416, l. 2: *Robert Smythe*: Robert Smythe (1613–c. 1664) was a neighbour of the Sidneys and an old friend; several members of the Sidney family married Smythes. Dorothy and Robert Smythe married in 1652 and had one child, Robert Smythe (1653–95).

p. 416, l. 4: *one son*: Robert Smythe (1653–95). This information comes from Arthur Collins's *Peerage of England*, 6 vols (London: W. Strahan, J. F and C. Rivington, 1756), vol. 1, p. 406.

p. 416, l. 6: *Charles II*: Charles II (1600–49; r. 1625–49).

p. 416, l. 7: *sacharissa*: Edmund Waller (1606–87) wrote a series of poems praising her as 'Sacharissa' between 1635 and 1638, concluding with a poem on her marriage. 'Sacharissa' was taken from 'sacharum', or sugar.

p. 416, l. 8: *fond of retirement*: This description is taken from Collins's *Peerage of England*, vol. 1, p. 406.

p. 416, ll. 10–12: *asked him 'when … young again'*: This tale is recounted in *The Works of Edmund Waller, Esq: in Verse and Prose*, ed. E. Fenton (Dublin: W. G. Jones, 1768), p. xiv.

p. 416, l. 12: *husband*: Hays refers here to her first husband, the Earl of Sunderland.

p. 416, ll. 13–14: *buried with him, in the same vault*: Dorothy was buried in the Spencer family chapel at Brington.

p. 416, l. 16: *Granger's*: *Granger's Biographical History of England* (1769) contains no entry on Dorothy Sidney Spencer. Hays gathered her information from Granger's entry on her husband Henry, Earl of Sunderland from Arthur Collins's entry on Sunderland in his *Peerage of England* and from the works of the poet Edmund Waller.

p. 416, l. 17: *COUNTESS DE LA SUZE*: La Suze, Henriette de Coligny, Countess of (1618–73), was born into an illustrious Protestant family, the Colignys. She was the daughter of Anne de Polignac (1598–1651) and Gaspard III of Coligny (1584–1646), second Marshal of Châtillon. Hays's entry is considerably shorter than that by Ann Thicknesse in *Sketches of the Lives and Writings of the Ladies of France* where she faithfully reproduces Joseph La Porte's entry which contains samples of the La Suze's poetry (*Histoire littéraire*, vol. 1, pp. 335–45). Interestingly, while Thicknesse starts her entry with an ambivalent assessment of La Suze's poetical work, followed by an account of her life, Hays, though she appears to have gleaned most of her research on Suze from her female predecessor, follows the more conventional lay-out proposed by La Croix in his *Dictionnaire historique portatif des femmes célèbres* (Paris: L. Cellot, 1769), vol. 3, and by the anonymous author of *Biographium Faemineum*, vol. 2, pp. 253–5.

p. 416, ll. 18–19: *count de Coligni*: Gaspard III of Coligny (1584–1646), second Marshal of Châtillon.

p. 416, l. 20: *the famous admiral Coligni*: the French Huguenot Gaspard II of Coligny (1519–72) was a prominent leader in the French wars of religion (1562–98).

p. 416, l. 21: *Thomas Hamilton*: a young Scottish nobleman, third Earl of Haddington (1626–45), who married the Comtesse de La Suze in 1643, and died of consumption at the young age of nineteen years.

p. 416, l. 22: *the count de la Suze*: Gaspard de Champagne (d. 1694), Count of Belfort, Ferrette and Suze, son of Louis de Champagne who besieged the town of Belfort in 1636 under Louis XIII. Gaspard La Suze, who had sided with the Prince of Condé during the Fronde (the French civil wars, 1649–53), lost the governorship of Belfort to the heirs of Cardinal Mazarin, chief minister to Louis XIV.

p. 416, l. 26: *Shut up in a country-house*: It was located in Le Mans (see E. Magne, *Femmes galantes du XVIIième siècle, Madame de La Suze (Henriette de Coligny) et la société précieuse* (Paris: Mercure de France, 1908), p. 34).

p. 417, l. 5: *Christina of Sweden*: Queen of Sweden (1626–89, r. 1632–54). She had close connections with the French court, and French men and women of letters, including Madeleine de Scudéry, a close friend of La Suze (see note to p. 418, ll. 26–7, below). Her 'secret' correspondence indicates she showed much sympathy for La Suze. It is also possible that the Queen, who converted to Catholicism, was partly inspired by the La Suze's own conversion (see note to p. 417, l. 6, below). See also Hays, *Female Biography*, vol. 3, pp. 288–314.

p. 417, l. 6: *changed her religion*: see de La Croix, *Dictionnaire historique*, vol. 3, p. 390. La Suze converted to the Catholic faith in 1653.

p. 417, l. 10: *divorce*: The divorce was a long, painstaking process (see Magne, *Femmes galantes*, pp. 235–9). In August 1661 it was granted to La Suze on the grounds of her husband's impotence (see the notarial act in Magne, *Femmes galantes*, pp. 270–3); however, he won his appeal, and the case was reopened and eventually settled on 27 August 1661, obliging La Suze to square accounts with him (see the notarial act in Magne, *Femmes galantes*, pp. 274–9).

p. 417, l. 18: *this whimsical anecdote*: Magne believes that this often-cited anecdote in historians' biographies is sheer fiction (*Femmes galantes*, p. 240, fn. 1).

p. 417, l. 20: *her woman*: not further identified.

p. 417, ll. 21–2: *the officer*: not further identified.

p. 417, ll. 23–7: *Sir,' said she … immediately withdrew.*: adapted from *Biographium Faemineum*, vol. 2, p. 254.

p. 418, l. 7: *Madame de Châtillon*: Elisabeth-Angélique de Montmorency-Bouteville (1627–95) became duchess of Châtillon (1627–95) through her marriage to La Suze's brother, Gaspard IV (d. 1649).

p. 418, l. 10: *Monsieur de la Feuillade*: François III d'Aubusson (1631–91); he was Marshall of France under Louis XIV, and was granted the title of Duke by the King. While a successful military man, he was considered a mediocre courtier.

p. 418, p. 12: *Benserude*: Isaac de Benserade (1613–91) was a renowned poet both at the French court and in the Parisian salons.

p. 418, ll. 13–16: *'You, madam, … without rhyme or reason.'*: see Thicknesse, *Sketches*, pp. 162–3; the anecdote is also related in *Biographium Faemineum*, vol. 2, p. 254.

p. 418, ll. 25–6: *Her poems are printed in a collection in four vols. 12mo.*: Hays probably got this information directly from *Biographium Faemineum*, vol. 2, p. 254. La Suze's poems were compiled in *Poésies de Madame La Suze* (Paris: Charles Sercy, 1668); her name also appears on the title page of another anthology, in which nine other pieces by her were printed. Her name is especially associated with the publication of a *Recueil de pièces galantes en prose et en vers* (Paris: Gabriel Quinet, 1664), known as *the Recueil La Suze-Pellisson*. Her popularity can be inferred from the sheer number of the revised and augmented re-editions of this anthology (see M. Dufour-Maître, *Les Précieuses, Naissance des femmes de lettres en France au XVIIe siècle*, 2nd edn (Paris: Honoré Champion, 2008), p. 739). La Suze is generally credited for re-introducing the elegy in seventeenth-century French poetry and for refining it.

p. 418, l. 26: *Pelisson*: Paul Pellisson (1624–93) was a highly regarded intellectual who wrote a history of the Académie française (*Histoire de l'Académie française*); as a result he became one of its most distinguished members in 1653. He was also an assiduous *habitué* of the salon hosted by his close friend, Madeleine de Scudéry (see note to p. 418, ll. 26–7, below).

p. 418, ll. 26–7: *madame de Scudery*: Hays refers to Madeleine de Scudéry (1607–1701), rather than Madame de Scudéry, who was the wife of her brother Georges. Madeleine was a prolific writer of fiction, dialogues and poetry, and is especially remembered for her multi-volume novels *Artamènes ou le Grand Cyrus* (1649–53) and *Clélie* (1654–60), in which she inserted her famous *Carte de tendre* which had been devised by herself for her friend Pellisson. See also Hays, *Female Biography*, vol. 6, pp. 388–92.

p. 419, l. 2: *Clelia*: *Clélie, histoire romance (1654–1661)* was translated into English (1656–61). Scudéry gives a portrait of La Suze in the eighth volume of Augustin Courbé's edition (see Scudéry, *Clélie* (Genève: Slatkine Reprint, 1973), vol. 8, pp. 894–5), and, following Thicknesse, Hays gives an excerpt in English (see note to p. 419, ll. 3–10, below).

p. 419, ll. 3–10: *'Hesiode, sleeping … a thousand charms.'*: This is a revised translation of Thicknesse's own rendering of La Porte's entry (see Thicknesse, *Sketches*, pp. 158–9).

p. 419, l. 3: *Hesoide*: this should read as Hesiod, the Greek poet (*c.* 750–650 BC).

p. 419, l. 6: *Calliope*: The muse of epic poetry in classical mythology.

p. 419, l. 9: *Venus*: The goddess of love in classical mythology.

p. 419, l. 10: *Charleval*: Charles Faucon de Ris (*c.* 1612/13–93), a love poet whose work for the most part seems to have been lost; what is left of it was rescued by an eighteenth-century scholar, Marc Lefevre, and was published in 1759 as *Poésies* (Michaud, J. Fr., *Biographie universelle, ancienne et moderne* (Paris: Michaud Frères, 1813), vol. 8, pp. 228–9).

p. 419, l. 14: *Sappho*: The Greek poetess (*c.* 630/12–*c.* 570 BC) whose poetry was rediscovered in the Renaissance. It was also the *nom de plume* by which Scudéry was known as salonnière and woman of letters. See also Hays, *Female Biography*, vol. 6, pp. 378–82.

p. 419, l. 21: *MARY*: Mary Herbert (née Sidney) (alt. Sydney) (1561–1621) was a poet, patron and translator.

p. 419, ll. 21–4: *daughter of sir Henry Sydney ... lady Mary ... John duke of Northumberland*: she was daughter of Sir Henry Sidney (1529–86) and Mary Dudley (*c.* 1530–86); granddaughter of John Dudley, Duke of Northumberland (1504–53).

p. 419, l. 25: *born about the middle of the sixteenth century*: she was born 27 October 1561 at Tickenhall, Worcestershire: see *ODNB*.

p. 419, l. 26: *reigns of Elizabeth and of James*: Elizabeth I (1533–1603; reigned in England from 1558); James VI of Scotland and I England (1566–1625; reigned in Scotland from 1567 and England from 1603).

p. 419, l. 27: *Sir Philip Sydney*: Sir Philip Sidney (1554–86); courtier and poet.

p. 420, l. 1: *Arcadia*: see note to p. 420, l. 17, below.

p. 420, ll. 1–2: *1576, married Henry earl of Pembroke*: Both *Biographium Faemineum*, vol. 2, p. 189 and Ballard, *Memoirs of British Ladies*, p. 249 have this erroneous date; she was married in 1577 to Henry Herbert (*c.* 1538–1601), second Earl of Pembroke; she became his third wife.

p. 420, ll. 2–6: *Three children were the fruit of this marriage ... who died young:* There were four children; William Herbert (1580–1630), Earl of Pembroke, who had no surviving legitimate children; the present family is descended from his brother Philip (1584–1650), Earl of Pembroke and Montgomery; Anne died in her early twenties; Katherine died at age three.

p. 420, l. 7: *Robert Dudley*: Robert Dudley (*c.* 1532–88), Earl of Leicester; her maternal uncle, favourite of Elizabeth I and influential literary patron.

p. 420, ll. 8–9: *Whose fortune ... he increased*: The dowry was £3,000.

p. 420, l. 17: *"The Countess of Pembroke's Arcadia"*: by Philip Sidney (London: William Ponsonbie, 1590).

p. 420, ll. 12–13: *highly ... talents*: Hays's original summation from her sources.

p. 420, ll. 18–19: *Mr. Abraham Fraunce devoted his poetic and literary labours*: Abraham Fraunce (alt. France; *c.* 1552–*c.* 1593), lawyer and poet; dedicated *Countess of Pembrokes Emmanuel* (1591), and *The Countess of Pembrokes Ivychurch* poems (1591 and 1592) to Mary Sidney.

p. 420, ll. 19–21: *talent ... cultivated:* Hays's original summation, emphasizing Mary Sidney's craft.

p. 420, ll. 23–4: *Wilton*: Wilton, near Salisbury; the Pembroke's country estate.

p. 420, ll. 21–2: *She translated from the Hebrew ... Psalms*: recognized as her greatest literary achievement, circulated widely at the time: see *ODNB*.

p. 420, l. 24: *picture*: engraving by Simon van de Passe (1618).

p. 420, l. 25–p. 421, l. 4: *also translated ... 12 mo.*: incomplete listing of her works from *Biographium Faemineum* and Ballard. *A Discourse of Life and Death* by Philippe de Mornay (1549–1623) first published with *Antonius: A Tragedy Written Also in French by Robert Garnier. Both Done in English by the Countess of Pembroke* (1592). Mary Sidney also translated Petrarch's 'Triumph of Death' and wrote at least three original poems: 'A Dialogue between Two Shepherds, Thenot and Piers, in Praise of Astrea', 'To the Angell Spirit of Sir Philip Sidney' and 'Even Now that Care' to Queen Elizabeth; perhaps also 'The Dolefull Lay of Clorinda'.

p. 420, l. 27: *Philip Morney*: see note to p. 420, l. 25–p. 421, l. 4, above.

p. 421, l. 4: *1595*: second printing of *Antonius*, with a different title.

p. 421, ll. 6–7: *Dr. Mouffet*: Thomas Moffet (alt. Moufet, Muffet) (1553–1604), author of *The Silkewormes and Their Flies* (1599), Pembroke family physician.

p. 421, l. 9: *Mr. Giles Jacob*: Giles Jacob (fl. 1686–1744), work referred to is *The Poetical Register: or, the Lives and Characters of all the English Poets. With an Account of Their Writings*, 2 vols (London: A. Bettesworth, W. Taylor, and J. Batley, 1723), vol. 1, p. 201.

p. 421, l. 12: *1602*: She died of smallpox on 25 September 1621; erroneous 1602 in *Biographium Faemineum*, vol. 2, p. 191.

p. 421, l. 17: *Ben Johnson*: Ben Jonson (1572–1637), poet and playwright.

p. 421, ll. 18–29: *"Under neath this ... her tomb."*: Epitaph attributed to Ben Jonson in *Biographium Faemineum*, vol. 2, p. 191, but written by William Browne (*c.* 1590–*c.* 1645), BL Lansdowne MS 777, fol. 43v.

p. 421, l. 27: *Niobe*: in Greek myths, lost six children. On Mount Sipylus her tears turned her into a column of stone.

p. 422, l. 1: *Sir Francis Osborn*: Francis Osborne (alt. Osborn) (1593–1659).

p. 422, ll. 1–2: *Memoirs of the Reign of James*: *Historical Memoires on the Reigns of Queen Elizabeth and King James* in *The Works of Francis Osborn* (1673; original 1658).

p. 422, ll. 3–16: *"She was that ... but untruth."*: from *Historical Memoires*, pp. 507–8. Osborn had personal knowledge from service to the Pembrokes: see *ODNB*.

p. 422, l. 16: *Wood*: Anthony Wood (alt. Anthony á Wood) (1632–95), antiquarian and author of *Athenae Oxonienses* (1691), the source for Hays.

p. 422, l. 16: *ascribes ... Sidney*: Philip Sidney composed metrical versions of Psalms 1–43; Mary Sidney completed the 150 Psalms.

p. 422, l. 21: *Mr. Hartington's Nugæ Antiquæ*: Hartington refers to Sir John Harington (*c.* 1588–1654); *Nugæ antiquæ: Being a Miscellaneous Collection of Original Papers in Prose and Verse*, 3 vols (London: Vernor and Hood, 1792).

p. 423, l. 1: *TANAQUIL*: She changed her name to Gaia Caecilia (called Gaia Cyrilla in Boccaccio's *On Famous Women*) when she arrived at Rome, although some Roman historians also commonly spelled her name *Caia Caecilia* or *Caia Cyrilla*. Under this name, she is the mythical source of various Roman wedding customs and a model of domestic life. She was highly skilled in working with wool. Queen Gaia was much admired by the Romans of her day; Pliny (*Natural History*, 8.194) says that a statue was dedicated to her as Gaia Caecilia in the temple of Semo Sancus. Tanaquil had a daughter, Tarquinia, and two sons, Lucius Tarquinius Superbus and Arruns Tarquinius.

p. 423, l. 2: *Tarquinius Priscus*: also known as Tarquin the Elder, Tarquinius Priscus was the legendary fifth king of Rome. He ruled from 616 to 579 BC. (See also note to p. 423, l. 12, below.)

p. 423, l. 4: *Lucumon*: He later changed his name to Tarquin. See note to p. 423, l. 12, below.

p. 423, l. 12: *her rank*: The daughter of an illustrious Etruscan family, Tanaquil thought her husband would make a good leader, but since he was the son of an immigrant, he would not be able to gain power in Tarquinii, where they lived. Tanaquil encouraged him to move to Rome, which at the time was not dominated by a strong local aristocracy. Tanaquil's prophecy was eventually realized for Tarquin; he became friends with King Ancus Marcius who made Tarquin guardian of his children. When the king died before his children were old enough to become successors to the throne, Tarquin used his popularity to be elected the fifth king of Rome.

p. 423, l. 22: *mount Janiculus*: the Janiculum hill, located on the west side of the Tiber river. It is not one of the famous seven hills of Rome.

p. 424, l. 3: *great fortune*: Tanaquil appears in the early legends of Rome as a woman endowed with prophetic powers, and was closely connected with the worship of the god of the hearth.

p. 424, l. 14: *Servius Tullius*: Tanaquil raised Servius Tullius, the sixth king of Rome, as her own child. When her husband King Tarquin was murdered, Tanaquil hid his death from her subjects, instead telling them that Tarquin appointed Servius as a temporary king until he got better. After gaining the people's respect and commanding the kingship, Servius and Tanaquil announced Tarquin's death.

p. 424, l. 26: *espoused the daughter of his benefactor*: Tarquinia.

p. 424, l. 28: *principality of Corniculum*: an ancient Latin town in the region of Latium (central Italy).

p. 425, l. 3: *a son*: Tarquinius Superbus, or Tarquin the Proud, who was the legendary seventh king of Rome. He ruled from 535 to 495 BC.

p. 425, l. 8: *Varro*: Marcus Terentius Varro (116–27 BC), Roman scholar and writer. Pliny (see note to p. 425, l. 14, below) records Varro's reference to Tanaquil (Pliny, *Natural History*, 8.194).

p. 425, l. 8: *Cicero*: Marcus Tullius Cicero (103–43 BC), Roman lawyer, orator, philosopher and politician; named an enemy of the state by the Second Triumvirate (Antony, Lepidus, Octavian) and murdered in 43 BC.

p. 425, l. 14: *Pliny*: Gaius Plinius Secundus, or Pliny the Elder (AD 23–79), a Roman writer, philosopher and military commander. He famously perished during the eruption of Vesuvius which buried the towns of Pompeii and Herculaneum.

p. 425, l. 24: *her girdle*: According to H. Malden, 'Caia Caecilia was possessed of magic powers, and wore a magic girdle. Her statue was preserved in the temple of the old Italian god, Sancus; and filings from the girdle of the statue were taken as amulets by persons in great danger. She was revered by the Roman matrons as the patroness of good housewifery and industry at the loom' (*History of Rome* (London: Baldwin and Cradock, 1830), vol. 2, p. 36).

p. 425, ll. 25–6: *having made important discoveries in medicine*: There is no evidence of this claim.

p. 426, ll. 2–3: Dius Fidius: the Roman god of oaths, associated with Jupiter and Semo Sancus.

p. 426, ll. 5–8: *"The admirable … ever to be forgotten."*: Jerome, *Against Jovinianus*, 1.49.

p. 426, l. 6: *St. Jerom*: Eusebius Sophronius Hieronymus, or Saint Jerome (*c.* AD 347–420), priest, theologian and historian. Recognized as a Doctor of the Church and a Christian saint, Jerome is best known for his translation of the Bible into Latin.

p. 426, l. 8: *(as Juvenal)*: Tanaquil was represented in the Roman traditions as a woman of high spirit, and accustomed to rule her husband; hence the name is used by the Latin poets to indicate generally any imperious consort. See Juvenal, *Satires*, 6.564.

p. 426, l. 14: *TELESILIA*: Her name is Telesilla: Greek Τελέσιλλα. Hays takes this error from *Biographium Faemineum*. She lived in the first half of the fifth century BC.

p. 426, ll. 15–16: *being advised by the oracle*: The source for the oracle story is Plutarch, *On the Bravery of Women*, 4.245c–d. The story may well have originated from something Telesilla said in her verse (in antiquity the biography of writers was largely drawn from their own work).

p. 426, l. 18: *such excellence*: Her poetry was admired in antiquity. See Antipater of Thessalonica, *Anthologia Palatina*, 9.26.5. Nine fragments of her poetry remain: see Plant, *Women Writers of Ancient Greece and Rome*, pp. 32–5.

p. 426, l. 19: *the Argive women to repel*: Cleomenes and Demaratus attacked Argos in 494 BC. Pausanias (2.20.7–8) tells us that Telesilla rallied slaves, the young, the old men and then the young women and drove off the Spartans who had earlier massacred the Argive fighting men (see also Plutarch, *On the Bravery of Women*, 4.245c–d). Herodotus describes the earlier massacre (6.77–83), but does not mention Telesilla or the role of the women or even an attack on the city itself. It is likely that the story is aetiological, invented later to account for a religious festival in which men and women swapped clothes (Polyaenus, *Stratagems*, 33; Pausanias, *On the Bravery of Women*, 4.245c–d). Eusebius dates Telesilla's fame to 451/50 BC; if he is right, it is unlikely she was born early enough to take part in the battle in 494 BC. It is more likely that she wrote about the battle and thus became associated with it (on this see Maximus of Tyre, *Orations*, 37.5). A statue of her holding a helmet with her books at her feet was made in the first century AD (Tatian, *Against the Greeks*, 33) and erected in the sanctuary of Aphrodite at Argos (Pausanias, 2.20).

p. 426, l. 20: *Cleomenes the Spartan king*: son of Anaxandridas, reigned 520–c. 489 BC. Sparta had two kings (Agiad and Eurypontid): he was the king of the Agiad line.

p. 426, l. 21: *king Demaratus*: son of Ariston, he reigned 515–491 BC; he was of the Eurypontid line.

p. 426, l. 21: *Pamphiliacum*: This was in Argos and was probably a sanctuary or a public building.

p. 427, l. 2: *A TRIPLE name*: Greek: Θεανώ.

p. 427, ll. 2–3: *The first of this name*: Hays follows the *Biographium Faemineum*, vol. 2, p. 258, in describing the poet first (*Biographium Faemineum* summarized the entry on Theano in the *Suda*); *Suda* lists her third.

p. 427, l. 3: *Theano Locrencis*: 'Locrencis' is a Latin adjective meaning 'Locrian'.

p. 427, l. 4: *the city of Locri*: There were two areas in Greece inhabited by Locrians, but the city of Locris was a colony of one of these in Magna Graeca (Italy). It was founded c. 680 BC and is now known as Locri.

p. 427, l. 4: *surnamed Melica*: 'Melica' means lyric poet.

p. 427, l. 5: *her songs and lyric poems*: The *Suda* adds that she wrote 'Locrian songs'. Eustathius (a Greek scholar of the twelfth century AD) in his *Commentary on the Iliad*, 2.327.10, also names the lyric Theano, but he does not cite any of her work. None of her work has survived.

p. 427, ll. 5–6: *The second*: The second Theano in Hays is also the second in the *Suda*, but the entry has been shortened.

p. 427, l. 6: *a poetess*: Hays calls this Theano a poetess too, but follows the *Biographium Faemineum* in calling attention to her reputation for poetry rather than philosophy. The *Suda* does state that a poem in epic meter was attributed to her; however, it sees her first and foremost as a philosopher, noting that she wrote *Philosophical Commentaries* and *Sayings*. Didymus (d. c. AD 10) said that Theano was the first woman to compose poems and cultivate philosophy. In the fourth and third centuries, and later, pseudonymous texts were written in Theano's name, incorporating Pythagorean philosophy and gaining some authority by the use of her name. See H. Thesleff, 'An Introduction to the Pythagorean Writings of the Hellenistic Period', *Acta Academiae Aboensis, Humaniora*, 24.3 (1961). Theano the poet was probably a namesake from Magna Graeca. Over time, the Theanos have been confused; the poet's texts have been ascribed to the Pythagorean Theano along with the later pseudonymous texts. For a defence of the attribution of the later texts to real women named Theano, see M. E. Waithe, *A History of Women Philosophers*, 4 vols (Dordrecht: M. Nijhoff, 1987), vol. 1, pp. 12–15, 41–55. For translations of extant works attributed to Theano and other Pythagorean women, see Plant, *Women Writers of Ancient Greece and Rome*, pp. 70–86.

p. 427, ll. 6–7: *said by some historians to have been the wife of Pythagoras*: Didymus believed that texts ascribed to Theano were written by the wife of Pythagoras (sixth century BC), but this is not correct. The *Suda* adds that she was the daughter of Pythonax, wife of Pythagoras and mother of Pythagoras's children, Telauges, Mnesarkhos, Myia and Arignote. This would place her in the sixth century BC. The *Suda* admits that this information was not secure, adding that some authorities said that this Theano was the wife of Brotinus and came from Croton. Other ancient sources reveal just how unreliable information about this Theano's life was. She is described variously as the wife or the daughter or pupil of Pythagoras; from Metapontum, Thuria, Cressa or Croton; her father was Leophron, Pythonax or Brontinus: see Iamblichus, *Life of Pythagoras*, 267, 132; *Suidas s.v.* Theano 1, Theano 2, Pythagoras; Diogenes Laertius, 8.42; Porphyry, *Life of Pythagoras*, 4, 19; Anonymous in Photius, 438b.31; Hermesianax in *Athenaeus*, 13.599a; Schol. in Plato, *Republic*, 600b.

p. 427, ll. 7–8: *The third, Theano Thuria, or Metapotino*: Hays's third Theano is the first listed in the *Suda*, where she is described as a Pythagorean and from Thuria or Metapontum. Both these cities are in Magna Graeca, as is Croton, where Pythagoras was said to have emigrated in 531 BC. He later moved to Metapontum.

p. 427, l. 9: *Carystius*: Carystus, according to the *Suda*.

p. 427, ll. 9–10: *Brantinus of Cretona*: Brantinus of Cretona probably refers to Brotinus (sometimes Brontinus) of Croton, a Pythagorean who is listed as a possible husband of two of the Theanos. Elsewhere we find him listed as the father of Theano (Diogenes Laertius, 8.42).

p. 427, l. 10: *daughter of the poet Lycophron*: *Suda* tells us that Theano was the daughter of Leophron. Lycophron was a Hellenistic poet of the third century BC. A Leophron was famous for winning chariot races at Olympia (late sixth to early fifth centuries BC).

p. 427, l. 11: *Suidas*: An encyclopedia compiled in the tenth century; the name of the work is now believed to be the *Suda*, previously this name, in the form Suidas, was treated as the title.

p. 427, ll. 11–13: *There are three epistles ... published*: Pseudonymous works; for translations see Plant, *Women Writers of Ancient Greece and Rome*, pp. 68–75.

p. 427, l. 14: *Aldus*: Aldo Manuzio, known as Aldus Manutius (1449–1515), an Italian humanist who founded the Aldine Press at Venice.

p. 427, l. 16: *Mrs. Thomas*: 1675–1731.

p. 427, l. 17: *Corinna*: 'the famous *Theban* Poetess who overcame PINDAR', as John Dryden explained when he offered the name to Thomas in a letter of 1699 (cited in Thomas, 'Life' [dated 31 October 1728, Fleet Prison], *Pylades and Corinna* (London: T. Curll, 1731), vol. 1, pp. l–lxxvii).

p. 427, l. 21: *her father*: Emmanuel Thomas (d. 1677), a lawyer at the Inner Temple.

p. 427, l. 24–p. 428, l. 1: *injudicious tenderness with which she was nurtured*: this and what follows paraphrases Thomas's 'Life,' *Pylades*, p. iv.

p. 428, l. 9: *Her mother*: also Elizabeth Thomas (née Osborne) (d. 1719) of Kent.

p. 428, l. 18: *economical lodgings in the country*: They retired to Surrey.

p. 428, l. 20: *a pretender to alchemy*: not identified.

p. 428, l. 22: *the philosopher's stone*: a stone with alchemical properties.

p. 428, l. 24: *three hundred pounds*: This was a small fortune at a time when a middle-class family needed above £100 per annum, and £500 per annum to ensure affluence. See C. Emsley, T. Hitchcock and R. Shoemaker, 'London History – Currency, Coinage and the Cost of Living', *Old Bailey Proceedings Online*, at http://www.oldbaileyonline.org, version 7.0 [accessed 15 August 2013].

p. 429, ll. 2–3: *Latin, arithmetic, and the mathematics*: in 'Life' she specifies 'Latin, *Writing*, and Arithmetic' and describes her extensive reading.

p. 429, l. 14: *Bloomsbury*: Thomas and her mother lived in Wynn's Court, Great Russell Street.

p. 429, l. 17: *duke of Montague*: Ralph Montagu, first Duke of Montagu (bap. 1638, d. 1709).

p. 429, l. 24–p. 430, l. 1: *'Be assured ... mutton.'*: This is a paraphrase of Thomas, 'Life', pp. lv–lvi.

p. 430, l. 5: *Mr. Freeman*: Montagu used this alias when visiting the Thomases house to keep the political nature of the meetings under cover.

p. 430, l. 8: *Jack and Tom, Will and Ned*: familiar covers for the gentlemen identified in notes to p. 430, ll. 10–11, p. 430, l. 11 and p. 430, ll. 11–12, below.

p. 430, ll. 10–11: *duke of Devonshire*: William Cavendish, Duke of Devonshire (1641–1707).

p. 430, l. 11: *lords Buckingham and Dorset*: John [Danvers] Villiers, styled third Earl of Buckingham (*c.* 1677–1723); and Charles Sackville, Earl of Dorset (1643–1706).

p. 430, ll. 11–12: *a viscount and his son, William Dutton Colt*: Sir William Dutton Colt (bap. 1646, d. 1693), and William Dutton Colt (d. 1698).

p. 430, ll. 16–17: *a projected revolution in the state*: an allusion to the Glorious Revolution of 1688 in which the Roman Catholic James II (1633–1701, r. 1685–8) was overthrown in favour of his Protestant daughter, Mary Stuart (1662–94, r. 1689–94) and her husband (and cousin), William of Orange (1650–1702, r. 1689–1702). The Colts, diplomats with strong European Protestant connections, Cavendish and Montagu, politicians who had favoured the exclusion of James II, and Villiers and Sackville, political power-brokers, all had vested interests in the outcome.

p. 430, l. 23: *closing of the Exchequer*: In 1672, Charles II raided the mint and closed the Exchequer or Treasury. The seized funds, advanced to the government by banks, represented the investments of over 10,000 people; widespread bankruptcy followed (see T. Harris, *Restoration: Charles II and his Kingdoms, 1660–1685* (Harmondsworth: Penguin, 2006)).

p. 431, ll. 1–2: *captain of the band of pensioners*: a group of nobles (the pensioners) enlisted to guard the monarch and enhance the spectacle of regal power; by the eighteenth century the tradition had a purely ceremonial function.

p. 431, ll. 2–3: *Mr. Gwynnet*: Richard Gwinnett (1675–1717), a consumptive, Oxford-educated minor playwright, Middle Temple member and family friend; failing to secure a position, he retired to his family estate in Gloucestershire, and maintained a sixteen-year engagement with Thomas.

p. 431, ll. 15–18: *his grace ... lure her from the paths of chastity*: This account of her attempted seduction by Montagu is described in 'Life', pp. lviii–lxiii.

p. 431, l. 22: *feelings of a mother*: according to Thomas, frustrated by the loss of a wealthy patron/suitor for her daughter, her mother was unsympathetic ('Life', pp. lxii).

p. 431, ll. 26–7: *mind of Corinna ... cultivated by a perusal of the best authors*: something Thomas takes pains to demonstrate in 'Life'.

p. 432, l. 3: *"The sons of interest deem romance."*: From the Scottish poet and friend of Pope, James Thomson, *Summer. A Poem* (London: Printed for J. Millan, 1727).

p. 432, l. 12: *his father*: George Gwinnett (1647–1724).

p. 432, ll. 24–7: *'Six months ... for ever.'*: Gwinnett in Thomas, 'Life', p. lxxiii.

p. 433, ll. 5–6: 'Sorrow ... ever since.': *Biographium Faemineum*, vol. 2, p. 202.

p. 433, l. 7: *deed of conveyance*: a lease and release or legal document for the transfer of property.

p. 433, l. 10: *his brother*: George Gwinnett.

p. 434, l. 16: *a pretended friend*: the 'false Friend' is unnamed in 'Life', p. lxxvi.

p. 434, ll. 16–17: *thrown into prison*: Thomas was committed to Fleet Prison (for debtors) from 1727 for three years. She stayed after the issue of her release warrant (June 1729), probably due to outstanding gaoler's fees.

p. 434, ll. 18–27: *In April, 1711 ... fever*: This account of Thomas's 'deplorable sufferings' after swallowing a chicken bone faithfully summarizes 'The surprizing Case of Mrs. Thomas, as it was given in, to the College of Physicians, 1730', appended to *Pylades and Corinna*, vol. 2: *The Honourable Lovers* (London: E. Curll, 1732), pp. 93–6. Dysentery is an intestinal inflammation causing severe diarrhoea and bleeding.

p. 435, l. 1: *the faculty*: Her doctors, Sir John Colbatch and Dr Samuel Garth (1660–1719), were members of the College of Physicians, and aspiring poets.

p. 435, l. 2: *ordered to Bath*: spa town in England, known for its healing waters.

p. 435, l. 17: *medicine*: The report to the College of Physicians specifies that 'Quicksilver', or mercury, a highly toxic element, was believed to have beneficial properties including internal cleansing; zealously advocated by 'Dr Quicksilver', College of Physicians member Dr Thomas Dover (bap. 1662, d. 1742).

p. 435, l. 18: *dropsy*: oedema or swelling of the stomach tissues.

p. 435, l. 27: *Mr. Pope*: Alexander Pope (1688–1744), a satirical Whig poet.

p. 435, l. 28: *Henry Cromwel, esq.*: Henry Cromwell (1659–1728), poet, translator and cousin to Oliver Cromwell.

p. 435, l. 28–p. 436, l. 1: *Cromwel ... letters*: Thomas sold Pope's juvenile correspondence (published in *Miscellanea*, 2 vols (London: E. Curll, 1726); see *The Dunciad*, ii, notes).

p. 436, l. 3: *Curl, the bookseller*: Edmund Curll (d. 1747), a successful London bookseller off the Strand who unscrupulously published literary works and ephemera without the formal permissions that were conventional in this pre-copyright age.

p. 436, ll. 7–8: *placing Corinna in ludicrous circumstances*: Pope mercilessly satirized Curll slipping in a huge 'lake' of Thomas's excreta (Pope, *The Dunciad* ii, pp. 69–76).

p. 436, l. 8: *the Dunciad*: Pope, *The Dunciad*.

p. 436, l. 13: *the church of St. Bride's*: Thomas was baptized and buried at St Bride's, Fleet Street (rebuilt 1672–5 under Christopher Wren).

p. 436, l. 14: *Her productions*: An anonymous poem on Dryden in *Luctus Britiannici* (1700), *Miscellany Poems* (London: T. Combes, 1722, 1726, 1727); and some correspondence sold to Curll.

p. 436, l. 17: *two volumes of letters*: *Pylates and Corinna*, 2 vols (London: Curll, 1731, 1732) also included miscellaneous documents and writings.

p. 436, l. 20: *THYMELE*: Her name is Greek: ϑυμέλη. Thymele is the Latin form of her name. Hays takes this entry directly from *Biographium Faemineum*, vol. 2, p. 264, though she does not cite her source here.

p. 436, l. 22: *Martial*: We can best date her as a contemporary of Martial (*c.* AD 40–104) and of Juvenal (AD 60–117). See mention of her in Martial, *Epigrams*, 1.4.5 and Juvenal, *Satires*, 1.36, 6.66, 8.197.

p. 436, ll. 22–3: *introduced ... a kind of dance*: Martial calls her a dancer in mime, not a poet or composer. Her name is Greek, but we only hear about her performing in Rome, especially with a famous mime artist named Latinus (Martial, *Epigrams*, 1.4.5, Juvenal, *Satires*, 1.36).

Roman mime was a popular form of theatrical entertainment in which actors (both male and female) did speak; the drama was normally farcical, and both improvised and more literary forms of mime are attested. Martial suggested that his form of lewd but playful humour was comparable to that of the performances of Thymele and Latinus.

p. 436, l. 24: *Themelinos*: In Classical Greek theatre, the altar to Dionysus, which was situated in the middle of the orchestra, was called the 'Thymele'. The derivation of the word comes from the word *thuô* (sacrifice). 'Thymele' later denoted the orchestra (the dancing space) and hence the chorus who danced there. Later still, when a form of stage was used, it came to mean that stage on which they performed. A form of the word, *Thymelikos*, was used to describe musicians and later actors. The use of the word to describe the altar to Dionysus in the theatre is much earlier than the date of the actress Thymele: we find it in Pratinus, a lyric poet of the fifth–fourth centuries BC (Pratin., Lyr., 1.2). Thus, Thymele seems to have taken a 'stage-name' that denotes her profession.

p. 437, l. 3: *Gualtherus Gruter*: Gualtherus *alt*. Gualterus Gruter; initiated a protest in Brussels against anti-Protestant discrimination. Protesters were later called 'gueux' (shrewd).

p. 437, l. 4: *Antwerp*: port in modern Belgium.

p. 437, ll. 4–5: *James Gruter*: James *alt*. Jan, Jean or John Gruter (1560–1627); scholar, writer and translator; studied at Caius College, Cambridge. Professor at the University of Wittenberg from 1586; he resigned for reasons of conscience; most important works appeared in Heidelberg after he moved there in 1592.

p. 437, ll. 7–8: *her religion*: she was a Calvinist when the Netherlands were under Spanish Catholic rule.

p. 437, l. 8: *the duchess of Parma*: Margaret of Parma (1522–86); governess of the Netherlands between 1559–67 and 1578–82.

p. 437, ll. 10–11: *Balthasor Venator*: German scholar and satirical poet (1594–1664); innovator of German-language poetry. With Martin Opitz, founded the Heidelberg circle; friend of Jan Gruter.

p. 437, l. 14: *Galen*: Aelius Galen *alt*. Galen of Pergamon, Greek physician and philosopher (129–*c*. 200*xc*. 216); his authority dominated Western medicine for 1,500 years.

p. 437, l. 18: *Cambridge ... Leyden*: Cambridge, in East Anglia, England, and Leiden, Netherlands; both centres of university learning during the northern-European Renaissance.

p. 437, l. 21: *daughter*: She had two younger brothers, George and Cooke. It seems likely that her mother died at a young age, and that she shared her brothers' lessons at home.

p. 437, l. 21: *George Tollet*: He held a succession of state administrative posts, initially in Ireland, and then in London. From 1702–14, he was Extra Commissioner of the Navy, with an annual salary of £500.

p. 437, ll. 22–3: *reigns of William and of Anne*: William of Orange (1650–1702) became king of England in 1689. He was succeeded by Queen Anne (1665–1714).

p. 437, l. 23: *born in 1694*: 11 March 1694.

p. 438, l. 3: *Latin*: Unusually for a woman, she wrote and translated Latin fluently, including the Latin aphorisms that Jane Grey had scratched in the wall of her cell at the Tower.

p. 438, ll. 8–9: *in the Tower*: As a Navy Board official, her father lived in the Tower precincts. Already a tourist site as well as a prison, the Tower housed not only the Crown Jewels and the Armoury, but also a menagerie, the Mint, an arsenal and army barracks. Her poetry indicates that she felt trapped in this noisy, claustrophobic environment.

p. 438, l. 10: *Stratford and Westham*: Before moving to Stratford (in Essex) and Westham (now West Ham), she lived in her father's country home, Betley Hall, in Staffordshire.

p. 438, ll. 11–12: *In 1755, a volume of her poems was printed*: see note to p. 438, l. 20, below.

p. 438, ll. 13–14: *Susanna, or Innocence Preserved*: Her other most famous poem was called 'From Anne Boleyn to King Henry VIII: An Epistle'.

p. 438, l. 15: *sir Isaac Newton*: Isaac Newton (1642–1727), natural philosopher most famous for his work on gravity and on optics. She wrote an elegy to Newton on the night of his death, and used well-informed Newtonian imagery in several of her poems.

p. 438, l. 16: *essays*: poems.

p. 438, l. 20: *after her decease*: An edition of her poems was published anonymously in 1724 (see *Poems on several occasions. With Anne Boleyn to King Henry Viii. An epistle* (London: Printed for John Clarke, 1724)). After she died, a more substantial collection was published, *Poems on Several Occasions. With Anne Boleyn to King Henry Viii. An epistle. By Mrs. Elizabeth Tollet* (London: Printed for John Clarke, 1755) with a revised version in about 1760. In 1756, about thirty of her poetic psalms were reproduced in an anthology: see H. Dell (ed.), *A Select Collection of the Psalms of David, as Imitated or Paraphrased by the Most Eminent English Poets* ... (London: Printed for the editor and sold by W. Griffin; S. Hooper, and by S. and P. Eaves, 1756).

p. 438, l. 23: *nephew ... Notes on Shakespeare*: George Tollet (bap. 1725, d. 1779); he contributed fifteen notes to the 1777 edition of Shakespeare by Samuel Johnson and George Steevens and over 400 to the ten-volume 1778 edition.

p. 439, l. 1: *TYMICHA*: 'Tymicha' in *Biographium Faemineum*, vol. 2, pp. 265–6; usually 'Timycha'. Greek: Τιμύχα. She lived *c.* 410–390 BC.

p. 439, l. 2: *Lacedæmonian*: Lacedaemonia (or Laconia) was a region of the south-eastern Peloponnese in which the city of Sparta was situated.

p. 439, l. 3: *Myllias*: a Pythagorean, but little is known of him. See Aelian, *Varia Historia*, 4.17 and Iamblicus, *On the Pythagorean Way of Life*, 143.

p. 439, l. 3: *Crotone*: a Greek city in Magna Graecia, Croton had traditional links to Pythagoras, as he founded his philosophical school there around 530 BC. While the school itself had been shut down, the city kept a tradition of Pythagorean philosophy.

p. 439, l. 4: *Jamblicus, in his Life of Pythagoras*: Iamblichus, a Neoplatonist philosopher from Chalcis, best known for this work, written *c.* AD 300. The title should be *On the Pythagorean Way of Life*.

p. 439, l. 5: *female Pythagoreans*: Found in *On the Pythagorean Way of Life*, 36. Theano is also on the list (see Hays, *Female Biography*, vol. 6, p. 425).

p. 439, l. 6: *Dionysius*: Dionysius seized power in Syracuse in 406 BC (Diodorus Siculus, 13.91–2). He attacked Magna Graecia, including Croton, in 390 BC (Diodorus Siculus, 14.100ff). Dionysius was renowned in antiquity for his cruelty (see e.g. Diodorus Siculus, 13.111–112). The story is told by Iamblichus, *On the Pythagorean Way of Life*, 31. He credits the story to two Greek historians whose work only survives in citations: Hippobotus, who wrote on the history of philosophy *c.* 200 BC, and Neanthes, who probably lived *c.* 290–220 BC. In the narrative, Dionysius had sent out his troops to capture Pythagoreans to learn about their mysteries: Timycha and her husband were caught near Tarentum while the rest of their party were slaughtered, as their escape route was blocked by a field of beans.

p. 439, l. 13: *beans*: The Pythagorean prohibition on eating beans is widely reported in antiquity but the reason for it remains a mystery. For the best explanation, see Cicero, *On Divination*, I.30.62.

p. 439, l. 20: *pregnancy*: not corroborated.

p. 439, ll. 23–4: *bit off her tongue*: No doubt the story is apocryphal: see the similar story motif in Hays's entry for Lionna (Hays, *Female Biography*, vol. 4, pp. 494–5) and compare, for example, with Plutarch, *Moralia*, 505e on Zeno.

p. 439, l. 27: *not sexual virtues*: This is Hays's conclusion and the only significant addition she makes to the entry from the *Biographium Faemineum*.

p. 440, l. 1: *Valeria*: Valeria Galeria (her full name is known from inscriptions) was the daughter of the Roman emperor Diocletian (see note to p. 440, l. 2, below) and Prisca (about whose background nothing is known).

p. 440, l. 2: *DIOCLETIAN*: Gaius Aurelius Valerius Diocletianus, a native of Illyricum, was emperor from AD 284–305.

p. 440, ll. 3–4: *Constantius and Galerius*: In AD 293, Diocletian created a 'tetrarchy' (four-man rule) intended to stabilize imperial government – with two *Caesars*, Flavius Valerius Constantius 'Chlorus' in the West and Galerius Valerius Maximianus in the East, to serve as 'deputies', and intended successors to the two *Augusti* (Marcus Aurelius Valerius Maximianus 'Herculius' and Diocletian, respectively). Constantius and Galerius became *Augusti* (emperors) in AD 305.

p. 440, l. 4: *Armentarius*: Galerius was a native of Illyricum, born in Dacia; he was ridiculed for initially following his father's profession as herdsman, *armentum* being the Latin for 'herd'. Galerius rose in rank through distinguished army service.

p. 440, l. 6: *Valeria in marriage*: Conventional wisdom has Valeria married to Galerius, 'Caesar' of the East, as part of her father's construction in AD 293 of the 'tetrarchy'. The marriage, however, had probably taken place by 289.

p. 440, l. 7: *a subject for a tragedy*: Hays's sole source, from whom she borrows in a more or less verbatim fashion, is Edward Gibbon's (1776) *Decline and Fall of the Roman Empire*, introduced by Christopher Dawson (London: Everyman's Library, J.M. Dent & Sons, 1910), vol. 1, ch. 14.

p. 440, l. 10: *the illegitimate son*: Candidianus (his fuller name was probably Gaius Valerius Candidianus) was born *c*. AD 297, was possibly a short-term co-ruler with Galerius, and was killed in 313.

p. 440, l. 10: *her husband*: see note to p. 440, l. 6, above.

p. 440, l. 12: *the death of her husband*: Galerius died in AD 311.

p. 440, l. 14: *Maximin*: Galerius Valerius Maximinus Daia, a native of Illyricum, was said to be born of peasant stock, to have served as a herdsman and to have risen through army service. He had been raised to the rank of *Caesar* by his maternal uncle Galerius in AD 305, and formally became emperor in 311 (though he had proclaimed himself such in 309 or 310).

p. 440, l. 15: *the wife of Maximin*: not further identified.

p. 440, l. 22: *To the persons commissioned to treat with her*: Lactantius (*On the Deaths of the Persecutors*, 39.3) speaks of unnamed envoys.

p. 440, l. 23–p. 441, l. 7: '*That, even could honour … faithful and affectionate wife.*': The source of this response is Lactantius (*On the Deaths of the Persecutors*, 39.4). The wording, with minor changes, is that of Gibbon.

p. 441, l. 15: *and her friends*: In trimming Gibbon's reference to Maximinus's persecution of Valeria's *friends* on false charges of adultery (an item drawn from Lactantius, *On the Deaths of the Persecutors*, 39–40), Hays introduces an error by calling it a false allegation against *Valeria* (see note to p. 439, l. 17, above).

p. 441, l. 18: *Prisca*: see note to p. 440, l. 1, above.

p. 441, l. 20: *a sequestered village*: Lactantius (*On the Deaths of the Persecutors*, 41.1) speaks of certain desert solitudes in Syria. Hays's wording is that of Gibbon.

p. 441, ll. 24–5: *having abdicated the purple*: The purple-dyed robe had become synonymous with imperial power. In using the metaphor Hays follows the language of Gibbon.

p. 441, ll. 25–6: *had retired to a private condition*: Having arranged the succession, Diocletian famously abdicated (1 May AD 305), retiring to his palace at Spalato (modern Split, in Croatia) on the Dalmatian coast.

p. 442, l. 11: *death of Maximin*: Maximinus Daia, at war with Licinius (see note to p. 442, l. 16, below), died in AD 313, his death ascribed, according to various reports (as Gibbon put it), 'to despair, to poison and to the divine justice' (*Decline and Fall of the Roman Empire*, ch. 14, p. 414).

p. 442, l. 16: *Licinius*: Valerius Licinianus Licinius, also said to be of Dacian peasant stock and a friend of the future emperor Galerius, was a Roman emperor (elevated by Galerius) from AD 308–24 (and executed the next year, by order of Constantine I, the son of Constantius Chlorus).

p. 442, l. 27: *Thessalonica*: Thessalonica, in northern Greece, had become the administrative capital of one-fourth of the Roman empire under Galerius.

p. 443, l. 10: *MADEMOISELLE DE LA VALLIÈRE*: born Françoise Louise de La Baume Le Blanc (1644–1710), commonly referred to by her second name, Louise. She was daughter to Laurent de La Baume Le Blanc (1611–51), Lord of la Vallière. Hays focuses on the anecdotal dimension of Vallière's life as royal mistress, but fails to mention her widely read *Réflexions sur la miséricorde de Dieu* (*Reflections on the Mercy of God*) written in 1671, first published in 1680 (see J. J. Conley, 'Mademoiselle de la Vallière: The Logic of Mercy', in *The Suspicion of Virtue: Women Philosophers in Neoclassical France* (Ithaca: Cornell University Press, 2002), pp. 97, 103, 105–20). She also paraphrased the *Cantique de David* (*Psalms*, see de La Croix, *Dictionnaire historique portatif des femmes célèbres* (Paris: L. Cellot, 1769), vol. 3, p. 442) and famously engaged in philosophical debates with distinguished men of letters (see Conley, 'The Logic of Mercy', pp. 97–123).

p. 443, l. 12: *Lewis XIV*: From 1661 to 1667, La Vallière was the favourite of King Louis XIV (1638–1715) at the beginning of his official reign as absolute monarch, and bore him four children, two of whom died in infancy.

p. 443, l. 18: *the lady of Gaston*: Possibly Marguerite de Lorraine (1615–72), the second wife of Gaston d'Orléans.

p. 443, ll. 18–19: *Her mother*: Françoise le Prevost (1615–86), a rich widow of Pierre Benard de Bezay who was a counsellor in the Paris Parliament.

p. 443, ll. 19–20: *her second husband St. Remi*: Jacques de Courtavel, marquis de Saint-Rémy (dates unknown) was her third husband.

p. 443, ll. 20–1: *Monsieur (Brother of Lewis XIV)*: Hays refers to Louis XIV's uncle, Gaston de France, also known as Gaston d'Orléans (1608–60), brother to Louis XIII, and former 'Frondeur', who lived in exile in his Château de Blois with his family.

p. 443, l. 22: *daughter-in-law*: Mademoiselle de La Vallière.

p. 443, l. 22: *Henrietta*: Henrietta of England (1644–70), daughter to King Charles I and Queen Maria Henrietta of France, and niece to Louis XIII. She married Louis XIV's youngest brother, Philip I (see note to p. 443, l. 25, below) in 1661. La Vallière became Henrietta's maid of honour in 1661 (Conley, 'The Logic of Mercy', p. 99), not long after the death of Gaston d'Orléans, when the latter's wife, Marguerite de Lorraine, was authorized to return to the Court.

p. 443, l. 24: *Charles the First*: Charles Stuart (1600–49) became Charles I when he was crowned King of England, Scotland and Ireland on 27 March 1625 upon the death of his father, King James I. His reign was marked by a series of disastrous civil wars and growing dissatisfaction at, and hostility towards, monarchical absolutism. He ruled until his death when he was deposed and executed for high treason under the aegis of political leader and Republican Oliver Cromwell.

p. 443, l. 25: *Monsieur*: Philip I (1640–1701), youngest brother of Louis XIV, husband of Henrietta of England.

p. 444, l. 1: *Blois, in the Court of Gaston*: the château de Blois in the Loire Valley was given to Gaston d'Orléans as a wedding gift in 1626.

p. 444, l. 2: *A gentleman of Bragela*: Not further identified. One possible source for this erroneous translation is *Histoire de Madame Henriette d'Angleterre* (1720) by Madame de la Fayette, in which 'un prénommé Bragelone' ('a certain Bragelone') is mentioned (see *Histoire de Madame Henriette d'Angleterre*, ed. C. Herrmann (Paris: Editions femmes, 1979), p. 57).

p. 444, ll. 8–11: *"She was a most ... were altogether captivating."*: This citation (see Anquetil's entry on La Vallière (*Memoirs of the Court* (Edinburgh: n.p., 1791), p. 44), was translated from the French citation attributed by de La Croix to 'the ingenious author of Madame de Maintenon's Mémoirs' (*Dictionnaire historique*, vol. 3, p. 439) – which was in fact written by herself.

p. 444, l. 12: *Choisy*: François-Timoléon de Choisy (1644–1724), an accomplished man of letters, who partly owed his reputation to his taste for cross-dressing as a woman. He wrote many religious and moral works, but is mainly known for his best-selling *Mémoires de Madame la comtesse des Barres, à madame la marquise de Lambert* (1732) and for his posthumous *Mémoires pour servir à l'histoire de Louis XIV* (1727), from which Hays's predecessor, Anquetil, drew part of his entry on Vallière.

p. 444, l. 13: *"And grace still more charming than beauty."*: This line, which is cited in English in the translation of L-P Anquetil's entry on La Vallière (*Memoirs of the Court of Lewis XIV during the reign of Lewis XIV, and the regency of the Duke of Orleans: by M. Anquetil, Regular Canon Of The Congregation Of France, &c. Translated from the French*, 2 vols (Edinburgh, n.p., 1791), vol. 1, p. 44), is by Jean de La Fontaine, not by Choisy.

p. 444, ll. 14–20: *"That La Valliere ... bitter regret and remorse."*: see Anquetil, *Memoirs of the Court of Lewis XIV*, vol. 1, p. 44.

p. 444, l. 14: *Anquetil in his Memoirs of the Court of Lewis XIV*: Louis-Pierre Anquetil (1723–1806), a highly regarded historian and professor of theology and literature. His scholarly works were re-edited several times throughout the nineteenth century, including his milestone study, *Louis XIV, sa cour et le régent*, 4 vols (Paris: Pierre Moutard, 1789) (see also note to p. 444, ll. 14–20, above).

p. 445, ll. 2–3: *Philip duke of Orleans*: see note to p. 441, l. 25, above.

p. 445, l. 8: *the queen-mother*: Anne of Austria, wife to Louis XIII, and mother to Louis XIV (1638–1715). Queen Consort of France and Navarre (1615–43), she acted as regent upon the death of Louis XIII from 1643 until 1661, when Chief Minister Cardinal Mazarin died and Louis XIV imposed himself as absolute monarch.

p. 445, ll. 19–20: *Madame De la Fayette*: Marie-Madeleine Pioche de La Vergne (1634–93), the author of the now canonic, psychological novel *The Princess of Clèves* (1678). Her *Histoire de Madame Henriette d'Angleterre* was published posthumously in 1720, and the several anecdotes mentioned here by Hays are related in the third part of this historical novel (*L'Histoire de Madame Henriette d'Angleterre*, pp. 55–73).

p. 445, ll. 22–3: *the countess de Soissons*: Olympia Mancini (1638–1708), niece to Cardinal Mazarin (1602–61), chief minister of Louis XIV, and sister to Maria Mancini (1639–1715), was Louis XIV's passionate first love. She was involved in several court intrigues, most notably the scandal known as the *Affaires des Poisons* in 1679 when she eventually plotted against Madame de Vallière, which led to her expulsion from the Court.

p. 445, l. 26: *the balls*: most notably the *Ballet des Saisons* in Fontainebleau (1661) in which she performed, and which was represented five times that year (Conley, 'The Logic of Mercy', pp. 77–8).

p. 446, ll. 19–20: *her brother*: Jean-François de la Baume Le Blanc (1642–76).

p. 446, l. 23: *the first duke De la Valliere*: Charles François de La Baume Le Blanc (*c.* 1665–1739) became duke de la Vallière in 1698.

p. 446, l. 24: *Fouquet*: Nicolas Fouquet (1615–80) was the Superintendent of Finances under Louis XIV from 1653 until 1661. He fell into disgrace because of his extravagant expenditures and excessive prodigality which were seen by the King as an affront to his own image as absolute monarch.

p. 447, l. 20: *convent in St. Cloud*: Critics seem to agree that she actually escaped to the Convent of Saint-Perrine, near Chaillot (see Bertière, *Les Reines de France*, p. 97 and J. Lair, *Louise de La Vallière and the Early Life of Louis XIV*, trans. E. C. Mayne, 4th edn (London: Hutchinson, 1908), pp. 91–2). However, she reportedly ran away from the court for having incensed the King who had grown suspicious of her friendship with Anne-Constance de Montalais. The latter had told her of Henrietta's love affair with the Comte de Guiche, which La Vallière had sworn to keep secret (Bertière, *Les Reines de France*, p. 97).

p. 448, ll. 1–4: '*Adieu, sister,*' ... *soon see me again!*': The anecdote is more or less taken from Anquetil's own account, *Memoirs of the Court of Lewis XIV*, vol. 1, p. 72.

p. 448, l. 11: *The ladies*: The most important figures in this plot were Olympe de Soissons and Henrietta of England, who were assisted by their respective male accomplices, the Marquis de Vardes and the Comte de Guiche.

p. 448, l. 21: *A forged letter*: the letter was written in French by The Marquis de Vardes and translated into Spanish by the Comte de Guiche, so Queen Marie-Thérèse could read it in her mother tongue. The letter was taken by mistake to the Queen Mother (Anne of Austria) who gave it to the King. The plot failed, but Olympe de Soissons told the Queen about Louis XIV's mistresses. This incident made the king's liaison with La Vallière public, and officially made her the king's favourite.

p. 448, l. 28: *madame de Navailles*: Suzanne de Beaudéan-Parabère (1627–1700) was Queen Anne of Austria's maid of honour, and became lady-in-waiting to Queen Marie-Thérèse in 1661, which gave her authority over the Queen's maids of honour.

p. 450, ll. 3–19: *The king thoroughly irritated by this answer ... in the household of the queen.*': This account is by Motteville and is cited in Anquetil, *Memoirs of the Court of Lewis XIV*, vol. 1, pp. 40–1.

p. 450, l. 10: *my husband*: Philippe de Montaud-Bénac de Navailles (1619–84) enjoyed a successful military career in the service of Louis XIII and Louis XIV, from 1635 until he retired in 1678 – despite falling into disgrace in 1664 due to his wife's involvement in court intrigues (see note to p. 450, ll. 3–19, above). He was made marshal of France in 1675. Since then, he has commonly been referred to as the 'Maréchal de Navailles'.

p. 451, ll. 10–11: *A virtuous and learned man*: This was probably the casuist, Claude Joli (1610–78), priest at the parish of saint-Nicolas-des-Champs in Paris, and author of ecclesiastic works. Later, he became Bishop of Agen. Lair spells his name 'Joly' (*Louise de La Vallière*, p. 107); however the name of the parish elucidates any possible confusion with another Claude Joli (1607–1700), a lawyer, then canon at Notre-Dame, and author of several moral, religious and political works.

p. 451, ll. 13–19: *"I saw her," ... worldly interest."*: Cited from Anquetil, *Memoirs of the Court of Lewis XIV*, vol. 1, p. 42.

p. 451, ll. 13–14: *madame de Motteville*: Françoise Bertaut de Motteville (*c.* 1621–89). See Hays, *Female Biography*, vol. 1, pp. *225–7.

p. 453, ll. 11–17: *"Had kings, ... which surround a throne."*: see Anquetil, *Memoirs of the Court of Lewis XIV*, vol. 1, p. 80.

p. 453, ll. 23–4: *her children*: In Autumn 1663, upon the discovery of her pregnancy, La Val-lière settled in the Palais Brion, the annexe of the Palais-Royal, where she gave birth to Charles (1663–5). After two years spent in the limelight of court life, she retired there again to give birth to two other children, Philippe (1665–6) and Marie-Anne (1666–1739). Upon the death of the Queen mother, she was given the title of Duchess de la Vallière, and de Vaujours.

p. 453, l. 26: *Mademoiselle de Blois*: Marie-Anne de Bourbon (1666–1739), La Vallière's first daughter, was legitimized by her father in 1667, and received the title of Mademoiselle de Blois.

p. 453, l. 27: *M. de Vemandois*: Louis de Bourbon (1667–83), La Vallière's second son was legitimized by his father in 1669, given the title of Count of Vermandois and made admi-ral of France.

p. 454, l. 3: *Maria Teresa*: Maria Teresa of Spain (1638–83) was daughter to Philip IV (1605–65), King of Spain and Portugal, and Elizabeth of France (1602–44); she married Louis XIV in 1660. Although this was not a happy marriage, the young queen became the protégée of her aunt, the Queen Mother, Anne of Austria.

p. 454, ll. 14–18: *'For my part,' ... his queen.'*: This quotation originated with Madame de Mon-tespan, and is cited in Anquetil, *Memoirs, of the Court of Lewis XIV*, vol. 1, p. 88.

p. 454, l. 19: *Madame de Montespan*: Françoise Athénaïs de Rochechouart de Mortemart, marquise de Montespan (1641–1707) was daughter to Gabriel de Rochechouart, Duke of Mortemart (1600–75) who had close connections with Louis XIII. She officially enjoyed the status of Royal mistress from 1667 until 1679 when the scandal of the *Affair of the Poisons* broke out (see note to p. 445, ll. 22–3, above), in which she was a prime suspect. The king, however, kept visiting her until 1691, by which time she retired to the Convent of the Dames de Saint Joseph which she had founded (Bertière, *Les Reines de France*, p. 306).

p. 454, ll. 19–20: *duke de Mortemart*: Gabriel de Rochechouart de Mortemart (see note to p. 454, l. 19, above).

p. 454, ll. 20–1: *her husband*: Louis Henri de Pardaillan de Gondrin (1640–91), a nobleman who came from a modest and obscure background. To provide for his own family, he enrolled in the King's army, but kept indebting himself, through bad luck rather than negligence. Deeply in love with his wife, the Marquise de Montespan, he became a laugh-ing stock at court when he grew jealous of the King's affair with her.

p. 455, l. 18: *the nuns of Chaillot*: At the Convent of Saint Perrine near Chaillot, where she retired in February 1671.

p. 455, l. 20: *Colbert*: Jean-Baptiste Colbert (1619–83), Minister of the Finances of France from 1665 until his death.

p. 455, l. 21: *Lazun*: Antoine Nompar de Caumont (1632–1723), Marquis de Lauzun, a sol-dier and courtier who was in love with Mlle de Montpensier, the daughter of Gaston d'Orléans.

p. 456, ll. 21–6: *'I have a letter ... syllable of it.'*: This anecdote originates with Mademoiselle de Montpensier, see *Mémoires de Mademoiselle de Montpensier, petite-fille de Henri IV,* ed.

A. Chéruel, 4 vols (Paris: Charpentier, 1858–9), vol. 1, p. 58, and is quoted in Anquetil, *Memoirs of the Court of Lewis XIV,* vol. 1, p. 101. On the accuracy of Hays's citation, see notes to p. 456, ll. 23–4 and p. 456, l. 27, below.

p. 456, ll. 23–4: *writing to Mademoiselle*: Hays seems to have slightly misinterpreted the passage: the Queen did not write to Montpensier, but, as Anquetil reports it, confided in her (Montpensier, *Mémoires*, p. 58; Anquetil, *Memoirs of the Court of Lewis XIV*, vol. 1, p. 101).

p. 456, l. 26: *has transferred his attentions to Madame de Montespan*: In Montpensier's original citation (*Mémoires*, p. 58), and in Antequil's fairly accurate rendering of her *Mémoires* (*Memoirs of the Court of Lewis XIV*, vol. 1, p. 101), Mme de Montausier (Julie d'Angennes (1607–71), the daughter of the famous salonnière, Mme de Rambouillet (1588–1665)), is also cited as a prime suspect in supporting Louis XIV's extramarital affairs.

p. 456, l. 27: *the writer*: In Montpensier's *Mémoires*, the 'writer' is not identified; and the translator of Anquetil's relation of the anecdote gives a literal rendering of the original, which points to the political intrigues and libellous attacks that pervaded late seventeenth-century court culture: 'the givers of the advice, whoever they were, lost their aims' (*Memoirs of the Court of Lewis XIV*, vol. 1, p. 101).

p. 457, l. 22: *another lady*: not further identified.

p. 457, ll. 24–6: *'When any thing ... made me suffer.'*: Cited from Anquetil, *Memoirs of the Court of Lewis XIV*, vol. 1, p. 160.

p. 458, ll. 17–23: *'Alas!' ... belong to any but God.'*: Cited from Anquetil, *Memoirs of the Court of Lewis XIV*, vol. 1, p. 161.

p. 458, l. 21: *St. Simon*: Louis de Rouvroy, duc de Saint Simon (1675–1755), a high profile diplomat. He is most notable for his controversial *Mémoires de la Cour de Louis XIV, ou l'observateur véridique sur les regnes de Louis XIV et sur les premieres epoques des regnes suivans,* which was published posthumously in 1788–9 and underwent many omissions until the full version was re-established in the 1823 revised edition.

p. 459, ll. 2–4: *'Happy region!'... forgotten!'*: Cited from Anquetil, *Memoirs of the Court of Lewis XIV*, vol. 1, p. 129.

p. 459, l. 3: *madame de Sevigné*: Marie de Rabutin-Chantal, marchioness de Sévigné (1626–96), was highly regarded by her contemporaries, both at court and in the salons. She left a substantial body of epistolary writings of historical and socio-cultural significance, consisting of her thirty-year correspondence with her daughter, which was published posthumously.

p. 459, l. 9: *The convent of the Carmelites*: a convent situated in Rue Saint Jacques, Paris.

p. 459, ll. 12–13: *under the name of Sister Louisa, of the order of Mercy*: Louise de la Miséricorde.

p. 459, ll. 18–21: *'Are you really ... but content.'*: Cited from Antequil, *Memoirs of the Court of Lewis XIV*, vol. 1, p. 162.

p. 459, l. 26: *the prince of Conti*: Louis Armand I de Bourbon-Conti (1661–85), son to Armand de Bourbon (1629–66), first prince of Conti, and Anne Marie Martinozzi (1637–72).

p. 460, l. 1: *the siege of Courtrai*: Courtray or Kortrijk is a Flemish town which was besieged by Marshal of France Sébastien Le Prestre de Vauban.

p. 460, l. 2: *the dauphin*: Louis de France (1661–1711), son of Louis XIV and Queen Marie-Thérèse.

p. 460, l. 7: the man with the iron mask: It has been speculated that the true identity of the man in the iron mask was Eustache Dauger, who died in prison in 1709 after nearly forty years of imprisonment.

p. 460, ll. 9–12: *'Alas, my God!' ... his birth?'*: This quotation originated with Montespan, and is quoted in Anquetil, *Memoirs of the Court of Lewis XIV*, vol. 1, p. 163.

p. 458, ll. 16–18: *'A dangerous cavern ... constantly multiplying.'*: in Sevigné, vol. 2, p. 221, cited from Anquetil, *Memoirs of the Court of Lewis XIV*, vol. 1, p. 172.

p. 460, ll. 24–5: *the duchess de Fontange*: Marie Angélique de Scorraille de Roussille (1661–81), who gave a birth to a stillborn, from which she was very much weakened. Subsequently, the King granted her the title of Duchesse de Fontanges. She retired to the abbey of Port Royal where she died from consumption (Bertière, *Les Reines de France*, p. 218).

p. 460, l. 27–p. 461, l. 5: *'She was so elated ... see her match!'*: This quotation originated with Sévigné, and is quoted from Anquetil, *Memoirs of the Court of Lewis XIV*, vol. 1, pp. 294–5.

p. 461, l. 9: *VETURIA*: The main sources for Veturia are Livy (2.39.1–40.12) and Valerius Maximus (5.2.1a).

p. 461, l. 9: *Coriolanus*: Gaius Marcius Coriolanus, fifth-century BC Roman general charged with misappropriation of public funds, convicted and permanently banished from Rome; he went into exile amongst the Volsci, became a commander in their army and marched on Rome.

p. 461, l. 10: *Volsci*: an Italic tribe prominent in the history of Roman expansion during the fifth century BC.

p. 461, l. 10: *Roman matrons*: *matrona* was the name given to a married woman held in esteem and belonging to the elite stratum of Roman society.

p. 461, ll. 15–16: *temple to the Fortune of Women*: founded at the fourth milestone outside the city of Rome, built in honour of Coriolanus's wife and mother (Veturia and Volumnia, respectively) for saving Rome from Coriolanus when he planned to attack the city. See Livy, 2.40; Augustine, *City of God*, 4.19; [Aurelius Victor], *De viris illustribus urbis Romae*, 19.3–5.

p. 462, l. 2: *Daughter to a physician*: Michel de la Vigne, renowned Doctor of Medicine.

p. 462, ll. 3–4: *Celebrated for her poetical taste and genius*: Anne de la Vigne also showed a great interest in the philosophy of René Descartes. See C. P. Goujet, *Bibliothèque Française ou Histoire de la Littérature Française*, 18 vols (Paris: H.C. Guerin et al., 1756), vol. 18, p. 165.

p. 462, l. 6: "Monsieur le Dauphin au Roi": the ode 'From the Prince to the King' (French), is a dialogue between the heir apparent and his father Louis XIV.

p. 462, ll. 10–11: *a little box, containing a lyre*: Most sources hold that the lyre was delivered in a coconut.

p. 462, ll. 14–21: *"Reçois donc. ... résonner sous la tienne"*: 'Receive, oh, beautiful heroine! / A lyre that Appollo / Intended specially for you. / Many a time, its illustrious sound / Has charmed the sacred valley / Through the strumming of a divine hand: / Only too happy would it be / To resonate also under yours' (French). Stanza from 'Ode to Climène' (Anon.).

p. 462, ll. 22–3: *a congratulatory ode*: Madeleine de Scudéry's 'Discourse on Glory' (1674) was awarded a prize for eloquence by the French Academy.

p. 462, l. 23: *mademoiselle de Scudery*: see Hays, *Female Biography*, vol. 6, pp. 388–92.

p. 462, ll. 24–5: *the ode ... published*: Published by Paul Pellisson (1624–93) in *History of the French Academy* (1672).

p. 463, ll. 1–2: *letter ... from* Les Champs Elisées: sent by Nicolas Pavillon (1597–1677), bishop of Alet.

p. 463, ll. 3–4: *several other poems*: most of de Vigne's poems, including her answer to Pavillon, were published in 1693 by Père Bouhours. See Goujet, *Bibliothèque Française*, vol. 18, note.

p. 463, l. 6: *a son*: not identified.

p. 463, l. 6: un peu borné: 'of confused intellects' (French).

p. 463, ll. 7–9: *'Quand j'ai fait … ma fille'*: 'When I conceived my daughter, I thought I was creating my son; and when I conceived my son, I thought I was creating my daughter' (French). A statement ubiquitously cited.

p. 463, l. 12: *MARY, COUNTESS OF WARWICK*: born Mary Boyle (1624–78). She wrote several works including a memoir, diaries, rules for a holy life and pious meditations. See *Memoir of Lady Warwick: also her Diary, from 1666–1672 and Extracts from Her Other Writings* (London: The Religious Tract Society, 1799).

p. 463, l. 14: *great earl of Cork*: Richard Boyle, first Earl of Cork (1566–1643). See *ODNB*.

p. 463, ll. 15–17: *Her mother … sir Geoffry Fenton*: Catherine Fenton (1588–1630), daughter of Geoffrey Fenton (1539–1605), translator and administrator of Ireland. Catherine's mother was Alice Weston (daughter of Dr Robert Weston, former Lord Chancellor of Ireland). See *ODNB*.

p. 463, l. 17: *Charles earl of Warwick*: Charles Rich, Earl of Warwick (1616–73), second son to the second Earl of Warwick (succeeded to fourth Earl of Warwick in 1659). The marriage took place at Shepperton near Hampton court, 21 July 1641. The couple had two children, Elizabeth (1642–c. 1643/4) and Charles (1643–64). See *ODNB*.

p. 463, ll. 18–20: *liberality … charitable uses*: see A. Walker, *Eureka, Eureka. The Virtuous Woman Found Her Loss Bewailed, and Character Exemplified in a Sermon Preached at Felsted in Essex, April 30, 1678* (London: Printed for Nathanael Ranew, 1678), p. 99.

p. 464, ll. 4–9: *alluding … twenty thousand*: see Walker, *Eureka, Eureka*, p. 90.

p. 464, ll. 11–12: *A. Walker … 8vo.*: Rev. Dr Anthony Walker had known the countess for thirty years. He was the chaplain to her father-in-law and her spiritual advisor. Walker, *Eureka, Eureka*; *Autobiography of Mary Countess of Warwick*, ed. T. Crofton Crocker (London: Printed for the Percy Society, 1848), p. 20; R. A. Anselment, 'Mary Countess of Warwick, and the Gift of Tears', *Seventeenth Century*, 22: 2 (Autumn, 2007), pp. 336–57, on p. 336.

p. 464, l. 14: *This lady, who was born*: Elizabeth Jane Weston, alt. Elizabetha Ioanna Westonia, Latin poet, was born in Chipping Norton, Oxfordshire, possibly in 1581 (d. 1612). Sources for the date of Weston's birth vary; her tombstone in St Thomas Cloister, Prague, records 2 November 1582, but baptism records at Chipping Norton suggest some time between 4 March and 31 October 1581. Hays notes she was alive in 1605. She was the second child of Jane Cooper (bap. 1563) and John Weston (d. 1582), after a son, John Francis (1580–1600). Hays's biography of Weston derives wholly from Ballard's *Memoirs of Several Ladies*, pp. 243–7. Ballard's chief source was most likely Thomas Fuller's *The History of the Worthies of England* (London, 1662). Hays's chief omissions from Ballard's account include the claim that '[Weston] is much better known abroad than at home' (Ballard, p. 243), and from wider biographical discussion, her education, variably described by some as 'polite' and 'gentile', and by others (including Weston herself) as unpropitious and materially straitened; and any direct literary interaction with Weston's solely Latinate output. Ballard, for instance, among other early biographers, utilizes a poem concerning the death of Weston's brother to demonstrate some Ovidian resemblances in her style.

p. 464, ll. 14–5: *the beginning of the reign of Elizabeth*: Elizabeth Tudor of England (1533–1603; r. 1558–1603) (See Hays, *Female Biography*, vol. 4, pp. 70–295). Hays, following Ballard, incorrectly suggests Weston's birth coincides with the early years of Elizabeth I's reign.

p. 464, ll. 15–16: *Dr. Fuller*: Thomas Fuller (*c.* 1607/8–61), clergyman and historian. Fuller's *Worthies* (see note to p. 464, l. 14, above), the first English biographical dictionary, provided an account of each county, noting biographies of illustrious inhabitants. Weston features in the account of Surrey, pp. 87–8. Fuller's praise for the 'eminent' Weston is far more extensive than either Ballard or Hays record. A summarized version of Fuller's description is in George Sandys *Anglorum Speculum* (1684).

p. 464, ll. 16–17: *branch of the ancient family of the Westons, of Sutton in Surrey*: Fuller found 'an Ancient and Worshipful Family of the *Westons* flourishing at *Sutton*' in Surrey, but noted that he was 'ready to remove her at the first information of the certain place of her Nativity', being keen to ensure 'her memory may not be *harbourless*' (*Worthies*, Surrey, p. 87). This connection with Surrey is not corroborated, but is explored by S. Bassnett, 'Revising a Biography: A New Interpretation of the Life of Elizabeth Jane Weston (Westonia), Based on her Autobiographical Poem on the Occasion of the Death of her Mother', *Cahiers élisabéthains*, 37 (1990), pp. 1–8.

p. 464, l. 18: *left England at an early age*: After her father's death, Weston's mother married Edward Kelley, close associate of the alchemist John Dee. In 1583, they travelled to Poland, along with John Dee and his family, and subsequently settled in Prague, where Kelley was appointed alchemist to Emperor Rudolf II. Weston and her brother remained in England with their grandparents and travelled to Prague a few years later.

p. 464, l. 20: *skilled in the languages, particularly in the Latin*: Weston was reportedly fluent in English, German, Italian, French and Czech, in addition to Latin. Her education was probably encouraged (and supported) by her stepfather. In a poem, she thanks her Latin tutor, John Hammond (Hammonius). However, Edward Kelley killed a courtier of Rudolf II in a duel in 1591, for which he was imprisoned. When he died around 1597, he left his family impoverished. It was Weston's resourceful turn to Latin poetry and correspondence, within the context of being an orphaned '*Virgo Angla*', that ignited continental recognition of her literary skill.

p. 464, ll. 22–3: *greatly esteemed by learned foreigners*: Ballard states, 'These performances gained her very great esteem; and made her taken notice of by some of the most learned foreigners of that time; who corresponded with her, and gave her great encomiums on that account' (*Memoirs of Several Ladies*, p. 243). Ballard possibly obtains his information from Fuller (among others), *The Worthies*, who states, 'It seems her fame was more known in foreign parts than at home' (p. 87); a list of those who praised Weston is in J. W. Binns, *Intellectual Culture in Elizabethan and Jacobean England: The Latin Writings of the Age* (Leeds: Francis Cairns, 1990), pp. 113–14.

p. 464, l. 23: *commended by Scaliger*: Joseph Scaliger (1540–1609), Dutch Protestant scholar. Scaliger corresponded with Weston, with whom he was most likely connected through her patron, von Baldhoven. Ballard provides an excerpt of Scaliger's praise: '*Penè priùs mihi contiget admirari ingenius tuum, quàm nosse*'. Among many laudatory poems and epistles, Heinsius described her as '*Deabus aequalem*', Gernadius described her as '*decimam musarum*', and Paul Melissus reportedly sent her a laurel wreath (signaling poetic honour). Scaliger's commendation is also reported in Edward Leigh's *Foelix Consortium* (1663), p. 363, along with Dousa's couplet on Weston; he includes Weston in his prefatory summary, listing 'learned women' as 'Queen Elizabeth, the Lady Jane Gray, and Weston' ('Epistle to the Reader'). Similar material is repeated in Leigh's *A treatise of religion and learning* (1656), p. 363; J. Norris, *Haec & hic; or, The feminine gender more worthy than the masculine* (1683), pp. 160–1.

p. 464, ll. 24–5: *complimented by Nicholas May in a Latin epigram*: Nicholas May's Latin epigram is quoted in full by Ballard, along with an English translation, *Memoirs of Several Ladies*, p. 244.

p. 464, l. 25–p. 465, l. 1: *placed by Mr. Evelyn in his* Numismata: John Evelyn (1620–1706), diarist and writer. Evelyn's *Numismata, a discourse of medals, ancient and modern* (London: B. Tooke, 1697). Weston features in 'some Instances of the Learned, Virtuous and Fair Sex': 'Mrs. *Weston,* who besides other things, writ a *Latin* Poem in praise of *Typography*', p. 264). Evelyn also mentions Weston in a letter to the Lord Chancellor on March 18, 1666–7, to add to his list of 'the Learned and Heroic persons of England'; she is added, along with Lady Jane Grey, to 'The Learned'.

p. 465, ll. 1–2: *Mr Philips*: Edward Philips (1630–*c.* 1696), writer and biographer, nephew of John Milton. In *Theatrum Poetarum* (London: C. Smith, 1675), an alphabetical list of (mostly English) ancient and modern poets, Philips describes Weston thus: '*Elizabetha Joanna Westoni,* an English Poetess of some repute in the esteem of *Farnabie,* who ranks her with Sir *Th. More, Alabaster, Drurie,* and other English writers of Latin Poetry' (p. 257).

p. 465, ll. 2–3: *ranked by Mr. Farnaby*: Thomas Farnaby (*c.* 1575–1647), schoolmaster, rhetorician, poet and classical scholar. Farnaby includes Weston ('Westonia'), the only woman and one of only seven English authors, among his list of Anglo-Latin poets in *Index poeticus* (London: Printed by Felix Kyngston, 1634), E4v.

p. 465, ll. 4–6: *translated several of the fables of Æsop in Latin verse*: Aesop (*c.* 620–560 BC), a Greek. There is no certain identification of him. Weston wrote several verse paraphrases of Aesop's fables, including the stories of the Lion and the Frog, the Eagle and the Tortoise, and the Sow and the Dog.

p. 465, ll. 6–7: *Latin poem in praise of typography*: Weston's poem is printed in *Parthenicon* (Prague, *c.* 1605–6). The poem is noted by Thomas Powell in *Humane Industry, or, A history of most manual arts deducing the original, progress, and improvement of them* (1661): 'Mrs. *Joan Elizabeth Weston,* one of the Muses of *England,* hath composed a Latine Poem (among sundry others of her compositions) in the praise of this art [printing], which is indeed the preserver of all other arts' (p. 68).

p. 465, ll. 7–9: *many poems and epistles ... collected and published*: Weston wrote letters to leading continental humanists, poets and patrons, most especially to von Baldhoven. Her correspondents included Justus Lipsius, Janus Dousa, Joseph Scaliger, Paul Melissus, Peter Lotichius, Daniel Heinsius, Jirí Carolides; she also wrote letters and poems to James I. Hays does not provide the titles of any of Weston's publications, which were: *Poemata* (Frankfurt-am-Oder, 1602) and *Parthenicon* (Prague, undated, *c.* 1605–6), the latter (meaning 'maidenly writings') reprinted the poems of the first volume and included a collection of letters; von Baldhoven was responsible for these publications, and for facilitating Weston's access to a wide network of scholars and writers across Europe. Ballard's sources could certainly have been the most recent editions of Weston's poetry, edited by Johann Kalckhoff in Frankfurt-am-Oder in 1723 and 1724. Ballard possibly sources his many quotations of encomium for Weston from this publication. Editions are also recorded as published at Leipzig, 1609, and Amsterdam, 1712.

p. 465, ll. 9–10: *married John Leon*: Johannes Leo of Eisenach, a lawyer and an agent of Christian van Anhalt at the imperial court. Weston married Leo in April 1603, and bore seven children (four sons and three daughters) before her death in 1612.

p. 465, ll. 11–13: *was living in 1605*: Hays's source is Ballard, *Memoirs of Several Ladies*, p. 245. Weston died on 23 November 1612, and was buried in Prague in St Thomas' Church.

p. 465, ll. 15–16: *sir Henry Lee*: Sir Henry Lee, third Baronet of Quarendon, Buckingham-shire (*c.* 1633–59) was an English nobleman who died of smallpox the same year that his wife, Anne Danvers (d. 1659), died from childbirth.

p. 465, l. 18: *the countess of Abingdon*: Eleanora Lee, Countess of Abingdon (1658–91) was an English noblewoman who married James Bertie, first Earl of Abingdon (1653–99).

p. 465, ll. 19–20: *Dryden*: John Dryden (1631–1700) was an English poet, playwright and literary critic. He was made Poet Laureate in 1668 by King Charles II (1630–85) but was dismissed by King William III (1650–1702) and Queen Mary II (1662–94) in 1688.

p. 465, l. 20: *"Eleonora"*: A poem published by John Dryden in 1692. The elegy was written for pay in honor of Eleanor Lee, the Countess of Abingdon, whom he had never met.

p. 465, l. 22: *Thomas*: Thomas Wharton, first Marquess of Wharton (1648–1715), was an English nobleman and politician who was well-liked despite his reputation for scandal.

p. 465, l. 24–p. 466, l. 1: *the collections of Dryden and Nichols*: Possibly *A Select Collection of Poems: with Notes, Biographical and Historical* (London: J. Nichols, 1780–2). Wharton's printed poems include 'On the Snuff of a Candle' (vol. 1, p. 51), 'Made in Sickness' (vol. 1, p. 51), 'Song' (vol. 1, p. 52) and 'The Lamentations of Jeremiah' (vol. 1, p. 53). John Nichols (1745–1826) was an English printer, writer and historian.

p. 466, l. 1: *The mother*: Anne St. John, Countess of Rochester (1614–96).

p. 466, ll. 1–2: *John Wilmot, earl of Rochester*: John Wilmot, second Earl of Rochester (1647–80), was an English poet, satirist and courtier. Upon his death, Wharton wrote 'An Elegy on the Death of the Earl of Rochester'.

p. 466, ll. 2–4: *"They were … as in blood."*: *Biographium Faemineum*, vol. 2, p. 270.

p. 466, l. 3: *Mr. Waller*: Edmund Waller (1606–87) was an English poet and politician who wrote a copy of verses, 'A Paraphrase on the Lord's Prayer, Written by Mrs. Wharton', to Wharton in response to her poem, 'A Paraphrase on the Lord's Prayer, Verses to Mr. Waller'. He is said to have written two cantos of divine poetry (possibly from 'Divine Poems', published in 1685) in response to reading Wharton's 'Paraphrase on the 53rd Chapter of Isaiah'.

p. 466, ll. 9–10: *"Love's Martyr, or Wit above Crowns"*: A tragedy in five acts written *c.* 1679 by Anne Wharton (*c.* 1632–85) and published posthumously. The work is centred around Ovid, a man who is in love with Julia, the daughter of Emperor Augustus.

p. 466, l. 12: *ANNE, COUNTESS OF WINCHELSEA*: 1661–1720. Note: Hays has two entries for Anne Finch: 'Anne Finch, Countess of Winchelsea', vol. 4, pp. 331–2 and 'Anne, Countess of Winchelsea', vol. 6, pp. 464–5. The biographies are complementary; this is the longer entry, containing a few more details about Finch's publication details.

p. 466, l. 13: *Sir William Kingsmill*: Sir William Kingsmill (1613–61) was a Hampshire gentleman with strong Royalist sympathies and Church of England loyalty. His family traced their lineage back four generations to an ancestor who saved the life of King John. His daughter Anne was born at Sydmonton Court near Kingsclere, the Kingsmill ancestral seat.

p. 466, l. 15: *duchess of York*: Maria Beatrice Anna Margherita Isabella d'Este, Mary of Modena (1658–1718); in 1673 married James, Duke of York, later James II (1633–1701; r. 1685–8), after his secret conversion to Catholicism around 1668.

p. 466, l. 15: *second wife*: James's first wife was Anne Hyde, a commoner, and mother of Mary II (1662–94, Queen of England, Scotland, and Ireland, 1689–94) and Anne (1665–1714, Queen of Great Britain and Ireland, 1702–14).

p. 466, l. 15: *James II*: James II (1633–1701) was the last Roman Catholic King of England, Scotland, and Ireland from 1685 to 1688, when he was deposed.

p. 466, l. 16: *Heneage*: Heneage Finch (1657–1726), Groom of the Bedchamber to James, Duke of York, who married Anne in 1684. When James acceded to the throne in 1685, Heneage remained his attendant. As a Jacobite, a loyal follower of James II and his line, Finch refused to take the oath of allegiance (to the monarch) and was debarred from the House of Lords.

p. 466, l. 16: *second son*: Heneage's grandmother had been created Countess of Winchelsea in 1628. Her title was passed on to her male heirs, but Heneage, the second son of the second earl, was unlikely to inherit it.

p. 466, ll. 16–17: *Heneage earl of Winchelsea*: In 1712, Charles Finch, Earl of Winchelsea, the son of Heneage's elder brother, died without progeny. His uncle Heneage became fifth Earl of Winchelsea and Anne Finch became Countess of Winchelsea.

p. 466, ll. 19–20: *"A new Miscellany of original Poems, on several Occasions"*: This collection is most likely to be Charles Gildon, *A New Collection of Poems for Several Occasions* (London: Peter Back and George Strathan, 1701). Anne Finch's Pindaric Ode, 'The Spleen' was originally published in this volume. Hays included different publication details here compared to her biographical entry for Finch in vol. 4, pp. 331–2.

p. 466, l. 20: *Charles Gildon*: Charles Gildon (1665–1724), writer, biographer and essayist.

p. 466, l. 22: *Nicholas Rowe*: Nicholas Rowe (1674–1718), dramatist and poet who became Poet Laureate of the United Kingdom in 1715. Anne Finch wrote the epilogue for Rowe's *The Tragedy of Jane Shore*, first performed in 1714.

p. 466, ll. 22–4: *"An Epistle ... her Friend"*: Nicolas Rowe's panegyric 'An Epistle to Flavia ...' accompanied Gildon's publication and contained a glowing tribute to Anne Finch.

p. 466, l. 25: *A collection ... was printed*: The title of this collection is *Miscellany Poems, on Several Occasions: Written by a Lady* (London: Printed for J[ohn] B[arber], 1713). While the first printing in 1713 was advertised as being 'Written by a Lady', the 1714 edition credited Anne, Countess of Winchilsea [*sic*], by name.

p. 467, l. 2: *"Aristomenes"*: 'Aristomenes: Or the Royal Shepherd. A Tragedy' was published along with eighty-six of Finch's poems in *Miscellany Poems, on Several Occasions* (1713) (see note to p. 466, l. 25, above).

p. 467, l. 3: *remain still unpublished*: *Miscellany Poems, on Several Occasions: Written by a Lady* was the only selection of poems published during Anne Finch's lifetime. *The Poems of Anne, Countess of Winchilsea* [*sic*], ed. M. Reynolds (Chicago, IL: University of Chicago Press, 1913) and *The Wellesley Manuscript Poems of Anne, Countess of Winchilsea* [sic], ed. J. M. Ellis d'Alessandro (Florence: J. M. E. d'Alessandro, 1988), added poems from hitherto unpublished manuscripts.

p. 467, l. 7: *ZENOBIA*: Julia Aurelia Zenobia; Zēnobía (Ζηνοβία) in Greek or Bat-Zabbai in Aramaic (*c.* AD 240–*c.* after 274).

p. 467, ll. 7–8: *descendant from the Macedonian kings*: Zenobia claimed to be a member of the Seleucid line, and so related to the Ptolemies, Macedonian rulers of Egypt. The main ancient source for her life is Trebellius Pollio, *Thirty Tyrants*; however, this work, part of the *Augustan History*, is considered unreliable as a historical source.

p. 467, l. 22: *an epitome of oriental history*: one of only a few references to a work of history composed by a woman in antiquity. The source, Trebellius Pollio, is unfortunately unreliable, and the history, if it existed, is not extant.

p. 467, l. 23: *Longinus*: A Greek grammarian and Platonic philosopher (*c.* AD 210–*c.* 272/3); he was executed by the Emperor Aurelianus after Zenobia's defeat (*Historia Augusta, Life of Aurelian*, 30).

p. 467, l. 24: *Homer*: (*c.* 750–*c.* 700 BC), Greek epic poet said to be the author of the *Iliad* and the *Odyssey*.

p. 467, l. 25: *Plato*: (427–347 BC), Athenian philosopher.

p. 468, l. 1: *Odenathus*: Lucius Septimius Odenathus; his Latin name shows his family had received citizenship under one of the Severan emperors. He was a pro-Roman ruler of Palmyra from AD 258 or earlier. Zenobia was his second wife. Bayle calls him a Saracen (meaning a non-Arab inhabitant of Roman Arabia) (*The Dictionary Historical and Critical of Mr. Peter Bayle* (1984), vol. 5, p. 603) after Procopius, *Wars*, 2.5.

p. 468, ll. 16–17: *Gallienus*: (AD 218–68); Emperor of Rome AD 253–68. See also note to p. 468, l. 17, below.

p. 468, l. 17: *the title of Augusta*: Odenathus and Zenobia supported the Roman emperor Gallienus against the usurper Quietus; Odenathus was rewarded with the title *totius Orientis imperator* (ruler of all the east). The honorific title *Augusta* was normally bestowed on the wife of the Roman emperor.

p. 468, ll. 21–2: *the Great King*: Odenathus and Zenobia had success against the Sassanid Persian Empire.

p. 468, l. 23: *Ctesiphon*: the capital of the Sassanid Persian empire: it was on the river Tigris (south of modern Baghdad).

p. 469, l. 2: *Mæonius*: This story comes from the unreliable *Historia Augusta* but was accepted by Hays's source, E. Gibbon, *The History of the Decline and Fall of the Roman Empire*, 6 vols, 2nd edn (W. Strahan and T. Cadell, 1776), vol. 1, p. 308. However, the *Historia Augusta* has another version in which Zenobia instigated the conspiracy against Odenathus in 266–7 to ensure that their son, Vaballathus, succeeded to the throne instead of Odenathus's son, Herodes or Hairan (*Thirty Tyrants*, 17; see also Zonaras, 12.24).

p. 469, l. 13: *Herod*: see note to p. 469, l. 2, above.

p. 469, l. 18: *the manes of her husband*: In Roman religion, the manes were spirits of the dead: the term could also be used of the spirit of a particular dead person. Gifts would normally be made to the manes of the dead, but not human sacrifice.

p. 469, ll. 26–7: *one of its generals*: not further identified.

p. 470, l. 12: *Bithynia*: a region in north-western Asia Minor which became a Roman province in 74 BC.

p. 470, l. 15: *Claudius*: Marcus Aurelius Claudius, generally referred to as Claudius Gothicus or Claudius II, was Roman emperor from 268–70.

p. 470, l. 25: *Cyrus*: Cyrus the Great (r. *c.* 559–530 BC), king of Persia and the founder of the Achaemenid Empire.

p. 470, l. 26: *her three sons*: Two of her sons, Herennianus and Timolaus, are mentioned in the *Historia Augusta* as ruling with Zenobia, (*Thirty Tyrants*, 27, 30.2); however, the son who succeeded Odenathus was Vaballathus Athenodorus (*Historia Augusta*: *Gallienus*, 13.2, *Aurelian*, 38.1).

p. 471, l. 5: *Aurelian*: Lucius Domitius Aurelianus, Roman Emperor from 270–5. For a fuller ancient account of the wars with Zenobia, see Zosimus (Zosimus, 1.50–61). Hays draws largely on Gibbon's account which she follows closely.

p. 471, l. 10: *Ancyra*: The modern city of Ankara.

p. 471, l. 11: *Tyana*: An ancient city in Anatolia; the ruins are in the modern town of Kemerhisar in Turkey.

p. 471, l. 14: *Apollonius*: a Greek Neopythagorean philosopher from Tyana; he lived in the first century AD and was well respected in antiquity for his philosophy and for miracles attributed to him.

p. 471, l. 17: *Antioch*: A Greek city in Syria of great significance in the Hellenistic and Roman east.

p. 471, ll. 26–7: *Two great battles*: Zenobia's troops fought at Immae, near Antioch in May 272 BC; the second defeat was in June/July at Emesa (Zosimus, 1.50–4).

p. 470, l. 3: *Zabdas*: The general who commanded Zenobia's forces at Antioch and Emesa.

p. 473, l. 5–p. 474, l. 2: *"The Roman people," ... in an original letter ... oppose her, &c."*: Hays quotes one letter from Gibbon, *The History of the Decline*, vol. 1, pp. 311–12, then switches to another (at 'It is, I hear, objected') from Bayle, *Dictionary Historical and Critical*, vol. 5, p. 603. The quotes come from Trebellius Pollio, *Thirty Tyrants*, 30.5 and Aurelian, *Historia Augusta*, 26.

p. 474, ll. 12–13: *the Persian monarch*: King of the Sassinad Empire or Neo-Persian Empire; Zenobia's husband had fought against the king.

p. 474, l. 17: *Sapor*: Shapur I King of the Sassanid Empire (reigned *c.* AD 240/42–70).

p. 474, l. 24: *Probus*: A successful Roman general who became emperor (reigned AD 276–82).

p. 475, ll. 18–22: *'Because, ... conqueror and sovereign.'*: Hays takes the quote from Gibbon, *The History of the Decline*, vol. 1, p. 313: Gibbon took it from *Thirty Tyrants*, 30.23.

p. 475, l. 21: *Aureolus*: A Roman cavalry commander; in AD 268 he attempted to become emperor, but failed, and was soon captured and killed.

p. 475, l. 24: *the courage of the heroine*: In this paragraph Hays follows Gibbon, but omits his pejorative comments on female courage: 'But as female fortitude is commonly artificial, so it is seldom steady or consistent'; and on the counsel she had been given, 'which governed the weakness of her sex' (*The History of the Decline*, vol. 1, p. 313).

p. 476, ll. 25–6: *The city of Zenobia ... an obscure town*: i.e. Palmyra; this was a prosperous Hellenistic city in Syria and the capital of Zenobia's kingdom.

p. 477, ll. 12–13: *Embassadors of Ethiopia, Arabia, Persia, Bactriana, India, and China*: not further identified.

p. 477, l. 22: *Ten martial heroines*: women dressed as men; from the account of Aurelian's triumph in AD 273 (*Historia Augusta: Life of Aurelian*, 34.1).

p. 478, l. 16: *her daughters*: Her other children, including daughters, are not named (Zonaras, 12, *Thirty Tyrants*, 30.27).

p. 478, l. 21: *Paul of Samoseta*: Bishop of Antioch (AD 260–8). He was condemned for his monarchianism, a belief in God being of one person. This final anachronistic note comes from Bayle, *Dictionary Historical and Critical*, vol. 5, p. 605.

p. 478, l. 26: *Or, according to some, four stags*: Gibbon has 'either four stags or four elephants' (*The History of the Decline*, vol. 1, p. 316).

Appendix 1: 'Memoirs of Mary Wollstonecraft'

p. 485, l. 5: *the vindicator of the Rights of Woman*: Mary Wollstonecraft (1759–97) is identified by her most controversial work at the time of her death, *A Vindication of the Rights of Woman, with Strictures on Political and Moral Subjects*, 2nd edn, corrected (London: J. Johnson, 1792). Hays likely worked from the second edition of this text, referred to hereafter as *Rights of Woman*.

p. 485, l. 7: *some events, of a peculiar nature, in her personal history*: Hays is most likely referring to the revelations in William Godwin's *Memoirs of the Author of the Rights of Woman* (London: Joseph Johnson, 1797), in which many learned for the first time that Wollstonecraft had had a child out of wedlock, and had twice attempted suicide, among other things. In part, Hays's obituary is an attempt to reframe the events of Wollstonecraft's life.

p. 486, ll. 24–5: *"for the sentiment that brutalized them"*: from *Rights of Woman*, ch. 5, p. 227, slightly misquoted. In this chapter, Wollstonecraft attempts to dismantle the literary sources of condescending and over-sentimentalized models of femininity and in this particular passage points out that even accomplished women writers concur with these 'sentiments'.

p. 486, ll. 26–7: *Edward-John ... Elizabeth Wollstonecraft*: Edward-John Wollstonecraft (1736–1803); Elizabeth Wollstonecraft (née Dickson) (1740–82). Like many of the biographical details in the 'Memoirs', the primary narrative of Wollstonecraft's life is drawn from W. Godwin, *Memoirs of the Author of a Vindication of the Rights of Woman*, 2nd edn, corrected (London: J. Johnson, 1798). This is the edition used in these notes.

p. 486, l. 28: *the Dixons*: Wollstonecraft's mother's family, of Ireland, whose surname was also spelled Dickson.

p. 486, l. 29: *her paternal grandfather*: Edward Wollstonecraft (1688–1765), a successful silk weaver in Spitalfields, to the east of London.

p. 486, l. 32: *three sons and three daughters*: There were in fact seven children. The four brothers of Mary Wollstonecraft were Edward, James, Charles and Henry. Her two sisters were Elizabeth (Eliza) and Everina.

p. 487, l. 8: *temper of her father*: As is clear in Godwin's *Memoirs*, upon which much of Hays's account relies, Wollstonecraft's father was abusive and intemperate. See the modern edition of *Memoirs of the Author of a Vindication of the Rights of Woman*, ed. P. Clemit and G. L. Walker (Toronto: Broadview, 2001).

p. 487, l. 35: *a day-school*: In *Vindication: A Life of Mary Wollstonecraft* (New York: Harper Collins, 2005), p. 11, Lyndall Gordon notes that Wollstonecraft attended several day schools in the neighbourhood of Walkington and Beverley in Yorkshire.

p. 488, l. 3: *Mr. Clare*: Likely Rev. Thomas Clare (1746–1809), who received a Doctorate of Divinity from Oxford.

p. 488, ll. 7–8: *The manners of this gentleman ... his habits peculiar*: Godwin writes that Mr Clare was 'a recluse' and proudly declared that he had worn the same pair of shoes for fourteen years (*Memoirs*, p. 49).

p. 488, l. 9: *the wife of Mr. Clare*: not further identified.

p. 488, l. 10: *Frances Blood*: Frances 'Fanny' Blood (1758–85), Wollstonecraft's dearest friend. Fanny died in Lisbon of consumption, Wollstonecraft at her bedside. This tragedy was memorialized in the semi-biographical first novel, *Mary: A Fiction* (London: Joseph Johnson, 1788), and affected Wollstonecraft for the rest of her life.

p. 488, ll. 12–13: *the younger children of her family*: Fanny Blood had six brothers and sisters.

p. 488, ll. 26–7: *Mr. Allen, two of whose daughters have been since married to the elder sons of the celebrated Josiah Wedgewood*: John Allen of Cresselly, father of Elizabeth Allen (1764–1846) and Jane Allen (1771–1836), who married, respectively, Josiah Wedgwood (1769–1843) and John Wedgwood (1766–1844), children of Josiah Wedgwood (1730–95), Dissenter, abolitionist, early industrialist and founder of the eponymous pottery company.

p. 489, l. 3: *Mrs. Dawson*: Sarah Dawson (née Regis) (d. 1814).

p. 489, ll. 4–5: *the peculiar humour of the lady*: In Godwin's *Memoirs*, p. 52, we learn that Mrs Dawson had had 'a variety of companions in succession', but that 'Mary was not discouraged by this information'.

p. 489, l. 12: *a lingering disease*: not further identified.

p. 489, l. 14: *her friend*: Fanny Blood.

p. 489, l. 22: *a married sister*: Wollstonecraft's sister, Eliza, who was now married to Meredith Bishop (not further identified).

p. 489, ll. 23–4: *lingering disorder*: not further identified.

p. 489, l. 33: *opening of a day-school*: This was a small school run by Wollstonecraft, her two sisters and Fanny Blood, originally started in Islington and then moved to Newington Green (*Memoirs*, p. 55).

p. 489, l. 35: *Newington-Green*: In Wollstonecraft's day, a village on the northern outskirts of London, today a suburb. This was one of the centres of intellectual and spiritual life for the 'Rational' Dissenters. Prominent residents at Newington were Richard Price and James Burgh (see notes to p. 490, l. 3 and p. 490, l. 25, below).

p. 490, l. 3: *Dr. Richard Price*: Richard Price (1723–91), leading Dissenter and influential moral philosopher. His key work is *A Review of the Principal Questions and Difficulties in Morals* (London: Printed for T. Cadell, 1758). Price engaged with the issue of innate moral sentiments, primarily in the 'moral sense' theory of Frances Hutcheson (1694–1746). Price gained notoriety with his public defence of the French Revolution in *Discourse on the Love of Our Country* (1790). Wollstonecraft applied Price's investigations to her rationalist analysis of culturally sanctioned notions of propriety for female behaviour and was among the first women writers to make explicit and radical use of contemporary moral philosophy.

p. 490, ll. 24–5: *Mrs. Burgh*: Hannah Burgh (née Harding) (d. 1788).

p. 490, l. 25: *the author of the Political Disquisitions*: James Burgh (1714–75), Dissenter and associate of Richard Price. His *Political Disquisitions* (Philadelphia: Printed by R. Bell and W. Woodhouse, 1774–5), a treatise on parliamentary reform and suffrage, influenced mid- to late-eighteenth-century reformist movements.

p. 490, l. 26: *John Hewlett*: John Hewlett (1762–1844), Anglican clergyman, biblical scholar and educator.

p. 490, ll. 27–8: *Dr. Johnson*: Samuel Johnson (1709–84), prominent eighteenth-century man of letters, author of numerous works of poetry, literary and political commentary and literary biography. From the point of view of Joseph Johnson and his circle, Samuel Johnson's political sympathies were reactionary. Despite some notoriously condescending comments, Johnson was an advocate for women writers.

p. 491, ll. 1–2: *Hugh Skeys ... Mrs. Skeys*: Hugh Skeys (d. 1810), an Irish merchant, who married Fanny Blood in 1785 and took her to Lisbon.

p. 491, l. 18: *a French ship*: not further identified.

p. 491, l. 32: *relations of her deceased friend*: Wollstonecraft sustained a lifelong correspondence with George Blood (1762–1844), Fanny's brother, and occasionally helped him with funds.

p. 492, ll. 2–4: *"Thoughts on the Education of Daughters' ... Mr. Johnson*: Wollstonecraft's first conduct book, published in 1787 by Joseph Johnson (1738–1809), Unitarian and publisher of numerous books of the reformist and Dissenting community. Johnson published all of Wollstonecraft's works and provided her with early support in London, as well as a steady income for her literary work.

p. 492, l. 10: *lord viscount Kingsborough*: John King, the Viscount Kingsborough (1754–99).

p. 492, l. 17: *Mr. Prior*: John Prior (1727–89), graduate of Eton and King's College, Cambridge, was Assistant Master at Eton. Mr and Mrs Prior showed Wollstonecraft many kindnesses after the failure of her school, and during an illness at this time.

p. 493, l. 4: *"Mary a Fiction"*: Wollstonecraft's first novel, published in London in 1788 by her friend and publisher, Joseph Johnson.

p. 493, l. 12: *her publisher*: Joseph Johnson; see note to p. 492, ll. 2–4, above.

p. 493, l. 21: *"The Cave of Fancy"*: A 'moral tale' in the vein of Samuel Johnson's *The History of Rasselas, Prince of Abissinia* (1759). Wollstonecraft never completed the work and it was published in *Posthumous Works of the Author of a Vindication of the Rights of Woman*, ed. W. Godwin, 4 vols (London: J. Johnson, 1798), as *Extract of the Cave of Fancy. A Tale*.

p. 493, l. 23: *"Original Stories from Real Life"*: (London: J. Johnson, 1788). This is a fictional account of a governess and two young children, expanding upon Wollstonecraft's educational philosophy. The first edition was illustrated by William Blake (1757–1827).

p. 493, ll. 27–8: *"The New Robinson"*: *The New Robinson Crusoe* (1788), a translation of *Le nouveau Robinson* (1783), apparently abandoned when another translation was published in 1788 by John Stockdale (London: Printed for J. Stockdale, 1750–1814).

p. 493, ll. 29–30: *"Young Grandison"*: *Young Grandison: A Series of Letters from Young Persons to Their Friends. Translated from the Dutch of Madame de Cambon. With Alterations and Improvements* (London: J. Johnson, 1790).

p. 493, l. 31: *Dr. Enfield's Speaker, "The Female Reader."*: William Enfield (1741–97), Unitarian minister and educator, wrote *The Speaker* (London: J. Johnson, 1774). *The Speaker* was an anthology of texts for elocution practice used in the Dissenting academies. Wollstonecraft was asked to write a version for women. *The Female Reader* (London: Joseph Johnson, 1789) was originally published under the name 'Mr Cresswick', and questions remain about Wollstonecraft's editorship of this anthology.

p. 493, l. 35: *An absurd report*: not further identified.

p. 494, ll. 2–3: *"the grave had closed"*: A common expression in the eighteenth century.

p. 494, l. 8: *the Analytical Review*: The periodical founded by Joseph Johnson and Thomas Christie (1761–96), known as a liberal publication as its contributors generally favoured reformists and supporters of the French Revolution.

p. 494, l. 11: *a work by Mons. Necker*: Jacques Necker (1732–1804), born in Switzerland, finance minister under Louis XVI, and father of the woman of letters, Germaine de Staël (1766–1817). *The Importance of Religious Opinions, Translated from the French of Mr. Necker* (London: J. Johnson, 1788) was Wollstonecraft's translation of Necker, *De l'importance des opinions religiueses* (1788).

p. 494, ll. 12–13: *Lavater's Physiognomy*: Johan Kaspar Lavater (1741–1801), Swiss poet, physiognomist and moralist writer, was a favourite of members of Joseph Johnson's circle. Wollstonecraft's translation and abridgement of his *Physiognamiche Fragmente* (Winterthur: H. Steiners, 1775–8) was left unfinished.

p. 494, ll. 13–14: *Salzmann's Elements of Morality*: Gotthilf Salzmann (1744–1811). Salzmann's *Moralishes elementarbuch* (Leipzig: S. L. Crusius, 1782) was translated by Wollstonecraft, *Elements of Morality, for the Use of Children; With an Introductory Address for Parents* (London: J. Johnson, 1790–1).

p. 494, ll. 17–18: *translating into German the Vindication of the Rights of Woman*: Salzmann returned the favour and translated *Rights of Woman*, published in German in 1793 (Leipzig).

p. 494, l. 35: *an orphan*: not further identified.

p. 494, l. 36: *a deceased friend*: not further identified.

p. 495, ll. 10–12: *George Anderson, accountant ... Dr. George Fordyce*: George Anderson (1760–96), accountant-general of the Board of Control; John Bonnycastle (c. 1750–1821), a professor of mathematics; Henry Fuseli (1741–1825), Swiss artist and writer and George Fordyce (1736–1802), physician, who treated Wollstonecraft after she gave birth to Mary Wollstonecraft Godwin (1797–1852), later the second wife of Percy Shelley (1792–1822), poet, philosopher and admirer of Godwin's philosophy.

p. 495, l. 24: *The French revolution*: Hays reflects the sentiments of British reformists and radicals at the start of the Revolution of 1789, in which the ancient estates of monarchical

France, that is, the court, the nobility and the high clergy were removed from power and replaced with a representative legislative body, the National Assembly.

p. 495, l. 32: *Mr. Burke's Reflections on the French Revolution*: Edmund Burke (1729–97) was a prominent Whig MP and formerly sympathetic with political positions held by Richard Price and other 'Rational' Dissenters, most notably their support for the American colonists. Towards the late 1780s, he became opposed to efforts to relieve the civil restrictions on the Dissenters and after 1789 was the most prominent critic of the French Revolution and its British supporters. In *Reflections on the Revolution in France, and on the Proceedings in Certain Societies in London Relative to that Event* (London: Printed for J. Dodsley, 1790), Burke makes the defining statement in favour of existing settlements on parliamentary representation and social hierarchies, a text that might be called foundational to modern Anglo-American conservatism.

p. 495, ll. 37–8: *foremost of the numerous answers provoked by this extraordinary production*: Hays is referring to Mary Wollstonecraft, *Vindication of the Rights of Men, in a Letter to the Right Honorable Edmund Burke* (London: J. Johnson, 1790), published anonymously and within weeks of Burke's *Reflections*.

p. 496, ll. 35–6: *Catharine Macauley's Treatise on Education*: Catharine Macaulay (1731–91) (see also Hays, *Female Biography*, vol. 5, pp. 287–307), celebrated woman of letters, author of numerous works of history, literary criticism, education and political commentary. Hays points out that Wollstonecraft drew some of her argumentation in *Rights of Woman* from Macaulay's *Letters on Education. With Observations on Religious and Metaphysical Subjects* (London: Printed for C. Dilly, 1790), in particular asserting that women's innate right to improvement derived from the 'sexless' soul. In this respect, Hays departs from her close adherence to the account of Wollstonecraft's life in Godwin's *Memoirs* of Wollstonecraft. Godwin emphasizes the 'deficien[cies]' in composition, and makes the claim that Wollstonecraft composed *Rights of Woman* in six weeks (Godwin, *Memoirs*, pp. 83, 84) (see also note to p. 497, ll. 29–30, below). Hays places the provenance of the ideas in the work within a legacy of women intellectuals. This is the key moment in Hays's 'Memoirs'.

p. 497, l. 26: *a second part was promised*: A second volume was never published, but a number of scholars have opined that Wollstonecraft's second, and unfinished novel, *The Wrongs of Woman, or Maria*, supplied some of the focus on legal and cultural restrictions upon women that Wollstonecraft had promised in *Rights of Woman*. *The Wrongs of Woman, or Maria* comprises volume 1 and 2 of *The Posthumous Works* published by Godwin.

p. 497, ll. 29–30: *In September 1791 ... to apartments in Store-Street*: Like Godwin, Hays places Wollstonecraft's move to her new home *after* the composition of *Rights of Woman*, leaving the impression that the work was written beforehand, and quickly. However, a letter dated 6 October 1791 confirms that she has relocated and proves that she was in the midst of *Rights of Woman*, 'a book that I am now writing'. See *The Collected Letters of Mary Wollstonecraft*, ed. J. Todd (New York: Columbia University Press, 2003), pp. 190–1. Clearly Wollstonecraft had been working on *Rights of Woman* throughout the year, for she indicates that she had begun to plan the work before Catharine Macaulay died in June of 1791 (*Rights of Woman*, ch. 5, p. 236).

p. 498, ll. 14–21: *"That romantic passion ... dimly seen"*: quoted from *Rights of Woman*, ch. 2, p. 61.

p. 498, l. 24: *a friend*: Mary Hays (1759–1843), novelist, reviewer and early feminist historian.

p. 498, ll. 24–5: *"to lose in public happiness the sense of private misery."*: This phrase is quoted from a letter from Wollstonecraft to Hays, *c.* April–May 1796 (*Collected Letters of Mary Wollstonecraft*, p. 340).

p. 498, l. 29: *some articles*: Wollstonecraft wrote reviews for the *Analytical Review* (London: Joseph Johnson and Thomas Christie, founded 1788) for all of her professional life, that is, from 1788 until her death in 1797. Hays refers to this period.

p. 498, l. 33: *Monsieur Fillietaz*: The son-in-law of Wollstonecraft's hostess, Madame Bregantz; otherwise not further identified. See Godwin, *Memoirs of the Author of A Vindication of the Rights of Woman* (2001), (n)p. 83.

p. 499, l. 9: *in letters, a series of observations*: published in the *Posthumous Works* as 'Letter: Introductory to a Series of Letters on the Present Character of the French Nation', dated 15 February 1793. See also *Collected Letters of Mary Wollstonecraft*, pp. 216–17.

p. 499, l. 12: *Thomas Paine*: (1737–1809), political writer and author of works in support of the American and French Revolutions.

p. 499, l. 14: *Helen Maria Williams*: (1762–1827), poet, novelist, translator, literary critic and author of a sympathetic account of the French Revolution, *Letters Written in France in the Summer 1790* (London: Cadell, 1790), which eventually went to eight volumes.

p. 499, ll. 18–22: *Brissotine party ... madame Roland, the heroine of the Girondists*: Brissotine and Girondist were both terms used for the dominant party in the early years of the Revolution. The Girondists were relatively moderate compared to the faction which came in with Robespierre in 1793, and suffered mass executions under that regime. Well-known sympathizers with this group were the Marquis de Condorcet (1743–94), philosopher, political theorist and author of a tract on women's rights, Thomas Paine and Madame Roland (1754–73). Madame Roland was a prominent intellectual and advocate of women's rights, and was executed in the wave of anti-Girondist reaction. See Hays, *Female Biography*, vol. 6, pp. 103–311.

p. 499, ll. 25–6: *Thomas Christie, author of a volume on the French revolution*: Thomas Christie (1761–96), Scottish medical student turned publisher, co-founder of the *Analytical Review* with Joseph Johnson and author of *Letters on the Revolution of France and the New Constitution Established by the French Assembly: Occasioned by the Publications of Edmund Burke and Alexander de Calonne*, 2 vols (London: J. Johnson, 1791).

p. 499, l. 27: *Gilbert Imlay*: (c. 1754–1828), an officer in the Continental Army under Washington, U.S. diplomat and author of *A Topographical Description of the Western Territory of North America* (London: J. Debrett, 1792). For recent scholarship on Imlay, see W. Verhoeven, *Gilbert Imlay: Citizen of the World* (London: Pickering & Chatto, 2008).

p. 500, l. 32–p. 501, l. 4: *"Fatigued during my youth ...enjoyment can give"*: From Wollstonecraft's letters to Imlay, published in the *Posthumous Works*, vol. 3, pp. 92–3. This is further evidence that Hays worked closely from Godwin's account. See also *Collected Letters of Mary Wollstonecraft*, pp. 222–339.

p. 501, ll. 5–15: *"You can scarcely ... to be born."*: Letter to Imlay, c. August 1793 (*Posthumous Works*, vol. 3, pp. 2–3).

p. 501, ll. 16–29: *"Recollection ... it divides."*: Letter to Imlay, 1793 (*Posthumous Works*, vol. 3, pp. 15–16).

p. 501, l. 30–p. 502, l. 2: *"Though I have ... browned by care!"*: Letter to Imlay, 31 December 1793 (*Posthumous Works*, vol. 3, pp. 22–3).

p. 501, l. 30: *captain —*: not further identified.

p. 502, ll. 3–26: *"I have just ... playfulness."*: Letter to Imlay, 1794 (*Posthumous Works*, vol. 3, pp. 28–9).

p. 502, ll. 22–3: *Voltaire's Man of Forty Crowns*: a translation of *L'Homme aux quarante écus* (1768), by Voltaire (1694–1778), a commentary on taxation.

p. 502, ll. 27–35: *"I am afraid ... affectionate."*: Letter to Imlay, 1794 (*Posthumous Works*, vol. 3, pp. 32–3).

p. 502, l. 36–p. 503, l. 4: *"What a picture ... round number."*: Letter to Imlay, 1794 (*Posthumous Works*, vol. 3, p. 37).

p. 503, ll. 5–13: *"You have, by your ... Yours truly."*: Letter to Imlay, 1794 (*Posthumous Works*, vol. 3, p. 42).

p. 503, ll. 14–26: *"Believe me ... society affords."*: Letter to Imlay, 22 September 1794 (*Posthumous Works*, vol. 3, p. 60).

p. 503, l. 36: *a gardener*: Lyndall Gordon notes that Wollstonecraft lived at a cottage owned or tended by a gardener who worked for the Fillietaz family (*Vindication: A Life*, p. 206).

p. 504, ll. 10–11: *the danger which now threatened her as an Englishwoman*: The Law of Suspects (17 September 1793) ordered the detainment of British nationals (*Memoirs*, (n)p. 86).

p. 504, ll. 13–14: *the ambassador of the United States*: Gouverneur Morris (1752–1816).

p. 505, ll. 14–15: *"tenderness and worth ... her heart"*: Letter to Imlay, 1794 (*Posthumous Works*, vol. 3, p. 42).

p. 505, l. 19: *Brissot, Vergniaud, and the twenty deputies*: Jacques Brissot (1754–93) and Pierre Vergniaud (1753–93), members of the Girondist faction, also known as the Brissotine faction, were arrested along with a number of deputies of the National Convention and executed.

p. 505, l. 22: *Robespierre*: Maximilien de Robespierre (1758–94), most notable in this context as the leader of the Jacobin faction during the French Revolution, which ousted the more moderate Girondists in March of 1793 and embarked on a policy of violent purges popularly known as the 'Terror'.

p. 505, ll. 26–7: *a daughter ... Frances*: Frances Imlay (1794–1816), whose life ended in suicide.

p. 506, ll. 14–35: *"I have been ... haunted my dreams."*: Letter to Imlay, 26 December 1794 (*Posthumous Works*, vol. 3, pp. 76–8).

p. 506, l. 36–p. 507, l. 14: *"Stay, my friend ... dark shades of the picture."*: Letter to Imlay, 28 December 1794 (*Posthumous Works*, vol. 3, pp. 81–3).

p. 507, ll. 15–26: *"I will own you that, ... to comfort me."*: Letter to Imlay, 29 December 1794 (*Posthumous Works*, vol. 3, pp. 86–7).

p. 507, ll. 27–33: *"I do not like this life ... principles of action."*: Letter to Imlay, 30 December 1794 (*Posthumous Works*, vol. 3, pp. 88–9).

p. 507, ll. 27–8: entre nous: 'between us', 'confidential' (French).

p. 507, l. 34–p. 508, l. 11: *"I consider fidelity ... sown with thorns."*: Letter to Imlay, 30 December 1794 (*Posthumous Works*, vol. 3, pp. 89–90).

p. 508, ll. 12–29: *"You left me indisposed, ... stripped of every charm."*: Letter to Imlay, 9 February 1795 (*Posthumous Works*, vol. 3, pp. 102–3).

p. 508, l. 30–p. 509, l. 7: *"When I determined ... his schemes"*: Letter to Imlay, 9 February 1795 (*Posthumous Works*, vol. 3, pp. 103–5).

p. 509, ll. 8–25: *"When you first ... very distinct."*: Letter to Imlay, 10 February 1795 (*Posthumous Works*, vol. 3, pp. 108–9).

p. 509, l. 26–p. 510, l. 4: *"Society fatigues me ... my bosom."*: Letter to Imlay, 19 February 1795 (*Posthumous Works*, vol. 3, pp. 111–12).

p. 510, ll. 1–2: *'the wind of heaven ... too rudely'*: Letter to Imlay, 19 February 1795 (*Posthumous Works*, vol. 3, pp. 111–12).

p. 510, ll. 8–23: *"Here I am ... anguish of disappointment."*: Letter to Imlay, 7 April 1795 (*Posthumous Works*, vol. 3, pp. 114–15).

p. 510, l. 30–p. 511, l. 16: *"I have laboured ... interrupted your peace."*: Letter to Imlay, 22 May 1795 (*Posthumous Works*, vol. 3, pp. 120–1).

p. 511, ll. 17–26: *"I will not distress you... electrified by sympathy."*: Letter to Imlay, 10 June 1795 (*Posthumous Works*, vol. 3, p. 124).

p. 511, ll. 27–31: *Why did she thus ... capable of enduring"*: Godwin, *Memoirs*, p. 124.

p. 512, l. 6: *a young actress*: not further identified.

p. 513, l. 8: *a female servant*: not further identified.

p. 513, ll. 12–13: *Letters from Scandinavia*: *Letters Written During a Short Residence in Sweden, Norway and Denmark* (London: J. Johnson, 1796).

p. 513, ll. 15–21: *"I am harassed ... unsophisticated heart."*: Letter to Imlay, 13 June 1795 (*Posthumous Works*, vol. 3, pp. 133–4).

p. 513, ll. 22–8: *"Do write ... closely together."*: Letter to Imlay, 13 June 1795 (*Posthumous Works*, vol. 3, p. 135).

p. 513, ll. 29–37: *"Often do I sigh ... God bless you!"*: Letter to Imlay, 14 June 1795 (*Posthumous Works*, vol. 3, p. 138).

p. 514, l. 1: *were not meant for the public eye*: There is scant evidence of Wollstonecraft's intentions concerning her letters; Hays is most likely relaying a conversation between the two women, and the comment here could be a hit at Godwin.

p. 514, ll. 3–12: *"The last time ... on my heart."*: Letter to Imlay, 15 June 1795 (*Posthumous Works*, vol. 3, pp. 139–40).

p. 514, ll. 13–25: *"What are you about? ... Adieu!"*: Letter to Imlay, 17 June 1795 (*Posthumous Works*, vol. 3, pp. 144–5).

p. 514, ll. 26–36: *"This is the fifth ... my expectations!"*: Letter to Imlay, 20 June 1795 (*Posthumous Works*, vol. 3, pp. 148–9).

p. 514, l. 33: *the North*: Wollstonecraft refers to her planned itinerary through Scandinavia. She wrote this letter from Gothenburg, Sweden and then travelled to the southern coast of Norway, including Frederiksten and Risor, where she confronted Imlay's debtor.

p. 514, l. 37–p. 515, l. 8: *"My friend ... never sleeps."*: Letter to Imlay, 29 June 1795 (*Posthumous Works*, vol. 3, p. 156).

p. 515, l. 4: *"How flat, dull, and unprofitable"*: Letter to Imlay, 27 June 1795 (*Posthumous Works*, vol. 3, p. 156).

pp. 515, l. 9–p. 516, l. 9: *"Believe me ... touch of disappointment."*: Letter to Imlay, 3 July 1795 (*Posthumous Works*, vol. 3, pp. 160–2).

p. 515, l. 19: *Brutus*: Referring to the stepson and betrayer of Julius Caesar, as he is depicted in Shakespeare's *Julius Caesar*.

p. 515, ll. 19–20: *"That the virtue ... an empty name"*: Letter to Imlay, 3 July 1795 (*Posthumous Works*, vol. 3, pp. 160–1).

p. 515, l. 27: *I allude to —*: not further identified.

p. 516, ll. 10–22: *"I shall not, ... it shall not last long."*: Letter to Imlay, 7 July 1795 (*Posthumous Works*, vol. 3, pp. 167–8).

p. 516, l. 23–p. 517, l. 11: *"I am now on my journey ... constant wretchedness."*: Letter to Imlay, 14 July 1795 (*Posthumous Works*, vol. 3, pp. 169–71).

p. 516, ll. 28–9: *"God will temper the winds to the shorn lamb!"*: Psalms 6:2.

p. 516, l. 32: *Lear*: referring to Shakespeare's *King Lear*.

p. 517, ll. 12–30: *"Write to me then ... nature and truth."*: Letter to Imlay, 30 July 1795 (*Posthumous Works*, vol. 3, pp. 173–5).

p. 517, l. 31–p. 518, l. 10: *"You tell me ... faculties are undisturbed."*: Letter to Imlay, 26 August 1795 (*Posthumous Works*, vol. 3, pp. 184–6).

p. 518, ll. 11–22: *"I am weary of travelling ... "Why am I thus abandoned?"*: Letter to Imlay, 6 September 1795 (*Posthumous Works*, vol. 3, pp. 188–9).

p. 518, ll. 23–35: *"By what criterion ... much less of friendship."*: Letter to Imlay, 27 September 1795 (*Posthumous Works*, vol. 4, pp. 1–2).

p. 518, l. 36–p. 519, l. 12: *"The tremendous power ... caprices of the moment."*: Letter to Imlay, 27 September 1795 (*Posthumous Works*, vol. 4, pp. 3–4).

p. 519, ll. 13–19: *"Do not keep me ... have an end!"*: Letter to Imlay, 4 October 1795 (*Posthumous Works*, vol. 4, p. 9).

p. 519, ll. 20–7: *"I must tell you ... the habit of my mind."*: Letter to Imlay, c. November 1795 (*Posthumous Works*, vol. 4, pp. 18–19).

p. 519, ll. 28–32: *"The grief I cannot conquer ... buried alive."*: Letter to Imlay, 27 November 1795 (*Posthumous Works*, vol. 4, p. 23).

p. 519, l. 33–p. 520, l. 14: *"My affection for you ... God bless you!"*: Letter to Imlay, 27 November 1795 (*Posthumous Works*, vol. 4, pp. 24–5).

p. 520, l. 15–p. 521, l. 2: *"Resentment, and even anger, ... forfeit my esteem."*: Letter to Imlay, 8 December 1795 (*Posthumous Works*, vol. 4, pp. 27–9).

p. 521, l. 16: *a servant*: not further identified.

p. 521, l. 18: *the house of the woman*: not further identified.

p. 521, l. 31: *"rests on human love."*: From the poem by Charles Lloyd (1775–1839), 'Lines', *Monthly Magazine and British Register*, 3 (May 1797), pp. 380–1.

p. 522, ll. 1–26: *"I write to you now ... deviation from rectitude."*: Letter to Imlay, 10 October 1795 (*Posthumous Works*, vol. 4, pp. 10–12). Hays has quoted this letter in its entirety.

p. 522, l. 2: *the maid*: not further identified.

p. 523, l. 1: *the bridge*: Putney Bridge.

p. 523, ll. 19–20: *"there, where the heart most exquisitely feels."*: From James Thompson (1700–48), *Tancred and Sigismunda, A Tragedy* (London: A. Millar, 1746), p. 28.

p. 523, l. 25: *a common friend*: not further identified.

p. 523, ll. 25–9: *"that the present wandering ... too fatal proofs."*: not further identified.

p. 523, l. 34–p. 524, l. 9: *"If we are ever ... a person that is dead."*: Letter to Imlay, c. October 1795. This letter, numbered 72 in Godwin's system, is missing from the *Posthumous Works* and is presented instead in his *Memoirs of the Author of a Vindication of the Rights of Woman*, pp. 142–3.

p. 524, ll. 17–18: *the lady*: not further identified.

p. 524, l. 30: *a common friend*: not further identified.

p. 525, ll. 13–16: *"It was not for the world (said she in a letter to a friend) ... in reality."*: A letter to Mary Hays, to be found in Godwin's *Memoirs*, p. 148. According to Todd, this letter should be dated c. April–May 1796 (*Collected Letters*, p. 340).

p. 525, l. 18: *a female friend*: not further identified.

p. 525, l. 33–p. 526, l. 6: *It is now finished ... strangely warped."*: Letter to Imlay, c. March 1796 (*Posthumous Works*, vol. 4, pp. 34–5).

p. 526, ll. 7–16: *"The sentiment in me ... I part with you in peace."*: Letter to Imlay, c. March 1796 (*Posthumous Works*, vol. 4, pp. 35–6).

p. 526, l. 22: *letters from Norway*: *Letters Written during a Short Residence in Sweden, Norway, and Denmark* (London: Joseph Johnson, 1796).

p. 526, l. 23: *a comedy sketched*: destroyed by Godwin after Wollstonecraft's death.

p. 526, ll. 31–6: *"Of what use are talents ... deadly nightshade."*: from W. Godwin, *Things as They Are; or The Adventures of Caleb Williams*, 3 vols (London: Crosby, 1794), vol. 3, p. 302.

p. 527, l. 30: *Mr. W. Godwin, a writer of distinguished talents*: This is the first time that William Godwin is mentioned by name. Godwin (1756–1836) was known as a radical political philosopher and novelist. His two most well-known works at the end of the eighteenth century were *An Enquiry Concerning Political Justice, and Its Influence on General Virtue and Happiness* (London: J. Robinson, 1793), and *Caleb Williams* (see note to p. 526, ll. 31–6, above).

p. 527, ll. 12–13: *some difference in their principles*: Reports of the first meeting of Wollstonecraft and Godwin are that she disliked his ideas.

p. 529, ll. 18–27: *"Those who are bold enough (said she in a letter to a friend) ... I rest on my own."*: The original letter has not been found, but this is certainly addressed to Hays. Todd surmises that this was written in April 1797 (*Collected Letters*, p. 410).

p. 530, ll. 4–16: *"She was a worshipper ... attempt to pourtray."*: From the *Memoirs*, pp. 171–2.

p. 530, l. 20: The Wrongs of Woman: published as a fragment in *Posthumous Works*, vols 1 and 2 (1798), in which it is titled *The Wrongs of Woman, or Maria; a Fragment*.

p. 530, ll. 24–5: *a series of letters on the management of infants*: published in *Posthumous Works*, vol. 4.

p. 530, l. 25: *a medical friend*: Dr Louis Poignard, French surgeon.

p. 530, l. 27: *a series of books for the instruction of children*: published in *Posthumous Works*, vol. 2, as 'Lessons'.

p. 530, l. 29: *her novel*: *The Wrongs of Woman, or Maria*.

p. 530, l. 36: *the Story of Jemima*: the companion and sometime servant of Maria in *The Wrongs of Woman*.

p. 531, ll. 15–16: *the defects in their professional education*: Historically, female midwives had attended births. This began to change with the invention of the forceps in the early seventeenth century, founding of maternity hospitals for the poor in the eighteenth century and Scottish surgeon William Smellie's (1697–1763) introduction of new and improved forceps. By 1797, male physicians attended 50 per cent of the births in England. Midwives were usually not trained in the use of forceps or allowed to deploy them.

p. 531, l. 17: *not to be a common case*: The placenta was not discharged during the birth, and had to be manually removed.

p. 533, ll. 2–4: *"sweet remembrance ... to rapture?"*: from one of the most widely read poems of the eighteenth century, *The Pleasures of Imagination* by Mark Akenside (1721–70), first published in 1744 and subsequently reprinted in hundreds of editions and collections. This quotation is from book 2, *The Pleasures of Imagination and Other Poems* (London: J. Dodsley, 1788), p. 68.

CONTRIBUTORS TO VOLUMES 8–10

VOLUME	SUBJECT	SCHOLAR(S)	RESEARCHER(S)
8	Madame Dacier	Peggy Schaller Elliott	
8	Elizabeth Dancy	Jaime Goodrich	Koren Whipp
8	Theodora Dante	Piera Carroli	
8	Damophila	Ian Plant	
8	Louisa Darbach [or Karsch]	Elisabeth Lenckos	Koren Whipp
8	Lady Eleanor Davies	Amanda L. Capern	
8	The Countess of Derby	Sandy Riley	
8	The Countess of Desmond	Melissa Ridley Elmes	
8	Dido	Jacqui Grainger	Daniella Polyak
8	Diotyma	Ian Plant	
8	Livia Drusilla	Diane Johnston	
8	Dorothea Dubois	Andrew Carpenter	
8	Mariæ Dupre	Véronique Larcade	Whitney Mannies
8	Ebba	Tracey-Anne Cooper	
8	Edesie	Ian Plant	
8	Egee'	Ian Plant	
8	Eleanor	Emily Sutherland	
8	Elizabeth, Queen of England	Philippa Gregory	Melissa Ridley Elmes, Koren Whipp, Theodra Bane, Lindsay Smith
8	Elizabeth of France	Marina Cano-López	Lindsay Smith
8	Elizabeth Elstob	Ruth Perry	
8	Ninon de l'Enclos	Véronique Larcade	
8	Emma	Arianne Chernock	
8	Eponina	Peter Mark Keegan	
8	Erinna	Ian Plant	
8	Maria D'Estrada	María Jesús Lorenzo-Modia	
8	Ethelfleda	Arianne Chernock	
8	Eurydice	Maria Mafalda Viana	
8	Eusebia	Peter Mark Keegan	
8	Lady Falconberg	Alan Marshall	

VOLUME	SUBJECT	SCHOLAR(S)	RESEARCHER(S)
8	Lady Elizabeth Fane	Claire Harman	
8	Fannia	J. Lea Beness and Tom Hillard	
8	Marie-Madeleine Pioche de la Vergne, comtesse de la Fayette	Abby E. Zanger	
8	Cassandra Fidele	Stella Cantini	
8	Sarah Fielding	Elisabeth Lenckos	Koren Whipp
8	Anne Finch, Countess of Winchelsea	Diana Barnes	
8	Mary Fischer	Carin Kuoni	
8	Margaret de Foix, Duchess D'Epernon	Jonathan Spangler	
8	Fulvia	Judy E. Gaughan	
8	Leonora Galligai	Elizabeth Hyde	
8	Lady Grace Gethin	Joanna Wharton	
8	Cecilia de Gonzaga	Silvia Giovanardi Byer	
8	Eleonora Gonzaga	Piera Carroli	Marta Facchini
8	Isabella de Gonzaga [Elisabetta Gonzaga]	Elizabeth A. Pallitto	Koren Whipp
8	Julia Gonzaga	Cinzia Recca	Koren Whipp
8	Lucretia Gonzaga	Cinzia Recca	
8	Lady Jane Gray	Philippa Gregory	Ashleigh Lay, Koren Whipp, Lindsay Smith
8	Constantia Grierson	Sarah Peterson Pittock	
8	Madame de Guercheville	Séverine Genieys-Kirk	
8	Jacquette Guillaume	Helena Bergmann	
8	Pernette du Guillet	Karen Simroth James	
8	Johanna Mary Bouviers, De La Mothe Guyon	Elizabeth C. Goldsmith	
8	Lady Anna Halket	Mary Spongberg	
8	Harriet Eusebia Harcourt	Ruth Scobie	
8	Elizabeth Hardwick	Lorna G. Barrow	
8	Lucia Haerin	Laura Schechter	
8	Lady Elizabeth Hastings	Anne Laurence	
8	Elizabeth Haywood	Nicola Parsons	
8	Helena Flavia	Peter Mark Keegan	
8	Heloise	Sally Livingston	Lindsay Smith, Koren Whipp
8	Helpes	Peter Mark Keegan	
8	Cecilia Heron	Koren Whipp	
8	Hersilia	Peter Mark Keegan	
8	Hildegurdis	Lisa LeBlanc	Daniella Polyak
8	Hipparchia	John Christian Laursen	

VOLUME	SUBJECT	SCHOLAR(S)	RESEARCHER(S)
8	Susanna Hopton	Amanda L. Capern	
8	Hortensia	J. Lea Beness and Tom Hillard	
8	Antonietta de la garde des Houlieres	Isabelle Mullet	
8	Ann Hyde	Nicola Parsons	
8	Hypatia	Ian Plant	
8	Jane, Queen of France	Rebecca J. Jacobs-Pollez	
8	Mary Catherine de Jardins	Isabelle Mullet	
8	Mary de Jars, Lady of Gournay	Séverine Genieys-Kirk	
8	Esther Inglis	Georgianna Ziegler	Koren Whipp
8	Isabella, Queen of Hungary	Teréz Oborni	
8	Juliana	Michelle M. Sauer	Rachel Ann Piwarski, Ruth Gripentrog
8	Julia Domna	John Christian Laursen	Koren Whipp
8	Anne Killigrew	Diana Barnes	
8	Katherine Killigrew	Claire McEachern	Koren Whipp
8	Louise Labe	Edith J. Benkov	
8	Catherine Landa	Cinzia Recca	
8	Mrs Jane Lane	John Sutton	Koren Whipp
8	Margaret Lambrun	Claire Harman	
8	Mary Leapor	Jane Rendall	
8	Elizabeth Legge	Helena Bergmann	
8	Leontium	Ian Plant	
8	Elizabeth, Countess of Lincoln	Sara Read	
8	Lionna	Ian Plant	
8	Jaquiline de Longvic, Duchess of Montpensier	Rebecca Nesvet	
8	Elizabeth Lucar	Melissa Ridley Elmes	
8	Lucretia	Imke Heuer	
8	Joanna, Lady Lumley	Rebecca Nesvet	
9	Mary, Queen of Scots	Maureen Meikle	Koren Whipp, Penny Whitworth, Lindsay Smith
9	Catherine Macaulay Graham	Mary Spongberg	
9	Maeroe	Ian Plant	
9	Julia Mœsa and Mammæ	Aureliana Di Rollo	
9	Madame de Maintenon	Helena Bergmann	
9	Margaret de Valois, Queen of Navarre	Barbara Stephenson	
9	Maria	Ian Plant	
9	Lucretia Marinelli	Christine M. Ristaino	

VOLUME	SUBJECT	SCHOLAR(S)	RESEARCHER(S)
9	Mary, Queen of Hungary	Orsolya Réthelyi	
9	Mary, an Anglo-Norman Poetess	Edith J. Benkov	
9	Damaris, Lady Masham	Mark Goldie	
9	Matoaks	Thelma Armstrong	Koren Whipp
9	Tarquinia Molsa	Marie Caruso	
9	The Hon. Mrs. Monk	Margaret Kelleher	Koren Whipp
9	Morata (Olympia Fulvia)	Elgin Kirsten Eckert	
9	Countess of Mountfort	Erin Jordan	
9	Magdelene de Saint Nectaire	Véronique Larcade	
9	The Duchess of Nemours	Sarah Hanley	Koren Whipp
9	Margaret Cavendish, Duchess of Newcastle	Amanda L. Capern	Penny Whitworth
9	Lady Frances Norton	David Alexander Rueger	
9	The Honourable Mrs. Dudley North	Begoña Lasa-Alvarez	
10	Octavia, Wife to Antony	Peter Mark Keegan	
10	Octavia, Wife to Nero	J. Lea Beness and Tom Hillard	Deborah Russell
10	Mrs. Oldfield	Nicola Parsons	
10	Maria Pacheco Padilla	Nieves Baranda	
10	Dorothy, Lady Pakington	Amanda L. Capern and Anne Laurence	
10	Anne de Parthenai	Kelly Digby Peebles	
10	Catherine de Parthenai	Séverine Genieys-Kirk	Katherine Boyd
10	Paulina	Diane Johnston	
10	Perilla	Peter Mark Keegan	
10	Susanna Perwich	Felicity James	
10	Phila	Ian Plant	
10	Philippa	Zina Petersen	Koren Whipp
10	Katherine Phillips	Sarah Peterson Pittock	
10	Lætitia Pilkington	Jane Rendall	
10	Mrs. Pix	Nicola Parsons	
10	Diana de Poitiers	Princess Michael of Kent	Lindsay Smith
10	Porcia	Diane Johnston	
10	Modesto Pozzo	Paola Malpezzi Price	Elena Testi
10	Praxilla	Ian Plant	
10	Proba	Peter Mark Keegan	
10	Renata, Duchess of Ferrara	Kelly Peebles	
10	Anne de Rohan	Séverine Genieys-Kirk	
10	Marie Eleonore de Rohan	Peggy Schaller Elliott	
10	Margaret Roper	Lorna G. Barrow	
10	Mary Roper	Jaime Goodrich	
10	Madame Roland	Koren Whipp and Katherine Boyd	Lindsay Smith, Ludmilla A. Simon

VOLUME	SUBJECT	SCHOLAR(S)	RESEARCHER(S)
10	Isabella de Rosares	María Jesús Lorenzo-Modia	
10	Elizabeth Rowe	Mihaela Mudure	Lindsay Smith
10	Claudia Rufina	Peter Mark Keegan	
10	Lady Russel [Elizabeth]	Claire McEachern	Koren Whipp
10	Lady Rachel Russel	Begoña Lasa-Alvarez	
10	Laura Sade	Rebecca Nesvet	
10	Sappho	Deborah Lyons	
10	Alexandra Scala	Elgin Kirsten Eckert	
10	Anna Maria Schurman	Brita Servaes	Kristen Stevens
10	Madeliene de Scudery	Helena Bergmann	
10	Anne de Seguier	Véronique Larcade	
10	Semiramis	Inês de Ornellas e Castro	Koren Whipp
10	Madame Seturman	Rebecca Nesvet	
10	The Marchioness de Sevigne	Abby E. Zanger	
10	Lady Arabella Seymour	Melissa Ridley Elmes	
10	Ladies Anne, Margaret, and Jane Seymour	Karen S. Keller	
10	Catherine Sforza	Joyce de Vries	
10	Isabella Sforza	Silvia Giovanardi Byer	Koren Whipp
10	Frances Sheridan	Abigail Burnham Bloom	
10	Sophronia	Peter Mark Keegan	
10	Sulpicia	Peter Mark Keegan	Deborah Russell
10	Dorothy, Countess of Sunderland	Margaret Hannay	
10	The Countess de la Suze	Séverine Genieys-Kirk	
10	Mary Sydney, Countess of Pembroke	Margaret Hannay	
10	Tanaquil	Diane Johnston	
10	Telesilia	Ian Plant	
10	Theano [Theano Locrencis; Theano of Crete; Theano Thuria or Metapotino]	Ian Plant	
10	Mrs. Thomas	Diana Barnes	Koren Whipp
10	Thymele	Ian Plant	
10	Catherine Tishem	Mihaela Mudure	
10	Elizabeth Tollet	Patricia Fara	
10	Tymicha	Ian Plant	
10	Valeria	J. Lea Beness and Tom Hillard	
10	Mademoiselle de la Valliere	Séverine Genieys-Kirk	
10	Veturia	Imke Heuer	
10	Mademoiselle de la Vigne	Helena Bergmann	
10	Mary, Countess of Warwick	Lorna G. Barrow	Lindsay Smith

VOLUME	SUBJECT	SCHOLAR(S)	RESEARCHER(S)
10	Elizabeth Jane Weston	Johanna Harris	
10	Anne Wharton	Lindsay Smith	
10	Anne, Countess of Winchelsea	Elisabeth Lenckos	
10	Zenobia	Ian Plant	
10	Appendix 1: Memoirs of Mary Wollstonecraft	Fiore Sireci	Lindsay Smith
10	Appendix 1: Headnote	Fiore Sireci	
10	Appendix 2 : The Sources for *Female Biography*	Mary Spongberg	

INDEX

Memoirs of Women Writers, Volume 10

Moretto, Marquis of, **9**.59
Morgan, Thomas, **8**.186
Morice, James, **8**.229, 230
Morley, George, Bishop of Winchester, 7.390–1, **10**.41, 43
Mornay, Philippe de, **10**.420
Morosini, Pellegrina, **6**.89
Morris, Edward, **1**.436
Morris, Dr Michael, **1**.380, 381
Morton, Agnes Leslie, Countess of, **9**.135
Morton, Archibald Douglas, fifth Earl of, **9**.230
Morton, James Douglas, fourth Earl of, **9**.36, 37, 79, 80, 82, 84, 86, 94, 102, 124–5, 128, 131, 133, 135, 136, 166, 196, 203, 205, 206, 207, 208, 209, 216, 217–18, 219, 220, 221, 225–6, 227–31, 285
Morton, John, Archbishop of Canterbury, **5**.360
Morwen, John, **10**.104
Moscow, Archbishop of, 7.76–7
Mosheim, Johann Lorenz von, **2**.289
Moss, Charles, Bishop of Bath and Wells, **2**.195, 274, 278, 295
Moss, Dr, **2**.278, 286, 288
Motraye, Aubry de la, **6**.248
Motte, Houdar de la, **8**.10, 19
Motteville, Françoise Bertaud, Madame de, **5**.120–1, 321–3, 7.299, **10**.451
Motteville, Nicolas Langlois, Lord de, **5**.321
Mottley, John, 7.278
Moulin, Peter du, **8**.39
Mount Cashel, Countess, **10**.492
Mount Edgcumbe, Emma Gilbert, Lady, **2**.80, 98, 156, 157
Mount Edgcumbe and Valletort, George Edgcumbe, Lord, **2**.155, 156, 185
Mountjoy, Charles Blount, eighth Baron, first Earl of Devonshire, **8**.245, 254, 263, 264, 272, 278, 279, 285
Mountjoy, William Blount, fourth Baron, **6**.167
Muller, Gerhard Freidrich, 7.161
Mulso family, 7.286
Mulso, Jane, 7.288
Mulso, John, 7.288
Münnich, Count Burkhard Christoph von, **6**.296–7, 325, 350–2, 354, 355, 356, 363, 391, 7.40, 65
Munsel, Mr, **1**.363
Murgatroyd, Jacob, 7.393
Murphy, Arthur, **1**.109, 224, 309
Murray, Thomas, **8**.387
Murray of Tullibardine, Sir William, **9**.128, 132
Musso, Cornelio, Bishop of Bitonto, **6**.213
Muys, Cornelis, **5**.31–2
Muzio, Girolamo, **5**.314
Myllias, **10**.439

Nantes, Louise-Françoise de Bourbon (later Duchess of Bourbon), **9**.335, 369, 379, 380, 435–6
Napoleonic Wars, **2**.328, 7.415
Narcussus, Tiberius Claudius, **5**.44, 51, 52–3, 55, 57
Nash, Dr, **9**.298
Nassau, Prince of, 7.226

Natalya Alekseyevna, Grand Duchess of Russia, 7.91, 133–4, 135
National Society for Promoting the Education of the Poor in the Principles of the Established Church, **3**.73
natural disasters, **4**.228
Nau de la Boisselière, Claude, **9**.227, 235, 252, 256, 260
Naudé, Gabriel, 7.297
Navailles, Philippe de Montraud-Bènac de, **10**.450, 452, 453
Navailles, Suzanne de Beaudéan-Parabère, Madame de, **10**.448–51, 452, 453
Necker, Jacques, **2**.189, **10**.494
Necker de Saussure, Albertine-Adrienne, **2**.451
Nelson, Robert, **3**.258–9
Nemours, Henri II of Savoy, Duke of, **9**.516
Nemours, Marie de Longueville, Princess of Neufchâtel, Duchess of, **9**.516–17
Nero, Emperor, **5**.41, 48, 50, 51, 53, 54, 56, 57–62, 64–5, 66, 67–71, 73–6, **6**.9, **10**.15, 16, 17–18, 19–230
Nestorians, **9**.417
Nestorius, Patriarch of Constantinople, **9**.417
Neufville, Nicolas de, **5**.259
Neuillant, Madame de, **9**.322–3, 324, 325
Nevers, François de Cleves, Duke of, **8**.499
Neville, Lady Anne, **5**.292
Neville, George, Archbishop of York, **5**.289, 290
Neville, Sir Henry, **8**.272
Neville, Lady Isabel, **5**.289
Neville, Sir Thomas, **5**.283
Newbury, First Battle of, **10**.415
Newbury, John, **3**.163
Newcastle, Henry Fiennes Pelham-Clinton, Duke of, **2**.50
Newcastle, Margaret Cavendish (née Lucas), Duchess of, **9**.517–26, **10**.539
Newcastle, William Cavendish, first Duke of, **5**.348, **9**.518–19, 523
Newson, Elizabeth, **2**.14
Newton, Elizabeth, **2**.46
Newton, Sir Isaac, **6**.54, 55, **10**.438
Newton, Mr, **2**.111
Newton, Mrs, **2**.165, 166, 176, 181, **3**.208, 209
Newton, Thomas, Bishop of Bristol, **2**.46, 88, 163, 165–8, 170–6, 181, 204–6, 254, 437
Neymar, General, 7.293
Nicephorus Gregoras, **8**.448, 449, 455
Nicholas V, Pope, **5**.196
Nicholas, Denton, 7.412–13
Nicholas, St, **5**.363
Nichols, J., **10**.466
Nicocles, King of Cyprus, **8**.506
Nicocrates of Cyrene, **5**.198, 199, 200, 202
Niemcewicz, Julian Ursyn, 7.257
Nifo, Agostino, **5**.308–9
Nigel, second Bishop of Ely, **5**.359
Niger (friend of Mark Antony), 7.348–9
Nine Years' War, **9**.374, 391, 409
Ninus, King of Assyria, **10**.395, 396, 397